JERRY F. HOUGH

DEMOCRATIZATION AND REVOLUTION IN THE USSR, 1985–1991

BROOKINGS INSTITUTION PRESS
Washington, D.C.

Library of Congress Cataloging-in-Publication Data

Hough, Jerry F., 1935–
 Democratization and revolution in the USSR, 1985–1991 /
 Jerry F. Hough.
  p. cm.
 Includes bibliographical references (p.) and index.
 ISBN 0-8157-3748-3 (cloth : alk. paper). —
 ISBN 0-8157-3749-1 (pbk. : alk. paper)
 1. Soviet Union—Politics and government—1985–1991.
 2. Post-communism—Soviet Union. I. Title.
 JN6500.H68 1997   96-44483
 947.085′4—dc21   CIP

9 8 7 6 5 4 3 2 1

 # 357235 86

Typeset in Times Roman

Composition by AlphaWebTech
Mechanicsville, Maryland

Printed by R. R. Donnelly and Sons Co.
Harrisonburg, Virginia

69638
JN
6500
.H68
1997

Foreword

AT THE BEGINNING OF THE 1980s some Western observers expected a new generation of party leaders to liberalize the Soviet system; others believed change was unlikely. Some thought that the Soviet Union, ruled by a military-industrial complex, was inexorably driven to world domination; others considered the Soviets obsessed only with equality and security.

Everyone was proved wrong. Members of the Central Committee of the Communist party in 1981—Mikhail Gorbachev, Boris Yeltsin, and Eduard Shevardnadze—went far beyond liberalization to introduce elements of democracy and the realizable right of secession from the Union. Concerns in the West over a Soviet drive for world domination and security may well have been exaggerated; the defense industry was not able even to defend its own existence, and when the awesome military and KGB attempted a coup d'état in 1991, they did not use force or arrest anyone.

Events moved so rapidly and were so incredible that few could keep up with them. Now time has passed, and more than seventy memoirs have been published in Russian on the Gorbachev period. In this book Jerry Hough reassesses the old and new evidence on the period and comes to striking conclusions that revise a number of his own earlier interpretations as well as those of others. Premier Nikolai Ryzhkov and his colleagues emerge in Hough's study as more serious economic reformers than we thought. Gorbachev, lacking a theory of economic transition, was from the beginning and against his better judgment driven to a de facto policy of shock therapy.

Hough treats the events of 1990-91 as a revolution, one as sweeping as the Bolshevik Revolution of 1917. He does not limit himself to writing a history of the period, but analyzes the implications of what happened for our general understanding of revolution, democratization, marketization, and political stability. His book, therefore, has great relevance for understanding developments in China and the third world, which have decades of difficult transition awaiting them if they are to become stable market economies and democratic societies.

Brookings received funding for this project from the Carnegie Corporation of New York, the John D. and Catherine T. MacArthur Foundation, and the Andrew W. Mellon Foundation. We greatly appreciate their support.

The views expressed here are those of the author and should not be attributed to the organizations whose assistance is acknowledged above or to the trustees, officers, or other staff members of the Brookings Institution.

Michael H. Armacost
President

May 1997
Washington, D.C.

Acknowledgements

THIS BOOK INCORPORATES the work of more than twenty years. A proper list of acknowledgments would fill pages, and I find it wiser to mention almost no one than to offend those left out. However, the influence of Sheila Fitzpatrick needs to be singled out. And George Breslauer and Timothy Colton had a dramatic impact on the structure and character of the book. David Laitin's comments at a late stage of the manuscript were also invaluable.

The contribution of hundreds of scholars and officials in the Soviet Union and now Russia cannot be acknowledged out of fear that the attention would be dangerous for them. But I do wish to mention a few. My friendship with Fedor Burlatsky goes back to the 1970s, with Nodari Simonia of the Institute of the World Economy and International Relations (IMEMO) to the late 1970s, and Viktor Sheinis, then of IMEMO and now of the political party Yabloko, to the early 1980s. Three men whom I met in the late 1980s had a direct influence on particular parts of the book: Vsevolod Vasilev, director of the Institute of Legislation, on the work of the USSR Congress and the Union Treaty; Mikhail Guboglo of the Institute of Ethnology and Anthropology on nationality policy; and Iosif Diskin of the Institute of Population Studies on the Russian Congress and the issues of economic reform after August 1991.

Although the book is critical of Mancur Olson's *Rise and Decline of Nations*, I want to acknowledge formally what will be apparent to the knowledgeable reader—that I consider myself a disciple of Olson and that my way of thinking has been deeply influenced by Olson's work. My criticism of Olson comes from the assumptions of that work.

ix

This book was edited at Brookings by James Schneider. Diane Chido Fisher provided research assistance. Melanie Allen, Julien Hartley, and Andrew Solomon verified its factual content, and Princeton Editorial Associates compiled the index.

My research was supported from many directions. I wish to thank the John D. and Catherine T. MacArthur Foundation and the Carnegie Corporation of New York for their support of the Center of East-West Trade, Investment, and Communication at Duke University and the exchanges with Russia it made possible. A grant from the Carnegie Corporation of New York enabled me, Timothy Colton, Jeffrey Hahn, and Blair Ruble to study the USSR legislature and the politics of the Yaroslavl national-territorial election. National Science Foundation grant SES 91-12-882 to Timothy Colton and me allowed the collection of roll call, biographical, and other data on the USSR and Russian legislature. The National Council for Research on the Soviet Union and Eastern Europe supported a project on central-local relations in the Soviet Union. The John D. and Catherine T. MacArthur Foundation, the Carnegie Corporation of New York, and National Science Foundation grants SBR 94-02548 and SBR 94-12-051 also provided major support for the 1993 election study that is cited in this book and that along with the 1995 and 1996 elections will be the focus of subsequent Brookings books.

J.F.H.

Contents

1. Introduction   1
   Competing Views of Revolution and Democratization   *5*
   The Soviet Revolution in Theoretical Perspective   *8*
   Implications for the Structure of the Book   *13*
   The Intellectual Assumptions of Reform   *16*

2. Prelude to Revolution   23
   The Social Base of the Communist Revolution   *25*
   Communism, Job Creation, and Economic Security   *31*
   Communism and Psychological Security   *37*
   The Equilibrium of the Mid-1970s   *41*
   The Changing Social Structure of the Brezhnev Period   *44*
   Elite Attitudes and Revolution   *51*
   Conclusion   *58*

3. Gorbachev's Ascent and the Circular Flow of Power   61
   Gorbachev's Path to Power   *64*
   The Circular Flow of Power   *80*
   Yury Andropov and the Kirilenko Machine   *86*
   Gorbachev and the Kirilenko Machine   *90*
   The Russian Republic and the Circular Flow of Power   *99*

4. The Tragedy of Economic Reform   103
   The Start of Economic Reform   *106*
   The Problem of Price Imbalances   *111*
   The Controversy over Price Reform   *114*

The Radical Economists and the Command-Administrative
  System   *118*
Gorbachev and Ryzhkov on Price Reform   *123*
Gorbachev and the Radical Economists   *135*

5. Democratization and the 1989 USSR Election   140
Political Liberalization   *142*
Democratization   *148*
The Creation of a New Legislature   *156*
The Candidates   *161*
Paradoxes of the 1989 USSR Election   *164*
The USSR Congress   *169*

6. Foreign and Domestic Policy and the Issue of
   Eastern Europe   175
Gorbachev's Foreign Policy Team   *177*
The Soviet Debate on Entente   *189*
Gorbachev's Foreign Policy   *192*
Attitudes toward Eastern Europe   *196*
Policy toward Eastern Europe   *198*
Conclusion   *209*

7. Soviet Federalism and the Problem of Russia   214
The Peculiarities of Soviet Federalism   *216*
Lenin's and Stalin's Policy on National Identity   *221*
The Non-Russian Republics   *227*
The National Identity of the Russians   *238*
The Economic Grievances of Russia   *241*
The Problem of the Autonomous Republics   *245*

8. The End of Communist Party Rule   249
Gorbachev's Other Options   *251*
The Communist Party and Economic Reform   *255*
Gorbachev and the Communist Party   *258*
The Anxiety of the Summer and Fall of 1989   *262*
The End of the Party's Leading Role   *266*
The Creation of a Presidency and the Destruction of the Party   *269*
The Failure of the Communists as a Parliamentary Party   *273*

9. The 1990 Russian Election   278
The Russian Legislature   *279*
The Candidates   *283*

The Election   *290*
Pre-Congress Negotiations and the Development of Group
   Politics   *298*
The Election of Boris Yeltsin as Chairman of the Supreme
   Soviet   *304*
The Moderate Majority   *308*

10. The Struggle between Gorbachev and Yeltsin   315
The Origins of the Conflict   *317*
The Comeback of Boris Yeltsin   *325*
Gorbachev's Calculations about Yeltsin   *329*
Yeltsin as Chairman of the Russian Supreme Soviet   *332*
Yeltsin and the Russian Congress   *335*

11. The Controversy over Economic Reform   341
The Growing Sophistication of the Economic Debate   *342*
The Failure of the Abalkin Plan   *348*
The Battle of Radicals and Conservatives   *352*
The Political Destruction of Nikolai Ryzhkov   *357*
The Craziness of the 500-Day Plan   *361*

12. The Union Treaty   373
Toward a Republic-Dominated Union   *374*
The Union Treaty   *376*
The "Subjects of the Federation"   *381*
The Russian Declaration of Sovereignty   *386*
The First Draft of the Union Treaty   *390*
The Hysteria of the Winter of 1990–91   *394*
Gorbachev's Position   *399*

13. The Russian Presidential Election and the August
Coup d'État   404
The Establishment of an Elected Russian President   *405*
The Alliance with Aleksandr Rutskoi   *410*
The Union Treaty and the Russian Presidency   *415*
The Election for President   *420*
The August Coup D'État   *422*
The Mystery of Gorbachev   *432*
The Mystery of the Conspirators' Plans   *437*
The Military and the Logic of Collective Action   *443*

14. Economic Options and the Breakup of the Union   449
    Gorbachev after the Coup *450*
    The Two Economic Strategies and Russian Independence *456*
    The Victory of the Burbulis-Gaidar Position *464*
    Dilemmas of the Democrats about Democracy *470*
    The Dissolution of the Soviet Union *477*
    The Mystery of the Soviet Military *483*

15. Conclusion   490
    The Character of the Second Russian Revolution *495*
    The Importance of Institutions and Incentives *504*
    Democracy and Democratization *510*
    The Implications for American Policy *518*

Index   527

Tables

1-1.   Indicators of Changing Living Standards, Selected Years,
       1970–90   16
2-1.   Attitudes toward Economic Reform, Survey Respondents
       Aged 18 to 59, by Level of Employment, December 1993   26
2-2.   Attitudes toward Privatization of State Property, Survey
       Respondents Aged 18 to 59, by Level of Employment,
       December 1993   27
2-3.   Distribution of Votes for Bolshevik Candidates for the
       Constituent Assembly, by Region, December 1917   29
2-4.   Soviet Citizens Completing Secondary Education or Higher,
       by Age Group, Selected Years, 1959–89   46
2-5.   Distribution of Workers by Type and Status of Occupation,
       1939, 1959, 1970   47
2-6.   Worker Attitudes toward the Communist Party, by Age Group
       and Size of Place of Residence, 1993   49
2-7.   Distribution of Employment, by Country and Sector, 1990   50
3-1.   Distribution of Male Officials Elected to the Central Committee
       and Central Auditing Commission, by Period of Birth and
       Economic Sector, 1981   67
3-2.   Employment and Age Distribution of Central Committee
       Voting Members, March 1985   79
5-1.   Occupations of Candidates in One-Candidate Elections,
       USSR and Russia, USSR Elections for Congress of People's
       Deputies, 1989   162

5-2. Candidates in Territorial Districts of Russia, by Size and
      Type of District, USSR Election for Congress of People's
      Deputies, 1989   163
5-3. Occupations of Candidates and Deputies from Russia in the
      USSR Legislature, 1984, 1989   164
5-4. Average Voting Score of USSR Council of Union Deputies,
      Second and Third Congresses, by Region and Population of
      Largest City in Electoral District   168
6-1. Central European Communist Leaders' Age and Years
      in Office   199
6-2. U.S. Investment in China, 1979–93   205
7-1. Population and Ethnicity of Union Republics, 1989   228
7-2. Assimilation in Ukraine, by Region, 1991   231
7-3. Indigenous Population in Central Asian Capitals, 1959, 1989   237
7-4. Russians Living in Republican Capitals Who Know the Local
      Language, 1979, 1989   241
7-5. Fluency in Local Language among Russians in Tashkent,
      1974, and Tallinn, 1974, 1988, by Length of Residence   242
7-6. Ethnic Composition of Population in the Autonomous
      Republics of the Russian Soviet Federated Socialist
      Republic, by Religion of the Indigenous Population, 1989   246
8-1. Characteristics of Obkom First Secretaries in the Russian
      Republic, 1985–91   275
9-1. Average Number of Candidates, 1989 USSR Election and
      1990 Russian Election, by Type of Russian District and
      Most Populous City   285
9-2. Occupations of Deputies in the Russian Supreme Soviet,
      1985, and the Congress of People's Deputies, 1990   287
9-3. Occupations of Candidates from Territorial Districts,
      by Population of Largest Town in District, Russian
      1990 Election   288
9-4. Distribution of Deputies, by Political Orientation, First
      Congress of People's Deputies, May–June 1990   296
9-5. Political Orientation of Deputies, by Size of City in Which
      They Were Elected, RSFSR Territorial Districts, March 1990   297
9-6. Actual and Ideal Numbers of Deputies to the Russian
      Congress of Deputies, According to Population and Eligible
      Voters, by Size of Largest City in the District, 1990   299
9-7. Pro-Yeltsin and Anti-Yeltsin Votes on Test Votes on Agenda,
      First Russian Congress of People's Deputies, May 1990   307
11-1. Income and Expenses of the Soviet Population, 1986–89   344

12-1. Distribution of Votes on Party Membership in the Military,
        First Congress of People's Deputies, by Deputy Views on
        Russian Sovereignty, May–June 1990   391

Figures
15-1. Economic Development and Democratization   517

CHAPTER ONE

Introduction

IN 1990 AND 1991 THE SOVIET UNION underwent one of the great revolutions in world history—the Second Russian Revolution, as it was called in a BBC special.[1] It lacked the dramatic violence, the storming of a Bastille or a Winter Palace, of other great revolutions. There were no irrepressible demonstrations, no rock-throwing mobs, no antigovernment guerilla actions. Yet the transformations in the political and economic systems, in ideology, social structure, and ethnic relations, and in relations with the international community were as sweeping as those produced by the Russian Revolution of 1917 and more sweeping than those of the French Revolution of 1789.

The Russian Revolution of 1990–91 was a true middle-class revolution, a revolution of the bureaucrats, of the bourgeois who managed the means of production. Most historians now emphasize that the "bourgeois revolutions" of the past were shouldered not by the bourgeoisie but by peasants fearful of their first exposure to market forces or, as I would be more inclined to emphasize, by people in transition from being country dwellers to being city dwellers.[2] Not surprisingly, revolutions based on the insecure

---

1. Angus Roxburgh, *The Second Russian Revolution: The Struggle for Power in the Kremlin* (Pharos Books, 1992).
2. This is particularly true if *bourgeoisie* is defined in Marxist terms: owners of the means of production rather than merchants of the service sector. Students of the Russian Revolution of 1917 often speak of the weak bourgeoisie, but this phrase is even more aptly applied to the French Revolution, or the American. Theda Skocpol, *States and Social Revolutions: A Comparative Analysis of France, Russia, and China* (Cambridge University Press, 1979), pp. 174–77. A country with little industry cannot have many owners of the industrial means of production.

1

and uneducated in transition were notably violent. But a revolution based on the middle class in a society with a nationalized economy need not be fought at the barricades. The revolutionaries are already working in the state system and can let it collapse from within.

Half a century ago Crane Brinton concluded that the key feature in a successful revolution was the elite classes' loss of self-confidence.

> When numerous and influential members of [a ruling] class begin to believe that they hold power unjustly, or that all men are brothers, equal in the eyes of eternal justice, or that the beliefs they were brought up on are silly, or that "after us the deluge," they are not likely to resist successfully any serious attacks on their social, economic and political position. . . . When those of them who [have] positions of political power [do] use force, they [use] it sporadically and ineffi-ciently. . . . It is almost safe to say that no government is likely to be overthrown until it loses the ability to make adequate use of its military and police powers.[3]

This is particularly likely to occur, as Karl Mannheim emphasized, when the old ideology no longer serves the interests of the elite.[4]

That is what happened in the Soviet Union in the late 1980s and early 1990s. Those who led the revolution of 1990–91, and that includes Mikhail Gorbachev and his advisers as well as Boris Yeltsin and his, came to accept Karl Marx's assumption that the state does not play a crucial or even useful role in economic performance, that it is parasitic and that planning can be achieved as it withers away. When it became clear that privatization was possible, the ambitious who were employed in the state and economic bureaucracies—and intellectuals in the professions—could see how they could personally benefit from a revolution that instituted private property and private business. Most had no interest in defending the collective interests of their bureaucracies, and the rest had little ability to do so.

This is, of course, not the conventional interpretation of the Russian Revolution of 1990–91. Although everyone now believes that a great revo-lution occurred in the Soviet Union, we never described events in such terms at the time. We saw only a struggle for and against reform. Although revolutions by definition must have revolutionaries, we saw only reformers. Revolutions usually bring extremists—the Robespierres, the Lenins, the Black Panthers in the semirevolution of the 1960s in the United States—to the forefront in their last stages, but we never asked who these extremists

---

3. Crane Brinton, *The Anatomy of Revolution* (Norton, 1938), pp. 40–41, 64–65, 288–89.

4. Karl Mannheim, *Ideology and Utopia* (Harcourt, Brace, Jovanovich, 1985).

might be in the latest Russian Revolution. Boris Yeltsin is never discussed for what he has been: a revolutionary on the scale of Lenin. Instead, those who acted as Robespierre—economists such as Yegor Gaidar and Boris Fedorov—continued to be called reformers.

In addition, those with the most to gain from a capitalist revolution, those with managerial experience in industry and the state economic institutions, were considered adamant and formidable opponents of the revolution or even of reform. They were not called managers or middle class, but bureaucrats and the *nomenklatura*. Even in the 1990s those who talked about "'nomenklatura privatization'" still improbably claimed that the bureaucrats who were being unfairly enriched were against the reforms that benefited them so much. Survey data showed them wrong.

The time has come to reassess the meaning of the events that occurred in the Soviet Union between 1985 and 1991. In retrospect, every Western scholar—certainly including me—understood parts of what happened and why but completely misunderstood other parts. The combination of insight and misjudgment varied wildly from observer to observer. The flow of events was so rapid and so unexpected that no one had time to step back and reflect upon what had transpired. Observers tended to retain their interpretations of events even after they had been proved incorrect and to combine them with interpretations of later events in contradictory ways. As a result, we are left with an odd collection of inconsistent memories, a melange of fact and fiction.

Now, however, enough time has passed to view events in perspective, to revise old judgments if necessary, try to put them in a coherent pattern, and begin to draw lessons. Most of the major participants of Soviet politics from 1985 to 1991 have written their memoirs about the period, and we can check statements made at the time against both these memories and the subsequent flow of events. That is the first purpose of this book. Those who know my earlier studies will recognize that many interpretations I advanced in the past are retained here but others have been revised in light of new evidence.

This book also has other purposes. Whatever the mistakes of specialists studying the Soviet Union, they were able to draw little guidance from the recent comparative studies of revolution and democratization. Political scientists have mostly abandoned the study of revolution, and the sociologists who have studied it recently have focused on communist and leftist revolutions in China, Vietnam, and other third world countries at early stages of industrial development. Recent studies of democratization, by contrast, have predominantly reflected the experience of southern Europe and Latin America in the 1970s and 1980s. These countries were at fairly advanced stages of industrial development and had actually begun to democratize a century before. Thus the studies actually explored, as Alfred Stepan has noted, redemocratization rather than the whole democratization process.[5]

Because the studies of democratization and revolution have described countries at very different stages of economic and political development, there has been little connection or cross-fertilization between them. Little has been said about democratization in Asian countries, which are at middle levels of industrial development and democratization at the end of the twentieth century.[6] The studies have been even less relevant for understanding the Soviet Union, an advanced industrial country with no experience of traditional democracy. It is symptomatic of the situation that six years after the introduction of democratic elections in the Soviet Union, comparativists generally ignore that experience and focus only on eastern Europe.[7]

Therefore a book on the Russian Revolution of 1990–91 is a natural place to begin integrating disparate theories of revolution and democratization and to focus more on the intermediate stages of democratization. Precisely because the countries of Asia at intermediate stages of development are likely to pose the greatest foreign policy challenges in the first half of the twenty-first century, this subject has immense relevance for U.S. foreign policy.

A second broad purpose of this book turns out to be more unexpected. The book concludes that the prime immediate cause of the revolution lay in the beliefs and unspoken assumptions of those at the very top of the economic and political hierarchies. The most surprising conclusion is that the private views of Mikhail Gorbachev and his top advisers were close to the announced opinions of the men in Boris Yeltsin's government who

5. Alfred Stepan, "Paths toward Redemocratization: Theoretical and Comparative Considerations," in Guillermo A. O'Donnell, Philipe C. Schmitter, and Laurence Whitehead, eds., *Transitions from Authoritarian Rule: Comparative Perspective* (Johns Hopkins University Press, 1986), pp. 64–68.

6. Indeed, Samuel P. Huntington, one of the leading scholars of the older generation, now associates democracy almost solely with the cultural values of Christianity, despite the experience of Moslem Turkey, Shinto Japan, and Hindu India. See *The Third Wave: Democratization in the Late Twentieth Century* (University of Oklahoma Press, 1991).

7. Peter Ordeshook is an exception, but he does not tie his work to societal developments or public opinion.

introduced shock therapy in 1992. It turns out not to have been merely a sign of opportunism that Yegor Gaidar could be the economics editor of *Pravda* under Gorbachev and then leader of the economic reform under Yeltsin. His assumptions were similar to those of both men.

In addition, the views of Soviet radicals who supported Gorbachev and then Yeltsin were similar to those of Western neoclassical economists. This was not an accident: both Marxism and neoclassical economics had their roots in the precorporate world of the early nineteenth century when government economic regulation and democracy were very much underdeveloped. Neither accommodated the complexities of modern corporate society, the institutional requirements of a modern market, or the institutional structure of democracy. For this reason the lessons of the latest Russian Revolution have direct relevance for the assumptions of the United States as it attempts to promote marketization and democracy abroad. And because economic and political reforms of the communist system in China were based on very different assumptions about the role of the state in economic development and democratization, it and the Soviet Union provide an especially valuable comparative test of theory.

Competing Views of Revolution and Democratization

Revolution and democratization can be viewed through two very different prisms. The popular view is that they are processes emanating from below. The most pragmatic definition of a revolution is that it is a major change of regime around which a great justifying mythology is created by the victors. It is depicted as a heroic triumph of good over evil, with the former rulers portrayed as brutally oppressive and the people as giving universal support to the revolutionaries, who are the decisive agents of change.

Democratization is popularly understood in like terms. Nearly all revolutions clothe themselves in democratic language, and in retrospect they are often seen as democratic, even when they quickly give way to authoritarian regimes. But popular demonstrations and protest meetings may occur under authoritarian regimes. When such regimes finally give way to democracies, the development is usually attributed to the most recent demonstrations.

The major theorists in the 1950s and 1960s saw revolution and democratization through such a prism, although in a highly sophisticated manner. Scholars who developed the theory of modernization argued that stable democracies were almost never sustainable in preindustrial societies, while dictatorships, other than in exceptional temporary cases such as Chile in the 1970s, were equally difficult to sustain once countries became industrialized and societies well educated. Within this modernization theory, scholars emphasized various factors as crucial in producing democracy: industrialization, increasing affluence, urbanization, higher levels of education, the development of a system of mass communication, the creation of a middle class, occupational differentiation, the growth of a political civic culture, and so forth. Yet all these factors were part of a general and interrelated societal process.

The postwar theory of revolution also emphasized social factors, values, and forces. In studies of modernization, revolution was more or less a residual category, the bad thing that could happen if government did not achieve the difficult balance between responding to social forces while still controlling and managing them. Marxist and neo-Marxist theorists emphasized the importance of class grievances and actions, the neo-Marxists more often focusing on peasants than on workers. Some sociologists gave prime attention to social movements, while others took a more psychological approach, emphasizing factors such as perceptions of relative deprivation and the effects of the J curve (an improvement of conditions after a downturn).[8]

Theda Skocpol has summarized "the shared image" presented by this generation of scholars:

> First, changes in social systems or societies give rise to grievances, social orientation, or new class or group interests and potentials for collective mobilization. Then there develops a purposive, mass-based movement—coalescing with the aid of ideology and organization—that consciously undertakes to overthrow the existing government and perhaps the entire social order. Finally, the revolutionary movement fights it out with the authorities or dominant class.[9]

In recent decades, however, most of those writing about revolution or democratization have deemphasized the importance of societal forces and movements and focused on decisions and actions taken or not taken by an elite. The title of Skocpol's influential 1979 book, *States and Social Revolution*, suggested she had returned to Brinton's emphasis on, in her words,

---

8. Charles Tilly, for example, emphasized social movements; see *From Mobilization to Revolution* (Reading, Mass.: Addison-Wesley, 1978). Ted Robert Gurr focused on people's perceptions; see *Why Men Rebel* (Princeton University Press, 1970).

9. Skocpol, *States and Social Revolutions*, pp. 14–15.

the importance of the "weakness" of the state to explain successful revolutions. "Before social revolutions could occur, the administrative and military power of these states had to break down." Revolutionary political crises only emerged once the old-regime states had broken.[10] She expressed the deepest skepticism about the concept of revolution from below: "the fact is that historically no successful social revolution has ever been 'made' by a mass-mobilizing, avowedly revolutionary movement."[11]

Mancur Olson, the economist who a quarter of a century ago wrote the classic book on the logic of collective action, recently described the implications of this logic for revolution.

When there are no free elections and governments are able and willing to use force, political outcomes do not mainly depend on the hearts and minds of the people—on what the various populations or nationalities want. Very often governments can be massively unpopular yet continue in power. . . . The logic of collective action keeps the huge number of people who don't like a regime from taking the actions that would overthrow it. . . . If such an individual makes a sacrifice to rebel against the regime that he despises, he will bear the full cost and risk of whatever he does to help overthrow the hated regime. Yet any benefits of what he does will automatically go to people throughout the society. . . . Even though the aggregate benefits to the group or population of overthrowing the regime are many times the total costs, each typical individual finds that his costs of working to overthrow an undemocratic regime are normally much greater than the benefits he would receive.[12]

Olson contends that "a dictator has power because he has a cadre of officials, police, and military officers who regularly obey his orders." And because the logic of collective action applies to them as well, they do not obey the dictator because of their beliefs but because of concrete incentives and disincentives—the ability of the regime to pay salaries, make promotions, and punish. But Olson also emphasizes the potential instability of dictatorial regimes.

If a government's operatives, and especially those in the police and the military, *believe* that they will be punished if they fail to carry out their orders and rewarded if they do, an autocracy is secure. If the cadre perceive that a dictatorship is invincible, it cannot be overthrown by its subjects. . . . Yet a regime whose power rests on nothing more than a shared perception can lose all of its power once perceptions change. And if the regime is even once observed to be weak,

10. Skocpol, *States and Social Revolutions*, p. 285.
11. Skocpol, *States and Social Revolutions*, p. 17.
12. Mancur Olson, "The Logic of Collective Action in Soviet-type Societies," *Journal of Soviet Nationalities*, vol. 1(Summer 1990), pp. 9, 10–11.

perceptions can change in the blink of an eye. . . . Since even the most awesome despotisms often rest on nothing more than a shared perception of their guards and administrators, they are, paradoxically, close to disorder and even to anarchy.[13]

Similarly, the leading theorists of democratization of the 1970s and the 1980s came to emphasize the crucial importance of the elites' decisions in the transition to democracy. The reintroduction of democracy into Latin America and southern Europe in those decades did not involve the dramatic overthrow of authoritarian rulers by popular uprisings. "Of the typologies of democratic transitions," Guiseppe Di Palma wrote, "the rarest ones originate in some sort of mobilization of society. The purest example of a democracy born directly out of an armed revolt of democratic forces (Costa Rica's 1948 revolt) is also the only one."[14]

The new students of democratization focused on the response of the leadership to opposition: "the emergence of splits between hard-liners and soft-liners within the circles of power, the ultimately unsuccessful attempts by authoritarian rulers to legitimate their rule by liberalizing rather than democratizing, the formation of coalitions pressing for democratic change between different and sometimes formerly divided political and social forces. . . ."[15]

The Soviet Revolution in Theoretical Perspective

When the Soviet experience is seen in terms of the two opposing theories of revolution and democratization, a remarkable result emerges: compelling confirmation of both.

Without question the best projections of the Soviet future in the 1950s and 1960s were made by the sociologists and political scientists who developed the theories of modernization. Today modernization theory is often considered passé by younger scholars, but its creators would recall

13. Olson, "Logic of Collective Action," pp. 14–17.
14. Guiseppe Di Palma, *To Craft Democracies: An Essay on Democratic Transitions* (University of California Press, 1990), p. 38.
15. See the introduction in Scott Mainwaring, Guillermo A. O'Donnell, and J. Samuel Valenzuela, eds. *Issues in Democratic Consolidation: The New South American Democracies in Comparative Perspectives* (University of Notre Dame Press, 1992), p. 4.

their predictions about the Soviet Union (and Latin America) with pride and would cite them as strong evidence of the validity of their approach.

As early as 1953 the political scientist Karl Deutsch warned colleagues who were focusing only on totalitarian controls that "the basic processes of political integration and disintegration occur on a more fundamental level than that of mere political, military, or police techniques, or of government-run propaganda." He emphasized the problems of "coordination of information channels and communication processes" and the "ability to maintain political cohesion and unity of decision-making under conditions of social, political, or economic strain." He pointed to the 1970s and 1980s as a time when Russia and China were likely to see "a diminution in 'classic' patterns of totalitarian behavior."[16]

In 1967 Talcott Parsons went so far as to call "democratic association" and "democratic government" one of the "evolutionary universals in society." Parsons was using the word *universal* not in an observational sense, but as a necessary part of the evolution of society: "a complex of structures and associated processes the development of which so increases the long-run adaptive capacity of living systems." Only those that "develop the complex can attain certain higher levels of general adaptive capacity."[17]

> The basic argument for considering democratic association a universal . . . is that, the larger and more complex a society becomes, the more important is effective political organization, not only in its administrative capacity, but also, and not least, in its support of a universalistic legal order. . . . No institutional form basically different from the democratic association can, *not* specifically *legitimize* authority and power in the most general sense, but *mediate consensus in its exercise* by particular persons and groups, and in the formation of particular binding policy decisions.[18]

Recognizing that others might claim this would not be true of communist regimes, he emphasized that "I do indeed predict that [communism] will prove to be unstable": "the Communist Party has everywhere emphasized its function in *educating* the people for the new society. In the long run its legitimacy will certainly be undermined if the party leadership continues to be unwilling to *trust* the people it has educated. . . . This can only mean that

16. Karl Deutsch, "Cracks in the Monolith: Possibilities and Patterns of Disintegration in Totalitarian Systems," in Carl J. Friedrich, ed., *Totalitarianism* (Harvard University Press, 1954), pp. 318, 330, 331.

17. Talcott Parsons, *Sociological Theory and Modern Society* (Free Press, 1967), pp. 493, 518.

18. Parsons, *Sociological Theory and Modern Society,* pp. 518–19.

eventually the single monolithic party must relinquish its monopoly of such responsibility."[19]

In the early 1950s Barrington Moore applied Max Weber's analysis of the consequences of the bureaucratization of modern society to the Soviet Union and suggested Soviet society would take on the characteristics of the rational-technical societies of the West.[20] Even W. W. Rostow's analysis of communism as "a disease of the transition," while alarmist in the short run, reminded people that in the long run transitions are transitory and that this should also be true of their diseases. My analysis from 1977 to 1988, based on the tenets of modernization theory, strongly pointed in the same direction.[21]

The theories with the worst predictive records were those that rejected the primary postulates of modernization theory. One theory denied the differentiation within the elite that modernization theory sees as a key element in political development. Its proponents saw the USSR as governed by a united, privileged ruling class: the bureaucracy, the nomenklatura, the partocracy. This concept was neo-Marxist, positing a ruling class composed primarily of the managers of the means of production. It described the political rulers as constituting an impotent "superstructure" that represented the interests of the ruling class. As in Marx's analysis of capitalism, evolution within the elite was considered impossible; change would occur only with its overthrow. Yet the Soviet system was overthrown by men such as Mikhail Gorbachev, Eduard Shevardnadze, and Boris Yeltsin who were at the very heart of Brezhnev's "partocracy."

A second antimodernization theory focused on the supposedly unchanging attitudes of the Russian people. Russians were considered authoritarian, xenophobic, and absorbed with security. Their "political culture" (to use the fashionable phrase) was judged relatively stable despite decades of industrialization, urbanization, and increased levels of education. Many of these theorists even spoke of a "social contract" between the workers and the

---

19. Parsons, *Sociological Theory and Modern Society*, pp. 518–519.

20. Barrington Moore, *Terror and Progress USSR: Some Sources of Change and Stability in the Soviet Dictatorship* (Harvard University Press, 1954). At the time, Moore was a close friend of Herbert Marcuse and shared his jaundiced view of modern "rational-technical" society. Moore could talk about an evolution of the Soviet Union to the American form of totalitarianism, but someone with a favorable view of Western society could see Moore's predictions in a positive light.

21. Jerry F. Hough, *Soviet Leadership in Transition* (Brookings, 1980), esp. chap. 2, pp. 16–36.

regime that featured workers' acquiescence to authoritarian rule in exchange for security. But it was precisely the workers of the large cities who consistently voted against the Communist party, even in 1996, after years of economic collapse.

Yet if the theory that the modernization of society is the engine of political change was successful in its predictions and the opposing theories unsuccessful, seldom has there been a revolution or process of democratization accompanied by so little direct pressure from society. There were few major protest movements or demonstrations and only one significant strike (and that a coal strike for "fair" or subsidized coal prices and wages, not market ones).

Before the July 1988 announcement of the intention to hold competitive elections in March 1989, ethnic unrest—and it was not widespread—almost always involved conflict between non-Russian groups.[22] In February 1988 a *New York Times* reporter wrote about the strongly anti-Soviet attitudes in the Baltics, but described the population as quiescent and resigned. A dissident with whom he talked saw little hope for the legalization of political parties in the foreseeable future.[23] When groups led by Ed Hewett of the Brookings Institution visited the Baltic republics in those years, they found economists far more passive than those in Moscow.

Soviet leaders seem to have felt little popular pressure. Rather, Aleksandr Yakovlev, Gorbachev's closest adviser, wrote of the passivity of the Russian people, as did Gorbachev himself. A major announced goal of democratization was "to activate the human factor," and it seems that this was, indeed, one of its major goals. Although the Central Committee members who elected Gorbachev general secretary knew they were voting for major reform, few suspected how far he would go. In his memoirs Yegor Ligachev, the second secretary from 1985 to 1988, talked about Gorbachev's having to use political shock therapy to conduct his revolution from above.

The competitive elections brought forth an outpouring of political activity, but it generally remained within the framework of normal democratic politics. Only in the Baltic republics and western Ukraine were there demonstrations suggesting mass support for secession, and the few tenta-

22. The only significant exception was a two-day demonstration in 1986 in the capital of Kazakhstan when the long-time ethnic Kazakh party leader was removed.
23. Phillip Taubman, "In Soviet Baltics, an Unintended Openness," *New York Times*, February 10, 1988, p. A8.

tive Soviet efforts to apply force in the Baltics were so successful that it is clear the secession movement could have been easily suppressed. Even democratic political activity remained a peculiarly elite pastime, and the groups that arose in the legislatures of both the Soviet Union and the Russian Soviet Federated Socialist Republic were accurately called factions, not parties. Very little effort was made to build parties that had local organizations and a mass following.

For all his high-profile activity, Boris Yeltsin was no more able to rally the people to political activity than were other political leaders. Although he took a strongly populist position, was skilled in playing on mass hopes and fears, and gathered substantial electoral support, the support did not translate into mass political action. When he called for a general strike at the time of the August 1991 coup d'état, no one responded. The crowds in front of the parliament building during the coup numbered only in the tens of thousands, and they became smaller at night when there was a danger of army action. Mass protests outside Moscow were even smaller.

Nor did popular pressure drive Yeltsin to dissolve the Soviet Union. A referendum in March 1991 overwhelmingly approved preservation of the USSR. Most of the opponents of a yes vote focused on the continued use of *Socialist* in the name of the country, arguing that it seemed to preclude major economic reforms. Seventy-six percent of the eligible voters turned out, and even with the issue of the preservation of the Union being confused with that of economic reform, 77 percent voted to maintain the status quo—71 percent in the Russian Republic and 70 percent in Ukraine.

The struggle between Gorbachev and Yeltsin in the last year and a half before the dissolution of the Soviet Union was a struggle within the political elite, not a battle between representatives of the masses. The old elite was profoundly anti-Yeltsin, and a great many high officials in the USSR government begged Gorbachev to take action against him. When he refused to unseat Yeltsin, the August 1991 coup was openly supported by the USSR vice president, premier, Gorbachev's chief of staff, the minister of defense, and the chairman of the KGB, and implicitly by virtually the entire cabinet but was ineffective because its leaders hoped Gorbachev would return.

The decision to break up the Soviet Union was made by the presidents of Russia, Ukraine, and Belorussia meeting secretly in Belorussia, but again it was a revolution from above with little planning or struggle. They were so little prepared they did not have copying machines to make multiple copies of the official documents to sign. Fortunately, they had several fax machines and were able to make copies by sending a fax of a document from one machine in the room to another. When the decision was announced, the military was apparently still willing to support Gorbachev if he asked, but he would not do so. There were no mass meetings to protest the dissolution of the Soviet Union, just as there had been few meetings outside the Baltic republics in favor of dissolution. As a visitor to Moscow in December 1991, I can testify to the eerie quiet in Red Square. On the evening of December 25 the Soviet flag flew atop the main Kremlin building facing Red Square. The next morning the Russian flag had replaced it with little ceremony. No one seemed to notice.

Implications for the Structure of the Book

The events in the Soviet Union from 1985 to 1991 dramatically support two interpretations that are usually considered mutually exclusive: that revolution and democratization are to be understood in terms of the values and actions (or inactions) of the highest officials and other significant participants in the political process, and that democratization and liberalization are consequences of the fundamental social changes produced by industrialization. Because support for both theories is undeniable, they must be complementary and reconcilable, not competing, as is usually assumed.

The nature of such a reconciliation is easy enough to see. On the one hand, recent studies of the transition to democracy have a timeless quality. Scholars such as Guiseppe Di Palma sometimes write as if stable democracy can be introduced anywhere at any time—Brazil, Haiti, Rwanda, Egypt under the Ptolmies—if only elites decide to introduce democracy and craft the transition carefully. This implication must be wrong. And indeed, the factors for change suggested by the theory of modernization provide clues as to when transitions are more or less likely to occur and when they are likely to be successful.

On the other hand, although modernization theory has a very successful record of predictions over the long term, it is much less successful for the near term. Latin America was mostly democratic in the mid-1960s, dictatorial in the mid-1970s, and democratic again in the mid-1980s. It was still democratic in the mid-1990s, but leading scholars were very pessimistic about the political systems' long-term stability. The sociological changes associated with modernization do not, then, have an immediate and linear effect in promoting democratization.

But surely theorists of modernization never made such an assumption. Modernization theorists always said that "transitional society" was politically unstable, and they understood that the transition took a long time. Nearly 200 years elapsed from Cromwell's revolt in England to the introduction of universal suffrage. The time between the French Revolution of 1789 and the establishment of stable democracy in the Fifth Republic after 1958 was nearly identical. Democratization in southern Europe and Latin America may be moving at a similar pace after beginning in the second half of the nineteenth century.

The problem with modernization theory is that it says little about the process by which a democratic political system is introduced or how "the political class" learns to function within democratic institutions. To be comprehensive, an analysis of the transition must explore the factors that make it so difficult for elites to establish stable democracy for such a long period and the factors that finally seem to make stability almost inevitable. This examination must incorporate the questions on process found in the studies on transition. And it must have a perspective of at least a century.

The implications for this book are apparent. First, of course, this is not the time for a sweeping comparison of democratization in Russia with that in the rest of the world. In the past three decades studies of democracy in Latin America have veered from pessimism about the chances for long-term stability to great optimism and back to pessimism, with the current moment always mistaken for the final outcome. The first studies of East European democratization often made too many assumptions about the longevity of early developments. Definitive judgments about a process that takes more than a century simply cannot be constructed from the observations of a few years or even decades. This is all the more true in Russia where the long-term pattern of democratization has been unique.[24]

Second, although a definitive overview of events cannot yet be produced, perestroika and the dissolution of the Soviet Union are far enough in the past to be analyzed seriously. And the outlines of the proper focus are

---

24. Democratization in Russia is likely to be seen as having begun in 1905, and the communist experience will probably be considered part of the process. But if constitutional democracy usually begins with a limited (one might almost say semiconstitutional) dictatorship and laws to protect John Locke's "life, liberty, and property," and features a slow increase in levels of education and rates of popular participation in politics, Russia has reversed this sequence. The communists spurred rapid increases in educational attainment and popular participation, but were atypical in denying the legitimacy of limited government or the protection of property rights.

clear if one accepts the assumptions of the previous two sections. Little space will be given to the popular political activity that was part of the events of the late 1980s and early 1990s. The informal networks, nationalist groups such as Rukh in Ukraine, coal strikes, acts of violence, demonstrations, speeches of Andrei Sakharov, and the like, while significant, were ultimately not determining factors of what happened.[25] In addition, the course of the events suggests that little effort be made to list and rank the "causes" of the revolution. The revolution was not "caused" by the state's poor economic performance, nationalist pressures from the Union republics, popular discontent over lack of freedom or consumer goods, or the very effort to liberalize a dictatorial regime.[26] The obstacles to effective collective action that kept people quiescent in the Brezhnev or Yeltsin eras were obviously formidable enough to prevent Gorbachev's loss of control if he had chosen different policies.

Clearly the key to the outcome is to be found at the top of the political system or "the state." Yet the state had control of the Soviet army, which was the most powerful in the world and had not been weakened in foreign or civil war. The state also had total control of the country's economy and finances and did not have to worry about the collection of taxes. Many observers claimed that economic growth had ceased and consumption was declining in the face of rising military expenditures, but this was simply revolutionary rhetoric, which is still too often accepted uncritically (table 1-1). The bureaucracy still functioned effectively—too effectively, many would have said.

The state was weak not because of objective factors but, as Crane Brinton and Mancur Olson would contend, because of the changing beliefs and assumptions and the loss of confidence of those at the top of the system. The problem was not the weakness of the state as such, but the weakness of the state of mind of those running the state. The Russian Revolution of 1990–91 did have preconditions, and these will be discussed. The social forces made evolution, not revolution, nearly inevitable. The book must concentrate on the intellectual assumptions that led the leadership to take

---

25. For a book that does emphasize popular political activity, see M. Steven Fish, *Democracy from Scratch: Opposition and Regime in the New Russian Revolution* (Princeton University Press, 1995).

26. It is true that revolution is usually preceded by liberalization and that liberalization unleashes forces that promote ever more radical change. But in most instances of liberalization the regime reins in radical change and revolution does not occur.

Table 1-1. *Indicators of Changing Living Standards, Selected Years,*
1970–90

Year	Meat consumption (kilograms per capita)	Urban housing (sq. meters per capita)	Possession of television sets (per family)	Possession of refrigerators (per family)	Production of electricity (kWh per capita)
1970	48	11.3	0.51	0.32	308
1975	57	12.6	0.74	0.61	414
1982	57	13.6	0.91	0.89	504
1990	67	15.3	1.11	1.00	906

Source: *Narodnoe khoziaistvo SSSR v 1975 g., Statisticheskii ezhegodnik* (Moscow: Statistika, 1976), pp. 7, 235, 577, 594, 595. *Narodnoe khoziaistvo SSSR v 1982 g. Statisticheskii ezhegodnik* (Moscow: Finansy i statistika, 1983), pp. 5, 141, 393, 411, 412. *Narodnoe khoziaistvo SSSR v 1990 g. Statisticheskii ezhegodnik* (Moscow: Finansy i statistika, 1991), pp. 67, 140, 141, 143, 189, 395.

the steps it did in reform and that led it to fail to resist the evident disintegration that began in 1990. This will be the focus of the book.

The Intellectual Assumptions of Reform

On the surface, Soviet leaders had relatively easy choices during the first decade of reform. Various communist countries had introduced various economic and political reforms, and the implications of their experience for the Soviet leaders seemed clear-cut. In the economic sphere the Soviet leaders needed to begin the painful process of reducing subsidies and allowing consumer prices to rise to market levels, but the universal lesson of economic reform in Eastern Europe and China was that reforming the service and agricultural sectors was much simpler than instituting industrial reform and always produced benefits for the entire population. That was where economic reform should start.

In the political sphere democracy and constitutionalism had to be introduced simultaneously. It seemed obvious to begin, as had Western and Pacific Rim countries, with proclaiming the principle of limited government, expanding individual freedom, reforming civil and commercial law, and introducing limited democratic institutions. The necessary price increases could be introduced without allowing the population to vote for populist opponents of such increases, and legal reforms could be introduced with a strong government in place to enforce contracts and protect private (or "cooperative") business. Such a policy might require some repression, but there was no reason to believe the Soviet Union would be any more unstable than China as a result.

Thus the Soviet leaders needed to pay attention to the steps East European countries took from the 1950s to the 1970s, not the steps they tried in the late 1980s after many years of transition. China offered an even more obvious model of reform. China was much more comparable to the Soviet Union in its size, lack of a democratic tradition, and the absence of any significant reform before the death of Mao Zedong in 1976. Although observers in the West were to contend that the mere attempt to reform a communist system was certain to lead to its quick collapse, the Chinese economy was growing 10 percent a year with partial but significant reform.[27] By 1985 the Chinese reforms had been under way for seven years and were to continue with great success for the next decade.

The Chinese leaders based their reforms on the postwar Asian model of economic and political development.[28] This model held that a strong state would long be needed for effective economic performance and that it was possible to reduce the economic role of the state and the state sector gradually rather than all at once. The Chinese also adopted other aspects of the Asian economic model, notably its combination of high tariffs and an export strategy that could protect infant industries while forcing them to compete with industries abroad.

The Chinese began economic reform in agriculture and the services, but even there they did so in a controlled manner. Private ownership and the free sale of agricultural land was not permitted, but land was leased to peasants on longer and longer terms, eventually with the right to transfer the lease. The system thus increasingly resembled private ownership, but some controls were retained, as was some ideological respectability. The regime bought a percentage of the peasants' production of important food items at low prices, essentially a form of taxation, and distributed the food to urban populations at low prices through a rationing system. The peasants were free to sell the rest of their produce at market prices. Thus as the city dwellers were guaranteed a minimum ration at a low price, the peasants had

27. See, for example, "Counter-revolution," *Economist*, December 3–9, 1994, pp. 23–27.
28. The Asian model, of course, had much in common with the mercantilism of Europe in the early stages of industrialization, although enormous differences in the levels of technological sophistication made the actual role of the state much different.

an incentive to maximize production and city dwellers to increase their earning power.

The Chinese leaders engaged in little privatization of state enterprises. If entrepreneurs were to enrich themselves, they were to do so by creating new enterprises. The leaders gave special priority to such activity in rural areas and small towns. Thus the basic structure of state industry and its complex incentive systems were retained, but an alternative system of structures and incentives was created for those who chose to work outside the existing system, although even these market arrangements were carefully delimited. Large-scale foreign investment was also encouraged.

In the political realm the Chinese leaders adopted Western and Asian models of democratization, beginning with the uneven, self-imposed limitations on government typical of the early stages of constitutionalism. The use of troops against the demonstrators in Tiananmen Square and the arrest of leading dissidents were typical of actions taken in authoritarian states undergoing liberalization. China is still far from being the liberal state that England was even in the early nineteenth century, but Chinese citizens are much freer in 1996 than they were ten years before. Observers now discuss "the rise of civil society" in contemporary China, a gradual change in the roles and functions of the official mass organizations, the development of independent institutions, and "a broader flowering of associational life."[29] The country even has competitive, if strictly controlled, elections. An earlier generation of scholars would have written about the evolution from a totalitarian to an authoritarian system.

Reforms based on the Chinese model obviously should not have been mechanically introduced in the Soviet Union. Because the Soviet population was more educated, a more liberal political regime would have been appropriate. And because the industrial sector was larger, more thought needed to be given to industrial reform. Yet many features of Chinese reform were directly relevant: emphasis on agricultural reform with distribution of products to the cities through a combination of rationing and market mechanisms, development of rural and small town small industry, price reforms that permit the reform of services, and implementation of an export strategy that encourages foreign companies to invest to produce components using a cheap and skilled labor force.

---

29. Gordon White, *Riding the Tiger: The Politics of Economic Reform in Post-Mao China* (Stanford University Press, 1993), pp. 217–19, 227.

There seems to have been a chance that the Soviet Union would adopt elements of the Chinese reforms. When Nikolai Ryzhkov became head of the Economics Department of the Central Committee under General Secretary Yury Andropov in 1982, they met once a week for a two- to three-hour talk. Ryzhkov became convinced that Andropov, had he lived for five more years, would have introduced something "close to the Chinese variant, with, of course, Russian specifics—a model in which the fundamental problems are under government control and the entire market system spins around [the government sector]."[30] As chairman of the Council of Ministers under Gorbachev, Ryzhkov thought in similar terms.

For reasons that are still obscure, Gorbachev apparently never seriously considered the Chinese model of reform, and the public (and apparently the private) debates on appropriate reforms were not couched in terms of "China" or "Poland." Gorbachev's chief adviser, Aleksandr Yakovlev, confessed in 1988 that he knew little about the Chinese reforms, and Gorbachev brushed aside those economists who did. But just as Leonid Brezhnev would not let his premier, Aleksei Kosygin, carry out his reform, Gorbachev followed the same course with Ryzhkov.

The Soviet program of economic and political reform was based on assumptions that were almost the polar opposites of Chinese assumptions. Although Gorbachev's and Yeltsin's policies are often described as sharply different, memoirs by government leaders indicate that Gorbachev and his closest advisers held most of the fundamental assumptions of what was to become Yeltsin's shock therapy. Intentionally or unintentionally, they began to introduce these reforms in 1988.[31]

That the Soviet and Chinese leaders chose such different ways to reform similar communist systems inevitably meant that the theoretical policy implications of the respective outcomes are of considerable interest and discussion. This debate is of even greater importance because the Soviet

---

30. Nikolai I. Ryzhkov, *Ia iz partii po imeni "Rossiia"* (Moscow: Obozrevatel', 1995), pp. 314–15.

31. In one interview Ryzhkov asserted that in the summer of 1987 Gorbachev wanted to smash everything at once and follow a revolutionary path, and that he began proposing the program Yegor Gaidar introduced in 1992. In another interview Ryzhkov said that "Gorbachev casts about from one side to the other and betrays everyone on the right and the left." This seems to have been Ryzhkov's most considered judgment. The shock therapy may have been the logical consequence of Gorbachev's policies in 1987, but it is unlikely he had such a vision at the time. Ryzhkov, *Ia iz partii po imeni "Rossiia,"* pp. 290–91, 316.

and Chinese reforms implicitly reflect differences in assumptions in one of the most important debates in American social studies—that on the relation of individual rationality, institutional structure, and the common good.

The Chinese economic reforms were based on the assumption, advanced by the Nobel laureate economist Douglass North, that institutions have a crucial impact on economic behavior and are a critical precondition for economic performance. By *institutions* North means not organizations but "the rules of the game in a society or, more formally . . . any form of constraint that human beings devise to shape human interaction." They are the "legal rules, organizational forms, enforcement, and norms of behavior." He does not use the phrase "legally established system of incentives," but this is what he has in mind.[32]

The communist economic and political system provided incentives that gave the individual full opportunity to move up the social and career ladders, but made access dependent on joining the Communist party and avoiding political dissidence. The institutions of the party became the main administrative structures of the country, and the desire to retain party membership became the major incentive to observe administrative discipline.

While they introduced reform, the Chinese kept this structure and its incentive system in place but supplemented it with a second system based on market incentives. They assumed, as had Mancur Olson in *The Logic of Collective Action,* that individuals often do not perceive enough self-interest to defend the interests of their group (or bureaucracy) and that appropriate incentives for individual bureaucrats would undermine their resistance to reform. They believed that bureaucrats and party officials who remained within the system would continue to be motivated to produce, and that others would want to enrich themselves in the private sector (and through corruption) so that the bureaucracy and party apparatus would not effectively resist economic reform.

By contrast, Gorbachev and his advisers seemed convinced that "the center"—the ministries, the apparatus, the bureaucracy—was implacably opposed to economic reform and that it would subvert and destroy any attempt at evolutionary reform. They coupled this assumption with the belief that reducing or destroying the power of the ministries would automatically "activate the human factor," permit the directors of various enter-

---

32. Douglass C. North, *Institutions, Institutional Change and Economic Performance* (Cambridge University Press, 1990), pp. 3, 33, 47.

prises to produce what the consumer wanted or, in the case of Yeltsin's advisers, create the conditions for a rebirth of Russia. They talked about crossing the chasm between socialism and capitalism in a single jump as if market institutions already existed on the other side. The rhetoric of those working to overthrow the old system contained a large dose of opportunistic populism, but memoirs show that many who spouted the rhetoric believed it themselves.

Russian economic reform was based on assumptions akin to those expressed in Mancur Olson's *Rise and Decline of Nations*, in some cases with explicit citations by Russian reformers and their American advisers.[33] This book assumed that the old institutions inevitably became rigid because they were subject to capture by small, powerful interest groups. They had to be deliberately destroyed to overcome their resistance to reform and provide a fresh soil in which new institutions and organizations (in Douglass North's use of the terms) could grow to provide the investment suggested by the new opportunities.

In the political sphere Gorbachev and his advisers believed that democratization would facilitate the destruction of old institutions, give legitimacy to radical economic reform, and preclude populists from organizing resistance to the retail price increases needed to achieve financial stability. Gorbachev introduced fully competitive elections into a deeply divided multiethnic state and allowed the most extreme examples of free speech to be broadcast by national television. He did not even couple elections with an insistence on the territorial integrity of the country, backed up by force if necessary, as had been done by Abraham Lincoln and a succession of democratic leaders in India. He was as heedless of constitutional restraints on his own behavior as Yeltsin was to be and was therefore oblivious to the necessity for developing in Soviet citizens respect for a constitution and laws.

Gorbachev was mistaken in fearing collective resistance to reform on the part of the bureaucracy and the party apparatus. The Chinese had a better conception of the relation of the individual and collective interests of the

---

33. Mancur Olson, *The Rise and Decline of Nations: Economic Growth, Stagflation, and Social Rigidities* (Yale University Press, 1982). For the argument in favor of Olson's ideas see Yegor Gaidar, *Ekonomicheskie reformy i ierarkhicheskie struktury* (Moscow: Nauka, 1990). Olson himself has been involved in consulting and conducting joint research with Gaidar. His advice follows solely from this book and supports shock therapy on the ground that destruction of old institutions is more productive than any effort to transform them.

bureaucrats. Gorbachev was also mistaken in believing that an economy and polity can continue to function acceptably if its basic rules, institutions, and incentive systems have been destroyed and and have not simultaneously been replaced by others. In such a situation the pursuit of individual self-interest produces chaos and anarchy. He did not understand that establishing and maintaining, by force if need be, such rules and incentive systems is the function of government.

The great debate of the future will concern the long-term implications of the very different decisions made by the Chinese and the Russians. Chinese economic reform has produced 10 percent annual growth for fifteen years, while on the surface, Russian reform has produced a disaster even greater than collectivization. The scale of the deterioration in living standards is highly controvertible, for supporters of the reform deny the accuracy of the official statistics that show GDP and living standards dropping some 50 percent. However, no one denies that consumption was maintained by a major cut in investment (some put the decrease at as much as 80 percent), and a careful calculation of the implications in the figures on age-specific mortality, which no one denies, shows that 2 million more people died in Russia alone than would have if the already extremely high rates of 1990 had been retained.[34] And so the grim statistics mount. Some observers believe conditions have been created for a market economy to flower; others think the situation will not improve until the state takes a much greater role in investment and regulation.

This is not a difference of opinion that will be resolved very soon, but it does involve what are likely to be crucial issues for the twenty-first century. Whatever happens in Russia, the problems that the U.S. government has faced in dealing with internal developments there are scarcely limited to Russia. The dilemmas that Mikhail Gorbachev faced in the 1980s and did not handle well will be those that leaders face around the world as they try to introduce constitutional democracy and market reforms. At least we can clarify the assumptions with which the Soviet leaders began so that we can know which assumptions are really being tested by events.

---

34. For the sources and calculations on death rates, see Jerry F. Hough, Evelyn Davidheiser, and Susan Goodrich Lehmann, *The 1996 Russian Presidential Election* (Brookings, 1996).

CHAPTER TWO

Prelude to Revolution

REVOLUTIONS ARE NOTORIOUSLY difficult to predict. Countless rulers and regimes have richly deserved to be overthrown but have remained in power for decades. Yet often when revolutions have occurred, they have not been anticipated even a few years before. In 1763 no one in the American colonies had even thought of independence. Russia had a revolution in 1905 and was performing poorly in World War I, but in January 1917 Lenin despaired of seeing a revolution there in his lifetime.

So it was in the Soviet Union in the 1980s. During Leonid Brezhnev's last years everyone could see the stagnation (*zastoi*) in the Soviet Union, to use Mikhail Gorbachev's term. It was easy to predict there would be an attempt to reinvigorate the system after Brezhnev's death. Although the communist countries had long been recognized as exceptions to the strong statistical relationship between social and economic development and democratization, those who accepted the tenets of modernization theory foresaw major liberalization when a new generation came to power. Any scholar who had studied the provincial party secretaries knew they hated the ministries and Gosplan; they would support a leader who attacked the power of these Moscow institutions. Anyone in contact with Moscow intellectuals knew the great majority wanted Western democracy, although almost always Western social democracy on the Swedish model.

But who would have forecast that Russia would lead the way in breaking up what conservatives all called the Russian Empire? Who would have foreseen that the Soviet army would permit the abandonment of Ukraine, the Transcaucasus, and Central Asia without a struggle, as well as the destruction of Soviet heavy and defense industries? Liberal and conservative alike would confidently have predicted a military and KGB coup d'état against any leader who was accepting the disintegration of the Soviet Union, but only a madman would have said these institutions would attempt such a coup without arrests or force.

Nevertheless, no great revolution occurs without a social base, and the Russian Revolution of 1990–91 was no different. Mass support for the 1917 Bolshevik Revolution and the communist regime was provided by those in transition to the city, those whom I call urban peasants. These were peasants already in contact with the city, often through part-time work, urban dwellers born in the countryside, and urban dwellers born to peasants who had moved to the city.

Since then, however, the Communist party had transformed the society in which it came to power. To an ever increasing degree, it destroyed the society's old social base. In 1926 only 12 percent of the Soviet people lived in cities with populations of more than 20,000 and only 7 percent in cities with populations of more than 100,000. In 1979 about 50 percent lived in cities of more than 20,000 people and 37 percent in cities of more than 100,000.[1] The population of the Russian Empire was little more than half literate in 1917, but Stalin saw mass technical education as the key to industrialization. A half century later under Brezhnev, expansion of the education system was given even greater priority than industrial growth. By 1980 more than three-quarters of those aged 20 to 29 had a high school diploma or better.

The social base of the 1990–91 revolution was, first of all, the large numbers of urbanized, well-educated, skilled workers and white-collar personnel who had been created by the Communist regime. To a large extent, theirs was a revolt to achieve more personal freedom: the right to travel freely abroad, to have access to Western culture, to enjoy a wider choice among consumer goods. To the extent that it was an economic revolution, it was inspired by the hope for a market economy and private property that did not exist, not a traditional revolution supported mostly by those anxious about the effects of a market that was already being introduced.

In the decade after 1985 there were to be two great economic victors. First, there were those in their twenties and thirties who were able to adjust to the new world of finance and business and make fortunes or at least high

1. *Narodnoe khoziastvo SSSR v 1989 g.* (Moscow: Finansy i statistiki, 1990), pp. 17, 25.

salaries within those worlds. Second, there were those in their forties and fifties in the old managerial elite—the *nomenklatura*—who were able to privatize state property and use their position either to export raw materials or obtain bribes by authorizing such exports (or imports).

From the beginning, Western observers recognized the support for the revolution by the first group, but the second was always treated as the major opponent of the revolution. In fact, however, as soon as the bureaucrats and the nomenklatura became confident that economic reform was possible, they understood how they could benefit and they supported it. A nationwide survey in Russia in December 1993 showed that administrative personnel as a whole had become the most enthusiastic proponents of radical reform and privatization, with top administrators more enthusiastic than younger and more junior ones (tables 2-1 and 2-2). Instead of fighting to preserve the system, the bureaucrats were willing to stand aside and let it collapse—indeed, to push reforms that would benefit themselves at the expense of the institutions for which they worked.[2]

The old assumptions about Soviet bureaucrats—really the Soviet middle class, because almost all of those with higher education worked in the state bureaucracy—have become part of the historical conventional wisdom. Even one of the most sophisticated students of the logic of Chinese reform dismisses the possibility that the Russians might have adopted the Chinese model because of the strength and presumed opposition to reform of the Russian bureaucracy.[3] If one is to understand both the Russian Revolution of 1990–91 and its theoretical implications, one must look at assumptions about its social bases with fresh eyes.

The Social Base of the Communist Revolution

In 1960 W. W. Rostow wrote that communism in this century was a "disease of the transition" from a rural to an urban society.[4] Only when the communist political and economic system is seen in these terms does one understand why it was durable for so long and then became increasingly

2. Joel Scott Hellman, ''Breaking the Bank: Bureaucrats and the Creation of Markets in a Transitional Economy,'' PhD dissertation, Columbia University, 1993.
3. Susan L. Shirk, *The Political Logic of Economic Reform in China* (University of California Press, 1993), pp. 11–14.
4. W. W. Rostow, *The Stages of Economic Growth: A Non-Communist Manifesto* (Cambridge University Press, 1960), pp. 162–64.

Table 2-1. *Attitudes toward Economic Reform, Survey Respondents Aged 18 to 59, by Level of Employment, December 1993*

Percent

Attitude	Profes- sionals	White collar	Workers	All managers	Higher- level managers	Medium- level managers	Lower- level managers
Favor quick transition	19	12	12	20	24	19	17
Favor gradual transition	56	53	40	55	57	59	55
Against market economy	12	14	20	13	9	11	13
Don't know	12	22	28	12	10	10	15

Sources: 1993 election survey conducted by Jerry F. Hough, Timothy Colton, and Susan Lehmann. For details of the survey see Jerry F. Hough, Evelyn Davidheiser, and Susan Goodrich Lehmann, *The 1996 Russian Presidential Election* (Brookings, 1996). Figures on the general occupations are from the weighted national sample. Those on different levels of managers are from the 34,000-respondent sample from the oblasts.

fragile with the rise of a new educated middle class. The communist system was a response to the psychological and economic problems of urban peasants, and the economic system established after the late 1920s provided many types of security for these people.

Successful communist revolutions did not occur in advanced industrial countries, as Karl Marx had predicted, but in countries at early stages of industrialization. This should not be surprising. Marx wrote *The Communist Manifesto* in 1848 when western Europe was at an early stage of industrialization, and he had an excellent sense of the grievances and psychology of workers at that time. Small wonder his analysis and his emotional appeals were attractive to others as they too reached the level of industrial development achieved by Europe in the middle of the nineteenth century. Russia's economy lagged a half century behind that of western Europe, and in the early twentieth century the Communist party in Russia represented a "working class" like that of western Europe at the time of *The Communist Manifesto*. The difference in outcome is largely explained by the fact that the armies of western Europe remained intact during the Revolution of 1848, whereas the Russian army was destroyed by World War I.

The nature of the early support for the communists was made clear in elections of deputies to local soviets in the summer of 1917 after the overthrow of the tsar and then of delegates to the Constituent Assembly in December 1917. In the large cities public opinion became polarized along

Table 2-2. *Attitudes toward Privatization of State Property, Survey Respondents Aged 18 to 59, by Level of Employment, December 1993*
Percent

Attitude	Profes- sionals	White collar	Workers	All managers	Higher- level managers	Medium- level managers	Lower- level managers
Accelerate tempo	24	15	15	25	31	25	21
Keep same tempo	24	23	17	21	26	25	24
Slow tempo	8	6	7	16	12	13	11
Stop privatization	9	13	15	9	10	12	14
Reverse privatization	7	9	10	8	8	7	7
Don't know	28	33	36	21	14	18	24

Source: See table 2-1.

class lines. Businessmen, professionals, and white-collar personnel supported the right; the workers (at least in Russia) swung behind the Bolsheviks. This gradually gave the Bolsheviks majority status in the large cities during the summer and fall of 1917.

Russia was, however, largely a peasant country. In the election to the Constituent Assembly, the Bolsheviks won 25 percent of the vote, while the peasant party, the Socialist Revolutionaries, received majority support.[5] Yet the peasant voting in the Constituent Assembly election was also split, and the nature of the split illuminated the Russian political landscape like a lightning bolt.

European Russia had two kinds of land: fertile black-earth land in southern Russia and non-black-earth land to the north. The black-earth areas were better able to absorb the population increase produced by improved medical care in the second half of the nineteenth century, at least with the help of considerable out-migration to Siberia and the new industries of the Donbass. These southern and eastern areas with "pure" peasant populations voted overwhelmingly for the Socialist Revolutionaries. In the non-black-earth areas the land simply could not provide enough food for the growing population. The men of the villages spent months of the year working in the city, often thousands of miles from home. These temporary migrants were so numerous they came to be given a special name: the

5. Jerry Hough and Merle Fainsod, *How the Soviet Union Is Governed* (Harvard University Press, 1979), pp. 71–72.

otkhodniki (those who left).[6] In the election to the Constituent Assembly, the rural areas in which *otkhodnichestvo* was a way of life did not vote like the peasants of the south but like their fellow workers in the city (table 2-3). In short, the half worker–half peasant of the northern Russian countryside voted in a way similar to the half worker–half peasant worker in the city.

It is not certain why Lenin's message appealed to these urban peasants: he was in exile before 1917, radio and television did not exist, and the Bolshevik party was illegal. We do not know which of his messages were heard inside Russia, which were most appealing, which statements were dismissed as campaign oratory, and which were taken as code for goals that could not be openly acknowledged.

Basically, however, the communist doctrine offered security and dignity to frightened people halfway between village and city, people no longer protected in communal society but exposed to the unpredictabilities of the market. It reassured those who were basically peasants in their values and thinking that they were not backward peasants but something special—the proletariat, the driving force of history. All economic value, the communists assured them, was produced by their labor, none by capital or the parasitical upper classes. The workers would introduce real paradise on earth: there would be so much production, it was said, that each could receive according to his needs, while at the same time the old sense of community of the peasant village would return.

In *State and Revolution* Lenin envisioned an economy without permanent divisions of labor: cooks could hold administrative posts, administrators could be cooks. In fact the Soviet leader deeply believed in the importance of specialized knowledge and administrative hierarchies.[7] But the movement of cooks into administrative posts occurred in another way: large numbers of people of lowly origins and even those who held lowly jobs as adults were promoted into low-level political positions and command positions in the Red Army during the civil war.

In the 1920s Leon Trotsky turned Marxist theory against the Soviet Union and insisted that the managers of the means of production—the bureaucrats—had seized power as had owners under capitalism and were

6. Sheila Fitzpatrick, *Stalin's Peasants: Resistance and Survival in the Russian Village after Collectivization* (Oxford University Press, 1994), pp. 21–23.

7. For a detailed and sophisticated discussion of this point, see Walter D. Connor, *Socialism, Politics, and Equality: Hierarchy and Change in Eastern Europe and the USSR* (Columbia University Press, 1979), chap. 8.

Table 2-3. *Distribution of Votes for Bolshevik Candidates for the Constituent Assembly, by Region, December 1917*

Region	Bolshevik vote	Total vote	Percent Bolshevik
Central and western			
Kostroma	223,353	550,990	40.5
Minsk	579,087	917,246	63.1
Moscow City	366,148	764,763	47.9
Moscow Province	337,492	597,374	56.5
Novgorod	203,658	486,418	41.9
Petrograd City	424,027	942,333	45.0
Petrograd Province	229,698	462,618	49.7
Pskov	139,690	441,117	31.7
Smolensk	361,062	658,234	54.9
Tula	219,297	477,585	45.9
Tver	362,687	606,437	59.8
Vitebsk	287,101	560,538	51.2
Vladimir	337,941	603,960	56.0
Yaroslavl	131,124	439,934	29.8
Black-earth, Kuban			
Don	205,497	1,406,620	14.6
Kursk	119,127	1,058,356	11.3
Orel	144,492	480,136	30.1[a]
Penza	54,731	636,247	8.6
Stavropol	17,430	327,916	5.3
Tambov	240,652	1,173,191	20.5
Taurida	15,642	524,750	3.0
Voronezh	151,517	1,097,977	13.8

Source: Oliver H. Radkey, *Russia Goes to the Polls: The Election to the Russian Constituent Assembly of 1917* (Cornell University Press, 1989), pp. 34, 78–79.

a. The northern part of the Orel Region is in the non–black-earth area; the southern part has better land.

exercising it to further their own interests. The political leader was just a representative of the ruling class: "The success which fell upon him was a surprise at first to Stalin himself. It was the friendly welcome of the new ruling group, trying to free itself from the old principles and from the control of the masses, and having need of a reliable arbiter in its inner affairs."[8] This was not only a misreading of the power relation between Joseph Stalin and the bureaucrats but of the realities of the social structure. The new bureaucrats were, in fact, the workers and low-level activists who constituted the Communist party during the 1917 revolution and civil war.

8. Leon Trotsky, *The Revolution Betrayed* (New York: Pathfinder Press, 1970), p. 93.

In that sense, in the 1920s the bureaucracy embodied the dictatorship of the proletariat.

In non-Marxist language Lenin's policy emphasized upward social mobility, but Lenin himself was suspicious of the newcomers to the cities and the peasant values they brought. By contrast, Stalin had no suspicion of the urban peasant. He accepted peasants and newcomers to the city into the party in great numbers as soon as Lenin died.[9] As he launched his industrialization program, Stalin rapidly expanded the system of higher education but virtually excluded children of white-collar parents unless they had earned proletarian status themselves.[10] Many of those admitted into college were workers and children of former workers in their mid-twenties who had already moved into low political work. It was precisely these *vydvizhentsy* (promoted ones) of the years of the First Five-Year Plan who were the major beneficiaries of the purge of 1936–39.[11]

The new managers began acting like bosses toward the workers, but the managers no doubt saw themselves as the real workers now running society and viewed the new workers streaming into the factories from the countryside as peasants in workers' clothes. Leonid Brezhnev, the son of a steelworker, was a typical beneficiary of the policy. Boris Yeltsin's father, a peasant's son who became an urban construction worker in his early twenties after the collectivization of his father's farm, was also typical of his generation of workers. The worker-managers received higher salaries and greater access to rationed goods and privileges than the new workers did and surely thought this was proper.[12] The new workers looked not so much for a workers' democracy but for the opportunity to become skilled workers and technicians and for their children to go to college and move into the managerial class.

9. T. H. Rigby, *Communist Party Membership in the USSR, 1917–1967* (Princeton University Press, 1968), pp. 120–31.

10. For example, Vyacheslav Malyshev, his top defense industry administrator after the war, was the son of a teacher but had a worker's job in industry for a year and was admitted into college on this basis. V. Chalmaev, *Malyshev* (Moscow: Molodaia gvardiia, 1978), pp. 14–17. After the purge, Andrei Zhdanov expressed Stalin's policy with the phrase, "the children are not judged by their parents."

11. See the discussion in Sheila Fitzpatrick, *Education and Social Mobility in the Soviet Union, 1921–1934* (Cambridge University Press, 1979), pp. 242–49.

12. For an excellent discussion of their values, see Vera Dunham, *In Stalin's Time: Middle Class Values in Soviet Fiction* (Duke University Press, 1990).

Communism, Job Creation, and Economic Security

Marx and Lenin said, and no doubt believed, that socialism and planning would be more productive than capitalism, but they were not disinterested economists. Instead of making abstract arguments about unequal distribution of income, they passionately denounced wealth and exploitation. They were moralists, deeply offended by the society in which they lived and eager to overthrow it through violent revolution. They talked primarily about class exploitation, about injustice and immorality, and in discussing industrial society they focused on exploitation of downtrodden industrial workers.

In *The Communist Manifesto* Marx was, in fact, writing about western Europe at a relatively early stage of industrial development and about a growing working class streaming into the city from the countryside. Those like himself and Charles Dickens who emphasized the difficulties in workers' lives at this time were no doubt right, but one needs to be careful not to fall into a trap of seeing the political actions of workers at this stage of economic development as a struggle of the bottom of society against the top.

Any serious student of social structure would name the peasantry as the lowest social stratum in industrializing countries. Even the mass of the farmers in a country such as the United States occupied a lower place on the social ladder than most urban dwellers did, including skilled industrial workers.[13] When those in agriculture are peasants rather than farmers, there is no doubt about their status. Scholars also recognize that the rural population, most of it composed of peasants, constitutes the overwhelming majority of the people in preindustrial society.

Taken together, these two observations have profound political implications that are seldom considered. First, if 80 percent of the people in a rural society are peasants and if skilled workers have higher status than peasants, then skilled workers occupy a high place on the social ladder of such societies. Because skilled workers also rank higher than unskilled labor in the cities, they must rank in the top 10 to 15 percent of the

---

13. Peter M. Blau and Otis Dudley Duncan, *The American Occupational Structure* (Wiley, 1967), pp. 122–23. The situation in the United States was complicated by the fact that so many industrial workers in the nineteenth and early twentieth centuries were immigrants. The discrepancy in status between occupation and ethnic origin was one of the sources of periodic political turmoil associated with nativism.

population in social status. If the upper class or upper stratum were defined in reasonable percentile terms—the top 20 percent of the population—the workers in such a society would be in that stratum. A proletarian revolution in a country such as Russia in 1917 is, therefore, a conflict within the upper stratum, not an uprising of the downtrodden at the bottom.

The problem with the new workers is that they were among the intelligent and certainly the most ambitious of peasant youth. They wanted to get ahead and ranked relatively high in the social hierarchy. Yet as Leonid Brezhnev bitterly remembered sixty years later, the men at the steel plant where his father worked were treated as if they were no better than peasants.

> Our family lived in the workers' settlement called the "Lower Colony.". . . To the southwest of the village, in the "Upper Colony," there was a totally different world. . . . Entry by the workers to the "Upper Colony" was strictly forbidden. . . . Cabs on pneumatic tires would roll up and important men and ladies get out of them. It was as if they were another breed of people—well-fed, well-groomed, and arrogant. An engineer dressed in a formal peak cap and coat with velvet collar would never shake hands with a worker, and the worker approaching an engineer or foreman was obliged to take off his hat. We workers' children could only look at "the clean public" strolling to the sounds of a string orchestra from behind the railings of the town park.[14]

When people of relatively high social status are treated in this manner, the resentment can be explosive.

Second, one of the most dangerous political groups in any political system consists of the ambitious, the intelligent, and the talented who are seeking to improve their economic and social positions but who believe their efforts are being blocked. Persons at the bottom of society who are not seeking to improve their positions do not have the motivation for sustained political action or, often, the capability to organize. But those who are upwardly mobile have both. Urban and semiurban peasants make a better base for revolutionary action than do rural peasants because urban dwellers are striving for upward mobility. The desire to rise in the economic hierarchy is also a crucial reason why the mass participants in revolutions are overwhelmingly young men between fifteen and twenty-two years old.[15]

In modern times many of the most explosive political situations have been created when one group, usually an ethnic or linguistic minority, has

---

14. Leonid Ilyich Brezhnev, *Memoirs* (Pergamon Press, 1982), p. 6.

15. For the implications of the dominant role of young men in revolutions, see Jerry F. Hough, "The Logic of Collective Action and the Pattern of Revolutionary Behavior," *Journal of Soviet Nationalities*, vol. 1 (Summer 1990), pp. 34–65.

found its upward mobility blocked and when the educational level of the group has become high enough to allow or encourage it to take action. This factor was a main element in the struggle of the French in Quebec against the English domination of Montreal, Catholics against Protestants in Northern Ireland, Moslems against Christians in Lebanon, and African Americans against a repressive and stagnant social system in the United States in the 1960s.[16]

But if by contrast a regime in an industrializing country tailors its appeals for mass support to those moving from the countryside into the city and especially into skilled industrial jobs, it is by definition seeking support among a very large group indeed. There is an enormous population of these migrating peasants from among whom upward mobility can take place, but a relatively small pool of workers who can move into higher positions. Those who are upwardly mobile normally support the regime they associate with this mobility, at least if it also provides the kinds of psychological and ideological satisfaction that one associates with the word *legitimacy.*

Social mobility need not mean rising from lowly origins into top professional and managerial jobs—the proverbial progress from log cabin to White House. People generally are satisfied with more modest movement. For the rank-and-file peasantry, getting a semiskilled job represents a long-term goal. The semiskilled worker dreams of a skilled position, the blue-collar worker a white-collar job, and so forth. This kind of limited movement is important to people as they ask themselves whether their status is higher than their fathers'.[17]

This acceptance of limited movement is one reason the Soviet system was so stable for so long. The peasants of 1917 did not have to become party secretaries or ministers to be satisfied with their opportunities for upward mobility. They did not need the cataclysmic mobility produced by the Great Purge of 1936–39. A two- or three-generation progress from peasant to skilled worker to technician or engineer and from there to a middle-management post was enough to satisfy tens of millions of peasants or their children. Some of their number did become factory managers, enter

16. The Palestinians on the West Bank and in the Gaza Strip are especially interesting. As long as they could migrate to the Gulf countries to find high-paid work, the area was quiescent. But when oil prices dropped and job growth on the Gulf dried up, the young men could not leave and the Intifada developed.

17. In the past a woman tended to compare the status of her husband with that of her father. Now a woman can have two reference points, her mother and her father, and the definition of upward mobility can become complicated.

the Politburo, and so forth, of course, which reinforced their sense that the path upward was open if only they and their children took advantage of opportunities.

Stalin's emphasis on heavy and defense industries was accompanied by incentives to ensure that the most ambitious and talented young people worked in them. The largest scholarships were given to students in engineering institutes preparing for heavy industry. Its workers, engineers, and managers received the highest wages and, because heavy industry received priority in the delivery of supplies, the highest bonuses for plan fulfillment. Investment in housing and other social amenities was disproportionately directed through heavy industry ministries and distributed to their employees.

Stalin's policy succeeded. Industry and defense employees were selected for high political and government positions. Leonid Brezhnev, Andrei Kirilenko, Dmitry Ustinov, and Nikolai Tikhonov were just such engineers and managers who reached the top of the political system. Thousands and thousands of their peers dominated the upper and middle levels of the political elite, including such future leaders as Boris Yeltsin, Nikolai Ryzhkov, Viktor Chernomyrdin, and Leonid Kuchma, the president of Ukraine.[18]

The Soviet socialist system also created a large number of workers' jobs with its rapid industrialization program, and at the same time protected the newcomers to the cities from the frightening unemployment, great disparities of income, and degrading conditions of the shanty towns typical of third world cities. Because the state paid wages, it could and did control the extremes of income found in a market economy. But in the first decades of the system, income was not as important as the provision of goods; and workers, at least workers in heavy industry, were assured access to the goods. After World War II, as money became more important, the differences between the incomes of workers and white-collar employees consistently narrowed.[19]

Many inside and outside the Soviet Union talked about bureaucratic privilege, but both in absolute terms and relative to others in their society, Soviet officials were far less privileged than their Western counterparts whom we call managers, businessmen, civil servants, or simply the middle

18. Kuchma was director of the factory that produced the SS-18 rocket.
19. Abram Bergson, *Planning and Performance in Socialist Economies: The USSR and Eastern Europe* (Boston: Unwin Hyman, 1989), p. 85.

class (such neutral terms were never used in Soviet political discourse). The income and nonmonetary privileges of a minister of the automobile industry did not remotely compare with those of a president of Chrysler or General Motors or even a midlevel manager in an American automobile factory. The introduction of the market economy in the 1990s would, however, greatly increase disparities in income distribution and relative privilege among Soviet citizens.

But even income statistics underestimate the extent of egalitarianism in the Soviet socialist system. The greatest income inequality in the noncommunist world is associated with ownership of property, toward which communists were always particularly hostile. Karl Marx insisted that ownership of the means of production was the root of all evil, and the *Communist Manifesto* made the abolition of private property the first element in the communists' program. Lenin's views were similar.

The Communist leadership often emphasized privileges and other nonmonetary payments over monetary ones. Western studies have focused on the inequities of this policy—preference on housing lists, access to closed stores, and the like—but in comparison with other countries, the egalitarian aspects were more important, at least in the cities.[20] The Soviet regime tried to move toward the Marxist ideal of "each according to his needs" by providing basic needs free or at steeply subsidized prices. Medical care and education, including higher education, was essentially free. Free medical care and higher education means very little without doctors and colleges, and the communist model involved a massive expansion of the medical and educational systems.

Other basic goods were provided at subsidized prices virtually anyone could afford. In the 1920s and 1930s food scarcities were handled by rationing most basic foodstuffs, with industrial workers given preference. Housing became extremely crowded, but rent became nominal. Cultural events and mass transportation were deeply subsidized. Bread in state stores was inexpensive. As per capita consumption of meat rose toward West European levels in the 1960s and 1970s, its price was not raised to reflect costs and, as shall be discussed in chapter 4, it came to be sold to consumers for less than one-third the amount the peasants were paid to produce it.

20. The classic journalistic description of this inequality is in Hedrick Smith, *The Russians* (Quadrangle, 1976).

After 1928 protection from unemployment was built into the planning system. In *State and Revolution* Lenin emphasized that the state should be preserved under socialism, using the analogies of the giant factory or the post office to illustrate his centralized vision of socialism. This was precisely what happened: plant managers did not have a sum of money with which to hire labor or buy supplies in the mixtures and at the places they desired. Instead, they were permitted a set number of lines or slots for employees, with basic salaries specified, and supplies were allocated directly from specified suppliers. The goods the plants produced were specified in their plan and allocated to specific enterprises or wholesale firms. Managers were judged by their fulfillment of their plan, not by total output or profit.

Once the decisions on number of employees, amount of supplies, and level of production were made, the enterprises and ministries were automatically allocated the money necessary to cover their expenses. That is, labor and supplies were essentially free to a manager if they were incorporated in the plan. The economic implications were that managers often cut corners on quality and avoided producing drastically new goods or using unfamiliar production processes. There were, of course, countervailing pressures, and the quality and sophistication of goods did gradually improve. Nevertheless, even in such a high-priority realm as weapons development, Soviet technological upgrading had an incremental character.[21]

The budgetary process was similar to that of bureaucracies around the world. Lower-level officials presented their requests for the following year, and higher officials decided which to approve. The logic of the budgetary system was clear: those in subordinate positions asked for more than they could ever hope to get, and those at higher levels pared down the requests.[22] The more raw materials and workers a director could get included in his plan for a given level of production, the looser the plan and the better his position. Managers were judged by whether they fulfilled their plan, not by their total output or profit.

---

21. Arthur J. Alexander, *Decision-Making in Soviet Weapons Procurement*, Adelphi Paper 147/8 (1978), pp. 24–26, 41–42. Also see the discussion in Jerry F. Hough, "The Historical Legacy in Soviet Weapons Development," in Jiri Valenta and William C. Potter, eds., *Soviet Decisionmaking for National Security* (London: Allen & Unwin, 1984), pp. 100–09.
22. The classic study of this appropriations process is Aaron B. Wildavsky, *The Politics of the Budgetary Process* (Little, Brown, 1964).

For this reason, demand for supplies and labor was essentially infinite. Because workers were cost free, managers had little incentive to fire inefficient ones and every incentive to demand more during budget planning. They had no reason to economize on labor; any request for fewer workers would become the base for the following year's plan, and the production goal would be correspondingly more difficult to fulfill. The system thus resulted in a perpetual labor shortage.

Least of all did Soviet plants have an incentive to demand labor-saving or energy-saving equipment from their suppliers. If, for example, plants received more efficient machinery, they would not make higher profits but would instead receive a smaller allocation of petroleum or workers for the following year. And, of course, the producer plants had no market incentive to manufacture complex new machinery. Fulfilling such a plan would depend on the successful production of new items with difficult start-up problems, but they would receive rewards no greater than those of plants producing the old items.

This system created problems as labor became well educated, the economy more complex, and economizing on skilled labor more desirable. In the early stages of industrialization, however, an incentive system that encouraged managers to hoard labor and train it (and that was coupled with a comprehensive system of night-school adult technical education at the plant) solved many social problems frequently found in the third world. Politically it generated strong support among the newcomers to the city who not only had job security, but also the opportunity for them and their children to receive more education and rise into managerial jobs.

Communism and Psychological Security

The promise of security was not limited to the economic sphere. Modern Americans like to think that everyone at all times and in all places wants democracy as we would define it and that dictatorship is universally unpopular. However, countries often confront severe difficulties in achieving full-scale stable democracy until they reach a high level of consumption. In the meantime, a dictatorship may prove attractive to many people and derive considerable popular support from very diverse societal groups. Such was the case in the Soviet Union for half a century.

First, to the extent government promotion of industry is associated with urban subsidies and undermines traditional rural values, peasants have a strong self-interest to vote against the policy and rural elite have a stronger interest to mobilize them to vote. Conversely, industrializing forces, including workers, often have strong reasons not to cede control of the political process to peasants, which is what would happen with a system based on majority rule. It is not a coincidence that west European countries did not generally adopt universal suffrage in the nineteenth century until society had become 50 percent urban and the Soviet Union remained a predominantly rural country for most of the Stalin period.

Second, democracy involves political uncertainty, tolerance of unpopular ideas, constant criticism of leaders and society, exposure to confusing interpretations of events and policy, and politicians seeking personal and partisan gain rather than the common good. Even in the United States these features of the democratic process lead to wide dissatisfaction. In countries with less educated populations, political uncertainty leads to deep-seated anxiety and a sense of ubiquitous conspiracy.[23]

When these psychological problems become associated with economic difficulties, they can lead to strong disillusionment with democracy. In January 1992, before Yeltsin's economic reforms, economic problems were already severe, but 50 percent of the respondents in a public opinion poll gave a positive rating to the Soviet system. This figure rose to 67 percent by April 1995. Only 26 percent of the respondents evaluated the current system of democratic and market reforms favorably.[24]

As Erich Fromm emphasized in *Escape from Freedom*, people in such situations may not want freedom but an escape from it.[25] Authoritarian populists with simple doctrinaire answers to all problems and with a recognizable devil figure to explain all difficulties can provide relief from uncertainty. Fromm explained the wide support received by Hitler in the late 1920s and early 1930s as a response to the insecurity and anxiety produced by German defeat in World War I, the runaway inflation that followed, and the depression of the early 1930s. Fromm also contended that the authori-

23. See the discussion by Bernard Bailyn, *The Ideological Origins of the American Revolution* (Harvard University Press, 1967), pp. 144–59, about conspiratorial thinking in Britain and the American colonies in the eighteenth century. This phenomenon is general at such periods.
24. John Thornhill, "Hard Times Help Russians to see Soviet Era in a New Light," *Financial Times*, August 17, 1995, p. 2.
25. Erich Fromm, *Escape from Freedom* (Holt, Rinehart and Winston, 1941).

tarianism and determinism of original Calvinist doctrine was attractive to those moving to the city in mid-sixteenth and seventeenth century Europe because of the breakup of the security of feudal society. The dogmatism and authoritarianism of Leninism had a similar appeal to people who were subjected to the insecurities of rapid industrialization, the breakup of the village commune, and defeats in the Russo-Japanese War and World War I.

Communism also appealed to Russians' hostility toward the West and its culture in the 1910s and 1920s. Americans were aware of the later anti-Americanism in the Soviet Union and communist movements in the third world, but Soviet leaders had always identified the internal class enemy with the external class enemy, especially at times of revolutionary transformation.[26] This association was partly a propagandistic effort to use patriotism against internal opponents and legitimate their suppression, but the argument touched a deeper chord.

The industrializing elite in non-Western countries usually adopts Western values and ways and, as in Iran, they arouse resentment for their rejection of traditional values as well as their economic privilege. The two resentments reinforce each other, but the Ayatollah Khomeini's emphasis on "satanism" and its tie to "the Great Satan" abroad suggests that the cultural factor may sometimes be more important than the economic one.[27] The importance of this factor in reinforcing class hatred in Russia is suggested by the passage in Brezhnev's autobiography quoted earlier.

Communist ideology played to these cultural resentments. Marx and Lenin not only condemned capitalism as an economic system, but also insisted that the superstructure of bourgeois society—its politics, culture, philosophy, values, religion—inevitably reflected the interests of owners of the means of production. This emphasis implied that because the culture of the modern West reflected the interests of exploiting capitalists, it had little intrinsic worth, let alone superiority over traditional values.

This theme was made most explicit in Marx's *Communist Manifesto*:

> The bourgeoisie, wherever it has got the upper hand, has put an end to all feudal, patriarchal, idyllic relations. It has . . . left remaining no other nexus between man

26. Sheila Fitzpatrick, "Cultural Revolution as Class War," in Fitzpatrick, *The Cultural Front: Power and Culture in Revolutionary Russia* (Cornell University Press, 1992), pp. 115–48; and Fitzpatrick, "The Foreign Threat during the First Five Year Plan," *Soviet Union*, no. 1 (1978), pp. 26–35.

27. The classic statement of this reinforcement is in David B. Truman's discussion of "overlapping group memberships" in *The Governmental Process: Political Interests and Public Opinion* (Knopf, 1951), pp. 157–67.

and man than naked self-interest, than callous "cash payment." It has
drowned the most heavenly ecstasies of religious fervor, of chivalrous enthu-
siasm, of philistine sentimentalism, in the icy water of egotistical calculation. . . . The bourgeoisie has stripped of its halo every occupation hitherto
honoured and looked up to with reverent awe. . . . [It] has torn away from the
family its sentimental veil, and has reduced the family relation to a mere
money relation.[28]

The American reformer Carl Schurz remembered "most distinctly the cutting disdain with which [Marx] pronounced the word 'bourgeois'; and as a
'bourgeois,' that is, a detestable example of the deepest mental and moral
degeneracy, he denounced everyone that dared to oppose his opinion."[29]

Lenin, for his part, showed little interest in contemporary Western culture, and his removal of the capital from Petrograd, Peter the Great's
"window on the West," to Moscow was only one sign of this feeling.[30] He
had also showed hostility toward foreign capital and the world economic
system in his crucial prerevolutionary work, *Imperialism—The Highest
Stage of Capitalism*. Lenin argued that Western capitalists had been able to
stave off revolution at home temporarily through exploiting colonies and
semicolonial areas. The raw materials of these areas were bought too
cheaply, the development of their manufacturing industry was stymied, and
foreign manufactured goods were sold to them at too high a price. Although
he treated Russia as an imperialist European power rather than a semicolonial country, it was the least developed major European power, and the
West, by implication, was charging it high prices for manufactured goods
and exploiting low prices for its grain and other raw materials.

In 1926 Stalin made the link between Russian development and foreign
exploitation explicit:

Tsarist Russia was an immense reserve of Western imperialism, not only in the
sense that it gave free entry to foreign capital, which controlled such basic
branches of Russia's national economy as the fuel and metal industries, but also
in the sense that it could supply the Western imperialists with millions of soldiers.
Remember the Russian army, fourteen million strong, which shed its blood on
the imperialist fronts to safeguard the staggering profits of the British and French
capitalists. Tsarism . . . was the agent of Western imperialism for squeezing out

28. Karl Marx, *The Communist Manifesto* (Norton, 1988), pp. 57–58.
29. Carl Schurz, *The Reminiscences of Carl Schurz*, vol. 1 (New York: McClure,
1907), p. 140.
30. Jerry F. Hough, *Russia and the West: Gorbachev and the Politics of Reform*
(Simon and Schuster, 1988), pp. 46–54.

of the population hundreds of millions by way of interest on loans obtained in Paris and London, Berlin and Brussels.[31]

The assertion that raw material prices were too low and those for imported consumer goods too high was certain to be appealing to people streaming into Russia's mines, steel mills, and textile factories.

The Equilibrium of the Mid-1970s

American memories of Leonid Brezhnev are of a wooden seventy-five-year-old whose slow, stilted speech on television bespoke such a loss of mental quickness that he became the butt of many jokes. In one such, he was said to have appeared on television slowly reading a TASS statement that the rumors of his death were false. In another he appeared on television slowly and ponderously reading a number of "oh's" from a paper. A fellow Politburo member tapped him on the shoulder to tell him he was reading the Olympic symbol, not his speech. Americans who saw him in private sometimes found him nearly comatose.[32] Brezhnev had surrounded himself with lieutenants of his generation. At the time of his death in November 1982 the nine men in the inner core of the Politburo who worked in Moscow averaged seventy-one years old. If Gorbachev is excluded, they averaged seventy-four, only two years younger than Brezhnev himself.

The result, Americans might have said, was that Soviet society was reflecting the age and infirmities of its leaders. The Soviet Union remained intolerant of Picasso and jazz, neither of which was politically threatening. Moscow did not have a single French or Italian restaurant. Although the rate of economic growth was falling, Brezhnev was afraid to introduce any domestic change for fear it would create the need for a new, more active leader. Gorbachev's word *stagnation* did not have a metaphysical meaning.

Yet if Brezhnev had retired in 1976 on his seventieth birthday, a year after his health began to fail, he would have gone down in history as a very effective leader. Speech and press in the Soviet Union, although still tightly

31. J. V. Stalin, "The Foundations of Leninism," in *Problems of Leninism* (Moscow: Foreign Language Publishing House, 1953), p. 20.

32. Robert M. Gates, *From the Shadows: The Ultimate Insider's Story of Five Presidents and How They Won the Cold War* (Simon and Schuster, 1996), pp. 116–17. Malcolm Toom, the American ambassador to Russia at the time, reported privately that one day he might be reasonably alert, while the next day he could hardly recognize people.

controlled, were freer in 1975 than when he came to power in 1964. He instituted a consumer revolution that provided many people with their first apartments and an increasing number of appliances. He introduced the principle of universal high school education and made significant progress in achieving it. In foreign policy he built the Soviet Union up to strategic equality with the United States. And he brought the country safely through the conflict with China and the Vietnam War while introducing detente with West Germany and then the United States.[33]

Partly as a result, the Soviet system seemed stable in the mid-1970s, a point on which all American observers agreed. There were, however, many ways to interpret this stability. Leading conservatives who were to be associated with the Reagan administration, denied any possibility of change, either through revolution or evolution. Richard Pipes argued that Russians were inherently authoritarian and aggressive, that they would always want to escape from freedom, and that the kind of dictatorship established in 1918 and in the 1970s rested on deep popular support.[34] William Odom described the Soviet system as focused on the goal of building up and projecting military force, which priority required the subordination of economic and social policy to military goals and the integration of military and society. He saw little possibility of the system changing, noting that the "requisites of military power . . . show every sign of continuing to dominate Soviet politics for the remainder of this century."[35] Mekhail Voslensky, a Soviet emigré, contended the Soviet Union was in the inexorable grip of a nomenklatura who were incapable of evolution but could not be challenged.[36] Jeane Kirkpatrick contrasted communist systems with authoritarian dictatorships, insisting the dictatorships could evolve toward democracy but that "the history of this century provides no grounds for expecting that radical totalitarian regimes will transform themselves."[37]

33. For evidence of Brezhnev's domestic achievements at this time, see Jerry F. Hough, "The Brezhnev Era: The Man and the System," *Problems of Communism*, vol. 25 (March-April 1976), pp. 6–15.

34. Richard Pipes, "Detente: Moscow's View*,*" in Richard Pipes, ed., *Soviet Strategy in Europe* (New York, 1976); and Pipes, "Response to Wladislaw G. Krasnow, *Russian Review*, vol. 38 (April 1979), pp. 192–97.

35. William E. Odom, "The 'Militarization' of Soviet Society," *Problems of Communism*, vol. 25 (September-October 1976), p. 33; and "Whither the Soviet Union," *Washington Quarterly*, vol. 4 (Spring 1981), pp. 30–49.

36. Mikhail Voslensky, *Nomenklatura: The Soviet Ruling Class* (Doubleday, 1984).

37. Jeane J. Kirkpatrick, *Dictatorships and Double Standards: Rationalism and Reason in Politics* (Simon and Schuster, 1982), p. 51.

Moderate and liberal analysts, who dominated the ranks of academic specialists, also contended that the authoritarianism of the mid-1970s Brezhnev regime rested on more than force. In the words of Linda Cook they argued that

> the post-Stalin regime and its working class made a tacit agreement to trade social security for political compliance, a 'social contract.' . . . The regime provided broad guarantees of full and secure employment, state-controlled and heavily subsidized prices for essential goods, fully socialized human services, and egalitarian wage policies. In exchange . . . Soviet workers consented to the party's extensive and monopolistic power, accepted state domination of the economy, and complied with authoritarian political norms.[38]

This second line of analysis suggested continued political stability but did not deny the possibility of all change. If the regime ceased to fulfill its part of the contract—if living standards did not rise or the regime had to change social policy to reinvigorate sagging economic growth—the workers' attitude could be expected to change. Moreover, all scholars in this group understood that younger workers, like younger college graduates, at a minimum wanted a milder authoritarianism: more toleration of rock and roll, Western movies, travel to the West, and the like. Indeed, Brezhnev was more lenient in these respects than his predecessors, and his successors were likely to be even more so. The movement of the Soviet Union toward an authoritarian regime such as Franco's in postwar Spain seemed quite possible.

A third interpretation of the mid-1970s stability suggested the possibility of far more drastic change. These scholars took seriously Rostow's statement that communism was a disease of the transition and assumed that transitions by definition do not last forever. If communism met the economic and psychological needs of the urban peasants and rested for its support on the mass of people who streamed into the city in the first half of the twentieth century, their children, who were born in the city, thoroughly urbanized, and much better educated than their parents and grandparents, could be expected to have different needs.

According to this third analysis, the Soviet Union had long since achieved societal wealth, urbanization, occupational differentiation, and a level of educational attainment that had been associated with liberalization

---

38. Linda J. Cook, *The Soviet Social Contract and Why It Failed: Welfare Policy and Workers' Politics from Brezhnev to Yeltsin* (Harvard University Press, 1993), pp. 1–2. References to relevant studies are in Cook's footnotes.

and democratization in the West and the third world. Historically, aging dictators such as Stalin, Franco, Ho Chi Minh, and Mao Zedong were not overthrown when they became wholly ineffective and when powerful societal forces wanted change. Rather, the forces manifested themselves during the succession crisis. In this view the stability of the late Brezhnev period was of a familiar type, and generational change in the leadership might have a powerful effect on the political system. This is the position of this book and is explored more fully in the rest of this chapter.

The Changing Social Structure of the Brezhnev Period

Throughout the 1980s many observers looked back at the failure of the reforms of Nikita Khrushchev and his premier, Aleksei Kosygin, and predicted a similar fate for the liberalizing moves of Mikhail Gorbachev. (They would have made the point more strongly by giving greater emphasis to the reforms of Georgy Malenkov.)[39] Their assumption was that the Russian people and Russian society had not changed and did not provide a social base for reform. Very few had any sense of the profound social changes that had occurred during the Brezhnev era.

Yet the number of people living in urban areas in the Soviet Union increased from 100 million in 1959 to 172 million in 1982, from 48 percent of the population to 64 percent. If the Moslem republics in the Soviet Union are excluded, the speed of urbanization was even more dramatic. Fifty-two percent of the population in the Russian republic was urban in 1959; this had risen to 71 percent by 1982.[40]

Educational attainment had changed even more dramatically. When Nikita Khrushchev was removed in 1964, only 17 percent of adults had a high school diploma or better; by the 1980s it was nearly 60 percent. An increase in average education level in the work force comes from the higher proportion of better-educated twenty-year-olds and the demise of the

---

39. See the discussion of Malenkov and Khrushchev in Hough, *Russia and the West*, pp. 130–37. The biography of Malenkov by his son makes a convincing case that he was a reformer on the model of Janos Kadar. A. G. Malenkov, *O moem otse Georgy Malenkov* (Moscow: Technoekos, 1992).

40. *Narodnoe khoziaistvo SSSR 1922–1982* (Moscow: Finansy i Statistika, 1982), pp. 12–13.

poorly educated elderly. Gradually the aging of the well-educated young changed the education levels at older age levels as well (table 2-4).

The occupational structure in the Soviet Union was also being transformed. A shrinking number of low-status jobs and the sharp increase in the number of high-status ones is a universal sign of industrializing society (table 2-5). It is the main reason large numbers of people believe they have enjoyed upward social mobility and that their society creates great opportunities for them. Scholars agree that this perception is a major source of political stability in modern industrial society.

Table 2-5, however, has implications that few political analysts consider. First, although the increase in the number of high-status jobs means that a large majority of the population can have higher-ranking jobs than their parents had and can see themselves as upwardly mobile, social mobility in the literal sense of ranking in the social hierarchy is a zero-sum game. If one leaves aside foreign immigration into low-status jobs and the retirement or death of administrative personnel at the top, the rise in the percentile ranking of some people must be accompanied by a decline in the ranking of others.

The inevitable consequence of the increase in the number of people in higher-status positions is a decline in the percentile ranking of those employed in a particular occupation. In the United States, for example, the median carpenter in 1940 ranked in the fiftieth percentile of employed men. Twenty years later the same person was in the thirty-third percentile because of the mass movement of men into higher-ranking occupations.[41]

During the Soviet period, data were not made available for a detailed analysis of occupational status, but the data in table 2-5 illustrate in rough terms what occurred to the relative status of the median skilled worker outside light industry. If such a worker was in the top tenth to fifteenth percentile of the population in 1917, he or she was in the twenty-first percentile in 1939, the twenty-ninth in 1959, and the forty-fourth in 1970.

The silent erosion in social standing is a significant cause of the vague sense of malaise observed in America in recent years. Middle-class Americans have known something is going wrong, but unaware of their social

41. I took the ranked list of census occupations found in Albert J. Reiss, *Occupations and Social Status* (Free Press, 1961), found the number of men employed in each in the 1940 and 1960 census, and calculated the percentile ranking of a number of the occupations. For an early discussion of the phenomenon, see Joseph A. Kahl, *The American Class Structure* (Rinehart, 1957).

Table 2-4. *Soviet Citizens Completing Secondary Education or Higher,*
by Age Group, Selected Years, 1959–89

Percent

Age group	1959	1970	1979	1989
20–29	22.6	52.6	75.3	91.8
30–39	20.6	33.3	60.2	86.0
40–49	13.1	24.0	35.5	67.6
50–59	9.2	15.7	26.7	39.8
60 and older	4.9	8.1	11.9	22.9
Average	15.8	28.0	54.2	63.1

Sources: Calculated from *Itogi vsesoiuznoi perepisi naseleniia 1959 goda. SSSR (svodnyi tom)* (Moscow: Gosstatizdat, 1962), pp. 74–75; *Itogi vsesoiuznoi perepisi naseleniia 1970 goda*, vol. 3 (Moscow: Statistika, 1972), pp. 6–7; and *Itogi vsesoiuznoi perepisi naseleniia, 1979*, vol. 3 (Moscow: Goskomstat SSSR, 1989), pt. 1, p. 17.

ranking in percentile terms, they have not been able to pinpoint the erosion. Instead they talk of a decline in values or they see immigrants as a threat. The problem has become particularly great for white men in recent decades because of the movement of a large number of women into higher-status jobs, which left correspondingly fewer positions open for men.

In the West there are various palliatives for silent status decline. Democracy provides a direct political outlet whereby people can vent their frustrations on individual officeholders rather than the political system or the elite as a whole. There are also indirect outlets. Those in middle occupations who are suffering the greatest decline in relative real status may join fundamentalist religions, become obsessed with guns for protection, be attracted to nativist movements, and so forth. Thus far, these outlets in the United States have not only deflected their resentment away from the economic system and the economic elite, but have turned the discontented into strong supporters of both against the government.[42]

The political problem in the Soviet Union was worse. As the number of people employed in agriculture decreases, the size of the pool in agriculture seeking upward mobility inevitably also shrinks. The pool of urban blue-collar workers seeking upward mobility correspondingly increases. The transition of the West to an automated service economy destroyed large numbers of unskilled and semiskilled jobs. The creation of high-status jobs in the service sector and the need for highly skilled workers to fill them provides opportunities for the growing number of ambitious and talented

42. The appeals, policy position, and social base of those such as Rush Limbaugh deserve far more serious study than they have received.

Table 2-5. *Distribution of Workers by Type and Status of Occupation, 1939, 1959, 1970*

	1939		1959		1970	
Type of occupation	millions	percent	millions	percent	millions	percent
Higher-education, white collar	4.860	3	8.115	4	14.790	6
Lower-education, white collar	6.720	11	10.650	14	26.030	22
Skilled labor in light industry	2.125	28	2.900	40	3.625	57
Skilled labor other than light industry	7.470	21	18.330	29	29.860	44
Higher-skilled labor in agriculture	2.690	40	3.500	56	3.925	70
Unskilled labor in agriculture	32.075	78	30.365	84	18.680	89
Medium-skilled labor	6.550	34	11.680	48	11.975	63
Least-skilled labor	9.935	49	10.450	63	8.075	74

Source: Based on Jerry F. Hough and Merle Fainsod, *How the Soviet Union Is Governed* (Harvard University Press, 1979), pp. 564–65; and author's calculations. The definitions and methodology are given there.

people in the working class who want higher-status jobs than those their parents have.[43] This is often decried as foreclosing opportunity for an underclass, which is true to some extent. However, the underclass is not politically dangerous.

In broad historical perspective the working class is not a critical political factor across several generations. The working class was politically dynamic and powerful in the early and middle stages of industrialization precisely because it contained such a large percentage of the ambitious, upwardly mobile members of society. But like Leonid Brezhnev, these people were former peasants or children of former peasants and retained many rural attitudes. By the second generation the dynamic, upwardly mobile, and politically dangerous workers were either eagerly moving into the middle class or sending their children to college to enter it.

The Soviet system was beautifully designed to provide upward mobility, security, and symbolic rewards when massive migration from the country-

43. The argument that this process cannot go on forever and that the children of college-educated parents may develop a dangerous sense of frustration is presented in Peter M. Blau, *Structural Contexts of Opportunities* (University of Chicago Press, 1994), pp. 197–200.

side to the city was occurring, but it was very ill equipped to deal with the status problems of a more advanced industrial society.

First, the lack of competitive elections meant that younger and middle-aged workers could not direct anger against an elected leader. Inevitably the elite and the system as a whole—the center, the bureaucrats, the nomenklatura—became the focus of frustration. Public opinion polls in the 1990s showed that older workers retained a sense of the Communist party as their representative, but that others saw it as the alien center. This was even truer of the advanced industrial workers in the major urban centers than of workers in smaller towns and in nonindustrial sectors (table 2-6).

Second, although the Soviet system was very well suited for the transition from a rural economy to an industrial one, it was not flexible enough to permit an effective transition to a service economy. Marxist-Leninist ideology focused exclusively on the means of production and treated services as "the nonproductive sector." This led to investment patterns and a wage structure that heavily discriminated against services. Ideology also focused on labor as the source of all value and gave little attention to the importance of management, which led to grossly understaffed bureaucracies both in the government and the economic enterprises compared with those in the West.[44] Indeed, a major reason that the bureaucracy was so bureaucratic and unresponsive to the citizenry was that it had far too few employees to do the work that was needed.

The country's leaders retained the values and biases of production engineers, which tended to perpetuate older priorities. The planning system reinforced the tendency by demanding that plant managers increase production every year. Although the advanced industrial countries began to reduce their production of textiles, steel, and other products of smokestack industries, production of them continued to increase in the Soviet Union.

As a result, the Soviet occupational structure in 1990 was very different from that of noncommunist countries. The percentage of the Soviet population employed in agriculture was similar to that in South Korea or Brazil, but nearly 50 percent of the population worked in industry, construction,

---

44. The Institute of USA and Canada calculated in 1986 that 41.4 million people in the United States, one-third of the labor force, are employed in administrative, staff, and white-collar work: 12.6 million managers, 1.7 million specialists, 2.0 million technicians, 17.7 million office workers, and 7.4 million sales personnel. The Soviet Union had 14.9 million such employees: 5.7 million leaders, 4.4 million specialists, and 2.1 million office workers. Leonid Abalkin, *Ne ispol'zovannyi shans: Poltora goda v pravitel'stve* (Moscow: Politizdat, 1991), pp. 55–56.

Table 2-6. *Worker Attitudes toward the Communist Party, by Age Group and Size of Place of Residence, 1993*

Percent

Age group	Positive	More positive than negative	More negative than positive	Negative
Total				
50–59	25.2	18.5	11.7	44.6
40–49	20.7	17.8	13.1	48.4
30–39	16.2	16.1	16.5	51.2
30 or younger	11.7	15.9	19.7	52.7
Cities of 200,000 to 1 million				
50–59	23.1	17.2	11.0	48.7
40–49	18.4	14.5	13.9	53.2
30–39	14.5	12.4	15.1	58.0
30 or younger	10.1	17.7	18.6	53.6
Cities larger than 1 million				
50–59	14.4	13.6	9.3	62.7
40–49	12.9	7.9	9.9	69.3
30–39	6.8	7.7	19.7	65.8
30 or younger	6.3	3.1	17.2	73.4

Source: See table 2-1.

and transportation, far greater than in either those countries or advanced industrial countries (table 2-7). The percentage employed in the services was much lower than in noncommunist countries, especially if education and health are excluded and "services" is used to refer primarily to consumer services.

The problem was even greater than these statistics indicate. In table 2-7 "manufacturing" includes production of everything from clothing to steel to pharmaceuticals to advanced electronics. But employment in the manufacturing sector in the Soviet Union remained concentrated disproportionately in coal, steel, rubber, textiles, tanks, artillery, and machinery. Moreover, in Western society manufacturing and construction positions are increasingly staff: secretarial, computer programmer, specialist in personnel and public relations, and so forth. Soviet industry, like the state bureaucracy, had many fewer such posts.

The economic consequences of the Soviet system were that productivity in the industrial sector remained low because of an excessive number of workers and that the quality of consumer services remained poor because they were understaffed. Less obvious but equally important, the Soviet Union was not creating enough high-status white-collar, managerial, and

Table 2-7. *Distribution of Employment, by Country and Sector, 1990*

Percent

Sector	Soviet Union	United States	Sweden	Korea	Brazil
Agriculture	18.2[a]	2.8	3.3	18.3	24.2
Manufacturing, mining, gas, electricity, water	28.3	19.9	22.2	27.7	17.0
Construction	10.0	6.5	6.9	7.4	6.3
Transport	8.2	5.6	7.1	5.1	3.8
Trade, restaurants, hotels	7.8	20.6[b]	14.4	21.7	11.6[c]
Community, social, personal services	25.1	33.2	37.4	14.6	31.1
Finance, real estate, insurance, business service	.6	11.3	8.6	5.2	6.0
Other	1.7	0	0.1	0	0

Source: Susan Goodrich Lehmann, "Costs and Opportunities of Marketization: An Analysis of Russian Employment and Unemployment," in Richard and Ida Harper Simpson, eds., *Research in the Sociology of Work*, vol. 5: *The Meaning of Work* (Greenwich, Conn.: JAI Press, 1995), p. 211. Based on International Labour Organization data.

a. Includes state farmers (*sovkhozniki*) and collective farmers (*kolkhozniki*).
b. Hotels are included under community, social, personal services.
c. Hotels and restaurants are included under community, social, personal services. Data are for 1988.

professional jobs into which the children of the blue-collar workers could move. In addition, professions such as law and medicine often received wages lower than those of skilled workers and for this reason were filled by women.

The fundamental problem with the communist industrial system is that it, not capitalism, developed the grave diggers about whom Marx had written. It was not the proletariat who served in this role but the children of the proletariat seeking upward mobility. As urbanization and education increased in the Soviet Union, the percentage of the bright and ambitious who sought upward mobility came less and less from the peasantry, simply because the percentage of peasants shrank. For demographic reasons alone, the largest group of potential upwardly mobile workers had to come from the urbanized children and grandchildren of the urban peasants. Yet upward mobility for the children of urban peasants meant moving into professional and managerial jobs, not into skilled blue-collar ones. The children and grandchildren of urban peasants in the West could move into sales, management, the professions, and open small businesses. Their Soviet counterparts were more restricted. Private business was prohibited, and jobs in sales, management, and the professions scarce and low-paying. The number of truly important hierarchical jobs was limited.

Older and middle-aged Soviet citizens were relatively content, but the ambitious and talented young were increasingly frustrated. If they were to have more opportunity in the 1970s and 1980s, they needed more and better-paid professional, staff, and entry-level managerial jobs. The most ambitious wanted the chance to enrich themselves in private business.

The lack of opportunity was especially serious because the psychological needs of Soviet citizens were also changing. Western values were not as upsetting for young urban dwellers as they had been for their parents and grandparents. Moreover, the very success of the political controls in shutting out frightening ideas from abroad or curtailing conflicts of opinion at home meant these children were raised in a much more secure environment than were previous generations. They had no need to identify with a reassuring political movement and charismatic dictator to escape from the chaos of war or economic depression. They needed to escape from the boring conformism of their lives. So that whereas their parents found the West menacing, even in the 1950s the Soviet young found it exotic and attractive, and they envied Western clothes, music, and movies. By the 1980s the twenty-year-olds of the 1950s were moving into their fifties. Westerners talked about the conservative bureaucrats of the Gorbachev era, but they forgot what these people had thought and believed in the 1950s and 1960s. It was not only the masses who were changing but also the elite, although with a time lag.

Elite Attitudes and Revolution

In the West the college-educated elite have constituted the heart of what is called the middle class, the people who in public opinion polls have provided the strongest support to democracy and tolerance. Most of these people are employed in the private sector. Most own property, at least their homes, by the age of thirty, and many own common stocks. They are employed in business, a number in small businesses of their own.

In the Soviet Union in the 1970s and 1980s virtually everyone with higher education worked for the state apparatus or for bureaucratized institutions that were subordinated to the central authorities. The path to higher wages and status was appointment to increasingly responsible administrative positions. This was true not only of those holding posts in the party and soviet apparatus, but of those in education, medicine, science, industry, and agriculture. Did this college-educated elite constitute a middle class and a force for liberalization? Or were they hidebound bureaucrats who would thwart change?

Trotsky's argument that the Soviet Union was ruled by bureaucrats was widely accepted by the Soviet intelligentsia and became the dominant view in the United States as well. Many labels were used—bureaucracy, partocracy, nomenklatura—but the implication of each was the same. If the bureaucratic ruling class was monolithic and self-contained, if it was parasitical and enjoyed great privileges acquired through the use of the totalitarian state that was its instrument, reforming the system from within was impossible. The exploited could improve their situation only by overthrowing the ruling class and its state. And naturally the bureaucrats would resist to their last bit of red tape.

Of course, the definition of *bureaucrat* or later *nomenklatura* was fuzzy. Everyone I knew in Moscow, whether dean of a university, head of a department of an institute, employee of a ministry or the Central Committee apparatus, or *Pravda* correspondent whose post was actually in the nomenklatura of the Central Committee, categorically denied he or she was a bureaucrat. But all were convinced that bureaucrats were pervasive, that they ruled, and that they were conservative. Anyone who thought seriously about bureaucrats gained the impression that they might comprise a few thousand people at a very high level in Moscow, plus some tens of thousands in the provinces; but even Gorbachev, a high party official and since 1971 a member of the Central Committee, talked and wrote as if he were not one of them.

Scholars who had contended that interest groups existed in the Soviet Union argued that image of rule by a united bureaucracy was wrong.[45] Even on matters on which the bureaucracy might have been united in interests and outlook, it scarcely seemed dominant. Thus both absolutely and in their share of society's income, managers lived much worse than their counterparts in the West, and their position was deteriorating. Moreover, they knew it. Cultural exchanges had given them an opportunity to travel and see just how well their counterparts lived. The excessive and growing egalitarianism of the Brezhnev era, as well as the continuing restrictions on foreign travel and exposure to foreign culture, were hard to reconcile with the image of an all-powerful bureaucracy.

---

45. See H. Gordon Skilling and Franklyn Griffiths, eds., *Interest Groups in Soviet Politics* (Princeton University Press, 1971).

In addition, the bureaucracy and the Communist party seemed on most matters neither united nor divorced from society. The bureaucracy and the party encompassed too many people of diverse interests to be monolithic. Virtually everyone in the Soviet Union worked for the state or statelike institutions, and half the men over the age of thirty who held a college diploma were members of the party.[46] And although the employment of all educated people by the state gave politics in the Soviet Union an institutional character, it also integrated society with the state.

To be sure, voluntary interest groups were not allowed to form. However, in the United States people take for granted that the American military is a societal group and a political interest group, a powerful one. Yet American military officers are all state employees, or bureaucrats, whose commissions are signed by the president. Similarly, in the Soviet Union, employees of the Ministry of Defense were both government bureaucrats and a societal group. Employees of the Ministry of Health and of the Ministry of the Automobile Industry were members of the state apparatus and the physicians' or automobile employees' segment of society, respectively.

In this view—and it is a basic thesis of this book—the intertwining of state and society, of the party and state apparatus, produced a thoroughly varied managerial stratum. This intertwining began in the first years of the Soviet period. In 1921 Nikolai Bukharin said, "The party, as it existed earlier, in the period of its illegality, when there was a single psychology and a single ideology, has split into a variety of separate columns. . . . Military workers, soviet workers, trade union workers, and party workers proper have organized together among themselves."[47] By the 1960s the officials of the party apparatus had become very professionalized in their educational and career backgrounds.[48]

Three cleavages existed within the "ruling class" in the 1970s, and in each case the group with the greatest potential for growth in power was deeply dissatisfied with the status quo. One cleavage was between the dominant group in the elite, the engineers from heavy industry, and other, less-favored elite groups. The major inequalities were not those between

---

46. Jerry F. Hough, *The Soviet Union and Social Science Theory* (Harvard University Press, 1977), pp. 130–31.

47. Quoted in Jeremy R. Azrael, *Managerial Power and Soviet Politics* (Harvard University Press, 1966), p. 65.

48. Hough, *Soviet Union and Social Science Theory*, pp. 71–108.

class strata (managers and workers, for example), but between employees in different economic sectors. Heavy industry was favored in all respects. There was no general bureaucratic privilege: most privileges were accorded high officials in politics and heavy industry but not those in the top bureaucratic jobs in education and the services or those in professions. People working in the service sector, including mid-level government and party officials, physicians, lawyers, and scientists, were paid less than skilled industrial workers.

In the 1950s and 1960s the less-favored elites were resentful, but their numbers were small and their political position weak. But in time their numbers increased, as did their status. By the 1980s, even large portions of the industrial elite were becoming restless. Steel, textiles, and other old-line industries were still favored, while computers, electronics, and other new industries remained underdeveloped. The Ministry of Railroads dominated transportation at the expense of investment in airlines, highway infrastructure, and trucking. Gorbachev's prime minister, Nikolai Ryzhkov, reported that the economic managers in the ministries and plants were particularly angered by the economic power concentrated in the party apparatus.[49]

The military elite was also unhappy, in this case about the level of technological sophistication of the weapons produced by the defense industry. The Soviet Union lagged twenty years behind the West in its ability to build solid-fuel intercontinental missiles, catch film ejected from satellites, and develop quiet nuclear submarines. But despite talk about the military's domination of the Soviet system, it was the defense industry that was successfully defending its interests in weapons development—interests that flowed from the logic of the planning system that created disincentives for innovation. As China underwent economic reform and rapid economic growth based on Western investment, the military was increasingly unhappy about its technological backwardness.

The head of the General Staff, Marshal Nikolai Ogarkov, began articulating these concerns publicly. When he wrote about changes in Western military strategy and weaponry, he prefaced his remarks with a quotation from Friedrich Engels: "Nothing depends on economic conditions so much as a country's army and navy. Weapons, structure, organization, tactics, and

49. Nikolai Ryzhkov, *Perestroika: istoriia predatel'stv* (Moscow: Novosti, 1992), p. 272. See also Vadim Medvedev, *V komande Gorbacheva* (Moscow: Vylina, 1994), p. 69.

strategy depend above all on the level of production and the means of communication that has been achieved at a given point in time."[50] Anyone familiar with the rules of censored Soviet debate knew that Ogarkov was sharply criticizing the policy of Leonid Brezhnev and Defense Minister Dmitry Ustinov and calling for major changes in economic policy.[51] The fact that he was allowed to publish in the leading Central Committee journal, *Kommunist*, demonstrated that he had powerful supporters in the Politburo itself.[52]

A second cleavage within the bureaucracy occurred along generational lines. Although Brezhnev and others of his class and generation may have looked through the fence with envy and resentment at the Westernized elite of the Upper Colony, the college students that foreigners began meeting in the 1950s had more favorable attitudes toward the West and also seemed less ideological in other respects. These attitudes infused the lowest levels of the bureaucracy as well.

In 1959 the British Sovietologist Edward Crankshaw observed, "Nothing in this world is more depressing to contemplate than the average Soviet official of high or low degree at present between the ages of forty and sixty [those in the Brezhnev and Chernenko generations]." He later commented,

> The Soviet Union's great hope lies in the young—those under thirty-five. . . . In a dozen professions in which Party control is particularly rigid—in the Foreign Service, in the Law, in journalism, in economics, in radio, in the higher civil service with its many branches, in the armed forces, in the university faculties, you will meet well-turned-out young men in their thirties, usually Party members, relaxed and easy in manner, often with a pleasantly ironical approach to life, and very much in touch with realities of every kind. . . .

50. "Voennaia nauka i zashchita sotsialisticheskogo otechestva," *Kommunist*, no. 7 (1978), p. 112. Quoted in Dale R. Herspring, *The Soviet High Command: Personalities and Politics* (Princeton University Press, 1990), p. 159. Also see the discussion on pp. 148–49. Soviet authors had to bolster their articles with an appropriate quotation from the ideological founding fathers. These quotations were chosen carefully to make a point.

51. Sergei Akhromeev, the first deputy head of the General Staff, reported strong tension between Ogarkov and Ustinov in early 1992. S. F. Akhromeev and G. M. Kornienko, *Glazami marshala i diplomata* (Moscow: Mezhdunarodnye otnoshenii, 1992), pp. 29-30.

52. Andropov was prominent among them. When Ogarkov repeated his points (and the quotation from Engels) in a featured interview in *Red Star* several months after Andropov's death, Chernenko removed him from office. See Jerry F. Hough, "Soviet Decision-Making on Defense," *Bulletin of the Atomic Scientists*, vol. 41 (August 1985), pp. 84–88. Both Andropov and Ogarkov had been stationed in Karelia during World War II.

I have been talking of the cream of the younger men beginning to rise in what
are called the liberal professions and the State and Party service. Until the last
decade young men of comparable ability would not have dreamt of this sort of
career.[53]

Westerners always understood that Soviet youth in the post-Stalin world
were different from their parents, but they nevertheless continued to believe
that the outlook of the middle and upper levels of the bureaucracy remained
unchanged. What they failed to consider was that twenty-year-olds become
fifty-year-olds after thirty years. By 1980 the students I had met in the
1950s had taken over the middle levels and much of the higher levels of the
bureaucracy and party apparatus.[54] Three members of Gorbachev's Politburo—policy adviser Aleksandr Yakovlev, KGB Chairman Viktor
Chebrikov, and Minister of Defense Dmitry Yazov—were born in 1923 and
thus had been Crankshaw's thirty-six-year-olds in 1959. The oldest member of Gorbachev's team, Yegor Ligachev, was thirty-nine in 1959;
Gorbachev and Yeltsin had been only twenty-eight and Foreign Minister
Eduard Shevardnadze thirty-one.

Yevgeny Yevtushenko, the semidissident poet of the 1950s, noticed the
transformation of the party elite when he talked in 1985 with the party first
secretary in Georgia who succeeded Shevardnadze:

I am used to talking with men in official posts who are all older than me and I
always see in their eyes that they regard me a disturber of the peace. . . . The first
thing [the Georgian first secretary] told me was that when he was a student he
managed to smuggle his way into the great hall of Tbilisi University to listen to a
poetry recital of mine. . . . Do you know what he said to me: "We grew up in the
spirit of your poetry." Then in the Urals I met the manager of a large metalworks,
so different from the people I was used to meeting that I could not help saying to
him: "Pardon me, but you are not in the least like a manager and do not have the
slightest appearance of a bureaucrat." Do you know what his answer was? "When
I was at high school I won a prize by reciting one of your poems against
bureaucrats."[55]

The third cleavage within the bureaucracy was between the ministries
and the officials in the provinces. The Soviet Union really was not so much

53. Edward Crankshaw, *Khrushchev's Russia* (Baltimore: Penguin Books, 1959),
pp. 91, 127, 130. I am grateful to Sheila Fitzpatrick for this reference.
    54. Jerry F. Hough, *Soviet Leadership in Transition* (Brookings, 1980), esp. chap. 4.
    55. Rodolfo Brancoli, interview with Yevgeny Yevtushenko, *La Repubblica*, Janu-
ary 18, 1986, pp. 20–21, in Foreign Broadcast Information Service, *Daily Report: Soviet
Union*, January 29, 1986, p. 6.

a Russian Empire as a Moscow Empire: Russian regions from Vladivostok to Leningrad were as tightly controlled as non-Russian republics, perhaps more so. Everything from their school curricula to their crop acreage to the types of goods they sold in their stores was determined in Moscow. Provincial government officials had no independent taxing power nor were they allocated money that they could distribute as they desired. Each local government department was subordinated both to the local government and to the ministry, and each obtained its financing from the ministerial chain of command. Virtually every article ever published by a regional party secretary in the central press and every speech given at a party congress complained about some ministerial decision.

In 1985 Tatiana Zaslavskaia, a reforming sociologist, argued that the real structure of bureaucratic power was very different from the formal structure. State officials, she believed, were divided among three groups: those at the highest levels of government; those in the middle, "the employees of the branch ministries and departments and their territorial administrations"; and "the employees of the enterprises." The problem in the Soviet Union was not a concentration of power at the top, but "the clear overgrowth (*gipertrofiia*) of the intermediate link and the relative weakness of the lower and often the higher links." Economic reform, she said, "raises the prestige and influence of the first and third level, and lowers that of the second." Press censorship prevented Zaslavskaia from discussing party officials, but she correctly implied that the ministries had usurped power from the top party leaders and that local party officials were in no better position than were the enterprises.[56]

When Yury Andropov became general secretary, only three of thirteen voting members of the Politburo worked outside Moscow. Excluding Gorbachev, the other nine members had worked in high political and administrative posts in Moscow for twenty-six years each. Andropov selected almost all his new lieutenants from the provinces. His number two man, Gorbachev, had been a Central Committee secretary for only four years and came from Stavropol. Two of his Central Committee secretaries, Grigory Romanov and Yegor Ligachev, came from Leningrad and Tomsk, respectively. A first deputy premier, Geidar Aliev, came from Azerbaidzhan; the head of the police, Vitaly Fedorchuk, from Ukraine; and Vitaly Vorotnikov, his premier of Russia, from Krasnodar. Aleksandr

56. Interview with T. I. Zaslavskaia, "Vybor strategii," *Izvestiia*, June 1, 1985, p. 3.

Yakovlev, his informal foreign policy adviser, had been in exile in Canada for a decade. These men became the heart of Gorbachev's team as well. This personnel policy was both a gesture to the provinces and a recognition that provincial officialdom had a reservoir of resentment against the old Moscow elite.

Conclusion

It is easy to identify the many factors that produced profound dissatisfaction with the political situation in the Soviet Union in the early 1980s both among the masses and the elites. The crucial inquiry is to discover the depth of the dissatisfaction and its target. Brezhnev's rule at the end of his life produced a disturbing political malaise at all levels, even, it turned out, in the Central Committee. Americans know how long four years can be in politics and how few presidents retain enough support to be reelected to a second term. Leonid Brezhnev had been in power for eighteen years when he died, and during the last six had become progressively so ill that his mental decline was clear to all television viewers. That the political elite could not or would not replace him led to the suspicion that the problem was stagnation not only in the Brezhnev administration but in the collective leadership and in the political system as a whole.

In principle the selection of Mikhail Gorbachev as leader and the introduction of such a popular new policy as perestroika could have dissipated some of this suspicion and malaise. Indeed, whatever else may be said about perestroika, it demonstrated that Brezhnev's obkom first secretaries could have the forward-looking views of a Mikhail Gorbachev, an Eduard Shevardnadze, or a Boris Yeltsin. It also demonstrated that the stagnation of the Brezhnev era was not inevitably perpetual.

But did the Brezhnev administration's loss of legitimacy otherwise extend to the system as a whole? No word is vaguer than *legitimacy* and no application of a word more difficult to determine. It would be simple to "demonstrate" the illegitimacy of the American political system in the 1990s with survey evidence of disillusionment and discontent, but no one expects an antidemocratic revolution in the near future. When discontent surfaces in other countries, it is very difficult to distinguish between grumbling and revolutionary discord.

Clearly the Soviet economic system and the elites running heavy industries had suffered a severe deterioration of support among educated citizens.

The West's lead in technological innovation and the Soviet Union's slow-ing rate of growth raised the most fundamental doubts about the legitimacy of Marxist assumptions about capitalism and socialism. The economic success of the Pacific Rim countries showed Lenin was wrong in believing that Russia's integration into the world economy would inexorably lead to economic stagnation.

It was just as clear that the legitimacy of ideology itself, in the sense of some true religion, was also being denied. Giuseppe Di Palma was later to speak of Brezhnev's "absolutization of the party" and his "determined effort to institutionalize a religion that had lost its god."[57] However, few close observers of the Soviet Union would have recognized such a charac-terization of the Brezhnev regime. I spoke of "institutional pluralism," Zbigniew Brzezinski of "oligarchical petrification," George Breslauer of "welfare-state authoritarianism." All these descriptions referred to the same phenomenon. The distinctive feature of Brezhnev was precisely that he had indeed lost the ideological fire of Nikita Khrushchev, not to speak of Stalin and Lenin. As a result, power had devolved from high party officials to the state or at least to specialized party-state complexes. But there was no evidence that any significant element in the population wanted to return to the ideological dogmas of the past.

In short, a very large segment of Soviet society—and the educated elite (the bureaucrats) even more than the masses—yearned for a freer society, greater access to the West, and a transition to a consumer-oriented econ-omy. They wanted a weakening of the detailed rule of all aspects of life by what Boris Yeltsin was to denounce as "the center."

But whatever Soviet citizens thought of Brezhnev's economic system, the vast majority believed in continuing nationalized heavy industry, social-ized medicine, and subsidized prices. Reformers seemed to be thinking of changes akin to those instituted by Janos Kadar's program in Hungary or the mixed economy of the New Economic Policy in the Soviet Union.

Neither did Russians—or indeed most non-Russians outside the Baltic republics–question the legitimacy of the Soviet Union as a country. This led most Western observers to take for granted that, behind the grumbling, Russians gave a grudging legitimacy to a one-party system—to be sure, a

---

57. Giuseppe Di Palma, "Totalitarian Exits," in H. E. Chehabi and Alfred Stepan, eds., *Politics, Society, and Democracy: Comparative Studies* (Boulder, Colo.: Westview Press, 1995), p. 242.

much looser one-party system—as something necessary to preserve the Union.[58]

Thus, despite the depth of the public's dissatisfaction with Brezhnev and his economic performance, or even because of it, Mikhail Gorbachev seemed in an ideal position when he came to power. He could use Brezhnev as a scapegoat for the country's problems and an explanation for all the sacrifices the people would have to make. He could use national defense and Marshal Ogarkov's arguments against the conservatives to justify fundamental economic reforms and changes in foreign policy. Indeed, Ronald Reagan's Strategic Defense Initiative was a godsend in dramatizing Ogarkov's argument about the connection between technology and defense. Then Gorbachev could use the need to preserve the Union as the justification for stopping liberalization short of full democratization. Strengthening national defense and preserving the Union seemed objectives certain to gain him strong military support for his program as a whole.

In the mid-1980s I envisioned Gorbachev's dreaming of standing on Lenin's mausoleum at the age of sixty-nine ushering in a new century and listening to people call him Mikhail the Great. Nothing that happened in the next decade either in Russia or the Soviet Union seems to indicate that the situation in 1985 was inevitably revolutionary or that introducing reforms into a communist regime must lead to chaos, at least within the time frame of one or two decades. China has managed for two decades to handle the ambiguity and contradictions of its partial transition to a market economy, and there is little reason to believe that such a reform could not have been equally successful in the Soviet Union.

Thus the problem is not just to look for the "causes" of the Revolution of 1990–91. There are more than enough causes for revolution in a great many political situations in which revolution does not occur. The real mystery is why Mikhail Gorbachev addressed the problems he inherited the way he did and created a revolutionary situation instead of defusing an incipient revolutionary one. In particular, why did he let the Soviet Union break apart without a struggle when most of the population, before and since, opposed a breakup and when the preservation of the Union was the natural rallying cry to legitimize the Communist party as well?

58. See, for example, Seweryn Bialer, *The Soviet Paradox: External Expansion, Internal Decline* (Knopf, 1986), pp. 136–37; and Hough and Fainsod, *How the Soviet Union Is Governed*, pp. 567–70. It is significant that neither of these books included the words *democracy* or *democratization* in their indexes.

CHAPTER THREE

Gorbachev's Ascent and the Circular Flow of Power

IN HIS LAST YEARS IN POWER, Leonid Brezhnev had become an incompetent leader. His cabinet was a collection of old men who lacked the will to alter the status quo by removing him. The country was falling behind the economic growth and competition of the United States, China, Japan, and Western Europe. Despite all this, the country was calm. There were no significant demonstrations or strikes, no effort in the Central Committee to remove Brezhnev, no attempted military coup. The social forces produced by modernization simply had no direct or decisive impact on the most important political and economic decisions made by the leadership during the late 1970s and early 1980s.

All observers agreed that in the past the office of Soviet leader had possessed such enormous power that a change of leaders had always produced significant changes in policy and in the way the political institutions functioned. But under Brezhnev policy seemed to reflect the interests and ideas of the party and bureaucratic structures. There had been few dramatic policy interventions from the political leadership against their interests.

What was the reason? Most observers believed that a fundamental change had occurred in the political system. They thought the bureaucracy or perhaps the collective leadership had come to dominate, or at least had achieved a position from which it could prevent a leader from dominating.[1]

---

1. The first important Western scholar to express this view was Zbigniew Brzezinski, "Victory of the Clerks," *New Republic*, November 14, 1984, pp. 15–18. See

In this view the Politburo, not the general secretary, now ruled, and Gorbachev had been selected by its aging and conservative members. He might be a pleasant young man with a new style but must have views that reflected those of a partocracy staunchly averse to meddling with the status quo.[2] Even if he had somehow managed to conceal more radical views, Gorbachev's support in the Politburo must be fragile and tentative. He would have to obtain four votes of approval from the other eight members to take any liberalizing action and would be easily stopped.

Opposing this view of the situation, a minority of Kremlin watchers believed that the basic power structure remained much as it had throughout the Soviet period: the slow process of policymaking and the economic and political stagnation that marked Brezhnev's later years actually reflected his desires. Far from exposing his weakness, the lack of change showed how powerful Brezhnev was, not how dominant the bureaucracy or the Communist party had become in obstructing change.

In this view, those who emphasized oligarchic or bureaucratic resistance to change failed to understand the problems of effective collective action by the bureaucracy—the difficulties in resisting change. In early 1957 Nikita Khrushchev had abolished the industrial ministries and established regional economic councils (*sovnarkozy*). The industrial ministers had been unable to stop him, even though he was also opposed by a majority of the members of the Presidium (as the Politburo was called at the time). Brezhnev had recreated the ministries, and in the 1980s it was unclear that they were any stronger than in 1957. Indeed, why should Soviet bureaucrats defend the interests of their bureaucracies by resisting economic liberalization or even privatization when promoting such reforms would enrich them as individuals? Why should local party officials, who favored decentralization of power in 1957, oppose it in 1987 when Chinese party officials had shown how the party apparatus could benefit from reform?

For these scholars the notion that some amorphous collective leadership can stay in power for decades without independent bases of power also seemed unrealistic. Institutional rules matter not only in providing the incentive systems in which members of the broader public make their decisions, but also in defining the struggle for power of potential leaders.

---

also Thane Gustafson and Dawn Mann, "Gorbachev's First Year: Building Power and Authority," *Problems of Communism*, vol. 35 (May–June 1986), pp. 1–2.

2. For a classic statement of this view, see Konstantin Simis, "The Gorbachev Generation," *Foreign Policy*, no. 59 (Summer 1985), pp. 3–21.

Some individual or group within the leadership would take advantage of the rules to upset the equilibrium and end the power of its other members.

In the Soviet Union, the observers in the minority contended, ultimate power was in the hands of the top party organs, and party rules defined the way leaders were selected. The rules specified that the general secretary was elected not by the Politburo but by the 300-member Central Committee, which also selected the Politburo. The rules and norms of the system had in turn transferred power over personnel selection to the general secretary. The Central Committee was selected by the Communist Party Congress, and the regional party secretaries had control over the delegates to it. But the regional secretaries were essentially appointed by the general secretary and became the core of his political machine in consolidating power in the top leadership. Robert Daniels called this system "the circular flow of power."[3]

In this minority reading of Soviet politics, the general secretary's chief lieutenant for personnel selection was always positioned to gain control of his former superior's political machine during the succession. Gorbachev was responsible for personnel selection under Yury Andropov and Konstantin Chernenko, and he used his position to build strong support in the Central Committee. This, not his malleability or a Politburo mistake, was the explanation for his selection as general secretary.

If this was indeed the situation, Gorbachev was from the beginning in a very powerful position vis-à-vis the Politburo. He would be in an even stronger position when a new Central Committee was elected at a Party Congress in early 1986. He had signaled his support for major innovations in policy, and like Khrushchev was likely to represent the resentments of the regions and their leaders against the central administration in Moscow.

The minority view proved to be right about the structure of power. Memoirs from across the political spectrum have testified to the crucial role of the Central Committee in Gorbachev's election and to his virtually unchallenged power in selecting personnel within the party apparatus. Gorbachev was able to remove the conservative Politburo members faster than any general secretary in history—three within a year and a fourth by

---

3. Robert V. Daniels, "Soviet Politics since Khrushchev," in John W. Strong, ed., *The Soviet Union under Brezhnev and Kosygin: The Transition Years* (Van Nostrand, Reinhold, 1971), p. 20. Also see the discussion in Jerry F. Hough and Merle Fainsod, *How the Soviet Union Is Governed* (Harvard University Press, 1979), pp. 144–46, 260–61, 454–55, 474–75.

June 1987. He achieved in one year something it took Stalin six years and Khrushchev four years.[4] The change was even greater one level lower: only two of seven candidate members of the Politburo in March 1986 had held this post a year earlier and only three of the eleven Central Committee secretaries besides Gorbachev.[5]

The structure of power within the Soviet Communist party is now mainly of historical interest, and some of the detail of this chapter will be too arcane for the nonspecialist.[6] Yet it is crucial to understand the basic point about Gorbachev's great power in 1985–86. Otherwise one would grossly exaggerate the ability of the conservative opposition to resist change, which Gorbachev's minions were emphasizing at the time to deflect criticism from him and to explain the decisions he was not taking. In addition, if one fails to understand the institutional source of Gorbachev's power, some of the crucial dilemmas he later faced, especially those associated with Boris Yeltsin and the Russian Republic, will not be understood.

Gorbachev's Path to Power

Mikhail Gorbachev was born in 1931 in a village in the fertile Stavropol Region. One grandfather resisted collectivization until 1933 when he was arrested and sent to forced labor in the Siberian timber industry. After two years of high-quality work there, he was freed, returned to his village, and became head of a pig farm in the village kolkhoz (collective farm). Gorbachev's other grandfather joined the Communist party and became the first chairman of the kolkhoz. As a reasonably high official, he was arrested in the Great Purge in 1937. He was never brought to trial but remained in

4. T. H. Rigby, "The Soviet Political Executive, 1917–1986," in Archie Brown, ed., *Political Leadership in the Soviet Union* (Indiana University Press, 1989), p. 48.

5. For the membership of the Politburo and Secretariat on the eve of Gorbachev's accession, see *Ezhegodnik Bol'shoi Sovetskoi Entsiklopediia 1984* (Moscow: Sovetskaia Entsiklopediia, 1984), p. 13. For the membership in March 1986, see *Ezhegodnik Bol'shoi Sovetskoi Entsiklopediia 1984* (Moscow: Sovetskaia Entsiklopediia, 1986), p. 15. By then the Politburo had been expanded from ten voting members to fourteen, so that the remaining pre-1985 members made up less than 40 percent of the body. Thus between 1988 and 1991 Gorbachev was able to introduce policy changes of the most sweeping character.

6. However, Boris Yeltsin created a legislative Federation Council that was modeled on the Central Committee and designed by similar mechanisms to ensure that the Russian president retained much of the power of the general secretary.

jail for fourteen months, after which he again was named kolkhoz chairman.[7]

Gorbachev was a member of a golden generation, those born between 1927 and 1933. Men born between 1918 and 1926 had been young adults during World War II, and millions had been killed at the front. Those who survived had forgotten their high school mathematics while in uniform, and unlike their American counterparts, had their college education irreparably disrupted in a country that usually required engineering and agronomic training for major managerial and political posts. Grigory Romanov, the leading Politburo member of this generation, was typical in obtaining his engineering education at night school.

Because those born after 1927 generally did not see service in the war, the number of men born from 1927 to 1931 who survived it was twice that of those born from 1921 to 1926. After the war Stalin for the first time introduced high-standard college education and gave little preference to class origin in college admission. Gorbachev's generation was the first to benefit widely from this policy.[8] These young elites began their administrative careers in the increasingly liberal atmosphere produced by de-Stalinization. They were the ones Edward Crankshaw described as "well-turned-out young men in their thirties, usually Party members, relaxed and

---

7. For the best weighing of evidence on the early life of Gorbachev and his wife, Raisa, see Archie Brown, *The Gorbachev Factor* (Oxford University Press, 1996), pp. 25–43. Gorbachev's memoirs describe his early years in some detail; see *Zhizn' i reformy* (Moscow: Novosti, 1995), pp. 31–98. The English edition, *Memoirs* (Doubleday, 1996), seems a direct translation of the Russian version, but with many passages cut or shortened. *Memoirs* also includes some very serious errors of translation or omission (see, for example, footnotes 58 and 67 below), but it is not known whether this is the fault of a translator or of a political sanitization of the memoirs by Gorbachev's people. Any serious scholar must use the Russian-language edition, and translations in this book will be mine from the Russian edition. For the benefit of the reader, the reference to the English edition will be added to references to the Russian edition throughout this volume, and deviations from the Russian edition will be noted. Gorbachev's early life is, for example, described on pp. 18–72 of *Memoirs*. The German-language version of the memoirs was published first and reportedly was assembled in Berlin by Germans from a mass of unintegrated materials sent the publisher. It possibly includes information not found in the Russian edition, but I do not have the knowledge of German to check it.

8. For a discussion of the socialization of Gorbachev and his generation, see Jerry F. Hough, *Soviet Leadership in Transition* (Brookings, 1980), pp. 57–60; and Hough, *Russia and the West: Gorbachev and the Politics of Reform* (Simon and Schuster, 1988), pp. 17–43.

easy in manner, often with a pleasantly ironical approach to life, and very much in touch with realities of every kind."[9]

By the early 1980s a generation gap had emerged in the middle levels of the party and state bureaucracy, especially the bureaucracy dealing with the economy. As officials of the older generation retired or died, they were disproportionately replaced not by men of Romanov's generation but by those of Gorbachev's. This distribution can be seen by examining the biographies of more than 450 high officials of the Soviet political system who were elected to the Central Committee and Central Auditing Commission at the 1981 Party Congress.[10]

As table 3-1 shows, by the 1980s many of the Soviet elite, even among the ministers, were men in their early fifties—that is, born after 1925.[11] The top of a bell-shaped curve of age distributions in 1981 should have been found among men in their late fifties (born between 1919 and 1925). If the seventy-year-olds (those born before 1912) are excluded, such a distribution did exist among officials in sectors—light industry and services, military, security, media, culture, education, and science—in which top technical education was not required. Of the 106 men at the central and subcentral level in these sectors, 28 were born between 1912 and 1918, 56 between 1919 and 1925, and 22 after 1925. The officials in general political work and in heavy industry, construction, and agriculture were distributed very differently: 86 born between 1912 and 1918, 71 between 1919 and 1925, and 124 after 1925.

Gorbachev himself was atypical among those seeking political power. He did not go to an engineering institute but studied law. He did so at the most prestigeous school in the country, Moscow University. He was on a fast track from the start.[12] He engaged in part-time Komsomol work in school and university and in 1955 entered full-time Komsomol work in his

9. Edward Crankshaw, *Khrushchev's Russia* (Baltimore: Penguin Books, 1959, pp. 90–91, 127, 130.

10. Election to the Central Committee or the Central Auditing Commission was an important status symbol for officials. The most important were named full members of the Central Committee, the next most important were named candidate members, and the next became members of the Auditing Commission.

11. There were only ten women among significant officials. Five were born between 1918 and 1925. They were in their early twenties during World War II, and they moved into lower political careers with particular ease then because the men were in the army.

12. Gorbachev himself remarks on his fast track in *Zhizn' i reformy*, vol. 1, pp. 410–11. The passage is not in *Memoirs*.

Table 3-1. *Distribution of Male Officials Elected to the Central Committee and Central Auditing Commission, by Period of Birth and Economic Sector, 1981*[a]

Percent

Sector	Before 1912	1912–18	1919–25	After 1925
Central Officials				
General political and economic	21	9	6	6
Heavy industry, construction, agriculture	16	25	14	24
Light and food industry and services	3	0	6	3
Military and security officers	13	12	9	1
Media, culture, education, science	8	7	5	4
Foreign policy	10	5	2	5
Total	71	58	42	43
Subcentral Officials				
Republican officials	1	24	22	36
Regional officials	0	28	29	58
Military and security officers	0	0	13	2
Foreign policy	0	0	11	2
Media, culture, science	2	4	10	5
Total	3	56	85	103

Source: *Ezhegodnik Bol'shoi sovetskoi entsiklopediia* (Moscow: Bol'shaia sovetskaia entsiklopediia, 1982), pp. 546–612.

a. Central party, governmental, and trade union officials specializing in industry, agriculture, culture, and so forth, are distributed into those respective categories.

native Stavropol krai (territory), an important agricultural province. He became Komsomol first secretary in 1958. In 1962 he transferred to the party organs. In 1966 at the age of thirty-five, he was first secretary of the Stavropol city party committee (in effect, its real mayor), in 1968 he became second secretary of the provincial party committee, and in 1970, at the age of thirty-nine, its first secretary. In 1971 he became the youngest official to be elected a full member of the Central Committee.

For a career politician, Stavropol was a fortunate place to work. The Central Committee second secretary, Mikhail Suslov, had been provincial party first secretary in Stavropol in the late 1930s and remained attached to the region. Yury Andropov, the chairman of the KGB, had been born in the region and continued to vacation there. Fedor Kulakov, the Stavropol first secretary who promoted Gorbachev into party work in the early 1960s, had worked closely with Chernenko in the Penza Region during the 1940s. In October 1964 Kulakov was brought to Moscow by Brezhnev to become head of the Agriculture Department of the Central Committee; eleven months later he was named Central Committee secretary for agriculture. Kulakov's ties with Chernenko were likely important in his promotion.

As a scholar who has studied the party apparatus and officials in the 1960s and 1970s in great detail, I find Gorbachev's memoirs on this period filled with sophisticated political judgments and insights. He showed extraordinary skill in courting the right officials at particular times and in using these connections to advance himself. He often called on Kulakov for help and developed very friendly relations with KGB chief Andropov. Gorbachev was also skilled in distancing himself from those who were falling into disfavor. Warned to avoid close contacts with Premier Aleksei Kosygin, he engineered a conflict with him almost immediately after becoming Central Committee secretary.[13]

By the end of his life, Kulakov had developed bad relations with Chernenko and other Politburo members, including Brezhnev. Although Kulakov had once been one of three or four men in the inner core whom Brezhnev invited to dine, he clearly offended Brezhnev for some reason.[14] When a Central Committee plenum was scheduled on agriculture in 1978, Kulakov was not included on the commission that prepared the materials, although he was the Central Committee secretary for agriculture.[15] All Politburo members were obligated by protocol to attend Kulakov's funeral and internment in the Kremlin wall in 1978, but none of those associated with Chernenko did so, including the Moscow first secretary. Andrei Kirilenko, Andrei Gromyko, and Dmitry Ustinov—the core of Andropov's team—were the most prominently featured in the funeral photograph and were joined at the funeral only by Arvid Pelshe and Kiril Mazurov from among the other Politburo members.[16] Kulakov presumably had switched his allegiance from Chernenko's faction to that headed by Kirilenko and Andropov. Gorbachev managed to quarrel with Kulakov at this time and mentioned it to other leaders.[17]

In 1978 Gorbachev was selected Central Committee secretary for agriculture to replace Kulakov. Westerners sometimes sneered at the post as no

13. Gorbachev, *Zhizn' i reformy*, vol. 1, pp. 29, 186–88; *Memoirs*, pp. 16–17, 115–16.
14. Yevgeny Chazov, *Zdorov'e i vlast': vospominaniia Kremlevskogo vracha* (Moscow: Novosti, 1992), p. 84.
15. Gorbachev, *Zhizn' i reformy*, vol. 1, pp. 19–20; *Memoirs*, pp. 7–8.
16. *Pravda*, July 19, 1978, p. 1.
17. Gorbachev, *Zhizn' i reformy*, vol. 1, pp. 17, 19–20; *Memoirs*, pp. 7–8. The strong passage on p. 17 of *Zhizn'* is omitted.

more than a graveyard for those with political hopes, but it was much more, as Gorbachev acknowledged in his memoirs:

> The post of secretary for agriculture was a key one in the structure of the Central Committee insofar as its occupant was constantly connected with the whole country, with the first secretaries of the republican central committees, the kraikoms, and the obkoms. And the corps of first secretaries was the patrimony (*votchina*) and base of support for the general secretary. This meant that Brezhnev had the final word in selecting this official.[18]

The following year Gorbachev was named a candidate member of the Politburo and in 1980 a full member.

In 1980 Gorbachev was forty-nine years old in a Politburo whose other voting members averaged seventy. Although Gorbachev has often been seen as nothing more than a protege of Andropov, this view is much too simple. The new regional secretaries were men of Gorbachev's age. Andropov, who became sixty-five in 1979, needed an ally in an important Central Committee post who could gain him the support of younger party officials. He no doubt thought of Gorbachev as a key element in building his support in the Central Committee, but the alliance, of course, also allowed Gorbachev to build his own support. Even within the Politburo, he spoke out on questions outside his area of responsibility, offending some of the older members.[19]

The next youngest Politburo member, Grigory Romanov, the first secretary of the Leningrad Obkom, was eight years older than Gorbachev, and the next two were thirteen and seventeen years older, respectively. Romanov, Gorbachev's most natural rival, had been an engineer who had worked for eight years in the defense industry before moving into party work. In the early and mid 1970s Brezhnev and Kosygin had told foreign leaders that Romanov was Brezhnev's likely successor.[20]

As Brezhnev's health deteriorated after 1975, however, the fact that Romanov, Fedor Kulakov, and Kiril Mazurov were the only logical successors in their fifties inevitably aroused great suspicion in Brezhnev and other potential successors of the older generation. While Mazurov was removed and Kulakov fell into deep disfavor, Romanov was effectively, although

18. Gorbachev, *Zhizn' i reformy*, vol. 1, p. 21; *Memoirs*, p. 9.
19. A. S. Cherniaev, *Shest' let s Gorbachevym* (Moscow: Progress, 1993), pp. 8–9. But Viktor Grishim claims he said little. V. V. Grishim, *Ot Kkrushcheva do Gorbacheva* (Moscow: Aspol, 1996), p. 69.
20. Valery Legostaev, *Tekhnologiia izmeny* (Moscow: Paleia, 1993), pp. 10–12.

almost surely unfairly, smeared through leaks to the Western media about his alleged drinking and other peccadillos in Leningrad such as the smashing of Hermitage china at his daughter's wedding.[21] Andropov made Romanov Central Committee secretary for the military-industrial complex in 1983, but that seemed simply a move to gain control of the Leningrad organization and put another person on the Politburo with such responsibilities to counterbalance Defense Minister Dmitry Ustinov.[22]

Gorbachev's great advantage when he was brought to Moscow was that he was only forty-seven at the time. Hence none of the older generation saw him as a threat either to Brezhnev or to themselves as the immediate successor to Brezhnev, but rather a counterweight to Romanov. Moreover, he seemed an ideal candidate to reassure his own generation that their values would eventually be reflected in policy. The sons of the elite were no longer going to engineering institutes unless they wanted to go into science; they did not want to begin their careers as foremen on the factory floor. Gorbachev's law degree suggested a man not so production oriented. The young adults in the Brezhnev period had been attracted to the so-called village writers who implicitly denounced the Soviet regime for sacrificing the countryside and the environment in the interest of industrialization. Gorbachev's rural background and career suggested an analogous set of priorities.

When Andropov was selected general secretary after Brezhnev died in November 1982, he had to give Chernenko responsibility for ideology and international relations within the Central Committee and award him the post of second secretary. (The second secretary chaired the Secretariat and in effect served as head of the White House staff.) However, Chernenko's chief personal assistant titled the chapter on 1983 in his memoirs "Exile

21. For a more sympathetic picture of Romanov, see Vladimir Soloyov and Elena Klepikova, *Behind the Kremlin Walls*, trans. Guy Daniels (Dodd, Mead, 1986). For a confirming version, see Legostaev, *Tekhnologiia izmeny*, pp. 12–15. During the late 1970s and early 1980s, Western correspondents privately admitted getting many of their leaks from correspondents of the Novosti news agency. The agency was being run by Lev Tolkunov, who had been Andropov's first deputy in the Socialist Countries Department in the early 1960s. Roy Medvedev, the sometime dissident, was a major source of information and disinformation to the West, and the head of the Fifth Administration of the KGB (the administration in charge of internal security) was protecting him. See Filipp Bobkov, *KGB i vlast'* (Veteran MP, 1995), p. 213. Legostaev reports that the rumors were also spread to other leaders in internal, secret documents. Brezhnev had to be involved in this.

22. Legostaev, *Tekhnologiia izmeny*, p. 29; Gorbachev, *Zhizn' i reformy*, vol. 1, p. 231. See *Memoirs*, p. 154, for a shortened version.

without Arrest." He asserts that Andropov decided "to push [Chernenko] into a corner" from the beginning and that Chernenko was "continually ignored and slighted."[23]

Gorbachev became Andropov's de facto second secretary, providing overall supervision of personnel selection, economic coordination, agriculture, and light industry. Gorbachev recommended Yegor Ligachev, a longtime friend, as head of the Organizational–Party Work Department, the number two post in personnel selection. Despite Chernenko's nominal responsibility for ideology, Gorbachev was chosen to present the key ideological speech on the anniversary of Lenin's birthday and, as shall be seen, sounded new ideological notes. Andropov treated him as his heir apparent, and Gorbachev claimed in his memoirs that Andropov's wife told Raisa Gorbachev after Andropov's funeral that her husband wanted Gorbachev to be his successor.[24]

If Andropov had lived another six months, his efforts and the decline in Chernenko's health surely would have brought success. When Andropov died in February 1984, even officials of the Central Committee apparatus had no idea who would have been selected general secretary. Many put the odds at 50 percent for Chernenko, 30 percent for Defense Minister Dmitry Ustinov, and 20 percent for Gorbachev. Gorbachev reports that he himself suggested Ustinov.[25] Even though it took four days for Chernenko to be elected, no information has emerged on the deliberations and the agreements that were reached.

Chernenko's lung disease was so advanced he could not utter a multi-syllable word without gasping for breath, and his wife was angry that he accepted the job.[26] Although the older leaders felt comfortable with a weak general secretary, they must have known that he would not live long and that public pressure for a younger successor would be extremely strong. This must have occurred to Gorbachev as well, and one agreement that was surely reached was that Gorbachev would retain all the duties Andropov had given him and also assume Chernenko's responsibility for ideology and foreign policy.

23. Viktor Pribytkov, *Apparat* (St. Petersburg: VIS, 1995), pp. 153–54.
24. Gorbachev, *Zhizn' i reformy*, vol. 1, p. 248; *Memoirs*, p. 154.
25. Legostaev, *Tekhnologiia izmeny*, p. 33; Gorbachev, *Zhizn' i reformy*, vol. 1, p. 231; *Memoirs*, p. 145, for a shortened version.
26. Pribytkov, *Apparat*, p. 64.

Chernenko and his allies would have liked to deny Gorbachev the chairmanship of the Secretariat after Andropov's death, and they made an effort to do so. However, the only other Central Committee secretary on the Politburo who could chair the Secretariat was Romanov, and Ustinov had a strong personal interest in preventing his rival in the national security realm from holding that key post. He blocked Romanov's appointment.[27] Chernenko might well have moved strongly to support Romanov after Ustinov's death in December 1994, but he was too ill and Gorbachev politically too strong by that point.

While Gorbachev became the nominal second secretary as well as the real one, Chernenko continually snubbed him in petty ways. Gorbachev was not formally named head of the Secretariat, although he was already filling the role. He was not allowed to take the traditional seat of the second secretary to the right of the general secretary at Politburo meetings, although this was finally granted grudgingly.[28] He was not permitted to take the second secretary's office in the Central Committee building until the very end of Chernenko's life. He was not made a member of the Defense Council.[29] Gorbachev was also often prevented from calling Politburo meetings, as was customary, and he was frequently bypassed on personnel decisions in favor of his subordinate, Ligachev, even though he was the Politburo member in charge of these matters.[30]

Gorbachev reported that all these "intrigues" strained his nerves "to the extreme."[31] Nevertheless, the few personnel decisions during this year pointed to the continued strength of the anti-Chernenko forces. In April 1985, for example, Boris Yeltsin, first secretary of the Sverdlovsk Obkom,

27. Gorbachev, *Zhizn' i reformy*, vol. 1, pp. 251–53; *Memoirs*, pp. 156–58; Legostaev, *Tekhnologiia izmeny*, p. 37.

28. Vadim Medvedev, *V komande Gorbacheva: Vzgliad iznutri* (Moscow: Bylina, 1994), pp. 16–17; and Valery Boldin, *Ten Years That Shook the World: The Gorbachev Era as Witnessed by His Chief of Staff*, trans. Evelyn Rossiter (Basic Books, 1994), pp. 45–46. Boldin was Gorbachev's assistant for agriculture, but in 1987 he was appointed head of the General Department, in effect the secretariat of the Secretariat, and the person in charge of the flow of documents in, out, and within the Central Committee. The post was one of the highest trust, and Boldin apparently was the closest of the aides to the Gorbachev family. Because he did not push a radical agenda, he sometimes saw a conservative side of Gorbachev and especially his wife, Raisa, that more radical assistants did not see or at least did not report.

29. Legostaev, *Tekhnologiia izmeny*, p. 48.

30. Boldin, *Ten Years That Shook the World*, pp. 45–54.

31. Gorbachev, *Zhizn' i reformy*, vol. 1, p. 253; *Memoirs*, p. 158. The period as a whole is described in *Zhizn'*, pp. 248–62; *Memoirs*, pp. 154–64.

was named a member of the Presidium of the Supreme Soviet, a symbolic honor but an extremely high one.[32] Gorbachev signaled his unhappiness with policy by failing to speak at a Central Committee session on agriculture or an important Politburo session on the 1985 plan and, as shall be discussed, by making a radical speech at an ideological conference in December 1984. On the day the conference was to convene, Chernenko phoned to suggest it be canceled, but Gorbachev reacted in a sharp and even unrestrained manner and Chernenko backed down.[33]

In 1985 the most plausible alternative to Gorbachev was Grigory Romanov, but Gorbachev was able to keep him out of sight and to keep rumors focused on Viktor Grishin. Grishin had become second secretary of the Moscow Obkom and voting member of the Central Committee in 1952, the last year of Stalin's life. He was named chairman of the USSR Trade Union Organization in 1957 and then served as first secretary (mayor) of Moscow for seventeen years after being selected in 1967. He was seventy-one years old in 1985, and even ten years earlier he had spoken of himself as being part of the older generation. Besides, whatever good qualities Grishin may have had, they did not include charisma and an inclination to innovate.[34]

By contrast, Gorbachev had been subtly conveying his radical intentions for some time. Under Brezhnev, for example, he signaled his orientation by using modern Scandinavian furniture in his Central Committee office.[35] But it was his speech on Lenin's birthday on April 22, 1983, that first drew notice. Although it expressed the usual themes of discipline, planning, and emphasis on heavy industry, it concluded with the striking new assertion that the articles Lenin wrote at the end of his life were "the essence of Leninism." This was an unmistakable endorsement of Lenin's New Economic Policy (NEP) and was followed by support for his ideas "about

32. Each yearbook (*ezhegodnik*) of the *Bol'shaia sovetskaia entsiklopediia* published the names of the current Presidium members. See, for example, p. 27 of the 1970 yearbook. The Presidium included its chairman, its secretary, the chairmen of the Supreme Soviet of the fifteen Union republics, and usually twenty or twenty-one other members. Most of the latter were chosen because they held a particular post, and they were replaced when they lost it. Yeltsin's selection marked the first time in this period that the Sverdlovsk secretary was named, and Sverdlovsk was the heart of the anti-Chernenko faction. See the 1984 yearbook, p. 9.

33. Gorbachev, *Zhizn' i reformy*, vol. 1, pp. 253–54. This incident and Gorbachev's discussion of the December speech is not in *Memoirs*.

34. For Grishin's autobiography see *Ot Krushcheva do Gorbacheva*.

35. This was reported by an Iowa banker, John Chrystal, who visited Gorbachev's office in the early 1980s.

taking objective economic laws more firmly into account . . . [and about] a skillful use of money-goods relations."[36] In June 1983 Gorbachev headed the delegation to the funeral of the Italian Communist party leader, Enrico Berlinguer, and in his speech said, "Dear Enrico, we never will forget your advice about the necessity of democratizing our country."[37]

Gorbachev's speech on December 10, 1984, at the ideological conference was described by the *New York Times* correspondent, Serge Schmemann, before his election: "[Gorbachev] was not simply calling, like all Soviet leaders these days, for greater efficiency and managerial innovation [but] for a transformation of the nation as radical as the one wrought by Stalin in the brutal industrialization drive of the 1930s."[38] Schmemann made his assessment on the basis of a truncated version of Gorbachev's speech printed in *Pravda*. When the actual speech became available in 1985, it turned out that Gorbachev had been even more radical than Schmemann had assumed.[39] Conservatives, including Chernenko, had fully understood its implications, which is why Chernenko had unsuccessfully tried to cancel the conference.

Although he later denied it, Viktor Grishin tried to position himself to succeed Chernenko, and he might have won out had the decision been made in the Politburo.[40] However, this time Gorbachev was determined to contest the nomination in the Central Committee if necessary. In early 1985

36. *Pravda*, April 23, 1983, pp. 1–2. In his 1987 book, *Perestroika: New Thinking for Our Country and the World* (Harper and Row, 1987), pp. 25–26, Gorbachev himself pointed to this speech to prove that perestroika had its origins well before 1985. For the classic Western argument that Lenin's last articles showed that he had accepted the NEP as the best long-term path to socialism and that Stalin's industrialization-collectivization program was a break with Leninism, see Moshe Lewin, *Lenin's Last Struggle*, trans. A. M. Sheridan Smith (Pantheon Books, 1968).

37. Fedor Burlatsky, *Russkie gosudari: Epokha reformatsii* (Moscow: Shark, 1996), p. 195.

38. Serge Schmemann, "The Emergence of Gorbachev," *New York Times Magazine*, March 3, 1985, p. 45.

39. Archie Brown of Oxford University quoted from and interpreted the full speech in "Gorbachev: New Man in the Kremlin," *Problems of Communism*, vol. 34 (May–June 1985), pp. 1–23. Brown read Gorbachev's speech in M. S. Gorbachev, *Zhivoe tvorchestvo naroda* (Moscow: Politizdat, 1984). For a discussion of the drafting of the speech, see Boldin, *Ten Years That Shook the World*, pp. 48–50. See also Medvedev, *V komande Gorbacheva*, pp. 21–23; and Gorbachev, *Zhizn' i reformy*, vol. 1, pp. 253–54. This is not in *Memoirs*.

40. For the denial see *Nezavisimaia gazeta*, February 16, 1991, p. 5. For the traditional view that the voting members of the Politburo were "the selectorate" that chose Gorbachev, see Brown, *Gorbachev Factor*, pp. 80, 83–87, 229.

Ligachev helped organize the obkom secretaries to support Gorbachev as the successor to Chernenko. "There was a kind of trade-off at work," Valery Boldin, another Gorbachev assistant, wrote, "with some of them wanting to stay in their jobs and others to move to Moscow. Pledges flowed freely, as the need arose."[41] Ligachev hinted at his own role when he said those were "alarming days" in which "absolutely other decisions" could have been taken had it not been for "a large group of [regional] first secretaries."[42] Boris Yeltsin told a correspondent in some detail that as first secretary of the Sverdlovsk Obkom he had been part of the effort to prevent the Politburo members from electing Grishin as general secretary and that the effort was made openly.

> A large number of obkom first secretaries agreed that of all the Politburo members, the man to be promoted to the post of general secretary had to be Gorbachev. He was the most energetic, the best educated, and the most suitable from the point of view of age. We decided to put our weight behind him. We conferred with several Politburo members . . . [and with] Ligachev. Our position coincided with his, because he was as afraid of Grishin as we were. Once it had become clear that this was the majority view, we decided that if any other candidate was put forward—Grishin, Romanov, or anyone else—we would oppose him en bloc. And defeat him.
>
> Evidently the discussions within the Politburo itself followed along these lines. Those Politburo members who attended that session were aware of our firm intentions, and Gromyko too supported our point of view. . . . Grishin and his supporters did not dare risk making a move; they realized that their chances were slim (or rather, to be precise, zero), and, therefore, Gorbachev's candidacy was put forward without any complications or problems.[43]

Yeltsin's recollections are precise and seem accurate. Nikolai Ryzhkov, in his memoirs, vehemently denied that this effort occurred, but the denial shows only that the Central Committee secretary in charge of economic

41. Boldin, *Ten Years That Shook the World*, pp. 60-61.
42. *XIX Vsesoiuznaia konferentsiia Kommunisticheskoi partii Sovetskogo Soiuza (28 iunia–1 iulia 1988 goda)*, vol. 2: *Stenograficheskii otchet* (Moscow: Politizdat, 1988), p. 86. Gorbachev, *Zhizn' i reformy*, vol. 1, pp. 260, 265–70, confirmed the role of the obkom secretaries and said he kept them informed earlier. See also *Memoirs*, pp. 163, 165–66, but the discussion is much abbreviated.
43. "Dialogi s Boris Yel'tsinym," in Andrei Karaulov, *Vokrug Kremlia: Kniga politicheskikh dialogov* (Moscow: Novosti, 1990), p. 104. Yegor Ligachev's assistant describes regional secretaries coming in independently and Yeltsin stating an intention to nominate Gorbachev, if necessary, only in the name of the Sverdlovsk party organization. Legostaev, *Tekhnologiia izmeny*, p. 50.

planning did not deal with regional secretaries on political decisions.[44] All that was necessary was to tell the opposition about the balance of forces within the Central Committee and to threaten a showdown. Indeed, when Boldin reported that the Politburo meeting of March 11 was scheduled for 3:00 P.M., he added that "the views of the participants of the plenum had to be ascertained no later than 3:00."[45]

When Chernenko died at 7:20 on the evening of March 10, 1985, Gorbachev moved with unseemly speed to secure his victory. The Politburo was convened at 9:30 without three of ten voting members present—the Kazakhstan and Ukrainian first secretaries and Grigory Romanov (who was not even told about the meeting until after it was over). The session was somewhat tense, but short.[46] Gorbachev was named chairman of the Chernenko funeral commission and convened a Politburo session for 3:00 P.M. the next day to discuss the candidates for general secretary and called the Central Committee plenary session for 5:00 P.M. The Politburo discussion of candidates was not meant to take long.

By midnight the military had the impression that a final decision had already been made, and Gorbachev's lieutenants worked through the night to ensure his support in the Central Committee was solid.[47] At some point, Foreign Minister Andrei Gromyko agreed to nominate Gorbachev as general secretary in exchange for being selected chairman of the Presidium of

44. Nikolai Ryzhkov, *Perestroika: istoriia predatel'stv* (Moscow: Novosti, 1992), pp. 80–81. Gorbachev said that Ligachev had responsibility for contact with the party officials on the Central Committee and Ryzhkov for contact with the "clan" of ministers on the Central Committee and solidifying their support. Gorbachev, *Zhizn' i reformy*, p. 267. *Memoirs*, p. 166, does not include the word *clan*.

45. Boldin, *Ten Years That Shook the World*, p. 61. Gorbachev said the Politburo met at 2:00 P.M., but all other sources agree on 3:00. Gorbachev, *Zhizn' i reformy*, vol. 1, p. 267; *Memoirs*, p. 166.

46. The best insider description of the process is Ye. K. Ligachev, *Zagadka Gorbacheva* (Novosibirsk: Interbuk, 1992), pp. 56–66. See also Boldin, *Ten Years That Shook the World*, pp. 57–64, and Angus Roxburgh, *The Second Russian Revolution: The Struggle for Power in the Kremlin* (Pharos Books, 1992), p. 23. Gorbachev has written that Gromyko had been allied against him in 1984 but that a reconciliation was effected shortly before Chernenko's death. Vladimir Kriuchkov, the first deputy chairman of the KGB (and future KGB chairman who would lead the August 1991 coup), whom Gorbachev calls a close friend of Aleksandr Yakovlev, was a key intermediary with Gromyko. Gorbachev, *Zhizn' i reformy*, vol. 1, pp. 251, 261, 264, 266–67; *Memoirs*, pp. 156, 164. The important information on pp. 261 and 266–67 in *Zhizn'*, including that on Yakovlev and Kriuchkov, is not in *Memoirs*.

47. S. F. Akhromeev and G. M. Kornienko, *Glazami marshala i diplomata* (Moscow: Mezhdunarodnye otnoshenii, 1992), p. 10.

the Supreme Soviet. Despite many rumors of conflict and debate in the Politburo and the Central Committee, Gorbachev was elected unanimously in both bodies without debate.[48]

Chernenko's death had not been announced in the newspapers of March 10. Thus both that news and his obituary appeared on March 11, along with the news of the election of his successor. All newspapers in the Soviet Union had the same first two pages that day, laid out in identical manner: page one had a report on the plenary session of the Central Committee, a picture of Gorbachev, and his biography, while page two informed the public of Chernenko's death and printed the medical bulletin and his obituary. Rumors, seemingly false, claimed that Gromyko had spoken of Gorbachev's "teeth of iron" in his nominating speech. The speed with which Gorbachev moved to have himself elected and the almost indecent way he handled the reporting of his predecessor's death gave the rumors credence. By all appearances, the Soviet Union had gained an extremely decisive and ruthless leader who was determined to act very quickly.

Indeed, one of Ligachev's assistants, who was intimately involved in the process, writes of a "seizure of power."[49] While this description is much overdrawn, Gorbachev was absolutely determined to avoid the four-day discussion that occurred between Andropov's death and Chernenko's election and to ensure that any possible contenders were presented with a fait accompli. His actions were more the result of anxiety than the presence of a real threat. It had been clear for weeks that Chernenko was dying. As Gorbachev reports, Central Committee officials were talking about nothing except the succession. The only hope of stopping Gorbachev was a Romanov-Grishin alliance in favor of Romanov, with appropriate offers to other leaders. For whatever reason that alliance had not been struck in the weeks before Chernenko's death, and it was highly unlikely to be struck in the few days afterwards.

The Central Committee members had reacted to Andropov's nomination by the Politburo in November 1982 with an ovation and to Konstantin Chernenko's in February 1984 with perfunctory applause, but they greeted

---

48. Legostaev, *Tekhnologiia izmeny*, pp. 47–49, but Gorbachev says the meeting was held at 11:00 P.M. Gorbachev, *Zhizn' i reformy*, vol. 1, pp. 264–65; *Memoirs*, p. 164. Others report the meeting as being over well before 11:00 when they arrived at the Kremlin. Legostaev's testimony is likely more reliable. Vadim Pechenev, *Vzlet i padenie Gorbacheva: Glazami ochevidtsa* (Moscow: Respublika, 1996), pp. 27–28.

49. Legostaev, *Tekhnologiia izmeny*, p. 49.

Gorbachev's nomination with an ovation larger than the one for Andropov.[50]

The 300 voting members of the Central Committee that named Gorbachev general secretary, it should be remembered, were the top officials in the country at the time the Central Committee was elected in 1981. They were not as old as the members of the Politburo, but they averaged sixty-four years of age in March 1985.[51] As table 3-2 shows, they were the heart of the top party-government-military nomenklatura. In 1985 nearly 15 percent had been retired or seriously demoted. Another 31 percent were central government and party officials, 28 percent were regional party and government officials, 7 percent were military officers on active duty and KGB officials, and 5 percent were former party officials in the diplomatic corps. Sixty percent were reelected to the Central Committee in 1986, and they presumably were the core of Gorbachev's support. This group averaged sixty-two years of age and had fewer central government officials, but except for the 44 retirees, they held much the same types of jobs.

Thus the support for change came not only from high levels of the party apparatus and bureaucracy, but also from the military and security organs. Gorbachev's hand was likely strengthened by the article, discussed earlier, written by Marshal Nikolai Ogarkov, head of the General Staff, and published in the Central Committee journal, *Kommunist.* Yury Andropov, KGB chairman from 1967 to 1982, was closely linked both with the military-industrial complex and the most powerful machine in the party apparatus, the one created by Brezhnev's closest long-time associate, Andrei Kirilenko. Gorbachev allied himself with the same power base, at least within the party apparatus.

Thus Gorbachev came to power selected by the party apparatus and the military-security complex, by people such as Yegor Ligachev and Nikolai Ryzhkov who were mislabeled conservative opponents of reform. The Central Committee did not imagine the scale, but they knew Gorbachev would introduce major reform. When he quoted Lenin's pro-NEP state-

---

50. Cherniaev, *Shest' let s Gorbachevym,* p. 29. See also Boldin, *Ten Years That Shook the World,* pp. 62–64.

51. In 1981, 319 persons had been elected voting members of the Central Committee, but by March 1985, 31 had died and 11 candidate members had been promoted to full membership to replace them. For their biographies, see 1981 *ezhegodnik,* pp. 564–611.

Table 3-2. *Employment and Age Distribution of Central Committee Voting Members, March 1985*

Percent unless otherwise specified

Type of employment	All members	Average year of birth	Members reelected in 1986	Members not reelected in 1986
Central party apparatus	9.0	1919	11.1	9.2
Central government apparatus[a]	22.0	1917	21.1	36.8
Other high political[b]	4.7	1922	5.6	5.3
Military and security[a]	6.7	1918	10.0	2.6
Republican and regional party	23.7	1924	29.4	23.7
Regional governmental	4.3	1920	5.0	5.3
Diplomats (former party)	4.7	1922	6.7	2.6
Professional diplomats	1.0	1924	1.7	0
Enterprise directors	0.3	1911	0	1.3
Natural science and design	2.7	1917	2.8	3.9
Workers and peasants[c]	6.3	1927	6.7	9.2
Retired or demoted	14.7	1914	...	...
Total	N=300	1920	N=180	N=76

Sources: The occupations of those reelected to the Central Committee in 1986 are in *Ezhegodnik Bol'shoi sovetskoi entsiklopediia, 1987* (Moscow: Bol'shaia sovetskaia entsiklopediia, 1987), pp. 548–99. The occupations of the others appear in various sources, notably Central Intelligence Agency, *Directory of Soviet Officials: National Organizations,* CR-84-13894 (Washington, November 1984), and the Soviet press.

a. The minister of defense and KGB chairman are placed among military and security officials, not central government. The military-security category includes seventeen military officers and three KGB officials.

b. "Other high political" includes those working in the trade unions, other "social organizations," party journals, and political-related social sciences.

c. Workers and peasants almost always hold foremanlike jobs.

ments in his 1983 speech, "the audience," he said, "enthusiastically supported this reference to Lenin's work."[52]

Obviously, large numbers of officials in the party apparatus were later deeply disturbed by the course that reform ultimately took. But the title of Ryzhkov's memoirs, *Perestroika: A History of Betrayals*, reflected his belief that *his* reforms were betrayed, not that his opposition was overcome. Ligachev later reported his happiness with the changes introduced through 1987, which were far more than most Westerners expected in 1985. But men such as Ligachev and Ryzhkov could not understand why Gorbachev deliberately introduced policies leading to the emasculation of the Communist party and then the disintegration of the Soviet Union itself. It is hard not to share their surprise.

52. Gorbachev, *Perestroika*, p. 12.

The Circular Flow of Power

Gorbachev was elected general secretary for many reasons. Society and the elite had changed drastically since 1964 when Brezhnev was elected, and a wide variety of people inside and outside the elite found the old rigidities and stagnation distasteful, even repulsive. The economic system was no longer functioning well even in comparison with communist countries such as Hungary, and it needed to be changed. Even conservatives understood that a new approach was necessary to hold the allegiance of the youth.[53] The USSR had been governed for a decade by leaders who were not only near seventy years old but who had been in disastrously poor health. The election of another elderly general secretary seemed risky.

At fifty-three Gorbachev was not that young—Bill Clinton was forty-six when he was elected president—but he was eight years younger than any other voting member of the Politburo. His education, career, and personality suggested he had the political skills to be a national and even international leader

In any political system, however, personality and policy are never enough to explain why a given individual becomes a leader. Organizational and institutional factors are also always crucial. In the American Democratic party, for example, since the abolition of the rule that the nominee must receive the vote of two-thirds of the delegates at the nominating convention, the nomination has been predetermined by the delegate selection process. Organizational considerations were no less important in the selection of a general secretary in the Soviet Union.

Gorbachev held the most strategic position in the system, the one giving him great power vis-à-vis the selection of the regional first secretaries. As has been seen, the basic structure of power inside the Communist party involved the election of the general secretary and members by a Central Committee that in turn was selected by a Party Congress whose delegates were controlled by the provincial secretaries who were supervised by the general secretary. Gorbachev's personal qualities explain why he had a dominant political position, but the position itself was crucial to his election.

53. For statements in the military press as early as 1965, see *Krasnaia zvezda*, November 25, 1965, p. 1, and December 18, 1975, p. 3. See also the discussion in Hough, *Soviet Leadership in Transition*, pp. 29–36, 103–08.

The circular flow of power was not some unintended consequence of party structure. It was deliberately instituted by Lenin in 1919 when the Politburo was created as the real cabinet within the party and the country's political structure. It was meant to accomplish just what it did—insulate him from Politburo influence. Lenin understood that if the leader were selected by the Politburo and removable by it, he would be politically dependent on its members. He needed an outside institution to which the Politburo was responsible, but which he controlled.

Since before the revolution, the party leader had been selected by the Central Committee, and the Central Committee was elected by a Party Congress composed of delegates elected in regional party organizations. This structure was well calculated to insulate the leader from other Moscow politicians, and the way to maintain the leader's independence from the Politburo was to subordinate it to the Central Committee as well. Then the leader would have a single problem: how to control the Party Congress. Delegates to the Party Congress were selected at the republican and provincial party conferences, and the delegates to these were selected at party conferences at the next lower territorial level. Lenin's first task was to ensure that the provincial leaders were loyal to him. His second was to see that the delegates to the Party Congress were under the control of the provincial leaders.

To accomplish this, Lenin established the principle that the provincial party secretaries, although ostensibly elected by their party organizations, were actually appointed (formally "recommended") from above. The provincial secretaries in turn recommended lower-level secretaries. Lenin then outlawed factions within the Communist party to prevent Politburo members from organizing slates of candidates to compete in the elections of delegates. Thus other Politburo members had little leverage in the Party Congress, and the selection of a delegation was effectively under the control of the regional first secretary, who led the delegation.

While Lenin was leader of the Politburo, he used Joseph Stalin as Central Committee secretary and then general secretary to control the selection of provincial first secretaries.[54] When Lenin died, the local secretaries not surprisingly proved to be loyal to Stalin. Stalin used this machine to control the Congress, the Central Committee it elected, and the Politburo

54. For direct testimony about Lenin's use of Stalin in 1922, see Anastas Mikoyan, *V nachale dvadtsatykh* (Moscow: Politizdat, 1975), pp. 140–41. The relevant quotation is translated in Hough and Fainsod, *How the Soviet Union Is Governed*, pp. 131–32.

and thereby consolidate his dictatorial rule. He continued to occupy the post of general secretary, and de facto it became the dominant position in the political system.

Although provincial first secretaries were officially approved by all the members of the Politburo, Yegor Ligachev's memoirs confirm what had long been clear: that there was "an unspoken, but strict subordination" in which Politburo members were never allowed to question or interfere in personnel decisions in policy realms where they did not have immediate responsibility. The only officials who could interfere in the selection of regional first secretaries were those explicitly supervising the party apparatus.[55] Viktor Grishin, Moscow first secretary and Politburo member, testified in like manner: "All proposals of the general secretary [on personnel] are accepted by other [Politburo] members. In this respect there is a certain discipline."[56] Fedor Burlatsky has noted that although Brezhnev often spoke last at Politburo sessions on policy questions, he always expressed his opinion first when he was interested in a personnel appointment. Naturally no one opposed him.[57]

There was, of course, another side to this power of the general secretary: as Gorbachev emphasized, he also had the right to remove obkom first secretaries.

> The [obkom] first secretary . . . was a key figure in the system of power. He received his post and huge power not from the people, not from a competitive election, but from the hand of Moscow—the Politburo, the Secretariat, and personally the general secretary. This was the basis for the duality and vulnerability of the position of the first secretary. Each knew full well that he would lose his post the moment he . . . lost the confidence of the general secretary.[58]

In these circumstances, the first secretaries continued to bring delegations to the Party Congress that were loyal to the general secretary. Indeed, the Organizational–Party Work Department of the Central Committee took a deep interest in persons who were named to the delegations, and it had to approve them. As expected, the delegates voted for a Central Committee that would support the general secretary, and they themselves comprised a

55. Ligachev, *Zagadka Gorbacheva*, p. 9.
56. *Nezavisimaia gazeta*, February 16, 1991, p. 5.
57. Fedor Burlatsky, *Vozhdi i sovetniki: O Khrushcheve, Andropove i ne tol'ko o nikh* (Moscow: Politizdat, 1990), pp. 292–93.
58. Gorbachev, *Zhizn' i reformy*, vol. 1, p. 123; *Memoirs*, p. 85. The English edition mistranslates *gensek* (the general secretary) as "the powers that be."

high percentage of the Central Committee members.[59] This gave the general secretary control over the Politburo, which was elected by the Central Committee.

Although up to two-thirds of the Central Committee members held high government, party apparatus, and military posts whose occupants almost automatically were named to the Central Committee, the general secretary had considerable influence in deciding who would be on the committee. One might have thought that the list of Central Committee members would be carefully negotiated among key members of the Politburo, but this seems not to have been so. One of his assistants has commented that in 1986 Gorbachev himself, with the help of his two chief assistants for personnel, Yegor Ligachev and Georgy Razumovsky, drew up the list of the Central Committee members to be elected at the Twenty-Seventh Party Congress.

> Most Politburo members simply did not know who would be elected and who would be dismissed. This secret, which was the basis of the leader's immense power, enabled him to decide the fate of the Central Committee and the Politburo as he wished. Few people realized that this highly important decision was the result of personal reflections. Since the general secretary determined who was to be on the Central Committee, its grateful members then duly elected him as their leader.[60]

This process also extended to the selection of Central Committee secretaries and perhaps even Politburo members.[61] In 1989, when Gorbachev was talking loudly about democratization of the Communist party, the Central Committee elected four new Central Committee secretaries to deal with agriculture, nationality questions, and Russian affairs. At a minimum, democratic elections would involve prior knowledge and discussion of candidates. Yet two of the new secretaries, both of whom were already members of the Central Committee, told a *Pravda* reporter they first learned, unexpectedly, that they were to be selected secretaries when Gorbachev announced their names in open plenum.[62] That this fact was then

59. For the changing percentages over time, see Hough and Fainsod, *How the Soviet Union Is Governed*, pp. 456–57.
60. Boldin, *Ten Years That Shook the World*, pp. 117–18.
61. Cherniaev claimed that no one had any idea who would be named to the Politburo in April 1985.
62. *Pravda*, September 23, 1989, p. 2, and September 28, 1989, p. 2. When interviewed a few days after the plenum, they still did not know what their responsibilities would be, and this information obviously was not given the plenum when it "elected" them. The Central Committee that elected Central Committee secretaries after the Twenty-Seventh Party Congress in 1986 was no better informed. V. A. Medvedev,

printed in *Pravda* was a signal that Gorbachev wanted others within the party apparatus to be clear about the extent of his power.

The general secretary obviously headed the Secretariat formally, but once he became unquestioned leader and gained responsibility for all national policy, he had little time for detailed oversight, let alone closely supervising the choice of personnel in the provinces. In practice the Central Committee Secretariat and apparatus came to serve many of the functions of the White House staff in the United States. As such, the general secretary needed a chief of staff, and one of the secretaries became a second secretary who chaired the weekly sessions of the Secretariat and assumed that role. The general secretary almost never attended sessions of the Secretariat.

In the Brezhnev period, Mikhail Suslov, who was four years older than Brezhnev and who oversaw ideological questions, served formally as second secretary and chaired the Secretariat, but he was more of a watchdog. The man who from 1964 through 1976 provided detailed supervision of personnel selection and oversight of the economy in the Secretariat was Andrei Kirilenko. From late 1976 to 1982 supervision of personnel selection was given to Konstantin Chernenko, while oversight of the economy remained with Kirilenko, although his memory was failing badly in Brezhnev's last years.[63] The general secretary occupied an office on the fifth floor of the main Central Committee building and the second secretary an adjoining office, the office that in memoirs is frequently described as "the famous Suslov office." But although it is seldom remarked, Kirilenko had his office on the fifth floor as well.[64]

The obvious danger for a general secretary was that the man supervising the political machine and playing a key role in selecting provincial party secretaries might gain the loyalty of the machine. Lenin's realization of this fact at the end of his life led to his virtually hysterical denunciation of Stalin and determination to move him to a less dangerous spot, and subsequent rulers took a series of steps to deal with the problem.

The leader therefore usually changed his lieutenant for personnel selection periodically and took pains to introduce checks and balances into the

---

Raspad: Kak on nazreval v 'mirovoi sisteme sotsializma' (Moscow: Mezhdunarodnye otnosheniia, 1994), pp. 17–19.

63. Medvedev, *V komande Gorbacheva*, p. 24; A. S. Cherniaev, *Moia zhizn' i moe vremia* (Mezhdunaiodroye ostnosheniia, 1995), p. 434; Gorbachev, *Zhizn' i reformy*, vol. 1, pp. 229–30; and *Memoirs*, p. 143.

64. N. I. Ryzhkov, *Desiat' let velikikh potriasenii* (Moscow: Kniga, Prosveshchenie, Miloserdie, 1995), p. 35.

system: division of responsibility or appointment of members of competing factions as chief lieutenant and a junior Central Committee secretary who served as his first deputy. Gorbachev has claimed that in the Brezhnev period some obkom secretaries were close to Fedor Kulakov, the Central Committee secretary for agriculture, who was surely being used as a counterweight to Kirilenko.[65] Gorbachev also commented that Kirilenko was always hostile to him.[66] This plus Gorbachev's ties with Andropov and Suslov, two others with Stavropol roots, was likely a reason that Brezhnev felt comfortable with Gorbachev in 1978 when he brought him into the Central Committee Secretariat and then the Politburo.

Brezhnev also took pains to ensure that new regional secretaries knew who had ultimate power. Both Gorbachev and Yeltsin have described the process by which they became obkom first secretaries and have indicated it was designed to emphasize Brezhnev's power. "I had conversations in turn," Gorbachev wrote, "with Kapitonov [the junior secretary for personnel], Kulakov [the secretary for agriculture and former first secretary in Stavropol], Kirilenko [the senior secretary for personnel], and Suslov [the leader of the Secretariat]." He then was taken to Brezhnev.[67] When Yeltsin was being appointed Sverdlovsk Oblast first secretary in 1976, he was taken up the hierarchical ladder in a similar way, although instead of Kulakov he met the Central Committee secretary who had been in Sverdlovsk.[68]

Although the general secretary took many such steps to ensure that he maintained control over his political machine, the lieutenant with the greatest power in personnel selection was still in a peculiarly strong position in the succession. Joseph Stalin held this post under Lenin, Khrushchev under Stalin in the last three years of the dictator's life, and Brezhnev in the last year of Khrushchev's rule. Chernenko held the job the last five or six years of Brezhnev's life, but Andropov had taken over the machine created by Chernenko's predecessor. When Andropov was elected second secretary in May 1982, it was widely assumed that he supervised ideological questions.

65. Gorbachev, *Zhizn' i reformy*, vol. 1, p. 141; not in *Memoirs*.
66. Gorbachev, *Zhizn' i reformy*, vol. 1, pp. 25–26; *Memoirs*, p. 13, presents a shortened version.
67. Gorbachev, *Zhizn' i reformy*, vol. 1, p. 123. Kirilenko is not included in the list in *Memoirs*, p. 85—an unlikely omission.
68. Boris Yeltsin, *Against the Grain: An Autobiography*, trans. Michael Glenny (Summit Books, 1990), p. 50.

According to Gorbachev, however, Brezhnev also gave him responsibility for personnel.[69] This was the job Gorbachev himself filled after 1983, and Andropov and Chernenko allowed him to choose a friend and supporter, Yegor Ligachev, as his chief deputy.[70] Moreover, even before 1983 Gorbachev had intimate contact with the regional party secretaries through his work as Central Committee secretary for agriculture. The limited life expectancy of the general secretaries in the early 1980s meant the younger regional secretaries were looking for a bandwagon on which to jump so they could develop ties with the likely leader of the future. Gorbachev was the obvious choice.

Yury Andropov and The Kirilenko Machine

Gorbachev had been able to select a number of regional secretaries while personnel secretary and had gained the support of others because of their common age. But he also made an alliance with the most powerful political machine in the Central Committee. It had been built by Brezhnev's long-time lieutenant, Andrei Kirilenko, and had been taken over by Andropov in the late 1970s. Kirilenko is an important figure in the political history of the 1970s and the 1980s, but he is almost forgotten now because Andropov, Gorbachev, and Yeltsin had a strong interest in keeping him forgotten. Precisely because of these ties, his importance must be discussed.

Given Lenin's abolition of factions in the party, the groups in the party apparatus had to be very informal. Strict, if unwritten, rules had been established forbidding social ties among Politburo and Secretariat members. As Nikolai Ryzhkov said, socializing among Politburo members and Central Committee secretaries was prohibited "so that there wouldn't be any 'blocs' or 'groups.'"[71] When Gorbachev became a Central Committee secretary in 1978, he was given a government dacha next to Andropov. Thinking to continue the friendly ties they had in Stavropol, he invited Andropov and his wife to dinner, but was quickly rebuffed. "I must refuse the invitation. . . . [Otherwise] the gossip will begin tomorrow: who?

---

69. Gorbachev, *Zhizn' i reformy*, vol. 1, p. 213; *Memoirs*, p. 132.
70. Ligachev, *Zagadka Gorbacheva*, pp. 8, 23; *Memoirs*, p. 132. Also see Cherniev, *Moia zhizn' i moe vremia*, p. 42.
71. Ryzhkov, *Ia iz partii po imeni "Rossiia,"* p. 411; Ryzhkov, *Desiat' let velikikh potriasenii*, p. 39.

where? why? what did they discuss? . . . We will still be on the road, and they will begin to report to Leonid Il'ich. I say this, first of all, Mikhail, for your benefit."[72]

Everyone has remarked on Gorbachev's lack of friends on the Politburo, but Ryzhkov noted that the old rule against Politburo socializing generally continued to be observed after 1985. None of the Politburo members visited each other's homes. Even an old college friend, Anatoly Luk'ianov, was never invited to Gorbachev's home during the perestroika period.[73]

The paradoxical consequence of this practice was to promote the creation of groupings along career lines. When officials were young, they had been able to develop personal ties and mutual trust. In the absence of personal contact, they tended to trust those who had appointed them or whom they had appointed. The most powerful informal faction was associated with the general secretary's chief lieutenant for selecting personnel in the provincial party apparatus—his patronage man.

The man who occupied this post from 1966 to late 1976 was Andrei Kirilenko. Kirilenko was born in 1906, the same year as Brezhnev, and graduated from the Rybinsk Aviation Industry Institute in 1936. He first worked with Brezhnev in the political organs in the army in 1941, but quickly moved into political work in the defense industry. He followed Brezhnev as regional first secretary in the Ukrainian steel and defense industry center of Dnepropetrovsk from 1950 to 1955. In 1955 Khrushchev was trying to take over the party organization in the Russian Republic and made Kirilenko obkom first secretary in Sverdlovsk, the major province in the Urals, with a heavy industrial and defense industry profile similar to Dnepropetrovsk.

In 1962 Kirilenko was put in charge of economic planning and personnel selection in the urban areas of Russia as first deputy head of the Bureau of the Central Committee for the RSFSR. The presence of a strong ally in this post was a major factor in Brezhnev's ability to organize the anti-Khrushchev coup of 1964. In 1966 Brezhnev abolished the bureau and made Kirilenko his chief lieutenant for supervision of the party apparatus and the central planning machinery. As a future Politburo member, Vadim Medvedev, has commented, Kirilenko "was concerned mainly with

72. Gorbachev, *Zhizn' i reformy*, vol. 1, p. 189; *Memoirs*, p. 122.
73. Jonathan Steele, *Eternal Russia: Yeltsin, Gorbachev, and the Mirage of Democracy* (Harvard University Press, 1994), p. 33.

strengthening the position of Brezhnev in the party apparatus."[74] These men were also, of course, often loyal to Kirilenko as well as to Brezhnev. Brezhnev learned from his overthrow of Khrushchev never to trust anyone fully. He had been party first secretary in Moldavia, and he used Konstantin Chernenko, who had been head of the Propaganda Department of the Central Committee there, as a counterweight to Kirilenko. Chernenko served as Brezhnev's personal assistant. Everyone describes Brezhnev and Chernenko as personally very close, as (in Nikolai Ryzhkov's words) "his faithful shadow . . . his faithful Pancho Sanchez."[75] Chernenko's personal assistant has stated that Brezhnev always referred to his lieutenants in public in the proper Russian manner—by their first and middle names together—but that he always called Chernenko by his nickname "Kostia," even in front of others. This assistant said that Brezhnev always wanted Chernenko with him when he went on vacation or to the dacha to relax. "[Brezhnev] was bored without him."[76] Americans at summit meetings considered him a flunky who was trying to ration Brezhnev's cigarettes and was given little respect by men such as Andrei Gromyko.[77] Behind the scenes, however, Chernenko filled a more crucial political role.

Among the most widely known examples of Brezhnev's policy of checks and balances were his choices of high-level KGB officials. The chairman of the KGB was Yury Andropov, who had close ties with a number of top leaders. He was born in Stavropol where Mikhail Suslov had been first secretary, was in school in Rybinsk at the same time as Kirilenko in the 1930s, was in Karelia during World War II when Marshal Nikolai Ogarkov fought there, and had worked with Brezhnev on East European questions.[78]

Yet Brezhnev still did not fully trust Andropov and surrounded him with three first deputies with conflicting loyalties. One was Grigory Tsinev, whom Brezhnev had known since the 1930s (Tsinev was in charge of military counterintelligence).[79] A second was Semen Tsvigun, who had worked in the KGB in Moldavia when Brezhnev and Chernenko worked there. The third was Viktor Chebrikov, who had been an officer in future

74. Medvedev, *V komande Gorbacheva*, p. 24.
75. Ryzhkov, *Desiat let' velikikh potriasenii*, p. 56.
76. Pribytkov, *Apparat*, pp. 59, 61.
77. This was conveyed to me by Helmut Sonnenfeldt.
78. For a book with a great deal of information on Andropov's work with Brezhnev written by one of his close assistants, see Burlatsky, *Vozhdi i sovetniki*.
79. Bobkov, *KGB i vlast'*, pp. 213, 254.

Defense Minister Andrei Grechko's army during World War II and who worked under Kirilenko in Dnepropetrovsk after the war.[80] Chebrikov reported in an interview that the first deputies could not even speak to each other without telling Andropov. Brezhnev was also worried about ties between the KGB and the military. His physician recalled a case when both Tsinev and Tsvigun rushed into Andropov's office when Dmitry Ustinov, Grechko's successor as defense minister, came to visit. Similar systems of checks and balances were found throughout the political system and involved other top leaders.

In the mid-1970s, when the rate of growth in the Soviet economy began to slow, Kirilenko and his associates wanted to take measures to restore growth, even if consumption and an egalitarian social policy had to be sacrificed. The fact that Kirilenko's associates included not only the biggest group of provincial secretaries but also the head of the general staff and the chairman of the KGB was deeply disturbing to Brezhnev. The Chernenko group supported Brezhnev's emphasis on consumption, egalitarianism, and social welfare. It is possible that the simmering conflict between them crystalized over whether to use oil revenues to purchase technology or grain.[81] In 1976 in a change surely associated with the conflict, Kirilenko was removed as Central Committee secretary for personnel and left in charge only of economic planning.

Chernenko became the personnel secretary. Yet while Chernenko supervised the lower party apparatus, he was not permitted to change enough personnel to build his own political machine. Thus the party secretaries appointed by Kirilenko over a dozen years remained largely in place. The machine came to follow the leadership of Yury Andropov, who had long personal ties with Kirilenko and Ogarkov.

Andropov's role in Brezhnev's last years was hinted at in a brief but extraordinary article in *Pravda* in 1978 just before Gorbachev was elected Central Committee secretary for agriculture. As Brezhnev's train passed through Stavropol, he met with three people at the station: Chernenko, Andropov, and Gorbachev.[82] It was more than a dramatic meeting of the

---

80. In an interview in October 1991 Chebrikov said proudly that his rise from private to major during the war was almost unprecedented, and he discussed Kirilenko with real warmth. Indeed, he refused the interview until I said that its main purpose was to talk about Kirilenko.

81. Ryzhkov, *Perestroika*, pp. 238–39.

82. *Pravda*, September 21, 1978, p. 1. For the strained nature of the meeting, see Gorbachev, *Zhizn' i reformy*, vol. 1, pp. 23–25; *Memoirs*, pp. 11–13.

final four general secretaries of the Communist party. Since mention of Andropov's presence was not required by protocol or even considered desirable because of his chairmanship of the KGB, the report was one of the signals meant to illuminate the political scene for insiders.[83] It showed that Andropov had assumed a broader political role. The next year Fedor Burlatsky, a former assistant to Andropov, commented privately that Andropov had moved into the inner circle of the leadership. Andropov was not just the representative of the military-security forces; he had taken over leadership of the group within the Communist party apparatus formerly headed by Andrei Kirilenko.

When Andropov became general secretary, he quickly relied on his connection with the Kirilenko machine. He named Nikolai Ryzhkov (former director of the biggest plant in Kirilenko's Sverdlovsk and then first deputy chairman of the USSR Gosplan under Kirilenko's supervision) Central Committee secretary heading the Economic Department of the Central Committee. Yegor Ligachev (Kirilenko's deputy in the Bureau of the Central Committee for the RSFSR in the mid-1960s) became head of the Organizational–Party Work Department of the Central Committee and junior secretary for personnel, and Viktor Chebrikov (Kirilenko's representative from Dnepropetrovsk as KGB first deputy chairman) became the new KGB chairman. Andropov selected Nikolai Sliun'kov, who had been deputy chairman of the USSR Gosplan, as first secretary in Belorussia. Vitaly Vorotnikov, a provincial party secretary in the Kirilenko mold who had become first deputy chairman of the Council of Ministers of the RSFSR before being exiled as ambassador to Cuba in 1977 when Kirilenko fell, was brought back and became chairman of the Council of Ministers of the Russian Republic. The first deputy head of the Organizational–Party Work Department of the Central Committee, and therefore number three in personnel selection behind Gorbachev and Ligachev, was Yevgeny Razumov, Kirilenko's long-time personal assistant.

Gorbachev and the Kirilenko Machine

Most of Gorbachev's own first appointments were political payoffs to members of the Kirilenko-Andropov machine. His actions clearly showed

---

83. For a discussion of such signals in elite communication, see Myron Rush, *The Rise of Khrushchev* (Washington: Public Affairs Press, 1958), pp. 88–94.

that the machine was a primary source of his power as it had been of Andropov's. Indeed, most of Gorbachev's appointments were the same men Andropov had chosen. Yegor Ligachev, Nikolai Ryzhkov, and Viktor Chebrikov were elected full members of the Politburo in April 1985. Ligachev became second secretary and chairman of the Secretariat and moved into Suslov's old office on the fifth floor. He had overall responsibility in the Central Committee Secretariat for personnel, ideology, foreign relations, and agriculture. Ryzhkov was soon named chairman of the Council of Ministers. Chebrikov retained his post as KGB chairman. Nikolai Sliun'kov was brought back from Belorussia in 1987 as Central Committee secretary in charge of the Economic Department of the Central Committee. Yevgeny Razumov remained first deputy head of the Organizational-Party Work Department of the Central Committee until 1990, at which time he was seventy-one years old.[84] The remaining Politburo member from Dnepropetrovsk, the aging and conservative Ukrainian first secretary, Vladimir Shcherbitsky, was kept in his post until the fall of 1989, a few months before his death. In addition, Boris Yeltsin, the first secretary of the Sverdlovsk Obkom, was made a Central Committee secretary and then a candidate member of the Politburo when he was put in charge of the Moscow party organization in December.

Two men, Yegor Ligachev and Nikolai Ryzhkov, were by far the most important of Gorbachev's lieutenants from the Kirilenko machine. Ligachev was born in 1920, eleven years before Gorbachev, and graduated from the Moscow Aviation Institute in 1943. After graduation, he quickly became a full-time Komsomol official and in the late 1940s served as first secretary of the Novosibirsk Komsomol Obkom.[85] Later he occupied mid-level party and soviet posts in Novosibirsk, including first secretary of the party committee in the district (*raion*) where the Siberian Academy of Sciences was being built. In 1961 he became deputy head of the Ideological Department of the Bureau of the Central Committee for the RSFSR. From 1965 to 1983 he worked as obkom first secretary in small and remote Tomsk in Siberia. In 1983 Andropov brought him to Moscow once more,

---

84. *Izvestiia TsK KPSS*, vol. 2 February, 1989, p. 95; and Evgeny Razumov, *Krushenie i nadezhdy: Politcheskie zametki* (Moscow: I. D. Sytin Fund, 1996), p. 191.

85. Ligachev was removed under a political cloud in 1949 because of suspicion about his marriage to the daughter of a general executed in 1937. Ligachev, *Zagadka Gorbacheva*, pp. 140–41.

this time as head of the Organizational–Party Work Department and junior Central Committee secretary for personnel.

The logic of Ligachev's appointment as Gorbachev's chief of staff and senior personnel secretary in April 1985 was clear. As a sixty-five-year-old moderate reformer, he was a perfect bridge to the older generation of provincial party leaders who were gradually being eased out of power. Having worked under Kirilenko, he solidified Gorbachev's ties with the machine, but he came from a small province and seemed not to have a large natural power base to challenge Gorbachev. He had a reputation for being very fair but strict and undiplomatic. Thus he was a natural "bad cop" chief of staff for a general secretary who was cultivating a "good cop" role for himself.

Much was to be said about the danger of a Ligachev opposition to Gorbachev in coming years, but this was grossly overdrawn. Ligachev was not allowed to select his own chief deputy (the junior Central Committee secretary for personnel and head of the Organizational–Party Work Department); instead, Gorbachev gave the post to Georgy Razumovsky, a party official from the Northern Caucasus with whom he was very close. Everyone assumed that as Ligachev's chief assistant Razumovsky was really the dominant figure in ensuring Gorbachev's control over the selection of provincial party secretaries. By 1990 Ligachev was more than fifteen years older than the average obkom party first secretary, and the secretaries seemed unlikely to bet on him as their long-term leader against Gorbachev. In fact, Ligachev was unable to stop Gorbachev from taking many actions of which he disapproved, ultimately including his own removal.

Ligachev had expressed amazement that he was given such a high position in Moscow at the age of sixty-three and then elected to the Politburo two years later. He had every reason to be grateful to Gorbachev as his patron and every reason to expect that he would be retired from the post of second secretary by the time of the next party congress, when he would be seventy. If he had been offered an honorific job around the time of his seventieth birthday (chairman of the Party Control Commission was just such an appropriate traditional post), he would not even have been offended.

Unlike Ligachev, Nikolai Ryzhkov was an archetypical Soviet industrial manager. Born in 1929, he went to work at a defense industry plant at the age of twenty-one. While filling a series of technical and managerial posts, he acquired an engineering education in night school. In 1971 he became director of Uralmash, one of the country's largest plants. In 1975 he was named first deputy minister of heavy and transportation machine building and in 1979 first deputy chairman of the USSR State Planning Committee (Gosplan) in charge of compiling the overall economic plan.

When Andropov became general secretary, he named Ryzhkov head of the Economics Department of the Central Committee (the new name for the Planning, Trade, and Financial Organs Department) and the Central Committee secretary who supervised that department. Ryzhkov therefore became the person in the Central Committee apparatus responsible for overseeing the major planning and financial organs, but not industry. He reported directly to Gorbachev, who was the senior Central Committee secretary in charge of planning. In April 1985 he became a member of the Politburo, and in September he replaced Nikolai Tikhonov as chairman of the Council of the Ministers—the head of the government.[86]

The Central Committee secretary for the economy from 1987 to 1990 was a third key member of the Kirilenko machine, Nikolai Sliun'kov. A Belorussian, Sliun'kov was director of the Minsk Tractor Works and then deputy chairman of Gosplan (the deputy in charge of agricultural machinery) and first secretary of the Belorussian Central Committee. He remains a shadowy figure. At the time, reform economists generally dismissed him as a conservative associated with Nikolai Ryzhkov, under whom he had served in Gosplan. He is seldom mentioned in memoirs. But in December 1989 he spoke at a Central Committee plenum calling for more radical economic reform, and he briefly appears in the memoir of one of Gorbachev's closest aides at this time as "an irreconcilable opponent" of Premier Ryzhkov.[87] Vladimir P. Mozhin, Sliun'kov's subordinate as first deputy head of the Economic Department of the Central Committee, reported that even behind the scenes Sliun'kov did not take an independent position; he followed the line of the general secretary.[88]

---

86. One peculiarity of the position of premier in the Soviet Union throughout the postwar period was that although the basic foreign policy, defense, security, and ideological (culture, publishing, and television-radio) ministries were subordinated to the government and to the premier, they were directly supervised by Central Committee officials, especially the general secretary and his chief assistant for ideology. See Medvedev, *V komande Gorbacheva*, p. 73; and M. Nenashev, *Poslednee pravitel'stvo SSSR: Lichnosti, Svidetel'stva, Dialogi* (Moscow: Krom, 1993), p. 198.

87. Anders Aslund, *Gorbachev's Struggle for Economic Reform* (Cornell University Press, 1989), pp. 41–44. See also *Pravda*, February 8, 1990, pp. 4–5; *Izvestiia TsK KPSS*, vol. 4, no. 303, 1990, pp. 49-51; and Cherniaev, *Shest' let s Gorbachevym*, p. 331.

88. Jerry Hough, interview with Vladimir Mozhin, January 12, 1995, Moscow.

The details of Gorbachev's alliance with the Kirilenko machine are not important for the average reader, but the implications are. First, the alliance meant that his power rested on people who had a strong network of ties in the Central Committee, the party apparatus, and the government. These were, however, men with whom he had worked closely for no more than three years. Although his lieutenants from the group, except for Boris Yeltsin, had not held important posts under Brezhnev and did not have substantial political stature, their lack of long-time ties with Gorbachev probably made him nervous about them. Because control over personnel selection in the party apparatus was the most sensitive of political questions, Gorbachev's relationship with Yegor Ligachev, the lieutenant for personnel selection, was certain to concern him most.

It was to be anticipated that Gorbachev, like earlier general secretaries, would try to create through other appointments a system of checks and balances to counter the influence of the Kirilenko machine. The traditional technique used by general secretaries was to select subordinates from geographic areas or political realms in which they had worked in the past. Gorbachev's selection of Razumovsky as Ligachev's deputy in personnel selection was only one of the appointees he made from his native south. The top agricultural administrator, who also held the post of first deputy premier, came from Gorbachev's own province of Stavropol, as did the chairman of the important oversight committee, the Committee of People's Control. The minister of foreign affairs, Eduard Shevardnadze, had worked all his life in Georgia, which borders Stavropol. The minister of internal affairs (the minister of the police) had come from the neighboring Chechen-Ingush Republic, while the Central Committee secretary in charge of the police had been Gorbachev's close college friend. Many of these officials, and others as well, had worked in the Young Communist League in the 1950s and 1960s when Gorbachev was a Komsomol secretary.[89]

Similarly, almost none of the men Gorbachev selected as ideological and political lieutenants had any connection with the Kirilenko machine. Many had received graduate degrees from Moscow University in the 1950s when Gorbachev attended, and many had worked in the Central Committee apparatus in foreign policy. They had all been young adults in the 1950s and

---

89. The top agricultural administrator was Vsevolod Murakhovsky, Sergei Maniakin was chairman of the People's Control Committee, and Aleksandr Vlasov was minister of internal affairs.

had been strongly affected by Nikita Khrushchev's de-Stalinization program in 1956.

The second implication of Gorbachev's alliance with the Kirilenko machine was that his chief lieutenants in economic affairs had managerial backgrounds. Prime Minister Nikolai Ryzhkov had been director of the huge Ural Machine Works. Nine of the thirteen deputy premiers he appointed were heavy industry or defense industry managers. Vladimir Dolgikh, the long-time Central Committee secretary for industry who remained in the post until 1988, was the former director of the Norilsk Metallurgy Combine. The Central Committee secretary for the defense industry had been a defense industry plant manager. The top economist in the group, albeit without any official party or government post, was Abel Aganbegian, a specialist on industry with ties to Siberian and Urals industrialists.

Gorbachev's democratic advisers were increasingly to describe Ligachev and Ryzhkov as the blackest reactionaries. Because the democratic advisers had greater control over the mass media and more contact with Westerners, the West generally accepted their point of view. However, one of the more unattractive features of politics is that lieutenants and assistants need to rely on persuasion for influence, and those with opposing views seem driven to vitriolic denunciation of each other. Nowhere was this more true than in the post-1985 Soviet Union. The democratic advisers distorted the positions of their opponents, and the opponents reciprocated.

In fact, a much more nuanced understanding is needed of the leaders associated with the Kirilenko machine, especially Ligachev and Ryzhkov. Economic reform in communist countries has usually begun in nonindustrial realms. Normally the transition to the market has been carefully controlled for years, even decades. Ryzhkov and Ligachev were not revolutionaries, but as long as they would accept or favor economic reform following the Hungarian and Chinese model, they were reformers in the sense that the word is normally used in the West. For example, Yelstin's chief economics reformer, Yegor Gaidar, considered himself radical and served on Ryzhkov's commission on economic reform under Chernenko and favored Hungarian economic reform.[90]

The real question is how the top Kirilenko-Andropov officials evaluated the Hungarian and Chinese experience. Janos Kadar had achieved a high level of popular approval with his semimarket policies in Hungary, while

---

90. Yegor Gaidar *Dni porazhenii i pobed* (Moscow: Vagrius, 1996), p. 34.

China was producing strong economic growth through reform. It is not credible that the Soviet political and economic leaders in the 1980s were divided between conservatives who wanted to retain Brezhnev's policies and reformers who wanted to introduce the Western economic system. Large numbers of the elite must have been looking at Hungary and China and seeing the Soviet future vaguely in those terms.

The major ideological debate of the early 1980s centered on the revision of Party Program that had been approved by Nikita Khrushchev in 1961. The program was wildly utopian in its assumption that the Soviet Union could go to full communism (withering away of the state, distribution by the principle "each according to his needs, from each according to his abilities," and so forth) in a short period. Its revision was highly sensitive because Khrushchev was often seen as a symbol of reform and because a group subordinated to Andropov had had a key role in drafting it. To discredit the old program was to attack Andropov.

For our present purposes, however, the interesting fact is the position of the "conservative" ideologists associated with Chernenko. Brezhnev had spoken of the Soviet Union as "real socialism" in a way that implied it needed little change. The new conservatives emphasized that the Soviet Union was at an early stage of socialism and that major changes would be needed within socialism before communism was achieved. It was scarcely a reactionary position, and the Chernenko aide in charge of redrafting the program, Vadim Pechenev, came to occupy a high post in the staff of President Boris Yeltsin.[91]

Andropov himself was probably among the supporters of the Hungarian or Chinese models. Gorbachev could not have called Lenin's last articles "the essence of Leninism" in his April 1983 speech had Andropov not approved. Indeed, Gorbachev has cryptically commented that his first efforts at drafting the speech were not successful and that he went back to rereading Lenin, especially the late Lenin. Probably it was Andropov himself who told him that his efforts were not a success. Andropov told a former assistant at this time that "you know, we are only beginning to unfold the reform. It is necessary to do a great deal, to change things sharply and thoroughly."[92]

---

91. For an excellent discussion of the issues, see Pechenev, *Vzlet i padenie Gorbacheva*, pp. 39–112, 131–44.
92. Gorbachev, *Zhizn' i reformy*, vol. 1, pp. 235–36; *Memoirs*, p. 148; and Georgy Shakhnazarov, *Tsena svobody: Reformatsiia Gorbacheva glazami ego pomoshchnika* (Moscow: Rossika, 1993), p. 32.

Gorbachev has insisted that "Andropov would not have gone for radical changes, just as Khrushchev could not do this." Gorbachev has even suggested that Andropov might thank his "lucky star that he died before encountering the problems that inevitably would have arisen on his path and created disillusionment in him and about him."[93] By 1995, however, Gorbachev defined radical reform as complete democratization and marketization and was trying to dampen speculation that Andropov would have been a more successful reformer than Gorbachev had been.

Nikolai Ryzhkov had a different judgment about Andropov. When he was Central Committee secretary in charge of the Economic Department in 1983, Andropov called him in once a week for a two- to three-hour conversation:

> Andropov was not a *rynochnik* [a proponent of complete marketization]. . . . If, as they say, God had given Yury Vladimirovich health and he had been able to work even five years, the fate of the country would have been different. He would have conducted things differently—something close to the Chinese variant with, of course, Russian specifics. This is a model in which the fundamental problems are under government control and the market system spins around it.[94]

Andropov, for example, told Ryzhkov to look into foreign investment in the Soviet Union.[95]

The younger members of the Kirilenko machine must also have been looking at the Chinese and Hungarian models. These men did, after all, support Gorbachev for general secretary rather than a man such as Grigory Romanov who had the typical engineering-managerial background of the Kirilenko party secretaries and seemed to favor the East German model of economic reform. Gorbachev had given enough signals that those who voted for him knew they were choosing reforms at least as radical as those in Hungary or China. Neither the Hungarian nor Chinese model was based on private ownership of land or totally free market pricing, and much of the moderate denunciation under perestroika of free market pricing and free sale of land should be seen in these terms, not as support for Brezhnev's economic system.

The Ryzhkov who emerges from the memoirs not only seems ready to have favored something like Hungarian and Chinese economic reform, but

93. Gorbachev, *Zhizn' i reformy*, vol. 1, p. 247; Memoirs, p. 153, but *lucky star* (*schaslivaia zvezda*) is translated as "it was his fate that he died."
94. Ryzhkov, *Ia iz partii po imeni "Rossii,"* pp. 314–15.
95. Ryzhkov, *Desiat' let velikikh potriasenii*, p. 50.

to have understood that the prerequisite for it was the rough price equilibrium found in Hungary, Czechoslovakia, and China, but that was absent in Poland when reform was attempted there and that had to be introduced under martial law in 1980. Premier Nikolai Ryzhkov said that as early as 1986 he and the rest of the leadership "were serious in thinking about turning the economy to the market." His only major dissatisfaction with policy during this period, he continued, was his inability to persuade Gorbachev to raise retail prices, as serious reform required.[96] Ryzhkov appointed a group of men with impressive financial credentials and experience to the financial posts crucial in economic reform. In 1990 when he moved into opposition to the 500-Day Plan, it was not because he was conservative but because he knew enough about the economic system to understand that the plan was certain to have catastrophic consequences.

Ligachev, all agree, was more conservative than Ryzhkov. But in his memoirs Ligachev strongly supported the formula of "different forms of socialist property," while being much more skeptical about "different forms of property."[97] Fedor Burlatsky, who knew him for a quarter of a century and was deeply committed to the democratic advisers, said that Ligachev would have readily accepted the Chinese agricultural reform because it involved leasing land, not outright private ownership.[98] As already noted, Ligachev wrote in his memoirs about his great happiness with the course of events through 1987, and later said that the entire leadership had agreed in 1986 not to use force to preserve communism in Eastern Europe.[99] He must have understood the implications of that decision. In 1989 he signaled his support for the kind of agricultural reform found in Czechoslovakia by visiting there and praising the reforms for three days just before a Central Committee plenum on agriculture.[100] The Czechoslovakian form of agricul-

96. Ryzhkov, *Perestroika*, p. 244.
97. Ligachev, *Zagadka Gorbacheva*, p. 106.
98. Burlatsky, *Russkie gosudari*, pp. 300–01.
99. Ligachev, *Zagadka Gorbacheva*, pp. 96, 103; and David Remnick, *Lenin's Tomb: The Last Days of the Soviet Empire* (Random House, 1993), p. 234. Yakovlev said the early statements about freedom of choice and noninterference were made "honestly and seriously even if some people perceived them otherwise at first." Aleksandr Yakovlev, *Muki, procheteniia, bytiia. Perestroika: nadezhdy i real'nosti* (Moscow: Novosti, 1991), p. 182.
100. William Drozdiak, "Gorbachev Farm Policy Challenged," *Washington Post*, March 13, 1989, p. A26.

tural organization was not the most radical in Eastern Europe, but it was more radical than anything Gorbachev was willing to introduce.[101] The crucial question, of course, was the policy that Gorbachev wanted to follow. The steps he took in 1985 and 1986 aroused little significant political opposition in the Politburo even though the measures were more radical than most Western observers expected in March 1985. If Gorbachev wanted to introduce the kind of reform found in Hungary or in China, the so-called conservatives of the Kirilenko team would not seriously have objected, and many would have actively applauded. But if the general secretary wanted to choose a different path of reform and loosen political controls drastically, members of the Kirilenko machine were likely to become increasingly unhappy. In that case Gorbachev had no other people in this reform team who understood much about economic reform or had a different model of transition.

The Russian Republic and the Circular Flow of Power

The scale of Gorbachev's problem with the Kirilenko machine should not, however, be exaggerated. All Soviet general secretaries came to power with the help of alliances with others. Once they became general secretary, they gained much greater power over personnel selection, and in time this enabled them to build their own machine and remove former allies from the leadership. Understanding the circular flow of power, other political leaders seldom challenged the general secretary; instead, they tried to win his favor. Most of the so-called opposition groups in Soviet history comprised men who were being eased out by the general secretary and were fruitlessly trying to defend themselves.

---

101. It is interesting to see how his spokesmen used Western media to create a misleading picture of Gorbachev, a picture that was then broadcast into Russia on foreign radio in an authoritative way but without evidence. Drozdiak, ''Gorbachev Farm Policy Challenged,'' p. A26; and Bill Keller, ''Gorbachev's Plan to Revive Farms Produces Opposition in Kremlin,'' *New York Times*, March 15, 1989, p. A1, had the same theme: potential conservative opposition to Gorbachev at the plenum. The reform program–free sale of land and decollectivization–was described as if it were Gorbachev's, but such a direct claim was not made by the two reports and would not have been accurate.

Consequently, a close student of the Soviet political system would have predicted that Gorbachev was keenly aware of the mechanisms that brought him to power and would know how to solve the problem posed by the power of the Kirilenko machine. Gorbachev would have been expected to follow a vigorous policy of replacing obkom first secretaries and removing the key members of the Kirilenko machine, especially Ligachev, from sensitive posts by the time of the next party congress, expected in 1991.

The predictions proved accurate. Gorbachev was extremely sensitive about the power of the Central Committee. According to Ligachev, he seemed to have had a "Khrushchev complex," a memory of the removal of Khrushchev as party leader by the Central Committee in 1964 and an almost irrational fear that the same might happen to him.[102] The clearest sign of this fear was his intense concern about the the Central Committee members who had been removed or retired from their regular jobs—the so-called lame ducks or dead souls—and might vote against him for that reason. He tried unsuccessfully to have them removed at the Nineteenth Party Conference in June 1988, then in April 1989 induced seventy-two of the voting members—nearly 25 percent of the total—to resign "voluntarily."[103]

But Gorbachev had one political problem that was never discussed by his lieutenants either openly or off the record and that was rarely recognized in the West. The delegations to the party congress were selected either at republican party conferences in the small republics or at oblast party conferences in the larger ones. (Moscow, Leningrad, and Kiev sent delegations independent of the surrounding oblast.) The principle of democratic centralism dictated the direct subordination of the obkom first secretaries to the republican party organization. Although the appointment of all obkom first secretaries always had to be approved by the all-Union Central Committee in Moscow, there was always the possibility they might become more loyal to the republican first secretary directly supervising them than to the general secretary.

The general secretaries tolerated this situation in Ukraine, Belorussia, Kazakhstan, and Uzbekistan, in part because the precedent was established when the party organizations of these republics were small and when they sent small delegations to the party congresses. Only Ukraine was likely to pose a problem because of its size. For a long time, Ukrainian questions

102. Ligachev, *Zagadka Gorbacheva*, pp. 108–09.
103. *Pravda*, April 26, 1989, p. 1.

were handled only in direct contacts between the general secretary and the Ukrainian first secretary. "It was not accepted that [other] Central Committee officials go into the oblasts of Ukraine, especially bypassing Kiev."[104] Both Khrushchev and Brezhnev had been party leaders in Ukraine and had a special knowledge of the officials in the party apparatus; and First Secretary Vladimir Shcherbitsky, from Brezhnev's Dnepropetrovsk, was careful to suppress any separatist movements.[105]

Gorbachev had no such ties to Ukraine, but in early 1987 his spokesmen leaked rumors that Shcherbitsky might be disloyal to the general secretary. In fact, Shcherbitsky had already responded to Central Committee criticism of his political base in Dnepropetrovsk by sacrificing for "defects in their work" the two obkom first secretaries with whom he had the closest career ties.[106] After this display of loyalty, Gorbachev kept the aging and conservative first secretary in his post until a few months before his death.

Russia was a different matter altogether. After the 1930s it had seventy to seventy-five oblasts and autonomous republics, and they selected more than half the delegates to the party congress. If such a large number of first secretaries of oblasts and autonomous republics were subordinated to a Russian first secretary, and were more loyal to him than to the general secretary, the Russians had a real possibility of removing the general secretary. General secretaries had always understood this, and they all solved the problem by creating a party structure without a Russian first secretary and with all obkom first secretaries in the Russian republic subordinated directly to the USSR Central Committee Secretariat.

Gorbachev, however, could not have introduced serious reform without decentralization of power to the republics and the transformation of the Soviet Union into a normal federation. This would require Russia to become a normal republic with the same institutions and powers as Ukraine or Uzbekistan. Either it would have to acquire a powerful Communist party

104. Medvedev, *V komande Gorbacheva*, p. 120.
105. Gorbachev, *Zhizn' i reformy*, vol. 1, pp. 232–33. *Memoirs*, p. 145, has a shortened version.
106. See Philip Taubman, "Gorbachev Push to Win Control in Ukraine Seen," *New York Times*, March 22, 1987, p. A1. The men sacrificed were Viktor G. Boiko, first secretary of the Dnepropetrovsk Obkom, and Viktor F. Dobrik, first secretary of the Lvov Obkom, who had come from Shcherbitsky's (and Brezhnev's) base city of Dneprodzerzhinsk. *Pravda*, March 18, 1987, p. 2; and March 21, 1987, p. 4. See *Pravda Ukrainy*, March 25, 1987; and July 11, 1987. See also Aleksandr Kapto, *Na perekrestakh zhizni: Politicheskie memuary* (Moscow: Sotsialisticheskii Zhurnal, 1996), pp. 62, 72.

organization and first secretary, or power would have to be taken from party organs in other republics. Not surprisingly, Gorbachev was strongly opposed to the creation of such an organization, but he had no alternative.[107] A Russian party organization was finally authorized in October 1989 and created in May 1990.

The creation of the post of Russian first secretary was certain to be disturbing to Gorbachev and to influence his thoughts about perestroika within the Communist party. Indeed, the most logical hypothesis about Gorbachev, although not necessarily a fully accurate one, is that he understood very early the threat that a Russian republican party organization and first secretary would pose to his political position. For this reason he began delegitimizing the Communist party at the first possible moment in order to move his base of power to the state. Given his confusion in 1990 and 1991, one is reluctant to attribute too much calculation to him in the early years. However, he certainly understood the problems the creation of a Russian party organization would cause him, and one must be aware of this crucial element of his calculations if his mental processes are to be understood.

---

107. Cherniaev, *Shest' let s Gorbachevym*, p. 297.

CHAPTER FOUR

The Tragedy of Economic Reform

LESS THAN SIX MONTHS into office, Mikhail Gorbachev told the editors of *Time* that he had a "grandiose" domestic program in mind. His language became more radical at the Twenty-Seventh Party Congress in February–March 1986. By July 1986 he had become still more radical, equating perestroika with revolution—in all spheres of life, not just the economy. In 1986 he backed his words with a series of laws and decrees that began the process of economic reform. The laws were all good early steps. From the fall of 1986 he increasingly emphasized democratization.

In his public speeches Gorbachev never acknowledged any contradiction between his various economic and political goals; he treated reform as seamless and indivisible. He never tried to present a theory of the transition or a strategy for reaching his goals in a logical manner. Economic reform was described as if it had no intermediate stage in which the state would play a powerful role. Political reform involved the immediate introduction of Western-style democracy.

Obviously serious economic reform required that careful consideration be given to the incentive system under which officials and the public operated. Economic incentives needed to be created that would push officials in the same direction that the exhortations were leading. Political incentives needed to correspond to economic incentives. Steps needed to be taken in careful sequence so that a new incentive system would be in place as the old one was destroyed. This was never done.

The leasing of land in China had worked well because the procurement and incentive systems were changed simultaneously. The peasants had to deliver part of their crop to the state at low prices, and the crop was then distributed to the urban population at low prices through rationing. The peasants were left with a third of their crop to sell at market prices. The introduction of leasing in the Soviet Union required similar changes. New cooperatives had to be given the chance to obtain supplies legally through some kind of wholesale trade system, and prices had to be brought more in line with market forces if managers were to be given the freedom to respond to them. Gorbachev did not introduce such changes in his early reforms.

It seemed impossible to believe that Gorbachev and his advisers were as naive as their statements about seamless reform and the impact of exhortation on the masses suggested. I was among those who thought the general secretary had an unacknowledged strategy and that he was using obfuscation to reduce opposition to painful measures. It seemed likely that once he had finished his consolidation of power he would "reluctantly" sacrifice full democracy to achieve other goals.

Nevertheless, Anatoly Dobrynin, former Soviet ambassador to the United States, observed that Gorbachev talked the same way within the Politburo.

> From 1986 to 1989, when I worked in the Politburo and participated in its deliberations, I never once heard Gorbachev present any broad and detailed plan for reforming the economy—whether one-year, or five-year, or some other kind of plan that had really been thought through. . . . At the start of reforms in 1986, Gorbachev explained his economic credo to the Politburo in this way: the Soviet economy certainly needed reforms, and although we did not know precisely how to achieve them, we must begin. He told the Politburo that they must all be guided by the words of Lenin: "The most important thing in any endeavor was to get involved in the fight and in that way learn what to do next." We got into a fight, all right, but for the years afterward even the new leaders of Russia did not know exactly what to do next.[1]

Apparently, Gorbachev did indeed think his radical language and the laws enacted in 1986 would by themselves have a dramatic impact. Valery Boldin, a speechwriter with agricultural experience, has commented in his memoirs that in an early speech the general secretary tried to claim that leasing agricultural land would ensure plenty of food in a year or two. When

---

1. Anatoly Dobrynin, *In Confidence: Moscow's Ambassador to America's Six Cold War Presidents (1962–1986)* (Times Books, 1995), pp. 636–37.

Boldin objected, Gorbachev answered, "Don't you know anything about the way peasants think? Just look how fast things moved in China, and we're no worse than them." He finally agreed to say that abundance would come only in two to three years.[2]

In his own memoirs Gorbachev attributed the lack of success of the early steps to resistance by the bureaucracy.

> The chief opposition to our plans were the leading structures of the ministries and departments, first of all the economic ones—Gosplan, the State Supply Committee, the Ministry of Finance, and the apparatus of the government. Then they closed ranks with the position of the party bureaucracy. No one dared to speak openly against reform . . . but they proposed halfway and ambiguous decisions that left many loopholes and even a direct possibility of a return to the past. . . . In fact, everything was explained very simply: they did not want to let the levers of power out of their hands.[3]

Gorbachev has also recalled that as early as April 24, 1986, he was telling the Politburo that the lack of progress was explained by the "gigantic party-state apparatus that, like a dam, lay on the path of reform." By the summer of 1986 he was making this accusation more strongly.[4] In the autumn he emphasized the theme in his speeches. His memoirs are filled with scornful references to the nomenklatura and the partocracy.

At the time Gorbachev's constant complaints about the bureaucrats appeared designed simply to justify his liberation from Politburo control. Yet his actions in 1990 and 1991 are difficult to explain except by assuming that he believed much of what he said. His leading assistants have provided indirect evidence of their own sincerity in their honest puzzlement that he did not adopt the 500-Day Plan, which involved destruction of the central government and economic shock therapy not unlike what occurred in December 1991 under Boris Yeltsin and Yegor Gaidar. What is difficult to understand is why he or they ever considered it.

It is possible that Dobrynin was right, that Gorbachev had no idea how to achieve economic reform, that he thought democracy would produce a legislature that would know what to do, and that he became increasingly demoralized. But it is also possible that in 1989 he genuinely came to

2. Valery Boldin, *Ten Years That Shook the World: The Gorbachev Era as Witnessed by His Chief of Staff*, trans. Evelyn Rossiter (Basic Books, 1994), pp. 75-76.

3. Mikhail Gorbachev, *Zhizn' i reformy*, vol. 1 (Moscow: Novosti, 1995), pp. 348, 352; *Memoirs* (Doubleday, 1996), pp. 227, 230.

4. Gorbachev, *Zhizn' i reformy*, vol. 1, pp. 298, 306; *Memoirs*, pp. 188, 194–95.

believe that the destruction of the nomenklatura and the command-administrative economic system would automatically create the conditions for the emergence of a well-functioning market. Either conjecture can explain the result: a belief that the central government needed to be dismantled.

One thing, however, is now absolutely certain from the memoirs. Gorbachev and his men grossly distorted the position of Premier Nikolai Ryzhkov, who was pushing for genuine economic reform in the mid- and late 1980s that they were resisting. Then Gorbachev was accused by Yeltsin's forces of becoming conservative at precisely the time he was becoming most radical. We never will move toward a better understanding of the history of Russian economic reform until the deliberate distortions promoted by both sides are cleared away.

The Start of Economic Reform

In the mid 1980s all members of the Soviet political elite agreed that decisive steps were needed to reverse the decline in the rate of economic growth and make the economic system more responsive to the consumer and more technologically innovative. While Westerners assumed that officialdom thought that tinkering with the old economic system or a little more investment would suffice, few officials could have been this naive.

Many in the elite had been to Eastern Europe and had seen a service sector that functioned much better than the one in the Soviet Union. They must have understood that at least this much structural change was needed in the economic sphere. Many knew that China was introducing major reforms in its economic system and achieving spectacular results. Few people—including, it turned out, few of the leaders—understood the details of East European and Chinese reform. Most had some vague notion of returning to the mixed Soviet system of the New Economic Policy of the 1920s, which they also did not understand. But whatever the confusion in their thinking, a great many educated people thought major change was necessary.

Gorbachev was certainly among them. His 1983 speech endorsing the ideas in Lenin's last articles and his December 1984 speech to the ideological conference signaled a commitment to major economic reform. Although the word he used to describe economic reform—*perestroika*—was the normal Russian word for reconstruction and never meant demolishing a structure and putting a new one in its place, during 1985 Gorbachev not only repeated his pre-1985 promises but used language that was increasingly radical.[5]

Gorbachev's first steps toward economic reform in 1985 were traditional: tightening discipline, attacking drunkenness, increasing investment in heavy industry. This program was generally summarized in the word *acceleration* (*uskorenie*). Goals for the 1986–90 Five-Year Plan, which had been approved in late 1984, were raised in 1985 to reflect the changes, but they were very optimistic and absolutely unrealistic so far as 1986 was concerned.[6]

Westerners generally treated the acceleration program with scorn, but it would have been an intelligent plan if it had been combined with reform of agriculture and the services sector and with the the necessary accompanying price adjustments. Even so the program was more successful than was acknowledged. Soviet economic reformers and their Western friends were afraid to praise it or say it had any beneficial effect, fearing that approval would undermine support for more radical reform. Indeed, a Central Committee secretary, Vadim Medvedev, has recalled that its early success did have this effect.

> In 1986, the economic situation in the country improved somewhat. This was naturally attributed to the positive influence of perestroika, and this was actually the case. . . . As a result, the growth in gross national product increased one-and-a-half times, from 2.4 percent to 3.3 percent, that of industrial production from 3.4 percent to 4.4 percent and agriculture from 0.2 percent to 5.3 percent. I think that this influenced the leadership, dampening its ardor . . . and lowered its decisiveness in conducting economic reform.[7]

Because world oil and gas prices—and thus export earnings—fell sharply in 1986 and 1987, the economic growth was doubly impressive.

Those who sincerely criticized the acceleration program and demanded its immediate transformation also failed to recognize the time limitations under which Gorbachev operated. The old Central Committee to which he was responsible remained in power until it could be replaced at the Twenty-

5. As Nikolai Ryzhkov points out, the phrase "acceleration of the perestroika of the economic mechanism" was in the decision of the Twenty-Fifth Party Congress in 1976, and he thinks that may have been its first such official use. *Desiat' let velikikh potriasenii* (Moscow: Kniga, Prosveshchenie, Miloserdie, 1995), p. 81.

6. Ed A. Hewett, "Gorbachev's Economic Strategy: A Preliminary Assessment," in Ed A. Hewett and Victor H. Winston, *Milestones in Glasnost and Perestroyka: The Economy* (Brookings, 1991), pp. 18–22.

7. Vadim Medvedev, *V komande Gorbacheva: Vzgliad iznutri* (Moscow: Bylina, 1994), p. 48.

Seventh Party Congress in March 1986. Because the Central Committee was composed of the top officials as of 1981—40 percent of them were retired or demoted by March 1986—Gorbachev understandably did not want to frighten them with a truly radical program.

Yet Soviet supplies allocation was totally centralized, and supply planning had to be initiated twelve to eighteen months in advance of delivery. Thus the supply plan not only for 1985 but also for 1986 was already in place when Gorbachev came to power in March 1985. Given the lead times built into the system, he had little choice at first but to limit himself to marginal reform efforts. Once major decisions were postponed until after March 1986, he again found himself locked into plans for 1987 that were essentially made at the end of 1985.

Given the political realities of 1985–86, the Twenty-Seventh Party Congress was the time for Gorbachev to begin to talk about further steps. At the end of 1985 Seweryn Bialer expressed skepticism about Gorbachev's intentions because he never used the East European codeword for radical transformation: *reforma* (reform).[8] As if to answer this criticism and make his intentions clearer, Gorbachev came out for "*radikal'naia* [radical] *reforma*" at the party congress: "It is impossible to limit ourselves to partial improvements. Radical reform is indispensable."[9]

In his speech to the party congress Gorbachev emphasized the importance of financial relations and prices and, most important, demanded that prices be linked not only to production costs, but also to "the consumption characteristics of goods [and] the degree of the balance of the goods produced with public needs and consumer demand." That is, prices had to be partly determined by market forces. He praised "cooperative property" and, for agriculture, called for leasing of the means of production, including land, by "brigades, links, and families."[10]

Gorbachev did not speak of the market or private property; instead he followed the Chinese example of using less threatening euphemisms such as "cooperatives," "leasing," or "money-goods relationship." (Even today China does not have "private ownership" of land in its agricultural reform.) He was right to emphasize leasing land within the collective farm rather

8. Seweryn Bialer and Joan Afferica, "The Genesis of Gorbachev's World," *Foreign Affairs*, vol. 64, no. 3 (1986), p. 611.

9. M. S. Gorbachev, *Izbrannye rechi i stat'i*, vol. 3 (Moscow: Politizdat, 1987), p. 212.

10. Gorbachev, *Izbrannye rechi i stat'i*, vol. 3, pp. 211–14.

than decollectivization and the free sale of land as the first step in agricultural reform. The lease could be extended to one hundred years and made transferrable, as it was in China, and the benefits of private farming could be obtained without unnecessary ideological battles and enormous social costs.

By the end of July 1986 Gorbachev began to present a vision of perestroika with increasing sweep. He said that perestroika would embody "transformations of no lesser scale" than Lenin's New Economic Policy in 1921 and Stalin's collectivization and First Five-Year Plan at the end of the 1920s.

> The present perestroika embraces not only the economy, but all other sides of social life: social relations, the political system, the spiritual-ideological sphere, the style and method of the work of the party and of all our cadres. *Perestroika* is a broad word. I would equate the words *perestroika* and *revolution*. Our transformations and reform . . . are a real revolution in all relationships in society, in the minds and hearts of the people, in their psychology and understanding of the contemporary period, and, first of all, in solving the tasks set by rapid scientific-technical progress. We should not be afraid to go boldly forward, to take risks, to take responsibility on ourselves. We will, as they say, make perestroika on the march, in the course of the active solution of economic and social problems.[11]

In 1986 and early 1987 a series of important laws were enacted that were experiments designed to open a road to the future, mostly through their ideological impact. From that perspective they were broad gauged. Agroindustrial enterprises were given autonomy in selling production that exceeded planned levels. The formation of small cooperatives that were not dominated by the government was legalized, and their freedom of activity was gradually expanded. Part-time private economic activity by individuals, and in some cases full-time activity, was permitted,. Various ministries and large enterprises were given freedom to engage in foreign trade outside the monopoly of the Ministry of Foreign Trade. And the right of foreigners to invest in the Soviet Union and to own property in the form of joint ventures was recognized.[12]

To be sure, reforming economists all said that these steps were insufficient. They were right. But that too was a necessary part of the process. It

11. Gorbachev, *Izbrannye rechi i stat'i*, vol. 4, pp. 36–37.
12. For a survey of the measures of 1986, see Philip Hanson, "The Shape of Gorbachev's Economic Reform," in Hewett and Winston, *Milestones in Glasnost and Perestroyka: The Economy*, pp. 59–65.

was impossible simply to introduce market reforms without ideological preparation. The Soviet people had been told for nearly seventy years that private property meant exploitation, that capitalists performed no useful function, and that the market meant only the right for producers to raise prices and make excess profits. They needed to be reeducated. Only if incomplete reforms were criticized and became the conservative alternative rather than the radical one would progress be made.

In fact, given the planning cycle, January 1, 1988, was the first time that really major economic reform could have begun, and the primary decisions needed to be made in late 1986. A Central Committee plenary session on economic reform was apparently planned for December 1986 and, as usual, a group was brought to the committee's dacha at Volynskoe to engage in a brainstorming session (*mosgovoi shturm*) and to draft the decisions and the speech of the leader. Most of those at Volynskoe were Central Committee officials, but other officials and some scholars were also included.[13]

Most Western correspondents were unaware of the monumental economic decisions being made in the fall of 1986, but on September 17 a long article by Patrick Cockburn of the *Financial Times* discussed the key issue. Titled "Now for the Prices Test," it pointed to the dismissal of Nikolai Glushkov, the conservative chairman of the State Committee of Prices, as a decisive step. Cockburn reported that a complete change in the price system was "neither feasible nor expected," but that reformers were looking at the East European system of fixed prices for necessities, free prices for luxuries, and maximum prices on other goods. "The Politburo's decisions over prices will be the best barometer of the balance of forces in the struggle between the economic radicals and conservatives within the Soviet leadership."[14] Cockburn was absolutely right, but it was only the memoirs of the 1990s that made clear who was on which side in the political balance of forces—that in practice Gorbachev was the leading conservative.

---

13. For a description of the setting, see Valentin Pavlov, *Upushchen li shans: finansovyi kliuch k rynku* (Moscow: Terra, 1995), p. 39.

14. Patrick Cockburn, ''Now for the Prices Test,'' *Financial Times*, September 17, 1986, p. 24.

The Problem of Price Imbalances

Before the 1917 revolution, Marx and Lenin said little about the organization and management of socialism, but they sometimes talked about abolishing money and replacing it by the direct distribution of goods. In any extreme form this hope was to be frustrated, especially in consumer transactions, but the striking thing about the Soviet economic system was how little importance money had and what large amounts of goods were distributed by nonmonetary means.[15]

During the late 1920s, Gosplan (the state planning committee) became the country's chief coordinating economic body instead of the Ministry of Finances. The political leadership determined policy on matters such as investment or consumption, the priority of sectors, and the like, and Gosplan's job was to translate these decisions into specific directives. Its main effort was to engage in "material balance" planning, or input-output balancing. It directed investment and divided production tasks among ministries so that supplies needed for one sector would be produced by others. Once the basic decisions on number of employees, supplies, and production were made, the enterprises and ministries were automatically assured the money necessary to cover their expenses.

Janos Kornai was to talk about this system as one of "soft budget restraint," but the phrase is misleading.[16] Once financial resources were allocated, they could result in severe restraints on wages and personnel, as the bitter complaints of managers against the Ministry of Finance throughout the Soviet period testified.[17] The key fact about money in the Soviet system was that, to use a comment popular after 1985, "the ruble was not internally convertible."

This was especially true of "accounting money" (*beznalichnye den'gi*), which was used in relations between state enterprises. If a manager had such rubles to buy steel, he could not use them to buy coal; if he had rubles

15. Gregory Grossman, "Gold and the Sword: Money in the Soviet Command Economy," in Henry Rosovsky, ed. *Industrialization in Two Systems: Essays in Honor of Alexander Gershchenkron* (Wiley, 1966), pp. 204–36.
16. Janos Kornai, *Economics of Shortage*, vol. 8 (Amsterdam: North-Holland, 1980), pp. 306–09.
17. There was a tendency to adjust "profits" of enterprises, but this was primarily to ensure that decisions on housing construction and other social expenditures could be financed.

to buy machinery from factory A, he could not use them to buy machinery from factory B. Other than through illegal means or (within limits) through negotiation with an assigned supplier, the only way to change suppliers was to obtain the authorizing directive or chit from the appropriate administrative agency. Such informal means were a prominent part of the Soviet system, but they affected only a small percentage of the goods being distributed.

Money did play an accounting role for state enterprises. Factories inevitably used a variety of supplies and produced a variety of goods whose value could not be aggregated unless they were given financial value. Prices were assigned to goods to create an aggregated measure against which to judge performance, including the extent to which the production plan was met, the extent to which costs were cut, and so on. These accounting prices generally had a cost-plus character—that is, they reflected costs plus a set percentage profit. They were, however, often set at artificial levels for policy reasons. These "irrational" prices did have some distorting impacts on decisions, but the essential fact about prices in the Soviet economic system was their minor influence.[18]

The basic difficulty with economic reform was that an economy in which money mattered only marginally would have to be transformed into one in which it was the crucial determination of action. The ruble would have to become convertible internally, and managers with rubles would have to be given the right to buy supplies as they wished. Subsidized prices would have to be brought more into line with market prices, especially prices of commodities that could be sold on the world market. The domestic price of petroleum, for example, remained at $2 a barrel for nearly a decade after the world price increase of 1973. Unless the price of oil was raised, managers with freedom to sell and buy goods could buy petroleum at the subsidized price and sell it abroad at market prices.

The most explosive political issue was the heavy subsidization of rent and utilities. Indeed, the subject was so explosive that it was hardly mentioned, let alone attacked, and it had barely been touched by 1996 when price liberalization had supposedly already occurred. Rent had remained stable for fifty years and covered only one-third of current operating and

---

18. In the existing sellers' market, cost-plus pricing led managers either to be indifferent to the basic costs of their products or to favor the production of larger, heavier items that contained more raw materials and therefore cost more.

maintenance costs, much less any of the original building costs.[19] The rent payment was based on square meters of floor space, not the quality or location of the apartment. If apartments were privatized, even by giving them away, inhabitants' assumption of operating costs would by itself cause major increases in housing payments. If young people without state apartments had to purchase apartments and make mortgage payments, their payments would be dramatically higher than the rents paid by old residents. Utility payments were also heavily subsidized and needed to be increased.

The problem most often discussed in the media was food prices. As grain prices were raised over the years, retail bread prices remained frozen. Bread came to cost the consumer less than the grain in it cost the state to produce or import. It was less expensive for peasants to feed their pigs bread bought from the store than to feed them the grain they themselves grew. Many other prices traditionally tied to bread prices were also too low.[20]

Meat prices were especially sensitive: price increases had triggered a riot in Novocherkassk in the Soviet Union in 1962 and several in Poland in the 1970s.[21] The state prices paid to farms for beef were raised eleven times between the early 1960s and 1987, but again the retail price remained unchanged.[22] By 1986, beef cost the state 5 rubles per kilogram to produce, while it was sold in the stores for a maximum of 2 rubles a kilogram for the best cuts. A considerable part of the production cost came in hard currency purchases of foreign feed grain.

Per capita meat consumption had risen from 58 kilograms a person in 1980 to 62 in 1985 and 67 in 1990. Yet because meat was underpriced both in relation to cost and demand, shortages often occurred in stores even as meat consumption approached West European levels. Russians were eating more meat than the country's economic performance justified, but the regime was receiving little credit. A survey in 1990 showed that only 18.9 percent of the people were satisfied with the supply of meat, a figure lower than that for any other food product.[23]

19. *Pravda*, February 8, 1988, pp. 1–2.
20. Pavlov, *Upushchen li shans*, pp. 63–64.
21. The riot in Novocherkassk was the product not only of price increases for meat but of simultaneous cuts in wages.
22. *Izvestiia*, May 20, 1987, p. 2.
23. *Narodnoe khoziaistvo SSSR v 1990 g., Statisticheskii ezhegodnik* (Moscow: Finansy i statistika, 1991), p. 141.

Food subsidies also produced an increasingly serious budget deficit and inflationary pressures. The deficit was small in the 1980s, but rose rapidly after 1985, reaching 100 billion rubles by 1989. It was supposed to rise another 30 percent during 1990 because of a planned increase in procurement prices. This would raise it to a fifth of the state budget and would threaten the country's financial stability.[24] Both then and under Boris Yeltsin, urban intellectuals called this a subsidy to the agricultural sector, but it really was a subsidy to the urban consumer.[25] If the price increase was to help reduce the urban subsidy, the question was whether the urban population would tolerate it.

The Controversy over Price Reform

In the mid-1980s radical and moderate economists generally argued that the price irrationalities of the Brezhnev period had to end and greater financial responsibility had to be introduced. In September 1985 Gorbachev indicated in Tselinograd, Kazakhstan, that he agreed.

The problem of securing food products for the population has still not been completely solved. The demand for some of them exceeds supply. This is connected with the fact that money incomes are growing more rapidly in our country than the production of food products. At the same time the state prices on the basic products have remained practically unchanged for two decades. Meat, for example, is sold in the stores at a price from two to three times lower than the expenditures the state expends on their production. Now this difference is covered by a state subsidy that costs almost 20 billion rubles a year. The sum, as you see, is impressive.[26]

Gorbachev's speechwriter and assistant for agriculture, Valery Boldin, said Gorbachev intended to make an even stronger case.[27] However, Boldin noted privately that although prices needed to be raised, no one had calcu-

---

24. Nikolai Ryzhkov, *Perestroika: istoriia predatel'stv* (Moscow: Novosti, 1992), pp. 313–14. Meat consumption is reported in *Narodnoe khoziaistvo SSSR v 1988 g.: Statisticheskii ezhegodnik*, (Moscow: Finansy i statistika, 1989), p. 118.

25. Talk about an agricultural subsidy was particularly misleading after 1991. Collective farms and private farmers were paid prices well below world market levels for their grain, but were charged world market prices for machinery and fertilizer. As a result, they could not purchase them, and grain production dropped to 50 percent of the level of the 1980s.

26. Gorbachev, *Izbrannye rechi i stat'i*, vol. 2, p. 404.

27. Boldin, *Ten Years That Shook the World*, p. 104.

lated the effects on other products and that Gorbachev should be careful. The passage was given a minor place in the speech, but those who remembered it (including me) thought it indicated Gorbachev was ready to make the needed price and agricultural reforms in 1987 or perhaps 1988. Sometimes a good memory can be a handicap.

There were, however, serious questions associated with allowing price increases, and they became the subject of intense controversy. One was whether the retail price increases were to be used to reduce the budget deficit and relieve inflationary pressures or were intended simply to bring administered prices closer to market prices and thereby reduce the shock when the market began to set prices. In the latter case the price increases could be offset by wage increases and would be relatively painless, but in the former the increases would have to reduce people's purchasing power.

The fundamental issue over which the political battle lines were drawn, however, was the method by which the increases would be introduced. Should the state adjust fixed prices to a more appropriate level as a first step, or should price changes be produced only through the introduction of market mechanisms and be allowed to vary with market forces? In the mid-twentieth century, Oskar Lange, a Polish economist, proposed a model of market socialism in which the planning organs would adjust prices in response to changing demand, but his ideas do not seem to have influenced the Soviet controversy in the 1980s.[28]

As might be expected, the State Committee of Prices, the institution responsible for establishing prices, favored the retention of administered prices. Nikolai Glushkov, the long-time chairman, was openly conservative about any type of price increase, but the long-time first deputy chairman, A. N. Komin, was vocal in insisting that goods and services not be sold below cost. Komin specifically referred to such sensitive items as rent and food.[29] When Glushkov was retired in the summer of 1986, he was replaced by the first deputy minister of finances, Valentin Pavlov, a strong supporter of Komin's position.

Because it was obvious that the sudden introduction of market-determined pricing would produce the type of chaos realized in Russia after 1991 and that the political leaders would never tolerate this in the second

---

28. For a recent discussion of this model and its possible relevance to Russia, see Pranab K. Bardhan and John E. Roemer, eds., *Market Socialism: The Current Debate* (Oxford University Press, 1993).

29. *Izvestiia*, May 20, 1987, p. 2.

half of the 1980s, an obvious position for a radical economist in the mid-1980s was to accept an administrative adjustment of prices as a first step and then to insist that price controls be loosened so prices could become increasingly demand oriented. The type of three-tier system of Eastern Europe was an obvious solution.

As late as June 1987 Patrick Cockburn could still report that "reform economists advocate state-fixed prices, but at a level which better reflects the balance between supply and demand and relieves the state of paying heavy subsidies."[30] This situation was, however, changing rapidly. The more radical economists always feared the cost-plus approach to pricing and the fixed prices of the State Committee of Prices. They thought prices should reflect demand as well as cost and should fluctuate with changes in supply and demand.

Moreover, those who were known in the West as radical economic reformers were becoming increasingly populist. Many of the best known, among them Nikolai Petrakov and Nikolai Shmelev, became adamant in their opposition to administrative price increases before market mechanisms were introduced. In practice this meant an indefinite postponement of increases and of any effort to reduce the burgeoning budget deficit and inflationary pressures. And many of their proposed measures—greater importation of consumer goods and the use of foreign loans to finance them, for example—would have worsened the situation.[31] When a group of Americans visited Komin's office in December 1987, he said that many volumes of corrected wholesale and retail price lists had been prepared and printed. Their introduction was simply awaiting a political decision. Both in print and in private, Komin was savage in his criticism of the radical economists who were opposing this decision.

The radical economists and the Westerners who talked with them used the words *price reform* to refer only to the introduction of a market economy as a price-setting mechanism. They insisted that the use of managed price changes to end subsidies and introduce fiscal responsibility was not

30. Patrick Cockburn, "Gorbachev and the Committee," *Financial Times*, June 24, 1987, p. 22.
31. Nikolai P. Shmelev, "Avansy i dolgi," *Novyi mir*, no. 63 (June 1987), pp. 142–58; and Shmelev, "Novye trevogi," *Novyi mir*, no. 64 (April 1988), pp. 160–75. Shmelev also took a conservative position in the debates on economic reform in the third world in the 1960s and 1970s, expressing profound suspicion of the market because of its impact on social justice. See Jerry F. Hough, *The Struggle for the Third World: Soviet Debates and American Options* (Brookings, 1986), p. 86.

reform. When Petrakov was offered the chairmanship of the State Committee of Prices in 1989, he declined it, officially on the grounds that the committee should be abolished.

The result of this conflict was that the best became the enemy of the good. Whatever the desirability of market pricing, in 1987 and 1988 it was still years in the future. Indeed, the "radical" 500-Day Plan proposed in 1990 began with the freezing of more than one hundred prices for 500 days, and some prices in 1996 were still far from those that would be established by the market. Thus to oppose the retail price increases introduced by the State Committee of Prices was, in effect, to oppose retail price increases altogether.

At a time when people's purchasing power was increasing rapidly, the so-called conservative economists were therefore proposing a tight money policy and price adjustments approved by the International Monetary Fund to create the conditions for radical reform. The so-called radical economists, in effect, were proposing the opposite.

Because Western economists were much more impressed by those who used "correct" market-oriented language than by those who studied the actual character of the corporate West or the transition to the market in Asia or the West, they enthusiastically supported those who espoused the ideology, even if it led to financial irresponsibility in the Soviet domestic political context. It was the "sophisticated" Soviet economists who spoke the Westerners' language (both figuratively and literally), who received staff positions in the international agencies, became consultants, or were invited to speak in the West. Thus support for fiscal irresponsibility at home won the support of populist domestic political leaders and was at the same time rewarded with large financial dividends from the leading apostles of fiscal responsibility in the West.

For this reason, economic debate inside the Soviet Union became extremely bitter and emotional. Leonid Abalkin, director of the Institute of Economics of the Academy of Sciences and later deputy chairman of the Council of Ministers in charge of economic reform, had a unique window on the political process. In his memoirs he described with wonder and sadness how his colleagues in one institution came to see those in the other as enemies (*vragi*, the old word used by Stalin). For the radical economists, bureaucrats were the root of all evil; the bureaucrats responded that scholars "knew nothing about life."[32] By the 1990s those not receiving the trips to

---

32. Leonid Abalkin, *Ne ispol'zovannyi shans: Poltora goda v pravitel'stve* (Moscow: Politizdat, 1991), p. 30.

the West and Western money also increasingly attributed their opponents' views to a desire to satisfy their patrons, whatever the cost for Russia. Instead of ignorance based on doctrinaire ideology, their patrons were mistakenly accused of a sophisticated policy of weakening Russia.

The Radical Economists and the Command-Administrative System

Both at the time and in retrospect, one of the strangest features of the Soviet debates on economic reform in the 1980s—and in the 1990s for that matter—was their truncated nature. They never included discussion of all the options for reform that might have been addressed, not even the most obvious.

The West was dominated by corporations that achieved high-quality production in assembly plants whose directors had less independence than the plant directors in the Soviet system. Eastern Europe and China had accumulated a great deal of experience with economic reform. There were positive lessons from the latter (a variety of agricultural reforms had proved successful) and disheartening ones (industrial reform was very difficult).

The most clear-cut cautionary lessons of the Polish economic reform of the 1970s were that postponing price increases in the midst of a deteriorating fiscal situation was even more dangerous than immediate increases, and that foreign borrowing to maintain consumption led to disaster.[33] Wladislaw Gomulka's successor, Edward Gierek, was removed when strikes spread in response to inflation that raged out of control in 1989.[34] The Polish experience also showed that even a political movement with the strength of Solidarity can be subdued by martial law and that price increases can be imposed under such martial law.

The economic debates surrounding perestroika, however, almost never alluded to the modern corporation and its assembly-line plants, let alone the economic policies of third world countries. No one looked at the successful

33. See the brilliant 1977 article by Richard Portes that not only explained why Polish economic policy was unsustainable but that pointed to 1980 as the year the house of cards was likely to collapse. "East Europe's Debt to the West: Interdependence is a Two-Way Street," *Foreign Affairs*, vol. 55 (July 1977), pp. 751–82.

34. For a survey of the politics of Polish reform in the 1970s, see Jerry F. Hough, *The Polish Crisis: American Policy Options* (Brookings, 1982).

economic program of Count Sergei Witte, the finance minister of Nicholas II in Russia in the 1890s, which was very relevant to the 1980s. Most striking of all, Gorbachev and the participants in the debates seemed oblivious to contemporary reform experiences in communist countries.[35] In his classic early book about Soviet economic reform, Ed Hewett noted that ''the extensive information available in the Soviet Union on other socialist economic systems has not greatly influenced the debate on economic reform in the USSR.'' He later reiterated, ''the Eastern European and Chinese reform experience seems to have had only limited influence on Soviet thinking in regard to reform strategy.''[36]

In the Brezhnev period the published debates among economists had focused almost exclusively on industry and its incentive systems because only these subjects were considered nonthreatening to the regime. The discussions remained much the same in the two years after Gorbachev was elected. Hewett's book, published in 1988, accurately reflected this focus in its almost exclusive attention to industry.

Because the press remained under tight censorship, the meaning of the truncation was unclear. Gorbachev early developed the practice of introducing the politically most sensitive reforms with little prior public discussion. When the decree legalizing joint ventures with foreigners was published in January 1987, the issue had not even been mentioned beforehand in the press. Moreover, the decree was published during a Central Committee plenary session that distracted attention from it.[37] Similarly, the law permitting privately owned cooperatives and individual labor was published to a drumroll of articles on the dangers of unearned income to reassure conservatives. If agricultural reform and price increases were to be introduced in 1987 or 1988, they would likely be announced in the same manner.

In this case, however, the published commentary reflected the behind-the-scenes reality. Little meaningful agricultural reform was to occur at any

35. An exception was Oleg Bogomolov, director of the Institute of the Economics of the World Socialist System, but even he was not an active participant in the published debates.

36. Ed A. Hewett, *Reforming the Soviet Economy: Equality versus Efficiency* (Brookings, 1988), pp. 300, 302.

37. This was deliberate. In November 1986 I was shown the decree and was told it would be published in mid-December, when the plenum was scheduled. The plenum was postponed, and the publication of the decree along with it.

time during Gorbachev's tenure in office or during Yeltsin's tenure either, at least through 1996.[38] Gorbachev did emphasize leasing collective property to large brigades, but he made few of the necessary changes in the procurement system and no price adjustments. In industry, virtually all attention was focused on the enterprise and its independence rather than on changes at ministry levels that were comparable to corporation headquarters. But if this focus had very conservative implications under Brezhnev, when a serious weakening of the position of the ministries was unthinkable, it became explosive when the dismantling of the ministries became a real possibility.

If economic reform was to concentrate on industry, there was, indeed, reason for very serious discussion. Anyone fearing public reaction to an increase in retail prices should have been terrified of industrial reform. The Soviet economic model strongly promoted egalitarianism and maximized the value of personal security, not only in its social policy and its protection against international market forces, but also in its incentive system for hiring labor and setting prices. Industrial economic reform meant that a system that encouraged managers to hoard labor had to be replaced by one that encouraged them to economize on labor. This meant toleration of unemployment and inflation in the prices of industrial goods. Yet the social consequences of radical industrial reform were little discussed in public and apparently given little consideration in the private political debates by the very people in the inner circles who worried incessantly about the social consequences of increases in food prices.

Once the radical economists began to oppose administered price increases and to justify this reaction by emphasizing their opponents' bureaucratic obsession with power, they were driven inexorably toward a simplified and abstract model of economic reform. If they would not accept administered price changes, they were scarcely likely to approve much more intrusive and subtle management of economic reform by central and republican institutions. Indeed, the reforming economists treated transitional measures that either rearranged the system (the re-creation of regional economic councils or sovnarkhozs favored by Premier Ryzhkov, for example), that accomplished good goals through administrative actions (a state-supported export strategy focused on important manufacturing indus-

---

38. Instead, the input of machinery and fertilizers into agriculture was cut drastically, and by 1995 the grain harvest had fallen to 63 million tons as compared with 120–130 tons in the 1980s.

tries), or that left a state sector in place (as did Chinese economic reform) as palliatives that the bureaucrats would use to throttle further reform.

Most radicals had Lenin's fear of reformism, of partial success. Just as Lenin thought welfare-state measures would undermine support for revolution, reforming economists seemed to fear that partial steps would be successful and would undermine support for future reform. For example, one of the major blows to perestroika was the collapse of oil prices after 1985 and consequent dwindling Soviet earnings in foreign currency. In a meeting with visiting U.S. congressmen in 1987–88, Georgy Arbatov expressed a view widespread among the reformers that the drop in world petroleum prices was a blessing for the Soviet Union: if partial reform and export earnings alleviated the problem, he said, the leaders might postpone thoroughgoing reform, but the absence of hard currency would force them to introduce more serious reform. It was a typical attitude.[39]

But if success achieved through partial measures could not be countenanced, if intermediate steps involving government management of the economy could not be contemplated, then by definition no intelligent theory of a transition was possible. Such a theory inevitably required a strong continuing role for the state. The radical economists gave no evidence of recognizing this.

If the radical reformers would not accept administered change, however, they needed another economic reform program. They could not emphasize the model of the modern corporation, which gives little power to its production plants, without admitting the crucial importance of corporate headquarters, that is, in Soviet terms, the ministry. For lack of any alternative, the reformers focused on the need for the independence of the enterprise from the ministry—in Western terms, the independence of the assembly plant from corporate headquarters. Indeed, they soon embraced privatization of the assembly plant, which in practice meant a return to the precorporate capitalism of the early nineteenth century.

39. Georgy Arbatov is an influential but tragic figure of the Gorbachev period. In the Brezhnev period he supervised the writing of the sections on domestic economy in Brezhnev's speeches, and they often were surprisingly bleak. Under Gorbachev he was driven to radical positions not in line with his basic instincts by the pressures to satisfy both those above him in the foreign policy and ideological establishment and the Americans with whom his job put him into contact. This included the appointment of the most irresponsible of the economists, Nikolai Shmelev, as his deputy director. Small wonder that at a time when dozens of memoirs about the Gorbachev period have been published, Arbatov ends his with 1985.

The proposals of the radical economists emphasized dismantling what one of them, Gavril Popov, called "the command-administrative system." They proposed to reduce ministries' staffs so that they would be less able to regulate the activity of the enterprises. Then the economists demanded the ministries be disbanded altogether. The ability of the local party organs to provide regional coordination of the economy, they said, must be ended by the abolition of Article VI of the Constitution. The empire must be transformed into a loose confederation or commonwealth.

The radicals acted as if they embraced the neo-Marxist view of the Soviet system. They seemed to believe the managers of the means of production under socialism constituted a united, privileged, repressive ruling class incapable of accepting evolution to any other economic system. Logically, therefore, the bureaucrats could be expected adamantly to oppose economic reform. For the radicals, then, only a revolutionary overthrow of the ruling class would achieve true reform. In economic terms this meant that only shock therapy was left as an alternative: destroy the old institutions and their controls on the economy and let new ones be built on their ruins. If enterprises were to be free and administrative controls on prices were counterproductive, there was little alternative to acceptance of monetarist doctrine in its extreme form as the solution to all problems. And, as will be discussed in chapter 11, the radical economists in fact adopted this position in 1989 and 1990.

In later years, both pro-Gorbachev and pro-Yeltsin spokesmen were to emphasize the difference between Gorbachev's economic reform of perestroika and Yeltsin's shock therapy. When Yeltsin introduced economic reform, he relied on economists such as Yegor Gaidar, who were in their thirties. The radical economists of the Gorbachev period were largely passed over, and they responded by criticizing Gaidar and his shock therapy.

In retrospect, however, the radical economists of both the Gorbachev and Yeltsin periods, as well as the two leaders themselves, seemed to assume that the destruction of the administrative-command system would by itself solve most problems and that independent enterprises would then produce economic abundance. Gaidar was more explicit in advocating this theory and Yeltsin more decisive in his actions, but surely the advice of men like Yakovlev, Petrakov, and Shmelev led to the same economic and political consequences as Yeltsin's program did in 1992 and 1993.

Gorbachev and Ryzhkov on Price Reform

Price reform was frequently discussed in the Soviet press, and the opposing positions of the economists were relatively easy to identify. There was, however, little evidence that the conflict extended into the leadership. As Anders Aslund, a careful observer of the press at that time, noted, the highest officials said almost nothing about prices or financial imbalance until 1990, and no difference was observable between Gorbachev and Premier Ryzhkov. Aslund concluded that the leadership as a whole was unsophisticated on issues of price reform.

> The Soviet financial crisis does not appear to have been . . . equally contentious within the leadership. The problem was rather that the leaders neglected reality and the quickly deteriorating financial balance for too long. . . . Gorbachev and Ryzhkov both spoke up late and did not reveal any differences of note. Nikolai Sliunkov expressed a different opinion, calling for a swift balancing of the economy in December 1989, but by then he had already lost most of his powers.[40]

The memoirs of the leaders, however, show that the press created a wrong impression. Ryzhkov had agreed with economists advocating immediate administrative price increases. Gorbachev, like the radical economists, had opposed them. After 1986 Gorbachev was treated by his supporters as a radical economic reformer, while Ryzhkov was increasingly denounced as a former plant manager who did not understand financial or economic matters. But whatever Ryzhkov may have thought about the market, from the beginning he clearly understood the need for greater fiscal responsibility, and he fought for it from 1986 onward. He understood the need for more "rational" prices. Gorbachev, by contrast, consistently opposed any price adjustments that would have prevented the inflationary pressures from getting out of control and would have eased the transition to the market.

In 1995 the memoirs of Valentin Pavlov and Gorbachev revealed for the first time that the subject of bread prices had arisen at the end of Brezhnev's life in conjunction with a large-scale food program designed to funnel more resources into agriculture. The program was, of course, close to Gorbachev's heart, and he has described at some length his difficult strug-

---

40. Anders Aslund, *Differences over Economics in the Soviet Leadership, 1988–1990*, report N-3277-A (Santa Monica, Calif.: Rand, 1991), p. vi.

gle to find funding for it.[41] He does not, however, mention that he actively supported increasing the retail price of bread. According to Pavlov, "almost all money received from an increase in bread prices should go to the development of the village [and this] became an integral part of the food program." This was the reason Gorbachev favored the increases.[42]

In July 1982 Brezhnev approved an increase in the price of bread that was scheduled to go into effect on January 15, 1983. But he died in November, and the increase was postponed indefinitely. Both Pavlov and Gorbachev agree in their memoirs that Brezhnev approved the increase and that it was reversed by Andropov. Both also agree that Gorbachev actively promoted the reversal, although Gorbachev says nothing about his earlier support for an increase.[43]

According to Pavlov, Gorbachev argued that no one would believe Brezhnev had approved the plan and that Andropov would be blamed for an unpopular decision at the beginning of his administration. According to Gorbachev, he and Nikolai Ryzhkov, the new Central Committee secretary for the economy, opposed the price increase both for economic and political reasons. Gorbachev claimed that Andropov was eager to go through with the price increase, but that he was finally persuaded otherwise by his insistent underlings.[44] It is hard to imagine that the sixty-eight-year-old former KGB chief relied on a new fifty-one-year-old subordinate for his political judgments, but Andropov probably decided that people needed to be better prepared for price increases by a new leader. His illness prevented any such effort.

The issue of price increases remained dormant during Konstantin Chernenko's year in office, but it was propelled onto the Politburo agenda by the antialcohol campaign begun in May 1985. The campaign was vigorously promoted by Gorbachev and Yegor Ligachev and strongly opposed by Ryzhkov, who supported Gosplan and the Ministry of Trade in their argument that the step could cost the state billions of rubles.[45] The antialcohol campaign was pursued vigorously and cut both alcohol sales and

41. Gorbachev, *Zhizn' i reformy*, vol. 1, pp. 204–11. *Memoirs*, pp. 127–30, contains a shortened version excising a long discussion of the trade-off of grain and defense expenditures.

42. Pavlov, *Upushchen li shans?*, p. 69.

43. Pavlov, *Upushchen li shans?*, pp. 69–72; Gorbachev, *Zhizn' i reformy*, vol. 1, pp. 234–35; *Memoirs*, p. 147.

44. Gorbachev, *Zhizn' i reformy*, vol. 1, p. 234; *Memoirs*, p. 147.

45. Boldin, *Ten Years That Shook the World*, pp. 101–02.

government revenues substantially. Although the campaign was marked by excesses and was universally condemned in Moscow and the West, it had much to recommend it if carried out moderately. Westernization and professionalization in Russian society demanded less use of alcohol, and the program was a useful symbol of the need for change. In addition, because alcohol was very expensive, the reduction in sales would greatly expand people's purchasing power.[46] This purchasing power would have been useful in lessening the financial blow of the badly needed increases in food prices, although pensions and wages of those with low incomes would also need to be raised to provide compensation for the most needy.

But the antialcohol campaign created potential problems as well as opportunities. It decreased government revenue at the same time that Gorbachev's insistence on acceleration and increased investments added to government expenditures. If the increase in purchasing power created by the reduction of alcohol sales were not somehow absorbed, then it would intensify inflationary pressures.

In 1985 almost everyone knew price increases were necessary in principle, but they apparently were first placed on the Politburo agenda in the fall of 1986. According to Gorbachev's close adviser, Anatoly Cherniaev, all the leading economic officials—Ryzhkov, the top two agricultural officials (Viktor Nikonov and Vsevolod Murakhovsky), and the Politburo member in charge of light industry (Aleksandra Biriukova)—favored retail price increases. Ryzhkov recalled that he was also supported by the Central Committee secretary for the defense industry (Lev Zaikov), the Central Committee secretary for the economy (Nikolai Sliunkov), and the premier of Russia (Vitaly Vorotnikov). The Central Committee secretary for Eastern Europe (Vadim Medvedev) said he took the same position. These high officials were joined by the top financial officials, but Gorbachev wavered.

Although he had advocated higher food prices in September 1985, Gorbachev now returned to the position he had expounded to Andropov in

---

46. This problem is usually described in terms of public finance. The government was deprived of tax revenue because alcohol was heavily taxed, it is said, and there was a need to cut food subsidies to reduce the budget deficit. This was a perfectly legitimate way to look at the problem, but it tended to reinforce the misleading impression, especially for Western economists advising the Russian government, that the Soviet Union and then Russia had a normal budgetary process and that financial problems could be solved by the usual monetary methods. Phrasing the question as a problem of purchasing power is more useful for understanding.

1982: the people should see benefits from perestroika before painful decisions were inflicted on them. According to Cherniaev, Gorbachev agreed with Ryzhkov on the need for price increases in December, but his top political lieutenants on the Politburo—both the more conservative Yegor Ligachev and the reforming Eduard Shevardnadze—opposed them. Gorbachev finally reversed himself and accepted their position.[47]

Cherniaev's testimony is precise on the positions of the leaders (except Aleksandr Yakovlev, who almost surely was aligned with Ligachev and Shevardnadze), but vague on the circumstances of the conflict. Valentin Pavlov has asserted that the occasion for the debate was a plenary session on economic reform scheduled for December 1986, the time a decision was needed for reform to go into effect in 1988. He said that Yakovlev was working closely with the group at Volynskoe and that Gorbachev also showed great interest in its work. Pavlov, however, reported that the plenum was suddenly canceled in mid-December and replaced by one on personnel and democratization to be held in January 1987.[48]

Pavlov, who was in the group preparing the decision and who describes its work in detail, seems credible on the issue, but Gorbachev's memoir does not mention any economic conflicts in 1986, and no one else refers to a proposed economic plenum in December. Indeed, in September 1986 Gorbachev had said that the next plenum would deal with personnel, and in his memoirs he claimed that work on the plenum began in early fall.[49] Leonid Abalkin did report that "a plenum on personnel was being prepared by the organizational department of the Central Committee [and] the economy was attached to it. Materials were written in two different sections of the dacha Volynskoe-2."[50] Abalkin says nothing about the timing of this decision or of the economics plenum, but his brief remark gives added credence to Pavlov's version.

Patrick Cockburn noted in early October that when Gorbachev returned from vacation in September, he talked much more about democratization than economic reform.[51] Fedor Burlatsky, a journalist who had a close

47. A. S. Cherniaev, *Shest' let s Gorbachevym* (Moscow: Progress, 1993), pp. 122–23.

48. Pavlov, *Upushchen li shans?*, pp. 38–48.

49. Gorbachev, *Zhizn' i reformy*, vol. 1, p. 307; *Memoirs*, p. 196.

50. Leonid Abalkin, *Na pereput'e: Razmyshlenniia o sud'bakh Rossii* (Moscow: Institute of Economics RAN, 1993), p. 221.

51 "Gorbachev Adviser Urges Political Reform," *Financial Times*, October 11, 1986, p. 2.

relationship with Yakovlev, was included in the group that went with Gorbachev to the summit with President Ronald Reagan in Reykjavik in October. At a press conference there Burlatsky emphasized that "without more democracy in the Soviet Union there could be no economic reform."[52] Vadim Medvedev says that work on a cadres plenum began in the fall, but that on November 19 Gorbachev widened its scope to include democratization.[53]

These various recollections are not necessarily incompatible. Gorbachev was to announce other Central Committee sessions, such as one on nationality issues, that were then postponed. Various groups often worked at Volynskoe on different subjects, and it may well have been that two plenums were being prepared simultaneously. Medvedev never says the cadres plenum would be next. The timing of the democratization plenum always seemed six months to a year early, given that no election was scheduled until March 1989, and Gorbachev may have been unsure which to hold first.

On Saturday December 20, Patrick Cockburn reported that a Central Committee plenum was scheduled the following week. On December 16 the Kazakh leader, Dinmukhamed Kunaev, had been removed, and riots broke out in Alma-Ata. Some 10,000 people participated, with 28 killed and 200 wounded.[54] It seems certain that the postponement of the plenum, whatever its topic, was caused by these riots. They also probably led Gorbachev to reverse himself on price increases, thinking that additional riots at this particular moment were particularly dangerous. The postponement of the plenum for a month is compatible with the mid-December change in theme about which Pavlov has written.

It is also possible that Gorbachev always preferred to hold the plenum on personnel and democratization first, while other Politburo members (for example, Ryzhkov) wanted to begin with an economic plenum.[55] Certainly Yakovlev and those associated with him wanted to emphasize political

---

52. Patrick Cockburn, "Gorbachev Targets Party Reform," *Financial Times*, October 9, 1986, p. 3.
53. Medvedev, *V komande Gorbacheva*, p. 43.
54. Andrei Grachev, *Kremlevskaia Khronika* (Moscow: EKSMO, 1994).
55. During the Brezhnev era, debates on the relationship of the political and economic spheres sometimes became codewords for the relative power of the Central Committee (Brezhnev) and the Council of Ministers (Kosygin). It would not be surprising if some people were seeing the issue in similar terms in 1986, all the more so because Ryzhkov was complaining about interference by the Central Committee Secretariat in the business of the Council of Ministers.

reform. Gorbachev has stated that the plenum had to be postponed two or three times, and his spokesmen claimed that the reason was conservative opposition to democratization.[56] It seems more likely that the conflict on price increases and disagreement over which plenum to hold first were the crucial issues.

If Gorbachev ever was tempted to begin with the economic plenum, his decision not to support price increases tilted him toward favoring the plenum on democratization. He cannot have wanted attention to be focused on an aspect of reform on which his resistance to price increases would be criticized in the West as the conservative one and Ryzhkov's considered the desirable one. The change to the plenum on democratization refocused attention on a matter on which Gorbachev had no problem claiming his position was in the forefront of the reform movement. This concern with image may have been decisive. No one among the reformers, let along Gorbachev, seemed to understand that democratization would redouble the political explosiveness of price increases. In any case, it was to be one of the most fateful decisions in the destruction of the Soviet Union.

Gorbachev's decision was not irreversible. The plenum on democratization did transform factory and farm managers into elected officials, temporarily freeing them from direct ministerial (but not local party) control.[57] The next logical step was an economic reform that would give them more power. In addition, a short-term drop in industrial output occurred in January and served as an argument to accelerate the reform process. The plenary session on economic reform was rescheduled for the summer of 1987, and the process of drafting the decision began once more in the first months of the year. At the beginning of March, Gorbachev began to have intensive conversations with economic officials and economists on the measures to be introduced.

Behind the scenes, two working groups were formed to draft the documents for the June plenum.[58] One, composed primarily of economists and middle-level Central Committee officials, but including Valentin Pavlov,

---

56. In February 1987 he said it had been postponed three times. M. S. Gorbachev, *Izbrannye rechi i stat'i*, (Moscow: Gospolitizdat, 1987), vol. 4, p. 428.

57. Paradoxically, it was the democratic election of managers that was reversed. Only 20 percent had been elected by late 1988, and Premier Ryzhkov announced the abolition of the practice in late 1989. Donald Filtzer, *Soviet Workers and the Collapse of Perestroika: The Soviet Labour Process and Gorbachev's Reforms, 1985–1991* (Cambridge University Press, 1994), p. 83.

58. Medvedev, *V komande Gorbacheva*, p. 49.

the reforming chairman of the State Committee of Prices, met in the dacha at Volynskoe to draft the general conception of reform and the text of Gorbachev's plenum speech. The group was led by Vadim Medvedev, Central Committee secretary for the socialist countries. Another group, composed of top government officials, met to draft decrees on the details of the economic mechanism and to discuss the financial situation and price reform. It was led by Nikolai Sliun'kov, Central Committee secretary for the economy.

The division of labor between the two groups proved unfortunate in the extreme. The economists working on the general conception were attracted to the idea of "regulating production through economic methods and norms."[59] Having no responsibility for detailed legislation, they produced a draft that, as critics charged, had a declarative nature. The government officials working on legislation for 1988 rightly worried that too much independence given prematurely to plant directors would lead to uncontrolled inflation and major disruptions in production. They insisted that the planning of production and the selection of recipients of specific supplies continue. But because their charge was to draft near-term legislation, their work had little long-term sweep or vision.

The professional self-interest and bias of the two groups were clear enough, and each began to emphasize the bias of the other. The fundamental problem, however, was that both groups were correct in their respective policy positions. The economists had a better understanding that shortages were produced by price imbalances rather than insufficient production. They better understood that increased production was not an achievement if goods were outdated or not the most appropriate products for the Soviet Union in the international division of labor at its stage of economic development. The government officials understood much better that the various parts of the economic system were tightly integrated and that changes in one element of the economy might have disastrous consequences in others–and for the economy as a whole–if they were not carefully coordinated.

The obvious solution was to let the government officials make the administrative adjustments in prices to reduce the subsidies and to take market considerations into account. The supply system could be gradually marketized by reducing the number of products produced and the proportion of "state orders" planned. Thus, steps toward introducing a market-

59. Medvedev, *V komande Gorbacheva*, pp. 48–49.

price mechanism could be introduced gradually—and easier steps they would be if prices were closer to market level before controls were loosened. If privatization was wanted, much was to be said for reintroducing the regional economic councils (*sovnarkozy*) of the Khrushchev era, for if republican officials controlled the factories, the pressure to destroy the central government and secede would have been eased. Indeed, Nikolai Ryzhkov favored the recreation of sovnarkhozis, although surely for different reasons.[60]

Gorbachev rejected all these options, and the reform package passed by the Central Committee in June 1987 pushed price changes well into the future. The decision referred to a "radical" price reform to be completed by 1990. New wholesale prices and tariff rates were to be introduced into industry, transportation, and communications on January 1, 1990, and new agricultural procurement prices on January 1, 1991. Reform in retail prices was mentioned, but no date for implementation was given.[61]

It is at this point in the history of perestroika that Gorbachev has been most dishonest in describing his thinking or that his thinking was the most confused. From 1986 to 1990, he became increasingly radical in his verbal support for economic reform, while Premier Nikolai Ryzhkov often spoke about the need for government controls to prevent chaos. The same split occurred behind the scenes. When the Law of State Enterprises was discussed at Politburo meetings—and Premier Ryzhkov says it was discussed repeatedly—the sessions were "stormy, nerve-racking, and long" and sometimes lasted seven or eight hours.

> [Gorbachev] in practice proposed to liquidate the existing mechanisms of economic administration without creating absolutely anything in their place. At first, I thought that Gorbachev simply didn't understand the essence of the question, but further conversations and particularly Politburo sessions on which these problems were discussed showed that he was consciously pursuing his line.
>
> Precisely the role of the state in the modern economy provoked the most frequent and furious arguments during the preparation of the draft of the law. . . . The ultraradicals demanded that the idea of the plan be totally rejected, asserting that the producers themselves would quickly understand everything and establish smooth, mutually profitable relations with each other. And nationwide tasks would be solved by themselves. Yakovlev, Medvedev, and Shevardnadze insisted on this point of view, and Gorbachev supported them. And it is necessary

---

60. Ryzhkov, *Desiat' let velikikh potriasenii*, pp. 66, 79.
61. See Gertrude E. Schroeder, "Anatomy of Gorbachev's Economic Reform," in Hewett and Winston, *Milestones in Glasnost and Perestroika: The Economy*, p. 211.

to say that their influence on the general secretary grew perceptibly. . . . I was supported by part of the Politburo members: Sliunkov, Zaikov, Vorotnikov, Nikonov, and others.[62]

At the end of 1987, according to Ligachev, Yakovlev, with Gorbachev's support, severely attacked the conservatism of the proposed state plan presented by Ryzhkov.[63]

The impression was created—and fostered in off-the-record statements by Gorbachev spokesmen—that Gorbachev was attempting serious economic reform but was being opposed by Politburo conservatives. Western scholars, including me, accepted this image of Politburo politics. But Gorbachev was proposing an extreme form of shock therapy yet insisting that there not be any shock. If he would not accept the relatively mild price increases under discussion in 1986–87, how could he have been serious about the far more disruptive costs of what he was proposing?

Just as the plan was being worked out in the fall of 1987, Ryzhkov again persistently raised the question about the reform of price formation: wholesale, procurement, and retail prices. "A system of measures was worked out to compensate the population. Let us move, [I argued] let us go from words to deeds. We have had enough hot air about reforms. . . . I was answered: wait, don't hurry, it is still not time, the people will not understand us. And not only politicians said this, but also scholars who had affirmed earlier that no economic reform was possible without a change in price formation."[64] Again, Ryzhkov was turned down, and then he was attacked for conservatism as a cover for Gorbachev's rejection of the crucial first steps of reform he proposed.

Ryzhkov continued to be supported by some of the most important institutions in the government, including the Ministry of Finance and the State Committee of Prices. Valentin Pavlov, chairman of the State Committee of Prices, wrote a forceful article in *Pravda* calling for price reform; it specifically mentioned the need for increases in oil and gas prices and a unified system of prices in the agroindustrial sector.[65]

The issue between Gorbachev and Ryzhkov was not economic reform, but the character of the transition to the market. Ryzhkov and the econo-

62. Ryzhkov, *Desiat' let velikikh potriasenii*, pp. 195–96, 199.
63. Ye. K. Ligachev, *Zagadka Gorbacheva* (Novosibirsk: Interbuk, 1992), pp. 290–93.
64. Ryzhkov, *Perestroika*, pp. 166, 244.
65. *Pravda*, August 25, 1987, p. 2.

mists associated with him had a serious plan for the transition, and even the Central Committee group at Volynskoe was proposing administered price increases. Medvedev, the committee secretary who led the group, expressed his regrets about not fighting more vigorously to overcome Gorbachev's resistance at this point.

Gorbachev's position was not consistent and surely was not honest. Officially, he was opposing immediate price increases on the grounds that the public should see results from perestroika before being subjected to the painful increases. Yet the sudden introduction of a market mechanism was certain to produce far more pain than gradual price increases. If he feared the pain caused by gradual increases, he cannot have wanted greater pain administered before the 1989 USSR and 1990 Russian elections. Consequently, he must have been giving lip service to radical economic reform in 1987 and 1988. Indeed, Viktor Gerashchenko, then chairman of the State Bank, was to charge that economic reform was postponed two years because of the impending elections.[66]

At the time it seemed that the bureaucrats and Ryzhkov were being used as scapegoats. Gorbachev had every incentive to deflect criticism from himself, while others were following the old Russian practice of saying the tsar was good and infallible but had bad lieutenants. Gorbachev seemed to be setting the stage for a purge of party and state officials and perhaps even the destruction of Central Committee and Politburo control over him that was to occur in the winter of 1989–90.

Yet when he did achieve an independent power base by the creation of the USSR presidency in 1990, Gorbachev showed great attraction to precisely those ideas of 1987 that seem most naive. His memoirs also vaguely refer to a single price increase being better than several and to the new mechanism being introduced by 1991. At a Politburo meeting in the spring of 1987, Lev Voronin, the first deputy premier,

> reported that by the end of the five-year plan [January 1991] 30 percent of material-technical supply would be transferred to wholesale trade. A discussion exploded—why 30 percent when the new economic mechanism should be completely working by the beginning of the next five-year plan? How is it possible to reconcile the preservation of 70% of the old system of distributing resources

66. Martin Wolfe "Model Central Banker," *Financial Times*, March 12, 1990, p. B11.

through "rationing" with the fact that there will be a new system of price formation?[67]

The kindest interpretation of Gorbachev's behavior in 1987 was that he had accepted the position of the International Monetary Fund on the relation of stabilization measures and elections: an election should be held and then the harshest stabilization actions introduced immediately afterward. Thus the leader could claim electoral legitimization for his actions, and the economy could be recovering by the time of the next election. Perhaps Gorbachev (or an adviser such as Yakovlev) really was thinking of shock therapy after the 1990 elections along the lines proposed in the 500-Day Plan in 1990. However, all the evidence suggests that although Gorbachev had rejected all alternatives but shock therapy, he was determined not to have the shock.

Gorbachev was either extraordinarily confused or extraordinarily naive. He was assuming that the introduction of a free market system into a socialist country enduring wild price imbalances would cause no more long-lasting pain than the introduction of a program to correct foreign trade imbalances into a country with a functioning market. He was probably being driven by tactical political considerations vis-à-vis other Politburo members, but was also wishfully reassuring himself that his actions seemed to correspond to the best Western advice.

In April 1988 the government again presented a multistage plan of price increases to the Politburo, but Gorbachev and others criticized it. The government apparently was instructed to present a plan with a more rapid and systematic introduction of price increases. In the ensuing two months, word of the program was leaked (no doubt by Gorbachev aides) and "a noisy campaign was raised in the press against the reform of prices, as if this contradicted the interests of the people." In a few weeks, Gorbachev said, "the radical democratic opposition" had engaged in such a level of "cheap populism" that "a transformation of public opinion categorically against a reform of prices and price formation had occurred." Almost all the leading economists also spoke out against price increases. Poor Gorbachev. With all the dictatorial powers of the general secretary at his disposal as well as the support of the conservative Council of Ministers and the bureau-

---

67. Gorbachev, *Zhizn' i reformy*, vol. 1. p. 352–53. This is not in *Memoirs*.

cracy, he could not resist the manipulation of public opinion by a tiny group of radicals in the party-controlled press. Once again, action was postponed.

In July 1988 Ryzhkov ostentatiously associated himself with Leonid Abalkin, one of the few important economists advocating fiscal responsibility while calling for radical reform.[68] Abalkin had written about the Japanese economic model and the Swedish form of socialism, and at the Nineteenth Party Conference had declared that "it is important to emphasize with total certainty that no radical transformation has occurred in the economy and that it remains in a condition of stagnation (*zastoi*)." The fundamental problem in economic reform, he said, was not the resistance of the bureaucratic apparatus, but "basic misconceptions about socialism and economics."[69] He also obliquely supported a multiparty system.

After Gorbachev sharply criticized Abalkin for "economic determinism," the economist found himself ostracized by other delegates in the intermissions of the conference. He was standing alone smoking when Premier Ryzhkov approached him directly and "held out his hand and didn't withdraw it for a long time." Ryzhkov asked Abalkin and his institute to prepare a report to the Presidium of the Council of Ministers by December. When this report was prepared, it put financial stabilization at the top of the agenda.[70]

Again the issue of price increases was raised, and again Gorbachev may have agreed to them. When a Central Committee plenum devoted to agricultural reform was opened on March 15, 1989, it strongly emphasized leasing and associated reforms. On the surface at least, the scheduling of the plenum between the 1989 USSR elections and the opening of the first USSR Congress of People's Deputies suggests that Gorbachev had decided to use the Congress to legitimize the price increases. However, Secretary of State James Baker came to Moscow on May 11–12, 1989, and strongly urged the general secretary to undertake price reform. According to Baker, Gorbachev expressed deep skepticism. Gorbachev's closest aide, who was present at the conversation, has described an even stronger negative reaction.[71]

---

68. Abalkin, *Ne izpol'zovannyi shans*, pp. 9–10.

69. *XIX vsesoiuznaia konferentsiia Kommunisticheskoi partii Sovetskogo Soiuza (28 iunia–1 iulia 1988 goda): Stenograficheskii otchet* (Moscow: Politizdat, 1988), vol. 1, pp. 115–19.

70. Abalkin, *Ne izpol'zovannyi shans*, pp. 10–11, 13–15.

71. Michael R. Beschloss and Strobe Talbott, *At the Highest Level: The Inside Story of the End of the Cold War* (Little, Brown, 1993), p. 65; and Cherniaev, *Shest' let s Gorbachevym*, p. 294.

Gorbachev was planning a trip to China on the eve of the Congress, the first trip there by a Soviet leader since the 1950s. The radical newspaper, *Izvestiia*, published a number of favorable articles on Chinese reform, including one by Theodore Shanin, a Western specialist on Russian agriculture.[72] Every sign indicated that Gorbachev was carefully setting the stage not only for a foreign policy reconciliation with China, but also passage of Chinese-style agricultural reform by the Congress of People's Deputies.

Three events intervened. First, the party suffered a number of defeats in the March 1989 elections, which will be discussed in the next chapter. Gorbachev must have wondered whether this was the right time for painful decisions.

Second, the demonstrations against the regime of Deng Xiaoping had begun in Tiananmen Square in Beijing on April 18 and were directed against price increases as much as against dictatorship. When Gorbachev visited Tiananmen Square on May 16, reports put the crowd at a million people. Four days later, martial law was imposed, and a month later troops were brought in. These events had a dramatic impact in Moscow. In the minds of Soviet intellectuals, the Chinese economic model became associated with the suppression of democracy.

Third, a major strike broke out in the Soviet coal industry on July 10, the first action on such a scale for decades.[73] The strike continued for two weeks, with full press coverage. Abalkin reported with scorn and despair that the Soviet leaders, including Gorbachev, were shaken and decided to buy peace at any cost.[74] Gorbachev later asserted that the radicals' incitement of the miners was a stab in the back and fatal for perestroika.[75] But the strong antiparty vote in the 1989 USSR congressional elections in the large cities must also have created the fear that strikes and demonstrations might spread to industrial workers as well.

Gorbachev and the Radical Economists

In later years Gorbachev tried to explain his mistakes in adopting economic reform by citing the conflicting advice he received from his econo-

72. *Izvestiia*, April 26, 1989, p. 2.
73. See Filtser, *Soviet Workers and the Collapse of Perestroika*, pp. 94–101.
74. Abalkin, *Ne ispol'zovannyi shans*, pp. 30–33.
75. Gorbachev, *Zhizn' i reformy*, vol. 1, p. 461; *Memoirs*, p. 309.

mists. In private he ruefully joked, "They say that Mitterrand has 100 lovers. One has AIDS, but he doesn't know which one. Bush has 100 bodyguards. One is a terrorist, but he doesn't know which one. Gorbachev has 100 economic advisors. One is smart, but he doesn't know which one."[76] And, of course, in his memoirs Gorbachev tried to blame his retreat from price reform on the pressure of public opinion created by "the cheap populism" of the economists.

Without question, Soviet economists were generally not ready to provide the intellectual base for market reform in 1985 and were especially unprepared to give advice on the complicated issues of the transition.[77] The old political system had forced them into compartmentalized work and prevented them from publishing on and discussing comprehensive models of change. Those who studied the outside world could not write on domestic economic questions except by indirection, and they could not write for an audience of domestic specialists. Perhaps most damaging of all, economists working on macroeconomic questions and industry were completely separated from those working on agriculture, who had very low status.

Yet Gorbachev was exaggerating wildly when he suggested he had to pick the one economist of a hundred who made sense. Economists working in the state apparatus with Ryzhkov were impressive and experienced men. They, not the radical economists, had worked in the foreign banking system and had experience with currency flows, the movement of commodity prices and exchange rates, and the relationship of the two to budget deficits and inflation. They were dismissed as conservatives or even bureaucrats because they worked in the government, but they were serious reforming economists.

Moreover, Abalkin, director of the Institute of Economics, remained consistent in urging price increases. He was close to the one economist in the Central Committee Secretariat, Vadim Medvedev, who himself favored price increases and criticizes himself in his memoirs for not promoting his position more vigorously. Oleg Bogomolov, the economist who knew Eastern Europe best, advocated an agriculture-first strategy and the East European model of reform. He spent a month in China in 1987 studying its

---

76. "Evolution in Europe: The Humor of Gorbachev," *New York Times*, November 29, 1990, p. A20. Four years later one of his assistants commented that he still often told the joke.

77. A prescient dissertation on economic debates of the Brezhnev period is Peter Austin Hauslohner, "Managing the Soviet Labor Market: Politics and Policymaking under Brezhnev," Ph.D. dissertation, University of Michigan, 1984.

reforms and prepared a memorandum on the subject for Gorbachev.[78]
Concentration on agricultural reform was advocated by the two most famous scholars from the Novosibirsk, the economist Abel Aganbegian and
the sociologist Tatiana Zaslavskaia.[79] Fedor Burlatsky, who had written
much about China in the late 1970s and early 1980s, proposed the Chinese
model in agriculture and other sectors.[80]

If a leader is uncertain and receives conflicting advice, his likely response is to choose familiar paths, follow the advice of those with practical
experience, and take the less radical alternative. All Westerners were advising Gorbachev to start with price adjustments and agricultural reform, but
the experience of Eastern Europe and China should have suggested this
path to him without outside advice.[81] Yet Gorbachev was not consulting
with Bogomolov, the one economist who was most consistent and open in
calling for agriculture-first reform and the adjustment in food prices that
this required. Gorbachev knew what Bogomolov was proposing, and he did
not want to hear it.

It is difficult to avoid the suspicion that Gorbachev was not so much
influenced by the radical economists as he was influencing them, at least on
the issue of price adjustments. Aganbegian, who stated flatly in 1990 that
perestroika should have begun in agriculture, explained the problem for an
economist such as himself: "People are tired of submitting proposals that
time after time go unclaimed, that are not understood, and that are given a
hostile reception."[82] He blamed unresponsive agricultural bureaucrats, but
it was obvious he was criticizing Gorbachev by criticizing "bureaucrats."

The radical economists were almost all directly or indirectly associated
with the Central Mathematical-Economics Institute, the one institute in the

78. Jonathan Steele, *Eternal Russia: Yeltsin, Gorbachev, and the Mirage of Democracy* (Harvard University Press, 1994), p. 95. Bogomolov was still advocating an
agriculture-first strategy in 1990. "Vostochnaia Europa i my," *Lituraturnaia gazeta,*
July 4, 1990, p. 15.

79. For Zaslavskaia's advocacy of an agriculture-first strategy, see *Izvestiia,* June 1,
1985, p. 3. As late as September 1986 she advocated the increases in meat prices needed
for this reform. T. Zaslavskaia, "Chelovecheskii faktor razvitiia ekonomiki i sotsial'naia
spravedlivost', *Kommunist,* no. 13 (September) 1986, pp. 71–72.

80. Fedor Burlatsky, *Russkie gosudari: Epokha reformatsii* (Moscow: Shark,
1996), pp. 201, 300–01.

81. As late as 1990 John David Galbraith was taking this position in "Est'li vykhod
iz krizis: Problemy perekhodnogo perioda" (Burlatsky interview with Galbraith),
Literaturnaia gazeta, February 14, 1990, p. 12.

82. *Sel'skaia zhizn',* September 22, 1990, p. 2.

country with real expertise on macroeconomics. They understood quite well the relationship of budgetary imbalances and inflationary pressures and the need to reduce state subsidies. It was unnatural for them to be supporting fiscal irresponsibility. Yet once Gorbachev made it clear he opposed price increases in the near and medium term, many economists suppressed their professional knowledge and courted him by presenting populist views he would find congenial. Indeed, the same impulse led them to come over to Yeltsin as he gained political power. Economists say that everyone is motivated by considerations of individual economic gain. Why should they themselves be any different?

The extraordinarily difficult thing to explain is the thinking of Gorbachev and his closest advisers. On the surface the answer is simple: the general secretary feared that the pain associated with price increases would lead to popular unrest and removal of the country's leader, as it had in Poland. In December 1987 a visiting group of American scholars pointedly and repeatedly asked Aganbegian why reform had not begun in agriculture. He put the point delicately: "We are opting for a painstakingly thorough approach, for, unlike in Poland and Hungary, there is no one to help us out if we miscalculate. We can only rely on ourselves."[83]

The "we" to whom Aganbegian was referring was Gorbachev; Aganbegian's position on price increases was closer to Ryzhkov's. He had been director of the Institute of the Organization of Industrial Production in Siberia, and his appointment reflected the influence of those such as Ryzhkov who came out of the Urals and Siberia. He was one of the few major economists to remain consistent in his position on prices until 1990.

The fear of popular unrest seemed exaggerated at the time and seems even more so after the people proved so patient in the face of simultaneous depression and inflation under Boris Yeltsin. Moreover, the lesson of Poland was that the postponement of hard fiscal decisions makes their implementation more, not less, explosive. But even if Gorbachev's excessive fear that price increases would produce rioting in the streets is perhaps understandable, the mystery is why he decided in 1988 to push through a democratization that would give the population the easier option of voting against price increases and other economic pain.

The conventional Western and Moscow interpretation is that Gorbachev was indecisive by character, but as Yegor Ligachev pointed out, this is not

---

83. Abel G. Aganbegian and others, "Basic Directions of Perestroyka," in Hewett and Winston, *Milestones in Glasnost and Perestroyka: The Economy*, p. 116.

accurate.[84] No general secretary was more ruthless in consolidating power within the Communist party in his first five years in office. Gorbachev was boldly decisive and consistent in forcing through democratization and a transformation of foreign policy despite strong opposition. All his former lieutenants, whether members of the Kirilenko machine or democratic advisers, remarked on his lack of loyalty and willingness to sacrifice people who no longer seemed useful to him.

Clearly Gorbachev had no theory of economic transition and something—including, no doubt, an exaggerated sense of the power of the bureaucracy—led him to hope that a market would automatically come into being if the old system were destroyed. His lack of conviction about how to conduct economic reform seems to have strengthened his commitment to democracy. Perhaps it would "activate the human factor" and lead to his exhortations being more effective. Perhaps elected deputies would have a better idea than he did of how to implement economic reform.

But as Gorbachev moved toward supporting freer and freer democratization, he turned out to have a conception of democracy that had no more institutional base than his conception of the market. He seemed to think of democracy in terms of the old village commune or Marx's utopian vision of the socialist future: a system in which people reason together and come to a consensus, not one in which leaders push through and legitimate their policies with close votes. Least of all did he understand that, just as do other forms of government, democracy ultimately rests on force. This is the subject of the next chapter.

84. Ligachev, *Zagadka Gorbacheva*, p. 291.

CHAPTER FIVE

Democratization and the 1989 USSR Election

THE EXPERIENCE OF THE WEST and the communist world strongly suggested economic reform would require political liberalization in Russia, at least as much as it did in China after 1978. The iron curtain could no longer be maintained in its old rigidity. Those in business-related endeavors had to be given greater freedom to read and travel if they were to import or export effectively. Entry into the computer and information age required fundamental changes in the system of prior censorship that had characterized the Soviet Union since the 1920s. The center had to give more power to local governments so that they could efficiently tax and regulate independent business.

It seemed likely this liberalization would be kept under strict control during the most difficult stages of economic reform because these stages can be painful for many segments of a population, especially for older people. An economic policy that benefits young men is not likely to produce uncontrollable demonstrations for these are the people who go into the streets. By contrast, voting turnout in elections is low among the young, but much higher among the middle-aged and older. The introduction of real democracy into a marketizing country gives power to those most inclined to want to slow the process, and it creates strong incentives for politicians to develop populist, antimarket programs.

Thus the more drastic the economic transformation Mikhail Gorbachev intended, the more strenuous should have been his attempts to maintain strong political control. When Serge Schmemann of the *New York Times* recognized that Gorbachev's speech in December 1984 promised "a transformation of the nation as radical as the one wrought by Stalin," he logically concluded that Gorbachev would be authoritarian.[1] Lenin had tightened his political control when he introduced his New Economic Policy in 1921. China had maintained strict political controls when introducing its reform. At the very least the Soviet leaders would want to do the same until they could be certain that the people would tolerate the price increases and other changes engendered by reform.

Constitutional democracy requires both majority rule and constitutional limits on the majority and the government it elects. The Soviet Union had few of the de facto limits on government found in normal dictatorships. The natural first step to constitutional democracy would be to establish an authoritarian constitutionalism (or liberal authoritarianism, if that phrase is preferred) and to create a semidemocratic legislature of the type found in the West in the eighteenth and nineteenth centuries and in much of Asia in the late twentieth century.

Within limits Gorbachev's policy for his first three years in office corresponded to these expectations. His policy of *glasnost* did involve liberalization, but the press remained under tight control in discussions of such sensitive topics as the Stalin past and nationalist grievances. When Boris Yeltsin broke with Gorbachev in the fall of 1987, he claimed the cause was that his rival gave economic reform primacy over political reform. The claim was plausible, both because of Yeltsin's caution on economic reform and Gorbachev's on political reform.

Nevertheless, the same Gorbachev who was afraid to raise subsidized food prices and who had introduced change in calculated doses during his first three years drastically loosened political restraints in the summer and fall of 1988. The most sensitive issues were discussed in such emotional terms that conservatives justly complained the traditional viewpoint seldom gained access to the mass media. Independent groups, which had been tolerated in a very limited way in 1987, were permitted to form almost without limitation, including separatist groups in the non-Russian republics. Then in December 1988 Gorbachev pushed through a decision mandating competitive legislative elections. When a substantial number of radical deputies were elected, they were given almost unlimited access to television.

1. Serge Schmemann, "The Emergence of Gorbachev," *New York Times Magazine*, March 3, 1985, p. 45.

There are many possible explanations for Gorbachev's striking retreat from authoritarianism. One is that he was dedicated to democratization as an end in itself (or perhaps came to this view in 1986), that he did not care about its consequences for economic reform and national unity, and that he introduced his program as soon as he could overcome the resistance of Politburo conservatives. A second explanation is that he did not know how to manage economic reform: he chose to democratize in hopes that elected representatives would know what to do and that democratization would distract attention from his reluctance to proceed with economic reform. Third, Gorbachev may have been transfixed by Yeltsin like a deer by oncoming headlights. To meet Yeltsin's criticisms and maintain a "centrist" position, he let Yeltsin drive him to poorly conceived decisions. Fourth, Gorbachev may have thought he was adopting a shrewd, even Machiavellian plan to free himself from control by the Central Committee and the Politburo, but misjudged the changes competitive elections would bring, and then for whatever reason decided not to bring the democratic institutions under tight control. Fifth, Gorbachev could have misunderstood the relationship between economic reform and democratization in a Soviet-style economy and adopted precisely the wrong political plan to achieve his goals. Finally, he may have had no understanding of the need for institutions and the incentives they create and enforce in a free society, let alone during a major social, economic, and political transition.

Each of these explanations no doubt contains elements of truth, some of them more and some less. And it is unlikely that historians will ever be able to assign them relative weights in an authoritative manner. At a minimum, however, the historical record needs to be clear. Gorbachev's followers have emphasized his total commitment to democracy, yet the 1989 election was closely controlled—nowhere more so than in the general secretary's home region of Stavropol—and he himself refused to run for president in 1990. Yeltsin's men countered that the free and democratic 1990 Russian election had not been free as they prepared the way to abolish the Supreme Soviet in 1993. If one is to try to analyze what happened, one needs to understand the strict limits of democratization through the spring of 1989 and the surprising extent of democracy permitted in the republics in 1990.

Political Liberalization

The Soviet political system was a dictatorship characterized by unusual levels of individual political participation and officially recognized group involvement in decision-drafting committees.[2] Yet it was also an unusually "illiberal" dictatorship. So-called authoritarian dictatorships generally come to embody informal constitutional restraints on the leader's ability to interfere, in John Locke's words, with "life, liberty, and property." Such dictatorships usually permit increasingly competitive legislative elections, although the legislatures have few powers and the elections may be suspended if they produce a result considered dangerous to the existence of the regime.

Lenin, however, rejected any concept of limited government, arguing that the representatives of the ruling class, including the workers, inevitably were unrestrained in defending class interests and that the workers *should* be unrestrained. Western scholars who distinguished between totalitarian and authoritarian dictatorships emphasized this absence of limitations on government, although they allowed their point to be obscured by their insistence on the crucial role of irrational terror and of a one-man dictatorship.

But Soviet elections were uncompetitive, and unauthorized public protest or gathering signatures on petitions was prohibited, even on subjects that were not politically sensitive.[3] Lenin, Joseph Stalin, and Nikita Khrushchev were ruthless in overriding society's preferences on important matters. Leonid Brezhnev rarely tried to transform society in unpopular ways (in practice, he tolerated mild forms of dissidence, especially cultural such as rock and roll and economic such as the so-called second economy with its illegal market activities), but he was unresponsive to public desires for any major change in policy.

It was apparent from his early days in office that at a minimum Mikhail Gorbachev wanted to transform the Soviet Union into a more familiar kind of authoritarian dictatorship. His first steps toward economic reform were dismissed by Westerners as ineffective, but they at least represented political liberalization in that they reduced government repression of the rights of private individuals to engage in independent economic activity. The policy of glasnost allowed individuals greater freedom to publish—and to read—ideas that were hithertofore prohibited. Democratization meant, first of all, a more tolerant attitude toward nonthreatening group activity.

2. Jerry F. Hough and Merle Fainsod, *How the Soviet Union Is Governed* (Harvard University Press, 1979), pp. 435–37.

3. Other communist countries usually permitted some very limited competition in their elections.

Gorbachev was determined to keep the political liberalization within strict limits. Glasnost sometimes meant the appearance of ideas—or more often hints of ideas—that were breathtaking in their departure from the Soviet past but still were limited in comparison with what was permitted in other authoritarian countries.[4] Moreover, press censorship was relaxed very gradually and carefully. It was announced in June 1986 that the power of the censor's office was being reduced, and the office was abolished altogether on August 1, 1990.[5] However, the more important censorship was always exercised informally by political officials, and it was relaxed slowly until mid-1988 and remained strong afterwards, although it was now turned increasingly against the conservatives.

Liberalization accelerated after the nuclear disaster at Chernobyl in April 1986.[6] Then in December 1986 the dissident Andrei Sakharov was released from exile in Gorkii, and it was promised that all other political prisoners would be freed. Because Sakharov had said and written many things that seemed deliberately designed to provoke arrest, his release implied there would be few types of political statements that would lead to arrest in the future, at least aside from those promoting republican separatism in the USSR.

The discussion of some major issues was still, however, kept under tight control, at least in published forums. One was the history of the Soviet period. Not until the spring of 1987 did names such as Leon Trotsky and Nikolai Bukharin begin to appear in the Soviet press, and then very occasionally and unobtrusively. In November 1987 Bukharin was officially

4. In September 1985, for example, the journal *Novyi mir* published an article by the poet Yevgeny Yevtushenko titled "Fuku," in which Stalin's system was implicitly compared with the fascist regimes of the past, and his chief of secret police, Lavrenty Beria, with Hitler. "Fuku" contained a poem that condemned borders and the iron curtain with such lines as "they say the greatest punishment for a tree is to become a border post. It was borders who invented customs-men, passports, and other shit." "Fuku" was published, it was said, because Aleksandr Yakovlev had given a direct order sanctioning it. Yevgeny Yevtushenko, "Fuku," *Novyi mir*, no. 9 (1985), pp. 3–58. The poem is translated in Yevgeny Yevtushenko, *Almost at the End* (Holt, 1986), pp. 40–42, 51. In the English version but not the Russian, Beria is cited by name.

5. R. W. Davies, *Soviet History in the Gorbachev Revolution*, (Indiana University Press, 1984), p. 130; and N. I. Ryzhkov, *Desiat' let velikikh potriasenii*, (Moscow: Kniga, Prosveshchenie, Miloserdie, 1995) p. 79.

6. I was part of the process. I had submitted a severe attack on secrecy to *Literaturnaia gazeta* several days before the disaster. I heard nothing about the fate of the article until August, when it suddenly appeared. Jerry Hough, "'Kogda priedet novoe pokolenie," *Literaturnaia gazeta*, August 27, 1986, p. 14.

discussed in a mildly favorable way as a person who had been wrong in the late 1920s but was to be praised for criticizing the unacceptable Trotsky.[7]

Until 1988 the issue of nationalism remained even more tightly closed. Westerners were later to say that Gorbachev had no inkling of the explosiveness of nationalist aspirations, but his actions before 1988 suggested otherwise. In January 1988 he had wanted Pope John Paul II to come to the Soviet Union the next summer for the celebration of the one thousandth anniversary of the introduction of Christianity into Russia, but he refused to accept the condition that the Pontiff be allowed to visit Catholic Lithuania. Gorbachev understood that Lithuania might be destabilized by the visit.

There was not a single article in the Central Committee journal, *Kommunist*, on a subject touching on nationalism until the fall of 1988, and then it dealt with languages of small population groups. The first major article, which appeared at the beginning of 1989, pointed to assimilation in the United States as the model for policy on national identity.[8] Not only did Gorbachev act as if he were afraid to permit these matters to be discussed in the press, but no first secretary had been changed in Moldavia, Ukraine, or the sensitive republics in the Baltics and the Transcaucasus other than in Georgia, where Eduard Shevardnadze had to be replaced when he was appointed foreign minister. Gorbachev was giving priority to men who had maintained order even if they were relatively conservative.

The same gradual liberalization occurred in book publishing, but it had its peculiarities. In 1987 a sociological survey was taken to discover which books the public most wanted to read. For the first time, the complete works of Russian authors (Aleksander Pushkin, Lev Tolstoy, Vladimir Mayakovsky) were published in sufficient number to satisfy demand. At the same time authors and books that could not be published in the past began to appear in increasing numbers and larger printings. As the months passed, the books that were published became more and more radical.

But there were problems. The USSR produced less than 35 kilograms of paper per person compared with 290 kilograms in the United States. The publication of classics cut into the publishers' ability to publish contemporary works. As economic conditions worsened, the output of the state

7. Gorbachev's speech on the seventieth anniversary of the revolution was the event that began the serious criticism of Soviet history and included the highly qualified praise of Bukharin. *Pravda*, November 3, 1987, pp. 2–5.

8. E. Zemal', "Narodnosti i ikh iazyki pri sotsializme," *Kommunist*, no. 15 (October 1988), pp. 64–72; and V. Tishkov, "Narody i gosudarstvo," *Kommunist*, no. 1 (January 1989), pp. 49–59.

publishers stood at 2.7 billion copies, but it had fallen by 700 million copies by 1990. The rise of private publishers explains some of the decline, but they published only 8 percent of the books printed in 1990. The problem for the reading public worsened further in 1991 when the $30 million hard currency appropriated for the purchase of foreign books, newspapers, and magazines was ended altogether.[9]

The same cautious approach was followed with respect to organized groups independent of the Communist party. During the Brezhnev years the number of independent groups had increased significantly, but only in the fall of 1986 was it recognized that they might be legitimate in some circumstances.[10] The press began cautiously to refer to unregistered groups (usually rock or pop groups, sports fan clubs, literary clubs, and the like), and in a way that was not wholly condemnatory. By 1987 avowedly political groups—the *neformalnye* or informals—began to develop and be tolerated.[11] In the summer of 1987 Boris Yeltsin as Moscow city first secretary tolerated a national convention of informal political groups in the city, but the Politburo decided to investigate this policy, and implicitly to criticize it. Yeltsin proposed a compromise whereby demonstrations could be held in Izmailovo Park as a kind of Hyde Park, but he then resigned, maybe because the compromise was not accepted, and moved on a path toward confrontation with Gorbachev.[12]

In Gorbachev's first years as general secretary the leadership had agreed to a gradual relaxation of controls on the press. Yegor Ligachev and Aleksandr Yakovlev were given joint responsibility for the press as a guarantee of this policy. By 1988, however, liberalization had reached a point at which consensus was certain to break down. Ligachev and those like him wanted to keep liberalization gradual; those such as Yakovlev wanted not only to accelerate it but supplement it with democratization. With a USSR election scheduled for March 1989, a decision on democratization could no

---

9. An excellent discussion of this period is found in the memoirs of the chairman of the State Committee for Publishing. Mikhail Nenashev, *Zalozhnik vremia: Zametki, razmyshleniia, sviditel'stva* (Moscow: Progress, 1993), pp. 199—217

10. S. Frederick Starr, "A Usable Past," *New Republic*, May 15, 1989, pp. 24–27; and Vera Tolz, *The USSR's Emerging Multiparty System*, Washington Papers 148 (Praeger, 1990), pp. 11–12.

11. For an excellent discussion of how the informal groups developed in Moscow, see Timothy J. Colton, *Moscow: Governing the Socialist Metropolis* (Harvard University Press, 1996).

12. Aleksandr N. Yakovlev, *Gor'kaia chasha: Bol'shevizm i Reformatsiia Rossii* (Yaroslavl': Verkhne-Volzhskoe Knizhnoe izdatel'stvo, 1994), p. 216.

longer be postponed. The result was a growing tension between the two groups of advisers as they struggled for Gorbachev's soul.

The tension came to a head on March 13, 1988, when *Sovetskaia Rossiia*, an organ of the Central Committee, published a one-page letter written by Nina Andreeva, an obscure Leningrad chemistry teacher, damning the position of the radical intellectuals.[13] The radicals contended that the article was an anti-perestroika, anti-Gorbachev manifesto sponsored by Ligachev (who has vehemently but not quite convincingly denied any responsibility).[14]

Without question Andreeva's letter was a manifesto against Yakovlev and his policy position. One of Gorbachev's closest aides has written that the general secretary and his wife, Raisa, originally found nothing wrong in the letter.[15] Gorbachev proved to be a man absolutely obsessed with deniability on unpopular political decisions, and the letter was published as he was preparing to leave for Yugoslavia. One even wonders whether he had read the letter beforehand, all the more so since he has said in his memoirs that it turned out to be very useful to him vis-à-vis Ligachev.[16] In any case, after a two-week interlude in which alarm over potential repression in Moscow soared, Gorbachev came firmly down on Yakovlev's side. A two-day Politburo session held at the end of March was devoted to denouncing the letter. Ligachev de facto lost his post as second secretary and head of the Secretariat.

Once the theses for the Nineteenth Party Conference were approved in May 1988, the Soviet press began to publish much more radical political ideas.[17] Delegates at the conference often spoke and acted in a relaxed and frank manner unprecedented in previous decades. One delegate called for the removal of some Politburo members, including Andrei Gromyko. Boris Yeltsin managed to have himself elected a delegate to the conference and marched to the platform and successfully demanded the chance to give a

---

13. *Sovetskaia Rossiia*, March 13, 1988.

14. For a radical interpretation of intent by A. S. Cherniaev, a close Yakovlev ally, see *Shest' let s Gorbachevym* (Moscow: Progress, 1993), pp. 199–209. For a similar interpretation in the Western press see David Remnick, *Lenin's Tomb: The Last Days of the Soviet Empire* (Random House, 1993), pp. 72–85. For Ligachev's version see Ye. K. Ligachev, *Zagadka Gorbacheva* (Novosibirsk: Interbuk, 1992), pp. 126–37.

15. Valery Boldin, *Ten Years That Shook the World: The Gorbachev Era as Witnessed by His Chief of Staff*, translated by Evelyn Rossiter (Basic Books, 1994), p. 168.

16. Mikhail S. Gorbachev, *Zhizn' i reformy*, vol. 1 (Moscow: Novosti, 1995), p. 387; *Memoirs* (Doubleday, 1996), p. 253.

17. *Pravda*, May 17, 1988, pp. 1–2.

speech. Ligachev answered him in open forum. Extensive television coverage focused on the drama and conflict of the conference.[18]

After the conference, the radicals gained freer access to the media, especially in denouncing the Stalin past. In June, Gorbachev removed the Estonian first secretary and allowed his successor to permit the formation of a noncommunist popular front, de facto a noncommunist party, at a time when the impending free elections virtually guaranteed the defeat of communist parties in those republics. By August the Baltic people were allowed openly to discuss the 1939 Molotov-Ribbentrop Pact and to claim that the incorporation of the Baltic republics was the illegal product of it.[19] When elections were held in 1989, the popular fronts in the Baltics were able to campaign freely.

By the summer of 1989 the first secretary of the Kirgizian Communist party complained that it seemed as if someone were deliberately trying to discredit the party. He did so in a closed party meeting and must have been shocked to see his frank statement—and the statements of other leaders—published in *Pravda*. The Kirgizian party leader knew full well that the general secretary had the power to determine the basic line that was to be followed by the Soviet media. It is not known whether he was trying to warn Gorbachev that this liberal line was delegitimating the party or whether he suspected the general secretary of such a policy. The Ukranian first secretary, Vlachimir Shecherbitsky, thought the latter.[20]

Democratization

In March 1985 in his acceptance speech after being elected general secretary, Gorbachev emphasized the need to change economic policy and then stated, "one of the basic tasks of the internal policy of the party is the further perfecting and development of democracy."[21] His only other mean-

18. See, for example, Philip Taubman, "Soviet Party Conference Delegates Turn Anger on Press and Economy," *New York Times*, June 30, 1988, p. A1; and Felicity Barringer, "Watching Party Meeting, Russians Are Wide-Eyed," *New York Times*, July 1, 1988, p. A1.

19. Rein Taagepera, "Estonia's Road to Independence," *Problems of Communism*, vol. 38 (November-December 1989), pp. 17–18.

20. *Pravda*, July 21, 1989, p. 2; and Vitaly Vrublevsky *Vladimir Shcherbitsky: Zapiski pomoshchikova: vospominaniia, dokumenty, slukhy, legendy, fakti* (Kiev: Dovira, 1993), p. 221.

21. M. S. Gorbachev, *Izbrannye rechi i stat'i*, vol. 2 (Moscow: Politizdat, 1987), p. 130.

ingful statement about democratization in 1985 was made on April 23 and was Delphic: "Socialist democracy cannot be understood abstractly.... The party will work to deepen the democratism of the Soviet system."[22]

The meaning of "democratism" was unclear. Gorbachev sometimes used it in his memoirs to refer to a boss who has an open relationship with subordinates. But every Soviet leader had a policy of introducing greater democracy while asserting that the Soviet system was already the most democratic in the world. Any reemphasis of democratization usually meant the removal of middle-level officials in order to consolidate the power of the dictator. Joseph Stalin even stage-managed the Great Purge of 1936–39 in these terms, first introducing a new democratic constitution in 1936, then launching the purge of the party apparatus with an attack on the entrenched regional party officials, who were said to be behaving in an undemocratic manner.[23]

At the Twenty-Seventh Party Congress in February 1986, Gorbachev referred to "necessary adjustments in our electoral practice," and in July he warned party, government, and economic officials that they would have to work "in conditions of widening democracy . . . activization of the human factor . . . and development of the responsibility of the people."[24] But once again the statements were vague and their meaning unclear. Indeed, speaking before the Polish legislature on July 11, 1988, he was to say, "I will tell you frankly, we did not come to an understanding of the necessity, even the inevitability, [of reforming the political system] at once. Both the lessons of the past and life itself, the experience of the first stages of perestroika, led us to this."[25]

In the autumn of 1986 Gorbachev changed the emphasis in his speeches from economic reform to political reform, and at the January 1987 Central Committee plenum on democratization he declared that "some comrades, as is evident, find it hard to understand that democratism is not simply a slogan, but the essence of perestroika." He commented in a speech that "the

---

22. Gorbachev, *Izbrannye rechi i stat'i*, vol. 2, pp. 165–66.
23. See in particular Stalin's speech to the Central Committee in February 1937. For the stenographic report on this plenum, see *Voprosy istorii*, nos. 2–12 (1992); no. 2 (1993); no. 3 (1993); nos. 5–9 (1993); no. 1 (1994); no. 2 (1994); no. 6 (1994); no. 8 (1994); and no. 10 (1994). J. Arch Getty, *Origins of the Great Purges: The Soviet Communist Party Reconsidered, 1933–1938* (Cambridge University Press, 1985), pp. 111–12, 153–63, 180–82, 204–06, is controversial in his conclusions, but unquestionably gives an accurate sense of the democratic theater that provided the setting for the conduct of the purge.
24. Gorbachev, *Izbrannye rechi i stat'i*, vol. 3, p. 234; and vol. 4, p. 49.
25. Gorbachev, *Izbrannye rechi i stat'i*, vol. 6, p. 429.

Politburo considers the perfecting of the Soviet electoral system the principal direction of democratizing our life." In addition, he noted that there were "comrades" who thought party secretaries could be elected in multi-candidate elections by secret ballot. He seemed to endorse the idea.[26]

In a 1991 BBC program Aleksandr Yakovlev, Ivan Frolov, and Georgy Shakhnazarov, Gorbachev's top political advisers, insisted that his words were all part of a long-range plan to introduce full democracy:

> According to [the advisers], Gorbachev was aware even in the autumn of 1986, when he first started speaking of democratization, that logically this must lead to the end of the one-party system; and from early 1988 he started working out a plan for step-by-step progress towards full, multi-party democracy. Only the timing and precise detail of that plan, according to these sources, was influenced by outside events. They say that Gorbachev encountered opposition within the Politburo at every stage; this forced him to adopt the tactics which led outsiders to believe he was only improvising.
>
> In early 1988 the 'inner circle'—Gorbachev, Yakovlev, and Gorbachev's radical aides, Ivan Frolov and Georgy Shakhnazarov—worked out their strategy for the ultimate introduction of multi-party democracy, with a view to putting the idea to the Nineteenth Party Conference in the summer. . . . His aide, Georgy Shakhnazarov, explains: "There are things which seem banal today but which you couldn't even mention then. Anyone who at that time had said openly that we were progressing towards cancelling the leading role of the Party and introducing a multi-party system, and that the Party might lose power, would have been swept aside."[27]

In 1990 Arkady Volsky told a Soviet newspaper that Gorbachev had wanted to introduce a multiparty system in 1988. When asked to elaborate, he cryptically advised the correspondent to ask Foreign Minister Eduard Shevardnadze.[28] Anatoly Luk'ianov told Jonathan Steele, the *Manchester Guardian* correspondent, that a multiparty system was discussed by the group preparing for the 1989 elections and that the proposal was presented three times to the Politburo, but was postponed to a later time.[29]

There are, however, various types of multiparty systems. Stalin had permitted multiple parties in many East European communist countries, but

26. Gorbachev, *Izbrannye rechi i stat'i*, vol. 4, pp. 320–23.

27. Angus Roxburgh, *The Second Russian Revolution: The Struggle for Power in the Kremlin* (Pharos Books, 1992), pp. 88–90.

28. Arkady Volsky, "Treugolnik s dvumi uglami," *Literaturnaia gazeta*, July 4, 1990, p. 2.

29. Jonathan Steele, *Eternal Russia: Yeltsin, Gorbachev, and the Mirage of Democracy* (Harvard University Press, 1994), p. 92.

they were under very tight control. Elections were freer in Poland and Hungary under Brezhnev, but not in a meaningful manner. Party systems also vary widely in noncommunist countries with competitive elections. They can include factions based on personalities, stable two-party systems, hegemonic one-party systems, such as that in Mexico in the mid-twentieth century and the rather different hegemonic one-party system of Japan between 1945 and the late 1980s, and the many parties of Israel. The weak Russian Duma after 1993 is typical of many "democratic" legislatures in the third world that have many parties but little power.

In a 1994 book Aleksandr Yakovlev reproduced substantial parts of a memorandum he sent Gorbachev in December 1985.[30] He called for the transformation of the Communist party into a Union of Communists consisting of two parties: a Socialist party and a People's Democracy party. The top official in the country would be a president elected for ten years by the people from candidates nominated by the two parties in the Union. The president would also be chairman of the united Politburo of the Union of Communists, but the country's premier would be the general secretary of the party in the union that won the election. The functions of the Supreme Soviet, he said, required thought, but were not a matter of principle.

The notion of two parties within a Union of Communists seemed confused, and perhaps he felt it a necessary concession to political reality. However, Yakovlev's language often seemed close to the utopianism of Nikita Khrushchev or even Lenin. There would be "a withering away of a series of state functions," "the real drawing of the masses into administration," "a deep democratization of economic life," "real participation of the masses in planning," "wide democracy in the economy combined with the centralized state administration of it." He concluded, "All this taken together will solve many problems which have to be solved. . . . Such questions as the activeness of the individual, the replacement of people, the struggle with inertia, etc., will be solved without special effort. The political culture of society will grow, and this means so will real stability."

If Yakovlev was thinking clearly, he was offering Gorbachev a semi-democratic, authoritarian regime that would establish structures that might afford the possibility of more meaningful choice to Gorbachev at the time of the succession. The two parties would have no choice but to nominate Gorbachev, for the party that failed to do so would surely lose and deny its

30. Yakovlev, *Gor'kaia chasha*, pp. 205–12.

leader the right to be premier. Assuming that several years would be required to change the constitution, create the parties, and hold the election, Gorbachev would be an elected president until shortly before the end of the century. As chairman of the united Politburo, he would not permit one of the parties to become highly oppositional to his rule. In short, the Union of Communists seemed not unlike an analogous institution in Yugoslavia that was more form than reality.

But Yakovlev may not, in fact, have been thinking clearly. The Khrushchevian language may have been the reality. Gorbachev and his advisers seemed to put great faith in an activated population, for when their exhortations did not produce immediate results, they seemed to assume that the only explanation must be resistance by the bureaucracy. The institutional proposals were probably not thought through, and one must be careful before assuming from their ex post facto interpretations that Yakovlev or other advisers were thinking of Western-style democracy from the beginning.

Even in his memoirs Georgy Shakhnazarov, Gorbachev's chief political adviser, stated that he thought private ownership of the media is incompatible with democracy.[31] In 1991 Gorbachev's advisers wanted to make the ex post facto pronouncements they considered the most advantageous at the time.

One fact is indisputable. When in the winter of 1989–90 Gorbachev decided to create an elected presidency, he had every opportunity to demand the election be held immediately. Instead he insisted that the first president be elected by the Congress of People's Deputies. This decision is impossible to reconcile with the image of a Gorbachev so committed to democracy that he was willing to pay any price to strengthen it. The decision is, in fact, hard to explain on any rational basis if he were going to permit elected officials in the republics. It was almost certain he could have won and established legitimacy for himself as an elected president for five years.

The tightly controlled "competitive" nominations in Gorbachev's home province of Stavropol, where the first secretary was completely loyal to Gorbachev and perestroika, also need to be explained if one posits a general secretary always committed to democracy. The territory (krai) had thirteen electoral districts: one large Council of Nationalities national-territorial district, seven territorial districts for the Council of the Union, and five

---

31. Georgy Shakhnazarov, *Tsena svobody: Reformatsiia Gorbacheva glazami ego pomoshcnika* (Moscow: Rossika, 1993).

additional national districts for the Karachaevo-Cherkess Autonomous Region located within the territory. Seven of the thirteen districts had single-candidate elections, including those with top party officials. In the others a factory manager ran against a factory manager, a collective farm chairman against a state farm director, an airplane pilot against a locomotive engineer, a factory worker against another factory worker, a shepherd against a tractor driver, and the head of the dermatology division of a sanatarium against a rank-and-file physician. Such elections in Eastern Europe had always meant pro forma choice.

Neither candidate received a majority in three of the contested elections, and in the second round, a factory worker ran unopposed in one of the districts, a collective-farm mechanic ran against the leader of a welders' brigade in another, and a worker ran against a state-farm brigade leader in the third. In none of the original elections or the reruns did a man oppose a woman. Thus it was predetermined that the delegation would include twelve men and four women.[32] Just conceivably this pattern was part of an elaborate ruse to fool the conservatives, but at a minimum it illustrates that general words about competitive elections can hide the reality of strict controls.

The January 1987 plenum was followed by a Politburo decision to hold experimental competitions in the local elections scheduled for June 1987. At the plenum Gorbachev had observed that most proposals for competitive elections had focused on multimember districts.[33] On February 26, 1987, the republics issued virtually identical decrees setting up experiments of that type.[34] Perhaps the leaders thought this experience was necessary before final decisions were made on the 1989 USSR elections, but the February 16 decree said that the 1987 experiment would be evaluated on January 1, 1990, nearly a year after the USSR election.

The local elections were held in June 1987 as scheduled, and 162 districts were chosen for the experiment. On average, 4 deputies were

---

32. The results of the elections were published in *Stavropolskaia pravda*, March 29, 1989, p. 1; and May 16, 1989, p. 1. The occupations of the losers were found in the reports of candidate nomination and registration from late January to early February.

33. Although it was not mentioned at the time, multimember districts had been used in Poland.

34. Jeffrey Hahn, "An Experiment in Competition: The 1987 Elections to the Local Soviets," *Slavic Review*, vol. 47 (Fall 1988), pp. 434–47. Also see Stephen White, "Reforming the Electoral System," in Walter Joyce and others, eds., *Gorbachev and Gorbachevism* (London: Frank Cass, 1989), pp. 1–17.

elected in each multimember district, with 5 candidates competing for the 4 vacancies. As usual, the voters had to cross out the names of candidates they did not want rather than mark the names of favored candidates. In practice, many voters crossed out no names. The seats were filled by the candidates who received the most votes, but if the next ranking candidate received more than 50 percent of the vote, he or she was declared a reserve deputy, a person who functioned as a deputy in all respects except the right to vote for legislation. In all, more than 120,000 candidates ran in the experimental districts; 94,000 were elected and 25,000 became reserve deputies. Only 600 received less than 50 percent of the vote and were defeated altogether.[35]

The most surprising feature of Gorbachev's speech on democratization in February 1987 was its reference to competitive elections of party officials. Because the appointment of regional secretaries was fundamental to the circular flow of power that emancipated the general secretary from the control of the Politburo and Central Committee, it was hard to believe that a general secretary consolidating his power against the Politburo and Central Committee would want to end it by having real elections. Indeed, after raising the idea Gorbachev immediately added, "Of course, the party should retain the firm principle that the decisions of higher organs are obligatory for all lower party committees, including on personnel questions."[36] If Gorbachev was behind the idea, however, he had surely already decided to change his base of power from the party apparatus to a presidency.

The first real movement toward democratization came at the Nineteenth Party Conference, June 28–July 1, 1988. Party conferences were permitted between congresses, but the previous one had been held in 1941. The conference was supposed to be the first example of greater democracy within the Communist party itself and the first to have conference delegates elected competitively. In fact, delegates sometimes were nominated in an open process, but the actual election of delegates at the district, city, and oblast levels was generally under tight control. As *Izvestiia* commentator Aleksandr Bovin stated, "the party apparatus has taken the preparation for the conference in its skilled hands, and, with minor exceptions, it smashed the young seedlings of party democracy."[37]

35. The numbers are drawn from Hahn, "Experiment in Competition," pp. 441–42.
36. Hahn, "Experiment in Competition," p. 441
37. Quoted in Philip Taubman, "Local Leaders Rebuff Backers of Gorbachev, *New York Times*, June 9, 1988, pp. A1, A9.

Although the drama at the party conference came in its televised speeches, the major policy change was Gorbachev's call in his opening speech for multicandidate elections and a restructuring of the Supreme Soviet.

> A decisive renewal of our electoral system is indispensable. Multicandidate elections were conducted in a series of districts during the last election [and] now it is necessary to go further. . . . We ought to guarantee the right of unlimited nomination of candidates, a wide and free discussion of them, [and] a strict observance of democratic procedure in the election. . . . In general, from now on the deputy corps should be formed . . . on the basis of a lively and free expression of the will of the electors.[38]

Gorbachev's chief advisers told BBC interviewers in 1991 that he had deliberately hidden his intention of introducing these changes at once and sprang them on the delegates at the very end of the conference.[39] The resolution on the timing of the election changes was, in fact, not introduced until the end of the conference, but everyone knew that the five-year mandate of the old Supreme Soviet ended in 1989 and that elections had to be held that year. Gorbachev's words in his opening speech cannot have been referring to the Supreme Soviet elections scheduled for 1994.

In his memoirs Yegor Ligachev has written that all the top leaders favored competitive elections; Nikolai Ryzhkov's memoirs also expressed strong support for them. The real question was the meaning of "unlimited nomination of candidates" and "democratic procedure in the election." Both Ligachev and Ryzhkov complained in their memoirs about the hurried and secretive way in which the rules for the elections were written under the direction of Aleksandr Yakovlev. Indeed, in an interview given after the publication of his memoirs, Ryzhkov said that at the time (and even more later) he favored the postponement of the election for a year so that a new constitution could be drafted.[40] Both Ligachev and Ryzhkov implied they believed the elections would be more tightly controlled than they proved to be.[41] The pattern of nominations in Stavropol suggests Gorbachev may have shared the same assumption and may have thought the results of the 1987 experiment would be repeated. We simply do not know.

38. Gorbachev, *Izbrannye rechi i stat'i*, vol. 6, pp. 361–62.
39. Roxburgh, *Second Russian Revolution*, pp. 101–02.
40. M. Nenashev, *Poslednee pravitel'stvo SSSR: Lichnosti, Svideltel'stva, Dialogi* (Moscow: Krom, 1993), p. 31.
41. Ligachev, *Zagadka Gorbacheva*, pp. 75–79. See also Nikolai Ryzhkov, *Perestroika: istoriia predatel'stv* (Moscow: Novosti, 1992), pp. 277–78.

The Creation of a New Legislature

In August 1988 the Presidium of the Supreme Soviet formed working groups to draft the constitutional amendments on the changes in government structure that were authorized by the Nineteenth Party Conference.[42] The working groups dealt with the various proposals, but serious issues were supposed to be referred to the Politburo for resolution. Both Ligachev and Ryzhkov were to complain in their memoirs about the cursory way in which the Politburo was drawn into the process.

The work was led by Anatoly Luk'ianov, a close Gorbachev adviser who had known him from their days together in the law school of Moscow University. Luk'ianov had worked in the Juridical Commission under the Council of Ministers and in 1961 moved into the apparatus of the Presidium of the Supreme Soviet. After about two years in the Central Committee apparatus, he was named head of the Secretariat of the Presidium of the Supreme Soviet in 1977. Luk'ianov had the classic career of a government apparatchik, but he focused his attention on questions of legislative organization. His short stint in the Central Committee apparatus was associated with drafting the 1977 constitution.[43] He is frequently described as one of those helping write speeches and documents in the late Brezhnev period.

In 1983 Lukianov had become first deputy head of the General Department of the Central Committee, the department handling all communications to and from the Central Committee apparatus. The head of the department, Klavdy Bogoliubov, was a follower of Chernenko, and Luk'ianov obviously was Gorbachev's watchdog. Lukianov became head of the General Department in 1985 and was elected a Central Committee secretary in 1987, supervising both this department and the department overseeing the police and the army. Thus when Boris Gromov was sent to command the army in Afghanistan, Luk'ianov was the Central Committee secretary with whom he met. Luk'ianov's office was on the fifth floor with the general secretary.[44]

Whether because he was expressing his personal conviction or was acting as Gorbachev's spokesman, Luk'ianov favored a new two-tier legis-

---

42. A good deal of information about this process is found in Michael E. Urban, *More Power to the Soviets: The Democratic Revolution in the USSR* (Aldershot, U.K.: Edward Elgar, 1990), pp. 46–87.

43. Shakhnazarov, *Tsena svobody*, p. 71.

44. B. V. Gromov, *Ogranichenyi kontingent* (Moscow: Progress, 1994), p. 251.

lative structure similar to that established by Lenin. In Lenin's government the supreme legislative body was the Congress of Soviets, which was convened once a year and remained in session for an average of one week. Between sessions, legislative power was vested in a smaller body called the Central Executive Committee (or VTsIK) that met four times during 1918, then twice a year for the rest of Lenin's life. The VTsIK's sessions lasted from one to fifteen days. The Congress had 649 deputies in 1917 and 2,214 in 1922; the Central Executive Committee increased from 200 to 386 deputies during the same period.[45]

A number of reformers, including Yakovlev and Shakhnazarov, favored the creation of a presidential system modeled after that in France. The idea was defended in print by their long-time friend Fedor Burlatsky, who claims a key role in its formulation.[46] It would include both a president and a premier, with the president elected by the people. In such a system Gorbachev would have ultimate power and Nikolai Ryzhkov could remain as premier.

Before the Nineteenth Party Conference, Gorbachev accepted Luk'ianov's basic proposal, arguing behind the scenes that if he were to become head of a presidential system, he would be accused of having dictatorial power. Lenin had ruled neither as general secretary (that was Stalin's job under Lenin) nor as chairman of the Congress of People's Deputies, but as chairman of the Council of People's Commissars (which was to become the Council of Ministers). Instead, Gorbachev chose to be chairman of the Congress, but it is not clear why he did so.

According to his assistant Georgy Shakhnazarov, Gorbachev had an emotional and even romantic attachment to the idea of a congress. And indeed, if he did have an idealized vision of democracy based on the peasant commune (people reasoning together in a peasant meeting under the leadership of wise older figures and resolving conflicts by consensus, not by force), the congress may have seemed such a consultative assembly. The

---

45. Julian Towster, *Political Power in the U.S.S.R., 1917–1947* (Oxford University Press, 1948), pp. 209–10, 226–29. Under Stalin, both bodies grew but met less frequently, until they were abolished by the adoption of the 1936 Constitution which replaced them with a bicameral Supreme Soviet.

46. Burlatsky was head of the working group preparing a new constitution for Khrushchev in the 1960s; the proposal for it included a full-time Supreme Soviet and an elected president. Fedor Burlatsky, *Vozhdi i sovetniki: O Khrushcheve, Andropove, i ne tol'ko o nikh* (Moscow: Politizdat, 1990), p. 177. Burlatsky published the proposal again in "O sovetskom parlamentarizme," *Literaturnaia gazeta*, no. 24 (June 15, 1988), p. 2.

role of chairman would fit him well in such a vision, and the congress would assume a considerable role in drafting legislation on economic reform and social policy and lending it legitmacy.

Gorbachev was probably also affected by several short-term political considerations. First, when he chose to become chairman of the Supreme Soviet, his action forced the retirement of the conservative Andrei Gromyko; if he had become chairman of the Council of Ministers like Lenin or Khrushchev, he would have had to replace or move his ally, Nikolai Ryzhkov. Second, if Gorbachev had already decided to end the power of the Politburo and Central Committee, as is probably the case, he may have wanted to wait to create a presidency so that the precedent of Politburo control over it would not have been established.

Whatever Gorbachev's motivation, the chairmanship of the Supreme Soviet had no executive power. It was a totally inadequate post from which to rule the country unless Gorbachev planned to remain the powerful general secretary of a ruling party, and he says in his memoirs he realized this in a few months.[47] A year and a half later he was to reverse his position opposing a presidency and establish one at the time he was destroying the power of the Politburo and Central Committee. Often Gorbachev seemed to be improvising, but the fact that he destroyed the Central Committee Secretariat in the fall of 1988 and was obsessed about lame ducks on the Central Committee gives credence to the hypothesis that at least on this particular question he was engaged in long-term thinking.

The legislature proposed by Gorbachev in 1988 consisted of two institutions. The dominant body was a 2,250-member Congress of People's Deputies that was to meet for a few days once a year. (The First Congress decided to meet twice a year and to lengthen the sessions to several weeks.) The secondary body was a working legislature of 542 deputies, in effect a large committee of the Congress misnamed the Supreme Soviet or the Supreme Council. It was to have two houses, a Soviet of the Union and a Soviet of Nationalities, and was to meet twice a year in sessions lasting from two to four months.

The Supreme Soviet was clearly meant to be a serious decisionmaking body, at least in the detailed drafting of legislation. Unlike its Russian counterparts formed in 1990 and 1993, it and its committees had the right to

---

47. Gorbachev, *Zhizn' i reformy*, vol. 1, p. 484; *Memoirs*, p. 318.

oversee ministerial behavior and to confirm cabinet officers.[48] The brevity of the congressional sessions suggested that the role of the Congress would be limited to the election of the Supreme Soviet and its chairman, the exercise of control over the Supreme Soviet if necessary, and the adoption of constitutional amendments.

Like the old Supreme Soviet, the Congress had 1,500 deputies elected in districts, half in territorial districts with more or less equal numbers of eligible voters, half in national-territorial districts that gave added representation to nationality-based territorial units.[49] The fifteen Union republics were each awarded 32 national-territorial seats, the twenty autonomous republics had 11 each, the eight autonomous regions 5 each, and the ten national districts 1 each.[50] Each of these territorial units was divided into the appropriate number of districts, and each district was to elect one deputy.[51]

The rules established for the selection of deputies to the Congress of People's Deputies were designed to keep the legislature under strict party control. The nomination rules ensured that deputies elected in the territorial and national-territorial districts would be politically moderate. Candidates could not put themselves on the ballot by collecting signatures on petitions.

48. For the role of the Supreme Soviet in cabinet confirmation in 1989, see Jerry F. Hough, "The Politics of Successful Economic Reform," *Soviet Economy*, vol. 5 (January–March 1989), pp. 29–34. For an excellent analysis of the committees, see Brendan Kiernan, *The End of Soviet Politics: Elections, Legislatures, and the Demise of the Communist Party* (Boulder, Colo.: Westview Press, 1993), pp. 89–136, 140–41.

49. The deputies to the old Supreme Soviet were elected in districts based on total population, not eligible voters. This change in rules resulted in less representation for areas with high birthrates in which adults made up a smaller percentage of the population. The high-fertility Moslem republics—those in Central Asia, Kazakhstan, and Azerbaidzhan—would have received 146 of 750 seats with distribution of seats by population; with distribution based on voters, they received 119 seats. V. A. Kolosov, N. V. Petrov, and L. V. Smirniagin, eds., *Vesna 89: Geografiia i anatomiia parlamentskikh vyborov* (Moscow: Progress, 1990), pp. 22–24.

50. Georg Brunner, "Elections in the Soviet Union," in Robert K. Furtak, ed., *Elections in Socialist States* (St. Martin's Press, 1990); Urban, *More Power to the Soviets*; and Stephen White, "'Democratization' in the USSR," *Soviet Studies*, vol. 42 (January 1990), pp. 3–24.

51. That is, normally a voter had the chance to cast a vote for two candidates, one running in the election for the territorial district in which he or she lived, the other running in the election for the national-territorial district in which he or she lived. The voter in an autonomous republic or district, however, "lived" in three districts: the territorial district, the national-territorial district of the autonomous unit, and the national-territorial district of the Union republic in which the autonomous unit was located.

They had to be nominated by production "work collectives," military units, or meetings of 500 citizens at the voters' place of residence. It was correctly assumed that the last mechanism was too clumsy to be used frequently and that production work collectives were not likely to nominate radicals.

In addition, the nominees had to pass through a second stage, a district meeting that approved or disapproved them for the ballot. This meeting could function in a variety of ways. One Moscow meeting voted to certify all fourteen candidates who were nominated; another controlled by the radicals approved two radicals and rejected the other eleven nominees.[52] In most cases, however, the meeting was under party control.

To further strengthen control over the Congress, the leadership added another 750 deputies to be selected by "public organizations." The Communist party, cooperatives (consumer coops and collective farms), and trade unions were each allocated 100 seats, while the Women's Committee, the Komsomol (Young Communist League), veterans' groups, creative unions, and scientific associations were each assigned 75. The remaining 75 were distributed among fifteen public organizations that ranged from the Red Cross (10 deputies) to the Stamp Collectors' Association (1).[53]

The public organizations were tightly controlled by the Communist party, and their deputies were expected to be conservative. Only 880 candidates were nominated for the 750 public-organization seats, and most were, in fact, conservatives. The only real drama occurred in the Academy of Science elections, where the members voted against the official slate and forced the Academy to nominate a number of radicals, including Andrei Sakharov, who then was elected.

The five Central Asian republics, together with the autonomous republics and autonomous oblasts, had 420 national-territorial seats, and these deputies were expected to accommodate Gorbachev's desires. Because constitutional amendments required two-thirds of all 2,250 deputies in the Congress, not just of the deputies present at the time of the vote, the Communist party was in a position to veto any threatening action, regardless of how the representatives of the territorial districts voted.

By all appearances, then, the purpose of the Congress was to establish a pliable institution to give Gorbachev a power base independent both of the Central Committee and the Supreme Soviet. If the full-time deputies of the

---

52. *Vecherniaia Moskva*, February 21, 1989, p. 1; and February 11, 1989, p. 2.

53. The number of seats assigned each public organization can be found in *Izvestiia*, December 28, 1988, p. 1.

Supreme Soviet developed an antiparty position, he could appeal to the deputies of the Congress, who were likely to be much more conservative. If the Central Committee challenged him, he could threaten to abandon the Communist party altogether and rely on the legitimacy of his elected post. All these expectations were met.

The Candidates

Although controls on nominations were not always as tight as those in Stavropol, they functioned on the whole as intended.[54] Originally 7,531 candidates were nominated for the 1,500 seats, but after the district meetings, only 2,895 were registered—1,449 in the 750 territorial districts and 1,446 in the national-territorial districts.[55] By the time of the election, the number had decreased to 2,851, presumably through withdrawals.

Because the Congress was to meet infrequently, its deputies could serve part time. Government and party officials, plant directors, and farm managers could be elected and still hold their regular jobs, and one-candidate elections were permitted to try to secure their election (table 5-1). In fact, 399 of the 1,500 districts had only one candidate, and another 952 had only two, often with a choice that was not meaningful.[56] Sixty percent of the one-candidate elections were designed to ensure the election of an important political or military figure; the others were intended to ensure some sociological balance to the regional delegation: the election of workers, peasants, or women.

Elections in areas such as Central Asia were under special control, but care was taken to ensure that the delegation from Russia would be conservative as well. Russia contained sixteen autonomous republics, five autonomous oblasts, and ten autonomous districts, and they elected nearly 88 percent of the republic's 243 national-territorial deputies. Even when the deputies in the territorial districts are added, more than 42 percent of Russia's 646 deputies, excluding those selected by the public organizations, came from the ethnically based regions. On the average, the deputies from the ethnic units were more conservative than the deputies elected from the regular oblasts.

54. See Urban, *More Power to the Soviets*, pp. 89–110.
55. *Izvestiia*, February 1, 1989, p. 1; and March 11, 1989, p. 1.
56. *Sovetskaia Rossiia*, April 5, 1989, p. 1.

Table 5-1. *Occupations of Candidates in One-Candidate Elections, USSR and Russia, USSR Election for Congress of People's Deputies, 1989*
Percent

Occupation	USSR	Russia
High political official	54	41
Medium political official	n.a.	4
High military and police	5	7
Enterprise directors	8	21
Middle manager and professional	10	13
Worker and peasant	18	14
Total candidates	399	159

Sources: USSR as a whole: *Sovetskaia Rossiia*, March 13, 1989, p. 1. (The figures only add to 95 percent in the original, too, and the missing deputies are probably enterprise directors in noneconomic posts such as school principal or hospital director.) Russia as a whole: data collected from regional press.
n.a. Not available.

Russia had almost an identical number of candidates per district as the non-Russian republics: 1.92 candidates each in the 646 districts in Russia compared with 1.89 each in the 854 districts in the other republics.[57] By this indicator, the controls on the nomination process in Russia were particularly strong in the nationality-based areas: 1.68 candidates in the territorial districts of such areas, 1.76 in the national-territorial districts, and 2.03 in territorial districts in the ethnic Russian areas.[58] They were also stronger in the territorial districts based on smaller towns than in the ones based on the largest cities (table 5-2).

Even when there were two or more candidates in a district, the extent of real choice is difficult to judge. As in Stavropol, it was possible to control the nominations so that voters were limited to a choice between two workers, two collective farm chairmen, or the like. Unlike the Russian republican election of 1990, there were many such limited choices in 1989.

Yet most competitive elections were not without all meaning, and results in some that seemed noncompetitive were misleading. For example, in the national-territorial district based on Moscow, a USSR minister ran against the director of the Moscow Auto Works and received 90 percent of the vote. If one did not know that the minister was Boris Yeltsin and that he was taking an antiparty position, one would say his 90 percent support showed the election was completely controlled. When a collective farm chairman

57. The Russian figure is given in *Sovetskaia Rossiia*, April 6, 1989, p. 1. The non-Russian figures were obtained by subtracting the Russian figures from the total.
58. These figures come from data collected from the regional press.

Table 5-2. *Candidates in Territorial Districts of Russia, by Size and Type of District, USSR Election for Congress of People's Deputies, 1989*
Percent unless otherwise specified

Size of largest city in district	Number of candidates				
	1	*2*	*3*	*more than 3*	*Total number*
Less than 25,000	52	48	0	0	21
25,000–49,999	38	60	0	2	55
50,000–99,999	33	62	5	0	85
100,000–199,999	15	77	7	2	60
200,000–499,999	11	67	17	5	60
500,000–999,999	15	78	4	2	46
1,000,000–2,000,000	3	81	11	6	36
Moscow and Leningrad	5	47	33	25	40
Total candidates	86	266	37	14	403

Source: The names and number of candidates from each district were gathered from the oblast press by Violetta Pavlovna Numiantseva in Moscow.

ran against a worker or a plant manager in a district with which an observer has no contact, it is easy to conclude that the voters had no choice. Often that must have been the case, but not always.

It is also difficult to distinguish between an election that has been controlled and one in which one or another candidate is simply inexperienced. Yeltsin managed to get over the hurdles to receive the nomination in the most sensitive district in the country. Many others simply could not figure out how to accomplish the task. When the occupations of the candidates and deputies of the 1989 election are compared with those of the wholly controlled election of 1984 and the essentially free election of 1990, the 1989 election seems a fairly normal transitional election in which people were learning to adjust to new rules.

In the past the occupations of those nominated in the one-candidate elections at the USSR level could be classified into two groups. More than one-third of the USSR deputies were Central Committee officials, ministers, obkom first secretaries, deputy ministers of defense, commanders of military districts, and so forth. A number of posts automatically conferred the status of USSR deputy on their holders. At the other extreme, one-half of the USSR deputies were workers and peasants, some 45 percent if managers of collective farms are excluded. As a result, there was very little room left for middle-level managers and professionals or even lesser party officials, plant managers, and farm chairmen (table 5-3).

In 1989 many high officials were nominated for the 750 seats allotted the public organizations and thus were not nominated in a district. Only 10.8

Table 5-3. *Occupations of Candidates and Deputies from Russia in the USSR Legislature, 1984, 1989*
Percent unless otherwise specified

Occupation	1984 deputies	1989 candidates	1989 deputies
High politicians	29.6	8.8	11.6
High military officers	3.5	1.9	1.9
Medium politicians	0.6	4.6	4.6
Medium military officers	0	1.5	2.8
Industrial directors	4.3	13.9	8.7
Agricultural directors	5.1	8.8	11.1
Science and media directors[a]	4.2	4.1	3.9
Other directors	1.8	3.7	4.5
Middle management[a]	7.5	13.4	13.3
Scholars and media[a]	0.3	7.0	10.7
Professionals	2.0	5.5	5.4
Workers	27.0	19.2	15.5
Peasants	14.2	7.3	5.2
Miscellaneous and unknown	0	0.2	0.7
Total number	1,226	624	n.a.

Source: See table 5-2 for 1989 and 1990 candidates. The list of deputies in 1984 was published in *Izvestia*.
n.a. Not available.
a. "Science and media directors" includes those employed in institutions of higher education and design bureaus. Those in middle-level management in science, colleges, design bureaus, and media are listed with "scholars and media."

percent of the nominees in the territorial districts and 12.7 percent of the elected deputies were in the "high official" category that had provided 33.1 percent of the deputies in the past. For various reasons the number of workers and peasants nominated was also much reduced. As a result, the number of nominees in the intermediate occupations expanded from 25.7 percent of the deputies in 1984 to 63.8 percent of the nominees and 65.8 percent of the deputies elected.

In contrast to 1990, a surprisingly small percentage of the intermediate nominees came from middle-level political jobs. Large numbers of people were still thinking of legislative elections and political work as they had in the past. Relatively few understood that the path to high political jobs in the future was going to pass along an electoral path rather than through jobs in the party apparatus, local government, and industry. The 1990 and 1993 elections were to reflect growing awareness of this probability, but the transition, as always, was gradual and incomplete.

Paradoxes of the 1989 USSR Election

When the ballots were counted, the Communist party turned out to have suffered some stunning setbacks. Leningrad sent nearly all its leaders down to defeat; Moscow elected a number of radicals. Most spectacularly, Boris Yeltsin achieved an overwhelming victory in the national-territorial district that included all of Moscow. He had managed to create a referendum on his 1987 removal as Moscow party first secretary, and he had won it hands down. In Russia as a whole, twenty-one of the fifty-five regional party first secretaries were defeated: four of the six party secretaries in the northwest region dominated by Leningrad and twelve of twenty in the Urals, Siberia, and the Far East. The commanders of the Moscow, Leningrad, and the Far East military districts ran in contested elections against fairly attractive candidates and lost. The party did better in many non-Russian republics, but very poorly in the Baltics and poorly in the Ukrainian capital of Kiev.[59]

Many of the worst defeats came in districts in which party officials were the only candidates on the ballot. A feature of the old election law that had once helped control elections was retained in the new law but operated very differently in a more competitive setting. Voters did not vote for a candidate by placing an X near his or her name but by crossing out the names of candidates not desired. (They did not have the option of writing in the name of another candidate.) If a majority of voters crossed out the name, the candidate was defeated, and a new election had to be held, with the nominating process still under the same set of controls. With only one candidate on the ballot, people could vote for him or her simply by depositing the ballot unmarked in the urn.

This procedure had been an inspired way to create the impression of choice in an election without one. If a mark had been required on the ballot, voters would have had to enter the voting booth and might have taken some undesirable action like voting against the candidate. Because a voter could deposit the ballot unmarked into the electoral urn, the only reason to go into the booth was to take the dissident step of crossing out the name of the official candidate. Not surprisingly, few chose to do so.

In 1989 the rules still specified that voters cross off the names of candidates they did not want and leave their preferred candidate standing. If they wanted, they could cross off the names of all the candidates. If there were more than two candidates and no one received a majority, a runoff between the two top vote getters was held. Only a plurality was required for victory in the runoff. If no one received a majority in a single-candidate or two-candidate election, however, a new election was required.

---

59. For a more detailed analysis of the 1989 election, see Hough, "Politics of Successful Economic Reform," pp. 14–24.

It was this rule that caused serious problems for the Communist party.[60] In the 1989 election no one feared to go into the electoral booth, at least in urban areas. Indeed, they had to do so if there was any competition in either the territorial or national-territorial election. Obviously if a majority of the voters crossed out the name of the only candidate on the ballot, he or she was defeated. This happened in a number of cases.

The most bizarre results occurred in relatively close two-candidate elections. If a candidate received 51 percent of the valid votes and the other 49 percent, a relatively small number of negative votes against both candidates would drop the apparent winner below 50 percent of all votes cast and both candidates would be defeated. In one election the chairman of the Moscow city soviet bested a plasterer, 84,701 votes to 49,526, but 196,000 persons had voted and he did not receive the necessary majority (111,282 voters crossed out his name while 146,457 crossed out hers.)[61]

Still, despite the spectacular defeats of some party officials, the Communist party won a sweeping victory. More than 87 percent of the deputies elected to the Congress were party members, and although some were radical, the vast majority were either moderate or conservative. Of the 191 party secretaries (not just first secretaries) of republican and regional committees on the ballot, 153 won. Among the 126 secretaries who ran unopposed, 120 won, while 32 of 65 secretaries won in contested elections.[62]

We take for granted that the Republican party in the United States usually does poorly in San Francisco and Chicago but still wins many elections, including those in California and Illinois as a whole. In the 1960s and 1970s the French and Italian communists won in many large cities, but never came close to power on the national level. On the surface, little worse happened to the Communist party in the Soviet Union in 1989. Once the election was over, only some 10 to 15 percent of the deputies of the Congress could be found to form an opposition "Interregional Group." Mikhail Gorbachev had enough votes not only to pass any legislation he wanted, but also to obtain the two-thirds majority he needed for any constitutional amendment.

---

60. When election rules were established after the dissolution of the Supreme Soviet in 1993, the runoff was abolished and victory awarded to the candidate with a simple plurality.

61. *Vecherniaia Moskva*, March 17, 1989, p. 2.

62. *Argumenty i fakty*, no. 21 (May 27–June 2, 1989), p. 8.

Gorbachev's apparent political problem was that the Congress might be too conservative to pass the economic reforms he wanted. But the conservatives were traditional party members and used to accepting party discipline. They were sometimes accused of scuttling a reform measure, but it never happened. The Congress did what he wanted. As shall be seen in the next section, Gorbachev voted more conservatively than the average conservative deputy. And Gorbachev remained general secretary with very firm control over the Communist party.

The election also brought personal benefits for Gorbachev, and the thought even occurred to some observers that he had engineered some of the defeats of party officials. Officials in the southern rural areas, which constituted the core of his political base, generally did well (table 5-4). They voted with Gorbachev in the Congress more often than those in the northern areas. The only plausible challenger to Gorbachev in the Politburo was Lev Zaikov, who supervised the security forces and the defense industry. As a former Leningrad first secretary who had replaced Yeltsin as first secretary in Moscow, Zaikov was humiliated by the election results in the two cities and soon stepped down as Moscow city party leader. Other major party defeats occurred in Siberia and the Urals, where officials often had links to Yegor Ligachev.

The defeat of a number of generals was also beneficial in disabusing the military of any notion that Soviet citizens saw them as saviors. Conservative Central Committee members now knew that if they tried to remove Gorbachev, he could abandon the party and retain his job as chairman of the Supreme Soviet. If conservatives in the Congress of People's Deputies tried to remove him and if he and Yeltsin joined in an appeal for popular support, the military had to worry whether it could control the streets. These elections may in fact have been a factor in the army's caution during the attempted August 1991 coup d'etat.

Still the elections were seen as a great defeat for the Communist party. Everyone focused on the party candidates who lost. Soviet democrats and Westerners could be accused of wishful thinking, but many party officials spoke in the same way. On June 20 the second secretary of the Moscow city party committee declared, "If we speak completely frankly, it is impossible not to see that we are engaged in a struggle for power."[63] The next day a plant director told the plenary session of the committee that "we Commu-

---

63. *Vecherniaia Moskva*, June 20, 1989, p. 2.

Table 5-4. *Average Voting Score of USSR Council of Union Deputies,*
Second and Third Congresses, by Region and Population of Largest City
in Electoral District

Population of largest city	Second Congress	Third Congress
Less than 50,000	−2,455	−69
50,000–199,999	2,068	5,992
200,000–499,999	8,475	9,540
500,000–999,999	6,217	7,724
1,000,000–2,000,000	14,938	8,894
Moscow and Leningrad	15,938	9,736
Average	5,187	6,195
Region[a]		
North	96.54	88.60
South	−2.85	30.31

Sources: The voting score of each deputy is printed in Giulietto Chiesa, with Douglas Taylor Northrop, *Transition to Democracy: Political Change in the Soviet Union, 1987–91* (University Press of New England, 1993). They were calculated by Northrop. I matched them with characteristics of the district.
a. Deputies are defined as being from the north or south depending on whether they were elected in a region whose capital was north or south of 55 degrees latitude. A high positive score is more radical; a low positive score or a negative one is more conservative.

nists are losing."[64] The first secretary of the Moscow committee worried that joining the party might be risky, not something to do for career reasons.[65] In a closed party meeting, Premier Ryzhkov said that "the party, practically speaking, is losing authority in the eyes of the people," while a regional first secretary in Siberia asserted, "The events in Kuzbass have thrown me into shock to a certain extent. I think that if Siberia has not stood firm; if people have been reeling even here, then we are almost on the brink."[66]

There were a number of reasons for this alarm. First, the party had been above public criticism for so long that any losses were a shock. The fact that the first prolonged strike in decades—among coal miners in Russia and Ukraine—was to break out during the session of the First Congress added to the psychological problem. The defeat of so many party secretaries was particularly disturbing to the defeated candidates and to those who realized that Gorbachev was emancipating himself from party control.

A second reason for unease was that the party had been often defeated in situations it thought were under control, which raised questions about the competence of its leadership. Many of the most spectacular defeats were of

64. *Moskovskaia pravda*, June 23, 1989, p. 4.
65. *Moskovskaia pravda*, June 22, 1989, p. 2.
66. *Pravda*, July 21, 1989, pp. 3, 4.

officials who were the only candidates on the ballot. When Ligachev wrote about excessive haste in drafting certain provisions of the electoral law, he no doubt had such instances in mind.

If the defeats in the Soviet elections had been an isolated event, the leaders might simply have focused on how to avoid them in the future, but the Eastern European Communist regimes were collapsing at the same time. The Polish electoral law of 1989 had been drafted to ensure that the Communists and their satellite parties controlled one house of the legislature and that President Wojciech Jaruzelski's tenure would last for at least five years. But on June 4, 1989, Solidarity won every seat in the lower house and all but one in the upper house, and the satellite parties were able to declare their independence. On August 24 a non-Communist was elected Polish premier. The concurrent collapse of Communist regimes in Eastern Europe must have left Soviet Communists with the feeling that the ground on which they were standing was shakier than the elections themselves suggested.

Finally, of course, the Communist party in the USSR had been a party of the industrial workers and big cities, with its strongest support in the industrial north and in the coalfields of the Donbass and its weakest in the peasant black-earth regions. Most Western analysts had posited an implicit social contract between the party and the industrial workers in which the workers accepted authoritarian rule in exchange for security and egalitarianism. Now the traditional party candidates had done poorly in the large industrial cities (table 5-4) and in the coal-mining districts, while they had swept the smaller cities, the south, and the countryside. This pattern of big-city rejection of the party would become even more pronounced in the elections for the Russian parliament. The Communist party never had strong support either among the intelligentsia or most professional groups. If it was now losing its working-class support, it would be in serious trouble if Russia was entering a revolutionary stage.

The USSR Congress

The USSR Congress of People's Deputies opened on May 25, 1989, an extraordinarily sensitive time for China and Poland, two of the most important communist countries. The demonstrations in Tiananmen Square had started on April 18 and were suppressed on June 3. The Polish elections that produced the Solidarity victory were held on June 4, while the Congress was still in session. The Soviet elections were destabilizing the communist world, and events in the communist world threatened to destabilize the Soviet Union. Yet nothing was done to reduce the effect of the Congress either at home or abroad. Its proceedings were broadcast live on daytime television. The programs drew so much public attention that one high Soviet official claimed they resulted in a 20 percent decrease in production.[67] The Congress exhibited enough high drama, confrontation, and intemperate personal denunciation to warrant its high ratings. Andrei Sakharov spoke eleven times during the sessions, often exceeding his time limit, and the radicals of the so-called Moscow group so dominated the proceedings that the other delegates often complained.[68] Moreover, the Supreme Soviet sessions were also televised, as were the sessions of the Moscow and Leningrad soviets on local television, and they all had this character.

The most serious study of the USSR Congress, that by Giulietto Chiesa, emphasizes this point: "However one judges the Congress . . . it must be admitted that the novelty of live, near-total television coverage affected the assembly greatly, and increased dramatically its already marked cultural impact. In discussing the Congress, we are not simply considering the convening of a new parliament. . . . The media dimension is crucial."[69]

The head of the State Committee of Television and Radio, a moderate liberal who had been insistently appointed by Gorbachev on the eve of the opening of the Congress in May 1989 and who was replaced in December 1990 by Leonid Kravchenko when Gorbachev seemed to move in a conservative direction, was dismayed at the coverage he was forced to carry:

My colleagues from Japanese, Finnish, and US television companies, professionals whom I met at that time, would frequently comment about the innovations in our television. . . . They told me frankly that it was important for them to study the unique phenomenon of the mass political psychosis which had not spared any sector of society and was being inflamed in a well-orchestrated and purposeful manner by the powerful media of radio and television. . . . Foreign journalists openly voiced their doubts about these "innovative experiments" by Soviet television. . . . [They] suggested that these experiments not only did little to

67. "Luk'ianov Details Curtailed Coverage," Moscow Domestic Service, June 27, 1989, in Foreign Broadcast Information Service, Daily Report: Soviet Union, June 27, 1989, p. 3.
68. For a discussion of the First Congress, see Giulietto Chiesa, with Douglas Taylor Northrop, Transition to Democracy: Political Change in the Soviet Union, 1987–1991 (University Press of New England, 1993), pp. 70–109.
69. Chiesa, Transition to Democracy, p. 71.

bolster public trust and aggravated disappointment but also instilled confusion in people's minds [and] lack of confidence. . . . I fully realized that the criticism was justified.[70]

He could, however, do nothing because the Congress dictated coverage and Gorbachev controlled the delegates.

Wisely or unwisely, Gorbachev wanted the opening of the first elected Congress in Soviet history to be a dramatic event. He seemed determined to use it to do precisely what he had been promising: "activate the human factor," shake the people from their lethargy, create "a school for democracy." Democracy—democratic discussion and negotiation—became an end in itself. He proclaimed his strategy on the third day: "I will try to find the middle ground so that points of view may be expressed and the atmosphere will remain calm. I believe this is the main objective."[71] All politicians use this type of language, but as time passed, it seemed as if Gorbachev really believed it.

But Gorbachev's approach to the democratic process had two egregious flaws. First, political activeness on a broad scale is never a permanent phenomenon. In any democratic country the percentage of politically attentive, let alone politically active, citizens is small. If elections do not produce responsive officials (or even officials who solve problems), people can become not only apathetic but even hostile to the democratic process itself. At a minimum, one of the consequences of democracy—indeed, one of the purposes—is to allow voters to turn their frustrations against the person in power rather than the system.

The second flaw was that seeking the middle ground come what may allows the middle ground to be defined by others. If the Lithuanian delegation walks out of the Congress, as they did on June 8, in protest against the establishment of a Supreme Court (literally a Commission on Constitutional Oversight) to adjudicate conflicts between the central government and the republics, one must respond to this protest with reason and an indefinite postponement of the creation of a Supreme Court with that power. If a conference of economic managers criticizes the Abalkin plan of economic reform, as one did in mid-October 1989, this was a legitimate position to which it was necessary to respond with reason and an eight-

70. Mikhail Nenashev, *An Ideal Betrayed* (London: Open Gate Press, 1995), pp. 89–91. For his appointment and removal, see Mikhail Nenashev, *Zalozhnik vremeni: Zametki, razmyshleniia, svidetel'stva* (Moscow: Progress, 1993), pp. 243–44, 307–09.
71. Chiesa, *Transition to Democracy*, p. 91.

month postponement of three crucial laws on economic reform. The problem was expecially great with Boris Yeltsin, who was not hesitant to take extreme positions that contradicted one another.

The original logic behind creating the Congress was, of course, to construct a government that had the legitimacy to introduce painful and unpopular economic reforms. As will be discussed in chapter 10, Premier Ryzhkov did appoint a much younger cabinet.[72] The persons in the most important economic and financial posts were the moderate reformers long associated with him. If they were now to be permitted to introduce the steps they had been advocating, the future looked hopeful. But if their reform was still to be denounced as unacceptable conservatism, Gorbachev had gone through the process of electing a controlled Congress for no apparent reason. If the government it selected was immediately to be damned, the Congress itself would quickly be discredited.

At first, the USSR Congress and Supreme Soviet did not recognize parties or political groups other than the Communists. Formal factions were recognized in the Russian Congress in May 1990, but only in December 1990 were they permitted in the USSR legislature. Yury Afanasev, one of the leaders of the radical Interregional Group, was allowed to present the manifesto of the group on the floor of the Congress.[73] At that time, eighteen groups were recognized; the largest was the Communists with 730 deputies, and the conservative Soiuz (Union) was second with 561. The radical Interregional Deputies Group had only 229 deputies. In the 542-deputy Supreme Soviet, there were twelve groups, with Soiuz having 110 deputies, Constructive Interaction 104, the Communists 94, Justice 71, and the Inter-Regional Group 59.[74]

The radical press often claimed that Soiuz dominated the USSR legislature and blocked Gorbachev's reform efforts, the subtext being that only the Russian government could take action. Yet the numbers cited in the last

72. Leonid Abalkin, *Ne ispol'zovannyi shans: Poltora goda v pravitel'stve* (Moscow: Politizdat, 1991), p. 27.

73. *Vtoroi s"ezd narodnykh deputatov SSSR [12–24 dekabria 1989 g.],* *Stenograficheskii otchet* (Moscow: Izdanie Verkhovnogo Soveta SSSR, 1990), vol. III, pp. 213–14, 397-400.

74. Brian Kiernan, *The End of Soviet Politics: Elections, Legislatures, and the Demise of the Communist Party* (Boulder, Colo.: Westview Press, 1993), pp. 141, 147–48. See also *Narodnyi deputaty,* no. 1, 1991. The best analysis of the work of the Congress is in an unpublished paper by Thomas Remington of Emory University, who will incorporate it in a forthcoming book on the evolution of the legislature in Russia.

paragraph belie such an analysis. Chiesa estimated that perhaps 950 of the deputies were reliably conservative and 440 were reformist, thus leaving some 850 in the middle.[75] But most of the conservative deputies, certainly the 363 from Kazakhstan and Central Asia who were the most conservative, accepted the principle of party discipline and would have voted with the general secretary on almost any question. Thus the numbers underestimate the support Gorbachev would have had for any reform plan.[76]

The most striking feature about Gorbachev's performance as a leader of the legislature was that he never tried to use the Communist party to organize the deputies or even part of them around a program. As shall be seen, he took policymaking power away from the Politburo and the Secretariat in early 1990, while still remaining general secretary. It would have been natural for him to give the Communist party a parliamentary role and to have it campaign on a program of preservation of the Union and a social democratic program more moderate than Yeltsin's. He made no such effort either at the USSR level or in the Russian legislature. The officials of Politburo and Central Committee apparatus in the legislature foundered with no role to play.[77]

Yet Gorbachev never identified himself with the radical Interregional Group, which contained some 250 deputies, and in his memoirs he was highly critical of "radical democrats." Indeed, his own roll call voting record was far more conservative than the average score of the Central Asian deputies and marginally more conservative than the scores of Yegor Ligachev and KGB chief Vladimir Kriuchkov.[78] He was eager to retain the reform label for himself, but he did nothing concrete to enact reforms.

Not only did Gorbachev fail to identify himself with any specific reform program (except democratization), he quickly moved to undermine the Congress and the Ryzhkov government it confirmed. The democrats wanted a less controlled nominating process in the republican elections, which led them to condemn the electoral procedures of the USSR elections. The media under the control of Gorbachev and his advisers carried such stories constantly, and the republics were allowed to introduce more liberal electoral laws. The denunciation of the Congress as undemocratic and of deputies who voted with Gorbachev as reactionary had a debilitating impact

75. Chiesa, *Transition to Democracy*, p. 107.
76. Chiesa, *Transition to Democracy*, p. 257.
77. This is well described in Nenashev, *Zalozhnik vremeni*, pp. 120–24.
78. Chiesa, *Transition to Democracy*, p. 263.

on its reputation and its ability to serve the purposes the general secretary originally had in mind for it. One might imagine this was part of a Machiavellian strategy except that in March 1990 he was to forgo a presidential election and have himself selected by the USSR Congress he was discrediting.

Gorbachev's failure to insist on a Supreme Court with the powers to impose decisions on the republics was followed by his failure to insist that republican constitutions and laws correspond to the federal constitution and laws. Long before the republican elections in 1990, virtually all republics had passed language laws that, whatever their virtues, were often inconsistent with the USSR Constitution.[79] Just at the time Gorbachev was talking about introducing a "government of laws" (*pravovoe gosudarstvo*), a war of laws broke out in which no laws, especially those passed by the new USSR Congress, received any respect. Then in the first months of 1990 Gorbachev agreed to renegotiate the basic treaty (the so-called Union Treaty between the republics that had established the Constitution), thereby undermining the constitutional right of the Congress to amend the Constitution and introduce new decentralized federal arrangements.

Gorbachev's major decision involved the republican elections scheduled for 1990. If the republican governments elected in the unanimous one-candidate elections in 1985 were becoming increasingly defiant, many governments placed in office by the free elections in 1990 were certain to be more so. If the 1989 election rules were instituted, however, the republican governments in all but a few areas would be moderate. But if the nomination and election processes were democratized, the legislatures surely would be more radical. This is a decision that will be discussed in chapter 7, but even at this point any reader understands how fraught with danger the situation was unless Gorbachev planned to move decisively to control it.

79. Albert S. Pigolkin and Marina S. Studenikova, "Republican Language Laws in the USSR: A Comparative Analysis," *Journal of Soviet Nationalities,* vol. 2 (Spring 1991), pp. 38–76.

CHAPTER SIX

Foreign and Domestic Policy and the Issue of Eastern Europe

IN NO COUNTRY has the connection between domestic and foreign policy been closer than in Russia in the nineteenth and twentieth centuries. The nineteenth-century Russian debates over foreign policy toward the West were, first of all, disagreements about the extent to which Russia should adopt Western values, institutions, and ways of life. In the twentieth century the confrontational policy of the Communist regime toward Western governments was, more than anything else, a reflection of hostility to Western values, institutions, and ways of life. Those struggling for political liberalization at home always saw it closely linked with a more open relationship to the outside world.[1]

Lenin had often recognized this connection by using Karl von Clausewitz's pronouncement that "foreign policy is a continuation of domestic policy, and vice versa." Normally Lenin's statement was cited by Soviet conservatives to argue that capitalist countries inevitably had a hostile foreign policy toward socialist ones. At the end of August 1985, however, Mikhail Gorbachev gave another gloss on the statement. He ended an interview to *Time* magazine with a prepared statement that deliberately teased his Western and Soviet audiences: "I would like to emphasize a point that has been the main one in our conversation. It has been rightly said that foreign policy is a continuation of domestic policy. If this

---

1. This is discussed in Jerry F. Hough, *Russia and the West: Gorbachev and the Politics of Reform* (Simon and Schuster, 1988).

175

is so, I ask you to ponder: if we have a grandiose program in the domestic sphere, then what are the external conditions in which we have an interest? I leave the answer to you."[2]

Gorbachev's comment had some notable features. The reference to "a grandiose program in the domestic sphere" was his most dramatic early declaration of an intention to pursue radical domestic reform. Second, a foreign policy that was a continuation of a "grandiose" change in domestic program logically should involve some grandiose change in foreign policy as well. Third, although he did not add "and vice versa" to his assertion that foreign policy was a continuation of domestic policy, he surely had it in mind.

Even Gorbachev's selection of personnel reflected the link between foreign policy and domestic policy. His foreign minister, Eduard Shevardnadze, had spent his entire career in domestic politics, while many of Gorbachev's closest assistants and advisers in domestic political matters had substantial foreign policy experience. Many of them had come out of the Central Committee apparatus and worked in the Soviet-dominated journal *Problemy mira i sotsializma* in Prague in the mid-1960s.[3] They found it easy to resurrect the utopianism of Marx and Lenin in the old ideology and to believe that society could be transformed by "jumping across a chasm in one leap." A Ligachev aide called them "*akademiki*" (academicians) in contrast to the "*praktiki*" (practitioners) in Premier Ryzhkov's team–former plant managers in economic posts and lifelong specialists in banking and finance.[4]

As long as Gorbachev wanted consensus, Ryzhkov's officials were, before 1990, in a position to block many of the most grandiose ideas of the general secretary's men in domestic policy. But the direct subordination of foreign policy to the general secretary meant the absence of any checks and balances in foreign policymaking. The professionals of the Ministry of Foreign Affairs were generally frozen out of policymaking, and the changes in foreign policy were, indeed, as grandiose as those in domestic policy that Gorbachev's advisers had in mind.

---

2. "An Interview with Gorbachev," *Time*, September 9, 1985, p. 29. The version of the interview published in the Soviet press was slightly different from the version in *Time*. This is my translation from the Soviet version, the most significant difference being the inclusion of *rightly* (*spravedlivo*). *Pravda*, September 2, 1985, p. 2.

3. A good description of this experience is found in A. S. Cherniaev, *Moia zhizn' i moe vremia* (Moscow: Mezhdunarodnye otnosheniia, 1995), pp. 225–36.

4. Valery Legostaev, *Tekhnologiia izmeny* (Moscow: Paleia, 1993), pp. 97-98.

Gorbachev's Foreign Policy Team

As was noted in chapter 3, Gorbachev had many subordinates on the Politburo who had in one way or another been linked with Andrei Kirilenko during their careers, but his political, ideological, and foreign policy advisers were men of a very different type. Most were intellectuals associated with Moscow institutes. They came from a very narrow age range: they had become adults during the de-Stalinization of the 1950s and were in their fifties at the start of the 1980s. They have generally testified to their belief in Stalin before 1953 and their deep disillusionment at the revelations about him after his death. They were disillusioned once more in the 1960s and 1970s when their hopes of the 1950s were dashed.

Eduard Shevardnadze

Gorbachev's most spectacular appointment in foreign policy, Eduard Shevardnadze, who was named as foreign minister in July 1985, was not an intellectual. His predecessor, Andrei Gromyko, had been foreign minister since 1957 and had held high foreign policy posts since 1940. It was no surprise that Gromyko was moved to the ceremonial post of chairman of the Presidium of the Supreme Soviet, but Shevardnadze's appointment was a complete surprise because he had no foreign policy experience other than participation in Politburo discussions as a candidate member since 1978.[5] Shevardnadze has testified to being as surprised as anyone else.[6]

Shevardnadze was born in 1928. Officially Georgian by nationality, he reportedly was of mixed parentage, with a heavy Greek element in his heritage. When Stalin launched a fierce xenophobic campaign in 1928, Shevardnadze's parents chose the Western name Eduard for their new son, implicitly and perhaps explicitly protesting such insularity. Until 1985 Shevardnadze spent his entire career in Georgia. In the late 1950s he still did not speak Russian smoothly.[7] He was first secretary of the Georgian Komsomol Central Committee from 1957 to 1961 and then was appointed

---

5. For Gromyko's reaction see Mikhail S. Gorbachev, *Zhizn' i reformy*, vol. 1 (Moscow: Novosti, 1995), p. 288; *Memoirs* (Doubleday, 1996), pp. 180–81.

6. Eduard Shevardnadze, *Moi vybor: V zashchitu demokratii i svobody* (Moscow: Novosti, 1993), p. 79.

7. Gorbachev, *Zhizn' i reformy*, vol. 1, p. 287; *Memoirs*, p. 180. This chapter includes no evidence on Shevardnadze's foreign policy role or views—or those of any of Gorbachev's lieutenants—because Gorbachev says not a word on the subject in his memoirs.

to a high office in the regular Georgian police (the Ministry of Internal Affairs). From 1965 to 1972 he served as Georgian Minister of Internal Affairs. He then became first secretary of the Georgian Communist Party Central Committee, a post he held for thirteen years.

The republic of Georgia and the province of Stavropol border one another. Shevardnadze and Gorbachev overlapped as Komsomol first secretaries from 1958 to 1961 in their respective regions and then as party first secretaries from 1972 to 1978. Shevardnadze was elected a candidate member of the Politburo in November 1978 at the same Central Committee session that named Gorbachev a Central Committee secretary. The two sat together on the party's ruling body after Gorbachev was elected to it in 1979. They not only met often over the years but also became friends.

In political terms Shevardnadze was a brilliant choice as foreign minister. His lack of ties with the foreign policy establishment signaled and facilitated a radical break with Andrei Gromyko's foreign policy. But because the new minister was a neutral and well-liked figure, Gromyko could not object as he would to an open critic of his policies. And since Shevardnadze was already a candidate member of the Politburo, his promotion to full membership was simple and gave Gorbachev a firm supporter on domestic policy as well. Shevardnadze actively supported domestic reform, speaking "clearly, and, as always, emotionally," according to a colleague, Vadim Medvedev.[8] In the Brezhnev period the major Georgian newspaper under Shevardnadze had taken a position strongly supporting reconciliation with the West.[9]

Anatoly Dobrynin

A second signal of a new attitude in foreign policy was the selection in March 1986 of Anatoly Dobrynin as secretary of the Central Committee and head of its International Department. The International Department had dealt not with government foreign policy but with relations with foreign

8. Vadim Medvedev, *V komande Gorbacheva: Vzgliad iznutri* (Moscow: Bylina, 1994), p. 71. In his memoirs Gorbachev said almost nothing about Shevardnadze as foreign minister, but he too noted he was "emotional." *Zhizn' i reformy*, vol. 1, p. 308; *Memoirs*, p. 197.

9. The republican press generally only published TASS dispatches in the Brezhnev era. However, TASS carried far more stories on its wire than any newspaper could publish. Some favorably reported Soviet peace efforts, while others criticized the behavior of foreign governments. If a Soviet newspaper published a disproportionate percentage of one type of story, it had a very different tone than did one that concentrated on the other type. Shevardnadze's *Zaria vostoka* carried a disproportionate percentage of stories on detente in Europe and peace efforts in the Middle East.

communists, left-wing political parties, and other nongovernmental organizations.[10] It had been headed since 1955 by Boris Ponomarev, an eighty-year-old who had worked in the Comintern from 1936 to 1941 and had been first deputy head of the International Department under Stalin after the war.

Dobrynin was born in 1919 and was an urbane professional diplomat who had been ambassador to the United States since 1962. He was a fixture of parties in Georgetown for two decades and was deeply unhappy about being forced to leave Washington.[11] Because he was so popular, Americans exaggerated the importance of his selection as Central Committee secretary and the liberal character of his views.

In fact, Dobrynin's foreign policy views were closer to the more conservative Yegor Ligachev's than to Gorbachev's. He had attended the Moscow Aviation Institute at the same time as Ligachev and was rising rapidly in a major airplane design bureau when he was sent to the Diplomatic Academy in 1944 against his will.[12] His memoirs only confirmed a point already clear—that he favored the controlled detente and stability produced by the division of Germany, not the radical change in foreign policy instituted in 1989. Dobrynin is scathing in his denunciation of what he sees as the incompetence of Gorbachev and Shevardnadze in foreign policy and their failure to insist on new security arrangements as a price for accepting the unification of Germany.[13] It was not surprising he was removed in 1988 as Gorbachev prepared to introduce drastic foreign policy changes.

Without any question, however, Dobrynin gave very low priority to the support for third world radical movements, which had complicated Soviet-American relations in the past. His selection as head of the International Department was a clear signal that Gorbachev also had little interest in third world revolutions. Indeed, Dobrynin tried to change the responsibility of the department's work to focus it more on the major questions of East-West relations, but he and his department were largely ignored.

Aleksandr Yakovlev

More important than either the selection of Shevardnadze or Dobrynin was the quieter appointment of Aleksandr N. Yakovlev as head of the

10. For Dobrynin's description of the role of the department, see Anatoly Dobrynin, *In Confidence: Moscow's Ambassador to America's Six Cold War Presidents (1962–1986)* (Times Books, 1995), p. 619–20.
11. Dobrynin, *In Confidence*, p. 601
12. Dobrynin, *In Confidence*, pp. 13–14.
13. Dobrynin, *In Confidence*, pp. 576, 623–32.

Propaganda Department in July 1985 and then as a Central Committee
secretary in March 1986. The relatively low status of Yakovlev's first
official post was misleading because, as Fedor Burlatsky commented privately in the summer of 1985, Yakovlev was becoming Gorbachev's closest adviser.[14] The then secretary for ideology of the Ukrainian Central
Committee reports that from the beginning Yakovlev did no dirty work
supervising propaganda, but was always "in the 'underground,' as was
called work on the most important documents in the suburbian dachas."[15]
In 1986 Yakovlev was one of two secretaries for ideology and a candidate
member of the Politburo.[16] A year later he became a full member of the
Politburo, overseeing ideology and foreign policy.

Both friend and foe agree that Yakovlev exhibited "a radical liberalism
that, in many respects, had an emotional-journalistic character and was not
distinguished by depth."[17] One speechwriter commented that Yakovlev had
worked out a program for radical change while ambassador to Canada and
that virtually all of Gorbachev's early speeches on perestroika were "based
on Yakovlev's thinking."[18] Dobrynin called him "Gorbachev's evil master-
mind."[19] Afterward Yakovlev said that he and Gorbachev agreed to transform the whole Soviet system from the beginning, and he treated himself as
the father of perestroika. Gorbachev always kept Yakovlev within strict
limits, even to the point of being offensive, and Anatoly Cherniaev has
expressed anger at Yakovlev for exaggerating his role to Westerners.[20] But

14. This was discussed in Jerry F. Hough, "Gorbachev's Strategy," *Foreign Affairs*,
vol. 64 (Fall 1985), pp. 52–53.
15. Aleksandr Kapto, *Na perekrestkakh zhizni: Politicheskie memuari* (Moscow:
Sotsial'no-politicheskii zhurnal, 1996), p. 160.
16. The other secretary was the conservative Mikhail Zimianin. Yakovlev supervised culture, publishing, and the media; Zimianin supervised science and education,
including the social sciences and history.
17. These are the words of his close ally, Medvedev, in *V komande Gorbacheva*, p.
20. Yakovlev has published no full memoirs himself. Like Gorbachev's other close
aides, he is almost totally absent from Gorbachev's memoirs as a foreign policy adviser
and appears only sporadically as a domestic policy adviser.
18. Valery Boldin, *Ten Years That Shook the World: The Gorbachev Era as Witnessed by His Chief of Staff*, trans. Evelyn Rossiter (Basic Books, 1994), pp. 73, 113.
19. Dobrynin, *In Confidence*, p. 618.
20. Boldin, *Ten Years that Shook the World*, pp. 159–60. See also A. S. Cherniaev,
Shest' let s Gorbachevym (Moscow: Progress, 1993), pp. 198–99. He was never allowed
to give the major ideological speech either on Lenin's birthday or the anniversary of the
revolution, and Yakovlev was especially offended in October 1989 when the assignment was given to the new Politburo member Vladimir Kriuchkov. Vladimir
Kriuchkov, *Lichnoe delo* (Moscow: Olimp, 1996), pt. 2, pp. 276–77.

certainly, as Ligachev said, Yakovlev's duties went far beyond his formal responsibilities for ideology and foreign policy. He had the crucial role in framing the 1989 election law and "was extremely active in working out the chief directions of economic policy."[21] Even while a candidate member of the Politburo, Yakovlev had an office on the fourth floor and then he was moved to the fifth. He was Gorbachev's "chief daily conversationist."[22]

Yakovlev was born in 1923, fought in World War II, and then quickly moved into party work in the Yaroslavl Obkom. In 1953 he was promoted into the Central Committee apparatus and worked in the committee's Propaganda Department for twenty years, with a three-year break to write a dissertation. Yakovlev served as head of the television and radio section late in the Khrushchev years and was promoted to first deputy head of its Propaganda Department under Brezhnev.[23] In 1973 he was appointed ambassador to Canada, a form of political exile. In 1958–59 he was sent to Columbia University for eight months on a Soviet-American scholarly exchange. His dissertation dealt with the American political system, and when he returned home, he participated actively in Soviet debates on the American system, debates that served as surrogates for discussions of the proper foreign policy for the Soviet Union to follow toward the United States. In these debates he was in the liberal-center part of the political spectrum.[24]

Most assume that Yakovlev was exiled to Canada because of a 1973 article critical of Russian chauvinism and non-Russian nationalism, but a number of officials of very different political persuasions say this was not the case. Although an official with a liberal reputation, Yakovlev had become, they assert, allied with the Moscow group around the archconservative Aleksandr Shelepin, and Brezhnev did not trust him.[25] If

21. Ye. K. Ligachev, *Zagadka Gorbacheva* (Novosibirsk: Interbuk, 1992), p 71.

22. Andrei Grachev, *Kremlevskaia khronika* (Moscow: EKSMO, 1994), pp. 94–95, 123, 140.

23. Aleksandr Yakovlev, *Muki, prochteniia, bytiia: Perestroika: nadezhdy i real'nosti* (Moscow: Novosti, 1991), pp. 57, 58, 64.

24. Franklyn Griffiths, "Images, Politics, and Learning in Soviet Behavior," Ph.D. dissertation, Columbia University, 1972, pp. 313–465. This is one of the truly important unpublished dissertations on the Soviet Union of the postwar period and must be read by anyone seriously interested in Soviet foreign policymaking toward the United States from the 1950s onward.

25. Medvedev, *V komande Gorbacheva*, pp. 19–20. The same information is found in Cherniaev, *Moia zhizn' i moe vremia*, p. 297, and in A. M. Aleksandrov-Agentov, *Ot Kollontai do Gorbacheva* (Moscow: Mezhdunarodnye otnosheniia, 1994), p. 256. Boris

so, Yakovlev was playing a complex political game. The liberal Georgy
Arbatov of the Institute of the USA and Canada, very close to Andropov,
frequently advocated Yakovlev's return to Moscow.[26] The fact that Andropov had come out of the same Yaroslavl party organization adds to the
suspicion that there was a link between the two men.

Gorbachev's and Yakovlev's paths first crossed publicly when
Gorbachev headed an agricultural delegation to Canada in 1983.[27] The
highlight of the trip was a question-and-answer session in the Canadian
parliament on foreign policy (in fact, Gorbachev spent only a day in the
agricultural provinces).[28] No doubt the main purpose of the trip was to test
Gorbachev in an unfamiliar foreign policy setting. As ambassador to Canada, Yakovlev accompanied Gorbachev throughout his tour, and
Gorbachev is likely to have been sent to Canada precisely because Andropov trusted Yakovlev's judgment. Two months after the trip, Andropov
brought Yakovlev back to a significant foreign policy post in Moscow:
director of the most important scholarly institute, the Institute of the World
Economy and International Relations (IMEMO). As IMEMO director,
Yakovlev became the de facto center of the opposition to the policy of
Foreign Minister Andrei Gromyko.

Vadim Medvedev

Before September 1988 the Central Committee apparatus had two departments dealing with international matters. One was called the International Department, but despite its name it had responsibility only for noncommunist countries and then only for relations with nongovernmental
bodies, most importantly Communist parties. The other, the Socialist Countries Department (or colloquially simply "the Department"), was in charge

---

Pankin, former editor of *Komsomol'skaia pravda* and therefore also a man with close
career ties to the Shelepin group, said that Yakovlev was extremely critical of Brezhnev
and his team when Pankin visited him in Canada. See *Sto oborvanykh dnei* (Moscow:
Sovershenno sekretno, 1993), p. 16.

26. Vadim Pechenev, *Vzlet i padenie Gorbacheva* (Moscow: Respublika, 1996),
p. 53.

27. Yakovlev reported that there had been some seemingly minor contact in the
1960s. *Muki, prochteniia, bytiia*, p. 63.

28. Bruce Ward, "MPs Suffer 'Spymania' Soviet Says," *Toronto Star*, May 18,
1983, p. A3; "MPs Misinformed: Russian," *Globe and Mail* (Toronto) May 18, 1983,
p. 8; and James Rusk, "Trudeau Invited to Visit Soviet Union," *Globe and Mail*
(Toronto), May 19, 1983, p. 8.

of relations with the countries the West called communist: China, Cuba, North Korea, Vietnam, Mongolia, and those in Eastern Europe. As Minister of Foreign Affairs, Gromyko dominated relations with the noncommunist world, but the Socialist Countries Department had a great deal of power in dealing with the communist countries.

In March 1986 Gorbachev changed the leadership of the Socialist Country Department, but in a way that was ambiguous. He named Vadim Medvedev Central Committee secretary and head of the department. Medvedev was an economist who also came from Yaroslav Oblast and who taught in Leningrad institutes of higher education for seventeen years before becoming the ideological secretary of the Leningrad city party committee in 1968. In 1970 he was named deputy head of the Propaganda Department of the Central Committee, working under Yakovlev who was first deputy head. In 1978 he was appointed rector of the Academy of Social Sciences of the Central Committee, and in 1983 he became head of the Science and Education Department of the Central Committee.

Both at that time and in subsequent memoirs, Medvedev emerges as less confrontational than Yakovlev but still radical enough in his ideological policy to arouse the ire of Politburo conservatives. Cherniaev treats him as very independent and radical, but a poor communicator.[29] Medvedev's memoirs, however, are the most precise and careful of any written on the perestroika period, and "poor communicator" probably refers to his tendency to smooth issues over and to back away from open conflict.

Medvedev's role in foreign policy is obscure. He wrote a separate memoir on Eastern Europe, but it contains none of the interesting detail of his discussion of domestic policy. Medvedev was in charge of the Central Committee group drafting economic reform at the Volynskoe dacha throughout the spring of 1987, and other references to him show him deeply involved in domestic policy. This activity took a great deal of his time. In addition, Gorbachev maintained a policy affirming the status quo in Eastern Europe until the fall of 1988, and the East European leaders were almost all old men unresponsive to change. Medvedev may, in fact, have had relatively little involvement in foreign policy as such because Eastern Europe was not on the agenda during his years of responsibility for it.

---

29. Cherniaev, *Shest' let s Gorbachevym*, pp. 235–36.

Anatoly Cherniaev

Gorbachev also had several personal assistants of great influence, although this was not obvious at the time.[30] The most important of these was Anatoly Cherniaev, appointed in February 1986. Although Cherniaev kept a very low profile, insiders emphasize the strength of his influence on both foreign and domestic policy. One very close Gorbachev assistant has commented that Cherniaev and Gorbachev "were practically twins."[31] In 1991 Gorbachev called him his "brother."[32] Cherniaev had begun working in the Central Committee at the same time as Yakovlev and has commented that they agreed 95 percent of the time. When Cherniaev became Gorbachev's assistant in 1986, his first piece of advice to his boss was to move toward urging the unification of Germany.[33] His memoirs confirm his deep involvement in domestic issues and his determination to denounce Stalinism fully and openly.[34]

Cherniaev graduated from the history department of Moscow University and in 1953, after three years of college teaching, went to work as an instructor in the Central Committee apparatus. He worked for several years in Prague on the journal *Problemy mira i sotsializma* and then returned to Moscow to work in the Socialist Country Department. In the late 1960s he was named leader of the group of consultants of the International Department, which had major responsibilities in writing leadership speeches and official documents. In 1970 he became deputy head of the International Department in charge of the British Commonwealth, but first of all Great Britain. He also was the deputy head of department who oversaw the group of consultants, and he continued to be drawn into work on documents and speeches.[35]

Cherniaev was an active participant in the ideological debates of the Brezhnev period. If those calling for moderate reform wrote about perfecting developed society, sometimes, to be sure, implying a great deal of perfection was necessary, Cherniaev wrote in 1968 about revolutionary

---

30. It would also not be obvious to a reader of Gorbachev's memoirs. He never makes a single meaningful reference to any of his assistants (*pomoshchniki*).
31. Boldin, *Ten Days That Shook the World*, p. 111.
32. Pankin, *Sto oborvanykh dnei*, p. 31.
33. Cherniaev, *Shest' let s Gorbachevym*, p. 66.
34. For other comments confirming Cherniaev's power and role, see Archie Brown, *The Gorbachev Factor* (Oxford University Press, 1996), pp. 98–99.
35. Cherniaev, *Moia zhizn' i moe vremia*, p. 267.

change. He later became involved in an esoteric but explosive debate with conservatives about the nature of the working class in which his position implied that relationship to the means of production was not decisive and that society was becoming postindustrial.[36] Fedor Burlatsky calls Cherniaev the "social democrat" in Gorbachev's team.[37]

Ivan Frolov

Ivan T. Frolov was never directly involved in making foreign policy, but in his "ideological" role, he developed ideas that were of direct relevance to it. In 1986 he was appointed editor of *Kommunist*, the Central Committee journal, and in 1987 he became Gorbachev's personal assistant for ideological questions. In 1989 he was named editor in chief of *Pravda* and Central Committee secretary for ideological questions.[38]

Frolov was born in 1929, graduated from Moscow University in 1953, and moved into philosophical and ideological work, focusing on the sensitive question of genetics.[39] He severely attacked the dogmatic pronouncements of Trofim Lysenko and his followers that had crippled Soviet genetics for decades and argued generally for the independence of science from ideological fetters.[40] A Western scholar called him "the most controversial of reform-minded Soviet philosophers."[41] From 1968 to 1977 he served as chief editor of *Voprosy filosofii*, the leading philosophical journal, but then for nearly a decade he was demoted to a number of minor posts.[42]

36. Cherniaev kept a diary throughout his official career—all in all, 24 volumes with a total of nearly 10,000 pages. His autobiography, *Moia zhizn' i moe vremia* deals only with the years before 1982, but in considerable detail. See pp. 239–40 and 247–57 for the ideological debates.

37. Fedor Burlatsky, *Russkie gosudari epokha reformatsii* (Moscow: Shark, 1996), p. 203.

38. Bill Keller, "Aide to Gorbachev Takes Pravda Helm," *New York Times*, October 20, 1989, p. A1.

39. For fuller discussion of his earlier background, see Hough, *Russia and the West*, pp. 24–25, 30.

40. Loren R. Graham, *Science and Philosophy in the Soviet Union* (Knopf, 1972), pp. 252–56.

41. Werner Hahn, *Postwar Soviet Politics: The Fall of Zhdanov and the Defeat of Moderation, 1946–1953* (Cornell University Press, 1982), pp. 169–81.

42. Loren R. Graham, *Science, Philosophy, and Human Behavior in the Soviet Union* (Columbia University Press, 1987), pp. 20–21; and *Ezhegodnik Bol'shoi sovetskoi entsiklopedii, 1987* (Moscow: Sovetskaia entsiklopediia, 1987), p. 593.

Increasingly in the 1970s Frolov turned from his focus on the philosophy of science to address the nature of values, environmentalism, disarmament, and bioethics. He deliberately chose issues that were not associated with class interests, thereby undermining the contention that politics centered on class conflict. He continually emphasized the importance of universal human values, which constituted a rejection of the traditional Marxist-Leninist view that values and morality were tied to class interests.

After 1985 Frolov's emphasis on universal values permeated Gorbachev's speeches and became the basis for what was known as the "deideologization" of foreign policy and the Soviet willingness to abandon communism in Eastern Europe. Frolov may have had an even more important long-term impact on Russian history when he named a young economist, Yegor Gaidar, as economics editor of *Kommunist* in 1987 and then took Gaidar with him to *Pravda* in 1989 as its economic editor. Gaidar was to become the architect of the economic shock therapy initiated by Boris Yeltsin.

Georgy Shakhnazarov

The most important appointment with respect to the Soviet Union's East European policy was not the selection of Vadim Medvedev as head of the Socialist Countries Department of the Central Committee, but the promotion of Georgy Shakhnazarov from deputy head of the department to first deputy head in 1986.[43] In early 1988 he became Gorbachev's personal assistant for domestic political affairs but was still deeply involved in promoting the democratization of Eastern Europe.

The old first deputy head of the Socialist Countries Department, Oleg Rakhmanin, was a conservative who had published a hard-line article on Eastern Europe in *Pravda* in the summer of 1985. Gorbachev was outraged. When Rakhmanin was removed in the fall of 1986, he was replaced with Shakhnazarov, an outspoken critic of the article.[44] On the surface

43. Georgy Shakhnazarov, *Tsena svobody: Reformatsiia Gorbacheva glazami ego pomoshchnika* (Moscow: Rossika, 1993), pp. 4–5, 21, 33, 95. Shakhnazarov was appointed a personal assistant on February 28, 1988. This was the time Nagorno-Karabakh was becoming explosive, and the fact that his ancestors had been major figures in Nagorno-Karabakh was probably a reason for his selection. *Tsena svobody*, pp. 208–09. For a description of him in the 1950s and 1960s, see Fedor Burlatsky, *Vozhdi i sovetniki: O Khrushcheve, Andropove i ne tol'ko o nikh* (Moscow: Politizdat, 1990), pp. 250–52, 262.

44. See his article written under the pseudonym, O. Vladimirov in *Pravda*, June 21, 1985. See also Cherniaev, *Shest' let s Gorbachevym*, pp. 49–51; and Raymond Garthoff, *The Great Transition: American-Soviet Relations and the End of the Cold War* (Brookings, 1994), pp. 569–71.

Shakhnazarov was an inappropriate replacement. He had been deputy head of the Socialist Countries Department of the Central Committee during the last ten years of Brezhnev's life and had been in charge of relations with Cuba, East Germany, and Poland. As might be expected, his public statements about these countries and about the Solidarity movement in Poland were not those normally associated with a dedicated democrat.

Shakhnazarov had, however, been a reformer since the beginning of the post-Stalin period. He was the first person in 1953 to question a central point of Stalin's dogmatism about American control over the foreign policy of other capitalist countries.[45] He was a close friend of Fedor Burlatsky, another young reformer. He moved into the party apparatus in early 1960, joining the group of consultants of the Socialist Countries Department that was headed by Burlatsky and that served Yury Andropov, then head of the department.[46] He and Burlatsky urged institution of the discipline of political science in the Soviet Union in 1965, and Shakhnazarov became chairman of the Soviet Political Science Association.

In 1972 Shakhnazarov wrote what Ronald Hill called "one of the most stimulating books of Soviet political science," one that "most clearly called for freedom of information."[47] Shakhnazarov emphasized the importance of freedom of information to promote both government efficiency and democracy and attacked the philosophical justification for censorship:

> When the state imposes specific restrictions and deprives a person of the possibility of acting or not acting according to his own judgement in this or that question, then, no matter in whose interests that restriction might be (in the interests of a minority, the majority, the whole society, including that person himself, who does not understand his real interests), the restriction of freedom remains a fact. It cannot be screened by arguments about the good of society, etc.[48]

If Shakhnazarov was to have a major impact on policy toward Eastern Europe, it was likely to be in promoting political liberalization. It turned out

45. See Jerry F. Hough, *The Struggle for the Third World: Soviet Debates and American Options* (Brookings, 1986), p. 117.
46. He was the only one of the group to occupy an important post under Gorbachev, but a number of other members were to be prominent reformers of the period: Burlatsky himself; Georgy Arbatov, director of the Institute of the USA and Canada; Oleg Bogomolov, director of the Institute of the Economies of the World Socialist System; Gennady Gerasimov, press secretary for Foreign Minister Shevardnadze and often informally for Gorbachev; and Aleksandr Bovin, commentator for *Izvestiia*.
47. Ronald J. Hill, *Soviet Politics, Political Science, and Reform* (Oxford, U.K.: Martin Robertson, 1980), pp. 108–09.
48. Quoted in Hill, *Soviet Politics, Political Science, and Reform*, p. 110.

that his greater role in promoting democratization in the Soviet Union and Eastern Europe came once he left the Socialist Countries Department.

Yevgeny Primakov

The last member of the inner foreign policy team, Yevgeny Primakov, had relatively little contact with Gorbachev at first, but became increasingly important as time passed—with much of his role being a domestic one. Primakov was a foreign correspondent who specialized in the Arab countries and became the *Pravda* editor for the Middle East. The American government was convinced that he simultaneously was working with the KGB, likely with good reason.[49] From 1970 to 1977 he served as the deputy director of the Institute of the World Economy and International Relations (IMEMO) of the Academy of the Sciences and supervised its study of the third world. Then from 1977 to 1985 he became director of the Institute of Oriental Studies. Throughout these years he was an important informal negotiator with the Arabs in the Middle East. In 1985 he replaced Aleksandr Yakovlev as director of IMEMO.

Primakov had many connections, but one of the least apparent was the first secretary of the Georgian party organization, Eduard Shevardnadze. Primakov had been raised in Tbilisi, Georgia, and had developed ties with Shevardnadze when the latter was Georgian first secretry. When Shevardnadze was informed of his forthcoming appointment as foreign minister, one of his aides called Primakov and said "Congratulations." When Primakov asked why, he was told of the appointment. Primakov was immediately appointed director of IMEMO, the premier foreign relations institute, so that Shevardnadze would have an institutional base for information and advice other than Gromyko's apparatus in the Ministry of Foreign Affairs

At the time of the Gulf War in the winter of 1990–91, Primakov was sent to Saddam Hussein to try to prevent the war from being launched, and he was treated in America as a pro-Arab, anti-American politician who was acting behind Gorbachev's back.[50] In fact, Gorbachev's abhorrence of the

49. See, for example, Jack Anderson and Michael Binstein, "Lord of the (Russian) Spies," *Washington Post*, March 17, 1994, p. C7; Anderson and Binstein, "Code Name 'Maxim,'" *Washington Post*, April 4, 1994, p. D1; and William Safire, "Rise of 'The Stepson,'" *New York Times*, January 15, 1996, p. 17.

50. For an extreme example of this misrepresentation of Primakov, see Safire, "Rise of 'The Stepson.'"

use of force at home was matched by his abhorrence of its use abroad, and he was deeply disturbed by Bush's policy.[51] Primakov was a natural adviser to Shevardnadze: he had long been known inside the Soviet establishment as a pro-American proponent of Arab-Israeli peace, although a man who had a more *realpolitik* view of foreign policy than either Gorbachev or Shevardnadze.[52]

In domestic policy Primakov was a fervent proponent of the Union. At the Nineteenth Party Conference, he strongly supported the principle of the leading role of the Communist party, arguing that its abolition could lead to "irreparable harm," a "frightful blow to perestroika" from nationalists. He advocated that promotion of personnel from within republics be supplemented by the shifting of administrators from republic to republic. Although he did not say so, this policy would guarantee that the language used throughout the administrative system would be Russian.[53] In June 1989 he was selected chairman of the Union of the USSR Supreme Soviet and in March 1990 a member of the Presidential Council. After the August 1991 coup, Primakov was named head of foreign intelligence. He was one of the few intimates of Gorbachev who retained a high post in the Yeltsin era. Indeed, in early 1996 he was named Russian minister of foreign affairs.

The Soviet Debate on Entente

The character of the people Gorbachev selected for his foreign policy team indicated that a major change in policy was intended. The question

51. Alessandra Stanley of the *New York Times* correctly noted that Primakov had been sent "on the instructions of Mr. Gorbachev." *New York Times*, January 13, 1996, p. 2. Gorbachev was frank in his memoirs about his unhappiness with the American military action in Iraq and about his own actions to stop it. *Zhizn' i reformy*, vol 2, pp. 243–46; *Memoirs*, pp. 555–56.

52. My contacts with Primakov went back to 1982 when I spent two months at the Institute of Oriental Studies working on Soviet-American relations in the Middle East. He was a hard man to meet, for he was shuttling back and forth between the PLO factions at the time. In private, however, he was contemptuous of the hard-line factions. My view of Primakov has also been shaped by a long friendship with Nodari Simoniia, a Georgian who was associated with him in the Institute of Oriental Studies and IMEMO for years.

53. *Pravda*, July 2, 1988, p. 8.

was the nature and extent of the change, for Dobrynin was obviously much more cautious than Yakovlev (and, it turned out, Shevardnadze).

The alternatives being discussed by Soviet foreign policy specialists in the 1970s and 1980s were far more complex than the West generally understood. During the 1970s Americans had seen the choice in U.S.-Soviet relations as detente or hard-line confrontation. In international relations, however, detente is a very limited concept, a relaxation of tension between adversaries. Its Russian translation, *razriadka*, implies lowering weapons, not unloading them. The French word that means warm and friendly relations was *entente*.

American liberals contended that detente was the liberal position in Soviet politics and that such proponents as Gromyko should be supported against their opponents. Some Americans genuinely thought of Soviet politics in these terms, but others wanted to go no further than detente in order to keep Germany divided and to deny that this option might be open. In fact, the conservative criticism of the Brezhnev-Gromyko detente policy, although it did exist, was grossly exaggerated. There were few forces in the Soviet Union more conservative than Brezhnev, Gromyko, and Ustinov, all of whom favored detente. The real alternative to detente was entente, and the conservative military criticism that was called antidetente in the West was really directed at the pro-entente position in the debate.

The Soviet Union and the United States had adopted policies of confrontation toward each other, but this confrontation screened a tacit alliance to keep Germany divided, Japan geostrategically subservient, and Eastern Europe under Soviet control—that is, to preserve the fruits of victory in World War II.[54] Gromyko wanted mild detente, a relaxation of tension, to ensure that confrontation did not get out of hand, but he strongly opposed entente for fear that it might destabilize the division of Europe.

In the Soviet Union before 1985 there were two acceptable ways to openly defend Gromyko's policy. One was to insist that "class" (the economic and social systems) determined foreign policy alliances and therefore that the division between Eastern and Western Europe was immutable. The second was to emphasize the dangers of German revanchism and Japanese militarism. The implication was that the division of Europe and

---

54. This situation is discussed in Jerry F. Hough, "Lessons for Western Theories of International Security and Foreign Relations," in Harley D. Balzer, ed., *Five Years That Shook the World: Gorbachev's Unfinished Revolution* (Boulder, Colo.: Westview Press, 1991), pp. 191–93.

American hegemony in Asia were desirable to keep Germany and Japan under control.

The most direct way to support entente with the West was to focus on matters that transcended class interests or economic systems: advocating disarmament, supporting human rights, protecting the environment.[55] Many Westerners dismissed those in the Soviet peace or disarmament movements as Brezhnev propagandists, but most of the proponents—Georgy Arbatov, for example—were in the pro-entente school. Their "propagandistic" criticisms of the American military were really indirect attacks on the Soviet military.

The safer way to attack Gromyko's policy from a pro-entente position was to emphasize the divisions within the Western alliance and the dangers of American aggression. The implication of these two positions was that the Western alliance was not impregnable and that it was less dangerous to court Germany than to leave it allied with the United States.[56]

Aleksandr Yakovlev was the foremost person to use this indirect method to criticize Gromyko from a pro-entente position. His first article after his return from Canada directly criticized politicians and analysts who attributed poor Soviet-American relations to "the personal characteristics of President Reagan." His 1984 book titled *From Truman to Reagan* was bleak in the extreme in its assessment of the United States. In Yakovlev's view all American presidents sought world domination: "Truman, Eisenhower, Kennedy, Nixon, as well as presidents before and after them." It was a profoundly pessimistic picture of American politics, because Kennedy had been idealized in the Soviet press, Nixon had launched detente, and "presidents before" Truman referred to Franklin Roosevelt, a person in the Soviet pantheon.[57]

Yet Yakovlev softened the threat implied in this view of the United States by emphasizing the limits on American power. "Because of the forced pace of the integration process in Western Europe and the rise of Japan to the level of a world economic power, these 'centers of force' create

---

55. For examples of this position, see Hough, *Struggle for the Third World*, pp. 219–20.

56. The debates in the early 1980s on this question are laid out in great detail in Jerry F. Hough, "Soviet Perspectives on European Security," *International Journal*, vol. 40 (Winter 1984–85), pp. 20–41.

57. Quoted in *Izvestiia*, October 7, 1983; and interview in *Komsomol'skaia pravda*, December 25, 1983. See also Aleksandr N. Yakovlev, *Ot Trumena do Reigana: Doktriny, real'nosti yadernogo veka* (Moscow: Molodaia gvardiia, 1984).

a real counterweight to the hegemony of the USA in the capitalist world." He treated Western Europe and Japan as "real components of international influence" whose interests were not served by Reagan's policy. The obvious implication was that the Soviet Union should be much more flexible in courting Western Europe and Japan. Yakovlev hinted at a more positive view of these countries by saying that the "the USA already can in no way be considered the symbol of 'youth, dynamism, and success' in the Western world."[58]

Yakovlev went even further in a page-long discussion, "Civilized Relations: A Necessity, a Reality, or a Utopia?," published in the Soviet press shortly after Gorbachev became general secretary. On the surface the phrase *civilized* (*tsivilizirovannye*) *relations* seemed unexceptionable, a more positive way of saying "peaceful coexistence." But in fact *civilization* had been a code word used by those undermining the validity of Marxism-Leninism. Marx and Lenin had emphasized class and stage of history in a way that implied the similarity of, for example, European and Chinese feudalism and European and Chinese capitalism. To emphasize "civilization" was to suggest continuities in China from feudalism and capitalism and their differences from European feudalism and capitalism. It was to deemphasize the role of class and ownership of property. Those who emphasized "civilized relations" were well aware of the implication.[59]

If Yakovlev was indeed to be Gorbachev's closest adviser and Gorbachev was to adopt Yakovlev's pro-entente position, then Gorbachev's question to the editors of *Time* magazine about the implications of his "grandiose" domestic program suggested there would be foreign policy changes more far-reaching than most Americans could imagine.

Gorbachev's Foreign Policy

When Gorbachev came to power, he uttered all the usual sentiments about the need for peace, disarmament, and improved relations with the United States. In his first years he followed a policy with which top Soviet

58. Aleksandr Yakovlev, "Imperializm: sopernichestvo i protivorechiia," *Pravda*, March 23, 1984, p. 3.
59. "Vostok-Zapad: Tsivilizirovannye otnosheniia, Neobkhodimost'?, real'nost'?, utopiia?" *Literaturnaia gazeta*, June 26, 1985, p. 2. The other participants were Fedor Burlatsky, *Literaturnaia gazeta* commentator, and Vadim Zagladin, first deputy head of the International Department of the Central Committee. See the general discussion in Hough, *Struggle for the Third World*, pp. 60–65.

leaders generally agreed: an opening to the West, more energetic arms control, and withdrawal of troops from Afghanistan.[60] Yet virtually every speech he made contained devastating criticisms of American foreign policy. President Reagan's Strategic Defense Initiative, he said repeatedly, demonstrated that the United States had adopted a first-strike strategy based on the most malevolent intentions.[61] Sometimes Gorbachev's language was considered evidence of an anti-Western policy, but his language was actually Yakovlev's and implied a reversal of Gromyko's policy in the direction of entente.

Gorbachev soon sent out other subtle signals of a change in policy. Brezhnev had focused on Eastern Europe in his early travel and discussions with foreigners. He did not travel to Western Europe until 1971 or the United States until 1973.[62] Gorbachev largely ignored Eastern Europe and as early as October 1985 traveled to Paris, the trip itself a signal of the priority of Western rather than Eastern Europe. More important, he and the media increasingly relied on a sentence he had first used when he spoke to the British Parliament in December 1984 before he became general secretary: "Europe is our common home." In Paris he returned to the theme: "Whatever aspect of the development of human civilization we take, the contribution made by the Europeans is immense. We live in the same house, though some use one entrance and the others another. We need to cooperate and develop communication within that house."[63]

At a dinner for the Italian Communist party general secretary on January 28, 1986, Gorbachev went out of his way to emphasize "the European aspect" of the Soviet plan as "exceptionally important for Europe itself and the whole world." He used the religious word *schism* (*raskol*) to describe the split in the world, but said that "precisely here [in Europe] all conditions now exist to overcome the *razobshchenost'* [alienation] between East and

60. Vladimir Kriuchkov, then head of foreign intelligence and a key participant in Afghan policy, claims that at first Gorbachev wanted to end the war quickly by accelerating military action on the ground but that six months later he was advocating ending the war by withdrawal. Yakovlev, Kriuchkov says, was for withdrawal without conditions. Kriuchkov, *Lichnoe delo*, pt. 2, pp. 223, 232–35.

61. Gorbachev noted that American scientists admitted the SDI could not hope to be effective enough to destroy thousands of rockets fired in a surprise Soviet first strike. He argued—not illogically—that "Star Wars" therefore must be intended to mop up any enfeebled Soviet response to an American first strike.

62. Aleksandrov-Agentov, *Ot Kollontai do Gorbacheva*, pp. 135–38, 180.

63. M. S. Gorbachev, *Izbrannye rechi i stat'i*, vol. 2 (Moscow: Politizdat, 1987), pp. 114, 441–42.

West."[64] In a speech to the Ministry of Foreign Affairs on May 23, 1996, he insisted that Europe should not be seen "through the prism of relations with the United States of America."[65]

Traditional Soviet analysis emphasized the difference between capitalist Western Europe and NATO, which were described as inherently exploitative, undemocratic, and aggressive, and socialist Eastern Europe, which was described as just, democratic, and peace loving. Contemporary West European culture was said to be violent, pornographic, and destructive of human values. Gorbachev's language did not distinguish between Eastern and Western Europe but clearly implied that European culture did not merely serve the interests of the ruling classes, as Marxism-Leninism claimed. On this point he was using Ivan Frolov's language about the existence of universal human values rather than values based on class.

Gorbachev made the same point obliquely when he met President Reagan in a summit meeting at Geneva in November 1985. His decision to meet in Western Europe was yet another signal of the importance of Europe, and while there he severely criticized the American president for his black-and-white view of the capitalist and socialist worlds.[66] He did not point out—but Soviet conservatives must have noticed—that traditional Marxism-Leninism treated the two worlds in the same way.

The phrase *common European home* (or *house*) was ambiguous in Russian. Americans are used to single-family homes; to them, such a common house occupied by different countries implies real intimacy. Although *house* (*dom*) can have this meaning in contemporary Russian usage, for most urban Soviet citizens an address such as dom 11 refers to a large apartment house, even an enormous apartment complex. People living in such a house live in separate apartments, each with its own lock and key. A common European house in that sense could mean only that it is not wise to drop an atomic bomb on your neighbor if he is living in the same apartment house.

Nevertheless, a common home was certainly a different image than the ones used for ideological confrontation. Whatever the precise meaning of the concept, Andrei Gromyko understood enough about its implications to

64. Gorbachev, *Izbrannye rechi i stat'i*, vol. 3, pp. 150–51.
65. Gorbachev, *Gody trudnykh reshenii* (Moscow: Al'fa-Print, 1993), pp. 46–55.
66. See "Excerpts from Gorbachev News Session: 'All Have a Stake,'" *New York Times*, November 22, 1985, p. 16.

be highly critical about it in private. Gromyko thought that "any house is built on solid ground," and he did not see such for "a single and universal building."[67]

At other times Gorbachev went much further. In Czechoslovakia in April 1987 he asserted, "Europe from the Atlantic to the Urals is also a historical and cultural category in a high, spiritual sense. Here world civilization has been enriched with the ideas of the Renaissance and the Enlightenment. . . . European culture, which has many faces, yet forms a single entity."[68] In Marx and Lenin the Renaissance and the Enlightenment reflected the interests of owning classes that were determined to establish and maintain their dominance and exploitation.

Although Americans were inclined to see such ideological phraseology as too abstract and esoteric to be significant, it was precisely its esoteric character that usually made it a reliable indicator. But how significant for Soviet policy toward Eastern Europe were the pronouncements about European civilization? If Europe was a single civilization, then logically Eastern Europe did not have to remain communist. In fact, the debate on Europeanization that had emerged during the 1970s and 1980s had precisely this implication.[69] On November 14, 1989, after the collapse of a number of communist regimes, Gorbachev made the point explicitly in his discussions with the French foreign minister. "It is time to recognize," he said, "that the contemporary world does not consist of two mutually exclusive civilizations, but of one general world in which human values and freedom of choice have primacy."[70]

The logic of Gorbachev's language was clear enough from the beginning: the Soviet Union should not intervene to suppress an anticommunist revolt in Eastern Europe. Moreover, if Gorbachev wanted the "common European home" of which he spoke and that was needed for economic reform, it would be impossible to keep the Germans divided against their will.[71] But when did he himself accept this logic? Cherniaev had advocated German reunification immediately after he had been appointed

---

67. Kapto, *Na perekrestkakh zhizni*, pp. 366–67.

68. *Pravda*, April 11, 1987.

69. Karen Dawisha, *Eastern Europe, Gorbachev, and Reform: The Great Challenge* (Cambridge University Press, 1988), pp. 189–92.

70. *Pravda*, November 15, 1989, p. 2.

71. See Jerry F. Hough, "Attack on Protectionism in the Soviet Union? A Comment," *International Organization*, vol. 40 (Spring 1986), pp. 502–03.

Gorbachev's foreign policy assistant in 1986. It is likely Gorbachev himself accepted the logic well before he told his colleagues in the Politburo.

Attitudes toward Eastern Europe

It had long been clear that the northern communist countries—Czecho-slovakia, East Germany, Hungary, and Poland—were inherently unstable, their governments ultimately maintained by the threat of Soviet interven-tion.[72] If these countries were going to have free elections and if Soviet troops would not intervene, the outcome was predictable.

From a geostrategic point of view, Gorbachev had every reason to change Soviet policy toward Eastern Europe. Eastern Europe had once been an important buffer zone when conflicts between Britain, France, and Germany periodically plunged Europe into war, but by 1985 the need for such a buffer had long since passed. Any danger to the Soviet Union came from intercontinental ballistic missiles that ignored all borders. Even a united Germany of 78 million persons would not be significantly more dangerous to the Soviet Union than a West Germany of 60 million.

In terms of economic policy, communist Eastern Europe had become a significant drain on resources, whereas relations with noncommunist coun-tries such as Finland and Austria and even West Germany had become economically beneficial. In addition, if the Soviet Union was to undertake serious economic reform, integration into the world economy would be indispensable. And as long as the West felt militarily threatened, it would never give Soviet industry access to, for example, the computer chips that were crucial for the domestic economy but also vital for the military. It was important, then, for the Soviet Union to do as Gorbachev promised at the Twenty-Seventh Party Congress: "We intend in the future to act so that no one will have the bases for fear, even imagined."[73]

---

72. The situation in the southern communist countries that had been part of the Ottoman Empire was more ambiguous. The communist regimes in Albania and Yugo-slavia had remained in power for several decades after they split with the Soviet Union and after their people no longer had to fear Soviet military intervention. Westerners knew Romania and Bulgaria were very different from Poland, Hungary, and Czechoslo-vakia, but knew little about them. The question about the future of East Germany—the remnant of the old Prussia—was whether West Germany would offer enough finan-cially to make unification attractive or compelling or whether the East Germans would want to be another independent German-speaking country such as Austria.

73. Gorbachev, *Izbrannye rechi i stat'i*, vol. 3, p. 248.

Each Soviet leader had been tested in Eastern Europe: Stalin in 1948 by Yugoslavia, Malenkov in 1953 by East Germany, Khrushchev in 1956 by Poland and Hungary, and Brezhnev in 1968 by Czechoslovakia and 1980 by Poland. It seemed certain that perestroika would unleash forces that would test Gorbachev as well. But how could he intervene militarily in Eastern Europe without creating a sense of threat in the West? Above all, how could he handle the problem of East Germany? Gorbachev had to reduce troops in East Germany to reduce the threat to the West, but if the East Germans began demonstrations, any action to suppress them was certain to destroy relations with West Germany. The first demonstrations after Stalin's death had occurred in East Germany.

The primary problem was that policy toward Eastern Europe always had profound domestic implications in the Soviet Union. The debate in 1947 and 1948 on the extent to which the East European "people's democracies" had to resemble the Soviet Union was really a debate on whether the Soviet Union itself could evolve in a more liberal direction after the war.[74] The question arose again in the first months after Stalin's death in 1953 as the party leaders debated how to respond to the riots in East Germany— specifically, whether to consider the neutralization of Germany, as they decided to do in Austria two years later.[75] The subsequent debates during the Khrushchev and Brezhnev eras about how much diversity to tolerate in Eastern Europe continued implicitly to focus on how much diversity to tolerate at home.

As the geostrategic importance of Eastern Europe declined, the main reason Soviet leaders came to fear the fall of the communist regimes was that their demise might destabilize communism at home. In 1980 Tomas Kolesnichenko, the *Pravda* correspondent in New York, spoke for most intellectuals when he stated privately that he hoped Solidarity in Poland would be successful so that such a trade union might be a legitimate

---

74. H. Gordon Skilling, "People's Democracy in Soviet Theory," *Soviet Studies*, vol. 3 (July 1951), pp. 16–33; and vol. 3 (October 1995), pp. 131–39. See also Jerry F. Hough, "Debates about the Postwar World," in Susan Linz, ed., *The Impact of World War II* (Totowa, N. J.: Rowman and Allanheld, 1985), pp. 266–74.

75. For the stenographic report of the July 1953 Central Committee plenum at which Beria was condemned for his policy toward Germany, see *Izvestiia TsK KPSS*, no. 1 (1991), pp. 139–214; and no. 2 (1991), pp. 141–208. For an earlier discussion of this subject, see Heinz Brandt, *The Search for a Third Way: My Path between East and West* (Doubleday, 1970), pp. 183–220. Brandt treats Malenkov and Beria as jointly committed to the policy, and surely he is right, but Malenkov was premier.

possibility in the Soviet Union. For precisely the same reason, the Brezhnev leadership was determined that Solidarity not be successful.

Thus when Gorbachev decided what type of elections to introduce in the Soviet Union in 1989 and what kind to tolerate in the republics in 1990, he knew that he was also dealing with policy toward Eastern Europe. The communist countries had generally been expected to follow the Soviet model. If free elections were a desirable part of communism in the Soviet Union, why should they be illegitimate in Poland? But by the same token, it was also predictable that the collapse of the communist regimes in Eastern Europe in the autumn of 1989 would embolden democrats and nationalists in the Soviet Union as the 1990 republican elections approached.

Policy toward Eastern Europe

At first the most striking thing about Gorbachev's policy in Eastern Europe was the lack of attention he gave the area. He seldom visited there and rarely alluded to the area in his speeches. Of course, in his first years in office he had no compelling reason to give much attention to it. Martial law had worked in Poland, and the rest of Eastern Europe seemed to be in a quiescent period.

Gorbachev's silence was reinforced by the fact that East European leaders, all but Wojciech Jaruzelski in their late sixties or seventies, had been in office for at least a decade and usually far longer and had proved adept at maintaining the status quo (table 6-1). Gorbachev had no desire to frighten Soviet conservatives with political change in Eastern Europe. Yet for the longer term the situation was extremely worrisome. He knew that East European leaders would not like the reforms he had in mind: he (and they) knew that his reforms would eventually destabilize their regimes.

Gorbachev's rare early comments on Eastern Europe were ambiguous and reflected divisions among his speechwriters. When East European leaders visited Moscow, the Socialist Countries Department of the Central Committee had the major responsibility for drafting Gorbachev's remarks. Because before 1986 the top officials of this department were conservative, the department prepared traditional remarks about socialist unity. These were absent from his other speeches, which were drafted by his general advisers, notably Yakovlev and Cherniaev.

In none of his statements, however, did Gorbachev ever reaffirm the right to intervene in Eastern Europe to preserve socialism. In an interview

Table 6-1. *Central European Communist Leaders' Age and Years in Office, January 1985*

Country	Leader	Age	Years in Office
Bulgaria	Todor Zhivkov	73	30
Czechoslovakia	Gustav Husak	71	16
East Germany	Erich Honecker	72	13
Hungary	Janos Kadar	72	28
Poland	Wojciech Jaruzelski	61	3
Romania	Nicolae Ceausescu	66	19

with *Pravda* published on April 7, 1985, only a month after he came to power, he introduced a theme that was to take on a new meaning as time passed: "It is impossible to ignore the interests of other states and, all the more, to try to deprive them of their rights to select their own path of development themselves."[76]

In 1990 Aleksandr Yakovlev told *Pravda* that the Soviet leaders had a clear-cut policy from the beginning:

> When we talked about freedom of choice of each people, that we did not intend to interfere in the internal affairs of other parties and countries or to impose our own ideas and approaches, these were words expressed honestly and seriously, even if this was not understood by some people. There were also lessons for us from the bitter experience of past interventions. We understood that August 1968 held back—indeed, threw back for two decades—the development not only of Czechoslovakia, but our own country as well. For years it strengthened the position of the most conservative forces in our own party and country.[77]

Yegor Ligachev also said the leaders had decided in 1985 or 1986 not to use military force against Eastern Europe, but it is not clear how many in the Politburo had thought through the implications.[78]

The first major signs of change in Eastern Europe appeared in 1988. Inflation in Poland rose by 51 percent and wages by 58 percent in the first half of the year. The result was one wave of strikes in April and then a second in August.[79] The failure of the strikes to spread more widely and to

76. Gorbachev, *Izbrannye stat'i i rechi*, vol. 2, p. 134.
77. *Pravda*, June 23, 1990. Reprinted in Yakovlev, *Muki prochteniia, bytiia*, p. 182.
78. David Remnick, *Lenin's Tomb: The Last Days of the Soviet Empire* (Random House, 1993), p. 234. In a 1991 interview with Raymond Garthoff, Ligachev reaffirmed that he had this position both earlier and in 1989. Garthoff, *Great Transition*, p. 605.
79. "Polish Cabinet, under Fire, Steps Down," *New York Times*, September 20, 1988, p. 3; and John Tagliabue, "Wanted in Poland: Less Money, More Goods," *New York Times*, September 26, 1988, p. 9.

take on a political character suggested that the revolutionary upsurge of the beginning of the decade had largely exhausted itself. But at a minimum, Poland had economic decisions to make that had major political implications.

In Hungary the long-time party leader, Janos Kadar, was removed as general secretary in May 1988 and replaced by Koroly Grosz. The Soviet Union showed no displeasure (in fact the Soviet leaders had been advocating the change since the spring).[80] Grosz spoke glowingly of Gorbachev and his democratization. But in the summer of 1988 he suggested that although independent parties and groups might be tolerated in Hungary, it would be half a dozen years before non-Communists would be permitted to win a national election.

In September 1988, however, a fundamental change occurred in Soviet politics. Premier Ryzhkov had long complained about the interference of the Central Committee departments and Secretariat in the detailed economic work of the government. In the summer Gorbachev had told the Politburo he had decided to agree with Ryzhkov's position.[81] He abolished the industrial departments of the Central Committee, along with the Secretariat as a collective institution and the post of head of the Secretariat (chief of staff for the general secretary).[82] There continued to be Central Committee secretaries, but virtually all of them were now placed in charge of a commission dealing with a particular policy area. Gorbachev may have talked as if he were making a concession to Ryzhkov, but this was scarcely what he had in mind. The immediate purpose of the reorganization was to begin the process of destroying the central institutions of the Communist party, including the Politburo.

A second purpose was to effect a number of personnel changes. The abolition of the post of head of the Secretariat officially destroyed Ligachev's job. Instead of being second secretary, he became the Central Committee secretary for agriculture. He was moved from the fifth floor to the third in the Central Committee building.[83] The Central Committee

80. See V. A. Medvedev, *Raspad: Kak on nazreval v 'mirovoi' sisteme sotsializma* (Moscow: Mezhdunarodnye otnosheniia, 1994), pp. 126–29.

81. Gorbachev, *Zhizn' i reformy*, vol. 1, pp. 396–97. This is not in *Memoirs*.

82. The industrial departments included heavy industry, defense industry, light and food industry, and transportation-communications.

83. V. I. Boldin, *Krushenie p"edestala: Shtrikhi k portretu M. Gorbacheva* (Moscow: Respublika, 1995), p. 94.

secretary for industry, Vladimir Dolgikh, a supporter of Chernenko, was retired.[84]

The most important personnel changes occurred in the sphere of international relations. Yakovlev became chairman of the International Relations Commission, and the International Department and Socialist Countries Department were merged. Medvedev, head of Socialist Countries, replaced Yakovlev as Central Committee secretary for ideology.[85] The conservative Dobrynin lost his job (officially he became consultant to Gorbachev, but he was to have little role in making or implementing foreign policy). Valentin Falin, a diplomat specializing in Germany and a long-time critic of Andrei Gromyko's policy, became head of the International Department.

At the same time, Gromyko was retired as chairman of the Presidium of the Supreme Soviet and replaced by Gorbachev. Viktor Chebrikov was removed as chairman of the KGB and made a Central Committee secretary in charge of the Legal Commission. This left him in charge of internal security, but he no longer had the foreign policy responsibilities of a KGB head. Andropov's long-time assistant and Yakovlev's friend, Vladimir Kriuchkov, the KGB deputy chairman for foreign intelligence, was appointed the new chairman of the KGB.[86] Any obstacles to a major change of policy in Europe had been removed.

As of 1996 Yakovlev had not written his full memoirs, and Vadim Medvedev and Georgy Shakhnazarov, the two other men very close to policy decisions on Eastern Europe, have been singularly uninformative discussing these decisions in their memoirs. Shakhnazarov, Gorbachev's personal assistant for Eastern Europe, wrote a chapter on the end of the ''socialist commonwealth'' that said more about thinking in the Brezhnev period than in 1988 and 1989. He asserted that the Soviet leaders had not

84. Dolgikh came from Krasnoiarsk, where Chernenko worked, and had been Grishin's candidate for premier.

85. The selection of Medvedev as chairman of the Ideological Commission was often said to reflect a move by Gorbachev toward the center on ideological questions because Medvedev was said to be more moderate than Yakovlev. In fact, Medvedev's beliefs were similar to those of Yakovlev, who remained deeply involved in domestic politics.

86. Gorbachev says that Yakovlev and Kriuchkov were "especially close at that moment" and that Yakovlev supported Kriuchkov's appointment "especially actively." *Zhizn' i reformy*, vol. 1, p. 409; and *Memoirs*, p. 267. Valery Boldin agrees. Boldin, *Krushenie p"edestala*, p. 238. Arbatov, closely associated with Andropov and Yakovlev, had proposed that Kriuchkov be named KBG chairman in 1982 when Andropov came to power. Cherniaev, *Moia zhizn' i moe vremia*, p. 444.

thought very much about the subject by the summer of 1988 and that Gorbachev had not found it simple "to come to a recognition of the truth about 1968 [in Czechoslovakia]."[87] Medvedev said nothing of importance about the period after September 1988 when he ceased to have direct responsibility for Eastern Europe. Gorbachev's memoirs are not much more revealing. Clearly, all of them have been afraid to discuss the matter: statements about their actions could be used against them after a conservative coup d'etat. The combination of silence and the desire for deniability strongly suggests that they had plans that needed to be denied.

In any case, events moved quickly. In his memoirs Shakhnazarov has reproduced several memorandums he wrote in October 1988. They indicate that the formation of the International Relations Commission was followed by conversations with a number of leaders of socialist countries and that the Politburo discussed the subject Eastern Europe on October 6. The Soviet leadership was thinking of the need for reform in Eastern Europe, and Shakhnazarov raised the hard questions. Would the Soviet Union help with the hard currency debts of bankrupt East European countries? Would it intervene militarily in a crisis? Was the West needed to help Eastern Europe out of its economic problems? What would be the cost? He does not indicate the responses of others—or of himself—but he asked the questions in a way that made a conservative answer very unattractive.[88]

In December 1988 Gorbachev appeared before the United Nations and announced a unilateral reduction of 500,000 Soviet troops, including six tank divisions in central Europe, in the next two years. Because the announcement was so dramatic, few observers noticed that he also mentioned a "deideologization of foreign policy" and once more endorsed "freedom of choice," this time "without exceptions."[89]

Gorbachev's pledge was particularly important because of the events occurring in Poland and Hungary. Almost at the same time as the September 1988 Central Committee plenum, Mieczyslaw Rakowski, a long-time Polish reformer, was named prime minister. Within a month his government had decided to open talks with the outlawed Solidarity movement. On January 27, 1989, a roundtable was formed of representatives of the Polish government, Solidarity, and the Catholic Church. Talks began on February 6, and on April 17 the roundtable agreed on the legalization of Solidarity

---

87. Shakhnazarov, *Tsena svobody*, p. 105.
88. Shakhnazarov, *Tsena svobody*, pp. 367–69, 371–72.
89. "Rech' M. S. Gorbacheva v OON," *Pravda*, December 8, 1988, p. 1.

and the holding of an election in June. In effect, General Jaruzelski was guaranteed the presidency for a number of years, while the Communists and their puppet parties were guaranteed half the seats on the legislature. The rest of the deputies were to be chosen in free elections.

In Hungary, Grosz moved quickly between November 1988 and January 1989 to legalize independent parties.[90] The legitimacy of the 1956 Soviet invasion and the status of Imre Nagy, the Hungarian leader whose support of democracy and withdrawal from the Warsaw Pact provoked the invasion, were the great symbolic issues in Hungarian politics. Nagy had been executed and his body buried in a secret grave. In January 1989 the Communist party declared that the 1956 rebellion had not been a counterrevolution, as previously stated. The pressure to rehabilitate Nagy and to give him a state funeral grew steadily. When a state funeral was held on June 16, 1989, it predictably turned into a huge demonstration in favor of democracy.

January and February 1989, it will be remembered, were the months of the first competitive election campaigns in the Soviet Union in more than sixty years, and the elections themselves were held in March. The fact that a number of Communist party officials were defeated and that Gorbachev then treated the outcome as basically a good thing inevitably had a major impact on other communist countries.

The most tragic result of democratization in the Soviet Union occurred in China. In mid-April, one month after the USSR election, a former Chinese Communist party leader, Hu Yaobang, died. Hu had been forced to resign in 1987 and was thought to have supported reform intellectuals. A student meeting held in Beijing to honor both him and democracy spilled into the centrally located Tiananmen Square. For six weeks, as the whole world watched, the square was the scene of continuing occupation and demonstrations, with protesters numbering in the hundreds of thousands. The demonstrators clearly hoped that the Chinese leaders would make concessions so as not to appear unattractive in the eyes of the world in comparison with the other communist leaders.

The Tiananmen demonstration was far more complex than most Westerners understood. At first the demonstrators were mostly students from elite families who were not only demonstrating for democracy, but also against the effects of economic reform on their incomes. Receiving finan-

90. Henry Kamm, "Hungary to Offer Multi-Party System, in Principle," *New York Times*, November 11, 1988, p. 16; and Kamm, "Hungary Eases Dissent Curbs," *New York Times*, January 12, 1989, p. 13.

cial aid and coming from families working in the state bureaucracy, they were being hurt by an inflationary spiral that was not being matched by a corresponding increase in college stipends and salaries in the state sector. Democracy, they understood, would increase the pressure for protection against market forces.

Li Peng, the moderately conservative premier, and Zhao Ziyang, the more moderate general secretary, were engaged in a struggle for power.[91] As a result, no action was taken against the demonstrators for more than a month. In mid-May Gorbachev came to Beijing for a historic meeting to end the thirty-year Soviet-Chinese conflict. When he visited Tiananmen Square on May 17, he praised the demonstration before a million protesters.

A few days after Gorbachev's departure, the Chinese regime introduced martial law in the central part of Beijing. It was five days before the opening of the USSR Congress of People's Deputies. The Beijing students understood the message that repression was coming, and the number of demonstrators fell sharply to about 10,000, most of whom were from the provinces. On June 3, the day before the Polish election that gave Solidarity a sweeping victory, the Chinese leaders sent tanks into Tiananmen Square to crush the remnants of the demonstration. The timing of their various actions showed that the Chinese leaders were, in fact, looking at the USSR Congress and the Polish elections, but the lesson they drew was far different from the one the demonstrators wanted.

Western governments and intellectuals condemned the repression in Tiananmen, and a flood of American investment may have been postponed (table 6-2). As the memories of Tiananmen faded, however, and it became clear that political unrest would not interfere with economic reform, American investment in China began to soar.

The Polish election resulted in a Solidarity victory even more overwhelming than anticipated: the movement won all the contested elections. As a result, the long-time puppet parties of the Communist party had no interest in remaining puppets. They joined with Solidarity, and on August 24, 1989, Tadeusz Mazowiecki, a non-Communist, was elected premier. Gorbachev had called Polish Prime Minister Rakowski beforehand and said that the Soviet Union would not intervene if a non-Communist were named by the parliament.

---

91. Nicholas D. Kristof, "China Party Chief Appears to Gain in Power Struggle," *New York Times*, May 14, 1989, p. 1; Kristof, "Power Struggle Goes on in Tense Beijing," *New York Times*, May 25, 1989, p. 1; and Kristof, "Chinese Hard-Liner Tightens Grip as Attacks on His Rival Multiply," *New York Times*, May 27, 1989, p. 1.

Table 6-2. *U.S. Investment in China, 1979–93*

Year	Investment (millions of dollars)	Number of contracts
1979–82	303	21
1983	478	25
1984	165	55
1985	1,152	101
1986	526	102
1987	360	103
1988	384	269
1989	645	276
1990	358	367
1991	548	684
1992	3,121	3,265
1993	6,813	6,750

Sources: *Almanac of China's Foreign Economic Relations and Trade* (Hong Kong, various years); U.S.-China Business Council; and Department of Commerce.

In the fall Gorbachev gave every indication of deliberately forcing the pace of the transformation of Eastern Europe. In early October he traveled to Berlin for the celebration of the fortieth anniversary of the establishment of the German Democratic Republic and "left no doubt at all about his belief in the need for far more radical reform of the system."[92] A day later the Hungarian Communist (Socialist Workers') party renamed itself the Socialist party. On October 18 it renounced the leading role of the party in the government, and the country changed from a "people's republic" to a republic. East German leader Erich Honecker resigned the same day. Demonstrations soon began in East Germany, and when no action was taken against the protesters, the demonstrations grew. On November 9 the Communist party decided to tear down the Berlin Wall. Gorbachev's press spokesman, Gennady Gerasimov, declared that "these changes are for the better. That is for sure."[93] Foreign minister Shevardnadze also said, "This was a reasonable and sensible decision. It ... corresponds to our own interest."[94] At the same time, the long-time Bulgarian leader, Todor Zhivkov, was forced to resign.

92. Quentin Peel, "Kremlin Agog at Pace of Change," *Financial Times*, November 11, 1989, p. 3.
93. Esther B. Fein, "Moscow Praises German Changes," *New York Times*, November 10, 1989, p. 16.
94. Quentin Peel, "Moscow Opposes German Unity," *Financial Times*, November 11, 1989, p. 1.

On November 16 R. W. Apple of the *New York Times* reported that the Soviet Union had warned the Czechs to introduce reform.[95] On October 25 the government resigned. Three days later the Communist party announced the end of one-party rule. In mid-December Gustav Husak, the party leader, agreed to step down as president, and on December 29 the playwright and long-time dissident Vaclav Havel was elected president pending national elections in June.[96]

In mid-December serious demonstrations began in Romania, and on December 16–17 the police opened fire on demonstrators in Timisoara. The repression encouraged the demonstration to spread to Bucharest and intensify. When the military withdrew its support from the government of Nicolae Ceausescu, it fell on December 22. On Christmas day Ceausescu and his wife were executed.[97]

The speed of events in Eastern Europe was remarkable. Many observers assumed that Gorbachev was caught unaware or that he expected the reform communists to win the free elections. Gorbachev's foreign press secretary, Gennady Gerasimov, who accompanied him everywhere abroad, still finds it hard to believe that Gorbachev thought the reform communists would be defeated so quickly. Otherwise, Gerasimov believes, Gorbachev would not have made some of the statements he did. Gerasimov reminds a Westerner that all Soviet officials, including himself, were so busy from morning to night that no one had any time to think, let alone rethink old assumptions.[98]

Yet Gerasimov is convinced that foreign policy was the exclusive province of Gorbachev and Shevardnadze and that Aleksandr Yakovlev played no role in it. This simply cannot be the case, all the more so in the crucial years when Yakovlev headed the International Relations Commission of the Central Committee. The then first deputy head of the Socialist Countries Department reports that even on questions of disarmament, the disagreement of the Ministry of Defense with the proposals of the Ministry of Foreign Affairs led to all decisions being "worked out in the triangle

95. R. W. Apple Jr., "A Soviet Warning on Foot-Dragging Is Given to Prague," *New York Times*, November 16, 1989, p. 1.

96. For a chronology of the events, see "Czechoslovakia's Seven Weeks of Drama," *New York Times*, December 30, 1989, p. 10.

97. For a chronology of the events, see "Rumania's 11 Days of Turmoil," *New York Times*, December 27, 1989, p. 11.

98. Jerry F. Hough, interview with Gennady Gerasimov, Duke University, November 30, 1995.

Gorbachev-Shevardnadze-Yakovlev."[99] Because Yakovlev and the people associated with him had fewer operational responsibilities, they had more time to think about events and policy. That had always been the function of the Central Committee apparatus, and Gerasimov's point about the lack of time for others to think may explain the great influence of those within the apparatus.

Gerasimov has also said that no outsider, even one as close to the process as he was, knows the thinking of the key participants. He was officially the press secretary of Eduard Shevardnadze and received informal briefings from him. Yet he has said he never knew what Shevardnadze really thought. The most important communications between top leaders, he said, usually took place on a special telephone line. When the general secretary called, a special ring filled the room, and everyone, including secretaries and assistants, had to leave immediately. No one other than the participants heard any part of the conversation, and there is no paper record for historians unless the KGB transcribed the conversations and preserved them.[100]

Nevertheless, after the results of the Polish election, Gorbachev cannot have been confident that the Hungarians and Czechs would vote for a Communist party that had been associated with the Soviet interventions in their countries. Yakovlev was telling people as early as 1987 that he looked for a Finlandization of Eastern Europe and had no hope Communists would win free elections in Eastern Europe.[101] The acceleration of the destabilization of the East European regimes occurred after the Polish election. Gorbachev's best hope was that the Communists would now be seen as Western social-democratic parties, but it was scarcely a bright hope in the short run. Only the executions in Romania were unexpected and unwanted. Boldin, the aide called "almost a member of the family," reported that "both

99. Kapto, *Na perekrestakh zhizni*, p. 131.

100. The same system was maintained under Boris Yeltsin after Russian independence. I was in the office of Vice President Aleksandr Rutskoi in March 1993 when a loud and unusual ring indicated a call from Yeltsin. We all left the room immediately and returned only after the call ended. Only later did we learn that it was a historic message that informed Rutskoi of Yeltsin's intention to take all power from the legislature. For the charge that Gorbachev had important meetings bugged, see Valentin Pavlov, *Upushchen li shans? Finansovyi kliuch k rynku* (Moscow: Terra, 1995), pp. 18, 22; and Boris Yeltsin, *The Struggle for Russia*, trans. Catherine A. Fitzpatrick (Times Books, 1994), pp. 38–39. Gorbachev has reported that he and his wife never had a serious conversation in his apartment or dacha for fear of it being recorded.

101. Jonathan Steele, *Eternal Russia: Yeltsin, Gorbachev, and the Mirage of Democracy* (Harvard University Press, 1994), p. 177.

Gorbachev and Raisa were really shocked and horrified by the death of Ceausescu and his wife."[102]

Probably the most surprising aspect of Gorbachev's policy toward Eastern Europe was the abrupt change in Soviet foreign economic policy that was part of the disintegration of communism in Eastern Europe. Trade between the Soviet Union and Eastern Europe had been substantial, but it had been integrated into the respective centralized plans. Because the trade was not a product of a competitive market, the prices were negotiated. The Soviet Union was shipping petroleum, natural gas, and raw materials to Eastern Europe and generally receiving manufactured goods that were not of a sufficient quality to be sold on the world market.

It was widely thought that this constituted a Soviet economic subsidy of Eastern Europe, and at a minimum the Soviet Union provided a market that prevented industrial unemployment in Eastern Europe. The Soviet Union decided to end this system abruptly and to conduct trade strictly according to market prices. This was a shock therapy for Eastern Europe as great or greater than their post-1989 economic reform policy. Eastern Europe was virtually forced to move toward the Western markets as quickly as possible. And whatever the theoretical balance of trade, the Soviet Union discovered it was benefiting from the "subsidized" trade as well. The loss of East European trade was a major factor in the Soviet economic problems of 1990 and 1991.[103] Eastern Europe was a major supplier of medicine to the Soviet Union, and its sudden loss was a major factor in the rapid decline of the Soviet health system.

It is even more a tenet of the conventional wisdom that Gorbachev did not want or expect a reunification of Germany in the foreseeable future. According to Hannes Adomeit, specialists on Germany in the Soviet foreign policy establishment did not expect reunification and did not think Gorbachev wanted it.[104] But this only demonstrates that leaders do not tell foreign policy specialists their innermost thoughts on politically sensitive subjects. Adomeit provided considerable evidence that Gorbachev and his closest advisers were talking about unification from an early period—1975 in Gorbachev's case—but chose to discount it.[105] Shakhnazarov claimed

102. Boldin, *Ten Years That Shook the World*, p. 141.

103. Ed A. Hewett with Clifford G. Gaddy, *Open for Business: Russia's Return to the Global Economy* (Brookings, 1992), pp. 51–52.

104. Hannes Adomeit, "Gorbachev, German Unification and the Collapse of Empire," *Post-Soviet Affairs*, vol. 10 (July-September, 1994), pp. 197–230.

105. Adomeit, "Gorbachev, German Unification, and the Collapse of Empire," p. 204.

that Gorbachev did not deliberately decide to "give back East Germany," but that he considered the Germans "one nation" (*natsiia*), which implied reunification, and was willing to let them set the pace.[106] Cherniaev has asserted that Gorbachev understood the need for German reunification by at least 1987.[107]

In fact, the way the postwar policy of de facto cooperation with the United States on the division of Europe was being repudiated and Europe was being treated as a whole made it obvious by 1986 that Gorbachev was considering fundamental changes indeed. One could imagine that he would back away from his commitment to free choice in Eastern Europe when faced with a hard choice. However, he clearly understood there was little point or little possibility in keeping Germany divided by force if Poland, Hungary, and Czechoslovakia were free. His caution in his public language was almost surely the result of a desire to avoid frightening Soviet conservatives, extract economic concessions from West Germany, and obtain some security guarantees. Perhaps the most interesting testimony came from Gorbachev's military adviser, Marshal Sergei Akhromeev. He was surprised by the number of trips that Gorbachev took to the major West European countries in 1989, and he concluded that Gorbachev expected change and wanted to find out the reaction of the West Europeans. In any case, Gorbachev never discussed the military implications of possible change in Eastern Europe with Akhromeev or, Akhromeev thought, with any other top officer. Gorbachev had already made up his mind on that question and did not want to hear the concerns of the military.[108]

Conclusion

If, as Gorbachev told the editors of *Time*, "foreign policy is a continuation of domestic policy," the stunning change in foreign policy in 1989 implied a domestic policy that was grandiose indeed. The 1989 USSR election had marked a major break with the past, but the USSR Congress of People's Deputies was under Gorbachev's tight political control. It re-

106. Shakhnazarov, *Tsena svobody*, p. 124.
107. "I can assert that in his soul he already then and even earlier was convinced that no improvement in international health . . . was possible without the solution of the German questions." Cherniaev, *Shest' let s Gorbachevym*, p. 154.
108. S. F. Akhromeev and G. M. Kornienko, *Glazami marshala i diplomata* (Moscow: Mezhdunarodnye otnoshenii, 1992), pp. 224, 226–27.

mained unclear how free the 1990 republican elections would be and how much independence the republics and their legislatures would be permitted. Economic reform had made little progress, but economic conditions were beginning to deteriorate and some type of economic reform would soon be on the agenda.

Gorbachev was, of course, being properly ambiguous in indicating how far he would go with democratization, economic reform, and foreign policy. The problem, however, was that the various components of the reform program were not fully compatible, especially radical economic reform and democratization. It was unclear what his sequence of moves would be, what his priorities would be, and what trade-offs he would accept.

Even more worrisome, Gorbachev did not seem to have the proper advisers to help him move to the next stage. This book has divided the discussion of his advisers between two chapters, a decision that is not simply a reflection of editorial convenience. The difference between the groups and their isolation from each other was apparent at an early stage, and the dynamics of their relationship led them to increasing mutual hostility and denunciation.

It is, of course, not unusual for leaders to surround themselves with advisers who hold different political views. Some leaders like the opportunity to hear different opinions and respond to them in ways that keep conflicting constituencies more or less satisfied. Gorbachev's desire to place himself between liberal and conservative elements was no less typical.

Gorbachev, however, had a fundamental problem. His moderate reformers, headed by Nikolai Ryzhkov and to a lesser extent Yegor Ligachev, had devised a generally consistent program to move the country in the direction of Hungarian and Chinese economic reform. When Ryzhkov had a chance in 1989, he appointed major reformers who were committed to his program as deputy premier for economic reform, deputy premier for foreign economic relations, minister of finances, chairman of the State Committee on Prices, chairman of the State Committee on Labor and Social Policy, chairman of the State Bank, and to a considerable extent chairman of Gosplan. Most members of this team were willing to introduce the price reforms necessary to produce financial stabilization and a smoothly functioning market in the service sector. The experience of Eastern Europe and China indicated that their program was almost certain to improve economic performance in agriculture, the services, and light industry, but unlikely to transform large state industries. Most of the moderate reformers also wanted a mildly authoritarian political system.[109]

The advocates of democracy who advised Gorbachev were eager to go much further than their rivals with political reform, although, of course, they probably are now exaggerating their early devotion to the scale of democratization that actually occurred. But whatever they wanted, it is clear they did not understand much about the mechanisms of democracy. They were between fifty-five and sixty-five years of age in 1986. The three most important—Yakovlev, Shakhnazarov, and Cherniaev—had begun working in the Central Committee apparatus more than a quarter of a century earlier, and the other three had gone to work there ten to twenty years before.

Like most revolutionaries, they had thought a lot about how to change the status quo and little about the details of what was to go in its place. The chairman of the State Committee of Television was to call the period one of liquidation of illiteracy about democracy (*likbez*), a reference to a campaign of the 1920s and 1930s.[110] Whether the political illiteracy was in fact liquidated in 1990 and 1991 is questionable, but it certainly existed in 1988 and 1989.

In addition, the democrats had little understanding of economic reform and seem to have given very little serious thought to the relationship between economic and political reform. Yakovlev confessed he knew little about China, and Ligachev caustically noted that Yakovlev never visited factories or learned about the economy first hand.[111] Cherniaev and Shakhnazarov seem to have made no effort to bring in economists who understood the West and East European economies with which the two had dealt. They also maintained little contact with jurists who specialized on the civil and commercial law required in a market.

Vadim Medvedev, the one member of the team who was an economist, should have performed important functions in economic reform. As Central Committee secretary for socialist countries from 1986 to 1988, he was the

109. Valentin Pavlov is the only one to discuss in his memoirs his preference for such a system, arguing that democracy inevitably follows economic reform, not the opposite. See *Upushchen li shans?* p. 49.

110. Mikhail Nenashev, *Zalozhnik vremeni: Zametki razmyshleniia, sviditel'stva* (Moscow: Progress, 1993).

111. Yakovlev, *Muki, prochteniia, bytiia*, p. 41; and Ligachev, *Zagadka Gorbacheva*, p. 71.

perfect person to study the economic experience of Eastern Europe and China, all the more so because one of the wisest economists was his former subordinate, Leonid Abalkin. Abalkin had worked for Vadim Medvedev before 1985 as head of the Political Economy Department of the Academy of Social Sciences, and Medvedev had had to fight to get Abalkin accepted in the post.[112] He probably was also influential in having Abalkin appointed director of the Institute of Economics of the Academy of Sciences in 1986.

It is not clear why Medvedev did not play a major role in economic reform. In the first three years of the Gorbachev period, he was a member and often chair of the major commissions on economic reform, but he seems to have served more as a speechwriter and drafter of documents. He strongly favored price reform in 1987, but by his own testimony fell silent on the subject after Gorbachev rejected his position.[113]

As director of the Institute of Economics, Abalkin appointed the radical economist Gavriil Popov editor of the institute's journal, *Voprosy Ekonomiki*. Abalkin was the first to criticize the one-party system at the Nineteenth Party Conference in 1988.[114] Yet he was allowed to become identified with Nikolai Ryzhkov, and the Soviet media under Yakovlev's supervision soon directed its fire at him. In his memoirs Cherniaev treats Abalkin as a "hostage" of Ryzhkov and a person without redeeming qualities.[115]

Medvedev, like Gorbachev's other trusted democratic advisers, never developed any real expertise on economic matters. Even in his 1994 memoirs Medvedev continued to hold primitive and contradictory views about economic reform. Although he was to endorse the 500-Day Plan of the summer of 1990 in his memoirs, he supported the opposing plan on the two main issues in dispute. He called for a compromise between the irreconcilables and even in his memoirs seemed puzzled that the protagonists did not agree.[116]

If Gorbachev had been his own strategist on the relation of economic and political reform, keeping different sets of advisers separate so as to maintain

112. Medvedev, *V komande Gorbacheva*, p. 11.
113. Medvedev, *V komande Gorbacheva*, p. 55.
114. This may have been the source of trouble. Gorbachev criticized him at the conference, and everyone except Ryzhkov snubbed him. Gorbachev may never have forgiven Abalkin for agreeing to serve as Ryzhkov's adviser.
115. Cherniaev, *Shest' let s Gorbachevym*, p. 369.
116. Medvedev, *V komande Gorbacheva*, pp. 158–63. Shakhnazarov, *Tsena svobody*, p. 190, also reports that he and the rest of Gorbachev's team did not understand Gorbachev's rejection of the 500-Day Plan. The great mystery is why they and Gorbachev ever considered accepting it, especially Shakhnazarov, a political scientist who favored a federal system.

a centrist position and retain power in his own hands, the situation might not have been so dangerous. But he began turning against the moderate reformers of the Kirilenko machine in 1989 and 1990. He allowed and encouraged their being labeled conservatives, even archconservatives, to paint himself as the centrist on the political spectrum. This left him at a far different point on the spectrum than he understood.

Gorbachev now had no one who could balance his democratic advisers. When in late 1990 he finally chose an economic adviser, Nikolai Petrakov, and then put Stanislav Shatalin, another economist, on the Presidential Council, they came from the abstract Central Mathematical-Economics Institute and quickly accepted Yeltsin's position on the totally unrealistic 500-Day Plan. They then publicly called on Gorbachev to resign when he rejected the plan. Yegor Gaidar, the economics editor of *Kommunist* and then *Pravda* from 1987 to 1990, was a protégé of Shatalin and made the same change of allegiance.

Because Gorbachev's democratic advisers were most knowledgeable on international relations and eager for a reconciliation with the West, they often saw domestic politics through that prism. They looked to the West, not China, for their models of reform—indeed, to an idealized United States rather than Western Europe. They wanted the Soviet Union to be a fully Western country both in its foreign policy and domestic institutions. They were especially sensitive to Western criticism and eager for Western approval. However, they had no sense of how many decades and even centuries lay behind the development of the market and democracy in the West. They wanted both immediately.

The most fundamental problem of all was that the democratic advisers advocated economic measures certain to lead to conditions that would require the use of force and other authoritarian measures to maintain stability. But they had naive definitions of democracy that included the complete repudiation of the use of force and other authoritarian measures.[117] All outside observers understood that this combination of views could lead to anarchy. The question was whether Gorbachev would break with his democratic advisers and end the anarchy with strong presidential rule.

---

117. Nenashev says that his generation—the children of the Twentieth Congress, the "sixtyers"—deserve detailed study. They were affected by Stalin's terror and by the 1968 invasion of Czechoslovakia. They often took to heart Khrushchev's utopianism and Marx's view of the future. Nenashev, *Zalozhnik vremeni*, pp. 33–34. Gorbachev has identified himself as a sixtyer and describes them in *Dekabr'—91: Moia pozitsiia* (Moscow: Novosti, 1992), p. 138.

CHAPTER SEVEN

Soviet Federalism and the Problem of Russia

FOR DECADES ALL Soviet leaders used words such as *democracy* and *peace* to cover behavior of a very different character from what the words normally indicate. Thus the leaders never admitted invading another country; instead, be it Finland in 1940, Hungary in 1956, Czechoslovakia in 1968, or Afghanistan in 1979, their troops were always invited in. Similarly, the Soviet Union never incorporated the Baltic states nor imposed communism on Eastern Europe: rather, 99 percent of the Baltic people voted for incorporation, and a similar percentage of those in Eastern Europe voted for communism. All the republics of the Soviet Union were sovereign and had their own ministries of foreign affairs. Ukraine and Belorussia were members of the United Nations.

As a consequence, when Mikhail Gorbachev began talking about democracy and freedom of choice for all peoples "without exception," his words had a familiar ring to any student of the Soviet Union, and they were given a very cynical interpretation. As it became increasingly clear, however, that he was using the words in a way different from his predecessors, the question became how far was he willing to go? Freedom of choice for Poles and Hungarians was one thing, but freedom of choice without exception implied Ukrainians, Uzbeks, Tatars, and Gagauz inside the Soviet Union as well. That would be something else.

As is discussed in the next chapter, Gorbachev had many options in the winter of 1989–90 in dealing with nationalities in the Soviet Union in the wake of the collapse of communism in eastern Europe. The option he actually chose seemed the most improbable of all, if for no other reason than it seemed certain to provoke a military coup d'etat.

To be sure, Gorbachev faced problems far more complex than Westerners generally recognized. He needed to decentralize power to the provinces if perestroika was to have meaning, but the peculiar structure of federalism in the Soviet Union made this task difficult. The political system was extraordinarily centralized, but the republics already had legal rights far beyond the regional units in a normal federal system: they were sovereign members of an alliance with the right to secede. A change in language alone could not give the republics anything they did not already have.

Indeed, from a legal point of view, the right path was a voluntary renegotiation of the terms of the alliance, and Gorbachev decided to pursue this policy. But this renegotiation promised to be politically difficult unless, as in the 1920s, the threat of the use of force hung over the talks. In such a case Gorbachev would be promising greater rights while de facto taking away the formal right to secede.

Gorbachev's largest problem was actually with the republic that had the fewest powers, the Russian Republic. Russia was a superfluous administrative link between the regions (*oblasts*) and the central government. Either the central government, the government of Russia, or the regional governments would have to be very weak. With the Soviet federal government controlling the integrated socialized economy and possessing a powerful military, with the oblasts to be strengthened through popular election of their officials, the Russian government seemed to have little to do. Yet the necessary creation of a Russian Communist party threatened to undermine the basic structure of political control on which the power of the general secretary rested.

Boris Yeltsin's political genius lay in perceiving that the USSR, not the Russian Republic, could be turned into the superfluous unit and that the USSR had a leader who might not successfully resist his efforts. More basically Yeltsin understood that the definitions of national identity and the federal system introduced by Lenin and Stalin made the system potentially unstable. Non-Russians had always considered Moscow a dominating center controlled by Russia, but Boris Yeltsin was able to convince Russians that they too had been dominated by the center and needed to be independent. He saw how to play upon Russians' economic grievances and the minor administrative role performed by the Russian Republic to turn Russia against the other republics and the center.

The peculiarities of Soviet federalism must be kept in mind if we are to comprehend not only Yeltsin's strategy for seizing power, but also Gorbachev's dilemmas. Westerners often sneered at him for not understanding the strength of nationalism, by which they meant the nationalism of non-Russians. In fact, he showed a good knowledge of this nationalism. Unlike his Western critics, however, he also understood that the really difficult national problem in the Soviet Union was posed by the Russians and their nationalism. Unfortunately, as Anatoly Cherniaev has commented, he understood this point because he came to accept Aleksandr Solzhenitsyn's argument that Lenin had sacrificed Russia for the interests of world revolution and ideology, and this undermined his self-confidence in his struggle with Boris Yeltsin.[1]

The Peculiarities of Soviet Federalism

Some have said the Soviet Union was the last empire, but this was simply propaganda. A large number of countries can be described in these terms. Country boundaries almost never correspond to ethnic borders in the third world, and in almost all these countries, one ethnic group is accused of having an imperial or assimilative position regarding the others—usually justly so. According to Myron Weiner,

> Hegemonic rather than accommodative ethnic politics characterize the new states. In country after country, a single ethnic group has taken control over the state and used its powers to exercise control over others. Indeed, among the multi-ethnic states, the process continues to be one of "nation-destroying," to use Walker Connor's term for the process by which the state attempts to assimilate, absorb, or crush ethnic groups that do not accept the legitimacy of the state within existing boundaries.[2]

The odd thing about the Soviet Union was the way Communist party leadership organized the empire or multiethnic country, whatever phrase one wants to use. The Soviet Union featured a strange combination of unprecedented overcentralization together with unprecedented legal rights

---

1. Anatoly. S. Cherniaev, *Shest' let s Gorbachevym* (Moscow: Progress, 1993), pp. 277–79.
2. Myron Weiner, "Political Change: Asia, Africa, and the Middle East," in Myron Weiner and Samuel P. Huntington, eds., *Understanding Political Development* (Little, Brown, 1987), p. 35.

for the republics. Article 15 of the 1936 Soviet Constitution said the republics were "sovereign" and had the right to secede from the Union. Beginning in 1944 each republic had a ministry of foreign affairs, and Stalin attempted to have each admitted to the United Nations in 1945. At the Yalta Conference, Franklin Roosevelt and Winston Churchill agreed that two of the republics, Ukraine and Belorussia, would be founding members, and they have since remained full members.

The structure of the Soviet federal system emerged from the interaction of Lenin's deep suspicion of federalism and his tactical political needs. The Russian and Austro-Hungarian Empires had featured a complex ethnic mosaic, and their social democrats had proposed many types of cultural and political autonomy and decentralization to deal with this situation. Lenin consistently opposed any dispersal of power to regions, cultural institutions, or workers' councils in factories, whether proposed in the form of municipalization, syndicalism, federalism, or the Renner-Bauer Plan for cultural autonomy. He argued that industrialization produced inexorable pressures for larger markets and for the fusion and assimilation of nations.

Lenin's 1917 work, *State and Revolution*, has often been interpreted as a utopian democratic document, but it is not. Amidst his talk about the eventual withering away of the state under communism, he emphasized that the state would continue to exist indefinitely in the socialist phase and power would have to be centralized.[3] *State and Revolution* contained a separate section on "the organization of the unity of the nation" that attacked the contention of men such as the German social democrat Eduard Bernstein that Marx had supported federalism.

Marx parted with Prudon and Bakunin precisely on the question of federalism. . . . Federalism flows in principle from petty bourgeois views of anarchism. Marx was a centralist. . . . Only people full of a Philistine "superstitious faith" in the state can confuse the destruction of the bourgeois state machine with the destruction of centralism. If the proletariat and the poorest peasantry take state power in their hands . . . [and] transfer private property in railroads, factories, land, and so forth to the *whole* nation, to the whole society, will this not be centralism? Will it not be the most consistent democratic centralism? . . . It simply cannot enter Bernstein's head that a voluntary centralism is possible.[4]

3. I owe this analysis to Cynthia Duff, a former fellow at the Center for East West Trade, Investment, and Communications, Duke University.
4. V. I. Lenin, "Gosudarstvo i revoliutsiia," in V. I. Lenin, *Polnoe sobranie sochinenii*, vol. 33 (Moscow: Politizdat, 1962), p. 53.

Such a view had little attraction for the non-Russians in the Russian Empire, and was not likely to promote successful revolution elsewhere in Europe. Lenin's solution to this political problem was to call for a centralized state in which the various nationalities had the right to secede, while at the same time making quite clear that the proletariat and its party would never choose to exercise this right. In his 1916 thesis on national self-determination he was frank about the tactical character of espousing the right of secession.

> The right of self-determination of nations . . . is in no way equivalent to a demand for secession, subdivision, and the formation of small states. . . . The closer we are to a democratic government and the full freedom of secession, the aspiration for secession in practice will be all the rarer and weaker. . . . The goal of socialism is not only the destruction of the splintering of mankind into small states and the isolation of nations, not only the bringing of nations together but even their fusion.

A note to the thesis added, "The freedom of separation is the best and only *political* means against the idiotic system of small states and national isolation, which, fortunately for mankind, are inevitably destroyed through the entire development of capitalism."[5]

Even the strength of nationalism manifested in the outbreak of World War I did nothing to change Lenin's position on the subject: the passage above was written two years after the war began. More important, his *Imperialism: The Highest Stage of Capitalism* blamed the war on rivalries within the capitalist elite, not on nationalism. The work emphasized the importance of supranational financial institutions in integrating the contemporary capitalist world.

After the overthrow of the tsar in March 1917, however, Lenin faced a serious political problem. He had predicted that the war would end in a worldwide socialist revolution, but such a revolution would not be facilitated by any suggestion that all peoples of the world would be ruled from Moscow. At the First All-Russian Congress of Soviets in June 1917, he proclaimed a new policy: "Let Russia be a union (alliance) of free republics."[6] *Soiuz* is always translated as *union* in this context, but in fact its first

---

5. Lenin, "Sotsialisticheskaia Revoliutsiia i pravo natsii na samoopredelenie (tezisy)," in Lenin, *Polnoe sobranie sochinenii*, vol. 27, pp. 255–56; and "Zametka k tezisam," vol. 27, p. 457.

6. Lenin, "Rech' o Voine: 9 (22) Iiunya," in Lenin, *Polnoe sobranie sochinenii*, vol. 32, p. 286.

definition in the standard dictionaries is *alliance*. The Allies in World War II were the *soiuzniki*.

After the November Revolution, the Bolsheviks controlled only the large cities of central Russia. Lenin had to organize the political system of the new country in a way that maintained control over this area but did not reduce the appeal of communism to outlying areas. Despite his reservations, he instituted a federal system. Indeed, the name he selected for the country was the Russian Soviet Federated Socialist Republic.

Lenin included only economically underdeveloped peoples and those living in the interior of Russia within the Russian Federation.[7] As socialist regimes were established in other areas, most did not become autonomous republics within the RSFSR, but separate soviet socialist republics. Such republics were established in Ukraine in December 1917, Belorussia in January 1919, Azerbaidzhan in April 1920, Armenia in November 1920, and Turkestan (what is now essentially Uzbekistan) in April 1921. These units were not formally subordinated to the Soviet government, but treaties of alliance were concluded with each of them as formally equal governments in late 1920 and early 1921.

When Lenin decided to create a federal system, he made another decision that has always been taken for granted by scholars but that was far from inevitable: he drew the boundaries of the main federal units along ethnic lines. Many in the Communist party favored the creation of federal units based on natural economic regions, with the ethnic composition of the population not being taken into account.[8] The idea had been formally proposed in the constitutional debates of April 1918 by Mikhail Reisner but was quickly rejected.

The leaders of many countries have made the opposite choice and have deliberately drawn boundaries to cut across ethnic-linguistic lines in an effort to undermine ethnic identities and power. In China, for example, members of the "Chinese" population speak languages as different as those found in Western Europe, but the regime insists the different languages are only dialects and their speakers are all Chinese, not separate nationalities. Provincial lines generally do not follow linguistic lines. In

---

7. Walter Russell Batsell, *Soviet Rule in Russia* (Macmillan, 1929), pp. 124–25, lists these autonomous republics or autonomous regions and the dates they were established.

8. Leon Trotsky, *Stalin: An Appraisal of the Man and His Influence* (Harper, 1941), p. 257.

Middle Eastern countries as diverse as Turkey, Iraq, and Iran, the Kurds find their identity as an ethnic group denied in similar fashion.

In 1918 Lenin's decisions had little immediate significance. Party organizations in non-Russian areas had always been subordinated to the central party institutions, and in 1919 the Eighth Party Congress bluntly reaffirmed this rule. The communist parties of the "independent" countries were given only the rights of a regional party committee, an obkom, of the Russian Federation. In practice the party leaders in the various parts of the country, non-Russian as well as Russian, were appointed from above. When a Ukrainian party congress elected an anti-Lenin central committee in 1920, Moscow simply declared it null and void and "elected" another one.[9]

The formality of alliance relations instead of incorporation in the RSFSR also meant little in government affairs.

> The alliance (*soiuznye*) treaties, concluded in late 1920 and early 1921 between the Soviet republics, incorporated the experience of the federative structure accumulated during the Civil War. . . . The treaties unified the state administration in the most important branches, and the united people's commissariats were included in the Council of People's Commissars of RSFSR. . . . Thus the legislative organs of the RSFSR . . . began, in fact, to act in two capacities: as organs of one of the republics (the RSFSR) and as all-federative (*obshchefederativnyi*) organs. . . . In 1921–1922 the united people's commissariats, as the higher organs of the RSFSR, gradually assumed the role of issuing decrees for the whole federation, which were reissued or "registered" in other republics in an obligatory manner.[10]

At the end of the Civil War in 1921, Lenin wanted to further regularize the political system. Such a step was necessary less to establish central control over the "independent" governments than to give them representation at the center and to increase their legitimacy as part of a federation rather than an empire. Stalin suggested that they simply be incorporated into the Russian Federation as autonomous regions, but Lenin thought this tactically unwise. He called for a formal, long-lasting alliance or union between these states.

A treaty was signed between the RSFSR, Ukraine, Belorussia, and the Transcaucasian Federation, which included Armenia, Azerbaidzhan, and Georgia, creating the Union of Soviet Socialist Republics—really an alli-

9. Robert Vincent Daniels, *The Conscience of the Revolution: Communist Opposition in Soviet Russia* (Harvard University Press, 1960), pp. 102–03.

10. V. M. Kuritsyn, *Stanovlenie sotsialiticheskoi zakonnosti* (Moscow: Nauka, 1983), pp. 155-156.

ance of Soviet socialist republics—on December 30, 1922.[11] Other republics were added over the years. When Stalin created a new Constitution in 1936, it did not mention the Union Treaty, but it formally recognized the "sovereignty" of the republics and their right to secede from the Union.

As long as a strong Communist party dominated the federal system, the formal powers of the republics did not matter. In the long run, however, the decision to draw federal boundaries on the basis of ethnicity was to have monumental consequences, all the more so when combined with the decision to grant sovereignty and the right of secession to the republics. The verbiage and legal forms were a time bomb if Moscow ever wanted to increase the powers of the republics. Because Ukraine and Belorussia were already members of the United Nations, why should membership be denied other republics, especially the larger Russian Republic? The admission of Ukraine and Belorussia to the United Nations was severely criticized by U.S. conservatives, but it was to have profound implications in the 1980s.

Lenin's and Stalin's Policy on National Identity

Most of the Soviet Union's problems involving national identity were typical of other industrializing countries. The language of the countryside is seldom the language of the city. Even in the United States Huckleberry Finn and Uncle Remus spoke very differently from Noah Webster. In the best of circumstances the question is whether peasants will assimilate the language and national identity of the city, as occurred in France a century ago, or whether their language and the national identity based on it becomes dominant, as occurred with the French in Quebec.[12]

In many modern countries the problem is more complex. There is no Nigerian, Indian, or Kuwaiti language or ethnic group. Because these countries include peoples of diverse ethnicities and languages, their governments have tried to create a sense of national identity not based on usual

11. The relevant documents and discussion of them are found in Batsell, *Soviet Rule in Russia*, pp. 300–20, 350–458, 521–36, 595–627. For a discussion of how the institutions functioned, see pp. 280–99.

12. Within the boundaries of modern France, "French was a foreign language for . . . almost half the children who would reach adulthood in the last quarter of the [nineteenth] century," and they knew more French than their parents and grandparents. Eugen Weber, *Peasants into Frenchmen: The Modernization of Rural France, 1870–1914* (Stanford University Press, 1976), p. 67.

definitions of nationality. People are taught that they are Americans rather than Irish or Italians, let alone Virginians, that they are Nigerians rather than Ibos, Kuwaitis rather than Arabs (or Iraqis). Obviously there have been leaders such as Jefferson Davis in the United States, Gamal Abdel Nasser in Egypt, and Saddam Hussein in Iraq who have spoken for different definitions of national identity. These examples remind us of the wisdom of the cynical statement based on European history: "a language is a dialect with the strongest army behind it," although David Laitin would add, "and with a strong education system." The same is true of national identity.

Perhaps the most surprising feature of Lenin's and Stalin's policy was that they made no effort to create a sense of suprarepublican national identity. In the Soviet Union, people had Soviet citizenship, but no designation such as American or Canadian was ever developed, let alone imposed, to refer to the inhabitants of the country as a whole. This definition of nationality may well have interrupted processes of Russification already under way. Russia had been largely synonymous with the Russian Empire, and in Russian, *Ukraine* means borderlands (in American terms, frontier) rather than a separate country. In 1991 Sergei Baburin, leader of a conservative congressional faction, was essentially correct when he charged that "the limitation of Russia to 'the RSFSR' . . . is the ideological inheritance of Lenin, Stalin, and Khrushchev."[13]

Lenin and Stalin defined national identity in terms of ethnicity and language rather than citizenship in the country or even republic. A Ukrainian was an ethnic Ukrainian wherever he or she lived, not a person who lived in Ukraine. When Stalin instituted domestic passports in the 1930s, he made the unnecessary decision to include nationality as information on it. Thus while citizens of the United States think of themselves as Americans regardless of ethnic origin, the Soviet state officially forced its citizens to think of themselves of Ukrainians, Uzbeks, Tadzhiks, Bashkirs, Jews, Russians, Germans, or Yakuts.

In comparative terms, the communists changed from a French (or American) definition of nationality to a German definition, but in a country with reasons to retain the French definition of the tsars.[14] Lenin probably decided

13. Interview with Sergei Baburin, "Zagovor sorvan, torzhestvuyet totalitarizm," *Rossiiskaia gazeta*, September 20, 1991, p. 2.

14. For the French and German definitions see Rogers Brubaker, *Citizenship and Nationhood in France and Germany* (Harvard University Press, 1992).

to emphasize an ethnic definition of nationality for the same tactical political reason he adopted federalism: it would make communism more acceptable to peoples still not under Moscow's control. Moreover, he seemed genuinely to believe that national identity was not an important matter; peoples of the Soviet Union would "fuse together" because of the economic unity of the country.[15] He seems to have assumed that as non-Russian villagers came into the Russian cities, they would adopt the Russian language and identity.

Certainly Lenin made little effort to recruit native-speaking members of the local nationalities into the Communist party and the local elite. Instead, one of his last political actions was to conduct a purge of the party that reduced its size by half between 1921 and 1923. He was deeply worried that "the factory workers of Russia have become far less proletarian in composition than before."[16] This suspicion of workers recently arrived from the countryside had ominous implications for the non-Russians who were still overwhelmingly peasants but who would begin coming into the city in great numbers during industrialization.

The most important republic was Ukraine, and there Lenin followed a strongly pro-Russification policy. He selected Khristian Rakovsky, one of the most pronounced Russifiers, as the head of the government. Dimitry Lebed, the second secretary of Ukraine at the beginning of 1923, expressed a view that may well have been that of Lenin himself: "Ukrainianizing the party . . . will serve the interests of the cultural movement of reactionary forces, since nationalization . . . means to adopt the lower culture of the village in preference to the higher culture of the city."[17]

Stalin made no assumption whatsoever that language and national identity were ephemeral. As early as 1921 he insisted that Ukrainianization must be supported. "It is clear that the Ukrainian nation exists, and the development of its culture is the obligation of Communists. It is impossible to go against history. It is clear that while Russian elements still predomi-

---

15. Interview with Yulian Bromlei, "Narod ne mozhet byt' malym," *Rabochaia Tribuna*, May 29, 1990, pp. 1, 2. See also Walker Connor, *The National Question in Marxist-Leninist Theory and Strategy* (Princeton University Press, 1984), pp. 36–38.

16. T. H. Rigby, *Communist Party Membership in the USSR, 1917–1967* (Princeton University Press, 1968), pp. 102–03.

17. Quoted in George Orest Liber, *Soviet Nationality Policy, Urban Growth, and Identity Change in the Ukrainian SSR, 1923–1934* (Cambridge University Press, 1992), pp. 38–40.

nate in Ukrainian cities, these cities will inevitably be Ukrainianized with the passage of time.''[18] Stalin extended this attitude to the Belorussians as well. They were one of the most rural and least nationally aware of the Soviet peoples, and the Belorussian language was close to Russian. As late as 1927, some 44 percent of the urban population in Belorussia was Jewish. Russians argued in the early 1920s that there was no need for a Belorussian republic. Stalin argued the opposite: ''Some forty years ago Riga was a German town; but since towns grew by drawing on the country, and the country is the preserver of nationality, Riga is now a purely Lettish town. Some fifty years ago all the towns of Hungary had a German character; now they are Magyarised. The same will happen with Belorussia, in the towns of which non-Belorussians still predominate.''[19]

In 1925 Stalin adopted a new formula: "socialist in content and national in form." He recognized that "a proletarian culture that is socialist in content accepts different forms and modes of expression in different peoples absorbed in a socialist construction, depending on differences in language, customs, etc."[20] This was not meaningless abstract language; it expressed a change in nationality policy. Six weeks after Lenin had been incapacitated by a stroke on March 10, 1923, Mikhail Frunze, the military commander in Ukraine, demanded a policy of Ukrainianization. On July 16 Vlas Chubar, a Ukrainian, replaced the Russifier Rakovsky as head of the government. Stalin officially proclaimed a policy of *korenizatsiia* (nativization) throughout the non-Russian areas.[21] The party organizations in each of the non-Russian territorial units were to recruit persons of the local nationality as rapidly as possible and promote them just as rapidly into the party administrative and political hierarchy. The policy was not one of nondiscrimination but of affirmative action.

When Lenin died, Stalin immediately changed policy on party admission with a massive and ironically named "Leninist enrollment" (*Leninskii prizyv*) of new members, dramatically reversing Lenin's membership policy in the name of honoring him. On January 1, 1924 (three weeks before Lenin's death), the number of members and candidate members stood at 472,000. By the beginning of 1933 there were 3,555,338. Stalin strongly

18. *Sotsial'nyi i natsional'nyi sostav VKP(b)* (Moscow: Gosudarstvennoe izdatel'stvo, 1928), p. 113.
19. I. V. Stalin, *Sochineniia*, vol. 5 (Moscow: Gospolitizdat, 1947), p. 49.
20. Stalin, *Sochineniia*, vol. 7, 138.
21. Liber, *Soviet Nationality Policy*, pp. 42–43.

emphasized class origin in party recruitment. By 1932 about 92 percent of all members were either workers or peasants, or had been so when they entered the party.[22] This policy had the most direct impact on non-Russians; the number in the party and the administrative elite who spoke non-Russian languages began to rise sharply.

When Stalin included nationality on the new domestic passports in 1934, the first decisions on national identity must have been subjective, tactical, or perhaps based on language.[23] Young people did not receive a passport until the age of sixteen, and after 1934 the nationality listed on their passport was not defined by their feelings but by the passport nationality of their parents. If both parents listed the same nationality, their children also had to list it. If the parents had different nationalities listed, the child could choose either of the two but not a different one.

This rule produced truly ridiculous cases by the 1980s. Parents in Moscow might speak Russian as their native language and be psychologically Russian, but they could have Ukrainian listed on their passport because of the origins of their own parents or grandparents. Their children had no choice but also to list themselves as Ukrainian even when they did not have the slightest connection or feeling of identity with Ukraine. It is hard to imagine a more foolish policy if the aim was long-term Russification or creation of a common sense of nationality. Robert Tucker has argued that Stalin identified psychologically with Russia,[24] but it is far more likely that he remained a Georgian at heart. This had a significant impact on his nationality policy.

At the end of his life Stalin reiterated his point of view when he intervened in a seemingly obscure scholarly dispute on linguistics. For political reasons—most immediately to insist that Eastern Europe follow the Soviet model in its entirety—he emphasized the primacy of the economic base over the social superstructure in the postwar period.[25] Some took this to

22. These figures are documented in Jerry F. Hough and Merle Fainsod, *How the Soviet Union Is Governed* (Harvard University Press, 1979), pp. 324–28.

23. For example, the number of Ukrainians fell from 31.2 million in the 1926 census to 28.1 million in the 1939 census, which is thought mostly to have been the result of redefinition of nationality. Frank Lorimer, *The Population of the Soviet Union: History and Prospects* (Geneva: League of Nations, 1946), pp. 137–39.

24. Robert C. Tucker, *Stalin as Revolutionary, 1879–1929* (Norton, 1973), pp. 137–43.

25. See Jerry F. Hough, *The Struggle for the Third World: Soviet Debates and American Options* (Brookings, 1986), pp. 110–14, 194–95.

mean that all parts of presocialist culture, including language differences, were part of the superstructure of previous class societies and therefore transitory. Stalin would have none of it: languages were part of the base, and by implication they and national differences were going to persist for a long time.[26]

The Brezhnev leadership seemed more sensitive to the problem of a common national identity than its predecessors. Brezhnev began speaking of "the formation of an historically new social and international community—the Soviet people (*narod*)." The Central Committee journal, *Kommunist*, and its editor began emphasizing Lenin's position on the "fusion" of nations. Nevertheless, at the time of the adoption of the 1977 Constitution, Brezhnev condemned those who went further and who proposed that the new Constitution refer to an "integral Soviet nation (*natsiia*)" or that it restrict the republics' sovereignty.[27]

The problem for the future was that many of the common experiences emphasized by Brezhnev to create a sense of a Soviet people were associated with the revolution, the establishment of a social system that was unique in the world, and a definition of human rights emphasizing social welfare. If central control were to be loosened and socialism were to be discredited, this effort to associate national identity with social and political achievements would backfire.

Even the name of the country posed a potential problem. Most country names are based on ethnicity, as is France, or, especially if they are multi-ethnic, on geography, as is the United States of America. But the names Union of Soviet Socialist Republics and Soviet Union had an ideological and political base. *Socialist* posed an obvious problem, but *Soviet* also did not refer to ethnic origin or a territory, but to the councils associated with an event, the Bolshevik Revolution. If socialism lost its popular support, a new name and a new base of legitimacy would have to be created—this in a country where no real attempt had been made to create a common sense of national identity.

---

26. The documents of the controversy are printed in *The Soviet Linguistic Controversy*, trans. John V. Murra, Robert M. Hankin, and Fred Holling (New York: King's Crown Press, 1951), with Stalin's statement found on pp. 70–76. Also see V. M. Alpatov, *Istoriia odnogo mifa: Marr i Marrizm* (Moscow: Nauka, 1991).

27. See the discussion and quotations in Connor, *National Question in Marxist-Leninist Theory*, pp. 402–07.

The Non-Russian Republics

The Union of Soviet Socialist Republics had four different types of ethnically based units—Union republics, autonomous republics, autonomous oblasts, and national districts. The Union republics were the "sovereign" units that officially formed the Soviet Union and were subordinated directly to the USSR government. Autonomous republics were subordinated to the Union republics, and autonomous oblasts and national districts were subordinated to the oblast governments in Russia.[28]

In general, the differences in types of names and subordination of ethnic units reflected the size of the ethnic group, but political factors were also important. Several smaller ethnic groups such as the Baltic peoples were given Union republic status to legitimize their incorporation into the Soviet Union.[29] Some Central Asian peoples whose numbers were small in the 1920s and 1930s were made separate Union republics, presumably because the leadership feared a large Turkic republic and wanted to strengthen separate national identities in the area. By contrast, the Bashkirs and Tatars, two very large ethnic groups in the center of Russia, were made autonomous republics inside Russia in hope that this action in addition to geography would facilitate Russification.

The Union republics were very different in land area and population. The Russian Republic was the size of the lower forty-eight American states and Canada combined, but Armenia was only marginally larger than the state of Maryland. As table 7-1 shows, the population of the Union republics in 1989 ranged from Russia's 147 million people (120 million of them Russians) to Estonia's 1.6 million (1.0 million of them Estonians).

This created one of the most serious obstacles to democratic decentralization. If the Soviet Union were to have a president or parliament selected on the principle of one person, one vote, Russia or Russia combined with Slavs living in other republics would have a strong majority of the voters. But if republics had equal power in voting, eight of them with 28.4 million people (10 percent of the country's population) could dominate.

28. Several autonomous oblasts in non-Russian Union republics were subordinated directly to their republics.
29. During the war with Finland in 1940, Stalin changed the Karelo-Finnish Republic from an autonomous republic to a Union republic because of the new territory and population it was expected to receive. In 1955 it was returned to the status of autonomous republic.

Table 7-1. *Population and Ethnicity of Union Republics, 1989*
Percent unless otherwise specified

Republic	Total population (in thousands)	Local nationality in republic	Russians in republic	Russians in capital
Slavic republics				
Russia	147,022	81.5	81.5	89.7
Ukraine	51,452	72.7	22.1	20.9
Belorussia	10,152	77.9	13.2	20.0
Baltics and Moldavia				
Moldavia	4,335	64.5	13.8	26.5
Lithuania	3,675	79.6	9.4	20.3
Latvia	2,667	52.0	34.0	47.4
Estonia	1,566	61.5	30.3	41.1
Central Asia and Kazakhstan				
Uzbekistan	19,810	71.4	8.3	34.0
Kazakhstan	16,464	39.7	37.8	59.2
Tadzhikistan	5,093	62.3	7.6	32.8
Kirgizia	4,258	52.4	21.5	55.9
Turkmenia	3,523	72.0	9.5	32.6
Transcaucasia				
Azerbaidzhan	7,021	82.7	5.6	18.0
Georgia	5,401	70.1	6.3	10.1
Armenia	3,305	93.3	1.6	2.0

Source: *Itogi vsesoiuznoi perepisi naseleniia 1989 goda. Tom VII. Natsional'nyi sostav naselenie SSSR* (Moscow: Finansy i statistika, 1991; and Minneapolis: East View, 1994), *Chast' 1*, pp. 66, 498; *Chast' 2*, pp. 6, 72, 154, 182, 192, 268, 296, 322, 444, 472, 484, 504, 516, 522, 524, 532, 536, 544, 548, 564, 592, 610, 636, 644, 646, 658, 690, 698.

All the Union republics, regardless of population, were legally equal, but with different histories, religions, levels of economic development, and ethnic mixes, they posed very different political problems. Table 7-1 classifies these republics into four groups, but even this involves oversimplifications. Moldavia does not fit easily into its category, and the Transcaucasian republics, while grouped administratively for years, includes three republics with different religions and traditions.

Ukraine and Belorussia

Without any question, the core Union republics in size and population were Russia, Ukraine, and Belorussia, the three Slavic republics. Together they comprised 209 million people, 73 percent of the population of the Soviet Union in 1989 (see table 7-1). Even in the 1950s John Armstrong could write that Stalin and Khrushchev treated them differently from other republics—as "younger brothers" who were more trusted.[30]

One of the crucial political questions of the early twentieth century in this region was whether these three peoples would become separate nations or basically one. The ethnic composition of the cities in Ukraine and Belorussia was largely Russian and Jewish; non-Russians showed a strong tendency to assimilate the Russian language. The countryside was populated by peasants who could be called Ukrainians and Belorussians, but who spoke a polyglot mixture of Russian, Ukrainian, Polish, Belorussian, and Lithuanian in the west and of Russian and Ukrainian in the east. "Ukrainian" peasants around Kharkov in the east could hardly understand the speech of "Ukrainian" peasants near Lvov in the west. As these peasants began to move in large numbers into the cities in the twentiethth century, the question was not whether they would have to adopt a new language, but which one—literary Ukrainian (or literary Belorussian) or literary Russian?

Belorussia was to be a republic that remained heavily Belorussian by national identification but whose citizens, or at least their children, had a strong tendency to become Russian speakers when they moved into the larger cities. In 1989 about 30 percent of Belorussians in the cities and 38 percent of those in Minsk spoke Russian as their native language. Another 27 percent of the Belorussian urban population was of another nationality, usually Russian, and almost all were either native speakers of Russian or well on their way to assimilation. Altogether the Russian speakers numbered approximately half the urban population.[31]

It is not surprising that the nationalist movement in Belorussia was to be the weakest among the republics outside central Asia. Belorussians consistently voted conservatively, and although nationalists attributed this conservatism to political control, the charge was mostly inaccurate. Indeed, after becoming independent, the Belorussians voted in 1994 to associate themselves with Russia once more.

Ukraine is a much more difficult republic to discuss because it is far more diverse than Belorussia. The eastern and southern regions are heavily urban and include a substantial proportion of Russians and Russified

30. John A. Armstrong, "The Ethnic Scene in the Soviet Union: The View of the Dictatorship," in Erich Goldhagen, ed., *Ethnic Minorities in the Soviet Union* (Praeger, 1968), pp. 14–21.

31. *Itogi vsesoiuznoi perepisi naseleniia 1989 goda. Tom VII. Natsional'ny sostav naselenie SSSR. Chast' 2* (Moscow: Finansy i statistika, 1991; and Minneapolis: East View, 1993), pp. 156–57, 182.

Ukrainians. The central regions have been the heartland of the Orthodox Ukrainian peasants. The area has begun to urbanize, but except for the capital of Kiev, it has included relatively small numbers of Russians. Although some Russification is under way, it remains very gradual. The western Ukraine was acquired by the Soviet Union in the Stalin-Hitler pact of 1939. Its percentage of Russians and Russified Ukrainians was very low, and the religion of the Ukrainians was not the Orthodox but the Uniate Church, which was closely associated with Roman Catholicism.

As table 7-2 shows, Russification was particularly notable in the cities of Ukraine. In 1989 about 34 percent of the urban population in Ukraine was not Ukrainian, and the great majority of these people spoke Russian as their native language. Virtually all their children spoke Russian as their native language. The other 66 percent of urban dwellers called themselves Ukrainians, but 19 percent spoke Russian as their native language.[32] As a result, only 54 percent of those in Ukrainian cities (and that includes small towns) would have Ukrainian as their native language. The figure was lower in the oblast capitals and other large industrial cities.

These official statistics on native language exaggerate the extent to which people use Ukrainian, especially in the larger cities. A survey conducted in Kharkov in January 1992 found that 60 percent of those persons who spoke Ukrainian as their primary language during childhood (and who presumably told the census taker Ukrainian is their native language) now speak Russian with their spouse; 67 percent of them speak Russian with their children.[33] As of 1989 only 25 percent of the children in Kiev went to Ukrainian-language schools.[34]

Western Ukraine (but not the provinces of Chernovitsy and Zakarpathia, which had been under Romanian and Hungarian control) was to become the center of the nationalist movement, Rukh. Americans sometimes talk loosely about western and eastern Ukraine as if they were equal in population, but this is far from the case. As table 7-2 shows, western Ukraine

---

32. This was true of only 2 percent of Ukrainians living in rural areas. *Itogi . . . Tom VII. Natsional'nyi sostav, Chast' 2*, pp. 12, 18.

33. Survey conducted by Jerry F. Hough and Susan Goodrich Lehmann, funded by the Carnegie Corporation. There were 2,000 respondents.

34. Dominique Arel, "The Parliamentary Blocs in the Ukrainian Supreme Soviet: Who and What Do They Represent?" *Journal of Soviet Nationalities*, vol. 1 (Winter 1990–91), p. 133. Arel's figures refer to the oblast as a whole, but the large cities are more Russified than the rural areas and small towns and an impression of the Russification can be gathered from the percentage of urban population in the regions.

Table 7-2. *Assimilation in Ukraine, by Region, 1991*
Percent unless otherwise specified

Region	Total population (millions)	Urban population	Ethnic Russians in urban population	Ukranians with Russian as native language	Urban citizens with Russian as native language	Capital citizens with Russian as native language	Percent supporting Union, March 1991
Kiev City	n.a.	100	21	21	—	21	45
Eastern	17.3	83	36	26	62	70	81
Southern	7.6	66	33	20	69	72	84
Central	14.3	54	9	4	22	22	79
Western	7.5	47	4	1	14	20	32
Others	2.1	42	5	2	30	38	61

Source: Dominque Arel, "The Parliamentary Blocs in the Ukranian Supreme Soviet: Who and What Do They Represent?" *Journal of Soviet Nationalities*, vol. 1 (Winter 1990–91), pp. 133–34.
n.a. Not available.

included only 7.5 million people, while the eastern and southern regions had 24.9 million.

Even if Ukraine became independent, it would be impossible to impose Ukrainian as the main language of instruction or business discourse in the east or center for a long period without risking a popular backlash. The eastern and southern cities were likely to be speaking Russian for decades, and the possibility of their secession or annexation by Russia would be real for years. Western Ukraine was certain to remain nationalistic.

The more rural central area posed an interesting puzzle. On the one hand, as its inhabitants moved into the larger cities, they could see a possibility of ensuring the predominance of the Ukrainian language in the cities, and they had an interest in doing so. On the other hand, the peasants were Orthodox, while western Ukraine was Uniate, a church closely associated with the Catholic Church.

In the past this religious difference had had an enormous significance. Although the Bolshevik Revolution took place in November 1917, it actually was won on the battleground during the Civil War. When Lenin tried to reconstitute the old Russian Empire during the Civil War, he succeeded in many areas but not all. Religion was crucial. Roman Catholic Poland and Lithuania, and Protestant Estonia, Finland, and Latvia became independent.

The "correct" border between Ukraine and Poland was ambiguous. In ethnic terms it was more or less that which British Lord Curzon proposed at the time of the Versailles Conference and which Stalin and Hitler imposed in 1939. In religious terms the border should have been further east because the westernmost Ukrainians were Uniate. If religion defined the border, these people should have been in Catholic Poland. When the border was determined on the battlefield in 1920, the Bolsheviks could not conquer the Catholic areas, and they remained within Catholic Poland until 1939. The Red Army must have received better support or tolerance from the Orthodox villages through which its units passed and less from the Catholic villages. In the 1980s the religious line remained an important political divide and the Catholic western Ukraine was more nationalist, but the relative impact of religion and language in central Ukraine remained unclear.

The Baltic Republics and Moldavia

Without any question, religion mattered in the Baltic states. Just as the Christian Serbs in Bosnia greatly feared being placed once more under the control of the Bosnian Moslems, and the Christian Armenians in Nagorno-Karabakh had a similar fear about the Moslem Azerbaidzhani, so the Protestant and Catholic peoples in Eastern Europe and the Soviet Union felt very restive under Orthodox control. This was to lead to secession by the Catholic Croats and Slovenes from the Orthodox Serbs in Yugoslavia and to a major secession movement in the Baltic republics.

The Baltic states had long been part of the Russian Empire, and the Latvian capital of Riga had been the empire's major western port. During the Civil War the three states gained their independence and maintained it during the interwar period. The Stalin-Hitler pact of 1939 acknowledged that they were within the Soviet sphere of influence and took the historical Lithuanian capital of Vilnius from Poland (where it was called Vilno, populated overwhelmingly by Poles and Jews) and gave it to the Soviet Union. In 1939 Stalin demanded defense treaties with the Baltic countries, and in 1940 he incorporated them into the Soviet Union.

The Baltic republics were always described as a unit in the West, and they were treated as a nearly insuperable problem for Moscow. In fact, the relationship among the Estonians, Latvians, and Lithuanians was somewhat tense, and little movement of people occurred among the three republics, especially between Catholic Lithuania and Protestant Estonia and Latvia. Thus in 1989 there were more Uzbeks in Vilnius, the capital of Lithuania, than Latvians and Estonians combined, and very few of any of the three.[35]

---

35. Mikhail Guboglo, "Demography and Language in the Capitals of the Union Republics," *Journal of Soviet Nationalities*, vol. 1 (Winter 1990–91), p. 16.

But whatever the political problems Moscow had in the Baltic areas, it did not face a military challenge in maintaining control. The three republics together totaled only 8 million people, less than 3 percent of the total population of the USSR. Besides, many of the urban areas of Latvia and Estonia contained a high proportion of Russian speakers. The northern city of Narva in Estonia was virtually all Russian, while the population of the second largest Latvian city, Daugavpils, was only 13 percent Latvian.[36]

The ethnic situation was mixed even in the capitals of the Baltic republics. The local population totaled more than 36 percent of the population in the capital in Latvia, 47 percent in Estonia, and 50 percent in Lithuania. Lithuania remained 32 percent rural and the proportion of Lithuanians in Vilnius was growing.[37] But in the Estonian and Latvian capitals the proportion of ethnic Estonians and Latvians was persistently declining (in 1959 about 60 percent of the population of Tallinn had been Estonian and 45 percent of the population of Riga had been Latvian). The sense that these trends might continue and lead to the permanent dominance of Russians in the republics and the gradual disappearance of the local nation and culture was a powerful emotional factor in the nationality movements, but the emotions were never strong enough to make significant armed resistance either likely or physically possible.

Moldavia was both similar to and different from the Baltic republics. Like the Lithuanian capital of Vilnius, the Moldavian capital of Kishinev had a population that was only 50 percent of the local nationality in 1989. But like Lithuania, Moldavia was rural, and Moldavians would eventually come to dominate the capital (in 1959 only 32 percent of Kishinev's population had been Moldavian). The eastern part of Moldavia had long been in Russia, but western Moldavia (known as Bessarabia) had been part of Romania between the wars. Western Moldavia was incorporated into the Soviet Union at essentially the same time as the Baltic republics.[38]

The divided history of Moldavia left its impact on the republic and on its independence movement. The major cities of pre-1940 Moldavia contained a very large percentage of Russians, Ukrainians, and (at least before the emigration of the 1970s and 1980s) Jews. Western Moldavia was more

---

36. Juris Dreifelds, "Immigration and Ethnicity in Latvia," *Journal of Soviet Nationalities*, vol. 1 (Winter 1990–91), p. 55.

37. *Naselenie SSSR, 1988: Statisticheskii ezhegodnik* (Moscow: Finansy i statistika, 1989), p. 22.

38. Guboglo, "Demography and Language," p. 7.

rural and more heavily Moldavian, although with Bulgarian and Gagauz minorities. The Moldavian language was essentially identical with Romanian, and the more radical nationalists demanded not independence but union with Romania. This was far more alarming to the Russian speakers of Moldavia than independence was to the Russian speakers of the Baltic republics. The major eastern cities were to establish their own Dneisterian republic to separate from Moldavia. General Aleksandr Lebed was to make his reputation with his military defense of this area from Moldavia's efforts to establish its authority there.

The Transcaucasus

The Transcaucasian republics were peculiar for many reasons. The three major peoples—Armenians, Azerbaidzhani, and Georgians—had civilizations that extended into antiquity, and they had strong senses of identity. In 1958 an Intourist guide in Georgia was very pointed in emphasizing to a visitor how much older the Georgian civilization was than that of Kievan Rus. He clearly meant to associate length of civilization with the extent to which a people was civilized at the present time.

The Transcaucasian peoples' long history had, however, led not to integration but to memories of ancient enemies. The Georgians and Armenians had their own Christian churches, and the Georgians historically had considered the Shiite Persians their feared oppressors. The Armenians had very bad memories of their relationship with the Turks. The Azerbaidzhani were Moslem Shiite Turks, and many lived across the border in Iran where they had assimilated into Iranian society. They engendered hostility from the Armenians and a combination of suspicion and disdain from the Georgians. A small enclave of Armenians lived within Azerbaidzhan and had been given a separate autonomous oblast called Nagorno-Karabakh, but it was administratively subordinated to Azerbaidzhan.[39] This created no serious problems when the political system was strongly centralized and Azerbaidzhan had relatively little power, but it was to prove explosive as the system became more decentralized in the late 1980s.

Despite the differences among the Transcaucasian peoples, they had been united into a Transcaucasian Federation before 1936. Stalin was a Georgian, and Lavrenty Beria was party first secretary of the federation from 1931 to 1936. Even after 1936 the party first secretaries of

---

39. In 1989 the region had 189,000 people.

Azerbaidzhan and Armenia were to be very close to Stalin and Beria. For this reason the Transcaucasian leaders were traditionally given more independence in running their own affairs than leaders in other republics.

The Armenians occupied a peculiar place within the Soviet Union. Like the Jews and Poles, they had traditionally been involved in trade and lived throughout the Soviet Union. They were the nationality with a Union republic, the largest percentage of whose number lived outside the republic.[40] Yet Armenia itself contained a very small percentage of Russians. Even in the capital of Yerevan, only 4 percent of the population was Russian in 1959 and just 2 percent in 1989. (The proportion of Armenians in Yerevan increased from 93 percent of the population to 97 percent during these years.) The Armenians in the diaspora had almost all assimilated to Russian, but almost no such assimilation occurred inside Armenia. More than 99 percent of the Armenians in Yerevan spoke Armenian as their native language in 1989, and 61 percent spoke Russian as a second language, up from 36 percent in 1959.[41]

The situation within Georgia was similar. The republic included several significant minorities in outlying regions (notably the Ossetians and the Abkhazians), but the capital, Tbilisi (formerly Tiflis) had been the major trade, military, and transportation center of the Transcaucasus and had always been a multiethnic city. In 1959 some 22 percent of the capital's population was Armenian, compared with 48 percent Georgian and 18 percent Russian. Thirty years later, however, the proportion of Georgians had risen to 66 percent, while that of the Armenians and Russians had declined to 12 percent and 10 percent, respectively.[42] Almost none of the Georgians spoke Russian as their native language and only one-third spoke it as a second language.

Azerbaidzhan had been the site of the first major oil field of the Russian Empire, and in the process it had acquired a substantial Russian working class. In 1959 about 35 percent of the population of Baku, the Azerbaidzhani capital, was Russian, 33 percent Azeri, and 21 percent Armenian. Yet as in Tbilisi, the percentage of the indigenous population in Baku had risen to 62 percent by 1989 and that of the Russians and Armenians had declined to 18 percent and 12 percent, respectively.[43] Similarly,

40. Armstrong, "Ethnic Scene in the Soviet Union," pp. 11–12.
41. Guboglo, "Demography and Language," pp. 22–23.
42. Guboglo, "Demography and Language," p. 26.
43. Guboglo, "Demography and Language," p. 25.

almost no Azeris had adopted Russian as their native language. In the growing unrest over Nagorno-Karabakh, Armenians increasingly fled from the Azerbaidzhan cities or were driven out.

Central Asia and Kazakhstan

The Georgians and Armenians were the most highly educated peoples with their own Union republics, and their republics had substantial industry. Central Asia and Kazakhstan were the most underdeveloped areas of the Soviet Union. The population was mostly Moslem and spoke a Turkish language (the Tadzhiks, however, were a Persian people who spoke a dialect of Farsi). The area contained considerable mining and metal processing, but the mainstay of the economy in central Asia and southern Kazakhstan was irrigated agriculture, especially cotton farming.

Central Asia (the republics of Kirgizia, Tadzhikistan, Turkmenia, and Uzbekistan) was 34.9 percent urban in 1959 and 38.0 percent in 1970. But because Brezhnev emphasized investment in irrigation in central Asia rather than in industry, the amount of irrigated land increased by 52 percent between 1965 and 1985. Without such an expansion of acreage, the rapidly growing population would have had to begin migrating in large numbers to the cities, or cotton production would have had to be replaced with food production for local subsistence.[44]

The expansion allowed the rural population to remain in the countryside, which was almost surely the purpose of the investment program. The population soared from 12.3 million people in 1970 to 19.8 million in 1989. The percentage of rural population actually rose from 59.3 percent in 1979 to 60.4 percent in 1989. Such a reversal was unique in world history.[45]

The Central Asian cities had been overwhelmingly ethnic Russian. In 1989 this remained true in some cases (table 7-3). Nevertheless, the rapid growth of the countryside meant that a major migration of people to the cities was eventually inevitable. Beginning in the 1970s, many Westerners saw imminent unrest and revolt in Central Asia, but modernization theory suggests that such developments are unlikely until the large-scale migration to the cities begins. The theory proved correct in the 1980s as the Central Asian republics were to be the only quiet ones during the revolution.

---

44. Gregory Gleason, "Marketization and Migration: The Politics of Cotton in Central Asia," *Journal of Soviet Nationalities*, vol. 1 (Summer 1990), pp. 73–74.
45. Gleason, "Marketization and Migration," pp. 73–74.

Table 7-3. *Indigenous Population in Central Asian Capitals, 1959, 1989*
Percent

Capitals	1959	1989
Alma-Ata, Kazakhstan	8.6	22.5
Ashkhabad, Turkmenia	29.8	50.8
Bishkek, Kirgizia	9.4	22.7
Dushanbe, Tadzhikistan	18.5	38.3
Tashkent, Uzbekistan	33.8	44.2

Source: Mikhail Guboglo, "Demography and Language in the Capitals of the Union Republics," *Journal of Soviet Nationalities*, vol. 1 (Winter 1990–91), pp. 29–33.

However, the theory suggests that for the future the situation looks ominous.

The one republic that differed distinctively from the others in Central Asia was Kazakhstan. It was a large republic with a population of 16.5 million. The southern oblasts were very similar to those in Central Asia; the northern oblasts, however, were heavily Slavic. The northern wheat-growing areas had been settled by Russians and Ukrainians in the mid-1950s during the Virgin Land program launched by Nikita Khrushchev, and large cities in the northern and central regions were populated mostly by Russians.

As a result, 39.7 percent of the people of Kazakhstan were Kazakhs, 37.8 percent were Russians, 5.8 percent Germans, and 5.4 percent Ukrainians.[46] The Kazakhs had a higher birthrate, the Germans were emigrating, and any end of agricultural subsidies would threaten the continued existence of the Virgin Lands and force the Russians off the land. One could imagine a sharp increase of tension in which Kazakh nationalists tried to accelerate the outflow of non-Kazakhs and quickly tip the ethnic balance. But one could also imagine an effort by the Russian government to annex the northern regions, especially if given a pretext by attacks on local Russians and Ukrainians. Fear of such a development should counteract the impulse to nationalist actions. The Kazakhstan leader, Nursultan Nazarbaev, seemed deeply aware of this fact and was to be the non-Russian leader most committed to the preservation of the Soviet Union. Still, the situation remained troublesome.

In general, however, the non-Russian but Russified and Westernized elites in Central Asia and Kazakhstan had to understand that they would be swept away like those in Iran if a political movement based on migrants

46. *Itogi . . . Tom VII. National'nyi sostav, Chast' 2*, p. 296.

from the countryside were victorious. Even after independence in 1991, the local urban elites had to understand that their fates were tied to Russians and Russia. Once the market began driving the local population off the farms, they surely would provide the base for a successful radical movement unless they were free to migrate to the north out of the republic.

The National Identity of the Russians

Most observers assumed that the main problem Gorbachev faced in reorganizing the Soviet federal system was that non-Russians had no countrywide sense of national entity, while their republics had formal powers well beyond those normal in a federal system. There seemed little glue to hold the country together once centrifugal forces were unleashed. This, however, was a superficial analysis. The centrifugal forces in the Soviet Union were less explosive than in most countries of the third world and were counterbalanced by a recognition of the tight economic integration of the country. The Soviet leadership had long followed a policy of affirmative action, which meant that the great majority of the non-Russians did not feel their careers blocked by the existing political system.

Gorbachev's really difficult nationality problem was posed by the Russians. Unless Russia were given the same rights and powers as the other republics, it alone would have to be administered directly by central institutions. Indeed, during 1990 and 1991 non-Russians were accused of making proposals that would have precisely that effect. Yet because in practice the central institutions were not likely to treat the other republics much differently from Russia, the establishment of a real federal system depended on Russia's becoming a normal republic. Whether the Soviet Union was to be communist or democratic, preventing the officials of Russia from dominating the federation would be a major difficulty.

The creation of a federal system was further complicated by problems faced by the Russians in adjusting to a new national identity as Russians. Communist leaders had long identified themselves with Russian patriotism and nationalism, but it was a superpower nationalism they had promoted, not an ethnically centered one. Lenin's distinctive contribution to Marxist theory was to emphasize an elite, highly centralized political party, and in the conditions in Russia at the time, this inevitably meant the strict subordination of non-Russian areas to Moscow. On other matters Lenin was also a strong centralizer. His opponents within the radical Marxist movement, the Mensheviks, consistently took the opposite side of the argument.

Lenin talked as if a successful Bolshevik Revolution were conditional on a world revolution that would leave Russia on the periphery. However, neither the Russians nor the non-Russians seem to have taken these statements seriously. Both voted as if they assumed that Lenin was really talking about the relationship of Moscow to the non-Russian areas after the revolution. At the 1902 Congress at which the split between Bolsheviks and Mensheviks occurred, the Russian delegates tended to support the Bolsheviks and non-Russians the Mensheviks. This difference in ethnic support was also apparent in the voting patterns for the deputies elected to the consultative parliament (the Duma) after the Revolution of 1905 and again in the December 1917 election of delegates to the Constituent Assembly (the Belorussians were an exception).

Stalin's passport policy meant that Russians identified themselves as *russkie*, but implicitly they identified their motherland (*rodina*) with the Soviet Union as a whole. Yury Arutiunian, the great Soviet ethnographer, pointed to the crucial indicator: the difference in the behavior of Russians and non-Russians when they moved to a different republic.

> [In Soviet ethnography] the concept of "nation" was applied to a "nationality" with its own territory that was unconditionally linked to its own culture. The various ethnic groups living outside their own republic behaved more like "nationalities" and were so treated in the literature. . . . We need to make an exception for the Russians in the Soviet Union, for in other republics as well as their own, they remained—at least until the most recent time—a nation with a united concept of an "all-Union" territory. Wherever they lived they actively used their own language and almost always clung only to their own culture.[47]

That is, when Russians moved into a non-Russian republic, they believed and acted as if they were at home. When Spaniards moved to Catalonia, they assumed that they and especially their children would need to learn Catalan even though Catalonia was still in Spain.[48] Russians in most non-Russian republics did not learn the local language, but assumed the local population should learn Russian.

---

47. Yuri Arutiunian, "Changing Values of Russians from Brezhnev to Gorbachev," *Journal of Soviet Nationalities*, vol. 2 (Summer 1991), p. 21.

48. David Laitin, "The Four Nationality Games and Soviet Politics," *Journal of Soviet Nationalities*, vol. 3 (Spring 1990), pp. 13–18.

In actuality, the Russians' knowledge of the local language varied greatly from republic to republic (table 7-4). If they were a tiny minority in the capital of a republic (and this was the case only in the Transcaucasian republics of Armenia, Georgia, and increasingly Azerbaidzhan), they learned the local language as a second language out of practical necessity. In the Slavic republics of Ukraine and Belorussia where the languages were very similar to Russian, they usually developed the ability to understand the local language, even if they did not speak it fluently. In the other republics, however, the percentage of bilingual speakers was extraordinarily low, and many bilingual "Russians" were really products of mixed marriages who had chosen to call themselves Russian. With such self-identification it is unlikely that their children would be as bilingual.

Although it might be thought that Russians answered census questions about fluency in a second language with excessive modesty, more sophisticated sociological surveys with more differentiated questions revealed surprisingly high numbers of Russian respondents in Tallinn and Tashkent who claimed no knowledge or very little knowledge of the local language (table 7-5).

If the status of the Union republics changed significantly, Russians living within them would be treated very differently. As early as autumn 1988 the republics were beginning to pass language laws that made strong demands on those not knowing the local language. Russians, like the English in Quebec, would have to adjust to language competence examinations in the job market, and they would be increasingly inconvenienced in other areas of life as well.[49] In addition, Russians would have to identify more with Russia as a republic; they would have to become *Rossiane* (inhabitants of the Russian republic) more than *Russkie*. The power of Russians over other peoples in the Soviet Union would be reduced.

Thus Russians needed to have the sense that they, like the peoples of other Union republics, would as a people be gaining from reform rather than losing. Otherwise they would be vulnerable to appeals to wounded national pride by right-wing extremists. Gorbachev seemed to understand this problem from the beginning. Because economic reform and the creation of a real federal system were going to benefit non-Russians disproportionately, he wanted to create support for reform by maximizing the

---

49. See Albert S. Pigolkin and Marina S. Studenikina, "Republican Language Laws in the USSR: A Comparative Analysis," *Journal of Soviet Nationalities*, vol. 3 (Spring 1991), pp. 38–76, for the complexity of the issues raised by the language laws.

Table 7-4. *Russians Living in Republican Capitals Who Know the Local Language, 1979, 1989*

	1988	1979		1989	
City and Republic	Percent intermarry[a]	Number of Russians	Percent bilingual[b]	Number of Russians	Percent bilingual[b]
Alma-Ata, Kazakhstan	7.5	590,932	0.5	660,522	0.6
Ashkhabad, Turkmenia	8.0	126,674	1.2	129,507	1.7
Baku, Azerbaidzhan	4.1	229,873	6.4	213,936	12.2
Bishkek, Kirgizia	6.4	323,595	0.6	340,799	0.6
Dushanbe, Tadzhikistan	11.5	192,016	1.4	194,459	2.3
Erevan, Armenia	3.0	26,141	38.3	21,754	43.3
Kiev, Ukraine	35.6	474,447	41.8	534,798	47.3
Kishinev, Moldavia	27.1	149,743	9.3	174,577	11.1
Minsk, Belorussia	34.6	277,166	23.3	316,471	24.8
Riga, Latvia	33.1	382,049	16.9	430,555	19.6
Tallinn, Estonia	16.1	162,714	12.2	197,187	15.4
Tashkent, Uzbekistan	7.3	674,440	3.9	699,262	3.5
Tbilisi, Georgia	13.1	129,122	24.4	124,825	34.5
Vilnius, Lithuania	13.2	105,618	25.6	116,618	31.6

Source: Census data from Guboglo, "Demography and Language" p. 40. Intermarriage data from "Data on Ethnic Intermarriages," *Journal of Soviet Nationalities*, vol. 1 (Summer 1990), pp. 170–71.
a. Percentages in this column are based on total population of each republic.
b. Bilingual means the respondent claimed to speak Russian freely (*svobodno*) either as a first or second language.

number of Russians on the Politburo. In that way ethnic Russians would be responsible for reducing Moscow's control over other peoples.

The Economic Grievances of Russia

The fact that the leaders of Russia had relatively little power in the Soviet Union had had few adverse consequences except for the leaders themselves. The Soviet system was overcentralized, and the creation of a strong Russian government between the central and regional institutions would have only concentrated more power in Moscow. The old system at least had the advantage that the regional Russian leaders dealt directly with the top decisionmakers in Moscow, not with second-echelon officials.

As long as the basic character of the Soviet system was not to be changed, the Russian regions resented not the absence of a powerful Russian republic but the presence of special status for the other Union republics, especially the small ones. Five years after he had ceased being oblast party first secretary in Sverdlovsk, Yury Petrov still fumed when compar-

Table 7-5. *Fluency in Local Language among Russians in Tashkent,*
1974, and Tallinn, 1974, 1988, by Length of Residence
Percent

Length of residence	Fully fluent	Fluent enough	Spoke with difficulty	Spoke with greater difficulty	Spoke not at all
Fluency in Uzbek, Tashkent, 1974[a]					
Less than 10 years	2	4	11	18	65
10 years or more	1	4	11	23	61
Native born	5	5	11	19	59
Fluency in Estonian, Tallinn, 1974					
Less than 10 years	1	5	14	12	68
10 years or more	3	7	18	28	44
Native born	16	22	28	24	10
Fluency in Estonian, Tallinn, 1988					
Less than 10 years	0	3	9	25	63
10 years or more	3	3	22	28	44
Native born	11	20	24	29	16

Source: Yuri Arutíunian, "Changing Values of Russias from Brezhnev to Gorbachev," *Journal of Soviet Nationalities*, vol. 2 (Summer 1991), pp. 26–27.
a. For fluency in Uzbek in Tashkent in 1988, figures by length of residence are not available, but the overall figures indicate little change. To the extent change has occurred, it seems 5 percent knew Uzbek fluently or fluently enough, 26 percent spoke with difficulty or great difficulty, and 69 percent did not speak Uzbek.

ing his position to that of the party first secretary of Estonia. Sverdlovsk region contained 4.7 million people in 1989 and was a major industrial center. Estonia had 1.6 million people and was economically insignificant.[50] Yet Estonia (like other Union republics) sent a large mission to Moscow to serve as the republic's lobby (and to take care of the first secretary and his hotel arrangements when he came to the capital). Sverdlovsk and its first secretary had no such representation in Moscow, and Petrov thought the situation outrageously unfair.[51]

Once the economic reform began, however, the situation changed. The Russians had long thought that the non-Russians, especially the non-Slavs, lived much better than themselves. This feeling had its roots in the days when Stalin had paid very low prices for grain, the basic agricultural product of Russia, and much higher prices for crops such as cotton, sunflower seeds, grapes, and fruits that were grown in the non-Russian south. Their belief was expressed in the popular *derevenchiki* (village writers) literature of the 1970s, but by the 1980s it had little basis in reality, except

50. *Itogi . . . Tom VII. Natsional'nyi sostav, Chast' 1*, p. 596.
51. Jerry Hough, interview with Yury Petrov, Duke University, April 25, 1993.

perhaps in Baltic, Georgian, and Armenian republics where the populace was highly educated.

After world oil prices shot up in the 1970s, the question arose as to whether the Russians might live better if they sold their oil and gas at market prices instead of at subsidized prices to the East Europeans and, especially, the non-Russian republics. But the subsidies, if any, were part of a network of prices, none of which reflected market values, and the issue was far too confusing to become politically salient. As long as foreign trade was centralized and the ruble was pegged at an artificially high value against the dollar, the world market price for commodities had little meaning for enterprises and regional officials. Russian resentments at the "wealthy" non-Russians arose primarily from the high prices the non-Russians charged for their fruits, vegetables, and spices at Russian collective farm markets and had little political relevance.

At the end of the 1980s and the beginning of the 1990s, however, significant changes occurred. One was psychological. A number of nationalists, especially in the Baltics, began to talk not only about Russian political domination but also Russian economic exploitation. As the USSR minister of finances at the time was later to complain bitterly, all republics in 1989 calculated that the goods they were exporting to other republics were worth more than those they were receiving.[52] The other republics were demanding "republican *khozraschet*" (essentially equitable prices for the goods that were imported and exported into the republics), and all believed, or at least said, this would be beneficial to them. The Russians, who had long been convinced that they were the exploited ones and who were the source of cheap oil and gas for other republics, had a strong urge to give the non-Russians what they wanted and let them suffer as they paid hard currency prices for Russian commodities.

A second change was produced by the law on enterprises of June 1987. The law gave the enterprises greater financial independence from the ministries and is best known for contributing to the unjustified expansion of wages in the last years of the Soviet Union. But it also reduced the role of the ministry in funding housing, day care, medical care, and other social needs of enterprise workers. These needs were now to be financed more out of the profits of the enterprise.

---

52. Valentin Pavlov, *Avgust iznutri. Gorbachevputch* (Moscow: Delovoi mir, 1993), p. 16.

Although the law did not end subsidies, it did give added importance to the prices enterprises were allowed to charge for their products. Enterprises that were selling overpriced goods found it easier to acquire profits and therefore funds to finance their workers' social needs. Those whose goods were underpriced had to plead for still greater subsidies to cover not only production, but social needs as well.

As early as the spring of 1989, *Sovetskaia Rossiia*, the conservative newspaper that carried the famous letter of Nina Andreeva, was publishing long articles about the economic imbalances between Russia and the republics. Gennady I. Fil'shin, head of the regional economics department of the major Irkutsk economics institute (and a future deputy premier of Russia), complained that the below-market pricing of timber had a deleterious effect on Russia that was felt with particular force in Siberia. With the greater financial independence of the enterprises, the low price of timber meant a lower standard of living for Siberian workers.[53] Fil'shin was a radical, but Nikolai I. Maslennikov, the conservative chairman of the Russian Gosplan, basically agreed: "I think that it is time to extend the slogan 'Each according to his labor' to territories [as well as to individuals]."[54]

For similar reasons the newspaper of the Ministry of Timber Industry was enthusiastic about economic sovereignty in 1990. Noting that Russia produced 92 percent of the country's timber and 98 percent of its wood pulp, it demanded market prices for these products.[55] On the eve of the First Congress it published a long interview with Sergei N. Baburin, a jurist from Omsk who was to be described as a reactionary in 1992. Baburin was passionate in his desire "to revive [*vosrozhdat'*] the real sovereignty of Russia." He favored the "liquidation of the dictatorship of Union ministries" and even supported the right of Russia to suspend USSR laws that contradicted the Russian Constitution.[56]

The third change at the end of the 1980s was the widening of the Soviet Union's opening to the world economy. As foreign trade became more decentralized and the opportunity, illegal as well as legal, arose to export commodities, producers became acutely aware of the hard-currency value

53. Interview with G. I. Fil'shin, "Khozraschet Sibiri," *Sovetskaia Rossiia*, March 24, 1989, p. 1.

54. Interview with N. Maslennikov, "Suverenitet na khozraschet," *Sovetskaia Rossiia*, April 21, 1989, p. 2.

55. V. Markov and V. Raskin, "Otkrytie I s"ezda narodnykh deputatov RSFSR," *Lesnaia promyshlennost'*, May 17, 1990, p. 1.

56. *Lesnaia promyshlennost'*, May 15, 1990, p. 1.

of their product. Indeed, when the ruble began to fall to artificially low levels against foreign currency, producers acquired an unrealistically optimistic view of the value of their goods.

Finally, of course, the expanding discussion of privatization made managers and workers realize that the loss of subsidized commodity prices would soon begin to have an impact on their personal wealth. In addition, the decision as to who would have the power to privatize—the USSR ministries or the republics—would be vital, for it would affect who would be in a position to distribute and obtain property. The 500-Day Plan, which came to dominate media discussion in the summer and early fall of 1990, dramatically affected the thinking of political and administrative officials. The plan called for rapid and total privatization. Even those who thought it unrealistic knew that if a plan allowing total privatization was being seriously discussed, substantial privatization was a real possibility.

The Problem of the Autonomous Republics

When Soviet leaders and reformers began to talk about returning power to the republics, most assumed that the discussion concerned the Union republics. Similarly, when the subject of privatizing state property was raised, it was followed by the obvious question: "Which state owned the property, the USSR or the republics?" It was generally assumed that *republics* meant *Union republics.*

But there was, of course, another kind of republic, the so-called autonomous republic and autonomous oblasts, which was subordinated not to the central government but to a Union republic or oblast. Twenty-one of twenty-eight of them were in Russia and contained 89 percent of the total population of such units in the country. But even these varied greatly in size, population, and ethnic composition (table 7-6). Many were small, but some were more populous than the Baltic republics. The leaders of these autonomous republics could ask why they should be treated differently from the Union republics.

Moreover, nearly 60 percent of the people (12.4 million of 21.5 million) of the autonomous republics in Russia were of a nationality other than the one that gave their republic its name, and a large proportion of them (9.1 million) were Russians.[57] As in the Baltic republics the nationalists in the autonomous republics were concerned that they were being outnumbered

57. See table 7-6 source note.

Table 7-6. *Ethnic Composition of Population in the Autonomous Republics of the Russian Soviet Federated Socialist Republic, and Religion of the Indigenous Population, 1989*

Autonomous republic	Total population	Percent Russian	Percent indigenous population	Percent indigenous population with Russian as native language	Percent indiginous population who speak Russian with mother
Nationalities that traditionally accepted Russian Orthodoxy					
Chuvashia	1,338,000	26.7	67.8	15.0	14.0
Karelia	790,000	73.6	10.0	48.3	33.0
Komi	1,251,000	57.7	23.3	25.6	29.0
Mari	749,000	47.5	43.3	11.6	22.0
Mordovia	964,000	60.8	32.5	11.5	20.0
N Osetia	632,000	29.9	53.0	1.8	18.0
Udmurtia	1,606,000	58.9	30.9	24.3	28.0
Yakutia	1,094,000	50.3	33.4	4.9	10.0
Nationalities that traditionally accepted Islam					
Bashkiria	3,943,000	39.3	21.9	4.6	12.0
Ch-Ing	1,270,000	23.1	70.7	0.2	1.0
Dagestan	1,802,000	9.2	80.2	0.8	7.0
Kab-Balk	754,000	31.9	57.6	1.1	7.0
Tataria	3,642,000	43.3	48.5	3.3	15.0
Nationalities that traditionally accepted Buddhism					
Buriatia	1,038,000	69.9	24.0	10.6	25.0
Kalmykia	323,000	37.7	45.4	3.9	52.0
Tuva	309,000	32.0	64.3	0.9	3.0

Source: *Itogi . . . Tom VII. Natsional'nyi sostav, Chast' 1*, pp. 104, 110, 116, 126, 136, 142, 148, 158, 164, 168, 178, 184, 190, 202, 206.

by other peoples within their own republics and that their ethnic group would be increasingly Russified. They demanded "sovereignty" equivalent to that of the Union republics. The question of whether republics within Russia could be sovereign within a truly sovereign Russia was to precipitate one of the thorniest political battles of 1990 and 1991. The fact that their peoples had been assigned a lower status than had those in a Union republic suggested to them only that they had been more mistreated by Stalin and deserved greater consideration.

Similarly, why should the governments of the Union republics be the only legitimate claimants to state property? One of the most vigorous legislators raising such questions was Vladislav Arzhinba, chair of the Presidium of the Supreme Soviet of the Abkhazia Autonomous Republic (population 525,000), but Bashkiria, Checheno-Ingushetia, Tataria, and

Yakutia, republics with significant oil, gold, or diamond resources were also vocal on the subject. It was not a coincidence that these four were to harbor the strongest independence movements.

It soon became clear that the claims of the autonomous republics had to be taken seriously. When Gorbachev announced in early 1988 that a plenary session of the Central Committee should be held on nationality policy, ethnic problems erupted almost immediately, but they were among the peoples of autonomous republics and regions (or peoples seeking such status), not the more nationalistic-oriented Union republics. The unrest, it should be noted, was not directed against Moscow or local Russians, but against the policy or feared policy of the local Union republic.

The reason was simple. Although no one knew how much Gorbachev would change nationality policy, everyone understood that the powers of the Union republics would be increased. This was frightening to minorities in these republics because the majority elites had been more insistent on the assimilation of small groups to their nationality and language than had distant Moscow. The minorities looked to Moscow as their protector against local authorities, and they wanted guarantees or even independence if these authorities were to be given greater power. The prospect of privatization intensified their concern: the Union republican authorities would surely discriminate against them in the distribution of property.

The first major demonstrations occurred in the autonomous oblast of Nagorno-Karabakh, populated mostly by ethnic Armenians but located within and subordinated to Azerbaidzhan, a republic based on a Moslem Turkish people. The Armenians feared that greater Azerbaidzhani power might lead to the kind of repression of Armenians seen in Turkey in the early twentieth century. The demonstrations intensified and became increasingly violent. The Abkhazy, a people who constituted only 18 percent of the population in the Abkhazian autonomous republic inside Georgia, began their own demonstrations, fearing that a stronger Georgia would conduct a policy of forced Georgification. Serious protests also arose among the Gagauz and Ukrainians in Moldavia and the Uzbeks in Kirgizia.

By 1990 little violence had occurred in the autonomous republics of the Russian Republic, but there had been a good deal of political unrest. (The serious problems with the Chechen-Ingush Autonomous Republic, which later split into the Chechnya and Ingushetia Republics, were to occur only as the Soviet Union began to collapse in the autumn of 1991.) Yet Russia had followed a vigorous policy of Russification within its autonomous republics, and there surely would be reactions in the future.

More immediately, as shall be discussed in chapter 12, the question of the autonomous republics of Russians was to become explosive in the Soviet political system in 1990 and 1991. In April 1990 Gorbachev was to have the autonomous republics and Union republics changed into equal republics in a quite unconstitutional manner. When he reopened the Union Treaty for renegotiation in the spring of 1990, each autonomous republic had representation equal to that of a Union republic. When Gorbachev was to turn the Federation Council into the most powerful collective organ in the country, it was to have thirty-four members (and soon more as other units became republics) instead of fifteen. Most important of all, those in Russia who were emotionally claiming that "the center" had unlimited power and had no concern for the interests of Russia now had a perfect, outrageous example with which to argue their case.

CHAPTER EIGHT

The End of Communist Party Rule

A MAJOR TECHNIQUE of any revolutionary group is to try to create the impression that revolution is inevitable and events are out of control. This the radicals associated with Boris Yeltsin did brilliantly. They not only persuaded the elite inside the Soviet Union but also most observers in the outside world. In retrospect the course of events from June 1988 to December 1991 seems inexorable. Mikhail Gorbachev was often described in the West as a man riding a tiger he could not control. Privately he used a play on the popular Russian phrase *poezd poshyol* (the train has left the station) by saying *protsess* (the process) *poshyol.*[1] In the Russian idiom, when a train leaves the station, it cannot be turned back. Gorbachev was saying that a process under way could not be stopped.

Policy, however, is not an irreversible train that must follow a predetermined route. It is almost always ambiguous and subject to modification. Scholars may debate whether the processes unleashed by perestroika were uncontrollable, but there can be no definitive evidence one way or another for a simple reason: Gorbachev never seriously tried to control the tiger. Instead he continually urged it on. In the rare case when force was applied, it seemed very effective.

1. Anatoly Luk'ianov, *Perevorot mnimyi i nastoiashchii* (Moscow: Manuskript, 1993), p. 46. Aleksandr Rutskoi also cites the phrase as a Gorbachev favorite. *Komsomol'skaia pravda,* January 17, 1992.

There were many points at which different decisions could have been made. For example, serious inflationary pressures in the second half of the 1980s could easily have been avoided. Indeed, it is inexcusable that retail prices were not raised in 1986 or 1987 and that mechanisms to encourage savings were not created. The 1989 USSR elections could have been more tightly controlled, and the sessions of the new Soviet Congress of People's Deputies could have been televised more selectively.

But if Gorbachev's miscalculations about the 1989 elections and the USSR Congress are understandable, the real mystery concerns his response to those elections and the collapse of communism in Eastern Europe. The events in Eastern Europe obviously would encourage democrats and nationalists in the Soviet Union as the 1990 republican elections approached. Gorbachev seemed likely to take special steps to ensure that the Soviet Union was not destabilized. Instead he acted in a way certain to destabilize it further. Then he recognized the illegitimacy of the Soviet Union by agreeing to renegotiate the Union Treaty. In the summer of 1990 he gave limited support to a 500-Day Plan that deprived the central government of all power of taxation.

In late 1991 many said Gorbachev failed because he lacked Yeltsin's courage in destroying the power of the party apparatus. In fact, although for some reason Gorbachev thought it tactically unwise to boast about what he had done, he destroyed the power of the Communist party and its apparatus in the winter of 1989–90. After the Twenty-Eighth Party Congress in July 1990 the Politburo no longer included Gorbachev's top political advisers, and it ceased to discuss policy questions. Gorbachev's personal assistants were no longer invited to Politburo meetings and no longer worked with it on its decisions.[2] When Yeltsin banned the party in August 1991 after the failed coup d'etat, he simply gave the coup de grace to an institution that was already moribund.

At the time, it seemed Gorbachev was deliberately fostering chaos to liberate himself from Politburo and Central Committee control and build support for a strong presidency with emergency powers. His behavior seemed deliberate, if Machiavellian, and it did achieve the hypothesized goals. Once he assumed the presidency, however, it seemed obvious he would use its powers to reestablish order, through martial law if necessary. But this did not occur and destabilization continued, leaving observers puzzled as to how to explain his behavior.

2. Georgy Shakhnazarov, *Tsena svobody: Reformatsiia Gorbacheva glazami ego pomoshchnika* (Moscow: Rossika, 1993), p. 252.

Gorbachev's Other Options

If the flow of events from March 1989 (or even earlier) to 1991 was inevitable, there is little to be analyzed. Revolution by definition was irresistably coming from below, and the leaders in the central government were powerless to prevent their overthrow. In reality, however, there were other options, and Gorbachev was making real choices.

Gorbachev's most obvious response to the surprising results in the 1989 USSR election would have been gradually to reduce media coverage of the new legislature and give his opponents little access to the state-controlled media. This was Yeltsin's response to defeat in the 1993 parliamentary (Duma) election. The man who imposed controls as head of central television in 1994 was the same Aleksandr Yakovlev who had controlled radio and television for Khrushchev, Brezhnev, and Gorbachev.

Similarly, Gorbachev could have instituted controls on the 1990 republican elections. When the first Duma elections after the Revolution of 1905 proved embarrassing for Tsar Nikolai II, he held new elections with tighter electoral rules. In Algeria in December 1991 the military responded to an electoral victory by Islamic fundamentalists in the first round of parliamentary elections by calling off the second round. After four years of struggle in which 40,000 persons died, a new election was held in 1995 and a moderate military-backed leader elected. These figures horrify us, but they pale in comparison with the millions killed by the collapse of the Soviet health system. It is not only Gorbachev who seeks deniability for events in Russia.

Gorbachev could have easily insisted on republican election laws that were identical with USSR law (which would have prevented a victory by pro-Yeltsin forces in Russia) or tightened control over nominations. Totally free elections, he could have said, give populist demagogues a chance to stir up unrest. His supporters could have quietly told the foreign press that free elections would give too much power to conservative older people who had the most to lose by economic reform. This argument would have returned to Russia almost immediately on the foreign airways. Gorbachev could have moved quickly to make subsidies to the large industrial enterprises explicit and well-publicized and then threatened either to close down the enterprises or call on the police and military in case disruptive strikes broke out.

Similarly, Gorbachev could have said that the integrated Soviet economy made separatism impossible until market-oriented reforms had taken effect.[3] India has maintained democracy for fifty years with more large nationalities and language groups than the Soviet Union. As Paul Brass has commented, India's central government "developed a set of consistent rules that were not all written down or consciously pursued, but that guided its actions" in maintaining democracy in a multiethnic country. This "made it possible for lasting, agreed solutions to be reached on some highly controversial cultural issues."

> Those four rules, stated concisely, were that no demand for political recognition of a religious group would be considered, that explicitly secessionist movements would not be tolerated and would be suppressed by force whenever necessary, that no capricious concessions would be made to the political demands of any linguistic, regional, or other culturally defined group, and that no political concessions to cultural groups in conflict would be made unless they had demonstrable support from both sides in the conflict.[4]

Gorbachev could also have said that political independence could be considered once normal economic relations were established, but that the republics and the enterprises first had to be given freedom from the domination of the Moscow ministries. He could have embraced Yegor Ligachev's view that a "multiparty system would mean the disintegration of the Soviet federation and . . . the Communist party is the only real political force that unites and consolidates all the peoples of the country."[5] He could have embraced Premier Ryzhkov's private advocacy of regional economic councils (*sovnarkhozy*) to administer industry.

Boris Yeltsin's populist attack against the party apparatus and price increases should have strengthened Gorbachev's incentive to adopt a semi-authoritarian position. As Yeltsin demonstrated he knew how to appeal to popular resentments, Gorbachev's logical strategy would have been to contend that Yeltsin and his program would permit the rise of separatist movements and parties in the non-Russian republics and would break up the Union. The argument could have been made with whatever degree of demagoguery was necessary.

If the military had been promised an improved defense industry and the young in all republics been given greater freedom and the opportunity to

---

3. The regime enacted a secession law with a five-year waiting or cooling-off period, which was all Gorbachev needed if he had stated flatly that early separation would not be tolerated.

4. Paul R. Brass, *Ethnicity and Nationalism: Theory and Comparison* (New Delhi: Sage Publications, 1991), pp. 168–69.

5. *Pravda*, July 21, 1989, p. 3.

enrich themselves, they would have seen Gorbachev's determination to keep radical nationalists, the trade unions, and the conservative middle-aged under control as a benefit. After the 1990 election the Soviet military pleaded with him to reinstitute controls over the republics. Indeed, after 1992 the strongest proponents of the free market—people who called themselves democrats—applauded Yeltsin's effort to establish a presidential dictatorship so he could push through economic reforms.

The allegedly conservative Communist party apparatus had been delighted at Nikita Khrushchev's decentralization of economic power with the creation of regional economic councils (*sovnarkhozy*). It would have had the same attitude toward market reforms that decentralized economic power to the regions and gave individual party officials the chance to acquire property. At least the party apparatus would have been delighted if its position had not been undermined by democratic elections. The "democrats" would have supported a semidictatorship if Gorbachev had given them jobs, for that is what they did under Yeltsin.

One group of Western analysts has recognized the effectiveness of force, but they have contended that Gorbachev could not afford to use it, that if he suppressed democracy and the non-Russian nationalities, he would have forfeited any economic relationship with the West. The West, however, was in no position to react if Gorbachev used moderate force and retained semidemocratic institutions. The West went ahead with detente toward East Germany in 1969–70, a time when the Soviet Union was sending weapons to Vietnam to kill American soldiers, and scarcely a year after Soviet troops entered Czechoslovakia. The United States has tolerated the Indian government's use of force to control its ethnic and religious conflicts. It went to war in the Persian Gulf to liberate Kuwait and protect Saudi Arabia, which is scarcely the embodiment of democracy and human rights. And it did not let the repression in Tiananmen Square affect the substance of its policy toward China. In 1993 the Clinton administration actively supported Boris Yeltsin in his power struggle with the Russian Supreme Soviet in March and again in September when he dissolved it.[6] The Bush and Clinton administrations would have done no less for Gorbachev as long as his

---

6. Richard L. Berke, "Clinton Defends Backing Yeltsin as Elected Chief," *New York Times*, March 13, 1993, p. A1; Keith Bradsher, "Clinton Gives Yeltsin Support, Saying Summit Is On," *New York Times*, March 14, 1993, p. A13; and Elaine Sciolino, "Showdown in Moscow: U.S. Supports Move by Russian Leader to Break Deadlock," *New York Times*, September 22, 1993, p. A1.

foreign policy remained the same and he exercised a modicum of decorum in his domestic repression.

Indeed, the Bush administration was publicly talking about stability in the Soviet Union in 1989, and in subtle ways it indicated its support for tightening control. On April 18, 1990, Gorbachev cut off oil supplies to Lithuania to reassert Moscow's authority. The Bush administration, of course, criticized this move, but on April 21 it moved to expel the leader of the Kashmir liberation movement from the United States as a terrorist and reversed America's nearly forty-year support for a plebiscite in Kashmir.[7] The administration was signaling that it saw a connection between the disintegration of the Soviet Union and the ethnic disintegration of third world multiethnic countries. The Clinton administration described Yeltsin's consolidation of authoritarian power in 1993 as essentially democratic and supported him in the 1996 presidential election despite his undemocratic control of the media and campaign finances.

Together these arguments seem so compelling that it was hard for me to believe Gorbachev would not be driven by them.[8] But instead he allowed the emotional and confrontational speeches of the First Congress of People's Deputies to be broadcast live on daytime television. The press was encouraged to exaggerate Soviet economic problems. (It is striking to compare the hysteria over the minor economic problems of 1989 with the quiet response of television to the horrendous depression of the 1990s.) Gorbachev did nothing to maintain control over the electoral process in any of the republics. Instead, except in the Russian Republic, he allowed republican leaders to handle the process as they wanted. In Russia he pushed through a thoroughgoing liberalization of nomination rules. He ended the power of the Communist party and discredited the Union. He continued to appoint subordinates in their fifties and ignored the thirty- and forty-year-olds whom Yeltsin was courting and would appoint. Gorbachev's actions seemed so bizarre that the sober, moderate Ryzhkov was to conclude there was a concerted plot to destroy the Communist party and the Soviet Union. It is easy to see how he might have gained such an impression.

---

7. Esther B. Fein, "Evolution in Europe: Lithuanians Say Moscow Has Cut Main Oil Pipeline; Growing Pressure," *New York Times*, April 18, 1990, p. A1; and Robert Pear, "State Dept. Moves to Expel Top Kashmir Separatist," *New York Times*, April 22, 1990, p. A17.

8. Indeed, I made this argument in Jerry F. Hough, "Gorbachev's Politics," *Foreign Affairs*, vol. 68 (Winter 1989–90), pp. 26–41.

The Communist Party and Economic Reform

Without question, any serious changes in the Soviet economic and political system would have required serious changes in the way the Communist party functioned. Because the party was the central administrative agency in the country, any decentralization of power to the provincial level would first demand decentralization of power within the party. In addition, the general secretary's base of power rested on his ability to appoint party secretaries in the republics and on their ability to control the delegations to the party congress. Any democratization that made the secretaries responsive to local political forces, let alone that resulted in the free election of delegates to the party congress, would destroy that base of power.

There were also more technical points about the structure and power of the Communist party that would have to be addressed in the course of economic reform. The Soviet system was based on incentives that spurred talented people to rise in the administrative system and encouraged them to avoid political dissidence. Party membership came to be required for all those in politically sensitive professions—military, police, journalism, diplomacy—and also for a wide range of administrative posts considered nonpolitical in the West. These included not only nearly all significant administrative civil service jobs in Moscow and the provinces but such posts as factory manager, farm manager, and usually shop head in large factories.

Party members were obliged to carry out all party directives. This became the basis for administrative subordination in the system. Industrial plants, colleges, the secret police, railroads, scientific institutes, and trade unions were not subordinated to local governments, but the fact that all their leaders were party members meant they were subject to party discipline. Because all institutions were headed by Communists and party rules subjected them to the decisions of the local party organs, these organs were turned by Stalin into the institutions that resolved many purely economic conflicts at the local level, even in such technical matters as procuring supplies.

Thus the real line of command did not go from the USSR Council of Ministers to the republican councils of ministers to the executive committees of the local soviets, but from the USSR Politburo to the republican party bureaus to the regional party bureaus. Indeed, because local government was not given authority, local party organs were the only institutions that could provide regional political and economic coordination.[9]

For this reason full-time party officials were usually chosen from among those with technical education and managerial experience in the economy. The lowest-level party organization was placed at work sites, and the party secretary in significant factories was always an engineer with administrative experience. The party apparatchik in the regional party organs, other than one in ideological work, normally was an engineer or agronomist who worked for some five to ten years in production before moving into party work. Boris Yeltsin was typical in that he worked for thirteen years as a construction administrator before being named head of the construction department of the Sverdlovsk regional party committee. From there he became secretary of the Sverdlovsk Party Committee and then its first secretary.

The potential flaw in this system was that people without the requisite intelligence, drive, and administrative ability might be admitted into the party because of ideological fervor or knowledge of Marxism-Leninism and would prove poor administrators. After the mid-1930s, however, this problem was solved by refusing to admit people into the party until they had proven themselves on the job (or in World War II, at the front). People often did not become party members until they were in their late twenties: Yeltsin became a member at the age of thirty-one when he was already a construction administrator. The deputies to the USSR Supreme Soviet from 1946 to 1970 had joined the party at the average age of twenty-nine.[10]

The postponement of the usual age of party admission was coupled with the policy of making membership almost automatic for any ambitious and high-performing person who did not engage in dissident political or religious activity. In practice the proportion of women who joined the party was relatively small, but party membership became widespread among men with high school and college diplomas. More than 50 percent of men older than age thirty who had a college education became party members.[11]

---

9. See Jerry F. Hough, *The Soviet Prefects: The Local Party Organs in Industrial Decision Making* (Harvard University Press, 1969).

10. The de facto division of labor in the Soviet family involved both spouses having full-time employment, with the woman combining her job with child rearing and the man combining his with the committee and civic work associated with party membership. For a discussion of gender and party membership, see Jerry F. Hough, *The Soviet Union and Social Science Theory* (Harvard University Press, 1977), pp. 128–33.

11. Hough, *Soviet Union and Social Science Theory*, pp. 126.

These de facto rules created a brilliantly structured set of incentives. Children were not punished for their parents' sins (Yeltsin's grandfather was a rich peasant and his father was imprisoned for criticism of the regime, but Yeltsin himself still was admitted to college during Stalin's regime and later into the party and the party apparatus). The ambitious and intelligent could rise as far as their talents would take them if they avoided political dissidence. Not surprisingly, most did avoid it, for the costs of collective oppositional action were extraordinarily high. The threat of expulsion from the party for failure to carry out orders gave administrative officials the most powerful incentive not to challenge orders from above.

This was a system that could not remain unchanged by marketization of the economy. Party membership could not be required of those in the private sector, and the state sector could not compete with the private sector for technical personnel if it required its personnel to assume the time-consuming burdens of party membership. As party membership became less vital for success, the incentives to avoid political dissidence would lessen.

Similarly, the primary party organization could not have a major role in managing privatized enterprises, and the regional party organs could scarcely be the proper instrument of regional economic coordination in a market economy in which many important people were no longer party members. Other institutions would have to be established to replace the party. A well-functioning legal system was one part of the answer, but so was improving the authority and quality of local government personnel.

There were several sensible lines of evolution for the Communist party. The party organizations could have gradually withdrawn from detailed production work. The party organization at the workplace could have retained an important managerial role if economic reform evolved in the direction of workers' self-management, but not otherwise.Local party organs could have remained the dominant political institution in the region—becoming machines such as Tammany Hall in New York City in the nineteenth century or Mayor Richard J. Daley's in Chicago in the mid-twentieth century. The local party organs still could have been concerned with economic development and have continued to have real access to resources and influence at higher echelons of the political system, or even control of semigovernmental banks at the local level. But their close involvement in management would have disappeared.

The Communist party could have been transformed into a parliamentary party. The focus of the lowest party organizations could have been shifted from the individual enterprise to the precinct, and party leaders could have been chosen from those who could appeal to consumers rather than from production-oriented managers. More and more decisions could have been made in government institutions rather than in the party bodies. The Communist leaders would have to learn to work more often within the government and perhaps even compete with other political parties for votes. If the party Central Committee and the Politburo were to remain important institutions, they could have come to be dominated by the Communist leaders in the legislatures and could have concentrated on coordinating party legislative strategy at the various territorial levels. (For example, after 1993 the Russian Communist party of Gennady Zyuganov had so little staff of its own that it relied on the staffs of the deputies in the Duma.)

There were, of course, other ways the party could change that made no sense. The functions of the party organs might be transformed without changing the type of personnel selected to staff its chief positions. The coordinating functions of local party organs might be ended before other mechanisms were created to take over the functions. Party officials might be subjected to competitive elections and then be damned if they were responsive to citizens' and especially workers' complaints about the pain of economic reform. The party organs and the Communists in the legislature might fail to develop a close relationship. For inexplicable reasons Gorbachev managed to take all these steps.

Gorbachev and the Communist Party

Mikhail Gorbachev seemed an unlikely candidate to destroy the Communist party. His grandfather had been chairman of a collective (*kolkhoz*) farm in the 1930s, and he himself had become a candidate member of the party at the unusually early age of nineteen and a full member at twenty-one.[12] He had worked in the party apparatus for thirty years, and in the early chapters of his memoirs he shows great respect for the men like himself in the post of regional first secretary. He had seen how the post had been used by different leaders and how it had been flexible enough to permit the rise of men such as Eduard Shevardnadze and himself. He certainly should have

---

12. He was admitted to the party because he earned a medal for his summer work as a combine driver and thus passed the work requirement for party membership. It is likely that he applied for membership in his home kolkhoz to facilitate his admission to Moscow University. Mikhail Gorbachev, *Zhizn' i reformy*, vol. 1 (Moscow: Novosti, 1995), pp. 56, 59; *Memoirs* (Doubleday, 1996), vol. 1, pp. 38, 41.

understood the vital economic functions the party performed. He seemed dedicated to socialism and the Union, although in more democratic form. Why would he want to dismantle the Communist party?

Many said that the party was incapable of accepting radical reform or of being transformed, but it never mounted meaningful resistance to anything Gorbachev wanted. Even in July 1990 when he had accepted the dismantling of communism and Soviet hegemony in eastern Europe, taken all power from the Politburo and Central Committee, introduced free elections in Russia, and produced growing economic and political chaos, the party congress voted for him as general secretary 3,411 to 1,116 and voted against the more conservative Yegor Ligachev as deputy general secretary 3,642 to 776.[13] The party secretaries were not damning Gorbachev for his reform policy but for having no consistent policy at all—for being passive.

Even with hindsight and evidence from the memoirs of those participating in the events, it is difficult to reconstruct Gorbachev's attitude toward the Communist party. His attitude toward Lenin did seem to evolve, and this may have had a major impact on his thinking about the party as an institution. His assistant and speechwriter Valery Boldin found him strongly under Lenin's influence, especially in 1986 and 1987, with Raisa Gorbachev reenforcing his tendencies in a pro-Lenin direction. "By virtue of her education and experience as a university lecturer on Marxist-Leninist philosophy, Raisa's views were those of a dedicated Communist, [and] she frequently upheld her convictions in private and in public." As Gorbachev often said, "Raisa was the head of 'our family party cell.'"[14]

Gorbachev's advisers generally want to portray him as a man long committed to democracy, and within limits this was true. Behind the scenes he said that he was "near to social democracy in his convictions," but he convinced his closest associates that this meant democratic socialism rather than the disappearance of the Communist party or socialism.[15] Radical advisers counseled him to split the party into two branches and lead the

13. Bill Keller, "Confronting Foes, Gorbachev Keeps Party Leadership," *New York Times*, July 11, 1990, p. A1; and *Pravda*, July 13, 1990, p. 1. *Pravda* was embarrassed by the number of votes against Gorbachev and did not print the totals.

14. Valery Boldin, *Ten Years That Shook the World: The Gorbachev Era as Witnessed by His Chief of Staff*, trans. Evelyn Rossiter (Basic Books, 1994), pp. 96, 85.

15. Interview with Anatoly Luk'ianov, *Sovetskaia Rossiia*, January 23, 1993, p. 1. Luk'ianov talked about his own support for "socialist orientation," a phrase applied to radical socialist regimes such as that in Angola in the Brezhnev period. Luk'ianov originally believed that Gorbachev was thinking in these terms as well.

more liberal one into electoral battle. He steadfastly refused. Georgy Shakhnazarov, who claimed to have been a social democrat since the 1960s and to have been one of many, has not said that Gorbachev was among their group at first.[16] Shakhnazarov noted that Gorbachev was very late in coming to a critical evaluation of Brezhnev's invasion of Czechoslovakia. One of Gorbachev's closest aides, Anatoly Cherniaev, speaks of the general secretary's "internal revolution."[17]

Cherniaev considered Gorbachev's reading of Aleksandr Solzhenitsyn's *Lenin in Zurich* in 1989 a landmark event. For the first time, he said, Gorbachev saw Lenin not only as a "person who could 'in general' be mistaken (sometimes even a genius can make mistakes), but one who probably made a mistake on a 'historic scale.'" According to Cherniaev, Gorbachev thought that Lenin had not cared for Russia as such but had used the country as a testing ground for world revolution.[18]

Ivan Frolov, one of Gorbachev's advisers, had long ago turned against Marx's insistence that values only reflected class interests and, in general, that the superstructure (culture) was a product of the economic base. Frolov's position was widely held and advanced in many forms by the liberal intellectuals of the Brezhnev period.[19] By the autumn of 1988, Aleksandr Yakovlev was telling a new assistant, Aleksandr Tsipko, that Marx had not simply exaggerated his point nor was he being misinterpreted: he was fundamentally wrong.[20]

Gorbachev was originally attracted to the idea of human values that transcended class, but at some point he likely moved closer to Yakovlev's conclusion. Tsipko was assigned the task of writing a criticism of Marx while working in the Central Committee apparatus. All the appropriate anti-Marxist literature was sent from the Lenin Library to the Central Committee building, and the librarians clearly knew what was being writ-

16. Shakhnazarov, *Tsena svobody*, pp. 171–72, 241–42.
17. Jonathan Steele, *Eternal Russia: Yeltsin, Gorbachev, and the Mirage of Democracy* (Harvard University Press, 1994), p. 20.
18. A. S. Cherniaev, *Shest' let s Gorbachevym* (Moscow: Progress, 1993), pp. 278–79.
19. Jerry F. Hough, *The Struggle for the Third World: Soviet Debates and American Options* (Brookings, 1986), pp. 119–27.
20. See the foreword by Aleksandr Tsipko, in Aleksandr Yakovlev, *Predislovie, obval, posleslovie* (Moscow: Novosti, 1992), p. 5. Tsipko has said privately that he does not know when Yakovlev came to this view.

ten. Tsipko is certain that Yakovlev was too cautious to permit this without Gorbachev's authorization.[21]

Whatever Gorbachev thought about the Communist party as a general institution, however, he certainly understood the way power worked within it. He understood that the Central Committee could vote him out of office, as it had voted out Nikita Khrushchev, and was acutely sensitive to the lack of power of lame ducks. He understood the importance of the circular flow of power (see chapter 2) and knew full well the dangers posed by the creation of the post of Russian first secretary and the subordination of the Russian provincial party apparatus to him.

Gorbachev knew he had little choice but to democratize the party if he were really going to democratize the country, for neither the various legislatures nor the republics could be democratic if they were tightly controlled by a centralized party hierarchy. Yet if lower party officials were subject to defeat in an election in which most voters were not party members, their first reaction would be that they could no longer depend on Moscow.[22] If so, this would destroy the power base of the general secretary.

Once the circular flow of power was destroyed, there were few administrative solutions to the general secretary's loss of control of the party. As Lenin had understood, the worst alternative for a general secretary would have been to give power to the Politburo. A better alternative, adopted at the party congress in July 1990 at Gorbachev's suggestion, was to have the general secretary elected by the party congress rather than by the Central Committee. This would make it very difficult to remove him in the five years between congresses. Yet it would eventually leave the general secretary subject to strong competition at the congress as other party leaders formed organized groups to compete for delegates.

Thus once it was decided to create a Russian party organization and permit free elections in the republics, Gorbachev needed to go beyond the circular flow of power in building his political base of support. His chairmanship of the Supreme Soviet gave him a second credible base, as the success of his threats to resign as general secretary testified. A presidency would be even more durable.

21. Jerry F. Hough, interview with Aleksandr Tsipko, May 17, 1996.

22. When the regional secretaries were told in 1988 that they should be chairmen of the regional soviets (and, therefore, would have to run in competitive elections), their first reaction, Shakhnazarov reported, was that they were no longer dependent on Moscow. Shakhnazarov, *Tsena svobody* p. 244.

Nevertheless, the preceding pages are filled with "if's," and they all seemed to lead in the direction of keeping democratization limited—to control elections, have a weak legislature such as the Duma under Boris Yeltsin, and insist on obedience to central laws. If he had taken power away from regional party secretaries, he could have instituted appointed governors, as Yeltsin did, and maintained tight financial controls on them. Indeed, Gorbachev said in his memoirs that "tactically it was more expedient to transfer power to the Soviets not in a jerk, but smoothly, gradually, so as not to lose the governability of the country."[23] It often is difficult to judge from Gorbachev's memoirs whether he is reporting his thinking at the time or making an ex post facto judgment, but this particular statement seems to be justifying his early limitations on democracy. The question is why he decided to change to an inexpedient policy that did, in fact, destroy the country's governability.

The Anxiety of the Summer and Fall of 1989

Of all the periods covered in this book, none has a stranger appearance in retrospect than the summer and fall of 1989. The Soviet public had elected a USSR Congress of People's Deputies that proved readily responsive to Gorbachev's desires. Although a number of regional party officials had been defeated in the election, this seemed only to suggest, as Moscow party leader Lev Zaikov said at the time, that party secretaries like himself who had been plant managers often were not natural politicians and had to be replaced by people with the skills needed in the new age.

The first serious conflicts concerning nationality erupted in 1988 and continued in 1989, but they involved clashes between non-Russians and were not directed against Russians or Moscow. Surprisingly, the Russian security forces were used sparingly; it seemed that Moscow might be deliberately letting non-Russians fight each other to prove that the central organization was needed as an arbiter and protector of the peace.

Yet Moscow intellectuals seemed near hysteria. In April 1989, when Georgians in Tbilisi organized a counterdemonstration against the Abkhazians who were demanding independence from Georgia, the army was used to disperse the crowds. Through some mistake, twenty persons

23. Gorbachev, *Zhizn' i reformy*, vol. 1, p. 451; *Memoirs*, vol. 1, p. 301.

were either crushed or died from crowd control gas in the ensuing melee. The incident was unfortunate but insignificant in comparison with similar events that occur repeatedly in democratic India.[24] There was no evidence the action would be the first in a series. Still, it became a cause célèbre involving charges and countercharges among Politburo members and a symbol to non-Russians of Moscow's repression.

Economic performance remained reasonably good in 1989—especially so compared with any year from 1990 through 1996. Industrial production was still rising slowly, and by the end of the year consumer goods production would be up 5.9 percent, non-food consumers' goods production up 7.7 percent, and retail trade up 8.4 percent.[25] Although the growth rate of heavy industry was slowly dropping toward zero, industrial production did not drop precipitously, as it would in the Yeltsin years when this development was to be hailed as desirable in promoting a transition to a consumer-oriented services economy.

There were economic problems to address, for economic growth at the end of the year was worse than at the beginning. Signs of inflationary pressure were starting to appear. A coal strike in the summer seemed to foreshadow more labor unrest. Yet in the fall of 1989 Gorbachev began talking more urgently about the need for economic reform. At the conclusion of a conference of economists in October he declared, "we are obliged to take the most radical, far-reaching measures" in economic reform.[26] It was at this time that Nikolai Sliun'kov, the Central Committee secretary for the economy who was said to lack an independent position and always to follow the Gorbachev line, became more radical.

The new Nikolai Ryzhkov government confirmed by the USSR Congress was much younger than its predecessor and contained serious economic reformers. Leonid Abalkin, who became deputy premier in charge of economic reform, presented a plan in October that included price increases and that the *Financial Times* termed the most radical since 1985. The government seemed ready to address economic reform, and if Gorbachev was willing to stand behind radical reform, real change seemed in the

---

24. The general in charge, Yury Rodionov, became the symbol of repression—no doubt unjustly. In July 1996 Yeltsin named him minister of defense.

25. Leonid Abalkin, *Ne ispol'zovannyi shans: Poltora goda v pravitel'stve* (Moscow: Politizdat, 1991), p. 94.

26. *Pravda*, October 24, 1989, p. 1; and October 30, 1989, p. 2.

offing. Certainly, it was much too early to insist the reform would be unsuccessful.

But at the end of the summer the Soviet press, encouraged by the political leaders, whipped up hysteria about the economy. The government was trying to get a ban on strikes through the Supreme Soviet, and it talked incessantly about the danger of insufficient fuel to get the country through the winter.[27] The Western press reflected the mood in Moscow. In October John Lloyd of the *Financial Times* described Gorbachev as "a man with a ruined economy."[28] In November Esther Fein of the *New York Times* wrote of the "dire economic backdrop."[29] None of this had any relationship to the economic reality of the time.

With the population possessing a great deal of purchasing power and being told that price increases were in the offing at some ill-defined point, the press hysteria had very predictable economic effects. Given the lack of investment opportunities and a savings bank interest rate much lower than the rate of inflation, excess money could be used for little else but consumption. Of course, severe retail shortages developed; even soap disappeared from the stores, although production was up 150 percent from the year before. All this deepened the sense of impending economic disaster.

When Premier Ryzhkov presented the government's plan to the Congress of People's Deputies on December 13, it included most major points of Abalkin's plan, but the two price increases were postponed by a year each.[30] The discussion on economic reform in the Congress was basically sober, but attention soon turned to such issues as the suppression of demonstrations in Tbilisi, which brought emotions to a boil. If Ryzhkov and his plan were treated gingerly in the Congress, they were denounced in the press for being conservative. The West was no different. It too had been deeply affected by the collapse of communism in Eastern Europe, and everything seemed possible. Reform in the Soviet Union was now judged from that utopian perspective. The *Financial Times* had called Abalkin radical a few months earlier, but now an editorial described the marginally more conservative speech by Ryshkov in the direst of terms:

27. Quentin Peel, "Kremlin Looks for Relief from the Economic Heat," *Financial Times*, October 4, 1989, p. 2.

28. John Lloyd, "The Many Roads from Socialism," *Financial Times*, October 14, 1989, p. 9.

29. Esther B. Fein, "'Unpopular Measures' Urged for Soviet Economy," *New York Times*, November 14, 1989, p. A23.

30. *Izvestiia*, December 14, 1989, pp. 2–4.

Mr. Nikolai Ryzhkov has made a chilling speech on the Soviet economy. It is not
the end, but it could be the beginning of the end of Soviet economic reform for
the present period. . . . Mr. Ryzhkov's speech was a conservative one, possibly
heralding a conservative reaction all along the line, with profound implications
for the country's external relations. . . . If . . . the retreat goes on . . . the ghosts of
the Soviet economic past, present, and yet to come will await the country's
leaders, more terrifyingly, more loaded with chains than before.[31]

It was a most remarkable judgment about a leadership that had just permitted the dismantling of the Berlin Wall and the end of communism throughout eastern Europe.

The Central Committee met on December 9, officially to discuss the
Ryzhkov plan, but in fact it was absorbed with the political situation. The
East European communist regimes were collapsing. The 1990 republican
elections would produce legislatures with very large numbers of anticommunist deputies in the Baltic republics, if nowhere else. In Russia itself,
according to the first secretary of the Leningrad obkom, "the reality of our
days is a stormy politization, and with it a polarization of positions, views,
and opinions."[32]

In the Central Committee at least, the main concern seemed to be the
lack of decisiveness of the leadership. At the December plenum the members of the committee all expressed their confidence in Gorbachev, but
everything they said betrayed their lack of confidence. An obkom first
secretary in Kazakhstan expressed the mood most dramatically when he
discussed a response of Viktor M. Chebrikov, former chairman of the KGB,
to a question from a Kazakh party official:

"There is a collapse of our federation, of our Union. . . . Don't you see this?"
[Chebrikov] said, "Yes, we in the Politburo see that there are many alarming
symptoms. We are doing everything to ensure that this collapse does not occur.
And if it does occur, Viktor Mikhailovich stated, then we [the current composition of the Politburo] will resign. Ever since this, my comrades and I have been
paralyzed by one question—is the Politburo confident about what it is doing? I
still cannot sleep."[33]

At the December 1989 plenum of the Central Committee (and periodically
from then on) Gorbachev did threaten to resign. This did not mean he would
step down as the country's leader. Rather, he was threatening to leave his

31. "Soviet Reform Deferred," *Financial Times*, December 15, 1989, p. 18.
32. *Izvestiia TsK KPSS*, no. 4 (April 1990), p. 40.
33. *Izvestiia TsK KPSS*, no. 4 (April 1990), p. 47.

post as head of the Communist party and rule the country from the post of president. In fact, he had already decided to make this move.

The End of the Party's Leading Role

In the fall of 1989 Gorbachev was keeping his intentions to himself. At the same time that he endorsed radical economic reform, his changes in Politburo membership pointed toward a conservative position. On September 19 several elderly and ineffective conservatives were removed from the Politburo but were replaced by Vladimir A. Kriuchkov, chairman of the KGB, and Yury D. Masliukov, chairman of Gosplan and first deputy chairman of the Council of Ministers. Boris K. Pugo, chairman of the Party Control Commission, was elected a candidate member.

Ryzhkov's plan pointed in the same more cautious direction, but Ryzhkov was not the leader of the country. If Gorbachev had ever praised the Abalkin plan, Ryzhkov and the Congress would have approved. Ryzhkov had always favored the price increases in the Abalkin plan that he had been forced to postpone. The postponement showed the hand of the general secretary at work.

Many members of the Central Committee were not convinced of Gorbachev's resolve for reform, but in fact he had reason to postpone difficult economic decisions in the winter of 1989–90. He was preparing to abolish Article 6 of the USSR Constitution that established the "leading" role of the Communist party and to create an elected presidency from which to rule. It made sense to postpone economic decisions until after he completed the consolidation of his power. Indeed, both at the time and in retrospect, it was easy to see the panic of late 1989 as the result of a deliberate campaign on the part of Gorbachev and his lieutenants in charge of the media to set the stage for abolishing Article 6, to extend extraordinary powers to Gorbachev as president, to legitimize radical economic reform that would be introduced after Gorbachev became president.

Through the decades Article 6 of the USSR Constitution had come to be seen as legitimizing the role played by the Communist party in the Soviet Union, but if read literally, it was vaguer than was commonly perceived: "The leading and guiding force of Soviet society and the nucleus of its political system, of all state organizations, is the Communist Party of the Soviet Union. . . . The Communist Party, armed with Marxism-Leninism, determines the general policy of the USSR [and] directs the great constructive work of the Soviet people.'' Article 6 did not outlaw other parties, although it certainly implied that they did not have the right to rule. Even more important, it did not specify how the Communist party would rule, that is, through a ruling party Politburo and general secretary rather than through party leaders who sat on the Council of Ministers.

Moreover, Article 6 did not demand tight discipline within the Communist party or the suppression of dissent within it. Given that all significant government and administrative officials were members of the party, its leading role could have meant no more than that certain important posts were reserved for party members. (The fact that the top officials of the Clinton administration were all Democrats does not mean that the Democratic National Committee became the ruling organ of the country in 1993 or that the chairman of the Democratic National Committee became the country's leader.) The leading role of the Communist party was also compatible with competitive primaries within the party or the competitive elections of the two branches of the party favored by Aleksandr Yakovlev in 1985.

Once it became clear that the republican elections in the most radical republics would be free, it seemed likely that non-Communists would win in at least a few. Either Soviet forces would have to intervene to maintain Communist party supremacy or Article 6 would have to be ignored or removed. If the Soviet leaders were willing to use Soviet forces to overturn an election result, they should have intervened earlier to keep the elections under control.

The logic of the situation was clear, and when the Congress of People's Deputies reopened on December 11, a number of deputies proposed putting the issue of Article 6 on the agenda. Gorbachev was "wary," "testy," and "temperamental" as he fought against the proposal.[34] He won, but by a surprisingly narrow margin of 1,139 to 839. Various Western correspondents discerned hints in Gorbachev's statements that he was going to yield on Article 6; it is likely that his aides were making the point privately to the correspondents in background briefings.[35] Indeed, one deputy who was a party official declared the party was only postponing the decision.[36]

34. Francis X. Clines, "Soviet Congress Reconvenes Today, the Joy of Spring Nipped in the Bud," *New York Times*, December 12, 1989, p. A18.
35. Francis X. Clines, "Signals from Gorbachev," *New York Times*, December 15, 1989, p. A18.
36. *Vtoroi (vneocherednoi) s''ezd narodnykh deputatov RSFSR (27 noiabria–15 dekabria goda): Stenograficheskii otchet* (Moscow: Respublika, 1992).

Gorbachev's aides reported he was agitated about this decision as late as January 1990. In 1993 they told a Canadian correspondent that they had to push him to the decision.[37] In fact, he had already made up his mind. Even as he was wavering in public, he was taking steps to transfer property and codes from party committees to government committees.[38] The abolition of Article 6 had long been urged by the group of advisers headed by Aleksandr Yakovlev, and Gorbachev may have been reasonably certain as early as 1988 that he would choose this option. It is probable that a primary reason for his 1989 decision to permit free republican elections was a desire to make the removal of Article 6 from the USSR Constitution virtually inevitable. The removal of Article 6, especially as interpreted by Gorbachev, was deeply controversial within the Politburo, and Gorbachev was maneuvering to ensure that the decision was inevitable before he could be accused of approving it.

On January 22 Gorbachev presented the Politburo with his program of political reform, which was drafted by Aleksandr Yakovlev. On the basis of leaks from Gorbachev's advisers, the Western press reported that the Politburo did not reach consensus because of conservative resistance to the removal of Article 6.[39] In fact, memoirs indicate that the really contentious issue was the nature of economic reform and price adjustments, with Ryzhkov and his deputy premiers unsuccessfully trying to push Gorbachev to attack the problem of financial stabilization. On January 30 Steve Hurst, head of CNN's Moscow bureau, reported on the basis of a leak that Gorbachev was thinking of resigning as general secretary and retaining only his state job. On February 4 Gorbachev permitted—and surely helped stimulate—a demonstration of 100,000 to 300,000 people in Moscow against Article 6.

It is not clear whether this orchestration was necessary. Premier Ryzhkov not unreasonably said that a multiparty system was already a fait accompli. On February 7, after a stormy session, the Central Committee agreed to modify Article 6. On March 13, 1990, the Congress of People's Deputies passed the necessary constitutional amendment.[40]

37. Donald Murray, *A Democracy of Despots* (Boulder, Colo.: Westview Press, 1995), pp. 82–87.

38. Cherniaev, *Shest' let s Gorbachevym*, p. 334.

39. Quentin Peel, "Gorbachev Threatened by Split in Soviet Leadership," *Financial Times*, January 24, 1990, p. 26.

40. For the changes see *Izvestiia*, March 16, 1990, pp. 2–3.

The Creation of a Presidency and the Destruction of the Party

At the same time that he abolished Article 6, Gorbachev decided to transform the structure of government and introduce a presidency. The structure he had introduced in 1989 was a strange form of parliamentary system with all power vested in the legislature but without a strong prime minister. In a normal parliamentary system the leader of the dominant party becomes the prime minister, and the Speaker is a more neutral figure. In the Soviet Union Gorbachev occupied the post of Speaker of the parliament. Officially he had to consult with the forty-two members of the Presidium of the Supreme Soviet to take such an action as introducing troops to quell riots in Azerbaidzhan.[41] This was a satisfactory arrangement if the Communists in the parliament were subject to party discipline, but it left the leader with few effective levers of executive power if party discipline weakened.

When Gorbachev decided to replace the parliamentary system with a presidential one, he chose one closer to the French system than to the American. The post of chairman of the Council of Ministers was retained, and like the post of French premier, its incumbent was responsible both to the president and the legislature. Ryzhkov remained chairman of the Council of Ministers until December 1990. Like the American president's cabinet, that of the USSR president had to be confirmed by the legislature. But in one respect he was less powerful than the American president: the Congress of People's Deputies was still "the supreme organ" of the government and had the exclusive right to change the constitution.[42]

When the system was replicated in independent Russia with an even stronger president who had the power to appoint cabinet ministers without confirmation by the Congress, Boris Yeltsin found the powers of the office too limited. When the Russian Congress disagreed with his choice of premier and with his policy, he did not adopt the policy of cohabitation with the legislature that was implied in the system and that Francois Mitterrand accepted in France. Instead, he dissolved the Congress. Limited power was a potential problem at the USSR level as well, but Gorbachev retained strong majority support within the USSR Congress until the Soviet Union was dissolved.

---

41. Murray, *Democracy of Despots*, p. 85.
42. For a good discussion of the strength of the Congress, see the defense of the new presidency by Anatoly Luk'ianov. *Izvestiia*, March 13, 1990, pp. 1–2.

The new president was supposed to be elected, but Gorbachev refused to submit to a popular election and demanded that the Congress of People's Deputies elect him president for the first five years. It was a fatal mistake when he had to face a Yeltsin who did run in an election in Russia in 1991 and could claim a legitimacy that Gorbachev had been afraid to seek. The double tragedy is that Gorbachev would have won in 1990. Yeltsin, his only opponent of any standing, was unlikely to run against him because he was unlikely to win. Gorbachev would have done very well outside the largest cities of Russia, and half the Russian electorate lived in villages and towns with a population smaller than 80,000 people. Moreover, half the votes were cast outside of Russia. Gorbachev was certain to run extremely well against the Russian nationalist Yeltsin in the populous republics of Belorussia, Kazakhstan, Ukraine, and in Central Asia. He would have received 90 to 95 percent of the vote in Kazakhstan and Central Asia.[43]

The real problem may have been the mechanism of the election. In drafts of the Union Treaty a president needed both a majority of republics and a majority of the popular vote to be elected. The decision, mentioned at the end of the last chapter, to equate the autonomous and Union republics may have been motivated by the thought that it would be easier to get a majority of thirty-four republics than of fifteen because of the generally conservative and compliant nature of the autonomous republics. But an immediate presidential election would have brought all these constitutional issues to a boil at a time when, wisely or not, Gorbachev wanted them dealt with in negotiations of a new Union Treaty.

The monumental event that occurred in the first months of 1990, however, was not the creation of a presidency or the abolition of Article 6, but the destruction of the power of the Communist party. Abolishing Article 6 meant only that other parties could compete and win in elections. The leadership had long recognized that the Baltic republics might have a much looser relationship with Moscow, perhaps analogous to that of Finland under the tsarist regime, and thus it did not matter that other parties might win in them. In Russia, eastern and central Ukraine, Belorussia, Kazakhstan, and Central Asia, the Communist party retained a solid core of support and the enormous political and economic resources to keep most

---

43. At the time of the March 1991 referendum, the Central Asian republics and Kazakhstan had 18 percent of the number of the electors of the three Slavic republics, but 21.5 percent of the actual votes the three republics cast in the election and 28 percent of the votes they cast in favor of the referendum. *Izvestiia*, March 27, 1991, p. 3.

ambitious politicians within the party. Those areas included 90 percent of the population of the USSR.

It was easy to imagine the Communist party in the Soviet Union serving the kind of function the ruling Institutional Revolutionary Party (PRI) served in Mexico, the Christian Democrats in the first four decades of postwar Italy, and the Liberal Democrats in the first four and a half decades of postwar Japan. It might lose some provincial and even big city elections and its control of the political system would loosen over the years, but there was no reason to believe this had to happen during Gorbachev's lifetime.

Although Article 6 said nothing about the relationship between the party organs and officials on the one hand and the members of the party on the other, Gorbachev's revolution in 1990 dealt with that very relationship. Successful perestroika no doubt required that the party organs gradually loosen party discipline, transfer more power to Communists working in the state organs, and concentrate more on electoral strategy. Nevertheless, party discipline within the British parliament or the Chicago political machine under Mayor Daley showed that parties could remain fairly centralized in a democratic political system with a free market.

Gorbachev, however, was able to force through his interpretation that the end of the leading role of the party meant the end of the leading role of party organs and the party first secretaries at each level. For himself this meant the end of the power of the Central Committee and Politburo to make policy decisions that had authority over him in his new presidential office. Indeed, even as the decision was being made, Gorbachev was bypassing the Politburo on the crucial matters of the future of eastern Europe and German unification.[44] In the fall of 1989 the plan proposed by the Ryzhkov government to the Congress of People's Deputies was not submitted to the Politburo beforehand for approval—an unprecedented act.[45]

Even more important in the short run was the end of the authority of provincial party organs over local institutions. The Communist party had been skillfully organized to perform vital functions in the existing political and economic system. Movement toward market reform would end the need for many of those functions and change the character of the party, but

---

44. For Germany, see Hannes Adomeit, "Gorbachev, German Unification, and the Collapse of Empire," *Post-Soviet Affairs*, vol. 10 (July–September 1994), pp. 217–19.
45. Mikhail Nenashev, *Poslednee pravitel'stvo SSSR: Lichnosti, Svidetel'stva, Dialogi* (Moscow: Krom, 1993), pp. 40–41; and Valentin Pavlov, *Upushchen li shans? Finansovyi kliuch k rynku* (Moscow: Terra, 1995), p. 152.

the party organs were dismantled before new institutions were created to perform their functions. As in the case of economic reform, Gorbachev seemed to give very little thought to the problems of the transition. The consequences were disastrous: the absence of an administrative organ that could provide economic coordination in the provinces was one of the main unrecognized factors in the increasing economic disintegration in 1990 and 1991.

The Democratic National Committee or the British Conservative party organization have no power to obligate government officials to carry out their decisions, and it is understandable that Gorbachev would want to turn the Central Committee into an institution analogous to them and create the type of subservient cabinet found in the United States. The truly surprising aspect of his decisions in early 1990 was that although he remained general secretary of the Communist party as well as president, he essentially abandoned the party as an instrument of his own rule.

First, Gorbachev seemed insensitive to the economic implications of the destruction of the power of the local party organs. The growing independence of the republics made the problem difficult to resolve, but there were interim solutions. The top government officials of provinces, cities, and counties could be appointed by the president, as was to occur in Georgia almost immediately and in Russia from the fall of 1991 through 1995 (and as was done in France). They could be given the authority of the old first secretaries, as was done in Russia. The party first secretaries could use control of local soviets to retain most of their old powers and functions, as was to occur in Ukraine, Central Asia, and Kazakhstan. If the central government retained significant financial resources, it would also have retained enormous influence with local officials. This became the main instrument of control of the Yeltsin government in 1996.[46]

The most serious problem occurred in Russia, especially once Boris Yeltsin became its leader. If the Russian government were to appoint the provincial leaders and they were to be loyal to a Yeltsin determined to break away from central control, Gorbachev would have great difficulty maintaining administrative control. If the new Russian Communist party were to oppose Gorbachev, it would only partially help him if the first secretaries retained de facto power.

Yet the events in Russia were not inevitable. The Russian Communist party was to be headed by Ivan Polozkov, who had worked closely with

46. Richard Sakwa, *Russian Politics and Society* (Routledge, 1993), pp. 179–200.

Gorbachev in southern Russia. Gorbachev did not take all power from the Russian party apparatus because it had moved into opposition; rather, it moved into opposition because he took all power from it. He seemed obsessed that the Russian first secretary would gain control of the circular flow of power. And he seemed not to realize that once the establishment of a presidency broke the circular flow of power, he could afford to give the Russian first secretary and the regional party officials the kind of power they had in Ukraine so long as they remained obligated to enforce central law.

Similarly, as will be seen, the victory of Yeltsin in Russia was far from inevitable. Gorbachev acted in a way that maximized Yeltsin's chances of becoming leader of Russia. He seemed to believe that Yeltsin could be useful to him on the one hand in giving Russians a more territorially based sense of national identity and on the other providing a Russian nationalist threat that could be used in balancing Russia and the other republics. He certainly could have arrested Yeltsin or removed him from power for insubordination if Yeltsin continued to violate central laws. (Think what would happen if an American state governor began acting as Yeltsin did.) Gorbachev's political calculations were flawed for reasons to be discussed later, but at a minimum it was certain that he was thinking in political terms and neglecting the administrative implications of what he was doing. He seemed totally unaware of the political problems that would be created by administrative disorder.

The Failure of the Communists as a Parliamentary Party

Whatever the consequences of the destruction of the Communist party apparatus as an administrative organization, the Communists seemed well placed to be an effective parliamentary party. By espousing nationalism limited to the republican level, Yeltsin was allowing Gorbachev and the Communists to support the necessity of a unified decentralized USSR for both security and economic reasons. By calling increasingly for radical economic reform, Yeltsin was allowing Gorbachev and the Communists to support a managed economic transition of the Chinese type that preserved economic growth and a social safety net. The appeals that Gennady Zyuganov used for the Russian Communist party in 1996 could easily and effectively have been used by Gorbachev in 1990—indeed, much more easily because he had the good will and support of the West.

In short, the Communists as a party were far better positioned than was Yeltsin to take a convincing populist stand or even a responsible social democratic one. The party needed to defend itself vigorously against the charge that it embodied the nomenklatura, but it could have proudly proclaimed its abandonment of its administrative role instead of remaining largely silent about it. It could have boasted that it remained a transforming party, but one that carefully considered the interests of the workers and the security of the country in new conditions. It could have convincingly claimed that it alone had the ability to carry through a coordinated legislative program in the USSR, republican, and local legislatures. A number of local Communist politicians did take such a position, but they were then denounced by the general secretary's men and the state media as being unacceptable conservatives.

Gorbachev never seriously tried to transform the Communist party into a collection of politicians who would work effectively in the new conditions. He did conduct a purge of the regional party secretaries, and he was helped in this by the defeats many of them suffered in the 1989 election. Yet the obvious implication of the election defeats and the abandonment of the party's administrative role was that party officials should be recruited from people with the skills of modern politicians rather than of plant managers. A key Ligachev aide advocated this in two articles in *Pravda* in May 1989.[47] It did not occur.

Obkom first secretaries were changed in 59 percent of the oblasts between January 1, 1989, and July 1990, almost all of them after the March 1989 election. The biographies of the new first secretaries gave all the appearance of centralized selection or at least selection according to central guidelines. An astonishing 82 percent had been born between 1935 and 1941, 94 percent between 1933 and 1941. When a new obkom first secretary was elected in Leningrad, Gorbachev attended the plenum and everyone made it clear that Boris V. Gidaspov was his man. The head of the local writers' union thanked Gorbachev for not sending in a *variag* [a Varangian, or outsider], and Gidaspov himself thanked Gorbachev for his election.[48]

It was remarkable how little changed in the biographies of the obkom first secretaries. Table 8-1 implies that younger men were being selected, but in this respect it is misleading. The first secretaries of January 1989

47. V. Legostaev, "Intellektual'noe dostoinstvo partii," *Pravda*, May 2, 1989, p. 2; and May 3, 1989, p. 2.

48. *Leningradskaia pravda*, July 14, 1989, pp. 1–3.

Table 8-1. *Characteristics of Obkom First Secretaries in the Russian Republic, 1985–91*
Percent unless otherwise specified

Year	Average year of birth	Average age at admission to party	Engineering education	Agronomy education	Five years or more work in production
March 1981	1923	25	54	30	57
(N = 56)					
March 1985 (named					
pre-83)	1924	25	57	27	60
(N = 40)					
March 1985 (named					
1983–84)	1931	26	69	31	50
(N = 16)					
January 1, 1989	1933	26	55	36	64
(N = 56)					
New secretaries					
1989–June 1990	1938	25	64	36	70
(N = 33)					

Source: The biographies of the party officials come from many sources. The earlier ones can be found in the 1981 and 1986 yearbooks of the *Bol'shaia sovetskaia entsiklopediia.* The later ones were published in the journal *Izvestiia TsK KPPS* that began publication in January 1989.

included people in place for some years. The new first secretaries averaged fifty-one years of age on January 1, 1990; the first secretaries appointed from 1985 to 1989 were fifty-two at the time of their selection.

The new first secretaries were engineers and agronomists in essentially the same proportions as before. The party was not naming fewer technocratic officials to compete in the new elections but men with even more managerial experience in production. The proportion of first secretaries that had at least five years of production experience rose to 70 percent for the first secretaries chosen in 1989 and the first half of 1990.

In only two respects did the experiences of the new first secretaries differ from those of their predecessors. First, in the past Gorbachev had often selected them from outside the oblast to solidify his control over it. After January 1, 1989, however, none of the new obkom first secretaries was an outsider. Second, the oblast formerly was dominated by its capital, and this dominance both reflected and was reflected in the fact that the top obkom officials usually had long worked in oblast-level institutions. In 1981, for example, the obkom first secretaries had worked in the capital in the oblast apparatus for an average seventeen years, not counting any previous work in the city. Although the new first secretaries of 1989–90 were insiders and came to their posts directly from oblast-level posts, they often had worked only a short time at the oblast level and came from smaller cities and county seats outside the oblast center.

In one sense the new pattern of personnel selection corresponded to the geographical locus of support of the Communist party. The party had done better in the small towns and countryside in the 1989 election than it had in the larger cities. The new first secretaries no doubt reflected better the mood of the average Communist voter than did people from the large cities. But the new first secretaries from small towns scarcely were the kind of politicians most likely to arrest the erosion of support in the large cities. If the party of the advanced industrial proletariat was to become the party of the old, the peasant, and the small town worker, it was in deep political difficulty.

Finally, no attempt was made to turn the Communist party into an effective parliamentary party. Those officials who voted with Mikhail Gorbachev dominated the USSR Congress of People's Deputies. Gorbachev, however, worked as a chairman of the Supreme Soviet who stood above parties, not as an American Speaker of the House who leads the majority party. Deputies with voting records very similar to Gorbachev's were damned as conservatives. Gorbachev made no effort to build a centrist coalition. He did not use the Politburo to hammer out party legislative strategy, but abandoned it altogether.

The same problem was to occur when the Russian Congress of People's Deputies assembled. One of the largest blocs in the Congress called itself the Communists of Russia. It seemed to have no meaningful contact with the new Russian Communist party or Gorbachev's all-Union Communist party. The founding congress of the Russian Communist party began just as the First Congress of People's Deputies ended, and the party leaders failed to elect most of the legislative leaders to the party Central Committee. There seemed to be little interaction between, for example, the Central Committee secretary for agrarian policy and the relatively conservative *agrarniki* (agrarian) faction in the Congress. There was little contact between Communist faction in the USSR Congress and the Communists of Russia in the Russian Congress.

But if the Communist party was not to become a parliamentary party and was not to be a leading organ, what role would it have? If regional party secretaries deprived of administrative duties were to be chosen from among small town officials with engineering and managerial experience, what were they supposed to do? If any responsiveness on their part to public fears about market forces was to be denounced as unacceptable conservatism, how were Communists to compete with other parties that were more sensitive to public opinion? It was difficult to avoid the sense that Gorbachev had no more feeling for democracy as an institution than he did for the market.

CHAPTER NINE

The 1990 Russian Election

ALTHOUGH BORIS YELTSIN'S stunning victory in Moscow in the 1989
USSR congressional election may have been the crucial psychological
moment in the Russian Revolution of 1990–91, the republican elections of
1990 were the crucial substantive event. Revolution from below is difficult
in the best of circumstances, and the Soviet population was passive. As
Mancur Olson has emphasized, the crucial element in a successful revolution is for officials with control over the power of appointment, financial
resources, and the means of repression to have the opportunity and incentive to take decisive independent action.[1]

The end of the power of the Central Committee, the Politburo, and the
Secretariat in early 1990 created the potential for lower officials to acquire
such independence. Officials at the oblast level were never able to do so,
but the 1990 republican elections created institutions at the republican
level with the necessary legitimacy and necessary control over finances.
These elections brought to the fore leaders who had proven to themselves
that they either knew how to appeal successfully to anti-Moscow feelings
or, especially in Central Asia, how to control local elections without
Moscow's help.

The major events were to occur in Russia, but they are poorly understood
in the West because the 1990 Russian republican election was later seriously distorted by Boris Yeltsin and his supporters. As they moved in 1992
and 1993 to destroy the Russian Congress elected in 1990, Yeltsin began to

---

1. Mancur Olson, "The Logic of Collective Action in Soviet-Type Societies,"
Journal of Soviet Nationalities, vol. 1 (Summer 1990), pp. 25–26.

denounce as undemocratic both the Russian legislature and the elections that produced it. Western observers tended to accept these criticisms because of memories of the semidemocratic 1989 USSR elections and the legislature they produced.

Yet the 1990 Russian elections were very democratic and the Russian legislature different from its USSR counterpart. Not only were the built-in conservative biases of the USSR legislature absent in the Russian legislature, but the nominating process was much freer and the election more competitive. The democratic political forces were better organized because a year had passed since the previous election. The 1990 Congress elected Boris Yeltsin chairman of the Supreme Soviet, passed a Declaration of Sovereignty that declared Russian laws superior to those of the USSR , and in April 1991, by a two-thirds vote, established a Russian presidency, knowing full well that Yeltsin would be elected president.

The 1990 election was free in Russia, but Yeltsin won with a program very different from the one he was to institute. Although pledging preservation of the Union and opposing price increases, he was to follow a contrary path on both measures. As long as neither Mikhail Gorbachev nor the military would impose restraints on him, the population faced the same problems of collective action in controlling an elected leader that they had with nonelected ones.

The Russian Legislature

In 1989 the Soviet leadership probably looked forward to the Russian election with equanimity. The radicals had won less than 20 percent of the seats in the USSR Congress of People's Deputies and seemed unlikely to win 50 percent of those in the Russian legislature. Presumably Gorbachev expected the 1990 Russian elections to produce a body of legislators somewhat more radical on the average than the USSR Congress, but one in which the moderates would have a majority and would elect a chairman acceptable to him. He likely already had in mind Aleksandr Vlasov, a former Komsomol secretary in Siberia in the 1960s and an obkom first secretary in a region bordering on Stavropol.

Boris Yeltsin was frustrated by his role in the USSR Congress, and he decided to transfer his base of power to the Russian republic and to run as a Russian deputy in the 1990 election. Most of the radical deputies in the USSR Congress thought the Russian Congress would be an even more unsatisfactory arena for him than the USSR Congress, and few left the

USSR Congress to run in the Russian election. Yeltsin's advisers believed the radicals were unlikely to win a majority.[2]

Unlike in other republics of the Soviet Union, the legislature established in the Russian Republic was built on the USSR model: a part-time Congress of People's Deputies and a full-time Supreme Soviet.[3] The Congress of People's Deputies had 1,068 deputies, 900 of them elected in districts with an equal number of eligible voters (the so-called territorial districts) and 168 in districts designed to give the nationality-based territorial units of Russia (the so-called national-territorial districts) greater representation. Each deputy had an equal vote in the Congress, giving the deputies elected in the territorial districts a large majority.

Of the 168 national-territorial deputies, half were elected in the ethnic Russian oblasts and half in the nationally based territorial units. Since only 57 such regions existed, the more populous Russian areas could be given more than one seat. For example, Moscow contained 3 percent of the population of the USSR and 6 percent of the population of Russia. The national-territorial district in which Boris Yeltsin had been elected in the 1989 USSR election embraced the entire 9 million people of the capital, and that district was but 1 of 750 national-territorial districts in the country. In 1990 Moscow was divided into 6 national-territorial districts—3.6 percent of the total. Together with its 59 territorial districts, Moscow had a total of 65 deputies, basically the appropriate number for its population.

The Supreme Soviet contained 256 deputies chosen from among congressional deputies. Half came from deputies elected in the 900 territorial districts and half from those elected in the 168 national-territorial districts. The Supreme Soviet was bicameral, with the deputies from the territorial districts forming the Soviet of the Republic and those from the national-territorial districts the Soviet of Nationalities.[4] Supreme Soviet legislation

2. Lev Sukhanov, *Tri goda s El'tsinym: Zapiski pervogo pomoshchnika* (Riga, Latvia: Vaga, 1992), p. 241.

3. The 1990 republican elections were held at different times, had different numbers of candidates per district, and different levels of turnout. See Stephen White, Graeme Gill, and Darrell Slider, *The Politics of Transition: Shaping a Post-Soviet Future* (Cambridge University Press, 1993), pp. 31–32. The extent to which the elections were really democratic also varied widely.

4. The word *soviet* (council) was confusing in official parlance in the USSR because it was used both for executive bodies (the Council of Ministers and the Federation Council) and legislatures (the Supreme Soviet). The rapid institutional change of 1989–91 left little time for the development of conventional usage to be codified, and the names of the institutions are variously translated into English.

required the approval both of the Soviet of the Republics and the Soviet of Nationalities. That is, a majority of the deputies elected both in the territorial and national-territorial districts had to vote for legislation if it was to pass.

The division of powers between the Congress and the Supreme Soviet was fairly straightforward. The Congress had the power to change the constitution, elect the chairman of the Supreme Soviet (the head of state, as in the original USSR Constitution), and override decisions of the Supreme Soviet. The Supreme Soviet had the right to select the chairman of the Council of Ministers, subject to confirmation by the Congress, but the major role of the Supreme Soviet was to pass legislation, also subject to congressional confirmation. Because the Congress was absorbed with institutional questions requiring constitutional change, the Supreme Soviet turned out to be relatively autonomous in its legislative behavior.

Although the two-tier legislature in the USSR was established to ensure conservative congressional control over the potentially more radical Supreme Soviet, this was not the case in Russia. The Russian Federation Soviet of Nationalities had to include 126 deputies from among the 168 national-territorial deputies, and the deputies were expected to be more conservative than the territorial-district deputies. Because the Soviet of Nationalities had a veto on Supreme Soviet action, everyone expected that the Supreme Soviet would be more conservative than the Congress.

The two-tier legislature was probably retained in Russia as a solution to an ethnic balance in the population that was very different from that in the Soviet Union as a whole. Non-Russians comprised nearly 50 percent of the USSR population, and it made intuitive sense to have a second house of any USSR legislature to give special representation to the ethnically based territories. However, more than 80 percent of the population of Russia was Russian, and only 14.5 percent of the population—21.6 million people in 1989—lived in the major federal units of Russia (the autonomous republics). For this reason it was unnatural to have a bicameral legislature in which one house was controlled by the ethnic units and had equal weight with the other house. In the past the Russian Supreme Soviet had only one house whose deputies were elected on the basis of population.[5]

5. In 1979 the autonomous republics accounted for 141 of the 975 deputies of the unicameral legislature, exactly the number warranted by their population. *Sovetskaia Rossiia*, December 9, 1979, pp. 1, 3–6. For the list of deputies elected in 1985 in each oblast and autonomous republic, see *Deputaty Verkhovnogo Soveta RSFSR: Odinnadtsatyi sozyv* (Moscow: Izvestiia, 1987), pp. 329–51. This book also provides biographies of the deputies.

By 1990, however, the idea of republican sovereignty was becoming very popular in the Union republics, including Russia. The Bashkir and Tatar republics together had more people than half the Union republics, and their leaders demanded sovereignty and even the right of secession. It was virtually inevitable that some kind of Soviet of Nationalities would be established within the Russian legislature to give them and other non-Russians more formal representation.

The two-tier system with 900 territorial districts and 168 national-territorial districts permitted additional representation for the republics, but not too much power. Because the territorial and national-territorial deputies each had a single and equal vote in the Congress and the passage of legislation did not require the agreement of the two types of deputies, the small number of national-territorial districts from non-Russian ethnic units (84) had a small impact on the balance of power in the Congress. The ethnically based units, by contrast, were given more formal and more substantial representation in the less powerful Supreme Soviet.

The major difference between the Russian and USSR legislatures, however, stemmed from the electoral laws that defined the way the candidates were nominated. All the changes were in a direction certain to produce a more democratic legislature in Russia than in the USSR.

First, seats were not set aside in the Russian Congress for public organizations, and all deputies were elected by the people. This removed the third of the deputies who were most likely to be conservative or under party control in the USSR Congress. Second, the national-territorial districts had elected one-third of the USSR deputies, and the national-territorial districts seriously overrepresented the villages and small towns at the expense of the larger cities. Some 420 of the 750 national-territorial districts were located in the five Central Asian Union republics and the autonomous republics and oblasts, units with 25 percent of the Soviet population. In Russia, by contrast, there were five times more territorial districts than national-territorial districts. Moreover, half the national-territorial districts were given to the basic Russian oblasts and the more populous oblasts were given greater representation. Thus while the national-territorial districts still overrepresented rural areas, this bias was much smaller than it was in the USSR Congress.

Third, although nominations in the 1990 election still were largely made by the "work collectives," many more different types of the collectives were given the power to nominate.[6] In the past the right to nominate

6. Candidates could be also nominated in a neighborhood caucus. The number of citizens required for a valid caucus was reduced from 500 in the 1989 election to 300.

candidates was largely limited to production labor collectives (notably those in industry, construction, and agriculture) and military units, but in 1990 the scientific and educational institutions were included in the labor collectives with this right. In the big cities in particular, many such institutions took advantage of this right, and large numbers of scholars and college instructors were nominated and elected. They usually were among the more radical candidates and deputies.

Finally, the district election committees that had served as an important filter in 1989 were transformed. The committees still had the responsibility of registering nominees, but could refuse to do so only if the election law had been violated. Indeed, the major complaints against the election committees were that they enforced the rules. Many people believed that the democratic rights of the majority should not be limited by legal technicalities such as a residence requirement any more than by dictation from the party apparatus. They sometimes nominated whoever they wanted and operated by the principle of "any means to achieve the end."[7] They were deeply offended when their candidate was not confirmed.[8]

The Candidates

There were many signs that the more democratic electoral rules led to a more democratic nominating process. First, by all outward appearances the process worked well.[9] More candidates were nominated in the 1,068 districts in the 1990 Russian election than in the 1,500 districts in the 1989 USSR election—8,254 or 7.7 per district as compared with 7,351 or 4.9 per district in 1989. More important, the screening process had drastically reduced the number of candidates from 4.9 to 1.9 per district in 1989, but only from 7.7 to 6.3 in 1990. The decrease in 1990 seems to have resulted

---

However, this was of little importance because only 2.5 percent of the candidates were nominated at their place of residence. *Argumenty i fakty*, no. 3, January 13–19, 1990, p. 8.

7. *Sovetskaia Rossiia*, February 25, 1990, p. 1; and *Krasnaia zvezda*, January 13, 1990, p. 1.

8. *Sovetskaia kul'tura*, January 20, 1990.

9. Some complaints did appear about apparatus control of the nomination of candidates for the oblast and city soviets that were being elected simultaneously. It was reported, for example, that fifty-one of the seventy-five seats for the city soviet and fifty-seven of the sixty-eight seats for the oblast soviet in Saratov had a single candidate. *Pravda*, February 5, 1990, p. 1.

almost totally from the voluntary withdrawal of candidates, rules violations, or candidates being nominated in more than one district. Only 3.6 percent of the districts had a single candidate.

Although the voter had little real choice in many of the rural and small town elections in 1989, this was not true in 1990. The territorial districts based on towns of less than 100,000 people had fewer candidates: 4.8 on the average, compared with more than 7.5 in cities with populations greater than 200,000, but 5 is a large number by normal standards (table 9-1).

A second indication that the 1990 elections were more democratic than the 1989 elections is the character of the nominees. When nominations are controlled, those in charge of the process try to make the nominees fairly representative in occupation, religion, ethnicity, and gender.[10] The party leaders in the Soviet Union were careful to ensure representation not only for women and non-Russian ethnic groups, but also for a range of occupations and age groups in the old legislatures.

The composition of the Russian Supreme Soviet elected in 1985 was typical for the period: 35 percent of the deputies were women, 44 percent were workers and peasants, 48 percent had less than a higher education, and 33 percent were not members of the Communist party.[11] (The non-elite categories overlapped, for most of the workers and peasants were women who were not party members.)[12] Deputies of a wide range of ages were selected: 20 percent younger than 30, 15 percent between 30 and 39, 24 percent between 40 and 49, 28 percent between 50 and 59, and 13 percent 60 or older. As was the case with the 1984 USSR Supreme Soviet, the occupational distribution of the deputies in the 1985 Russian Supreme Soviet was bimodal. More than a third (36 percent) of the deputies were high officials: 5 percent USSR officials, 7 percent RSFSR officials, 5 percent military and security generals, and 19 percent important regional soviet and party officials. Another 8 percent were directors of economic enterprises. A virtually identical 44 percent were work-

---

10. Gerhard Loewenberg, "The New Political Leadership of Central Europe: The Example of the New Hungarian National Assembly," in Thomas F. Remington, ed., *Parliaments in Transition: The New Legislative Politics in the Former USSR and Eastern Europe* (Boulder, Colo.: Westview Press, 1994), p. 32.

11. *Deputaty Verkhovnogo Soveta RSFSR*, pp. 3–4. The age breakdown of those older than fifty was calculated from the biographies in this book.

12. Regina A. Smyth, "Ideological vs. Regional Cleavages: Do the Radicals Control the RSFSR Parliament?" *Journal of Soviet Nationalities*, vol. 1 (Fall 1990), p. 116.

Table 9-1. *Average Number of Candidates, 1989 USSR Election and 1990*
Russian Election, by Type of Russian District and Most Populous City

Population of largest city and average number of electors	1989 USSR territorial district (Russia only)	1990 RSFSR territorial district	1990 RSFSR national-territorial district
Less than 25,000	1.5	4.7	...
25,000–49,999	1.7	4.9	5.9
50,000–99,999	1.7	4.9	6.0
100,000–199,000	2.0	5.7	6.5
200,000–499,000	2.2	7.4	7.6
500,000–999,000	1.9	7.5	8.1
1,000,000–2,000,000	2.2	7.8	10.0
Leningrad	2.4	7.5	10.7
Moscow	3.1	8.4	10.5

Sources: The cities in the electoral districts are found in *Izvestiia*, November 8, 1988, pp. 1–8; *Sovetskaia Rossiiak*, November 11, 1989, pp. 2–7; and *Itogi Vsesoiuznoi perepisi*, vol. 1: *Chislennost' irazmeshchenie naseleniia* (Moscow: Goskomstat SSSR; and Minneapolis: East View Publishing, 1992) pt. 1, pp 13–197. The names of all candidates in each electoral district, and therefore, the number were collected by Violetta Rumiantsev from the regional press in Moscow libraries.

ers and peasants.[13] As a result, only 20 percent of the deputies held interme-diate occupations, and 4 percent of them were mid-level agricultural man-agers who officially were called collective farmers.

The phrase "high official" had a very precise meaning in this context. The party leadership used election to the soviets as an important status symbol for its officials: top officials were elected to the USSR Supreme Soviet, the next level to the republican soviets, the next level to the oblast soviets, and so forth. The same categories of officials tended to be elected time after time to a particular level of soviet.

Thus first secretaries of all oblast party committees (obkoms) and the chairmen of the executive committees of the soviets in the largest regions were elected deputies to the USSR Supreme Soviet. The second secretaries of the oblast party committees, the chairmen of the executive committees of the soviets in the middle-sized and small oblasts, as well as the first deputy chairmen of the executive committees of the regional oblast soviets in the large oblasts were elected deputies of the Russian Supreme Soviet. The party first secretaries in the largest capital cities were elected USSR depu-ties and those in the next largest were named Russian deputies. Command-

13. It was officially stated that 50.1 percent were workers and collective farmers, but collective farmers included farm administrative personnel—chairman, chief agron-omists, brigadiers, and so forth.

ers of military districts usually were elected USSR deputies, while heads of the political administrations of the military districts were usually elected to the Russian Supreme Soviet. Plant directors and farm managers were elected in reasonably large numbers, but invariably they were administering very important plants and farms.

There is no full information on the candidates of 1990, but only 7.6 percent were women, 8.7 percent workers, and 3.1 percent peasants. Only 5.5 percent of the candidates were younger than age 30, and 3.0 percent older than 60.[14] Only 161 of the deputies of the 1985 Russian Supreme Soviet even ran in the 1990 election.

Detailed information is available about the occupations of all candidates in 1990, and they were very different from the candidates of 1985. Only 5 percent of the candidates elected in 1990 had political, government, and military jobs important enough to be counted among the 36 percent of the candidates and deputies who were important officials in 1985. At the same time, the proportion of workers and peasants decreased from 44 percent of the candidates (and deputies) in 1985 to 10 percent in 1990 (table 9-2). The major fact about the candidates and deputies of 1990 is the great increase in the number in intermediate, white-collar occupations from middle-level officials down to nonadministrative professionals. In 1985 nearly half of the 20 percent of the deputies in this category were directors of enterprises. Seventy-five percent of the candidates were in these middle categories in 1990, and one-quarter in the middle group were enterprise directors. In 1985 virtually all the military officers among the deputies held the rank of lieutenant general or colonel general (or the equivalent in other services); in 1990 most held lower ranks.[15]

The occupational distribution of candidates did differ by the size of the largest city or town within the district (table 9-3). Almost half of the nominees in Moscow—245 of them—worked in scientific institutions, design bureaus, colleges, publishing, and journalism. Only 59 were directors or chief editors of these institutions. (To be more precise, the Moscow elections were dominated by the city's male intellectuals; only 27 of the 497 candidates were women.) An additional 16 candidates worked in public health and in education below the college level. Leningrad was similar, although it had a higher percentage of nominees from industry.

---

14. *Izvestiia*, February 3, 1990, p. 1.

15. Army officers who taught in the military academies are counted as nonadministrative professionals in this analysis. If they were included in the military category, the percentage of lower- and middle-ranking officers in the category would be even greater.

Table 9-2. *Occupations of Deputies in the Russian Supreme Soviet, 1985,*
and the Congress of People's Deputies, 1990
Percent

Post or occupation[a]	1985 deputies and candidates	1990 congressional candidates (territorial districts)	1990 congressional deputies
Higher political officials	31	4	14
Higher military-security	5	1	2
Lower military-security	0	7	6
Middle regional officials	2	12	13
Directors of economic enterprises	8	19	20
Directors of institutes, schools, hopsitals, other	2	9	10
Middle-level administrators, including agriculture	7	14	9
	5	1	1
Nonadministrative professionals	1	21	20
Workers	30	9	5
Peasants	14	1	1
Miscellaneous	0	3	1

Sources: For the official statistics on the 1985 deputies, see *Deputaty Verkhovnogo Soveta RSFSR, Odinnadtsatyi sozyv* (Moscow: Izvestiia, 1987), p. 3. For 1990, see *Izvestiia,* February 3, 1990, p. 11; and TASS, March 1, 1990. The numbers and occupations of deputies were collected by Violetta Rumiantseva from the oblast press.
a. "Higher political official" is defined as one who held a post traditionally warranting election to the RSFSR or USSR Supreme Soviet. Lower-level administrators in higher educaiton, science, and the media are included among "nonadministrative professionals."

The nominees in the smaller towns and cities were very different from those in Moscow and Leningrad. In districts whose largest town had less than 25,000 people, only 8.3 percent of the candidates worked in science, higher education, publishing, or journalism, compared with 49.3 percent in Moscow. More than 60 percent of the candidates in districts in which the largest town had less than 25,000 people were political, government, military, and economic officials at the enterprise level or above, compared with 27 percent in Moscow. As table 9-3 shows, the cities between these two extremes also had occupational distributions of candidates that were between the extremes.

Table 9-3 does not, of course, demonstrate that voters had a real choice, and confident generalizations about the nominating process in the large number of districts in the Soviet Union are impossible. However, the lists of all the candidates in all the districts, together with the percentage of the vote received by each, were published in the local press, and they provide some sense of the character of the election. Chapter 5 noted the nature of the 1989 USSR elections in the Stavropol region: collective farmer running

Table 9-3. Occupations of Candidates from Territorial Districts, by Population of Largest Town in District, Russian 1990 Election

Percent

Occupation	Largest city of district								
	Less than 25,000	25,000–50,000	50,000–100,000	100,000–199,000	200,000–499,000	500,000–999,000	More than 1 million	Leningrad	Moscow
Higher political	9.7	7.9	4.0	1.7	2.0	2.7	1.6	1.7	3.2
Higher military-security	0.7	0.5	1.3	0.7	0.3	0.4	0.5	0.4	0.8
Medium military-security	6.7	7.4	6.2	6.3	7.7	6.6	6.6	8.8	6.4
Medium political	15.9	16.4	11.2	13.4	9.2	10.8	13.3	8.0	11.7
Director industrial enterprise	10.4	15.1	16.8	16.6	12.5	11.1	12.1	7.5	4.8
Director agricultural enterprise	18.4	13.9	8.1	2.9	2.4	1.2	0	0	0.2
Medium industrial administration	4.0	9.2	11.7	13.9	13.2	10.9	11.0	9.7	4.4
Medium agricultural administration	4.1	2.9	1.9	1.2	0.3	0.4	0.2	0.4	.0
Director, science, education, or media institution	4.4	1.9	1.6	2.7	3.3	4.2	4.0	4.6	11.9
Director, other institution	4.3	4.9	6.9	4.1	6.4	6.3	4.9	2.5	2.4
Medium administrator	1.8	3.0	7.1	3.2	3.2	2.3	1.6	3.8	2.2
Lower science, college, or journalist	4.7	5.0	9.4	8.5	15.3	19.2	25.0	35.3	37.4
Other professional	5.7	7.1	10.5	6.6	7.2	5.9	5.9	4.6	4.8
Worker	5.2	2.7	0.9	12.4	13.6	12.1	8.4	5.0	4.2
Peasant	3.2	1.4	2.0	0.5	0.1	0.4	0.0	0.0	0.0
Miscellaneous	1.0	0.5	0.4	3.4	3.2	4.6	4.9	7.1	5.4
Unknown	0.7	0	0	1.7	0.3	0.9	0	0	0

Sources: See table 9-1.

against collective farmer, worker against worker, and so forth. The 1989 elections in the rural areas frequently left the same impression, but this is not the case in the 1990 Russian elections.

Even the large number of officials in the countryside does not indicate a lack of choice there or in small towns. First, of course, 40 percent of the candidates had positions less important than that of enterprise director. Second, even when choice was limited to government and farm officials, that fact does not prove the elections were controlled. In most countries voters who do not wish to elect revolutionaries normally elect candidates with experience. The fact that Ronald Reagan and Bill Clinton were state governors did not make their presidential elections undemocratic. In addition, categories such as officials and enterprise directors hide candidates of very different natures, including many who are far from the type of nomenklatura who had been elected deputies in the past. For example, the county (*raion*) party first secretary, who was a very powerful figure in his county, looked far less imposing in an electoral district containing four to eight raions, only one of which was his own. In the other counties of the district, most voters probably did not know his name, and they and the local party apparatus might fear that his election as a Russian deputy would give his raion an advantage over theirs in resource allocation.

Consider District 296 in Briansk oblast, an agricultural area whose largest town (Karachev) had 22,000 inhabitants. By my classification the four candidates in its election were two political officials, an industrial enterprise director, and an agricultural enterprise director. One political official was first deputy chairman of the executive committee of the Briansk oblast soviet, a post usually warranting election to the obkom party bureau but ranking perhaps eighth among top oblast officials. The other political official was the deputy chairman of the executive committee of a county soviet whose largest town had 14,000 inhabitants. The factory manager was the director of a furniture factory in a town with 11,000 people. Nothing is known about the collective farm chairman except that he came in fourth in the election with 7 percent of the vote. The winner was the county official, Vladimir A. Barabanov. He turned out to be a radical in the Congress, but even if he had been a conservative, he would not have been the winner in a controlled election.[16]

16. *Brianskii Rabochii*, March 23, 1990, p. 1.

In other cases when voters were given less choice, one cannot be certain about the reasons. For example, districts in the Northern Osetian and the Kabardino-Balkar Autonomous Republics each had a first deputy chairman of the Soviet KGB as their single candidate.[17] Was this the result of control of the nomination process, or were other potential candidates simply afraid to enter the race? In other races in which top local officials ran, was the nominating process controlled, were other candidates induced or pressured not to run, or did other potential candidates simply believe they did not have a chance to win? Probably each of these calculations was made in different districts, but one should remember that pressure not to run or disinclination to be a candidate is a normal part of democracy. Well-established members of the U.S. Congress often face nominal opposition at best in their districts.

The Election

The turnout in the 1990 Russian election was lower than that in Russia in the 1989 USSR election—77 percent as against 87 percent.[18] The fact that the number of candidates in the 1990 Russian election was much larger than it had been in the USSR 1989 election made it much more difficult for a candidate to receive an absolute majority of the votes, but it also simplified matters in subsequent rounds.[19] As in 1989, a new election had to be held if the winner in a one-candidate or two-candidate election did not receive a majority. In 1990 there were only 30 districts where the election had to be repeated because no candidate received a majority. A runoff between the top two candidates was required in 913 multicandidate districts, and a plurality was sufficient for a victory in a runoff.[20]

In the runoffs, voter turnout dropped to 69 percent, and it was below the required 50 percent in some instances.[21] By the time the First Congress opened on May 15, two months after the election, nine seats were still vacant. Another three deputies were elected in the next few months, but after several more attempts to obtain the required 50 percent turnout in the

---

17. These were Genii E. Ageev in national-territorial district 98 in Kabardino-Balkaria and Filipp D. Bobkov from national-territorial district 122 in North Osetia.

18. *Izvestiia*, April 5, 1989, p. 1. Turnout in the USSR as a whole was 89.8 percent.

19. This happened in only 121 districts, and 1 of these elections was declared void because of election irregularities.

20. *Izvestiia*, March 14, 1990, p. 1.

21. *Sovetskaia Rossiia*, March 28, 1990, p. 1.

remaining districts, the authorities gave up and left the seats vacant. As a result, the Congress of People's Deputies never had more than 1,062 deputies, not the 1,068 specified in the Constitution. As deputies died and often were not replaced because it was impossible to get a 50 percent turnout, the number of deputies continued to decline; by 1993 there were 1,038.[22]

Few major claims of vote fraud surfaced after the election. Both sides made the usual array of complaints about illegal campaign expenses and press bias; most of the charges by both sides seem accurate. Because the financial limits in the election law were unrealistically low, all serious candidates, both radical and conservative, used the photocopying facilities and paper of the institutions supporting them. The newly liberated press had relatively little sense of the need for balanced political coverage, so there was plenty of bias on both sides, depending on the viewpoint of the editors.

It is uncertain that any of this mattered much. In 1990 the basic issues of the election were clear. Did the voter want to vote against the party apparatus and the system it oversaw? Were the radicals demanding too much change too rapidly or representing alien values, or both? Voters were not likely to be greatly influenced by biased press coverage or the quantity of leaflets distributed in choosing between a radical candidate and a conservative. Indeed, in the Leningrad election of 1989 many voters had been so antiapparatus that they would vote against a candidate precisely because he had high-quality leaflets or support by the local party newspaper.

The Yaroslavl national-territorial election seems typical. Viacheslav Shchepotkin, deputy editor of *Izvestiia* in charge of parliamentary reporting, ran against three other candidates, one of them Vladimir A. Kovalev, the first deputy chairman of the executive committee of the oblast soviet in charge of agriculture. Shchepotkin was the top vote getter in the first round, with 175,000 votes against 163,000 for Kovalev and 155,000 and 95,000 for the other two candidates, respectively. He then lost in the second round and complained bitterly in *Izvestiia* about unfairness in the local press and party machine support for Kovalev.[23] No doubt Shchepotkin's complaint about the press and party machine was accurate, but the voters surely knew

---

22. When Yeltsin became president, for example, his seat in Sverdlovsk became open, and it was impossible to elect a successor. The number of deputies was that on the computerized Supreme Soviet directory of Congress deputies in June 1993. The directory was provided to the author by Iosif Diskin.

23. *Izvestiia*, April 3, 1990, p. 3.

that Kovalev was a top local government official who was on the bureau of the oblast party committee, while his opponent was a radical-democratic Moscow editor. The choice was clear, and a few dirty tricks were not likely to affect the outcome.

In the politics of Yaroslavl Oblast, a central issue was the dominance of rural regions by the capital city, which contained 40 percent of the population. The voting for the oblast soviet suggested that neither the radicals nor Yaroslavl city had a majority among the voters. A Moscow editor supported by the urban democrats received almost exactly the percentage of votes that would have been predicted from a knowledge of the mood of the oblast.[24]

The Absence of Parties

The strongest impression gained from looking at the lists of candidates across the country, reading reports of the campaigns, and analyzing the results, including those from rural areas and small towns, is of a very democratic election in Russia in 1990. Certainly, it does not seem to have been rigged in favor of the old elite. Even when high political officials were nominated, they often lost.

The major defect in the 1990 election was not too little choice, but too much—too many candidates, not too few. Voters in Moscow and Leningrad received two ballots for the Russian legislature, one with an average of eight candidates for the local territorial district and one of ten or eleven candidates for the national-territorial district. They also received ballots for simultaneous elections to the local soviet. Even in the rural areas, two ballots with five candidates apiece were not a simple matter for the average citizen.

As in the 1989 election, a substantial number of voters crossed out the names of all candidates. In 1989 this practice frequently seemed a protest against a single candidate or an unsatisfactory selection of candidates in a two-candidate election. In 1990 the percentage of "none of the above" ballots increased with the number of candidates. It seemed more a protest against the impossibility of making an intelligent choice than one against the candidates themselves, an impression that was reinforced in the 1993 legislature (Duma) that had simultaneous party and district elections.[25] Only

24. Jerry F. Hough, "Political Cleavages in Yaroslavl Politics," in Remington, ed., *Parliaments in Transition*, pp. 75–96.
25. In the Duma, half the seats were selected by proportional representation and party list and half in districts.

4.3 percent voted against all in the party election where there was a wide choice between well-known parties, but 15 to 20 percent voted against all in the district elections, which featured candidates with little opportunity to develop name recognition.[26]

The problem in the nominating process was the lack of parties, which could have given the voters signals about the programs of the candidates, at least on the first round. Gorbachev did not abolish Article 6 on the leading role of the Communist party until after the nominations for the Russian Congress were over. Thus only the Communists had the right to nominate candidates, and the Communist party of the Russian Federation was not created until June 1990. The USSR Communist party chose not to fulfill the nominating role of a political party.

The only nationwide political group independent of the Communist party in 1989 was the Interregional Group of USSR Deputies, but it did not make a coordinated effort to nominate candidates for the Russian Congress. Loose groupings, however, did form during the campaign. The two most prominent were the Russian Patriotic Bloc, essentially composed of right-wing nationalists, and the Democratic Russia group in conjunction with Elections-90, which supported the establishment of democracy and a market economy.[27] The names they informally applied to themselves were the patriots and the democrats.[28]

The Patriotic Bloc created a great deal of alarm in the West during the campaign, but it had virtually no success.[29] Democratic Russia proved far more important. It was established before the election in January and by February 20 was supporting more than 5,000 candidates for the various soviets.[30] Consisting primarily of urban intellectuals and low-level admin-

26. See the discussion in Jerry F. Hough, "The Russian Election of 1993: Public Attitudes toward Economic Reform and Democratization," *Post-Soviet Affairs*, vol. 10, no. 1 (1994), p. 32. The hypothesis that the "votes against all" were usually a protest against unknown candidates is further suggested by the fact that "none of the above" defeated the top vote getter in thirty-one of the thirty-five contests for the Moscow City Duma where the candidates were even more obscure. *Pravda*, January 4, 1994, p. 2.

27. For a very well documented discussion of the groups and political organizations that formed during the Russian campaign, see Brendan Kiernan, *The End of Soviet Politics: Elections, Legislatures, and the Demise of the Communist Party* (Boulder, Colo.: Westview Press, 1993), pp. 161–71.

28. *Sovetskaia kul'tura*, February 10, 1990, p. 3.

29. See, for example, Bill Keller, "Yearning for an Iron Hand," *New York Times Magazine*, January 28, 1990, pp. 18ff.

30. *Argumenty i fakty*, no. 8, February 24–March 2, 1990, p. 8.

istrators, the democrats rested organizationally on the many informal groups that had sprung up in large cities since 1987. Democratic Russia could not provide any direct support to the candidates associated with it because the election law prohibited any private individual or organization from providing financial support for a candidate's campaign.[31] In fact, the democrats were most noted for their lack of organization and their internal conflicts. The most important role of Democratic Russia was to be the organizational base it provided for the pro-Yeltsin forces as they prepared for the First Congress after the election.

The nomination process thus seemed individualistic and personality driven. It is striking how often candidates of similar background and views chose to compete in the same district. With an absolute majority of the votes cast required for victory on the first round, candidates naturally assumed that a runoff would be required in multicandidate elections. They often used the first round as a primary to determine the strongest candidate of a particular viewpoint or even to gain name recognition for a subsequent local political career.

In the runoff, political forces often rallied behind a candidate of a particular point of view. The case in Yaroslavl has already been mentioned. A subsequent chapter will describe how conservative and moderate forces united behind a moderate conservative, Colonel Aleksandr Rutskoi, who had been in second place on the first ballot behind a radical priest. In many other cases it was a more radical or reformist candidate who benefited. Here too, however, the phenomenon tended to have a local character.

The Election Results

The lack of nationwide parties in the 1990 election meant that no one could be certain who had won the election once it was over. Vitaly Vorotnikov, the Politburo member in charge of the Russian Republic, estimated that 20–23 percent of the deputies were supported by Democratic Russia.[32] The Russian Congress of People's Deputies clearly was going to have a far stronger radical-reformist character than the USSR Congress, but the views of many deputies would not be known until key congressional

---

31. The state allocated each candidate a wholly inadequate 350 rubles for the campaign, and each candidate was permitted to specify five official full-time campaign workers whose salary was to be paid by his or her employer during the campaign.

32. *Pravda*, March 26, 1990, p. 2.

votes were taken. Even when the Congress opened, Western reporters thought Yeltsin might have only a third of the vote.[33]

The First Congress turned out to be very closely balanced between pro-Yeltsin and anti-Yeltsin forces. Pronounced radicals comprised slightly more than a third of the deputies, while strong conservatives were slightly less numerous. The most thorough Moscow analyst puts the percentage of those on the left at 52 percent of the deputies and those on the right at 48 percent, and that estimate seems essentially correct (see table 9-4). The distribution resembled a U-shaped curve, but when Yeltsin adopted a relatively accommodating posture toward the deputies, he could achieve his major goals.

The one piece of information on the deputies that was known from the first was their occupations. When the deputies who held major political, administrative, and managerial jobs turned out to be more conservative than those without administrative posts, observers writing about the election, who all supported the democratic side, focused on this fact in their analysis and political polemics (the two were identical). They charged that the anti-Yeltsin forces were the undemocratic, antireform bureaucrats, and partocrats; the pro-Yeltsin forces were those who came from the people and represented them.

The analyses were certainly right in pointing to a high correlation between occupation and voting at the First Congress, but it is crucial to remember the distinctions discussed previously between the officials of 1985 and 1990. The more conservative half of the Congress was dominated by officials, but not those at the level of the old nomenklatura, the old Communist elite. Only 16 percent of the 1990 deputies occupied the type of political and military posts that warranted election to the Supreme Soviet in 1985. Similarly, only 18 percent of deputies in 1990 were fifty-five years of age or older compared with 80 percent in 1985. Many of the deputies who were being classed as nomenklatura were very low-level nomenklatura, if at all, and only a few percent were really "the old Communist nomenklatura."

Districts, Public Opinion, and the Election

What does the correlation between occupation and political views in the Russian Congress mean? People normally look for experience when voting

33. Bill Keller, "Revolution in Europe; To Gorbachev Anxieties, Add Yeltsin Candidacy," *New York Times*, May 17, 1990, p. 10.

Table 9-4. *Distribution of Deputies, by Political Orientation, First Congress of People's Deputies, May–June 1990*

Political orientation	Number	Percent
Extreme radicals	281	26.6
Radicals	118	11.2
Moderate radicals	70	6.6
Left center	77	7.3
Right center	95	9.0
Moderate conservatives	110	10.5
Conservatives	118	11.2
Extreme conservatives	187	17.7

Sources: The roll-call analysis was done by Aleksandr Sobianin. His calculations for each deputy at each session of various RSFSR Congresses are found in Michael Makfol and N. Petrov, *Politicheskii al'manakh Rossii 1995* (Moscow: Moskovskii Tsenr Karnegi, 1995), pp. 700–18.

for national leaders or representatives. Russian voters wanting either the status quo or, more likely, gradual reform were similar. Candidates who had been outside the political system would be most likely to launch a populist attack on the bureaucracy since their opponents had been working within the system. It would be natural for voters deeply disenchanted with the system to vote for persons not working within it.

But when the radicals dominated the Russian government after independence, it was natural for 50 percent of the deputies elected on the list of the radical Russia's Choice party in 1993 to be high officials. The very conservative deputies on the list of Vladimir Zhirinovsky's Liberal Democratic party included almost no officials. Not occupation as such but relationship to the current insiders determined whether a candidate was radical or conservative.

The important element both in 1990 and 1993 was not the occupation of the deputies, but the views of those who elected them. The difference among deputies that was to be durable in all Russian elections was the character of the electoral districts.[34] As in 1989, as has been seen, southern regions elected more conservative deputies than did more northern ones (see table 5-4). The southern regions were more rural, and people in villages and smaller towns voted more conservatively than did those in larger cities (table 9-5).[35] In Moscow 70 percent of the victorious candidates worked in

34. For the 1993 election, see Hough, "Russian Election of 1993," pp. 1–37. For a comparison of the 1993 and 1995 elections, see Hough, Evelyn Davidheiser, and Susan Goodrich Lehmann, *The 1996 Russian Presidential Election* (Brookings, 1996).

35. Smyth, "Ideological vs. Regional Cleavages," pp. 142–49.

Table 9-5. *Political Orientation of Deputies, by Size of City in Which They Were Elected, RSFSR Territorial Districts, March 1990*

Population of largest city in electoral district	Radical deputies	Moderate deputies	Conservative deputies	Cases
Less than 25,000	17	29	90	136
25,000–49,000	40	36	91	167
50,000–99,000	51	42	60	153
100,000–199,000	24	19	24	67
200,000–499,000	50	30	34	114
500,000–999,000	52	23	17	92
1,000,000 or more	35	22	13	70
Leningrad	27	1	2	30
Moscow	52	5	0	57

Sources: See tables 9-1 and 9-4.

scientific institutions, design bureaus, colleges, publishing, and journalism, and virtually all of them voted as extreme radicals at the First Congress of People's Deputies. It is the Moscow voter who should be the center of analysis, not so much the occupation of the candidate elected.

In general, radical analysts wrote as if it were self-evident that conservative deputies who were nomenklatura by definition were not elected democratically. Implicitly, the radicals were saying that the elections in the villages and small towns were not authentic. They sometimes spoke loosely about the control of the collective farm chairmen and the rural elites but presented no evidence that the outcomes in the rural areas and the small towns did not reflect public opinion. In fact, as has been seen, rural districts were competitive. The weakness of the Agrarian party in the 1993 and 1995 elections confirmed the lack of control by the rural elite.

There was also no evidence of gerrymandering in favor of rural areas. District lines generally followed city and county boundaries. Although district size varied, it seemed to introduce little bias into the Congress.[36] The key decision taken was designed to reduce the rural overrepresentation produced by the creation of national-territorial districts. As in 1989, territorial districts were based on number of electors rather than population, a decision that discriminated against areas—generally rural—with a disproportionate number of people younger than eighteen years of age.

36. The average district had 115,000 eligible voters, but only 48 percent of the districts contained between the 103,500 and 126,500 eligible voters that would be necessary to remain within the 10 percent deviation that is considered legally acceptable in the United States.

The persons living in the 548 districts in which the largest city had less than 250,000 people "should" have received 543 deputies if eligible voters were the criterion and 572 if population were (table 9-6). The figures in the 352 districts based on larger cities were 357 and 330, respectively. Once territorial and national-territorial districts were added together, each economic region received almost exactly the same number of seats as it would have if there were no national-territorial districts and if districts were based on population rather than eligible voters.

There is also no reason to see much control in the elections in the districts, at least not that significantly reduced radical representation. The large number of candidates in the rural areas, the consistency in the conservatism in their voting across times (and in their views as revealed by public opinion polls),[37] and their support for Zhirinovsky in 1993 instead of the Agrarian party of the rural elite all strongly suggest that the rural elections were legitimate and democratic, not the result of elite control.

The fact that radicals did not want to recognize was that more than half of the population lived in cities and towns with less than 100,000 people. To say that the Congress (or later the Duma) was not legitimate because it reflected the views of the people living in such places was to say that their opinions were not legitimate. The radicals were saying that the "real" opinion of the masses had to be revolutionary. It was a very Leninist definition of democracy.

By the end of 1994, alarmed radicals were speaking of Moscow and St. Petersburg as democratic cities isolated in a communist-fascist sea. Yet a major survey taken in December 1993 showed that the countryside and small towns continued to favor democratic values and institutions.[38] They also retained their deep hostility to the political center of power in Moscow that was continuing to suppress them. By ignoring the fact that a democracy must be responsive to the majority of the population, the Yeltsin government, the radicals, and the West that supported them had created a political situation that was, indeed, frightening.

Pre-Congress Negotiations and the Development of Group Politics

Television coverage of the First USSR Congress gave the impression of great radical strength, but in fact the Interregional Group was too small to

37. See Hough, "Russian Election of 1993," pp. 23–27.
38. Hough, "Russian Election of 1993," pp. 11–15.

Table 9-6. *Actual and Ideal Numbers of Deputies to the Russian*
Congress of Deputies, According to Population and Eligible Voters,
by Size of Largest City in the District, 1990

	Actual number of deputies	Eligible voters (thousands)	Ideal number of deputies	Total population (thousands)	Ideal number of deputies
Moscow	59	6,890	60	8,967	55
Leningrad	31	3,727	32	5,026	31
Other large cities					
(500,000 or larger)	164	19,496	162	24,819	152
Medium cities					
(250,000–499,000)	98	11,417	103	14,833	92
Less than 250,000	548	62,064	543	93,377	572

Sources: See table 9-1.

be a significant factor in the legislative life of the Congress. The Congress was dominated by forces that were called conservatives by the radical press but that voted less conservatively than Mikhail Gorbachev.

It was clear from the beginning that the Russian Congress would be very different not only in the balance of the political forces within it, but also in the way it operated. A correspondent for *Komsomol'skaia pravda* caught the major difference in one of his first reports on the Congress.

Strains have appeared in the political melody of the Russian Congress that were never heard previously. Take this example. A deputy gets up and introduces a suggestion from the deputy group "Smena." Another makes a proposal from "Democratic Russia." And listen carefully. No one fell into a swoon or began to wail about schism, about opposition, about the danger of factional deviation. Compare this with the USSR Congress. They only hinted at an interregional deputy group, and noise erupted. They tried to talk about a multiparty system. Uproar.[39]

For someone long familiar with the Soviet Union it was, indeed, breath-taking. A central feature of Lenin's ideology had been the denial of the legitimacy of diverse interests and their political representation. Lenin and his successors did acknowledge the legitimacy of debate over the correct policy to be followed in a particular case. Commissions were always formed to draft decisions and laws, and they played an important role in policymaking.[40] They included representatives of different interested (*zainteresonnye*) government agencies and often of relevant Communist-

39. *Komsomol'skaia pravda*, May 17, 1990, p. 1.
40. Jerry F. Hough and Merle Fainsod, *How the Soviet Union Is Governed* (Harvard University Press, 1979), pp. 435–37, 536.

controlled social organizations that represented broad groups—trade unions, the Young Communist League. But Lenin had believed that political organizations and parties that "represented other classes" had no right to exist. He also believed that a "trade union consciousness" of workers served the interests of the capitalist class and had no more right to be represented in the political process than did defense of capitalist interests. He was utterly contemptuous of "parliamentarianism" (debate and political struggle among different parties) in a legislature.

The formation of political groups in the Congress of People's Deputies began even before it opened. Moscow had elected a large number of radical democratic deputies, and they began meeting soon after the election. Very quickly they were joined by others from outside Moscow. The inner core met in the office of the Committee of Construction of the USSR Supreme Soviet. The chairman of the committee was Boris Yeltsin, while the secretary was Mikhail Bocharov, a close associate of Yeltsin. Yeltsin never attended these meetings, but Bocharov was a key figure. He became the leader of a deputies' group, which was called Democratic Russia.[41]

On March 31 and April 1, Bocharov convened a meeting of deputies to form Democratic Russia as a formal organization. Two hundred deputies attended. Bocharov emphasized that Democratic Russia was not a party but "an association of deputies" and claimed that 370 supported the association.[42] When the first organizational meeting of deputies was held on March 30, only 215 deputies appeared, and this number fell to 189 at the second meeting on April 14.[43] However, Bocharov's claim of support corresponded fairly closely to Democratic Russia's actual voting strength.[44]

Democratic Russia formed working groups to devise a comprehensive program. On April 14 at its second meeting it adopted draft declarations on

41. Mikhail Chelnokov, *Rossiia bez Soiuza, Rossiia bez Rossii: zapiski deputata rasstrelianogo Parlamenta* (Moscow: Novaia sloboda, 1994), pp. 23–24.

42. TASS, April 1, 1990, in Foreign Broadcast Information Service, *Daily Report: Soviet Union*, April 2, 1990, p. 104 (hereafter, FBIS, *Soviet Union*). See also "Konferentsiia bloka 'Demokraticheskaia Rossiia,'" *Argumenty i fakty*, no. 14, April 7–13, 1990, p. 4.

43. *Sovetskaia Rossiia*, May 10, 1990, p. 2 (this source dates the organizational meeting as April 30, but that is wrong and a misprint). Nazimova and V. Sheinis, "Deputatskii korpus: shto novogo?" *Argumenty i fakty*, no. 17, April 28–May 4, 1990, p. 1.

44. *Sovetskaia Rossiia*, May 10, 1990, p. 2. Nazimova and Sheinis, "Deputatskii korpus," put the support at 30 to 35 percent of the deputies.

Russian sovereignty and the supremacy of Russian laws over USSR laws in Russian territory that were to be presented to the Congress.[45] It nominated Boris Yeltsin as its candidate for chairman of the Supreme Soviet.

Soviet legislatures had always functioned formally according to democratic rules, which included confirming (really rubber-stamping) the legislative agenda by a meeting of representatives from each of the regions before the opening of the session. A preparatory commission of similar type was formed for the First Congress of People's Deputies of Russia. It consisted of ninety-three members, including one representative from each of the eighty-one regions and districts.[46]

The official preparatory commission met from April 4 to April 20 and was unable to agree on the agenda.[47] The party leaders wanted the Congress to concentrate on electing a Supreme Soviet and then adjourn. The deputies in Democratic Russia who were on the commission wanted to expand the agenda, and some of their positions—the inclusion of a discussion of a declaration of sovereignty, constitutional amendments, and the working out of undefined legislation on the agenda—were accepted.[48] Some seemingly obscure procedural questions also remained controversial.

Both sides agreed to create a second preparatory commission, a "conference of representatives" that included ideological and occupational groups as well as regional ones.[49] It was the first dramatic and official acknowledgement that ideological and policy groups would not only be tolerated but would have to be active participants in the legislative process if acceptable compromises were to be found. This commission, too, could not agree on the agenda, and it had to be decided on the floor of the Congress.

The existence of groups in the Congress itself was recognized in congressional rules that were endorsed by both sides. Any fifty deputies were permitted to form an organized group or faction (*fraktsii*) and to register it officially. Each deputy was free to join up to five factions. By the beginning of the First Congress, more than twenty groups had officially registered;

<hr />

45. *Argumenty i fakty*, no. 16, April 17–20, 1990, p. 4.
46. *Sovetskaia Rossiia*, April 5, 1990, p. 2; April 8, 1990, p. 3; and May 10, 1990, p. 2.
47. *Sovetskaia Rossiia*, April 5, 1990, p. 2.
48. See the agenda published in *Izvestiia*, May 16, 1990, p. 1.
49. *Pervyi s"ezd narodnykh deputatov RSFSR (16 maia–22 iunia goda): Stenograficheskii otchet*, vol. 1 (Moscow: Respublika, 1992), p. 54.

two weeks later the number had risen to twenty-nine and then by the Second Congress in November to thirty-two.[50]

There were three major types of registered groups.[51] The first, with twelve groups, was occupational: the *agrarniki* (officially "food and health") from the rural sector; military and KGB officers; journalists of Glasnost; the Worker-Peasant Union; Educators, Scientific, and Cultural Workers; Transportation, Communications, and Computers (in practice, only Transportation and Communications); Medical Workers; Legal System Workers; Economics and Management Specialists; Municipal Services Workers; Industry (really industrial managers); and Soviets and Local Self-Administration.

The character of the occupational groups varied. Some functioned as traditional interest groups. For example, the day before the Congress opened, the deputies listed as railroaders were invited to the Ministry of Transportation, and the ministerial leaders "called on them decisively to defend the interests of the workers of the branch."[52] The preparatory commission had decided to propose a single standing committee of the Congress for industry, transportation, and other branches of the economy, but the railroad deputies thought it crucial to have a separate committee for transportation and communications, and the central goal of the deputies' group was to lobby for one.[53] At the end of the Congress the newspaper of the railroad industry reported that this goal had been achieved.[54] In practice, the standing committee replaced the deputy's group as the significant interest group of the industry, and the deputy's group faded.

Other occupational groups often adopted a broader role, promoting the general policy line thought to be in the interest of the group. Thus the military group, the *agrarniki*, and the industrialists became powerful and long-lasting groups that served as the spokesmen for broad policy positions on the conservative and center-right of the political spectrum.

---

50. *Trud*, May 19, 1990, p. 1; *Pervyi s"ezd*, vol. 3, p. 263; and *Vtoroi (vneocherednoi) s"ezd narodnykh deputatov RSFSR (27 noiabria–15 dekabria 1990 goda): Stenografichesky otchet*, vol. 1 (Moscow: Respublika, 1992), p. 212.

51. The names and numbers of the registered groups were announced on the floor of the Congress. The following list is drawn from this source. See *Pervyi s"ezd*, vol. 2, pp. 266–67, 407, 460; and vol. 3, p. 263. One of the groups cannot be found, but presumably it was the Non-Black-Earth Group, which is mentioned elsewhere.

52. *Gudok*, May 20, 1990, p. 1; and May 17, 1990, p. 1.

53. *Gudok*, May 27, 1990, p. 1.

54. *Gudok*, June 20, 1990, p. 1.

A second type of registered group had a territorial base. All the regional delegations met for a number of purposes (for example, the election of Supreme Soviet deputies), but except for the large Moscow group with sixty-four deputies, the only territorial groups to register officials were superregional ones. These were Central Russia, Far East and Zaibaikal, Non-Black-Earth, the North, Siberia, Urals, the autononous republics and territorial units, and Democratic Autonomy.[55] Most of the territorial groups were relatively inactive, but that for the North and above all that representing the autonomous republics and territorial units played important parts in the legislative process.

The striking phenomenon in 1991 was the legalization of a third type of group that was openly political and not based on a defined institutional or territorial interest. As preparations for the Congress were being made, a number of political parties were formed.[56] None, however, had more than a few deputies at the Congress. Only one of their leaders, Nikolai Travkin, played any significant independent role in the organization or conduct of the Congress—or, indeed, in Russian political life.

The political group that was significant was that formed within the legislature, not outside. Some of the groups seemed frivolous and were never heard from again. Five, however, became serious participants in legislative activities: Etika, Non-Party, Independent Deputies, Independent Trade Unions, and especially Smena. The two most important political groupings of this type at the First Congress, Democratic Russia and the Communists of Russia, were actually umbrella organizations that each originally claimed more than a third of the deputies.

Most of Democratic Russia's supporters did not register with it officially (it formally had only 66 members) but were associated with other factions.[57] Despite its loose organization, however, the group functioned very effectively in supporting Yeltsin and his agenda in the first few congresses. Communists of Russia formed in response to Democratic Russia. In a sense it was misnamed, for nearly 90 percent of all deputies were members of the Communist party at the time of the election, including three-quarters of the

55. *Pervyi s"ezd*, vol. 2, pp. 266–67; vol. 1, p. 407; vol. 2, p. 460; and vol. 3, p. 263.
56. These parties are described in M. Steven Fish, *Democracy from Scratch: Opposition and Regime in the New Russian Revolution* (Princeton University Press, 1995), pp. 80–136.
57. *Pervyi s"ezd*, vol. 2, p. 267.

400 most radical deputies supporting Democratic Russia.[58] In fact, Communists of Russia, which embraced 355 deputies, consisted of the more conservative Communists.[59]

The conflict between Democratic Russia and Communists of Russia was to be very emotional, and spokespersons for each used caricatures in describing the other. In fact, both blocs were deeply divided. From the beginning, Democratic Russia was an uneasy alliance of radicals and reformers; the group tore apart near the end of the Congress and gradually disintegrated in the years after the election. Similarly, Communists of Russia included both archconservatives who were bitter opponents of Mikhail Gorbachev and others who were strong Gorbachev supporters.

Despite the divisions within the two large groups, a cochairman of Communists of Russia could still talk after the Second Congress of People's Deputies in December 1990 about the existence of thirty-two different groups in parliament, but there were two sides on the barricades.[60] Democratic Russia and the Communists of Russia both behaved at the First Congress like Western parties, attempting to organize the agenda, nominate their candidate for chairman, and enact their special programs. The two groups were at the barricades, for the issues on which they differed concerned the basic structure of society.

The Election of Boris Yeltsin as Chairman of the Supreme Soviet

In April, Tat'iana Ivanova, deputy chairman of the Presidium of the Russian Supreme Soviet, expressed the leadership's hope that the First Congress might last for seven to ten days.[61] Thus, as a radical stated, the leaders wanted the Congress to serve as "a college of electors." It would select the Supreme Soviet, confirm the government, and leave policymaking to the two of them. The conservatives expected the Supreme Soviet to be more conservative than the Congress because of the greater weight of the national-territorial deputies in it. The deputies associated with Democratic Russia agreed with the government leaders on this point, which led them to

58. In the early summer 39 deputies left the Communist party, reducing the percentage of Communists among all deputies to 86 percent and among the 400 most radical to 66 percent.

59. *Pervyi s"ezd*, vol. 2, p. 267.

60. *Vtoroi s"ezd*, p. 212; and *Pravda*, January 26, 1991, p. 2.

61. *Sovetskaia Rossiia*, March 29, 1990, p. 2.

want a much more active Congress that made policy decisions. It wanted the Congress to be in session for three to four weeks.[62]

The pre-Congress conflict between Democratic Russia and the leadership focused on the agenda. The agenda had to be decided at the very beginning of the Congress and would require a recorded roll call vote. The situation was thus a perfect test to gain a sense of relative strength, to find out the positions of many deputies, and to decide what deals could be cut with opposing or wavering delegates. The first two points on the proposed agenda—the election of the Mandate Commission and the adoption of the temporary Rules of the Congress—were not controversial. The question of whether the election of the chairman of the Supreme Soviet would be the third item, however, produced "one of the very sharpest" disagreements.[63]

The leadership had not unreasonably proposed that the election of the chairman of the Supreme Soviet follow the adoption of the temporary rules so that he could chair the rest of the session. Democratic Russia wanted item three to be a report on the social-economic and political situation of Russia by Aleksandr Vlasov, the chairman of the Council of Ministers. Vlasov was likely to be the Communist candidate for chairman of the Supreme Soviet, and the leaders of Democratic Russia hoped that his report about the difficulties during his tenure—and the ensuing criticisms by deputies—would embarrass him and undermine support for his election as chairman of the Supreme Soviet.[64]

As predicted, the first major test vote between the pro-Yeltsin and the anti-Yeltsin forces at the Russian Congress was the proposal to elect the chairman of the Supreme Soviet before hearing Vlasov's report. It was defeated when 499 deputies voted for it and 504 voted against or abstained. A second vote was held immediately on the proposal to have the report of the chairman of the Council of Ministers presented before the election of the chairman of the Supreme Soviet. It carried, 551 to 441, and there were 16 abstentions.[65]

62. *Rabochaia tribuna,* April 17, 1990, p. 1.

63. *Pervyi s''ezd,* vol. 1, p. 54.

64. *Pervyi s''ezd,* vol. 1, pp. 54–55; and Chelnikov, *Rossiia bez Soiuza, Rossiia bez Rossii,* pp. 28–29.

65. Because a bill had to receive a majority of all deputies, not just the deputies present and voting yes or no, an absence or an abstention had the same effect on the outcome as a negative vote. When a deputy abstained, the vote can be included with the no's, but one cannot know whether an absence had no meaning, whether it reflected a disinclination to be counted, or whether it was a conscious (if silent) no vote.

On the surface it seemed that when the first test vote failed, some 50 of the moderates shifted to the pro-Yeltsin side to prevent a deadlock. When the actual roll calls on these two votes are analyzed together, however, only 825 of the 1,059 deputies maintained a consistent position. A total of 128 deputies, not 50, shifted to support Yeltsin on the second vote, but 78 voted against him who had either been pro-Yeltsin or absent on the first vote. Although the second vote was held immediately after the first, only 24 deputies were recorded absent on both votes, not 50 or more (see table 9-7).

There were various causes for the turnaround: lack of organization on one side or the other and in some cases simple technical mistakes in electronic voting in the first vote or the second. (In the Second Congress deputies were still having problems mastering the technology of casting a vote.) But some groups in the Congress were probably sending subtle signals to the Yeltsin leadership as part of a sophisticated process of coalition formation.

For example, the former autonomous republics had 69 deputies who were Russians and 101 from the native population. On the first ballot 51 percent of the Russian deputies from the autonomous republics and 58 percent of the native deputies supported the Yeltsin position. On the second the support of the Russian deputies from the autonomous republics for Yeltsin rose to 58 percent, while that of the native deputies fell to 38 percent. One cannot be sure, but it is likely that some of the deputies of the native nationalities were signaling that the price of their support for Yeltsin would be the election of one of their own, the Chechen Ruslan Khasbulatov, as first deputy chairman of the Supreme Soviet.

The vote on the agenda suggested Yeltsin's chances of being elected chairman of the Supreme Soviet were very good. They improved even more on May 24, the day before the nominations for Russian Supreme Soviet. The chairman of the USSR Council of Ministers, Nikolai Ryzhkov, announced his economic program, including price increases for bread as of June 1 with further increases scheduled for January 1, 1991. Moscovites flooded the stores to buy bread.

In a speech on May 25 Yeltsin was able to support his candidacy for chairmanship with an strong denunciation of the price increases as an "antipeople's policy Russia should not adopt." He spoke in sweeping terms about his program. "We ought to take radical decisions. The republic should independently concern itself with domestic and foreign policy." He laid out a comprehensive policy that, whatever its pluses and minuses (it

Table 9-7. *Pro-Yeltsin and Anti-Yeltsin Votes on Test Votes on Agenda,*
First Russian Congress of Peoples' Deputies, May 1990

	Pro-Yeltsin second vote	Anti-Yeltsin second vote	Absent	Total
Pro-Yeltsin first vote	423	67	14	504
Anti-Yeltsin first vote	107	378	14	499
Absent first vote	21	11	24	56
Total	551	456	52	1,059

Source: *Pervgi S"ezd narodnykh deputatov RSFSR* (16 maia–22 *iunia 1990* goda): *Stenograficheskii otahet* (Moscow: Respublika, 1992), vol. 6.

was a classic populist policy promising the most radical reform with no pain for the people), was appropriate for an independent state. He talked as if the Union government did not exist, or rather as if it had abdicated because of its indecisiveness, and he laid out specific proposals on investment, defense production, abolition of the draft, and the like.[66]

The Politburo of the Communist party was said to have recommended three candidates for chairman of the Russian Supreme Soviet: Yury A. Manaenkov (chairman of the Russian bureau of the Central Committee), Aleksandr Vlasov (chairman of the Russian Council of Ministers), and Ivan Polozkov (a conservative regional party secretary who was to be elected first secretary of the Russian Communist party in June).[67] Manaenkov and Vlasov withdrew their names from consideration after being nominated, leaving Polozkov to run against Yeltsin. A relative unknown was also a candidate.

The election was conducted by secret ballot, and the familiar rules were in effect. Deputies did not vote directly for a candidate, but crossed out the names of candidates they did not want. A winning candidate had to receive the votes of an absolute majority of the deputies. Since the opening of the Congress, one more deputy had been elected and registered, increasing the number from 1,059 to 1,060 and the number of votes required to win from 530 to 531.

On May 25 in the first round of voting, 497 deputies voted for Yeltsin and 535 against him. Polozkov received 473 yes votes and 559 no votes; the unknown was defeated 32 to 1,000. Because the three candidates received

66. *Pervyi s"ezd*, vol. 2, pp. 232–40.
67. *Pervyi s"ezd*, vol. 2, p. 204.

a total of 1,002 yes votes and 1,034 deputies had voted in the election, 32 deputies had crossed out the names of all three candidates.

The election rules specified a runoff between the two top candidates, and it took place on May 26. Yeltsin gained six votes, but still was defeated 503 to 529; Polozkov lost 16 votes and was defeated 458 to 574. This time 1,032 deputies had voted. Because Yeltsin and Polozkov received only 961 yes votes between them, the number of deputies who had crossed out both names had risen to 71.

On May 28 a new election was held. Yeltsin was nominated once more, but Polozkov dropped out and was replaced by Aleksandr Vlasov as the Communist nominee. It was to be said that Vlasov had discredited himself by refusing to run the first time, but presumably he thought he would come in third in a race with Yeltsin and Polozkov and would be irrevocably dropped in the runoff.

Yeltsin tried to reassure the conservatives. "I never spoke for the separation of Russia, but for the sovereignty of Russia, for the equal rights of all republics . . . so that the republics would be strong and by this strengthen our Union. . . . I am for a united army." He promised a coalition government and said the chairman of the Supreme Soviet should only rule for two years instead of five. The economic program "in this very complicated transitional period" should be worked out in conjunction with the Russian Congress or Supreme Soviet.[68]

Yeltsin's appeal proved successful. On May 29 Vlasov received 467 yes votes and 570 no; 535 deputies voted yes for Yeltsin and 502 crossed out his name. Yeltsin had won with four votes to spare.[69]

The Moderate Majority

When the First Russian Congress of People's Deputies opened, its sessions turned stormy. "'Noise in the hall'—this notation is found on almost every page of the stenographic record," a newspaper reported. "'Soon the hall will need megaphones instead of microphones,' one of the deputies said, shaking his head."[70] Most of this was broadcast on television, and

68. *Pervyi s"ezd*, vol. 2, pp. 381–83.
69. *Pervyi s"ezd*, vol. 2, p. 445.
70. *Sovetskaia Rossiia*, May 18, 1990, p. 1.

deputies reported receiving telephone calls from their families at home expressing wonder at what was happening.

These statements reflected the anger of the conservative and moderate observers at the Democratic Russia deputies and the unprofessional atmosphere they created. The Democratic Russia deputies had come into politics through the democratic process: demonstrations, speeches, meetings, elections. The English word *meeting* (*miting*) came to be used for nonofficial political gatherings with fiery speeches, and Democratic Russia deputies often retained a *miting* style, a strong tendency to be confrontational, agitational, and emotional. This style was said by TASS to have pervaded even the faction's own organizational meeting.[71]

The correspondent of the military newspaper reported that "the second day of work of the Congress of People's Deputies was little different from the first day. White heat, passions, meetinglike emotions, mutual claims against each other, disagreements."[72] A railroad engineer made the same point to the railroad newspaper: "The work of the Congress thus far does not leave a very good impression. There are few constructive propositions, and questions are decided slowly. I am struck by the improper conduct of the deputies: they shout, they stomp their feet, they tear microphones from each others' hands, and they march out of the hall in groups."[73]

The sessions themselves, and certainly the television coverage of them, were almost totally dominated by the radicals, especially those from Moscow and Leningrad. Congressional rules gave deputies the microphone in the order they requested it, and Democratic Russia deputies had figured how to exploit the situation. They simply made their requests en masse at the beginning of the session before the debate began. One conservative deputy, the head of the Osetr River port, said that he submitted his request to speak an hour after the agenda was established and found himself among the second hundred in the line. In disgust he gave his speech to the newspaper of the water transportation employees to publish.[74]

The rules were changed to give the factions a greater role in regulating access to the debate so that different views could be presented fairly.[75] But the Russian Congress remained a raucous body until its dissolution in

71. TASS, April 8, 1990 in FBIS, *Soviet Union*, April 12, 1990, p. 108.
72. *Krasnaia zvezda*, May 18, 1990, p. 1.
73. *Gudok*, May 23, 1990, p. 1.
74. *Vodnyi transport*, May 31, 1990, p. 1.
75. See, for example, *Piatyi s"ezd*, vol. 1, p. 145.

September 1993. In 1990 the conservatives made most of the complaints because they were losing the major battles. When Yeltsin supporters became a minority and the conservatives began beating their leader at his populist game, the democrats began reacting with the same outrage as the conservatives had at the First Congress. In his 1994 autobiography Yeltsin wrote about the legislature in a way that suggested he found Lenin's view of "parliamentarianism" congenial.

> Khasbulatov's leadership stunted the growth [of the first parliament] and turned some of the normal deputies into a political machine. It's too bad. . . . [However,] there is an opinion that our former parliament was a freak in the wonderful family of parliaments of the world, all of which were intelligent, decorous, and utterly democratic. But that's not completely the case. The words *congressman*, *deputy*, or *senator* in various languages are not surrounded by such a glowing halo. We have only to recall Mark Twain to realize that this elected body has long been associated in the minds of Western people with corruption, official sloth, and an inflated and empty self-importance. While this claim may be disputed, no one can deny that parliamentary activity is constantly beset with scandals and exposes.
> . . . When you have fifteen hundred people in a hall, that's not a parliament or a senate but a popular assembly. It's difficult to make any decision because there are numerous factions trying to recruit adherents, plus a huge number of independent deputies. It's an arena of ruthless political scrapping, spasms of little groups forming, personal ambitions being flaunted. Most of all, it's hysterics, overheated emotions, and a matter of who can shout the loudest. It's pointless to speak with a quiet voice; the laws of large auditoriums and the psychological factors of speaking to a crowd (in this case, a crowd of popularly elected representatives) begin to operate.[76]

In fact, this view, as well as the earlier conservative criticism of the First Congress, was greatly overdrawn. The new legislature had certainly not developed a clublike, gentlemanly atmosphere, but this was scarcely unique in world history. In the United States the debate over approving the Jay Treaty of 1794 brought into focus the sharp class, regional, and foreign policy conflicts in early American politics. The descriptions of the debate have a familiar ring to students of contemporary Russia. "The Republicans claimed that the Treaty put us completely in the hands of Great Britain, that it was a betrayal of our Revolution: the Federalists claimed that opposition to the Treaty came only from those who were the tools of France."[77] The

76. Boris Yeltsin, *The Struggle for Russia*, trans. Catherine A. Fitzpatrick (Times Books, 1994), pp. 188–89.
77. Joseph Charles, "The Jay Treaty: The Origins of the American Party System," *William and Mary Quarterly*, vol. 12 (1955), pp. 613–14.

lack of legislative or even political experience among so many deputies added another explosive element to the mixture.

The "nomenklatura deputies" did not have much more relevant political experience than the democrats. Those who did have political and administrative experience were usually factory managers, collective farm chairmen, military officers, or county or small town politicians in a system without elective politics. The conservative leaders in the Russian Congress included Sergei Baburin, Igor Bratishchev, and Nikolai Pavlov, who were college professors at the beginning of 1990; Aleksandr Rutskoi, a combat pilot in Afghanistan; Boris Tarasov, chief political officer of the small Volga Military District; and Ivan Rybkin, a borough party secretary in Volgograd. These posts scarcely provided much preparation to be national political leaders, let alone in an elected legislature.

Nevertheless, the radical character and the amount of disorder of the First Congress—or the conservative character of the Congress in 1992 and 1993—should not be exaggerated. Despite all the chaos on the floor, decisions did get made. And the seemingly irrational behavior did not mean that serious decisions were irrational. In fact, decisions consistently reflected the balance of the legislature. Many test votes showed the majority in Congress was basically stable.

The reason that disorder and conflict was so often overcome was that "conciliation commissions" of representatives of different factions were created as matter of course to reach compromises. They often had surprising success. One leader of a conservative faction, Sergei Baburin, wrote in March 1991, a time of severe confrontation between Yeltsin and Gorbachev, ''When deputies fight out their battles at the microphones in an atmosphere of emotional fervor, it seems that they are irreconcilable. When, however, they begin to converse in the smokers' room, it turns out that the differences are considerably fewer and that they are entirely surmountable. The deputies themselves are then astonished: look, we can negotiate.''[78]

The leaders of the Communists of Russia had little trouble working with radical deputies and finding compromises with them in the conciliation commissions, but they wanted to resolve issues off the floor of the Congress. They often had an aversion to open factions or interest groups that far transcended that expressed by James Madison in his famous Federalist

78. *Pravda*, March 19, 1991, p. 3.

Paper No. 10. Their assumptions were succinctly expressed by two TASS reporters in an article on the tendency for deputies to meet in factions on all issues: "One may ask if deputies divided into such groups can express the interests of all the people in Russia and of all the workers? Indeed the bulk of the population consists of workers, peasants, and part of the intellectuals who do not belong to any bloc or are in any group. They work and hope for almost nothing any longer. Perhaps because deputies split up into factions which are at odds with each other."[79]

In fact, the biggest mistake of Communists of Russia was that they often made too many compromises with Yeltsin. One of the faction's leaders, Boris Tarasov, was to say at the end of the year, "At first we had many illusions. We supposed that we would act within the framework of a democratic process, but events at the Congress, and especially in the post-Congress period showed that we have been dealing with a political struggle for power."[80] To some extent Tarasov was saying he had not recognized that some of the Democratic Russia members were engaged in revolutionary action rather than reform politics, but he was also recognizing that Communists of Russia did not understand the rules of the game of normal public democratic politics.

Although roll call analysis has its difficulties, the distribution of views in the First Congress is clear. Indeed, the first two votes on the the agenda make the point without any sophisticated analysis: 423 deputies were consistently pro-Yeltsin, 378 were consistently anti-Yeltsin, and some 250 switched sides and were in the middle. That distribution of forces remained throughout the First Congress.

Even though a majority of the deputies voted for Yeltsin for chairman of the Supreme Soviet, the moderates seemed determined to demonstrate both their control of the Congress and their dissatisfaction with the radicals. When Yeltsin proposed a constitutional drafting commission for ratification by the Congress, for example, its proposed sixty-three members were much more radical than the average deputy. The Congress changed the rules to allow each region to nominate and elect one member of the

---

79. Health care workers were demonstrating with placards to demand an increase in the health care budget. Immediately, the deputies gathered in faction meetings to decide how to respond. For the reporters this symbolized everything that was wrong with the new system. *Sel'skaia zhizn'*, November 1, 1990, p. 3.

80. *Rabochaia tribuna*, December 1, 1990, p. 2.

commission. As a result, only half of Yeltsin's nominees were elected, and the final commission was only marginally more radical than the Congress.[81]

Similarly, Yeltsin had to promise before his election that he would select deputy chairmen of the Supreme Soviet and chairmen of the two houses of Congress who represented a spectrum of views. The Communist candidate for one deputy chairmanship was quickly elected, as was the candidate for the deputy chairmanship reserved specifically for a woman (a moderate, Svetlana Goriacheva). A Democratic Russia activist, a leader of an informal group from Yeltsin's Sverdlovsk, and another conservative became the other deputy chairmen. It was agreed that the first deputy chairman would be a radical and Yeltsin loyalist, but Yeltsin supported his chief legal adviser, Sergei Shakhrai, while others voted for Ruslan Khasbulatov, the radical Moscow economist of Chechen origin. Khasbulatov eventually prevailed as a non-Russian who would be acceptable to Moscow.[82]

The anger of the congressional majority toward the radicals came out most clearly in the election of deputies to the Supreme Soviet. Seats in the Supreme Soviet were awarded to regions on the basis of their population, and the deputies' groups from each region were supposed to nominate those from within the group they wanted for their quota.[83] But the Congress elected the Supreme Soviet deputies, and, as usual, undesired candidates on the ballot were crossed off. Thus although a region might nominate only as many deputies to the Supreme Soviet as it had seats in its quota, the Congress could defeat any and all nominees by denying them a majority.

Even uncontested nominees normally received from 200 to 350 no votes but, with a few exceptions, congressional moderates approved the nominees, whether conservative or radical, of the regional deputies' groups.

81. Smyth, "Ideological vs. Regional Cleavages," pp. 128–29.
82. In February 1992 five of the six (but not the radical Khasbulatov) protested against Yeltsin's conduct as chairman. In the mythology of the future, these five were all to become hard-liners, along with Khasbulatov, who supported Yeltsin vigorously throughout 1990 and the first two-thirds of 1991. See Alessandra Stanley, "Hacks Are Back," *New York Times Magazine*, May 26, 1996, p. 29. In the new history Aleksandr Rutskori, who signed the democratic manifesto of 1991, becomes a signer of the hard-line manifesto because he broke with Yeltsin (p. 46).
83. There were anomalies here, as in the determination of the number of deputies in the Supreme Soviet. For example, a deputy from Moscow Oblast complained that it deserved to have 3.6 places in the Soviet of Nationalities and 6.1 in the Soviet of the Republic by its population, but was assigned only 3 and 5, respectively. *Pervyi s"ezd*, vol. 3, p. 446.

However, alternative candidates were nominated in 60 percent of the regions. They were almost always from the radical wing of deputies, when the radicals could not agree on a common delegation.[84] This practice angered congressional moderates, who voted in sufficient numbers against all the nominees from these areas to ensure that none was elected. The more radical deputies received particularly large numbers of negative votes. The deadlock continued for several weeks, and the Supreme Soviet that gathered to elect a premier on June 15 still included only 205 deputies, with none from Moscow, Leningrad, or Kemerovo, three of the regions with severe conflicts.

Two major candidates, Mikhail Bocharov, chairman of Democratic Russia, and Ivan S. Silaev, a former USSR minister of the aviation industry, were nominated for chairman of the Council of Ministers. Bocharov, Yeltsin's candidate, received 86 votes, while Silaev, the candidate of the conservatives, received 119. Silaev's total was one vote short of the necessary majority, and Bocharov was certain to have the support of most of the deputies from Moscow, Leningrad, and Kemerovo when they were elected. However, the Yeltsin forces assumed that Silaev was too close to victory to be stopped, and after a short consultation, proposed Silaev's unanimous election.[85]

For the Yeltsin forces, however, only two things really mattered. One was the election of Yeltsin as chairman, and even then he was clear that he wanted a change in the Constitution and popular election of a president within a year. The government arrangements in the interim were not all that important. The second priority was a declaration of sovereignty that would give Russia the right to override federal laws. As will be discussed in chapter 12, the Congress gave him such a declaration with the provision he desired. For the revolution that was all that was needed.

84. The report on the nominations is found in *Pervyi s"ezd*, vol. 3, pp. 371–446.
85. *Sovetskaia Rossiia*, June 16, 1990, p. 1.

CHAPTER TEN

The Struggle between Gorbachev and Yeltsin

REVOLUTIONS ARE USUALLY DESCRIBED in superhuman terms. The state being overthrown is painted larger than life both by its opponents and its supporters. Revolutionaries are said to be heroic or demonic, and ideologies, classes, and social forces stride across the historical canvas. The events of the revolution are retold in painstaking detail, and it is claimed the revolution transformed the course of history, for good or for evil.

Yet great revolutionaries such as Giuseppe Garibaldi or Vladimir Lenin are very human—fascinating combinations of self-confidence and insecurity, charm and oversensitivity, calculation and passion. And the fate of revolutions is often determined by decisions and acts—or by the failure to decide and act—of a small number of people at the top. As these people interact, their egos and the personal competition between them come to play a far larger role than is usually recognized.

In no case was this more true than in the Russian Revolution of 1990–91. The central conflict was often more a personal duel between Mikhail Gorbachev and Boris Yeltsin than it was a conflict between great ideas or institutions. This means that the calculations of the two personalities were crucial, but nothing is more difficult to understand. Part of the problem is that all great leaders dissemble, and this was certainly true of Gorbachev. At the end of December 1989 the new editor of *Pravda* cautioned a *Financial Times* reporter that while Gorbachev is "an open man," this "does not mean he has on his tongue what he has on his mind. Not at all. He is a very

315

complicated man."[1] For their part, great populist leaders such as Yeltsin instinctively say what their audiences want to hear and do not ask themselves whether they themselves believe what they are saying.

Another characteristic of revolutions is that events begin to move so fast and old assumptions become so irrelevant that the human mind cannot process all the new information. Herbert Simon and James G. March contended thirty years ago that decisionmakers even in stable settings must "satisfice" rather than optimize because of the impossibility of mastering all the relevant information.[2] The problem becomes infinitely worse in a revolutionary situation, but satisficing is no longer adequate. The leader may be a more or less rational actor on many decisions, but when the number of them, especially unfamiliar ones, multiplies, he finds it increasingly difficult to remember that the assumptions behind decision A contradict the assumptions behind decision B and that the combination of the two seemingly rational decisions is irrational. Gorbachev's press agent, it may be recalled, cautioned that everybody was so busy that they had no time to think.

The months from the end of 1989 through the fall of 1990 constituted just such a period. The collapse of communism in Eastern Europe, the end of the power of the Politburo and the Communist Party Central Committee, the first republican elections with noncommunist victories in the Baltics and a free election in Russia, the populist Yeltsin challenge, the 500-Day Plan and the drive toward radical economic reform—these events were so momentous that their analysis covers a number of chapters. Yet they were occurring simultaneously, and the leaders had to try to think through their implications when the implications were interrelated but often unknowable.

The great problem for the analyst of a revolution is judging which facts and assumptions the actors are keeping straight at a particular time. Often the actors see connections between decisions, try to follow a sophisticated strategy in linking decisions, and actually succeed to a considerable extent. At other times they forget connections. At still other times (and this began

1. Quentin Peel, "Hero to All but His Own People," *Financial Times*, December 30, 1989, p. 13.

2. James G. March and Herbert A. Simon, *Organizations* (John Wiley, 1958), p. 205.

to happen to Gorbachev in 1990), they can become tired or depressed and their minds may essentially shut down for a while.[3]

The Origins of the Conflict

Yeltsin was born in a village in the Urals in 1931, the same year as Gorbachev. His grandfather was a well-to-do peasant.[4] After the family farm was destroyed in collectivization, his father and uncle, both in their twenties, fled to the city of Kazan as construction workers. When Boris was three, his father and uncle were arrested for criticizing the regime at a construction site and were sentenced to three years in a labor camp. After his release, Yeltsin's father served as a worker at the Berezniki Chemical Combine.[5]

In 1950 Yeltsin entered the civil engineering department of Sverdlovsk Polytechnical Institute and graduated in 1955, the same year Gorbachev earned his law degree. After graduation he became a construction foreman in Sverdlovsk. His career progressed rapidly: he was promoted to senior foreman, chief engineer of a construction trust, and then head of a city construction trust. In 1963 he became chief engineer and then head of the housing construction combine of Sverdlovsk.[6]

3. One of the great paradoxes of the Bolshevik Revolution is that Lenin became nonfunctional in the week before the revolution, but this did not matter. Robert Vincent Daniels, *Red October* (Scribner, 1967), p. 106. Yeltsin continually disappeared at important times from 1990 onward, but it will be some time before full information on his behavior will become available.

4. According to a police report, "Before the revolution [the grandfather's] homestead was of the kulak type. He owned a watermill and a windmill. He owned a threshing machine, he owned permanent farmhands, he owned about twelve hectares of cropland, he owned a harvester and a binder, and he owned about five horses and about four cows." Boris Yeltsin, *The Struggle for Russia*, trans. Catherine A. Fitzpatrick (Times Books, 1994), pp. 94–95.

5. In fact, the labor camp to which Yeltsin's father was sent probably was at the Berezniki construction site, and he simply moved from the camp section of the site to the free section when his imprisonment was over. For the way the system worked at the construction of the Magnitogorsk Metallurgy Works, see John Scott, *Behind the Urals: An American Worker in Russia's City of Steel* (Indiana University Press, 1989).

6. For Yeltsin's early life, see his *Against the Grain: An Autobiography* (Summit, 1990), pp. 15–30, 34–45.

Yeltsin has commented that, as a construction official, he was "constantly engaged in party work outside working hours."[7] He was clearly seeking full-time party work, and in 1968 he was named head of the construction department of the Sverdlovsk Regional Party Committee (*obkom*) and then in 1975 Sverdlovsk Obkom secretary for construction—positions usually filled by a manager such as himself and ones that involved detailed management responsibilities. In 1976 he received an unusual promotion—selection as first secretary of the Sverdlovsk Obkom, bypassing the usual intermediate position of second secretary or chairman of the executive committee of the regional soviet.

Sverdlovsk was one of the most populous regions in the country, a center of heavy industry and the defense industry, and one of the two political bases of Andrei Kirilenko, Leonid Brezhnev's long-time chief deputy. Yeltsin became one of the most important obkom first secretaries in the country. In 1985 when these secretaries insisted on Gorbachev's election as general secretary, he was one of the leaders of the group. He was brought to Moscow, first as head of the Construction Department of the Central Committee and then as Central Committee secretary for construction. Yeltsin felt deeply offended, for he, Gorbachev, and Yegor Ligachev had all been obkom first secretaries (the equivalent of U.S. state governors) under Brezhnev, and his region had been by far the most important of the three. Now he had a trivial job, while Gorbachev and Ligachev were the top two figures in the party apparatus.

Yeltsin's job was, however, to be a holding position for the crucial job he was to receive in December 1985—first secretary of the Moscow city party committee (*gorkom*).[8] In 1926 Stalin had taken over the Leningrad party organization by naming a friend from the Transcaucasus, Sergei Kirov, as first secretary of the Leningrad party organization. This, no doubt, was how Yeltsin's appointment was seen in 1985. By all appearances, he was chosen Moscow city party first secretary so that a trusted outside member of the Kirilenko political machine could clean out the most important party organization of the opposing faction. (Viktor Grishin, the conser-

7. Yeltsin, *Against the Grain*, p. 55.
8. Gorbachev commented in his memoirs that he was planning Yeltsin's selection as Moscow first secretary at least as early as June 1985. There is, however, no evidence he told Yeltsin of his intentions. Mikhail Gorbachev, *Zhizn' i reformy*, vol. 1 (Moscow: Novosti, 1995), p. 292; *Memoirs* (Doubleday, 1996), p. 184.

vative associate of Chernenko, had been Moscow first secretary since 1967.)

Yeltsin was supported by Ligachev, the most powerful member of the Kirilenko machine in the Gorbachev entourage. Ligachev said in public and in private that he had personally recommended Yeltsin, and this claim is unchallenged.[9] Vadim Medvedev claimed that "Yegor insisted that Boris be brought from Sverdlovsk" and that he "thought Yeltsin would be his man in Moscow."[10] By contrast, Nikolai Ryzhkov, who had been director of the Ural Machinery Works while Yeltsin was an obkom secretary, told Gorbachev, "He will cause you only grief. I would not recommend him."[11]

Although Yeltsin was supported by the more conservative Ligachev, his speech at the Twenty-Seventh Party Congress in February-March 1986 was multifaceted. On the one hand, his comments were traditional. He complained about the weakening of party influence on literature and art. His proposals for action had little to do with democracy, economic mechanisms, or a lesser role for the party apparatus. "The medicine is constant control of each official from above and from below—and not formal control. Discipline should be sharply raised, and demands made. The work of each individual leader should be subjected to principled, sometimes even harsh evaluations." On the other hand, the speech sounded notes attractive to reformers. It contained a strong populist attack on the party apparatus and privilege, on "bureaucratism, social injustice, and abuses," on "dual morality," and especially on "special privileges for leaders."[12] It even attacked the Organizational–Party Work Department of the Central Committee at the time Ligachev headed it.

Gorbachev's political advisor and expert on Eastern Europe, Georgy Shakhnazarov, has commented he "heard the speech with ecstasy."

9. *Izvestiia TsK KPSS*, no. 2 (February 1989), p. 242; and *XIX vsesoiuznaia konferentsiia Kommunisticheskoi partii Sovetskogo Soiuza [28 iunia–1 iulia], Stenograficheskii otchet*, vol. 1 (Moscow: Politizdat, 1988), p. 82. See the discussion in Angus Roxburgh, *The Second Russian Revolution: The Struggle for Power in the Kremlin* (Pharos Books, 1992), pp. 29–30.

10. Vadim Medvedev, *V komande Gorbacheva: Vzgliad iznutri* (Moscow: Bylina, 1994), pp. 66–67. Gorbachev agrees on Ligachev's complete confidence in Yeltsin. *Zhizn' i reformy*, vol. 1, pp. 291–92; *Memoirs*, p. 184.

11. Gorbachev, *Zhizn' i reformy*, vol. 1, p. 291; *Memoirs*, p. 184. See also Nikolai Ryzhkov, *Desiat' let velikikh potriasenii* (Moscow: Kniga Prosveshchenie Miloserdie, 1995), pp. 137–39.

12. *Pravda*, February 27, 1986, pp. 2–3.

In the first intermission [I] expressed the opinion to colleagues that Gorbachev had received a strong ally who could be used as a kind of battering ram for democratic reforms. With his fighting temperament . . . Yeltsin could speak more assertively and daringly since he was not responsible for policy, and Gorbachev would look at the reaction and either support the hothead or rebuke him for excessive speed.[13]

Medvedev considered Yeltsin useful to Gorbachev for the same reason. Gorbachev must have felt unusually blessed at the chance to satisfy both Ligachev and his democratic advisers with the same appointment.

As Moscow first secretary, Yeltsin did not make a favorable impression on intellectuals. He began a large-scale purge of party officials selected by Grishin and launched a well-publicized attack on corruption. Yet he never acted as if he were enthusiastic about the private and cooperative enterprises that were beginning to be introduced, and he gave no indication that he considered them the path to prosperity. Instead, his favorite method of reform was to pound the table. When things were not corrected immediately, his response was to conduct a renewed purge of lower officials.[14] At the end of 1986 Yeltsin's relations with Gorbachev began to deteriorate, but the details of the conflict, let alone the thinking of the two men, have deliberately been kept secret by both Yeltsin's and Gorbachev's forces. Yeltsin's letter of resignation of September 12, 1987, and various speeches by other leaders indicated the conflict had been brewing for some time. Gorbachev claims that in December 1986 and January 1987 he had reprimanded Yeltsin for resorting excessively to purges.[15]

When on January 19, 1987, the Politburo discussed Gorbachev's report to the forthcoming Central Committee plenum on democratization, Yeltsin spoke somewhat more critically than others and said the report exaggerated the changes that had occurred since Gorbachev's election. Medvedev passed a note to Aleksandr Yakovlev saying, "evidently he is to the left of us and that is good." Yakovlev wrote back, "Good, but I felt sometimes a posturing that I don't like." Medvedev replied, "Perhaps, but that is his role."

In his concluding words, Gorbachev . . . briefly, but fairly seriously answered Yeltsin's remarks, saying that, of course, it is wrong to fall into self-satisfaction

---

13. Georgy Shakhnazarov, *Tsena svobody: Reformatsiia Gorbacheva glazami ego pomoshchnika* (Moscow: Rossika, 1993), pp. 155–56.
14. For such a contemporary analysis of him by a Moscow radical who was to become mayor of Moscow, see Gavril Popov, *Moscow News*, December 20, 1987.
15. *XIX vsesoiuznaia konferentsiia*, vol. 2, p. 182.

and even more into self-glorification, but at the same time it would be incorrect to minimize the significance of the transformation occurring in the country. He emphasized that we need perestroika, but not "pereshaking" as some hotheads sometimes understand it.

None of this went outside the bounds of normal discussions in the Politburo, but Boris Nikolaevich took the criticism badly. Everyone parted, but he remained sitting in his chair, not hiding his hurt. We had to call a doctor, but it seems that his help was not needed.[16]

At the June plenum of the Central Committee on economic reform, Yeltsin spoke and criticized Gorbachev from a leftist (radical) perspective.[17] Gorbachev said that nobody at the plenum supported Yeltsin.[18] However, almost no information has been published on the contents of his speech. It is not even mentioned in Yeltsin's memoirs or biographies. Gorbachev said that Yeltsin attacked the speed of perestroika and the work of the Secretariat and Ligachev.[19] Rumors suggested that Yeltsin had attacked Raisa Gorbachev at the October plenum, but this was universally denied. A knowledgeable source close to Yeltsin who does not want to be identified said that he did so at the unmentionable June plenum.

Yeltsin's attack on Ligachev and the Secretariat was to be understood on a number of levels. The Moscow first secretary, Medvedev comments, had always dealt directly with the general secretary, and Yeltsin, as a candidate member of the Politburo, resented reporting to the second secretary like any other provincial party secretary.[20] In addition, of course, Ligachev was serving as Gorbachev's chief of staff and conveying, bluntly by all accounts, messages to underlings that Gorbachev preferred not to convey himself. In August 1986 and July 1987 the Politburo and secretariat had criticized the Moscow leadership for its defects in organizing vegetable deliveries to the capital, but the real issue was Yeltsin's toleration of "informal groups" and political demonstrations in Moscow.[21]

As the relations of Gorbachev and Yeltsin worsened during 1987, false rumors abounded that Yeltsin was one of Gorbachev's closest, pro-reform

---

16. Medvedev, *V komande Gorbacheva*, pp. 46–47.

17. At this stage of perestroika, *left* meant radical and *right* meant conservative. In the 1990s the meaning of these terms was reversed and came to be used as they were in the West: *right* meant promarket and *left* meant prosocialist or at least more favorable to social welfare measures.

18. *Izvestiia TsK KPSS*, no. 2 (February 1989), pp. 283, 284.

19. Gorbachev, *Zhizn' i reformy*, vol. 1, p. 356. Not in *Memoirs*.

20. Medvedev, *V komande Gorbacheva*, p. 67.

21. *Izvestiia TsK KPSS*, no. 2 (February 1989), p. 244.

allies on the Politburo. No doubt, Gorbachev considered the rumors an attempt by Yeltsin to gain popular support. As Yeltsin began giving interviews and citing embarrassing facts in public (for example, the number of political prisoners), he created the impression of a man who wanted to stake out a personal political position for himself.

While Gorbachev was on vacation in the south in the summer of 1987, Ligachev chaired Politburo meetings. At the September 10 meeting he criticized Yeltsin (probably at Gorbachev's behest) and organized a Central Committee commission of inquiry to investigate the Moscow demonstrations.[22] On September 12 Yeltsin sent Gorbachev his letter of resignation. He insisted with wounded innocence that a decision on political demonstrations was within the competence of the city government—no doubt the first time such a claim had been made in the Soviet Union in more than sixty years. The decision to create a Central Committee commission to investigate the situation, he said, was "incomprehensible."[23] In his letter Yeltsin referred to "an increasing number of unpleasant situations" because of his directness in speaking out at Politburo sessions, and he criticized "the mastodons and dinosaurs" on the party ruling body.[24] As a result, he virtually stopped speaking at the Politburo.[25]

Yeltsin claimed an explosion occurred at a Politburo session that discussed Gorbachev's speech for the seventieth anniversary of the revolution. He said that he made some twenty suggestions for change in the speech and that Gorbachev left the room for thirty minutes. When he returned, he launched a tirade directed at Yeltsin personally.[26] Gorbachev has commented that his exchanges with Yeltsin on unspecified subjects at unspecified times were heated.[27] But Medvedev, who seems the most careful and accurate of the memoirists, categorically denies the incident occurred.

Cherniaev, Medvedev, and Gorbachev agree in their memoirs that Yeltsin's attack on the main theme of the November 1987 speech—how to discuss the Stalinist past—came from the conservative side of the political

22. Roxburgh, *Second Russian Revolution*, p. 71.

23. The letter is reprinted in Yeltsin, *Against the Grain*, pp. 178–81.

24. Gorbachev, *Zhizn' i reformy*, vol. 1, p. 371; *Memoirs*, p. 243; and Yeltsin, *Against the Grain*, p. 179.

25. Yeltsin, *Against the Grain*, pp. 178–79; and *Izvestiia TsK KPSS*, no. 2 (February 1989), pp. 242, 257, 259.

26. Yeltsin, *Against the Grain*, pp. 128–29.

27. *Moskovskaia pravda*, November 11, 1987.

spectrum.[28] According to Medvedev, who took notes on the Politburo speeches on the anniversary report,

> Yeltsin, like some other orators, objected to the transfer of emphasis from the October revolution to the February one. He spoke about the necessity of having "a whole section" about the role of Lenin in the report. . . . He criticized the report for the fact that the whole period of the Civil War was excluded and proposed to reduce the number of judgments about the party opposition until the conclusions of the Politburo commission [investigating the matter] were received.[29]

These comments were likely the cause of Gorbachev's exasperated remark, "Now he accuses us of going too fast, now of not going fast enough. It is whatever is convenient to him, depending on his mood."[30]

Given the extraordinary secrecy about these events, it is not surprising that no one even today can be sure about the reasons for the Yeltsin-Gorbachev conflict. In his 1989 memoirs and a 1990 interview, Yeltsin indicated the issue was the most basic imaginable: he thought Gorbachev was pushing economic reform too fast and that political reform should precede it. "The absolute insistence on the primacy of economic factors—to the detriment of the social and political dimensions—has affected the general strategy of perestroika."[31]

In 1989 and 1990 such comments were self-serving, but they do correspond to the statements already cited. Whatever change Gorbachev had made in his priorities in December 1986, they were not reflected in his speeches or actions in 1987. It is, however, unclear what Yeltsin meant by political reforms, especially since he was conservative on the question of discussing the past. As late as his speech at the Nineteenth Party Conference in June 1988, he spoke out against a multiparty system and in favor of socialism. His memoirs read as if he thought an attack on the party apparatus and its privileges would have been all that was needed to ensure perestroika's success (indeed, at one point he says so).[32]

28. Gorbachev, *Zhizn' i reformy*, vol. 1, p. 368; *Memoirs*, p. 241; Medvedev, *V komande Gorbacheva*, pp. 61–62; and A. S. Cherniaev, *Shest' let s Gorbachevym* (Moscow: Progress, 1993), p. 177.

29. Medvedev, *V komande Gorbacheva*, pp. 61–62.

30. *Izvestiia TsK KPSS*, no. 2 (February 1989), p. 284.

31. Yeltsin, *Against the Grain*, p. 170; and Yeltsin, "Ia vse-taki optimist," *Argumenty i fakty*, no. 9, March 3–March 9, 1990, p. 4.

32. Yeltsin, *Against the Grain*, p. 164.

The meaning of Yeltsin's resignation letter has been the subject of debate. Gorbachev says they had agreed to postpone discussion of Yeltsin's resignation until after the celebration of the seventieth anniversary of the revolution in November 1987. Yeltsin claims that he and Gorbachev had agreed to discuss the subject in a few weeks, not after the anniversary, and that he took Gorbachev's silence as evidence that Gorbachev was ignoring the resignation and even planning to attack him.

Obviously, however, if Yeltsin had wondered about Gorbachev's reaction, all he had to do was ask. If he had wanted a broader discussion, he certainly could have raised the issue at the Politburo. Medvedev not unreasonably concluded, "Yeltsin consciously took the route of unleashing a public conflict."[33] However, during the Yeltsin era a number of officials "resigned" primarily to get a vote of confidence from Yeltsin—and often did. Perhaps this was Yeltsin's regular style, and he expected Gorbachev to respond to his letter of resignation by pleading with him to stay. When Gorbachev failed to do so, Yelstin may have been offended.

In any case, Yeltsin utterly disrupted the October 21 Central Committee plenary session devoted to the celebration. There was not to be any discussion of the report. In an emotional statement he denounced Gorbachev and Ligachev personally and resigned as a Politburo member.[34] Yeltsin acted as if he thought that he could remain Moscow first secretary and so requested in a letter to Gorbachev on November 3, but that, of course, was impossible.[35]

As the news leaked out, it overshadowed the anniversary. Gorbachev considered Yeltsin's action an unethical and disrespectful violation of an agreement that spoiled a major celebration.[36] The leadership responded to Yeltsin in kind both at the plenum itself and then in public at the session of the Moscow city committee that removed him as first secretary. He was summoned to the committee meeting from the hospital where he was

33. Medvedev, *V komande Gorbacheva*, p. 65.
34. The speech was published in *Izvestiia TsK KPSS*, no. 2 (1989), pp. 239–41. Many wondered whether it had been altered when published, but the person in charge of Central Committee documents asserts that although amended by Yeltsin in minor ways, it is "an accurate rendering of what he said." Valery Boldin, *Ten Years That Shook the World: The Gorbachev Era as Witnessed by His Chief of Staff*, trans. Evelyn Rossiter (Basic Books, 1994), p. 235.
35. Gorbachev, *Zhizn' i reformy*, vol. 1, p. 373; *Memoirs*, p. 246; and Boldin, *Ten Years That Shook the World*, p. 236.
36. *Izvestiia TsK KPSS*, no. 2 (February 1989), p. 282.

staying because of a heart attack in his own version or a fake suicide attempt with scissors in Gorbachev's version.[37] The city newspaper *Moskovskaia Pravda* carried eight pages of attack, all so heavy-handed that it succeeded only in building sympathy and support for Yeltsin, and Gorbachev compounded the mistake by attending the session himself and thus associating himself with the criticism.

At the October plenum, Gorbachev and his allies explained Yeltsin's rebellion in personal terms. For many (Aleksandr Yakovlev, for example), Yeltsin was reacting immaturely to "petty offenses." For others (such as his longtime acquaintance from the Urals, prime minister Nikolai Ryzhkov), he was driven by "ambition pure and simple," combined with a craving of attention—especially from the West. Gorbachev himself emphasized Yeltsin's ambition.[38]

At the time, I thought Yeltsin's break with Gorbachev reflected his judgment that the major challenge to the general secretary was going to come from the radical democrats, not the conservatives as was usually assumed. In this view Yeltsin's action showed his determination to lead that challenge.[39] In subsequent years he seemed a complex combination of calculation, political instinct, and personal sensitivity. All these factors played a role in his 1987 decision as well, but calculation and political instinct surely were the dominant ones.

The Comeback of Boris Yeltsin

After the plenum Yeltsin was offered and accepted the post of first deputy chairman of the State Committee for Construction (a post of ministerial rank). He was told by Gorbachev that he never would be allowed to return to politics. He has given his reaction in his memoirs.

37. Gorbachev, *Zhizn' i reformy*, p. 374; and *Memoirs*, p. 246. A very well informed journalist who interviewed many leaders agrees with Gorbachev's version. Andrei Karaulov, *Plokhoi mal'chik: Grustnaia kniga* (Moscow: Sovershenno sekretno, 1996), p. 105. Gorbachev's version is also supported in some detail in Aleksandr Kapto, *Na perekrestakh zhizni: Politicheskie memuary* (Moscow: Sotsialisticheskii-politicheskii zhurnal, 1996), p. 186. As later events were to indicate, Yeltsin used "heart attack" to refer to attacks of angina or heartbeat irregularities. Yeltsin, *Against the Grain*, p. 199.

38. *Izvestiia TsK KPSS*, no. 2 (February 1989), pp. 256–57, 263, 282, 284.

39. Jerry F. Hough, "The Tentacles of Soviet Reform," *New York Times*, November 18, 1987, p. A35.

People have often asked me—and later I asked myself the same question—why didn't Gorbachev decide to get me out of the way once and for all [in 1987]. . . . I could easily have been pensioned off or sent as ambassador to some faraway country. Yet Gorbachev let me stay in Moscow, gave me a relatively high placed job, and, in effect, kept a determined opponent close by him. It is my belief that if Gorbachev didn't have a Yeltsin, he would have had to invent one. . . . In this real-life production, the parts have been appropriately cast, as in a well-directed play. There is the conservative Ligachev, who plays the villain; there is Yeltsin, the bully-boy, the madcap radical; and the wise omniscient hero is Gorbachev himself. That, evidently, is how he sees it.[40]

Yeltsin said the eighteen months following his removal from the Politburo were a black time, a nightmare, and a friendly biography provides confirming details.[41] Nevertheless, Gorbachev found the threat to keep him out of politics incompatible with the democratization begun in the year after Yeltsin was removed. Yeltsin began granting interviews to foreign correspondents in 1988 and then ran as a delegate to the Nineteenth Party Conference in 1988 and a deputy to the USSR Congress in 1989. Gorbachev had to decide whether to change the new democratic rules of the game or permit him to reemerge politically. Gorbachev was lured into letting him return out of his own dedication to democratization, his overconfidence, or his belief that Yeltsin was serving some useful functions for him.

When Yeltsin sought to be a delegate to the Nineteenth Party Conference, he was rejected by important party organizations and was finally put on the delegation of the Karelian republic, which was seated in the back of the balcony. (Although expelled from the Politburo, he remained a governmental minister and a member of the Central Committee; it was difficult to deny him a seat at the conference altogether.) His requests to speak at the conference were turned down, but on the last day he dramatically stood at the foot of the platform and waited until he was allowed to speak.

Yeltsin asked for political rehabilitation, but implicitly on conditions that were unacceptable. He called for an acceleration of perestroika, but again in terms that tended to be limited to an attack on the apparatus. He strongly criticized its authoritarianism and secrecy and demanded full democracy within the party. He emphasized the need for a full accounting of party

40. Yeltsin, *Against the Grain*, p. 202.
41. Yeltsin, *Against the Grain*, pp. 203–05. See also Vladimir Solovyov and Elena Klepikova, *Boris Yeltsin: A Political Biography*, trans. David Gurevich (Putnam's, 1992), pp. 82–92; and Yeltsin, *Struggle for Russia*, pp. 15–16.

funds in a way that implied they were being spent mainly on apparatchik privileges.[42]

On national television, Ligachev took the podium to answer the charges. He was deeply offended both by Yeltsin's speech and by earlier personal attacks. The struggle among Gorbachev's advisers had become so emotional and even paranoid that Cherniaev was to describe this speech in his diary as a subtle and comprehensive attack on perestroika as a whole.[43] In fact, Ligachev's speech was disorganized, personal, and emotional, and it gives little evidence of being crafted for any subtle purpose.[44] It was a venting of frustration. As a result, Ligachev's accurate criticisms (for example, of the very low pay of officials) were lost, and his effort to answer Yeltsin before a nationwide audience only dramatized Yeltsin's daring. The result was that Yeltsin "had become more than ever a national figure, a symbol of resistance to the party *apparat*."[45]

As the USSR 1989 elections approached, Yeltsin and his advisers carefully planned ways to circumvent the control the party apparatus was trying to impose on the nomination process. He succeeded in getting himself nominated in the most important district in the country, national-territorial district no. 1, which embraced Moscow. Running against the director of the Moscow Automobile Works, he won nearly 90 percent of the vote in the city where he had been removed as party first secretary a year and a half before.

The scale of Yeltsin's victory in the 1989 election was probably the decisive event in the revolution of 1990–91, for it apparently undermined Gorbachev's self-confidence. The general secretary no longer seemed to believe he represented the country's desire for change. He often acted as if he accepted that Yeltsin spoke for public and intellectual opinion. Essentially recognizing Yeltsin's legitimacy, he found himself unable to deal effectively with him.

Yet except for a psychological victory, Yeltsin had achieved little. The USSR Congress of People's Deputies was the legislature Gorbachev had wanted. Radicals were to say that the Congress was conservative, but the congressional majority and Gorbachev voted much the same. The Interre-

42. *XIX vsesoiuznaia konferentsiia*, vol. 2, pp. 55–62.
43. Cherniaev, *Shest' let s Gorbachevym*, pp. 217–19.
44. *XIX vsesoiuznaia konferentsiia*, vol. 2, pp. 82–88.
45. John Morrison, *Boris Yeltsin: From Bolshevik to Democrat* (Dutton, 1991), p. 84. This is the best biography of Yeltsin written from the point of view of the Moscow intelligentsia who were optimistic about him in 1990.

gional Group was able to make its points to the public because it was allowed access to television, but it was too small to have an impact on legislation. Andrei Sakharov had the intellectual stature and the program to be the real leader of the opposition to Gorbachev. Yeltsin seemed to have no policy agenda that he wanted to push.

During these months Yeltsin was writing his autobiography, and when it was published in early 1990, John Lloyd, the respected reporter of the *Financial Times*, wrote a review with which it was hard to disagree either then or now.

> Boris Yeltsin's biography inspires fear. You end it fearful that the Soviet Union is incapable of producing a political class. By his own account, the main opponent to Mikhail Gorbachev has no programme, no critique beyond a demagogic condemnation of privilege . . . and no useful insights into his country's plight. . . . Cunning, vainglorious, with a huge thirst for power, and a shrewd nose for finding it, the Soviet Union—or at least Russia—may one day come to this man. The biography does not convince that it would be better that it did.[46]

Lloyd was certainly right about the thirst for power. Yeltsin found the USSR Congress too restraining and moved his base of political power to the Russian Republic. It was a bold step. The Russian Republic seemed a superfluous administrative stage between the central government and the oblasts. If authority was to be decentralized to the state level (in American terms), if state governors were to be elected and not appointed, and if the central government was to retain the kind of economic and security responsibilities exercised by the U.S. government, what role was to be played by the Russian government? In addition, it seemed unlikely that the radicals would win enough seats to elect Yeltsin chairman of the Russian Supreme Soviet, and some close advisers suggested he seek to become mayor of Moscow.[47] He therefore seemed to have little to gain from moving his base to the Russian Congress. Only Mikhail Bocharov, who was to be Yeltsin's candidate to be chairman of the Council of Ministers at the First Congress, decided to leave the USSR Congress with him. But they were exceptions among the democrats in the Congress.

46. John Lloyd, "Yeltsin's Vain Russian Hope," *Financial Times*, March 15, 1990, p. 22.

47. Lev Sukhanov, *Tri goda s El'tsinym: Zapiski pervogo pomoshchnika* (Riga, Latvia: Vaga, 1992), p. 241.

Gorbachev's Calculations about Yeltsin

From 1988 to 1991 Gorbachev seemed to have an extraordinary relationship with Yeltsin. By all reports he was very hostile to Yeltsin and Yeltsin reciprocated, although Yeltsin's hostility was strongly mixed with contempt.

The general secretary's political advisor Georgy Shakhnazarov has said that Gorbachev was absolutely determined to stop Yeltsin's election as chairman of the Russian Supreme Soviet, but that he was overconfident of his ability: Gorbachev was like "an outstanding grandmaster in chess [who] loses a game to an average master because he did not take him seriously."

> Undoubtedly, Gorbachev saw Yeltsin as his future chief competitor [but he had] a low opinion about his intelligence and his other qualities. . . . An optimist by nature . . . he was forever certain that anything would turn out well for himself, and so he did not prepare for the worst. . . . During the period of our work, I almost never saw him afraid or apprehensive about the future in a way that led him to take additional precautions.[48]

Gorbachev no doubt did underestimate Yeltsin, but it is important to understand the nature of his miscalculations. He publicly opposed Yeltsin's election, but if Gorbachev was acting with the slightest rationality in April and May of 1990, he had decided he wanted Yeltsin to be chairman of the Russian Supreme Soviet. This almost surely was one of those instances in which, as Ivan Frolov had commented, what Gorbachev had on his tongue was not what he had on his mind. Gorbachev apparently accepted the argument of Shakhnazarov and Medvedev that a radical Yeltsin was useful in allowing him to maintain the image of a reformer while still seeming to occupy a centrist position.

Every step Gorbachev took in April and May 1990 strengthened Yeltsin's position. Some might have been simple political misjudgments—for example, a decision made against all advice to go to the Russian Congress and argue against Yeltsin's election.[49] Others may have been the result of genuine overconfidence—for example, the decision to nominate competent but not exciting candidates to oppose Yeltsin in the election for Supreme Soviet chairman. (In addition, Gorbachev may have feared that a strong candidate such as Vadim Bakatin would have been a greater threat than Yeltsin.)

---

48. Shakhnazarov, *Tsena svobody*, pp. 156, 158, 159.
49. Shakhnazarov, *Tsena svobody*, p. 159.

Two of Gorbachev's decisions are, however, extremely difficult to explain as simple miscalculations. The first was constitutionally inexcusable—all the more so for a leader trained at Moscow State University as a lawyer—and explosive in Russian politics. On April 26, 1990, Gorbachev had the USSR Congress pass an unconstitutional law that, in effect, subordinated Russia's autonomous republics directly to the Soviet Union.[50] If the law had been serious, it would have given independence to 15 percent of Russia's population and 28 percent of its territory without Russia's consent and without the required amendment to the Constitution. Nothing was more certain to arouse Russia's fury about being impotent and dominated by the center and to build support for a politician emphasizing the need to give the Russian Republic more power over its own fate.

The second action was to permit Premier Ryzhkov to introduce on May 23, the day before the opening of the Russian Congress of People's Deputies, the economic reform package containing the long-postponed price increases on bread. By then political maneuvering had shown the Congress was evenly divided. Gorbachev always had an exaggerated fear of the public's potential reaction to food price increases, and the rush of people to buy bread before the price was raised was the tamest reaction that could have been expected. It was even less surprising that Yeltsin would denounce the price increase and that undecided deputies would be tempted to take the politically popular decision to oppose it.

In 1991 Anatoly Lukianov commented that Yeltsin was popular precisely because he was out of power and could be irresponsible. If he had responsibility, he would have to face hard choices, and hard choices are bound to offend someone.[51] Such arguments must have had weight in 1990 as well. Gorbachev must have thought that Yeltsin would find being leader of Russia very confining. Russia was still subordinate to the USSR, and ultimately—or at least so Gorbachev must have assumed—it would have to function within the framework of central laws and decisions. Yeltsin would have responsibility for the difficult and unpopular decisions on economic reform, but he would not really be in control.

In addition, Gorbachev loved to try to create a centrist position for himself, and the old balance between left and right in the Politburo had been destroyed with the destruction of the positions of Ryzhkov and Ligachev.

---

50. This is discussed at length in chapter 11.
51. For the expression of the view by Gorbachev himself in the fall of 1991, see p. 456.

Gorbachev began to emphasize the power of the Federation Council and change the Politburo to a republic-dominated body. He seemed to think that he could now balance Yeltsin and the non-Russian republics.

The general secretary seemed to understand that the Russians needed a sense that political and economic reform benefited Russia as well as other republics. Russia needed to be a strong republic to give its people a sense of ethnic pride, and the people needed to be pushed toward accepting market prices by the argument that Russia was receiving too little for the petroleum, natural gas, timber, and other natural resources that it shipped to other republics. Moreover, if the republics were to have important roles in conducting economic reform, it was vital for Russia to have a strong pro-reform government. Although economic reform could proceed slowly in some republics, it had to be introduced effectively in Russia if it was to succeed. This required a Russian government that would follow through.

Thus from Gorbachev's point of view, Russia needed a strong leader who would loudly proclaim that it had been exploited by the old system, that greater independence and sovereignty were required to make it equal to the other republics. This leader should emphasize Russian pride and rebirth (*vozrozhdenie*) He should call for radical reform so that he would have the responsibility for the pain reform was certain to bring. Ideally this leader should not be a member of the Communist party, for the party could then move into a social-democratic position: favoring reform but critical of the Russian government for its failure to support social-welfare programs. Thus Yeltsin could define the radical position, while Gorbachev could regulate the speed at which the country moved toward reform and could maintain a moderate image.

In addition, Gorbachev must have thought that the more Yeltsin emphasized Russian sovereignty and power—which he was certain to do in a crude, populist way—the more he would frighten the other republics and make it less likely that they would support him as a replacement for Gorbachev. The presence of large numbers of Russians in most of the republics and local nationalists' fear that Moscow might intervene in case of civil war would also restrain the republics in their drive for independence.

This calculation was a sophisticated way to control the actions of many republics. The Baltic republics were confident that they could become fully independent and part of the West, but others were much more worried. In March 1991 Nursultan Nazarbaev, the president of Kazakhstan, was to be very critical of a Yeltsin speech that promoted confederation: "What is he proposing? That the country be headed by the Federation Council? . . . There would be no leader of the state, there would be no center at all. Then what, is he proposing that all republics become part of a Russian empire? This also is unacceptable."[52] Nazarbaev was, in fact, right that a confederation without a strong central government would leave power in the hands of the Russian economic organs and ministry of defense.

In principle, the judgment attributed to Gorbachev is a highly sophisticated one. The strategy could even have been brilliant. However, it needed two further features that turned out to be absent.

First, Gorbachev needed a concrete, centrist plan he was trying to push through. Instead, he was thinking of politics as a process in which politicians occupied a particular place in policymaking and operated under the kind of restraint he had observed throughout his life in Soviet politics. Thus he could let them define the center. However, Yeltsin understood democracy and he was a master populist who did not hesitate to advance the most inconsistent ideas if they seemed popular. But when Yeltin took contradictory radical positions, any attempt by Gorbachev to take a centrist position meant moving toward him on all of them. Gorbachev would declare that some new Yeltsin proposal was extremely ill advised—and often rightly so—but then would move into a centrist position with regard to it. As Yeltsin took contradictory positions, Gorbachev inevitably seemed contradictory and indecisive. Because Gorbachev had responsibility, such responses were disastrous.

Second, Gorbachev's reluctance to use force left the non-Russian republics with no alternatives. If he had promised to use force against Yeltsin if his demands and violation of central legislation became too unreasonable, the non-Russian republics could have functioned in a normal bargaining environment. But if Gorbachev was not going to stand up to Yeltsin regardless of his actions, independence was the only hope of the non-Russian republics to be free of Yeltsin's dictation. When the population of the non-Russian republics saw rising inflation in Russia, they could also have the illusion that independence might insulate them from Russia's economic problems.

Yeltsin as Chairman of the Russian Supreme Soviet

In June 1990 Gorbachev was preparing for the Twenty-Eighth Party Congress, accelerating economic reform, and beginning to negotiate a new

52. *Argumenty i fakty*, no. 9, March 1991, p. 2.

Union Treaty. Boris Yeltsin was beginning to function as the leader of the Russian government. Although his election as chairman of the Russian Supreme Soviet was a remarkable achievement, he had won a very unsatisfactory post from which to lead the republic. The chairman of the Russian Supreme Soviet, like the chairman of the USSR Supreme Soviet when Gorbachev held that post, was head of state, who "represents it both inside the republic and in international relations." Nevertheless, the executive power was vested in the chairman of the Council of Ministers, who was elected by the Supreme Soviet, not appointed by its chairman.

Yeltsin solved the problem in a breathtakingly easy manner. He never really tried to govern Russia in the normal sense of the word. From the beginning he acted as a national politician, the equal of Gorbachev at the very least. "The pyramid [of government] must be turned upside down," he asserted, and he continually spoke about a political structure in which the republics had enormous power and the USSR government virtually none. Republican laws would be superior to those of the USSR. Russia would set its own prices in bilateral negotiations with the republics, and it would take control of its own oil and gas fields to ensure it could do this. Yeltsin demanded and obtained substantial control over the banking system.

Because economic reform was the key to destroying the financial power of the central ministries and acquiring control over property, Yeltsin focused on it. He continually attacked the price increases of the Ryzhkov government and promised "another transition to the market that does not lead to a deterioration in the standard of living."[53] At the end of July a *New York Times* correspondent commented that Yeltsin's appointment of thirty-two-year-old Boris Fedorov as minister of finance created the image of Russia as "a center of youth and fresh ideas." The major fresh idea Yeltsin embraced was a 500-Day Plan that promised complete financial stabilization and privatization within its first hundred days of implementation. "Mr. Yeltsin's economists insist that they can dismantle the state economic monopoly and create a market without the shock of sharp price rises or unemployment," Bill Keller reported in the *New York Times*.[54]

Throughout, Yeltsin demonstrated a strong sense of theater and managed always to be at the center of attention. He believed, as he said in his

<hr />

53. Press conference, May 30, 1990, in Foreign Broadcast Information Service, *Daily Report: Soviet Union*, May 31, 1990.

54. Bill Keller, "As Yeltsin Sets Quick Tempo, Gorbachev Tries to Keep Beat," *New York Times*, July 25, 1990, p. A6.

memoirs, that "in politics, everything is symbolic," and he was a master of symbolic politics.[55] He said nothing about leaving the Communist party until the end of the Twenty-Eighth Party Congress. Then he provided its most dramatic moment as he resigned from the party (so he could be subordinated only to "the will of the people") and strode out of the conference hall. When the destruction of the local party organs removed the traditional administrative mechanism for bringing in the harvest and threatened the successful gathering of a bumper crop, Yeltsin promised that Russia would award vouchers for consumer goods for the best farmers. The vouchers would be backed by a Russian republican fund for consumer goods (the fund did not then exist and never would). When the autonomous republics complained that Russia was aggrandizing too much power, Yeltsin told them to take as much power as they wanted.

Gorbachev seemed to play continually into Yeltsin's hands. When the general secretary supported a renegotiation of the Union Treaty, he implicitly acknowledged that the old Union was illegitimate and that any republican demand for something totally new was an acceptable position rather than a treasonable attack on the USSR. When Yeltsin supported the 500-Day Plan, Gorbachev agreed to form a USSR-RSFSR commission to draft an economic program and allowed it to be dominated by economists favoring the plan. The media treated the plan not only as reasonable, which it was not (see chapter 12), but as ideal. It so dominated Moscow discussion that Westerners who listed all its defects still treated it as the best plan available.[56]

Gorbachev's strategy seemed clear at the time and in retrospect still does. He wanted Yeltsin to be associated with plans for the Union and the economy that were obviously too extreme so that he could counter them with a conservative alternative (usually Premier Ryzhkov's) and then himself propose a more moderate and reasonable compromise. The problem was that Yeltsin and his supporters always treated their own plan as the moderate, even painless, alternative—indeed the only alternative. Then when Gorbachev tried to move toward a more moderate position, Yeltsin would condemn him severely for indecision and hesitation.

55. Yeltsin, Struggle for Russia, p. 123.
56. Marshall I. Goldman, "Boris Yeltsin: At Least He Has a Plan," New York Times, September 16, 1990, p. C11; and Bill Keller, "Hesitation on the Soviet Economy," New York Times, September 13, 1990, p. A1.

If the intellectuals and the media had damned Yeltsin's plans, if Gorbachev had been populist in turning Russian nationalism against Yeltsin, Yeltsin's strategy would not have worked. But when Gorbachev turned against Ryzhkov, the premier's economic plan, and the bureaucracy, he left himself with no economic plan of his own and no ideology about the necessary role of central government in economic life. Many intellectuals endorsed Yeltsin or were silent about the grave defects of his plans because they recognized his popular support, were in despair about Gorbachev, hoped or even assumed that they could control Yeltsin if he came to power, or simply thought they could benefit personally.

Yeltsin and the Russian Congress

In 1992 and 1993 a dramatic struggle for power between Yeltsin and the Russian Congress of People's Deputies played itself out before the world and was ended by Yeltsin's shelling of the parliament building. It is tempting to assume this confrontation dated from 1990, but this would be wrong. In 1990 the Russian Supreme Soviet supported Yeltsin and passed irresponsible acts that contradicted central laws and created legal anarchy. Ruslan Khasbulatov was in the forefront of those supporting Yeltsin's most radical statements and actions.

In theory, there could have been major executive-legislative conflict over the legislation. The Presidium, which consisted of the chairmen and deputy chairmen of the Russian Supreme Soviet and its houses and the committee chairmen, was the ruling body of the Supreme Soviet. It was an active legislative body, meeting eighteen times in the first six months after its creation in 1990 and enacting 124 decrees and decisions. In the first nine months of 1991 it met forty-eight times and and passed 910 laws.[57] The Russian Constitution did not make it clear whether the chairman or the Presidium of the Supreme Soviet was authorized to oversee the government and the chairman of the Council of Ministers. In Russia in 1990 these problems were exacerbated by the Supreme Soviet's rejection of Mikhail Bocharov, Yeltsin's candidate for prime minister, and the election of Ivan Silaev, a representative of the military-industrial complex who did not share Yeltsin's goal of dismantling the central government.

57. Sergei Filatov, "Trudnye problemy parlamenta Rossii," *Narodnyi deputat*, no. 17 (562) (1991), p. 13.

The potential for conflict between executive and legislature was intensi-fied by Yeltsin's driving concern with status and power and his extreme sensitivity to slights, real and imagined. He must have found it particularly galling to be elected chairman of the Russian Supreme Soviet just months after Gorbachev had freed himself from that post at the USSR level and become a president with far greater executive power. In addition, if Yeltsin had found it difficult to subordinate himself to Gorbachev and Ligachev, who had been obkom first secretaries in less important oblasts than Sverdlovsk, he had an even greater problem in considering the leaders of the Supreme Soviet equals. After serving as governor (obkom first secre-tary) of one of the most important regions from 1976 to 1985 and leader of Moscow from 1985 to 1987, he had received almost 90 percent of the vote in Moscow in the 1989 election to be USSR deputy and in Sverdlovsk in the 1990 election to be Russian deputy. The Supreme Soviet leaders had all been unimportant figures a year earlier.[58]

Yet a classic conflict between the executive and legislature in Russia failed to develop. The Supreme Soviet was expected to be conservative, but this proved not to be the case. The radicals' fears about the conservatism of deputies elected from national-territorial districts were more a reaction to their memories of the 1989 USSR election than to the reality of the 1990 Russian election. The Supreme Soviet deputies elected in June 1990 were only marginally more conservative than the congressional deputies: 4.35 instead of 4.25 on a 1-to-8 scale in which 3 was moderate radical, 4 was left-center, and 5 center-right.[59] They were prepared to support Yeltsin.

This situation occurred in part because many deputies worked only part time. Membership in the Supreme Soviet proved a mixed blessing for many deputies.[60] The more moderate and conservative congressional deputies often held important jobs as party or local soviet officials, plant managers, collective farm chairmen, or the like, and they were reluctant to give up

---

58. Yeltsin's closest allies in the Congress—Gennady Burbulis, Ruslan Khasbulatov, Sergei Shakhrai, and Sergei Filatov—were college professors or depart-ment heads in institutes two years before. Most of the conservative leaders, including Sergei Baburin, Nikolai Pavlov, and Igor Bratishchev, had the same background. Ivan Rybkin was a borough party secretary.

59. Author's calculations based on the source for table 9-4.

60. This was also true of the USSR Supreme Soviet. In December 1990, when the first scheduled rotation of its members occurred, roughly 40 percent of the deputies had to be replaced, not the 20 percent originally envisaged when democracy was introduced in the Soviet Union. *Izvestiia*, December 18, 1990; *Komsomol'skaia pravda*, December 27, 1990; and *Sovetskaia Rossiia*, January 8, 1991.

these posts to serve as full-time legislators. The deputies who chose to work full time in the legislature thus came disproportionately from those who formed the more liberal and radical factions. If the first Supreme Soviet elected in 1990 had an average liberal-conservative score of 4.35, the 244 Supreme Soviet deputies in June 1992 had an average score of 3.83 in their First Congress voting. By 1992 some 368 deputies were working in the legislature full time. They had an average score of 3.26 in their First Congress voting; the committee chairmen averaged 3.39.[61]

Conflict between Yeltsin and the legislature also failed to develop because Yeltsin's efforts to establish an elected presidency and emancipate himself from legislative control required changes in the Russian Constitution, and attention to these issues dominated the sessions of the Congress. By default, the Supreme Soviet took over much of the legislative function. In the short run at least, the legislation and budgetary acts it passed were relatively unimportant. Before December 1991 the Russian legislature did not have much real power because Russia itself did not have much power. The legislature had declared its laws superior to those of the USSR, but the "war of laws" only meant that few people had respect for any law, USSR or Russian.

The legislation passed by the Supreme Soviet tended to be more symbolic and propagandistic than regulatory. Laws were often drafted by the interest groups most directly involved and usually expressed wishes rather than reality. Thus the Health Committee, dominated by deputies who were physicians, drafted a medical insurance law to obtain more funds for health care. The Agricultural Committee, dominated by deputies from the agrarian sector, drafted laws that greatly increased investment in the countryside. Neither could be funded. New laws frequently contradicted each other, and their language was often so imprecise that neither administrators nor the courts could determine their meaning.[62] Whatever the advantages and dis-

---

61. The Supreme Soviet had a computerized directory of all congressional deputies, with biographical data, addresses, committee assignments, and so forth, that was updated continually. In June 1992 Iosif Diskin obtained a copy of this directory for me. The data on deputy work comes from this source and the roll call data from the source for table 9-4.

62. Jurists of the Institute of Legislation, which was long responsible for providing expertise in drafting legislation, reported that lawyers often were not drawn in during drafting, not even as technicians charged with the responsibility of getting the intentions of the drafters expressed in juridically correct language.

advantages of this process, and a case could be made for either, it reduced conflict between the legislature and the president.

The Russian legislature especially lacked power in budgetary matters. As Aleksei A. Ponomarev, chairman of a subcommittee of the Committee on Social Development and Agrarian Affairs, said of the formation of the 1991 budget:

> The day before yesterday, on November 28, I once again was in the Ministry of Finances of the Russian Federation. I became convinced that it is impossible to decide many questions there, since the USSR Ministry of Finances is conducting this work independently from the Union republics—one can say, in secret. The difficult work that is going on in the USSR Supreme Soviet and government and in the Russian Supreme Soviet and government is unfortunately uncoordinated. Such lack of agreement creates bottleneck situations on key questions in the formation of the budget of the Russian Federation. It does not permit us to put the ideas of the Declaration of Sovereignty of Russia into practice, or even to take the first concrete steps in defining the basic policy about the path to a market economy. I think it indispensable: first, to create a joint working commission of the deputies of the USSR and RSFSR deputies and specialists of both Ministries of Finances, and, second, to give information to the Congress about the course of work in forming the budgets.[63]

Because the budget had little meaning, there was little reason for fighting over it.

Yet for all the lack of executive-legislative competition over legislation in 1990–91, Yeltsin's relations with other leaders of the Russian Congress were not without problems. The basic problem was Yeltsin's struggle with Gorbachev and the difficulty this created for the officials with whom he worked, most of whom were closer to Gorbachev than they were to him. As both supporters and opponents acknowledged, Yeltsin was focusing on his struggle with Gorbachev and his own campaign to create a presidency and to have himself elected to it. In January 1990 he began vigorously to support the idea of a president in Russia as well as in the USSR, and in May he talked about remaining chairman of the Supreme Soviet for no more than a year.[64] He was staking out populist, independent, and confrontational positions as part of this campaign. By assembling a team of radical advisers for his presidential run, he was abusing, or at least stretching, the powers of the chairman of the Supreme Soviet.

---

63. *Vtoroi (vneocherednoi) s"ezd narodnykh deputatov RSFSR (27 noiabria–15 dekabria goda) Stenograficheskii otchet*, vol. 1 (Moscow: Republic, 1992), p. 394.
64. See his interview in *Moscow News*, no. 2, January 14, 1990.

The first group whose frustration boiled over was the reforming econo-mists in the Russian government. Yeltsin's populist economic positions undermined any effort to introduce financial stability. He proclaimed his intention of introducing the 500-Day Plan in Russia but did nothing to follow up. Grigory Yavlinsky, the deputy premier in charge of economic reform and a sincere monetarist who believed that control of the money supply could solve all problems, resigned. Boris Fedorov, the minister of finance, resigned soon after and made a devastating criticism of the govern-ment in an interview with *Izvestiia.* Although Ivan Silaev formally headed the government, Fedorov's criticisms were directed at Yeltsin's policies:

> In practice, the government of which I am a member does not have its own policy, but flows with the current. Only we, it is necessary to recognize honestly, do this with less competence and knowledge that the Union government. . . . The activity of the government is permeated with populism. It strives to please everyone, and for this we constantly are giving out money and privileges, which simply leads to the bankruptcy of Russia.[65]

The leaders of the legislature had begun to feel just as frustrated. In February 1991 Svetlana Goriacheva, the centrist deputy chairman of the Supreme Soviet, issued a statement signed by her and five other of the seven top officials of the Supreme Soviet that expressed their grievances about Yeltsin. Only Ruslan Khasbulatov remained loyal to Yeltsin and did not sign.

> The relationship within the Supreme Soviet leadership is such that the chairman always acts on his own, without consulting with others or even notifying them. Very few in the Supreme Soviet are privy to the affairs and plans of our chairman. There is no collectivism in his work. . . . All of us who signed this statement belonged to different political currents. . . . We have tried so many times to establish cooperation. Now we understand that we have exhausted all the means of trying to return him to reason.[66]

The unmentioned impetus for the statement was Yeltsin's frontal attack against Gorbachev in January 1991 in the wake of the general secretary's actions to thwart the independence movement in Lithuania. Gorbachev was trying to maneuver the debate on economic reform and the Union Treaty in

---

65. *Izvestiia,* December 27, 1990, p. 5. This is the same Boris Fedorov who returned to government as deputy premier after the removal of Yegor Gaidar in December 1992.

66. For the text of the statement, see *Ekonomika i zhizn',* no. 9 (February 1991), p. 1. For the grievances of the group see *Sovetskaia Rossiia,* March 23, 1991; *Sel'skaia zhizn',* March 19, 1991; *Pravda,* March 22, 1991; and *Krasnaia zvezda,* March 14, 1991.

a direction that would keep Russia and the other republics in the Union and that would make Yeltsin responsible for hard decisions on economic reform. Because the congressional leaders and the great majority of the deputies were eager for a Gorbachev-Yeltsin reconciliation, they were willing to give Yeltsin the elected presidency he wanted if he would agree to the basic deal that Gorbachev wanted.

Gorbachev was thinking of a compromise that would preserve the Union and give Yeltsin substantial power and status within it. But Yeltsin was not looking for a compromise. He was following a revolutionary policy that would bring him to ultimate power, and he came to understand that this was possible only if Russia seceded from the USSR. It was a daring strategy, one that easily could have cost him his life in case of a military coup, but he was willing to take great risks for an unmatchable gain. Gorbachev was never willing to imprison or kill Yeltsin, and he never learned how to turn populism and nationalism against him. Gorbachev's continuing faith that there was some kind of reasonable compromise in a situation in which none existed left him helpless as events played themselves out.

CHAPTER ELEVEN

The Controversy over Economic Reform

MIKHAIL GORBACHEV AND HIS SPOKESMEN always linked democratization with economic reform. Democracy, they said, was necessary to "activate the human factor," "shake the public out of its lethargy," and "wake up society," all of which were required to develop the initiative needed for a market economy to flourish.[1] In addition, they asserted, democratically elected institutions were necessary to break the resistance of the bureaucracy and the party apparatus to economic reform. Gorbachev himself made the point to U.S. Secretary of State James Baker in May 1989: "To break up the old managerial attitudes and to defeat the old administrative system, some kind of move to political reform is necessary."[2]

Movement on economic reform had stalled in 1988 and the first half of 1989, when Gorbachev had decided political reform took priority. The corollary was that he would refocus attention on economic reform once the 1989 USSR elections were over. And indeed, after the elections Premier Nikolai Ryzhkov appointed Leonid Abalkin, an economic reformer, as deputy premier and chairman of the Commission on Economic Reform. New faces, also people with a strong reforming bent, were appointed to head the three main financial organs—the Ministry of Finance, State Com-

---

1. Mikhail Gorbachev, *Zhizn' i reformy*, vol. 1 (Moscow: Novosti, 1995), pp. 281, 426; *Memoirs* (Doubleday, 1996), pp. 175, 220.
2. James A. Baker III with Thomas M. DeFrank, *The Politics of Diplomacy: Revolution, War, and Peace, 1989–1992* (Putnam, 1995), pp. 81–82.

mittee on Prices, and State Bank. A young moderate reformer was named chairman of Gosplan and another deputy premier for foreign economic relations.

Nevertheless, the leader of the country—the dictator by any reasonable definition of the term—was not Ryzhkov, but Gorbachev. Ryzhkov's choices for his government's members had to be cleared with Gorbachev and his lieutenants in the Central Committee Secretariat, whose role was "decisive."[3] At least some were chosen on the "initiative" of the Central Committee. For two years before the election Gorbachev had resisted pressure from Ryzhkov and his advisers for retail price increases and fiscal responsibility. He had advocated the rapid dismantling of the administrative system. Would he now allow the premier and his new ministers to introduce economic reform in the gradual manner they thought necessary?

Gorbachev had never permitted the Politburo's dissention over price reform to be publicized and thus had never explained his position. Even his 1995 memoirs do not illuminate his thinking. The radical economists were much clearer and louder. They criticized administered increases on the grounds they were half measures that would maintain and even strengthen the bureaucracy. Given this attitude toward administered increases, they would never approve the more intrusive administrative measures Ryzhkov, or the Chinese, thought necessary during a long transition to a market economy. If Gorbachev's position coincided with that of these economists, Ryzhkov would endure a painful year. Still, at least the general secretary would be driven to reveal what he meant by radical reform.

The Growing Sophistication of the Economic Debate

Gorbachev should have adjusted retail prices earlier, but by 1989 it was obvious that serious measures needed to be taken. The urban food subsidy continued to grow, and the 1987 Law on State Enterprise, which had been meant to decentralize industrial production decisions, had unexpectedly fueled inflation. Immediately after the law's passage, radical economists had worried that the ministries' continued control of plan fulfillment and supplies would make the law meaningless. In fact, the enterprises turned out to have more independence than expected, especially in handling their

3. Mikhail Nenashev, *Poslednee pravitel'stvo SSSR: Lichnosti, Svidetel'stva, Dialogi* (Moscow: Krom, 1993), p. 21.

finances.[4] In the past, "real" transferrable (*nalichnye*) money in an enterprise's account was kept separate from accounting money (*beznalichnye*) that was used to "pay" other enterprises for supplies that had been allocated. The Law on the Enterprise gave directors of enterprises some freedom to turn the accounting money (funny money in U.S. jargon) into cash that could be paid to employees as wages. Thus they were able to expand the real money supply in the country.

This increased freedom allowed the directors to raise wages far faster than they could increase productivity, paving the way for inflation. They began to take advantage of their monopoly positions to raise prices on profitable products and cut production of necessary but less profitable items. The ministries were unable or unwilling to exercise control, and they were not forced to do so. The level of production did not decline in 1988 and most of 1989, but the increase in wages and the failure to control the food subsidies meant that the population had progressively larger amounts of money at their disposal (table 11-1).

Gorbachev's decision to hold a Central Committee plenum on agricultural reform in March 1989 just before the opening of the First Congress of People's Deputies seemed to imply that he would back raising retail food prices and reducing the urban food subsidy. He would presumably put Ryzhkov and his advisers in charge of economic reform, allow them to propose the economic measures they thought necessary, use his strong majority in the Congress to pass the measures and other needed legislation, and let price increases provide the base for the beginning of agricultural reform the plenum had promised. If the reform worked out, Gorbachev was the leader and would get credit; if problems arose, the elected Congress provided political cover and Ryzhkov was the perfect scapegoat.

In the first stage of his operation Premier Ryzhkov nominated a new cabinet, which, except for nine conservatives, was accepted by the First Congress after a lively confirmation process.[5] Leonid Abalkin's appoint-

---

4. Anders Aslund, *Gorbachev's Struggle for Economic Reform*, 2d ed. (Cornell University Press, 1991), pp. 187, 196. The early pages of this book, which are little changed from the first edition, present the earlier interpretation of this law by the radicals of 1988.

5. For the cabinet and the votes for and against each in the confirmation process, see Jerry F. Hough, "The Politics of Successful Economic Reform," *Soviet Economy*, vol. 5 (January–March 1989), pp. 29–34. See also Eugene Huskey, "Executive-Legislative Relations," in Eugene Huskey, ed., *Executive Power and Soviet Politics: The Rise and Decline of the Soviet State* (Armonk, N. Y.: M. E. Sharpe, 1992), pp. 85–89.

Table 11-1. *Income and Expenses of the Soviet Population, 1986–89*
Billions of rubles

Year	Income	Expenditures	Excess
1986	435.3	407.3	28.0
1987	452.1	420.1	32.0
1988	493.5	451.6	41.9
1989	558.0	496.2	61.8

Source: Leonid Abalkin, *Ne ispol'zovannyi shans: Poltora goda v pravitel'stve* (Moscow: Politizdat, 1991), p. 93.

ment as deputy prime minister brought a top economist high into government for the first time, and his chairmanship of the State Commission of the Council of Ministers on Economic Reform gave him the responsibility to urge reform. The men appointed minister of finance and chairmen of the State Committee on Prices, the State Bank, the Committee on Labor and Social Forces, and the State Committee of Statistics were soon to be denounced as hidebound conservatives by the radicals, but they were impressive reformers with a sophisticated knowledge of economics. Valentin Pavlov, the minister of finance, clearly understood that economic planning based on the central manipulation of economic levers instead of the central distribution of goods would mean a shift of power from the institution that distributed goods (Gosplan) to the institution that controlled money (the Ministry of Finance). As he said in his memoirs, all financial officials by their nature and self-interest are promarket (*rynochniki*).[6] Pavlov was determined to preside over marketization: he had been a vigorous public proponent of price increases and subsidy adjustments as early as 1987.

When foreigners were taken to the Ministry of Finance in 1987, the deputy minister to whom they were introduced as the economic reformer was Viacheslav Senchagov. He now became chairman of the State Committee on Prices. The new chairman of the USSR State Bank, Viktor Gerashchenko, had eleven years of experience in Soviet financial institutions abroad. He was to be falsely charged with being responsible for monetary expansion in the Yeltsin years and was denounced as incompetent.[7] But in 1990 the *Financial Times* would praise him as "a model central

6. Valentin Pavlov, *Upushchen li shans? Finansovyi kliuch k rynku* (Moscow: Terra, 1995), pp. 4–5.
7. Anders Aslund, *How Russia Became a Market Economy* (Brookings, 1995), p. 98.

banker" and "a banker with revolutionary ideas."[8] (After 1991 he was simply carrying out the policy of the Yeltsin government and was being used as a scapegoat.)

The coal strike in the summer of 1989, however, once more frightened the leadership away from retail price increases, and the basic dilemmas of 1987 took sharper form.[9] The differences among economic reformers on how to resolve them also reemerged, but now Soviet economists had talked more with Westerners. Radical and conservative reformers retained their old positions, but now they defended them in more sophisticated or at least more fashionable language.

The radical economists faced the same difficulties in 1989 as in 1987. Either out of sincere belief or a desire to retain Gorbachev's support, they opposed both the price increases and administrative controls that Premier Ryzhkov wanted to help balance the budget and bring prices more in line with market values. This, however, left the radical economists in a more difficult position in 1989 than in 1987, for now the inflationary pressures cried out for action. The immediate introduction of market pricing would produce even more inflation, but it was politically unacceptable to admit this. So, deprived of a defensible opposition to controlled price increases, the radical economists desperately needed some program.

Having rejected both a change in fiscal policy and the use of government regulation, the radicals were driven to a monetarist solution: inflation must be the result of excess money supply, and the problem could be easily solved by bringing the money supply under control. This Nikolai Petrakov was to say in the first half of 1990. In this opinion the radical economists were, of course, encouraged by many Western economists who understood nothing about the Soviet system but were confident their theory had universal applicability.

Radicals and their Western allies came to insist on the existence of a huge "monetary overhang" as the source of inflationary pressure in the Soviet Union. The picture, however, was grossly overdrawn. First, the overhang was not large by Western standards. The money supply was put

8. Martin Wolf, "Model Central Banker," *Financial Times*, March 12, 1990, p. B11; and Wolf, "Soviet Banker with Revolutionary Ideas," *Financial Times*, March 22, 1990, p. C9.

9. Leonid Abalkin, *Ne ispol'zovannyi shans: Poltora goda v pravitel'stve* (Moscow: Politizdat, 1991), p. 32.

at 585 billion rubles, 445 billion in private hands (100 billion in cash and 345 billion in savings accounts) and 140 billion in the hands of enterprises (20 billion in cash and 120 billion in bank accounts). The State Committee of Statistics estimated the overhang at the start of 1990 at 165 billion rubles, close to 40 percent of consumer spending.[10] These seemed large numbers, but the overhang was manageable: the money supply was 60 percent of gross national product, the same percentage as in the United States and less than the 70 percent of West Germany and the United Kingdom and the 100 percent of Japan.[11] The Soviet economy did not have checking accounts or credit cards, so the public had to hold money either in cash or savings accounts. The cash in the hands of the population was only some 350 rubles a person, less than two months' average salary.

Because there were no checking accounts, savings accounts were used both as the depository for consumption funds and for long-term savings. Valentin Pavlov commented that people took an average 70 percent of their funds out of their savings accounts during the year but returned even more so that the accounts were higher at year's end.[12] But however savings in the USSR were counted, Viktor Gerashchenko, chairman of the USSR State Bank, reported that they were almost the lowest among the developed countries.[13]

The nature of money supply was also far more complex than most realized. Money supply is always an artificial construct, even in the West. It does not refer to all money that people could conceivably spend, but generally only to that which is not frozen in savings. As the differences between the proponents of M1, M2, and M3 show, the category of frozen savings is not and cannot be precisely defined. If the population of a country with a market economy becomes panicked for some reason, the real supply of money in their hands and the real inflationary pressures can be much higher than in more normal times. "Frozen" assets can be turned into cash and used for consumption. Thus the crucial factor in controlling inflation is to induce people to save rather than consume.

In the Soviet Union virtually all investment came from the government. There were no private stores or factories, little private housing in the large

10. Martin Wolf, "The Fall of the Rouble," *Financial Times*, April 18, 1990, p. 23. As of the summer of 1994, checking accounts still had not been introduced.

11. Wolf, "Fall of the Rouble," p. 23.

12. Pavlov, *Upushchen li shans*? p. 242.

13. *Izvestiia*, October 5, 1989, p. 1.

cities, no stocks or bonds. Other than dachas (summer cottages), jewelry, and perhaps art, people's significant financial assets were in cash. A crucial element in economic reform was to create capital markets that privatized investment. Inevitably this required that people have money or access to loans to invest, which in turn required a huge increase in funds at their disposal.

For this reason the economists associated with Ryzhkov and Abalkin were contemptuous of simple monetarist solutions. When asked if the problem was not too much money in the Soviet Union but too little because of the need for investment, Leonard B. Vid, first deputy chairman of Gosplan for economic reform, raised his right hand and formed a circle with his thumb and index finger, the international sign for "right on."[14] The problem was how to expand the country's liquid assets, very broadly defined, while preventing the population from pouring the money into consumption.

For the economists associated with Ryzhkov and Abalkin the answer was to create incentives to save and invest. Some of the needed measures seemed self-evident. As Abel Aganbegian told the *Financial Times* in October 1989, it was scarcely surprising that Soviet consumers were rushing to buy goods when the inflation rate was 9 percent and they earned 2 to 3 percent interest on their saving accounts. Clearly the interest rate on saving accounts needed to be raised.[15] Others suggested issuing state bonds (Leonid Abalkin), selling housing and other property (Oleg Bogomolov), or selling apartments and dachas (Viktor Gerashchenko).[16] These men feared that a focus on money supply alone would distract attention from balancing the budget and creating incentives to save.

Those who take private investment and savings for granted and do not understand the complexity of introducing private investment in a country such as the Soviet Union sneer at the Ryzhkov-oriented economists for their "complete ignorance of macroeconomics."[17] In fact, it was Ryzhkov's economists, not their opponents, who understood the macroeconomics of Soviet society. Those in Russia and the West who were focusing on money supply in Russia without thinking about investment were doing so as a way

14. Jerry F. Hough, interview with Leonard B. Vid, Duke University, March 22, 1990.

15. John Lloyd, "Aganbegyan Aims to Clear Air on Soviet Economy," *Financial Times*, October 3, 1989, p. 3.

16. *Izvestiia*, September 11, 1989; September 23, 1989; and October 5, 1989, p. 1.

17. Aslund, *How Russia Became a Market Economy*, p. 75.

to distract attention from their opposition to the price increases that were necessary for fiscal responsibility.

This position led the radical Russian economists to a strong antisavings bias. They simply considered savings accounts part of the money supply. By this definition an increase in interest rates would automatically expand the money supply. If the higher rates led people to hold more money in savings accounts, this would have the same effect. Savings were therefore defined as inflationary.

Often it is difficult to distinguish between the genuine beliefs of the radicals and their opportunistic rhetoric. However, they clearly believed monetarist doctrine on money supply. When Yegor Gaidar came to power as deputy prime minister in charge of economic policy in 1991 and liberalized prices, he resisted all efforts to index savings accounts or raise interest rates to cover the rate of inflation. He considered liquidation of money in savings as part of the effort to reduce the monetary hangover. It was not until the fall of 1994 that Boris Yeltsin finally admitted that an increase in savings was beneficial.

In presenting alternative proposals to reduce excess purchasing power, some economists such as Nikolai Shmelev proposed massive foreign loans for the government to purchase consumer goods abroad and soak up the excess money. These proposals would have made the situation worse, or at best were an argument to get loans from the West that failed to solve any problem.[18] Because such a policy would not affect the core problem—wages that were rising much faster than productivity—it would at best be a temporary palliative unless either the market or administrative controls brought wages under control. The loans would leave the Soviet Union with higher debt and interest payments that would reduce its ability to purchase consumer goods in the future. The policy of maintaining consumption through foreign loans had been a prescription for disaster in Poland in the 1970s and was certain to be one in the Soviet Union.

The Failure of the Abalkin Plan

Once the new government was installed, Leonid Abalkin began putting together a comprehensive plan of economic reform that included price increases and privatization to be introduced over a six-year period. After he presented it in November 1989, Quentin Peel of the *Financial Times* called

18. Nikolai Shmelev, "Novye Trevogi," *Novyi mir*, April 1988, pp. 168–70.

it "the most radical document on the future of Soviet economic reform yet to emerge."[19] Anders Aslund, normally scornful of Abalkin in his book, commented, "The Abalkin program acknowledged that the market must take precedence over the plan. . . . It established that an efficient market must be characterized by free prices and competition. The value of stock exchanges and a convertible currency, hallmarks of a real market economy, were readily appreciated. No one who wanted to be taken seriously dared call for central planning any longer."[20]

Abalkin then presented his plan to a conference of economists and managers who met in the Kremlin from November 13 to 15 with Gorbachev and Ryzhkov in the audience. More than 250 people spoke at the plenary sessions and smaller meetings.[21] The criticism from both the left and the right was emotional, and it shocked Abalkin.[22] The conference had the same impact on the leadership.

The most obvious consequence of the conservative criticism was Gorbachev's retreat on three draft laws for economic reform—one on property, one on leasing, and one on land—that he had been ready to submit to the Supreme Soviet. He proposed that they be postponed until the spring of 1990, and in fact they were postponed until the summer.[23] The more important impact of the conservative criticism was indirect: Gorbachev never backed the Abalkin plan, and Ryzhkov was compelled to present a more conservative one to the Second USSR Congress of People's Deputies in December 1989.

When Ryzhkov presented the new plan, it included most of Abalkin's ideas, but the wholesale price increases were postponed until 1991 and retail price increases were not mentioned.[24] Nevertheless, the government proceeded with an increase in procurement prices paid to peasants, an

---

19. For the strong praise for the plan by Ed Hewett of the Brookings Institution, see Quentin Peel, "The Battle Lines Are Drawn," *Financial Times,* November 20, 1989, p. 24; and Peter Passell, "New Soviet Blueprint Seeks a Middle Road," *New York Times,* December 9, 1989, p. 35.

20. Aslund, *How Russia Became a Market Economy,* p. 37.

21. Abalkin, *Ne ispol'zovanny shans,* pp. 77–79. The stenographic report of the conference was published as L. I. Abalkin and A. I. Miliukov, eds., *Ekonomicheskaia reforma: poisk reshenii* (Moscow: Politizdat, 1990).

22. Abalkin, *Ne ispol'zovannyi shans,* p. 85.

23. Giulietto Chiesa with Douglas Taylor Northrup, *Transition to Democracy: Political Change in the Soviet Union, 1987–1991* (University Press of New England, 1993), pp. 116–17, 139–40.

24. *Izvestiia,* December 14, 1989, pp. 2–4.

action that of course raised the amount of the urban food subsidy even further. With prices still frozen and inflationary pressure rising, Ryzhkov correctly emphasized the interim need for strong government controls to prevent further economic disintegration.

Ryzhkov and the government plan were denounced by Gorbachev's spokesmen and Moscow intellectuals for being too conservative, a criticism that was echoed in the West. Yet whatever one thought about the plan, it was wrong to call it the Ryzhkov plan. Gorbachev was the country's leader, not the technocratic Ryzhkov, and Gorbachev had been preventing Ryzhkov from making the price adjustments the premier wanted. Ryzhkov's retreat on price increases—the heart of the retreat from Abalkin's plan—was the result of Gorbachev's refusal to support the plan and such price increases.

In Russia one always criticized the tsar's lieutenants, not the tsar, for the tsar's decision, and Ryzhkov was indeed being so criticized. Historians have the duty to sort out reality from the political chaff. Gorbachev had the power to dictate his own plan. As general secretary he had demonstrated that he had enough power to introduce competitive elections, permit a strongly antiparty tone in the Soviet press (against both Ligachev's and Ryzhkov's vigorous objections), destabilize the communist regimes in Eastern Europe, and initiate unilateral disarmament. If he did not like Abalkin's or Ryzhkov's plans, he could have had the radical Stanislav Shatalin, who became his informal adviser on economic and other matters between the end of 1988 and the beginning of 1989, or someone else develop another.[25]

Gorbachev showed the same lack of commitment to economic reform in his behavior in the Congress and the Supreme Soviet. He had political control over more than two-thirds of the deputies, but he did nothing to prevent them from taking irresponsibly populist positions. The Congress supported the Ryzhkov plan 1,532 to 419, with 44 abstentions. Yet the Supreme Soviet rejected a law on decentralization of power because it left the economy too centralized, then rejected an increase in cigarette, beer, and luxury goods prices that was the government's modest attempt to reduce the budget deficit.

Gorbachev's memoirs do not explain his own thinking at this time except indirectly, but thinking he attributes to the government was probably his own.

---

25. Gorbachev, *Zhizn' i reformy*, vol. 1, p. 572; *Memoirs*, p. 379.

I think the chief role was played by the vacillation that existed then, the lack of certainty that the decision expected from parliament would permit the rapid improvement of the economic situation. Imagine, almost every day leaders of different spheres of production and culture break through your secretary to warn against hurried steps. The press is full of alarmist commentaries and forecasts. The workers with their periodic strikes give you to understand that they will not tolerate attacks on their already low living standards. Radicals sharpen their teeth, foreseeing the failure of "the Gorbachev reforms." And the government itself passively waits for the completion of the endless discussions in the parliamentary committees, as if to drag out "the pause" in order not to be involved in a risky enterprise.[26]

Perhaps Gorbachev would have backed down if Ryzhkov had insisted on putting his plan into action, especially if the whole government had threatened to resign as Minister of Finances Pavlov proposed. But one of the most difficult matters to judge is the extent of Ryzhkov's commitment to the government plan. Some ministers considered him more cautious on economic reform than Abalkin, and there may be truth to this assessment.[27] Nevertheless, Pavlov, who was in closer contact with him, seemed nearer the mark when he observed, "Ryzhkov oriented himself too much on the third floor":

In the Kremlin ... Gorbachev's office and the Politburo meeting room were located on the third floor. Directly under them, and with exactly the same floor plan, was located the Presidium of the Council of Ministers. ... It is possible I didn't know everything and didn't understand everything, but it seemed to me that Nikolai Ivanovich could have shown much more independence in taking social-economic measures. ... Almost every time it turned out in the final analysis that Ryzhkov went upstairs with one opinion and returned from the third floor with another.[28]

But the floor plan of the Kremlin made the subordination of the premier, first to the general secretary and then to the president, absolutely clear. As many subordinates later said, Ryzhkov was too honorable or gentlemanly (*poriadochno*) in his behavior, and he would not break the rules of cabinet secrecy. Yet after 1987 it is not clear such an action would have done him much good. Radical economists had already declared price increases retrograde, and they were attributing any gradualism to bureaucratic self-interest. Gorbachev was supporting them behind the scenes. When

26. Gorbachev, *Zhizn' i reformy*, vol. 1, p. 570; *Memoirs*, pp. 376–77.
27. Nenashev, *Poslednee pravitel'stvo SSSR*, p. 70.
28. Pavlov, *Upushchen li shans?* pp. 24–25.

Ryzhkov did go public with his position on prices in May 1990, Gorbachev abandoned him and Yeltsin savaged him.

The speeches of the members of the Central Committee at the December 1989 plenum showed that they understood that the problem was Gorbachev. The first secretary of the Moscow Obkom (a USSR minister of agriculture from 1976 to 1986 and a man usually called a conservative) probably spoke for the majority of the Central Committee:

> [The Ryzhkov plan] foresees the implementation of extraordinary, extremely necessary, but so-called unpopular measures. We are sure that if it is lucidly explained to people why they are needed, they will understand and support. But these measures will become still more unpopular and will subvert confidence in the leadership of the country and party if they are conducted with the same indecisiveness, wavering, and inconsistency that were seen in price reform, cooperatives, leaseholds, transition to wholesale trade, and the establishment of state orders (*goszakazy*).[29]

The Battle of Radicals and Conservatives

It made some political sense for Gorbachev to postpone his decisions on economic reform in the fall of 1989. If he wanted to portray himself as a strong leader, a logical course of action was to wait until he occupied his new presidency and the Russian elections were over and then move decisively, as he promised on March 27, 1990, to introduce "concrete measures to radicalize economic reform," including "the formation of a normal full-blooded market."[30] The contending camps of radical and conservative economists understood that Gorbachev's assumption of the presidency followed by the republican elections set the stage for major economic decisions. They argued hard for their programs, which, of course, retained their starkly different prescriptions for how to begin the reform.

In December 1989 Gorbachev had finally selected an economist as a personal assistant. Instead of a neutral, he chose Nikolai Petrakov, the leader of the radicals, whom Ed Hewett correctly called "a kind of Russian Milton Friedman."[31] Petrakov began to speak out repeatedly in public. On

---

29. The stenographic report of the plenary session was published in *Izvestiia TsK KPSS*, no. 4 (1990), pp. 25–112. The official was Valentin K. Mesiats.

30. For an editorial that saw the situation in these terms, see *Financial Times*, March 12, 1990, p. 4.

31. Ed A. Hewett, "Capitalism's Chances: A U.S. Expert's View: Prognosis for Soviet Economy Is Grave, but Improving," *New York Times*, March 25, 1990, p. D3. See Quentin Peel, "Pro-Market Adviser for Gorbachev," *Financial Times*, January 6-7, 1990, p. 1, for the first report on his appointment.

Radio Moscow he attacked the Ryzhkov government, hinting that Ryzhkov should resign. He called for the abolition of all industrial ministries. He repeated his positions about the need to focus on the exchange rate and demonopolization, and created a sense of urgency by saying that a package of measures must and would be introduced by presidential decree within one hundred days.[32] According to Hewett, who was close to him at this time, Petrakov favored freeing prices and adopting a tight money policy that would, he expected, produce stabilization by the end of 1990 and growth in 1991.[33]

Aleksandr Yakovlev also advocated a radical program of economic reform, which he presented to Gorbachev in private:

> The chief obstacle to perestroika and all your [Gorbachev's] policy is the Politburo, then the Central Committee plenum. There is no reason to convene them so often . . . convene the Congress of People's Deputies and establish presidential power. For the time being, let the Congress elect you president . . . then you [will] concentrate all power in your hands. . . . Before the Central Committee plenum set for February 5–6, go on television and appeal directly to the people. Say you take on yourself all responsibility for a program of extraordinary measures: land to the peasants, factories to the workers, real independence to the republics, a union of independent states instead of a Union state, a multiparty system and full renunciation of the Communist party of a monopoly on power, a sharp reduction of the apparatus, large loans from the West, military reform (toss out the generals and put lieutenant colonels in their place), begin to take troops out of Eastern Europe, liquidate the industrial ministries . . . freedom to private enterprise.[34]

Neither Petrakov nor Yakovlev ever presented a comprehensive reform plan to the public. Indeed, a year and a half later Yakovlev spoke with exasperation to an interviewer on the subject: "The recipes are very simple. We don't need new programs. Everyone is filled up to here with them. How many times is it possible to say that the private farming is more effective, that a rental enterprise works better?" His explanation for the failure of reform and his solution remained just as simple:

> I don't agree that we have a crisis. There is a crisis of the old stuctures, but not a crisis provoked by perestroika. . . . Do you really think the ministries and depart-

---

32. Quentin Peel, "Gorbachev Aide Attacks 'Insane' Financial Policy," *Financial Times*, March 17, 1990, p. 2; and Peel, "A Strongman of the People," *Financial Times*, March 17, 1990, p. 7.

33. Hewett, "Prognosis for Soviet Economy," p. 3.

34. A. S. Cherniaev, *Shest' let s Gorbachevym: po dnevnikovym zapisiam* (Moscow: Progress-Kul'tura, 1993), pp. 330–31.

ments will yield the road to entrepeneurs? Or that the Ministry of Agiculture will let farmers live? They think very simply: "Either we or them!" This is the collapse of old structures. If we do not get rid of them, perestroika will perish and the right wing will take its revenge.[35]

In the late summer of 1990 Yakovlev and Petrakov basically agreed with a program supported by the Russian government. This plan had its origins in February 1990, when three young economists—Aleksei Mikhailov, Grigory Yavlinsky, and Mikhail Zadornov—developed a radical 400-Day Program. The name of the plan reflected the length of time declared necessary to create a market economy. Mikhail Bocharov, the head of Democratic Russia who was to be Yeltsin's candidate for Russian premier, took the plan, added several days to each stage to lengthen it to 500 days because the number had a better ring, and made it his basic campaign document. Yavlinsky took the leading role in redrafting and was named deputy premier for economic reform in the Russian Federation government headed by Ivan Silaev that was formed in early June 1990. He was essentially the counterpart to Abalkin in the USSR government.

A young Central Committee official close to Aleksandr Yakovlev insists that the 500-Day Plan was really Petrakov's. When the presidency was being created in early 1990, two groups of specialists worked in the Central Committee dacha. One under Georgy Shakhnazarov was drafting the law on the presidency, while the other under Petrakov and Grigory Yavlinsky worked on the economic program.[36]

Meanwhile, the opposing group of economists had also been active. In mid-February, Abalkin and Yury Masliukov, the chairman of Gosplan, wrote a memorandum calling for a radical package of measures to be introduced on July 1, 1990, or January 1, 1991. They began developing such a package to be presented to the Supreme Soviet.[37]

The government economists continued to promote their cautious approach to reform. Viktor Gerashchenko, the chairman of the State Bank, and Pavlov advocated measures to promote savings, with Gerashchenko emphasizing the sale of housing and Pavlov the sale of bonds. Gerashchenko poured scorn on the idea that the Soviet Union could follow

---

35. Aleksandr Yakovlev, ". . . My sami sdelaem tak, shto oni voz'mut verkh," in Andrei Karaulov, *Vokrug Kremlia* (Moscow: Slovo, 1993), pt. 2, pp. 274, 273.

36. Andrei Grachev, *Kremlevskaia khronika* (Moscow: EKSMO, 1994), pp. 137, 139. Grachev was to become Gorbachev's press secretary in September.

37. Abalkin, *Ne ispol'zovannyi shans*, pp. 121–24, 131–36.

Petrakov's advice to work out a realistic exchange rate for the ruble as long as prices were so heavily subsidized. Otherwise enterprise directors would simply purchase underpriced raw materials and export them at world market prices.

For this reason alone, Gerashchenko contended, "the decision to put the price reform under the table is unforgivable. . . . We have lost two years."[38] He blamed fear of popular reaction produced by the introduction of elections. Gerashchenko's position was sound, but it was not the most diplomatic thing to say publicly to Gorbachev and Petrakov (Petrakov had favored that "unforgivable" decision that Gorbachev had made). Gerashchenko's indiscretion probably reflected his conviction that nothing was changing for the better.

At the December 1989 plenum of the Central Committee, Nikolai Sliun'kov, chairman of the Central Committee Commission on Economic and Social Affairs, had spoken out in alarm about the financial situation. In the autumn of 1987 he had been the only high official in the Central Committee Politburo to support the government's program to reform prices.[39] Now, ill and about to retire, he returned to the fray one last time. At the end of January 1990 he and the Economic Department of the Central Committee prepared a memorandum for Gorbachev that, in the general secretary's words, called for "not a partial, but comprehensive reform of price formation . . . a reform of wholesale and procurement prices in the middle of 1990 and a reform of retail prices at the beginning of 1991." Medvedev supported him.[40] Cherniaev described Sliunkov's position as anti-Ryzhkov, and it was no doubt described in those terms to Gorbachev, but it seemed in many ways to support the government economists.[41]

It is not absolutely clear whether Petrakov was speaking, as he claimed, for himself or for the president when he called for radical change and hinted at Ryzhkov's resignation. Usually it is nonsensical to raise such a matter about the newly appointed personal assistant of a president, all the more so because Petrakov was spending hours and even days with Gorbachev in

38. Wolf, "Model Central Banker," p. B11; and Wolf, "Soviet Banker," p. A23.
39. Pavlov, *Upushchen li shans?* pp. 78–79.
40. Gorbachev, *Zhizn' i reformy*, vol. 1, p. 568; *Memoirs*, p. 376.
41. For Sliun'kov's speech, see *Izvestiia TsK KPSS*, no. 4 (1990), pp. 49–51. Sliun'kov strongly supported one savings measure, the sale of housing, that Ryzhkov opposed. Nikolai I. Ryzhkov, *Ia iz partii po imeni "Rossiia"* (Moscow: Obozrevatel', 1995), p. 216.

early 1990 discussing economic reform.[42] Yet because of the increasing lack of discipline and the irresponsibility within the Soviet political system the matter must be addressed. Indeed, a year or so after his appointment, Petrakov resigned because he disagreed with Gorbachev's economic policy, and within a month he (along with Stanislav Shatalin, the economist on the Presidential Council) had signed a public statement calling for Gorbachev's resignation.

Nevertheless, although Gorbachev may have had little commitment to Petrakov's ideas, he knew that Petrakov's relations with Ryzhkov had deteriorated badly after 1987, In his memoirs Ryzhkov described Petrakov in the most critical and even bitter terms.[43] Gorbachev must at least have known how Ryzhkov would perceive Petrakov's appointment and his public position. Because Gorbachev did not stop Petrakov's stream of public statements, he clearly wanted them made.[44]

On February 7, 1990, the Central Committee approved an official party program that called for "radical economic reform," including a market economy and the possibility of individual ownership of the means of production.[45] The program endorsed "a restructuring of price formation," "financial stability," "a structural change of the economy in favor of the consumer sector," and "a deep restructuring of property relations [with recognition] of a multiplicity of its forms . . . including individual ownership of the means of production." The program said, rightly from a Western perspective, that there must be central leadership of the economy, but primarily "through prices, taxes, interest rates, credit, and so forth."

The party program emphasized the need to achieve financial stabilization not only through the reduction of subsidies, but also by measures to increase savings: "the encouragement of deposits in savings banks through a rise in interest rates, the development of insurance, the issuing of favorable state loan obligations, the sale of housing, the payment in advance for the future acquisition of long-term consumer goods, the sale of stocks and other securities."

The program even began by giving priority to reforming the agricultural sector. Its concessions to the conservatives were mostly in the language in

42. Hewett, "Prognosis for Soviet Economy," p. 3.
43. Nikolai Ryzhkov, *Perestroika: istoria predatel'stv* (Moscow: Novosti, 1992), pp. 323–24.
44. Gorbachev piously told his assistants how much he valued Ryzhkov and wanted to retain him, but all his actions in 1990 spoke of opposite intentions.
45. *Izvestiia*, February 13, 1990, pp. 1–2.

which statements were couched. "Private property" was not endorsed, only "individual property"; the center "led" the economy instead of regulating it. As in the Chinese agricultural reform, the free sale of land was not permitted, but its individual use and inheritance was allowed.

Thus the new program fully committed the Communist party to radical economic reform and included almost everything that could be desired. This resulted from the fact that it contained the ideas and phrases of both contending camps of reforming economists. In itself the inclusiveness was not a major problem. Abalkin was a radical, as a *Financial Times* editorial and others recognized at the time (but not six months later), while Petrakov was to denounce Gaidar's shock therapy when it was introduced in early 1992. But the two sets of ideas could be combined only by beginning with government-controlled price adjustments and other transitional steps, which had been the crucial issue for three years. The program said nothing about implementing transitional steps and therefore solved nothing in the conflict.

The Political Destruction of Nikolai Ryzhkov

Because little more than six months passed between the confirmation of Premier Ryzhkov's cabinet by the Congress of People's Deputies in July 1989 and Petrakov's suggestion that Ryzhkov resign, it is difficult to believe that Gorbachev ever expected Ryzhkov to be more than a scapegoat. Indeed, even before Petrakov's statements, as Ryzhkov, Abalkin, and Pavlov all correctly assert, the press, which basically remained under the control of the Central Committee, especially Yakovlev and Medvedev, had become very critical of the Ryzhkov government.

The tension exploded in the spring of 1990. On April 17 and 18 Masliukov and Abalkin presented their economic reform plan as an official government proposal to a joint session of the Presidential Council and the Federation Council. The report laid out a multistage movement toward a market economy, beginning with immediate increases in food prices and then introducing increasingly radical measures on January 1, 1991, and January 1, 1992.

The discussion in the Presidential Council and the Federation Council was "extremely stormy" (Ryzhkov's phrase), and the government was ordered to make its plan more concrete and to return in a month.[46] Although

---

46. Nikolai I. Ryzhkov, *Desiat' let velikikh potriasenii* (Moscow: Assotsiatsiia Kniga Prosveshchenie Miloserdie, 1995), p. 420.

Ryzhkov has implied he was being criticized, Gorbachev complained that "the academicians and directors of the institutes" had appeared at the session with positions that seemed more progovernment. They began to speak out against an underevaluation of the role of centralized leadership. One person he must have had in mind was his adviser of over a year, Stanislav Shatalin. On May 2 Shatalin published an article in *Literaturnaia gazeta* titled "Let's Not Lose Our Head!" in which he warned against impatience and asserted that shock therapy was inadvisable until the political and organizational infrastructure of a market had been created. Shatalin's protegé Yegor Gaidar, who now headed an institute, contemptuously called the 500-Day Plan a "sugary fairy tale" in his memoirs. Gaider said the plan did have a useful political side, and that side must have been the removal of Ryzhkov.[47]

On May 22 the two councils examined the new plan and entrusted the government with the responsibility of presenting it to the USSR Supreme Soviet on May 24, the day before the Russian Congress was to open. As Ryzhkov bitterly observed, they never actually endorsed the program, just its presentation.[48]

Ryzhkov's presentation would be televised to a national audience and would announce price increases. Yet Gorbachev not only never publicly associated himself with the proposals for retail price increases, but at the Twenty-Eighth Party Congress in June he would declare in a statement not in the draft of his written speech that "it was absurd to begin economic reform with price increases."[49] Ryzhkov claimed that Gorbachev had agreed that price increases were necessary, but Gorbachev claimed in his memoir that "it is still difficult to explain why Ryzhkov more than a half year before the price increases decided to announce them on television. Evidently his nerves failed him."[50]

In fact, either Gorbachev's memory or his honesty failed. The program Ryzhkov submitted to the Presidential Council and the Federation Council included immediate food price increases. The councils had instructed him to give a report to the Supreme Soviet and, therefore, television. The two

---

47. Stanislav Shatalin "Ne teriat' golovy!" *Literaturnaia gazeta*, May 2, 1990; and Yegor Gaidar, *Dni porazhenii i pobed* (Moscow: Vagrius, 1996), p. 68, and, in general, pp. 64–70.

48. Ryzhkov, *Desiat' let velikikh potriasenii*, p. 420.

49. For Ryzhkov's discussion of this and Gorbachev's reaction afterward, see Ryzhkov, *Perestroika*, p. 311.

50. Ryzhkov, *Perestroika*, pp. 310–11; Gorbachev, *Zhizn' i reformy*, p. 570; and *Memoirs*, p. 377.

bodies, both chaired by Gorbachev, had first postponed final consideration of the plan until mid-May and then approved May 24 as the day Ryzhkov should present it. This was the eve of Yeltsin's battle to be elected chairman of the Russian Supreme Soviet. Ryzhkov would never have had the authority to announce such a potentially explosive measure on his own at this crucial political moment.[51] Gorbachev had been delaying the decision on price increases for four years, and it would have been simple to postpone the announcement until after the Supreme Soviet election to avoid giving Yeltsin a popular issue. No one, least of all Ryzhkov, would have questioned Gorbachev's right to ask for such a delay. Characteristically, Gorbachev simply went abroad at the crucial moment, this time to a summit meeting in the United States.

When Ryzhkov made his report to the Supreme Soviet, the result was predictable. The public rushed out to buy bread before the prices went up, and bread disappeared from the shelves of stores for several days.[52] The measure was sharply denounced by Boris Yeltsin as an "antipeople's policy [that] Russia should not adopt." The government postponed price increases until January 1, 1991, and the Supreme Soviet ordered the government to rework its plan and present it once more on September 1.

Gorbachev clearly was making two political judgments. First, economic production was down 2 percent in the first eight months of 1990 and inflation was rising rapidly. He had decided to blame Premier Ryzhkov and his government. All pro-Gorbachev intellectuals were opposing price increases and calling for massive privatization and destruction of the central ministries that Ryzhkov led. By postponing the price increases until January 1, Gorbachev could persuade himself that he had turned that decision into the moderate ("centrist") alternative between Ryzhkov's April proposal and Yeltsin's rejection of all price increases.

Second, although Georgy Shakhnazarov says Gorbachav was overconfident,[53] the timing of Ryzhkov's presentation made no sense if Gorbachev was determined to defeat Yeltsin's bid to become chairman of the Russian Supreme Soviet. The president must have known Ryzhkov's announcement would help Yeltsin in his effort, and he must have decided that this was in his interest.

51. Georgy Shakhnazarov, *Tsena svobody: Reformatsiia Gorbacheva glazami ego pomoshchnika* (Moscow: Rossika, 1993), pp. 157–58.

52. Esther B. Fein, "Rising Food Prices Stir Panic Buying in Soviet Markets," *New York Times*, May 26, 1990, p. A1.

53. *Pervyi s"ezd narodnykh deputatov RSFSR (16 maia–22 iunia goda): Stenograficheskiy otchet*, vol. 2 (Moscow: Respublika, 1992), p. 234.

The campaign to destroy Ryzhkov and move toward agreement with Yeltsin reached a new level on July 27. Ryzhkov and Abalkin were preparing their economic program for the September 1 deadline set by the Supreme Soviet. Meanwhile Grigory Yavlinsky, deputy premier for economic reform in the new Russian government, began working on his reform plan. Yavlinsky, perhaps on the initiative of Yeltsin, who was now chairman of the Russian Supreme Soviet, proposed to Gorbachev that the two efforts be combined.[54] Gorbachev agreed, and on July 27 he and Yeltsin created a new working group, which was given responsibility for "the preparation of an agreed-upon conception of a program of transition to a market economy as the basis for the economic section of the Union Treaty." The unpublished version of the agreement went further, referring to "the preparation of a transition of the country to a market economy, taking the Russian proposal as the basis of the negotiations."[55]

The group was headed by Stanislav Shatalin, the radical economist who was on the Presidential Council. Only two government economists, Abalkin and Yevgeny Yasin, were named to the group, but Abalkin refused.[56] Yavlinsky and Petrakov were also members, but the other six were unknown young economists closely associated with the position of the Russian radicals. (Two of them, Zadornov and Mikhailov, had written the 400-Day Plan.)

When Gorbachev presented the proposed agreement with Yeltsin to Ryzhkov to sign, Ryzhkov was horrified. He considered the document to be the product of Petrakov's antigovernment program and realized the group was dominated by radicals who opposed him. A separate group of anti-Ryzhkov economists was being publicly instructed by the leaders of the USSR and Russia (including Ryzhkov, if he signed) to draft another economic reform program. Ryzhkov's and Abalkin's program was being dismissed as inadequate before it was even drafted. Ryzhkov did not want to sign, but Abalkin (and apparently another deputy premier, Stepan Sitarian) persuaded him that if he did not sign, he would be blamed for promoting conflict between Yeltsin and Gorbachev.[57]

54. Gorbachev, *Zhizn' i reformy*, vol. 1, p. 572; *Memoirs*, p. 378.
55. See Ryzhkov, *Ia iz partii po imeni "Rossiia,"* p. 231. That day Gorbachev also met with a number of radical economists and journalists. *Pravda*, July 28, 1990 , p. 1. For the decree, see *Sovetskaia Rossiia*, August 5, 1990, p. 1.
56. See Yavlinsky's interview in *Soiuz*, no. 37 (1990).
57. Ryzhkov, *Perestroika*, pp. 322–25.

The work of the Shatalin group was the subject of continual press coverage during August. Almost all the stories were favorable, while almost all references to the government group were unfavorable. Yet no one had seen either plan, for neither was yet drafted. On August 31 the radio talk show *Top Priority* perfectly illustrated the general line. The guests were two scholars of the Institute of the United States and Canada. One, Sergei Plekhanov, was forthright in his views:

> There needs to be a consensus between the center and the Republics, and it is not accidental that when the work of this joint Gorbachev-Yeltsin Commission on economic reform began to move forward immediately, the Council of Ministers—the Ryzhkov government—began to kind of throw spanners in the works, right, diminishing the importance, trying to denigrate the importance of the Gorbachev-Yeltsin Commission, saying now well look, it's we who are in charge, these guys don't know anything, and so on. Which means that serious work is going on in the Yeltsin-Gorbachev Commission.

The other guest, Andrei Kortunov, carefully avoided all judgments on the economic substance of the plan but was clear on one point: "No program proposed by the Ryzhkov government now can be accepted by the society, even the most radical reform, because people—let's face it—people simply do not trust the Ryzhkov government and they will not accept anything that will come out of this government. It has no legitimacy."[58]

The Craziness of the 500-Day Plan

Stanislav Shatalin, like so many of the radicals of the late 1980s, had a distinguished party pedigree. His father had risen to the level of party obkom second secretary, and his uncle, Nikolai Shatalin, had been Georgy Malenkov's chief lieutenant for personnel selection in the late 1940s and early 1950s and a Politburo member from 1952 to 1955. He was finally removed as Central Committee secretary for personnel when Malenkov fell from favor in 1955. Stanislav remembers sitting on Malenkov's knee while on vacation with his uncle.[59]

---

58. "Panel Assesses Gorbachev-Yeltsin 'Interaction,'" Moscow World Service, 2200 GMT, August 31, 1990, in Foreign Broadcast Information Service, *Daily Report: Soviet Union*, September 4, 1990, p. 58 (hereafter FBIS, *Soviet Union*).

59. Jerry F. Hough, interview with Stanislav Shatalin, October 10, 1990. In a July 1991 interview, Shatalin told an interviewer that he was "from a party family" and at a high enough level to know as a fact that Khrushchev had denounced Stalin in 1956 to win the support of Marshal Zhukov and the army. Stanislav Shatalin, "Tebe nado byt' prem'erom," in Karaulov, *Vokrug Kremlia*, pt. 2, p. 190.

During the late 1960s and early 1970s, Shatalin had become involved with a radical group of economists at the Central Economics-Mathematical Institute, including the institute director, Nikolai Fedorenko, and Petrakov. Because they opposed the 1965 reforms of Aleksei Kosygin for their excessively administrative character, they began to develop mathematical models whose application, they thought, would lead to self-regulation of the economy.[60] Two of Shatalin's young proteges, Yegor Gaidar and Aleksandr Shokhin, were to become the leading economic reformers in the first government of independent Russia.

The assignment given the Shatalin group in July 1990 was twofold. On the one hand, it was to present an economic reform plan on September 1 to compete with the government plan. On the other hand, the official task of the group was to prepare "an agreed-upon conception of a program of transition to a market economy as the basis for the economic section of the Union Treaty." That these tasks were fundamentally incompatible was noted by few observers in the West, and Gorbachev himself seems to have been confused about what he wanted from the group.

The negotiation of the Union Treaty—essentially a new constitution—will be discussed in the next chapter, but one point needs emphasis here. The economic section of the Treaty was to deal with the most fundamental aspect of the relation between the central government and the republics: the relative economic power of the central and republican governments and the system of taxation to finance the central government. Whatever the merits of the Shatalin group, it was extraordinarily ill suited to deal with such a crucial constitutional matter. Macroeconomic economists have little expertise on federal systems. In addition, the economists of the working group were Muscovites, and a majority were associated with the Russian government. At a minimum a constitutional committee should have included balanced representation from the republics. Other union republics sent representatives, but they served more as observers and had little influence on the outcome. Shatalin himself recognized that it would have been good to consult with President Nazarbaev of Kazakhstan and Ukrainian leaders but that there was no time.[61]

60. Richard W. Judy, "The Economists," in H. Gordon Skilling and Franklyn Griffiths, eds., *Interest Groups in Soviet Politics* (Princeton University Press, 1971), pp. 213, 240–47. For an extremely unfavorable description of the group, see Pavlov, *Upushchen li shans?* pp. 257–59.

61. Shatalin, "Tebe nado byt' prem'erom," p. 192.

Moreover, no one was making any effort to coordinate the activity of the Shatalin group with the legal scholars drafting the Union Treaty. Participants agree that the negotiations on economic reform and on the Union Treaty were entirely unrelated. The economists did not even seem to have informal contact with the drafters of the treaty. Shatalin, the economist on the Presidential Council, said privately that he had never discussed his plan or the questions of the taxing power of the government with Grigory Revenko, the member of Gorbachev's Presidential Council supervising the negotiation of the treaty.[62] In July academician Vladimir Kudriavtsev, chairman of the committee drafting the USSR Constitution and the key scholar working on the Union Treaty, made the identical point in reverse, saying privately that he never talked with Leonid Abalkin, the key man in the government dealing with economic reform. Abalkin asserted in an interview that he had never been consulted on the Union Treaty negotiations, although in memoirs he said that he talked with Revenko while on vacation in August 1991 after he had left office.[63]

Yet while they were dealing with the most fundamental of constitutional questions, Shatalin's group of young economists was also drafting a plan with a great deal of short-term economic detail to compete with the government plan. Ryzhkov was to note the incongruity of the demand that a group working on the Union Treaty submit a short-run economic plan by September 1.[64] The 500-Day Plan was to become a document of more than four hundred pages; it was not condensible into a short section in a treaty or constitution.

But if the plan was detailed, it was fatally affected by the responsibility of dealing with constitutional questions. Thus, taken literally, much of the 500-Day Plan was laughable. For example, both total privatization and total monetary stabilization were to be completed by the end of the first one hundred days. But the plan did not indicate the principle by which privatization would occur (through vouchers, for instance, or something else such as workers' ownership) and of course, no preparations had been made for either step. A three-month deadline was physically impossible if the measures were to be more than symbolic. The plan was filled with such wild utopianism.

Even on the level of minor detail–and a document of four hundred pages has a great deal of detail–the plan had many qualifications and inconsisten-

62. Jerry F. Hough, interview with Stanislav Shatalin, October 10, 1991.
63. Leonid Abalkin, *K tseli cherez krizis. Spustia god* (Moscow: Luch, 1992), p. 121.
64. Ryzhkov, *Perestroika*, p. 325.

cies. Some of its most dishonest features were little more than verbal games. The radicals had damned the government for beginning reform by raising prices and claimed they would retain price controls on 100 necessities. Yet they would free other prices, and they knew very well that this would produce serious inflation, including major price increases for necessities.[65] Informally, its proponents acknowledged the first five hundred days would only see the first steps toward a market economy.

If all the qualifications and informal statements were taken as the reality of the 500-Day Plan, the economic differences between it and the government plan were not as large as they seemed. According to Pavlov, 90 percent of the plan was taken verbatim from one of the early drafts of the government's plan, but with the brakes taken off.[66] The government's plan called for rapid changes in the economy during the transitional year of 1991, and then an acceleration of reform, including privatization, in January 1992. In fact, much of the "bad" inflation that was to mark 1991 was the result of deliberate policy and had many of the characteristics of the "good" price liberalization of 1992. The five hundred days that gave the plan its name would end in mid-1992 if it were adopted in September 1990. If the plan were really intended to be more gradual than promised, it and the government plan might bring the economy to similar points at that time. And finally, of course, both plans, as was true of all of Gorbachev's and Yeltsin's plans from 1985 to 1996, essentially ignored agriculture.[67]

The real differences between the government plan and the 500-Day Plan flowed from the charge to the Shatalin group to draft a section of the Union Treaty. The differences were political and involved radically different images of the federation. The 500-Day Plan gave all taxing powers to the republics, which would decide how much to allocate to the central government. The plan proclaimed the priority of republican laws over Union ones. Indeed, even its emphasis on immediate and total privatization had profound political implications. The government plan promised more gradual privatization that would begin in the trade and services sectors and be the responsibility of local government. Total privatization would include large-

---

65. Aslund, *Gorbachev's Struggle for Economic Reform*, 2d ed., pp. 214–16. For example, because price controls were to be put on only one kind of bread, bakeries would cease to produce it and concentrate on types without price controls.

66. Pavlov, *Upushchen li shans?* pp. 261–62.

67. The 500-Day Plan mentioned private farmers and private ownership of land, but the radicals admitted these were essentially talking points. No one believed that the cities could be fed at a tolerable price with a sudden privatization of agriculture.

scale industry and wholesale trade, and it would be in the hands of the republics if the central ministries were destroyed.

The advocacy of total privatization meant that during the transition period, the industrial plants and wholesale trade agencies of the State Supply Committee would have to be under control of the republics. If the plan were actually introduced more slowly but the transfer of property to republican control remained very rapid, the republics might be forced to become smaller versions of the central government for some time. One could imagine how Russia might take over USSR officials and institutions, but the administrative capabilities even of a Ukraine, let alone smaller republics, would be totally inadequate.

Indeed, the 500-Day Plan was vague about the very existence or power of central economic organs. On August 21 Ryzhkov and Abalkin had a three-hour discussion with the drafters of the plan. Abalkin repeatedly asked the proponents of the plan whether the Union would have a government, but he received no answer.[68] He concluded that its purpose was "the quiet liquidation of the USSR, replacing a federal state with an economic union of independent states."[69]

There were some features in the plan that suggested a continuing economic role for the central government. Moreover, the sovereign republics could delegate unspecified powers to the center, and in theory those powers could be the same that the sovereign republics had delegated to the Union in 1924. If Russia had a leader with a different policy and if the Soviet Union had a leader with a different personality, it was easy to imagine that the kind of economic functions exercised by the U.S. government would be ceded to the USSR government.

Yet when critics of the 500-Day Plan accused its authors of making the central government impotent, the answers were not reassuring. Shatalin was not atypical in his comment on September 11 to *Komsomol'skaia pravda*: "The center is, if you like, an executive committee, fulfilling the wishes of all the states united together. Sometimes its is said, 'The president of the country . . . Why are you making this figure a puppet?' That is idiotic. Look: defense, state security, the Ministry of Internal Affairs, energy, space, strategic transport, a single foreign policy.'"[70] The answer seemed to suggest that the central government had no role in economic policy.

68. Abalkin, *Ne ispol'zovannyi shans*, pp. 206–07.
69. Abalkin, *Ne ispol'zovannyi shans*, p. 206. Ryzhkov also emphasizes this point and says he made it sharply at the meeting. *Desiat' let velikikh potriasenii*, pp. 377, 439.
70. *Komsomol'skaia pravda*, September 11, 1990, p. 1.

When the 500-Day Plan did mention central financial powers, it was unclear whether this meant the central government would have the exclusive monetary powers of a Federal Reserve Board in the United States or a national bank in Western Europe, even though the emphasis on monetary stabilization assumed a strong such organ. Ukraine was talking about an independent currency, and the Russian parliament had passed a law setting up a financial and credit system independent of the central government. It assumed Russia would collect all taxes in Russia and itself decide what to transmit to the central government. The chairman of the State Bank and the minister of finance saw that an independent Russian financial system meant an acceleration of the loss of control over the money supply and told Gorbachev he must use his constitutional power to annul or suspend this law. Pavlov prepared the needed decree. Gorbachev called a conference of Russian and Soviet financial officials in the old Politburo meeting room, but after hearing the face-to-face arguments, he refused to sign the decree.[71]

Some drafters of the 500-Day Plan—Yavlinsky for example—perhaps thought the central government would exercise its power to impose strict limitations of money supply and that money supply alone would restrain the republics. If so, they were naive about the populist policies the republics could take and the political pressures on the central government to create the money to cover these expenditures. During the coming months, Yeltsin increased payments to various groups and withheld increasing amounts of tax money from the central government. In principle, the central government could have controlled the money supply, but the consequence would have been a severe depression and Gorbachev would have received the blame. Yavlinsky soon lost his naiveté and resigned from the Yeltsin government over its lack of fiscal responsibility.

The plan's drafters had also given little thought to the problems of tax collection in a transition from public to private ownership of the economy. Taxing socialist enterprises was easy, but how were taxes to be collected from private entities if there were no tax collection agency? The plan's drafters had given even less thought to the interaction of the concentration of all power of taxation in the republics with the problems of budgetary balance at a time when shock therapy was producing a sharp drop in production and therefore in tax revenues.

71. Pavlov, *Upushchen li shans?* pp. 100–01, 106–07, 130–35.

The 500-Day Plan seriously weakened the power of the central government and created the kind of financial starvation of the government that scholars associate with successful revolution. Because of this Pavlov makes the reasonable judgment that Gorbachev's refusal to sign the decree on tax collection was the key event in the breakup of the Soviet Union. Yet the plan's success depended on tight control of the money supply, and this could not be achieved without strong USSR government enforcement of controls, which the plan was destroying. And, of course, if the economy deteriorated because of its highly integrated character, some government agency was needed to provide a safety net. That safety net was to be introduced between the 300th and 400th day, although subsidies to industry and agriculture were to be ended between the 200th and 300th day and massive unemployment would begin then. I said the plan was laughable; it would have been better to say ludicrous.

If the 500-Day Plan is to be explained logically, its drafters must have wanted to break up the Soviet Union and give the Russian government many of its powers. At some point in 1990 or the first half of 1991, Yeltsin and some of his closest advisers (notably Gennady Burbulis) did in fact understand the consequences of the actions they were advocating. However, this was not true of a number of important participants such as Shatalin and especially Yavlinsky. Ruslan Khasbulatov, the first deputy chairman of the Russian Supreme Soviet, who was vigorously supporting Russian sovereignty and the seizure of central finances at this time, became an open supporter of the Union in the second half of 1991 and had always supported it.

It is hard to know what was going through the minds of these men, and their assumptions may have varied. When pushed very hard on the subject of taxation and the Union in an October 1990 interview, Shatalin spoke like a dogmatic Marxist who thought politics would be determined by economics, that a common economic market would automatically produce a common political authority.[72] When talking to the *New York Times* at this time, he expressed great faith in the degree of interdependence among the republics, but also stated his belief that Russia was the republic most committed to the federation and could keep the others in line.[73] Similar arguments were being made in Moscow. According to one critic, "Today we often have

---

72. Jerry F. Hough, interview with Stanislav Shatalin, October 10, 1990.
73. Peter Passel, "Russia Rules, But Gently," *New York Times*, October 17, 1990, p. D2.

occasion to hear that there is no need to worry about the fate of the Union, that the one power that will bind it together is market relations."[74] It was the ultimate example of the disdain for institutions shown throughout the period.

An even more decisive factor was that nearly everyone assumed the breakup of the Soviet Union was unthinkable. It was, therefore, something about which no thinking was done. If the question ever arose, few must have thought it conceivable that the military or the KGB would permit the Union to disintegrate. Those analysts of the CIA who were convinced by 1990 that Gorbachev was in deep trouble were talking about the likelihood of a conservative coup d'état.[75] The panic in the winter of 1990–91 over the possibility of dictatorship showed that many in Moscow were thinking the same way.

Many in Russia therefore believed that Yeltsin must be posturing and would stop short of the abyss. Indeed, he was being very careful about not burning bridges. As a consequence, other Soviet politicians often felt comfortable themselves in posturing. There was in the Russian Congress the combination of bombast and seeming chaos with reasonable compromises in its reconciliation committees. Many economists followed the same pattern. Abalkin was to report in conversation that, like Petrakov and Yavlinsky, Shatalin always supported an independent power of taxation for the central government in private, but that he moved in the direction of denying it to the central government to gain the support of the republics, especially of Yeltsin, for their plans.[76] They spoke irresponsibly in the belief that others would prevent the implications of their words from being carried to fruition.

Gorbachev's thought process at this time is the most mysterious of all. Negotiations on the Union Treaty and 500-Day Plan seemed brilliant strategies to undermine the Union, destroy the central government, and give enormous power to the government of Russia and Boris Yeltsin personally. But why would Gorbachev choose to follow this path? Many conservatives could think of no better answer than that he and his chief advisers were CIA agents, and one can understand their problem in finding another explana-

74. "We Must Create a New Union," *Rabochaia Tribuna*, October 23, 1990, p. 2, in FBIS, *Soviet Union*, November 13, 1990, p. 42.

75. Bruce D. Berkowitz and Jeffrey T. Richelson, "The CIA Vindicated: The Soviet Collapse *Was* Predicted," *National Interest*, no. 41 (Fall 1995), pp. 36–47.

76. Jerry F. Hough, interview with Leonid Abalkin, September 29, 1990.

tion.[77] Yet even the conservatives' suspicion is inconsistent with the fact that the Bush administration seemed much more interested in Soviet stability than did the Soviet president.

Gorbachev wrote as if he were reassured because Yavlinsky had worked in Abalkin's group and Shatalin, whom he definitely considered pro-Union, was the first name in the list of the working members of the group and therefore its leader. The former fact seemed to suggest that the two plans could be reconciled, while the latter suggested the group would be loyal.[78] Gorbachev commented that when he went on vacation, he maintained contact with the Shatalin group through Petrakov. He almost never called Ryzhkov or showed interest in his plan.[79]

Then, according to Gorbachev, he read about conflict between the Shatalin and Abalkin groups in the press, returned to Moscow early, and called a joint session of the Presidential Council and Federation Council for August 30–31. In his memoirs he damns the plan of the Shatalin group, which lacked independent taxing power for the federal government and perhaps a federal government altogether.[80] Yet he still told the Supreme Soviet on September 11 or 12, "If you ask me, I am more impressed by the Shatalin program."[81] It is all mindboggling, especially considering that the general secretary was a lawyer and was working with the best legal specialists (all pro-Union) drafting the Union Treaty and a new Constitution.

Part of the answer was tactical. Gorbachev and his democratic advisers were absorbed with discrediting Ryzhkov and replacing him because of his

77. In 1993 Vladimir Kriuchkov, former head of the KGB, said there was firm evidence that Aleksandr Yakovlev was an agent and that he, Kriuchkov, had presented this evidence to Gorbachev in 1990. See *Sovetskaia Rossiia*, February 13, 1993, pp. 1, 5; March 6, 1993, p. 1; and March 11, 1993, p. 4. Enormous suspicion remains among high officials. General Varennikov not only believes Kriuchkov's charges, but thinks the deaths of Andropov, Chernenko, and Ustinov were suspicious. Valentin Varennikov, *Sud'ba i sovest'* (Moscow: Paleia, 1993), pp. 10, 12, 24–25, 62. Valentin Pavlov's book, *Upushchen li shans?*, is filled with dark hints that Gorbachev was working under somebody's direction, and even the careful Nikolai Ryzhkov has indicated he may have used the word *treason (predatel'stvo)* in his memoirs in a literal sense. Aleksandr Lebed suggests that the August 1991 coup was somehow President Bush's work.

78. Gorbachev, *Zhizn' i reformy*, vol. 1, pp. 571–73. *Memoirs*, pp. 378–79, cuts most of the discussion in the original.

79. Ryzhkov, *Desiat' let velikikh potriasenii*, pp. 440–46.

80. Gorbachev, *Zhizn' i reformy*, vol. 1, pp. 573–76; and *Memoirs*, 380–82.

81. Moscow Television, September 11, 1990, in FBIS, *Soviet Union,* September 12, 1990, p. 39.

alleged responsibility for economic policy. Moreover, Gorbachev must have had some notion of positioning himself as a centrist between a 500-Day Plan that was too radical and a government plan that was too conservative. He saw how confusion over economic reform, coupled with economic crisis, could be used to get the Supreme Soviet to grant him emergency powers.

In addition, Gorbachev was trying to be crafty. Almost immediately upon his return to Moscow, he moved to integrate the government plan and the 500-Day Plan. He asked Abel Aganbegian to perform the task. The Aganbegian plan was treated by both Western and Soviet media as virtually identical to the Shatalin plan, and it therefore served to further discredit Ryzhkov. However, Aganbegian had prepared an analysis for the government in August that Ryzhkov considered progovernment.[82] His September plan sided with the government plan on the two main issues at stake: recognition of the supremacy of republican legislation and the denial of independent taxing power for the Union government.[83] The USSR Supreme Soviet, having received all three plans, said on September 24 that the plans should be integrated and gave Gorbachev the emergency powers he wanted to do it and a month to report.

Gorbachev gave Shatalin, Abalkin, Petrakov, and Aganbegian the duty of working out a presidential draft, but Shatalin, according to Gorbachev, had left for the United States, ostensibly for medical treatment.[84] Again Ryzhkov was not consulted. First Abalkin, then Aganbegian and Petrakov, and then Gorbachev himself worked on the program. It was presented to the Supreme Soviet on October 15.[85]

In November Gorbachev finally rejected the 500-Day Plan and, as shall be seen, presented a draft of the Union Treaty that preserved a strong government, but *before then* he had moved toward much more radical economic reform. On October 4 a presidential decree had stated 30 percent of wholesale prices would be set freely, 30 percent would be free to rise to a ceiling, and 40 percent would be fixed at a higher level. Retail prices on most goods were raised, and retail prices on luxury goods were set free.

82. Ryzhkov, *Desiat' let velikikh potriasenii*, p. 440.
83. Shatalin on television, September 18, 1990 in FBIS, *Soviet Union*, September 19, 1990, p. 46; Gorbachev, *Zhizn' i reformy*, vol. 1, p. 578; *Memoirs*, p. 384.
84. In fact, Shatalin went to America on a speaking tour to cash in on his fame at $5,000 a speech. It was during this tour that he appeared at Duke University and gave the interviews cited in this book.
85. Gorbachev, *Zhizn' i reformy*, vol. 1, pp. 578–79; *Memoirs*, p. 384.

Russia passed a law to block the price increases inside Russia and increased agricultural procurement prices.

In many ways it seemed a nice set of tactical moves. Gorbachev had moved to a radical economic reform much like Abalkin had been proposing, but had used the 500-Day Plan to position himself as a centrist. He had allowed Yeltsin and his team call for a total dismantling of the Soviet Union and then himself had moved toward a new Union Treaty that would feature a democratic federalism. As has been seen, he got rid of his most radical advisers but also Premier Ryzhkov, and he moved toward the center in personnel selection as well as policy.

Predictably, on October 16 Yeltsin gave his most confrontational speech up to that time, claiming that Gorbachev was determined to preserve the Soviet command-administrative system and limit the sovereignty of Russia. Westerners who were spokesmen of the Yeltsin radicals concluded in December 1990 that "Gorbachev no longer stands for democratization and marketization, but the opposite."[86]

But there was something in Gorbachev's attitude that went beyond tactics. His closest advisers—Yakovlev, Cherniaev, Shakhnazarov, Medvedev, and probably Shevardnadze—were strong supporters of the 500-Day Plan. Yakovlev was basically to break with Gorbachev when the president rejected the plan, and Cherniaev and Medvedev expressed support for the plan in their memoirs several years later. They were deeply attracted to the idea of a very loose federal or even confederal system in which the non-Russians genuinely saw the advantages of cooperation and accepted it. They understood that the non-Russians would never believe federal arrangements had any real meaning so long as the USSR ministries played such a dominant role in the economy.

It was to be said that Gorbachev and his advisers never understood the depth and strength of nationalism and the desire for independence. This criticism is wrong. Instead, they thought non-Russian nationalism was so strong that major concessions had to be made to win the trust of the non-Russian republics. Indeed, if the republics should move toward some prosperous economic union, federation, or confederation in the next decade, future historians may look at the enormous costs of the late 1980s and first half of the 1990s as a trivial price to pay for the change in psychology, the recognition of common interests, that permitted voluntary reintegration.

86. Aslund, *Gorbachev's Struggle for Economic Reform*, 2d ed., p. 223.

Gorbachev's mistakes seem to have been of two types. First, he really did seem to accept many of the assumptions found in the Western arms control literature of the Brezhnev period. This literature focused on misunderstanding and a perception of threat as a major cause of hostility and developed nonthreatening gestures to overcome this problem. Gorbachev seemed to think that if he made nonthreatening and reassuring gestures to Yeltsin and the non-Russians, they would be more willing to compromise with him. He was probably paying a severe price for having too many close advisers from the foreign policy community of the 1970s.

Second, and most important, Gorbachev did not understand the problems of collective action. He thought that economic interests, especially an understanding of the economic consequences of disintegration, would balance the impetus of nationalism. The vote in the March 1991 referendum showed that he was correct in his assumptions about public opinion. The problem was that the economic incentives of privatization for bureaucrats and the political incentives for officials such as Yeltsin and Ukrainian President Leonid Kravchuk as individuals were far more decisive than the collective interest in economic prosperity. Unless Gorbachev or the military were to control republican leaders, the people for whom the collective interests were more important had no ability to defend them.

CHAPTER TWELVE

The Union Treaty

THERE WERE MANY revolutions in the Soviet Union in 1990 and 1991. The overthrow of governments or even of political systems is not unusual, and they are seldom called revolutions. The collapse of the Communist party was bound to be a more momentous event because of the thoroughly nationalized nature of the country and the party's control of all organized life. Yet the establishment of a strong presidency, a strong Ministry of Finance, and the central appointment of state governors—all features of Boris Yeltsin's independent Russia after 1991—could have created a political system with enough in common with the communist system to provoke serious discussions on what, if anything, had changed. Many hybrids were possible; after all, China has been called a communist dictatorship even though Deng Xiaoping never held a party post and did not sit on the party Politburo or Central Committee for years.

The truly unexpected, perhaps unique, revolution in the Soviet Union was that which broke it into fifteen separate countries. Many called the Soviet Union the last empire and suggested that it should disintegrate as easily as the British and French Empires. Yet these had not dissolved without years of struggle, often armed struggle, to preserve them. Moreover, the word *empire* is normally used to describe geographically widespread political units in which persons of the home ethnicity constitute a very small percentage of the population of outlying units. Geographically compact "empires" such as the Soviet Union, especially those with large numbers of the home ethnic group living in the different territorial units, are normally called multiethnic countries. As Donald Horowitz has pointed out, there were many separatist movements in such countries between 1945

373

and 1990, but only one was successful: in Bangladesh where the secession was supported by the Indian army.[1]

The Soviet Union had the most powerful army in the world, and it had in no manner been weakened by defeat in war. The non-Russian republics showed none of the violence directed against the dominant ethnic group that is a constant feature of life in India, Sri Lanka, and Sudan. Indeed, significant anti-Russian demonstrations occurred only in the Baltic republics, and the Baltic peoples never resisted military force. In normal parlance the Soviet Union had an extraordinarily strong state, indeed too strong with too powerful a bureaucracy and with total control over finances because it "owned" all economic enterprises. The Soviet Union collapsed because its leaders made no effort to enforce its laws and allowed the republics to take over all tax collection. Ultimately it was Russia that ended "the Russian Empire" by seceding from it.

Mikhail Gorbachev seemed genuinely committed to the idea of a more decentralized federation of the republics of the Soviet Union, perhaps without the Baltic republics. The military and the security forces seemed even more committed to federation. Yet neither did anything to prevent the dissolution of the country. In fact, Gorbachev accelerated the disintegration by the bizarre manner in which he tried to renegotiate a more democratic federation through a new Union Treaty.

Toward a Republic-Dominated Union

Power in the USSR had always had been divided and delegated on two principles, one territorial or horizontal, the other branch (*otrasl'*) or vertical. The chief territorial units were called "sovereign" and were even given ministries of foreign affairs, but in practice they were not as powerful as the branch institutions, especially the USSR ministries and state committees.

The clearest evidence of the dominance of the branch institutions was the organization of the Central Committee apparatus, Gosplan, the trade unions, the Young Communist League (the Komsomol), and so forth, along branch lines. Gosplan and the Central Committee had agricultural departments, the Komsomol a rural youth department, and the trade unions an Agricultural Workers Trade Union. They supposedly controlled the various

---

1. Donald L. Horowitz, *Ethnic Groups in Conflict* (University of California Press, 1985), p. 265.

agricultural ministries, but in fact they were staffed by agricultural specialists and became members of a powerful branch complex. The situation was similar in other branches, and each had its de facto representive on the Secretariat and Politburo.

Leonid Brezhnev's passivity in policymaking meant that a great deal of power devolved to these bureaucratic complexes, at least within the limits established by his disinclination to make changes at the end of his life. The result was described by Tatiana Zaslavskaia, a sociologist, as the domination of the middle levels of power over the upper (the Politburo) and the lower (the local party organs).[2] This structure was described in many ways by Westerners, but the question was how to explain it.[3] Did it simply reflect the manner in which Brezhnev chose to rule, or did it reflect the unchallengeable power of the bureaucracy?

Mikhail Gorbachev and his closest advisers shared or came to accept many of the assumptions that the bureaucracy was all-powerful. Gorbachev thought the bureaucracy could be defeated, but the method he chose—"political shock therapy," Yegor Ligachev called it—implied a belief that the defeat had to be administered by direct attack and had to be complete or else the bureaucracy would regain its power.[4] In June 1985 Gorbachev had argued that decisions to widen the independence of the enterprises had been thwarted because "some ministries . . . are able to so 'swaddle' the independence of the enterprises and interpret the decisions of the Central Committee and government in such a way that in practice nothing at all remains of these principles after all the departmental recommendations and instructions."[5] As seen in earlier chapters, he increasingly seemed to think that such behavior was inherent in the system.

But if a political system based on the priority of the power of the branch ministries was to be transformed, something was needed to replace it. A natural alternative was a system in which greater power was concentrated in the republics and regions. During 1990, in fact, Gorbachev moved in such a direction. In July the Politburo was changed into a body of twenty-

2. *Izvestiia*, June 1, 1985, p. 3.
3. A second issue was whether the bureaucracy was united, as the analyses of bureaucratic ossification and nomenklatura argued, or whether there were significant cleavages, as the analysis of institutional pluralism argued.
4. Ye. K. Ligachev, *Zagadka Gorbacheva* (Novosibirsk: Interbuk, 1992), pp. 75, 298–99.
5. Mikhail S. Gorbachev, *Izbrannye rechi i stat'i*, vol. 2 (Moscow: Politizdat, 1987), p. 272.

five persons, fifteen of whom were first secretaries of the party committees of the Union republics. In November Gorbachev took power away from the Council of Ministers and purportedly gave it to a Federation Council composed of republican leaders.

But what was to be the relationship among the republics? During the autumn of 1988 a "war of laws" began to develop between them and the central government. On November 16 the Supreme Soviet of Estonia passed a declaration of sovereignty that proclaimed the primacy of its law over the Union laws and constitution, and such actions were to multiply. On January 18, 1989, Estonia passed a language law that contravened USSR legislation and constitution, and ten more republics followed in the next sixteen months.[6]

Clearly, new rules had to be established and then enforced. Most of the changes could have been in the framework of the provisions of the existing Constitution, which was quite democratic on paper. And many changes, such as those in the system of taxation, would normally have been introduced by legislation, not constitutional amendment. If changes were desired in government structures, they could be introduced through constitutional amendments, as the creation of the Congress of People's Deputies had been in 1989 and the introduction of the presidency in 1990.

But the 1936 Constitution had been called the Stalin Constitution, and the 1977 Constitution the Brezhnev Constitution; Gorbachev wanted a constitution associated with himself personally that would be the first of a truly democratic Soviet Union. Moreover, the non-Russian republics would likely consider new federal arrangements more legitimate if they were embodied in a new constitution than in one amended by the Congress of Peoples' Deputies, even if the provisions of the two were identical. Thus it was not surprising that the First Congress of People's Deputies created a constitutional commission, headed by academician Vladimir Kudriavtsev, to draft a new constitution.

The Union Treaty

Within nine months of the establishment of the constitutional commission, however, Gorbachev decided to negotiate a new constitution in a

---

6. Albert S. Pigolkin and Marina S. Studenikina, "Republican Language Laws in the USSR: A Comparative Analysis," *Journal of Soviet Nationalities*, vol. 2 (Spring 1991), p. 39.

different way: through the renegotiation of the Union Treaty that had established the USSR in 1922. The word *soiuz* in Russian is normally translated *alliance*, rather than *union*. Formally the country was an alliance of sovereign states: the Alliance of Socialist Soviet Republics. In 1988 Baltic scholars contended that because their republics had been incorporated in 1940 and had not signed the Union Treaty, a new one was required to legitimate the Union.[7] The Estonian Supreme Soviet formally proposed a Union Treaty in November and the Communist party central committees of the three Baltic republics endorsed it during preparations for a plenum of the all-Union Central Committee on Interethnic Relations.[8]

In December the Moscow leadership decided to create a working group to examine this demand. Officially called the Working Group for the Preparation of Proposals on the Division of Competency between the USSR and the Republics, it included a representative from each Union republic (but no autonomous republic) and was headed by Georgy S. Tarazevich, chairman of the Presidium of the Supreme Soviet of Belorussia.[9] The Tarazevich Commission was given the task of drafting the "Law on the Division of Powers between the USSR and the Union Republics," and worked out rather traditional plans for decentralization of power.[10]

In the new USSR Congress of People's Deputies, the radical Interregional Group supported the idea of a Union Treaty, but the idea made little

7. For a statement by an Estonian scholar to this effect at a September 1988 roundtable in the Institute of State and Law in Moscow, see "Demokratizatsiia sovetskogo obshchestva i gosudarstvenno-pravovye aspekty natsional'nykh otnoshenii v SSSR," *Sovetskoe gosudarstvo i pravo,* no. 1 (1989), p. 41.

8. I. S. Muksinov, "Sovetskii federalizm i kompleksnoe ekonomicheskoe i sotsial'noe razvitie soiuznoi respubliki," *Sovetskoe gosudarstvo i pravo,* no. 10 (1989), p. 7.

9. The decree was enacted on December 28 and was published, together with the list of its members, in *Vedomosti Verkhovnogo Soveta Soiuza Sovetskikh Sotsialisticheskikh Respublik,* no. 1, January 4, 1989, pp. 12–13. Belorussia had been one of the republics to acquire territory from Poland in the Hitler-Stalin Pact of 1939, and Tarazevich had special reason to be sensitive to the area's nationality problems. He had been born in the region of Belorussia adjoining Lithuania, had gone to college in Lvov in western Ukraine, where he married a Ukrainian, then had worked most of his life in party organs in Minsk, the Russified capital of Belorussia. In 1990 he still spoke Russian like a Ukrainian. Jerry F. Hough, interview with Georgy S. Tarazevich, Moscow, June 28, 1990.

10. For reports on its sessions, see *Izvestiia,* March 6, 1989, p. 2; and March 21, 1989, p. 2.

progress during 1989.[11] As late as September the platform of the Communist party supported "radical transformations in the Soviet federation." It declared a new Union Treaty unnecessary and suggested a new declaration in the Constitution.[12] At a conference convened to discuss the powers of the republics and the advisability of a new Union Treaty, scholars from Latvia and Tataria argued in favor of the treaty, but the major Moscow scholars were opposed. All the participants, it was said, agreed that the federation needed to be perfected, not transformed into a confederation.[13]

Gorbachev wrote that he began to consult seriously about the Union Treaty only at the end of 1989.[14] In his report to the Central Committee on February 5, 1990, he briefly mentioned the "development of the treaty (dogovornyi) principle" in the creation of a federal system and thus signaled a decision to move forward quickly. By March 21 the prospective Law on the Division of Powers between the USSR and the Union Republics, already on the legislative agenda, had been made the vehicle for initiating the negotiation of the treaty.[15] The title of the draft law was changed to "The Law on the Renewal of the Union Treaty and the Division of Powers between the USSR and the Union Republics."

Tarazevich told the Supreme Soviet that the very idea of combining the law on distribution of power with the renewal of the Union Treaty had arisen only "recently." One deputy complained that the text of the draft had been completed several days before it was presented and, as Tarazevich

11. V. B. Isakov, chairman of the Supreme Soviet of the Russian Republic, was later to discuss the group's support, complaining on Moscow television that "this idea [is] now being discredited by the democrats themselves." "RSFSR Officials Examine Union Treaty," Moscow Central Television, 1851 GMT, March 15, 1991, in Foreign Broadcast Information Service, Daily Report: Soviet Union, March 26, 1991, supplement, pp. 1–2 (hereafter FBIS, Soviet Union).

12. Izvestiia, September 24, 1989, pp. 1–2. The draft program was published on August 17, 1989. The press had carried on a substantial discussion of its features in July. See Pravda, July 12, 1989, p. 3.

13. For a short summary of the conference, see "Pravovye problemy natsional'nykh otnoshenii v SSSR," Sovetskoe gosudarstvo i pravo, no. 5 (1989), pp. 137–43. The proceedings were published in Pravovye problemy garmonizatsii mezhnatsional'nykh otnoshneii v SSSR, Zasedanie 25/27 ianvaria 1989 g., Minsk (Moscow: VNII sovetskogo gosudarstvennogo stroitel'stva i zakonodatel'stva, 1989).

14. Mikhail Gorbachev, Zhizn' i reformy, vol. 1 (Moscow: Novosti, 1995), p. 518. This does not appear in Gorbachev, Memoirs (Doubleday, 1996).

15. See the report of the session of the Presidium of the Supreme Soviet, Russian Radio, March 20, 1990, in FBIS, Soviet Union, March 21, 1990, pp. 40–41.

admitted, the text had not even been redrafted to reflect the new presidential structure.[16]

It is unclear why Gorbachev had suddenly changed his mind and agreed to renegotiate the Union Treaty. In his memoirs he treated the decision as inevitable: "[In] the so-called war of laws, the republics agreed to recognize only those legislative acts that were approved by their parliaments. Central authority was becoming subverted in a fundamental way. It was becoming obvious . . . that it was necessary to conclude a new Union Treaty."[17]

The potential advantages of such a treaty were in fact obvious enough. The central government was deeply distrusted in non-Russian republics. Both non-Russian nationalists and Moscow radicals were denouncing the USSR Congress of People's Deputies as conservative, and neither would accept constitutional amendments passed by it as legitimate. If the republics would accept a new Union Treaty, then one should be signed to end questions about the legitimacy of the Union.

The long-term potential advantages of a Union Treaty were, however, the major disadvantages of negotiating one. If the republics were free to join the Union voluntarily, they also had to be free not to join. Indeed, Gorbachev was implicitly admitting that the Union would not be legitimate unless this option were real. By March 1990 those republics that had originally called for a new Union Treaty were electing officials who wanted no part of one.

Moreover, the procedure of negotiating the treaty implied the need for consensus. A revision of the Constitution by the Congress of People's Deputies could have been decided by a two-thirds vote, but a Union Treaty negotiated outside the framework of the legislature made each republic an independent actor. The draft that was prepared would be sent to the republics not for ratification, as had occurred with the U.S. Constitution, but for comments and suggestions for revision. The direction of these suggestions was easy enough to predict.

Gorbachev's assistant Georgy Shakhnazarov, after proposing in December 1990 that a new Union Treaty be sought and quickly signed and then calling in May for its conclusion within a few weeks, had by June 28 come

16. *Biulleten'*, no. 4, pp. 8, 11; and Moscow Domestic Service, March 21, 1990, in FBIS, *Soviet Union*, March 22, 1990, p. 34.
17. Gorbachev, *Zhizn' i reformy*, vol. 1, p. 491; *Memoirs*, p. 325.

to understand that eagerness on Gorbachev's part was fatally weakening his bargaining position. He then wrote to Gorbachev.

It seems to me that we now must reevaluate in principle our position on the schedule for concluding the Union Treaty. In practice we are in the power of a framework of thought based on the assumption that this Treaty will save statehood and will allow us to bring perestroika to a conclusion. From this point of view, a delay with it is a catastrophe. Such a mood at the Union level is acutely felt in the republics. Those who are for the Union use [the Treaty] as a hostage to trade for greater rights for themselves. Those like Rukh who are against the Union use it to enforce nationalist campaigns.

It is untrue that a delay with the signature of the Union Treaty will lead to disaster. Instead there is every basis to think it would work out for the best. . . . As soon as the Ukrainians and Russians feel . . . that we find a certain advantage in a delay in the signing of the Treaty, they will start to worry. . . . If it becomes clear that things are dragging out, the public will begin to be agitated and pressure the republican rulers.[18]

At best the process of obtaining agreement would take several years.[19] The analogy with the old Union Treaty, "negotiated" when Moscow was in total control and could prevent any republican resistance, suggested a very long process indeed. The treaty signed on December 29, 1922, had twenty-six articles, but the Union Treaty that became part of the Constitution on January 31, 1924, had seventy-two, and because of amendments and changes the text was "substantially different."[20] After the treaty was signed, it had to be cleared with the republican legislatures, and a new and more detailed constitution had to be negotiated on the basis of it.

At the time there seemed a logical, if cynical, explanation for Gorbachev's behavior. Tarazevich said privately that people assumed Russia, Ukraine, and Belorussia would stay together, in which case the other republics could be easily handled. If Gorbachev made this assumption, he may have been happy that the Union Treaty negotiations would drag out for years and be inconclusive. That would serve only to postpone the new Constitution that would require him to submit himself to a popular election. In addition, the 500-Day Plan for economic reform that was introduced in 1990 was so unrealistic that it seemed certain to discredit Boris Yeltsin and

18. Georgy Shakhnazarov, *Tsena svobody: Reformatsiia Gorbacheva glazami ego pomoshchnika* (Moscow: Rossika, 1993), pp. 535, 542–43.

19. For such an argument made as an objection to the Union Treaty by a scholarly insider, see B. Lazarev, "Soiuznyi dogovor," *Sovety narodnyh deputatov*, no. 6 (1989), pp. 22–23. This article contains a useful history of the original treaty.

20. Lazarev, "Soiuznyi dogovor," p. 20.

his radical reformers who were backing it and who were Gorbachev's primary opposition. It seemed likely Gorbachev would move decisively on some intermediate course of changing the federal structure and reforming the economy once these two points had become clear to everyone.

The "Subjects of the Federation"

Long before a Union Treaty would be completed, another matter would have to be faced. Who would have the right to participate in the negotiations? Most assumed that the treaty would be renegotiated by its original members, the so-called Union republics. However, other ethnic groups, some of them larger than groups within Union republics, had autonomous republics. That they had been assigned lower status by Stalin seemed to strengthen their case to participate in the renegotiation rather than preclude them.

This problem was "solved" by Gorbachev with a high-handed and unconstitutional change in the status of the autonomous republics of Russia. A seemingly innocuous USSR Supreme Soviet law of April 26, 1990, the Law on the Division of Powers between the USSR and the Subjects of the Federation, formally broadened the powers of republican governments, but did so in a way that was explosive. The terms *Union republic* and *autonomous republic* disappeared, and *subjects of the federation,* which was said to encompass both kinds of republics, was inserted. Both former types of republics were subordinated directly to the USSR government.[21] In 1991 a number of autonomous oblasts also transformed themselves into republics.

The law of April 26 had been foreshadowed by a law of April 10 entitled Basis of Economic Relationships between the Soviet Union, the Union Republic, and Autonomous Republics, which implicitly treated the Union republics and the autonomous republics as if they were equal.[22] The major stimulus for the new laws was the decision to deprive republican and local party organs of the power to serve as the chief regional economic coordinators. The authority of the republican and local government organs had to be strengthened so that they could fill the old role of the party organs.

The equation of the union republics and autonomous republics was, however, not a necessary consequence of this action, but of the political

21. *Izvestiia,* May 3, 1990, pp. 1–2.
22. *Izvestiia,* April 14, 1990, pp. 1–2.

fears of radical and liberal reformers. In the past the oblast party organs were the powerful provincial institutions in Russia and Ukraine, but reformers were very suspicious of democratically elected oblast governments. As is often the case in the United States, the balance of power in such "state" governments would often be held not by the people in the major city of the region but by those living in the outlying areas. The outlying areas in Russia were less supportive of radical reform than the larger cities, and the reformers wanted to reduce the power of the "state" level. To solve this problem, reformers supported a Law on Local Self-Government and the Local Economy that gave most power to city (and rural county) governments. Such a law was passed on April 9, 1990.[23] It was not a coincidence that the law of April 10 was passed the next day, for it and the law of April 26 were intimately connected with the law on local self-government.[24]

None of these three laws had any practical significance in the short and medium run because the system of taxation remained centralized and left the oblast subordinated to Moscow and the city subordinated to the oblast (the same remained true in early 1997). The Law on Local Self-Government and the Local Economy did, however, create an enormous political problem with the autonomous republics. Although the Soviet political system had been highly centralized, the party first secretaries of the Union republics and the oblasts had been important political figures. The autonomous republics had been little different from oblasts, and their actual governing body—their party organ—even had the same name as that of the regular oblast (obkom or oblast committee).[25] Except for giving the autonomous republics more autonomy on cultural questions, Moscow had not treated them and the oblasts differently, and had little reason to do so.

Thus if the Law on Local Self-Government and the Local Economy would take power away from the oblasts, it would take it away from the autonomous republics as well. Even as an abstract principle, this was

23. Izvestiia, April 14, 1990, pp. 1–2.
24. Izvestiia, April 16, 1990, pp. 1–2. I owe my understanding of the intricacies of these laws to one of the participants in the drafting process, Boris Krylov of the Institute of Legislation.
25. In my book The Soviet Prefects: The Local Party Organs in Industrial Decision-Making (Harvard University Press, 1969), on the role of the local party organs in industrial decisionmaking, I used examples or evidence about party organs in the oblasts and autonomous republics interchangeably.

politically unacceptable in the new conditions. The ethnic Russians usually constituted a majority of the population of the capital cities in the autonomous republics, and granting them de facto independence from the republics would leave the republics virtually powerless in their own capitals. The legal equation of the autonomous republic with the Union republic avoided this problem.

In practice the autonomous republics remained administratively subordinate to the respective Union republics, as everyone expected, and the laws might have been ignored had not Gorbachev decided to renegotiate the Union Treaty. Leaders of the autonomous republics had long been insisting on the right to participate in the process, and now this question was resolved by fiat. If there were only republics without a qualifying adjective, representatives of all would participate in the renegotiation of the federal relationship as a matter of course. It is highly likely that the prior knowledge that the twenty relatively conservative autonomous republics would outnumber the fifteen Union republics was a key reason Gorbachev agreed to renegotiate the Union Treaty.

The substance of the negotiations was also certain to be affected. The Union republics already had been given "sovereignty," but the autonomous republics had not. Indeed, conservatives had advocated sovereignty for the Union republics in the 1977 Constitution precisely in order to emphasize their superiority to their autonomous republics. The first draft of the 1977 Constitution had not included a clause proclaiming the Union republics sovereign, but one was added to the final draft at the suggestion of a relatively conservative Russian law professor at Moscow University.[26] The professor had no thought of promoting the independence of Russia from the USSR, but wanted to distinguish between the sovereign Union republics and the nonsovereign autonomous republics. His goal was simply to reaffirm the unquestioned dominance of Russia over its autonomous republics.[27] In fact, the proclamation of the sovereignty of Russia and the other

26. The final version of Article 76 reads, "A Union republic is a sovereign Soviet socialist state that has united with other Soviet republics in the Union of the Soviet Socialist Republics," and Article 81 adds that "the sovereign rights of the Union republics are preserved by the USSR."

27. *Izvestiia*, September 21, 1977, p. 2. This man, D. L. Zlatopol'sky, later wrote a good short history of republican sovereignty in Soviet constitutional history: "Natsional'naia gosudarstvennost' soiuznykh respublik: nekotorye aktual'nye problemy," *Sovetskoe gosudarstvo i pravo*, no. 4 (1989), pp. 14–20.

Union republics was associated with a more vigorous policy of Russification in the autonomous republics.[28]

In the new political conditions the former Union republics obviously could not be deprived of their "sovereignty," and the equation of Union and autonomous republics conferred such sovereignty on the latter as well. Thus even the most conservative draft of the Union Treaty—that of November 1990—called each of the republics (including former autonomous republics) a "sovereign federal state" with the "full plenitude of state power" on its territory. The March 1991 draft declared that the republics were "full members of the international community" with the right to establish diplomatic relations with foreign countries and participate in international organizations. In the negotiations the representatives of the former autonomous republics always advocated maximum independence from the former Union republics in which they were located.

In addition, some practical matters in the Union Treaty took on wholly different meanings because of the expansion of the number of republics. For example, all drafts of the Union Treaty said that the president must receive a majority of the popular vote and win in a majority of the republics to be elected. If *republics* meant Union republics, eight of fifteen republics had to support a presidential candidate. If the term included all republics, it meant nineteen of thirty-six republics.[29] The governments of Russia and Ukraine became insignificant on any body, such as the Federation Council, in which each republic had one participant and one vote.

The law of April 26, 1990 was published on May 3, less than two weeks before the opening of the Russian Congress. As Russian politicians then and later repeatedly complained, the Supreme Soviet law was amending the Constitution in a most fundamental way, but without going through the amendment process, which required a two-thirds vote in the Congress of People's Deputies.[30] Especially since the Union Treaty negotiations empha-

---

28. Brian Silver, "Social Mobilization and the Russification of Soviet Nationalities," *American Political Science Review*, vol. 68 (1974), pp. 52–53, 59–64; and Silver, "Language Policy and the Linguistic Russification of Soviet Nationalities," in Jeremy R. Azrael, ed., *Soviet Nationality Policies and Practices* (Praeger, 1978), pp. 258–59.

29. Moreover, as Gorbachev's assistant G. Shakhnazarov warned him in a January 1991 memorandum, the number threatened to increase because the smaller ethnic units were beginning to transform themselves into republics. Shakhnazarov, *Tsena Svobody*, p. 508.

30. For a statement a year later by Ruslan Khasbulatov, the first deputy chairman of the RSFSR Supreme Soviet, see "Khasbulatov Comments on Yeltsin Speech, Treaty," Moscow Radio Rossii, 1230 GMT, March 13, 1991, in FBIS, *Soviet Union*, March 14,

sized the implications of the law, no other action could have so dramatized Yeltsin's claim that the center ignored and repressed Russia and that Russia needed a strong leader and the right to abrogate USSR laws on Russian territory. Gorbachev could not have been so blind as not to see the implications for Yeltsin's chances.

From the beginning, cynics believed that Gorbachev had accepted the redefinition of the power of the autonomous republics to have a bargaining chip he could use in his contest with Yeltsin. The more Yeltsin emphasized sovereign rights for Russia, the more he would promote the sovereign rights of the former autonomous republics within Russia. This might be a restraining influence on him. In addition, Gorbachev would ultimately be able to trade the chip away: he could eventually agree to sell out the rights of the autonomous republics if Yeltsin would sign the Union Treaty.

As shall be seen, Gorbachev did in fact betray the autonomous republics in May 1991, and Yeltsin did agree to sign the treaty. Yet Gorbachev was wrong in thinking that Yeltsin would be restrained by the fear of creating a precedent for the autonomous republics. He demanded all rights for Russia and, like a good populist, told the autonomous republics they could have maximum sovereignty as well. Once the Soviet Union was dissolved, he signed a Federation Treaty with the republics giving them sovereignty, and then when he dissolved the Russian Congress in 1993, he simply instituted a new constitution that did not mention the sovereignty guaranteed by the Federation Treaty. His chief advisers—no doubt with his encouragement— urged the transformation of the republics into oblasts with no national rights whatsoever.

Gorbachev's scorn for constitutional procedures on such a crucial matter undermined his effort to insist on respect for law and on legal restraints on government that he needed to foster in his attempts both to introduce constitutional democracy and to restrain Yeltsin. He only succeeded in inflaming Russian nationalism and discrediting the central government in Russia. And, of course, his promotion of the election of Yeltsin as chairman of the Russian Supreme Soviet was a sound strategy only if he knew how to hold him responsible once in that post.

1991, pp. 72–74. The chairman of the Soviet of Nationalities acknowledged that the law required a change in the Constitution and promised that this would be done at the next Congress of People's Deputies. *Pravda*, May 29, 1990, p. 3. It never was, no doubt because Gorbachev did not want the change institutionalized but was planning to betray the autonomous republics in the endgame negotiations with Yeltsin.

The Russian Declaration of Sovereignty

In 1989 and 1990 all the Union republics passed declarations of sovereignty, and Boris Yeltsin put great emphasis on one for Russia. The declaration itself did not have great significance, for Russia, like the other Union republics, was already sovereign according to the 1977 USSR Constitution. Not surprisingly, the declaration finally passed with 907 votes in favor, 12 votes against, and 9 abstentions. The harder decisions involved the wording of the document, particularly the question of whether Russia had the right to contravene USSR laws on Russian territory.

In Soviet legal language, the word *suverenitet* never had the sweeping meaning of the English *sovereignty*. Stalin was not using a word he thought had much meaning when he gave the sovereign republics ministries of foreign affairs. The "sovereignty" described in the 1977 Constitution was strictly limited. Article 76 stated that the "Union republic independently exercises state power on its territory outside the boundaries defined in Article 73." As can be imagined, Article 73 defined the boundaries of central authority very broadly in twelve points, the last of which was "the settlement of other questions of all-Union significance."[31]

When, however, nationalists were allowed to speak out in 1988, many in the Baltic republics began demanding that sovereignty be defined in its Western sense. In 1988 the Popular Front of Estonia declared that "sovereignty is [only] possible when the priority of the Union republic over the Union as a whole is clearly established." It insisted that a confederation be created. This did not, however, mean sovereignty would now be defined precisely in political discourse. It meant the opposite. A Soviet scholar summarized the situation in the summer of 1991.

> The problem of sovereignty has attracted great attention. They speak about the sovereignty of individual territories, of individual local soviets, and even of deputies. They speak about the unity of the sovereignties of the USSR and the Union republics, about the full state sovereignty of the republics, about the sovereignty of the USSR as a sum of the sovereignties of the republics, about the limited sovereignty of republics, about limitations of the sovereign rights of the republics, and so forth.[32]

31. *Izvestiia*, October 8, 1977, pp. 4–5.
32. A. A. Golovko, quoted in "'Kruglyi stol' zhurnala 'Sovetskoe gosudarstvo i pravo,'" *Sovetskoe gosudarstvo i pravo*, no. 9 (1991), pp. 12–13.

The substance of the Russian Declaration of Sovereignty was the subject of long and difficult negotiations. The declaration was first discussed on May 17, 1990, and went through an elaborate drafting process. Various versions were repeatedly sent to the Editorial Commission for reconciliation. The voting on individual articles and amendments took a week.[33]

Several sharply contrasting conceptions of sovereignty lay hidden behind the nearly unanimous support for the term in the declaration. One group spoke about "economic sovereignty." Although radicals were to say non-Russian exploitation of Russia justified independence from the Soviet Union, economic sovereignty became a code term for a more conservative definition of sovereignty as greater freedom from the central ministries and equity in the trade balance between republics. Thus Sergei Baburin, the deputy from Omsk who was a fervent advocate of Russian sovereignty, combined his support of economic reform and market pricing with a strong pro-Union position: "In the final analysis [only real Russian sovereignty] will save the Union as a whole."[34] That is, most of those talking about economic sovereignty were making a point to non-Russians about the subsidized raw materials they were receiving, but those Russians were willing to make the economic sacrifice in intermediate terms if the non-Russians would adopt a moderate position on the Union.

The second definition of sovereignty, "political sovereignty," could have a meaning applauded by conservatives: the need for Russia to create a complete set of political institutions: Communist party organization, Young Communist League (Komsomol), trade unions, KGB, Academy of Sciences. But the reformers were afraid of the creation of such Russian institutions, for the Moscow city organizations would be directly subordinated to their counterparts in Russia, which were more conservative than Gorbachev's USSR Central Committee and the organizations under its control.

Political sovereignty became the rallying cry of the radicals and came to mean either full republican independence or great autonomy within a confederation. Boris Yeltsin always claimed he was only seeking a more equitable role for Russia within the Soviet Union. Yet, as envisioned by

33. Regina A. Smyth, "Ideological vs. Regional Cleavage: Do the Radicals Control the RSFSR Parliament?" *Journal of Soviet Nationalities*, vol. 1 (Fall 1990), pp. 122–23.
34. *Lesnaia promyshlennost'*, May 15, 1990, p. 1. At the First Congress of People's Deputies, Baburin's voting behavior ranked him in the left-center group by the Sobianin-Yurev voting scale, but in November he was one of the founders of the Rossiia faction that emphasized the preservation of the Soviet Union as a country.

him, strengthening Russian political sovereignty included increasing the importance and responsibilities of the Russian Ministry of Foreign Affairs. Russia, he said, should be able to conclude foreign economic agreements, cultural exchanges, and the like with other countries.[35] Others spoke of representation in the United Nations.[36]

The open call for full Russian independence was slower to be voiced. Russian nationalists had always been divided between what Roman Szporluk called the empire savers and the nation builders. Most nationalists envisioned Russian national destiny as being the head of a large multiethnic state (or perhaps even a third Rome, providing leadership for the whole world), but there had always been an element in the Slavophilism or Pan-Slavism of ethnic nationalism that did not want Russia's distinctiveness diluted by non-Russians, or at least non-Slavs. This had traditionally been a right-wing position, and it recently had been reiterated by the conservative Aleksandr Solzhenitsyn.[37] In the summer of 1989 Szporluk noted only that some radical activists were beginning to take the position.[38]

Proponents of rapid marketization and democratization identified with radical definitions of sovereignty. They tended to equate the central government with powerful economic ministries and believed the government needed to be dismantled if the ministries were to be destroyed. Those who wanted a rapid transition to the market argued that Russia would be greatly benefited by market pricing of its energy and raw resources. They hoped this argument would increase Russians' acceptance of radical market reform. They could even conclude that Russia would be better off economically without the republics and should get rid of them.

Finally, as Yeltsin began appointing young promarket radicals to top posts and Gorbachev continued to rely on men in their fifties and sixties, the young saw that decentralization of power to the republican level would give them personal control over privatization. That such control might well lead to personal riches surely also occurred to them.

35. *Rabochaia tribuna*, May 20, 1990, p. 1.
36. *Rabochaia tribuna*, May 16, 1990, p. 1.
37. See Aleksandr Solzhenitsyn, *Rebuilding Russia: Reflections and Tentative Proposals* (Farrar, Straus & Giroux, 1991), p. 8, for his proposal of a Russian Union of Little Russians, Great Russians, and White Russians. For his argument that the concept of a separate Ukrainian people is artificial, see pp. 14–19. The book was first published in the USSR in September 1990.
38. Roman Szporluk, "Dilemmas of Russian Nationalism," *Problems of Communism*, vol. 37 (July–August 1989), p. 25.

The main policy battle of the First Congress was fought on an amendment to article 5 to the Declaration of Sovereignty of the Russian Federation. The exact wording was negotiated over many days in a reconciliation commission, and finally took in the following form: "In order to secure political, economic, and legal guarantees of the sovereignty of the RSFSR, it is decreed that . . . the RSFSR Constitution and the laws of the RSFSR are supreme on the whole territory of the RSFSR. Acts of the USSR that contradict the sovereign rights of the RSFSR are suspended by the republic on its territory. Differences between the republic and the Union are resolved in a manner established by the Union Treaty."[39]

On the surface the exact meaning of the amendment depended on the Union Treaty's provisions for resolving differences between the Union and a republic. But no one expected the treaty to be signed and ratified very soon. The real meaning of the amendment was to be determined by the willingness of the central government to permit its decrees to be suspended. There were to be dramatic Russian Supreme Soviet laws later in the year—one taking control of the gold and diamonds on Russian lands, for example—that had little meaning because the central government ignored them. On other matters a "war of laws" broke out in the winter of 1990–91 because Gorbachev would not accept repeated advice to declare a state of emergency and enforce the supremacy of USSR laws.[40]

Article 5 was finally passed 540 to 302, with 217 absentees. The vote was much closer than it seemed, for the majority needed for passage was 530 votes. Many absentees were conservative and moderate deputies who preferred to vote against the amendment by their absence rather than by being recorded.

One aspect of the vote hinted at problems to come in later congresses. Radicals considered some matters as part of a package aimed at destroying the dominance of central party and economic institutions, and a radical scholar constructed an index out of six votes to define the political position of deputies in the Congress.[41] One was Amendment 5, while two of the most important of the others prohibited political parties (notably the Communists) from having units in the military and the police organs. Moderates and even conservatives, however, could have very different combinations

---

39. *Sovetskaia Rossiia*, June 14, 1990, p. 1.
40. See the discussion in Anatoly Luk'ianov, *Perevorot mnimyi i nastoiashchii* (Moscow: Manuskript, 1993), pp. 17–18.
41. *Argumenty i fakty*, no. 29, July 21–27, 1990.

of views, and the distribution of votes on these two issues was far wider than it had been on the agenda test votes (table 12-1). (In this cross-tabulation I used the vote on political membership in the military because there were twenty fewer absentees.)

The 342 generally consistent prosovereignty and antiparty deputies were the usual Democratic Russia Bloc. The conservatives, however, were much more fragmented. There were 343 "consistent" conservative votes if one counts the 52 antisovereignty deputies who were absent on the party vote and the 95 pro-party deputies who were absent on the sovereignty vote. (In overall terms, such a judgment about the absentees is accurate, but it obviously exaggerates the number of consistent deputies by including some who were absent for other reasons.) There were, however, 198 deputies who were radical on sovereignty and conservative on party membership, and 133 deputies who were conservative on sovereignty and radical on party membership.

The two inconsistent groups had very different social bases. Some of the urban intelligentsia were nervous about security agencies' independence from the party. As a result, 41 of the professional and lower-level administrators in education, science, and so forth were more radical on the question of allowing party membership among the military and police, and only 32 were more radical on sovereignty. By contrast, three occupational groups—party and soviet officials, high security officials, and enterprise directors in agriculture—were generally extremely conservative on the question of party organs in the military. Only 24 in this group were more radical on party organs, while 83 were more radical on sovereignty. This tendency was particularly strong in the rural areas and small towns, and the vote on this issue in 1990 foreshadowed the emergence of the conservative coalition of 1992 and 1993.

The First Draft of the Union Treaty

As has been seen, the negotiation of the Union Treaty and the 500-Day Plan began simultaneously in the summer of 1990. The drafting committee of the 500-Day Plan was dominated by supporters of the Russian government, and naturally it emphasized granting great power—indeed, virtually total power—to the Union republics. The legal transformation of the Union and autonomous republics in April into republics had, however, resulted in

Table 12-1. *Distribution of Votes on Party Membership in the Military,
First Congress of People's Deputies, by Deputy Views on Russian
Sovereignty, May–June 1990*

	Antiparty	Proparty	Absent	Total
Prosovereignty	342	157	41	540
Antisovereignty	54	196	52	302
Absent	79	95	43	217
Total	475	448	136	1,059

Source: *Pervyi s"ezd narodnykh deputatov RSFSR (16 maia–22 iunia 1990 goda): Stenograficheskii otchet* (Moscow: Respublika, 1992), vol. 6.

both sending representatives to the Union Treaty negotiation.[42] There were fifteen former Union republics and twenty-one former autonomous republics, and the latter were highly suspicious of the former. Any Union Treaty drafted by majority vote was certain to be very different from the 500-Day Plan on the question of the relative power of the central and Union republic governments.

At the same time that the press was emphasizing and praising the 500-Day Plan, the leading figures in the negotiation of the Union Treaty were holding periodic meetings with journalists.[43] On September 25 the chairman of the Union of Nationalists gave a report to the Supreme Soviet that discussed many of the issues, while at the beginning of November, the Federation Council called for an acceleration of the preparation of a draft.[44]

While the negotiations for the Union Treaty and the 500-Day Plan were being kept parallel in the sense of being separate from each other, they obviously were also parallel in a time sense. The leadership was quietly reminding the public that the 500-Day Plan was not the final word on the issue of republican power, and it wanted a draft of the treaty ready at the time Gorbachev rejected the 500-Day Plan and presented his own economic reform plan.

On November 24, 1990, a week after Gorbachev finally rejected the 500-Day Plan and presented his own economic program to the Supreme Soviet, the first draft of the Union Treaty was suddenly published.[45] The

42. This point was emphasized by Gorbachev's two main representatives in the negotiations, V. Kudriavtsev and B. Topornin. *Izvestiia*, June 18, 1990, p. 3.

43. *Izvestiia*, July 14, 1990, p. 2; and September 5, 1990, p. 2.

44. *Izvestiia*, September 26, 1990, p. 2; and November 2, 1990, p. 2.

45. *Izvestiia*, November 24, 1990, pp. 1–2.

draft was described in the West as a centralizers' document, which it certainly was in comparison with Shatalin's proposals. However, negotiations on the treaty began on the basis of the March 21 draft of the Law on the Division of Power between the USSR and the Union Republics, and the November draft provided considerable more power to the republics than the Tarazevich Commission had proposed the previous March.

The major difference of the November draft treaty, however, came in the new power it gave the former autonomous republics. The title of the original law, the Division of Responsibilities between the Union and the Union Republics, implied that the autonomous republics, let alone the lesser territorial units, would be strictly subordinated to the Union republics. Now, as the chairman of the Soviet of Nationalities stated on December 3, the Union Treaty draft made "virtually no distinction between Union and autonomous republics."[46]

The outcome of the negotiations had been predetermined by the character of the participants. Because the negotiations included more autonomous republics than Union republics, the representatives of the autonomous republics were certain to have a dominant role in equating Union republics and autonomous republics as simply republics. As a result, the first draft reflected their desires. The primary concern of the autonomous republics was recognition of ethnic rights. This the November 1990 draft did. Indeed, the second house of the legislature, called the Soviet of Nationalities, provided representation to all nationalities in the Soviet Union, not just those with territorial units. The autonomous republics, as has been seen, were even more suspicious of the Union republics than of the central government and did not want to be left at the mercy of the former. The autonomous republics had little fear of a fairly strong center, viewing it as protection against the Union republics that were closer and more threatening.

For this reason the leaders of the autonomous republics were ecstatic with the first draft of the Union Treaty. Mintimer Shaimiev, chairman of the Supreme Soviet of Tatarstan, declared, "Since the document under discussion speaks of the Union of Soviet Sovereign Republics, we are ready to sign it."[47] The symbolic issue for both the former autonomous republics and

46. "3 Dec. Session Detailed," Moscow Television Service, 2045 GMT, December 3, 1990, in FBIS, *Soviet Union*, December 4, 1990, p. 14.

47. "Republic Leaders Comment on Draft," *Komsomolskaia pravda*, December 2, 1990, in FBIS, *Soviet Union*, December, 3, 1990, p. 47.

Russia was the order of the signatures. The leaders of the republics wanted the signatures in alphabetical order to signify their independence. Russia wanted either the Union republics to sign for their autonomous republics or the autonomous republics to sign in a subordinate manner.

The draft of the Union Treaty, however, contained clauses that were still in dispute. It was to be sent to the supreme soviets of the republics for comment, and not surprisingly, all would demand greater powers for the republics. In 1991, when the fourth published draft was scheduled to be signed (an event that the August 1991 coup was timed to forestall), Vladimir Lukin, the head of a committee of the Russian Supreme Soviet, noted that even this would be far from the final stage.

> For some reason, it is taken for granted by the press and by the public that the Treaty of Union will be based on the draft prepared in Novo-Ogarevo. This is not so. In fact, the latest text of the draft is to be thoroughly analyzed and revised in all the parliaments of the constituent republics concerned. . . . As of right now, a number of the draft's provisions are unacceptable to certain republics.
>
> We shall certainly keep improving the Treaty by amending it and adding extra supplements and protocols to it. After all, the US Constitution's formative period lasted for a decade after the declaration of independence, and this had no adverse effect on the quality of that country's democracy. After the draft version of the Treaty of the Union is agreed upon, work will begin in earnest.[48]

Boris Yeltsin, like other Russian leaders, always spoke as if he took Russia's signing of a Union Treaty as a given. Yet he pushed for a confederation in which very few powers would be left to the central government. Together with Ukraine, he held out for the complete republican control over the powers of taxation in Shatalin's 500-Day Plan. Because Gorbachev, as well as poorer republics hoping for redistribution of wealth from the richer ones, seemed unlikely to accept this proposal, the stage seemed set for endless deadlock.

From Gorbachev's point of view, delay was not necessarily bad. While negotiations were dragging on, he could quickly introduce changes in central government–republican relations and the structure of the executive branch through constitutional amendment, legislation, or presidential decree. Indeed, that is precisely what happened through the spring and summer of 1990. Before the signing of the Union Treaty, a series of "interim" arrangements were instituted through Supreme Soviet legislation and pres-

48. Vladimir Lukin, "London Is within Easy Reach of Novo-Ogarevo," *New Times*, no. 27 (July 9–15, 1991), pp. 8–9.

idential decrees: April 3, conditions of republican withdrawal from the USSR; April 26, subjects of federation; April 26, rights of citizens outside their national boundaries; July 29, relations of Union and republican organs on financial questions during preparation of the Union Treaty; August 9, formation of the fund of state property of the USSR.[49]

The publication of the first draft of the Union Treaty was itself accompanied by drastic constitutional change sprung on the country without notice and passed by the Congress of People's Deputies in a few weeks. The draft described new political institutions, and most were simply instituted immediately. The Council of Ministers was replaced by a Cabinet of Ministers, the Presidential Council was abolished, a new Security Council and post of vice president were created, and the Federation Council was strengthened.

The governmental structure was becoming disorderly.[50] But for all the talk about his losing control of the USSR Congress to the conservatives, Gorbachev still could get the support of two-thirds of the members to push through a new organizational structure that further strengthened his hand in the executive branch. In addition, the change from Council of Ministers to Cabinet of Ministers meant that the head of the cabinet had to be confirmed, and Gorbachev could claim that he could not appoint Ryzhkov to the new post because the Federation Council would not agree.[51] Ryzhkov was deeply offended because he was told of the change in structure thirty minutes before it was announced publicly.[52]

The Hysteria of the Winter of 1990–91

For reasons that remain obscure, Gorbachev's November 16 speech and the publication of the first draft of the Union Treaty on November 24 were followed by hysterical fear among Moscow intellectuals that he had allied with the far right and that dictatorship was imminent. Yet Gorbachev had

49. B. S. Krylov, I. N. Kuznetsov, and N. A. Mikhaleva, "Kontseptsiia soiuznogo dogovora," *Sovetskoe gosudarstvo i pravo*, no. 10 (1990), p. 4.

50. On government disorderliness see the warnings in a number of Shakhnazarov memorandums to Gorbachev at the time. *Tsena svobody*, pp. 509–12.

51. For Gorbachev's claim that this was important, see *Zhizn' i reformy*, vol. 1, p. 586; *Memoirs*, pp. 390–91

52. Nikolai Ryzhkov, *Desiat' let velikikh postriasenii* (Moscow: Kniga, Prosveshchenie, Miloserdie, 1995), pp. 22–24.

done little more than reject a commonwealth that would have left no power to the central government. This was predictable and was defined as conservative only by those demanding the breakup of the Soviet Union. Because he remained emphatic in his commitment to economic reform and decentralization of power and because the only real consequence of the reorganization of November 1990 was the replacement of Ryzhkov, the bête noire of the liberals, one might have thought that the liberals would have been measured in their reaction.

One reason they were not was that Gorbachev filled key positions—the director of TASS, the minister of justice, and most important, the minister and first deputy minister of internal affairs—with conservative appointees. Vadim Bakatin, the liberal minister of internal affairs was replaced by Boris Pugo, a former KGB official, while Boris Gromov, the leading general of the Afghan war, became first deputy minister of internal affairs and head of the internal troops.

Gorbachev had also not been defending the leading liberals, who had embraced the 500-Day Plan fully, from conservative attack. Aleksandr Yakovlev distanced himself from the president, and on December 20 Gorbachev's long-time friend Foreign Minister Eduard Shevardnadze, who supposedly was slated to take over domestic nationality affairs, resigned with a warning of the danger of dictatorship. In addition, Nikolai Petrakov, Gorbachev's personal assistant for economics, resigned, also presumably over the 500-Day Plan.

Another reason for alarm may have been that Gorbachev did succeed in obtaining emergency powers from the USSR Fourth Congress of People's Deputies. His November 16 speech before the USSR Supreme Soviet included a powerful and perhaps threatening appeal for the preservation of the Union: "I am decisively against the fragmentation of the state, against the recarving of territory, the destruction of the eternal ties of peoples. My own bitter experience, already washed by the blood of our people, makes it easier for me to say that we cannot separate. We will not go down this path."[53] He called for a referendum to support the Union. Boris Yeltsin had made a confrontational speech before the Russian Congress on October 16, and the two men seemed headed toward a showdown in which Gorbachev might well use the military.

53. *Izvestiia*, November 17, 1990, p. 1.

Vladimir Kriuchkov, the chairman of the KGB, and a number of leading generals also spoke out in threatening terms. Kriuchkov appeared on television asserting that "the threat of the collapse of the Soviet Union has emerged" and that the efforts in this direction were "well thought through" and that "some of them are enjoying lavish moral and material support from abroad." He declared, "on instructions of the USSR president," that the KGB would fulfill its obligation to maintain state security.[54]

Within a week, a "galaxy" of top military officers and civilians circulated an open letter to Gorbachev proposing action against rebellious republics: "If constitutional methods prove ineffective against separatists, criminal speculators, and the paramilitary forces that are continuing to spill the blood of the people, we suggest instituting a state of emergency and presidential rule in zones of major conflict." The signers included the head of the General Staff, the commander of the ground forces, the commander of the navy, and the commander of the MVD troops, as well as the patriarch of the Russian Orthodox Church and the liberal minister of culture.[55]

At the beginning of 1991, Soviet security forces were used to storm a television station in Lithuania, and fourteen deaths ensued.[56] At the time, blame was placed on local units and local right-wing extremists, but it was later revealed that the unit involved was the elite A or Alfa unit of the KGB, which was subordinated directly to the chairman of the KGB. Alfa must have been ordered into action by central officials and almost surely with Gorbachev's approval. In his Russian-language memoirs Gorbachev denied responsibility and reported the denials of his top ministers, but by the time of the publication of the English-language version, a group of Alfa veterans had published a book that could not be ignored. In the English-language version Gorbachev asserted that the chairman of the KGB and minister of defense must have been involved.[57] However, it is hard to believe that

54. Moscow television, December 11, 1990, in FBIS, *Soviet Union*, December 12, 1990, p. 32.
55. The statement was published in the Italian newspaper *La Repubblica* by December 15. Vilnius International Service, December 15, 1990, pp. 33-34. The signers indicated were mentioned by Paris AFP, December 19, 1990, in FBIS, *Soviet Union*, December 19, 1990, pp. 44-45. The statement and the word *galaxy* are from Bill Keller, "Gorbachev Urged to Consider Crackdown in Republics," *New York Times,* December 20, 1990, p. A3.
56. Craig R. Whitney, "Gorbachev Puts Blame for Clash on Lithuanians," *New York Times*, January 15, 1991, p. A1; and Frances X. Clines, "Disarray in Moscow," *New York Times*, January 15, 1991, p. A6.
57. Gorbachev, *Zhizn' i reformy*, vol. 2, p. 507; *Memoirs*, pp. 578–79.

Gorbachev did not know what units were involved within hours of the attack and that he would not have taken corrective action if he considered it warranted.[58]

Vladimir Kriuchkov described the events leading up to the Lithuanian attack in some detail in his memoirs, and his version is convincing. He insisted that a company of Alfa was sent to Lithuania "with the sanction of the highest leaders of the country."

> Moreover, my deputies and I were criticized at different conferences more than once for "inaction" in the face of the threat of the unconstitutional exist of the Baltic republics from the USSR. Gorbachev himself threw such an accusation at us. . . . The situation in Lithuania, and in general in the Baltic republics, was discussed at the highest level daily. These were working discussions, larger gatherings, the exchange of opinions with the USSR president in small groups. . . . At the end of December a decision was taken at a conference (soveshchanie) in Gorbachev's office to apply force against the actions of extremists in Latvia and Lithuania. . . . Gorbachev was decisive, but this did not increase confidence [that he would not waver]. By the way, [foreign minister] Shevardnadze was at this meeting and supported the variant of force. . . . Gorbachev gave an instruction to Yazov, [minister of internal affairs] Pugo, and me to accelerate the preparation of concrete measures, but by the evening he made an adjustment: "Don't get hot-headed, study the situation more delicately, weigh everything, and we will discuss it again." In the words of [his chief of staff] Boldin, Gorbachev had a long conversation with Yakovlev prior to this. . . .
>
> The sharp worsening of the situation required President Gorbachev on January 10 . . . to give an instruction of defense minister Yazov, minister of internal affairs Pugo, and me as chairman of the Committee of State Security to apply force and send to Vilnius a small group of the KGB subdivision known as Alfa. The group should act with subdivisions of the Ministery of Defense and the Ministery of Internal Affairs depending on circumstances.[59]

Gorbachev made no effort to install a new government in Lithuania or to follow up troop action in a way that suggested a broader plan. He denied responsibility for the action, but he did nothing to punish the perpetrators. Presumably he was trying to suggest to the Lithuanians and to radicals everywhere that there were forces in Moscow that would take decisive action and that he did not have the power to stop them or criticize them.

---

58. The information about Alfa was published in the West, for example, in John B. Dunlop, *The Rise of Russia and the Fall of the Soviet Empire* (Princeton University Press, 1995), p. 238.

59. Vladimir Kriuchkov, *Lichnoe delo* (Moscow: Olimp, 1996), pt. 2, pp. 28–31.

The result was that Gorbachev angered everyone. Liberals treated the action as a sign of the imminent dictatorship they had been predicting since November. The departure of Eduard Shevardnadze, Aleksandr Yakovlev, and Nikolai Petrakov suddenly looked like a protest by insiders who knew what was coming. Democratic Russia, the umbrella radical-liberal political group in the Russian Congress, called for his resignation and a general strike.

Yeltsin joined in the protest. "I have formed the impression that this is the beginning of a powerful attack on democracy," he said on January 15.[60] Two days earlier he had characterized the use of force in Lithuania as "another bloody wound on our already lacerated body" and predicted the republic would become the "next Afghanistan."[61] Yeltsin especially denounced the use of Russian draftees in ethnic conflicts without the approval of the Russian parliament, a use that the parliament had prohibited in October. He flew to Tallinn, Estonia, and issued a joint statement with the chairmen of the legislatures of the three Baltic republics denouncing the central government's action. The statement included a clause announcing that it was sent directly to the United Nations.[62] When he returned from the Baltics, Yeltsin held a press conference at which he said he had been giving increasing thought to the subject and that "we . . . evidently will not succeed in defining sovereignty without a Russian army."[63]

Conservatives were no less upset than liberals. They deeply disapproved Gorbachev's refusal to be decisive and especially his decision to leave the army and other security forces open to what they considered an unfounded flood of criticism. Colonel Aleksandr Rutskoi, who was to be a major political actor from 1991 to 1993, expressed a widespread feeling in his usual forceful language: "Stupidities! Anyone who has served in the armed forces understands perfectly well that the head of a garrison never gives such orders. . . . And even the minister of defense never gives such orders."[64]

---

60. Radio Rossii Network, January 15, 1991, in FBIS, *Soviet Union*, January 16, 1991, p. 92.
61. Radio Rossii Network, January 13, 1991, in FBIS, *Soviet Union*, January 14, 1991, p. 92.
62. For the text of the statement, see Riga Domestic Service, in FBIS, *Soviet Union*, January 14, 1991, p. 91.
63. Radio Rossii Network, January 15, 1991, in FBIS, *Soviet Union*, January 16, 1991, p. 93.
64. The speech was republished in *Argumenty i fakty*, no. 4, January 1991, p. 2.

Gorbachev's Position

By early 1991 radical political analysts in Moscow argued that the center of the political spectrum had disappeared. Public opinion, they said, had polarized, and Gorbachev had to identify with one pole or the other. When he moved in a more conservative direction, this meant by definition that he had come to oppose democratization and reform altogether. His only hope, they said, was to shift back to the other pole—to embrace the radical revolutionaries.

Without any doubt, the politically most vocal members of society had become polarized, but this did not mean a polarization of society as a whole or even of the politically aware members of it. Gorbachev had moved the center of public opinion to an acceptance of the market that seemed unlikely five years earlier. However, all significant political actors, including Boris Yeltsin, publicly opposed shock therapy, and this reflected their judgment about the state of public opinion.

The public held the same kind of centrist views about the preservation of the Soviet Union. Most wanted an ill-defined decentralization of the political system, and all significant political actors, including Boris Yeltsin, pledged support for the Union, although a transformed one. More than 70 percent of the Russian population were to vote for the retention of the Soviet Union in March 1991, and six years later only 20 percent of Russians surveyed thought the breakup of the Soviet Union had been useful or more useful than harmful.

The public and the majority of the politically aware wanted a centrist reforming program, but even more they wanted a leader who would be decisive in formulating a viable program and pushing it through. If he sometimes exercised a strong hand against separatists and radicals, this would more likely build support than undercut it. But the activists were polarized, and Gorbachev would find it absolutely impossible to find a centrist position by building consensus among them.

Thus at the end of 1990 Gorbachev in fact seemed to have created the secure and centrist position for which he had been maneuvering. He had emancipated himself from Politburo and Central Committee control, he had removed the most important members of the Kirilenko machine with whom he had come to power, and he had rid himself of the most extreme radicals in his entourage. The police and media were in reliable hands.

He also retained solid control of the USSR Congress of People's Deputies. His only real problem in the Congress came from a new conservative group that called itself Union, but the name suggested that a presidential policy of maintaining the Union would keep the group under control. Moreover, Gorbachev had put into the premiership an impressive figure in Valentin Pavlov. Pavlov was a financial specialist who had been fighting for years for price reform and who favored the authoritarian introduction of the market found in much of Asia. As shall be seen in chapter 14, plans were being worked out to replace the ministries with "holding companies," "corporations," and "banks." While they were to be tightly controlled at first, they seemed a sensible way to begin the transition to privatization and gradual independence.

In Lithuania, Gorbachev had chosen a good case to defend the principle of maintenance of the Union. Lithuanian leaders were, in fact, acting in an extreme manner, and Lithuania was too small and too vulnerable to resist. In the spring of 1991 Gorbachev was to bring Lithuania to de facto subservience through an oil boycott. Moreover, he had chosen an ideal time to send the Alfa unit to Lithuania. The United States had launched a war against Iraq over Sadam Hussein's invasion of Kuwait and was trying to handle the problem of the Kurds without threatening the territorial integrity of Turkey. It was in no position to offend Gorbachev, especially over the attempted secession of an ethnic minority.

Although Ryzhkov had been removed and Leonid Abalkin had resigned as deputy premier for economic reform, both convenient scapegoats for the economic difficulties, all the reforming professionals of the Ryzhkov government remained in place. They were joined by a new first deputy premier of like mind, Vladimir Shcherbakov, who had been working as chairman of the State Committee for Labor and Social Problems. Stalin had removed Trotsky, but then had introduced his policy as he removed the opposition on the right headed by Nikolai Bukharin. Gorbachev was now in a position to introduce Ryzhkov's program as he removed the opposition headed by Aleksandr Yakovlev.

But, in fact, in 1991 Gorbachev simply repeated the scenario that he had followed in 1990. The Cabinet of Ministers was formally subordinated to the president, and he had selected a premier who had championed strong presidential rule.[65] Yet Gorbachev never tried to turn it into his own cabinet in any meaningful sense and never even was to preside over it. When asked what lessons to draw from the experience of the Cabinet of Ministers, one

---

65. Gorbachev, *Zhizn' i reformy*, vol. 1, p. 579; *Memoirs*, p. 384.

of its members, the minister of geology, responded, "I would advise not to try to utilize the experience of the Cabinet of Ministers, for, in my opinion there is simply no such experience."[66] The cabinet functioned under Premier Pavlov's leadership, and it tried to carry out the same administrative and planning functions performed by Ryzhkov's Council of Ministers. However, its orders were carried out even less frequently as the administrative structure disintegrated, and the loss of the central control over finances (see chapter 13) meant that it could not even draft a meaningful budget.

Gorbachev's main interest in his new Cabinet of Ministers was control of its Kremlin offices. As already seen, the central offices of the Council of Ministers had been located on the second floor of the Kremlin building in which the Politburo, and then the president, had occupied the third floor. Indeed, the party offices had been directly over the government offices to symbolize the government's subordination to the party. As soon as Pavlov was installed as premier, Gorbachev ordered the government out of the Kremlin so that its second floor rooms could be taken over by officials of the presidential apparatus.[67]

The Pavlov cabinet, like Ryzhkov's, drafted a stabilization and economic reform plan, but Gorbachev ignored it and Yeltsin denounced it as conservative. The early summer of 1991 featured the same farce as the summer of 1990. Now, however, the unrealistic radical panacea was a "grand bargain" drafted in substantial part by Yavlinsky and a group of Harvard scholars, while the Pavlov program was treated with as much scorn as the Ryzhkov plan a year earlier.

The one new post introduced in the winter of 1990–91 was that of vice president. Once again Gorbachev made no attempt to make it serve a useful function. He wrote in his memoirs that he offered Ryzhkov the vice presidency, but that is confirmed nowhere else.[68] Gorbachev chose Gennady Yanaev, who had been a Komsomol official from the 1960s to the late 1970s concerned with international relations. In the perestroika period he had served briefly as chairman of a trade union and then leader of the Communist faction in the USSR Congress of People's Deputies.

<hr>

66. Mikhail Nenashev, *Poslednee pravitel'stvo SSSR: Lichnosti, svidetel'stva, dialogi* (Moscow: Krom, 1993), p. 105.

67. Valentin Pavlov, *Upushchen li shans? Finansovyi kliuch k rynku* (Moscow: Terra, 1995), pp. 157–63. As can be imagined, Pavlov was bitter about the policy and unsuccessfully tried to resist.

68. Gorbachev, *Zhizn' i reformy*, vol. 2, p. 532. Not in *Memoirs*.

Yanaev was not an impressive figure—although no more unimpressive than many American vice presidents—but his experience suggested he might be used as liaison with the legislature. Instead, he was assigned the nonrole of the less impressive American vice presidents and would likely have been a footnote in history had he not been forced against his will to become acting president by the August 1991 coup d'état.

The chief collective organ in the system after November 1991, the Federation Council, was headed by the president and included the vice president and the heads of the republics. This meant the heads of all thirty-six republics, not just the fifteen former Union republics, although apparently Gorbachev was slow to invite the former autonomous republics to attend.[69]

The Federation Council was created, it was said, "to determine the basic directions of the Union's domestic and foreign policy and to coordinate the activity of the republics."

> The Federation Council coordinates the activities of the higher organs of state authority and administration of the Union and the republics, looks out for observation of the Union Treaty, determines measures for carrying out the national policy of the Union state, secures the participation of the republics in the solution of questions of all-Union significance, and works out recommendations for the solution of arguments and the regulation of conflict situations in international relations.[70]

The Federation Council seemed the replacement for the Politburo, but its power was ill defined. Gorbachev's personal assistant for political affairs, Georgy Shakhnazarov, reported to his boss with alarm that some republics wanted it to have the power of the Politburo and to have an interepublican committee as its operational organ. Shakhnazarov told the Western press that "the President will have the last word, but I think 90 percent, if not all decisions, will be made on the basis of consensus."[71] Most observers expected Gorbachev to use his new powers to establish authoritarian rule;

---

69. A Shakhnazarov memorandum of January 18, 1991, reported to Gorbachev that the leaders of the former autonomous republics were dissatisfied that they had not been invited to the first session of the Federation Council and that this omission needed to be corrected. *Tsena svobody*, p. 508.

70. *Izvestiia*, November 24, 1990, p. 2.

71. Bill Keller, "Soviets Adopt Emergency Plan to Center Power in Gorbachev and Leaders of the Republics," *New York Times*, November 81, 1990, p. A1. Shakhnazarov was warning Gorbachev privately against allowing the Federation Council from being turned into a Politburo. *Tsena svobody*, p. 509.

instead, Shakhnazarov turned out to be more accurate than he hoped. Gorbachev seemed unwilling to make any decision that the republics—particularly the leader of the Russian Republic—did not approve.

If Gorbachev was not to follow up the attack on Lithuania with an insistence, backed up by martial law if necessary, that all republics obey central laws and give the central government control over its finances, if he was going to weaken his new cabinet and premier and not use them to work out and impose an economic reform program, then he was leaving himself with only one alternative. He needed some grand compromise with Yeltsin that would give each of them much of what they wanted.

But Yeltsin was damning the central government for raising any prices and not having a radical enough reform. He was conducting such an irresponsible financial policy that his deputy minister for economic reform and his finance minister had resigned in disgust after less than six months in office. He was insisting on the supremacy of republican laws over central laws. He had been highly offended by Gorbachev's treatment of him between mid-1985 and mid-1987, and he had disrupted the November 1987 celebration of the seventieth anniversary of the Bolshevik Revolution in an offensive manner. Gorbachev had responded in kind. Both had bitter memories that were frequently expressed in their behavior and language. One can argue about the rights and wrongs in the Gorbachev-Yeltsin relationship, but what was difficult to imagine was a grand bargain that left Yeltsin in a subordinate position and that was not marked by his constant effort to reverse the situation.

CHAPTER THIRTEEN

The Russian Presidential Election and the August Coup D'État

AT ONE LEVEL, the political steps Mikhail Gorbachev took in late 1989 and late 1990 seemed brilliant. Worried that the creation of the Russian Communist party would compromise the basic mechanism on which his power depended, he managed to liberate himself from the control of the Politburo and the party's Central Committee. In March 1990 he was given the presidency that he wanted, and in September he maneuvered to ensure that the office was awarded strong emergency powers.

In November 1990, after several months of high drama over the wildly utopian 500-Day economic program that could have led to the dissolution of the Soviet Union, Gorbachev presented his own plan and a draft of a Union Treaty that involved some decentralization of power but the mainte- nance of a strong federal state. He scheduled a referendum on the Union for March 1991 and appointed some conservative lieutenants in a way that suggested he was willing to use the powers of the presidency decisively. The panic in Moscow about impending dictatorship always seemed over- drawn, but Gorbachev did seem ready to move to end the chaos of the war of laws.

In March 1991 Gorbachev won the referendum on the USSR with 70 percent of the vote, and in April he and the Congress obtained the conces- sions they wanted from Boris Yeltsin to institute a Russian presidency. At almost any time during the year—and maybe as late as November and December—Gorbachev could have introduced the dictatorship that Moscow intellectuals expected at the beginning of the year or simply have ordered the temporary emergency rule that many of his advisers proposed. Yet within nine months of the March 1991 referendum the Soviet Union was dissolved and Gorbachev's post abolished, and he was out of power.

Gorbachev's advisers and supporters have stated that everything was going well with the decision to sign the Union Treaty on August 20 and that the attempted coup d'état caused the disintegration of the country. This version of events is not accurate. The coup occurred because Gorbachev allowed Yeltsin to take control of all finances and economic enterprises in Russia, including the Tiumen oil fields. Gorbachev's policy would have led to the same outcome that was to occur after the coup. But when the coup itself was as ineffective as Gorbachev in his worst moments, the disintegration of the Soviet Union proceeded to its conclusion.

It was an extraordinary turn of events. Gorbachev had seemed ruthless in consolidating his power within the Communist party and destroying the power of the most important party institutions. He seemed dedicated to the Union, but he put up no resistance as Yeltsin, the man he seemed to hate most in the world, stripped him of all his powers in as humiliating a manner as possible. Even today many of those closely associated with him remain mystified by his thinking, and Westerners too can only guess.

The Establishment of an Elected Russian President

Everyone agrees that the key event in 1991 in the disintegration of the Soviet Union was the election of Boris Yeltsin as president of Russia on June 12 by a wide margin. This gave him a legitimacy that Gorbachev lacked, and it gave him an executive post from which he could take drastic (and unconstitutional) actions without worrying about hesitation by the Russian legislature. When he assumed control of the military forces in Russia during the coup and demanded they obey his orders, he created a legal situation that permitted them to act contrary to the orders of their constituted commanders.

Although this interpretation of events is generally accepted, most observers take Yeltsin's election as president for granted. That election was, however, a very improbable event. Yeltsin had been elected chairman of the Russian Supreme Soviet by four votes in the Congress of People's Deputies, and a presidency could be established only by a constitutional amendment that required two-thirds of the votes of all the deputies, not just of those present. Nearly a third of the deputies were implacably opposed to Yeltsin, and the centrist third included large numbers who were Gorbachev supporters. Democratic Russia was shrinking.

In addition, Gorbachev seemingly had no interest in giving Yeltsin an electoral legitimacy he himself lacked. The Congress had no institutional interest in giving the headstrong Yeltsin a power base independent of itself. As long as he was chairman of the Supreme Soviet, he could be removed by 50 percent of the deputies. As president he could be removed only by impeachment, and that required two-thirds of the deputies. As he moved to dissolve the Congress in 1993, the conservatives and moderates could mobilize over two-thirds of the deputies who were present to defend the old constitution, but only 62 percent of the total deputies.

How had the improbable, if not the impossible, occurred? How had the presidency received the necessary two-thirds vote? The first key event was a pair of referendums held in March 1991. One, as has been seen, dealt with the preservation of the Union. The other, added to the Russian ballot by Yeltsin, asked whether the population wanted to establish an elected president. The preservation of the Union had been approved by 76.4 percent of the voters, 71.3 percent of those in the Russian Soviet Federated Socialist Republic, and 70.2 percent of those in Ukraine.[1] Yeltsin received almost identical support in Russia for an elected presidency: 69.85 percent in favor.[2]

Neither referendum was legally binding, and it would have been easy to delay the introduction of an elected president indefinitely. A new constitution was required that defined the president's office, the organization of the executive branch, and the relative powers of president, premier (if there was to be one), and the Congress and Supreme Soviet. This promised to be a lengthy process at best, and it was logical to combine the restructuring of the executive with the merger of the Congress and Supreme Soviet into a one-stage bicameral legislature, as nearly everyone was advocating. Yet the key decision was taken within several weeks of the referendum, the law on

---

1. *Izvestiia*, March 27, 1991, p. 3. Six republics refused to conduct the referendum officially: Armenia, Estonia, Georgia, Latvia, Lithuania, and Moldavia. Their participation would have reduced the yes vote to some extent, but the number of their citizens was small and the effect would have been minor.

2. *Izvestiia*, March 16, 1991, p. 2.

the presidency adopted a month later, and the presidential election itself held only three months after the referendum after an extraordinarily abbreviated campaign.

Paradoxically, the movement toward an elected president began in February 1991 when, as described in chapter 10, six of the seven leaders of the Supreme Soviet issued an angry statement denouncing Yeltsin for his arrogance and irresponsibility.

> The relationship within the Supreme Soviet leadership is such that the chairman always acts on his own, without consulting with others or even notifying them. Very few in the Supreme Soviet are privy to the affairs and plans of our chairman. There is no collectivism in his work. . . . All of us who signed this statement belonged to different political currents. . . . We have tried so many times to establish cooperation. Now we understand that we have exhausted all the means of trying to return him to reason.[3]

Only Ruslan Khasbulatov, first deputy chairman of the Supreme Soviet, and ten of the twenty-four committee chairmen supported Yeltsin.[4] Even Khasbulatov distanced himself from the Russian president's most extreme statements by trying to explain them in less threatening terms. Yeltsin's decision to join the three Baltic states in an appeal to the United Nations was "not a felicitous act," Khasbulatov said.

The conservative deputies were far more emotional at Yeltsin's attack on Gorbachev. A group of 282 deputies signed a statement demanding the immediate convening of an extraordinary congress to deal with the situation. Radicals were to claim that the conservatives had called for the congressional session to overthrow Yeltsin, if not directly, then through promotion of a legislative stalemate that would lead to strong action.[5] However, the six leaders who criticized Yeltsin always denied the intention to remove him, and they were only demanding the convening of a congress that was already in the works. On January 4, 1991, more than a week before the crisis, the Supreme Soviet had called for a Third Congress at the end of

---

3. For the text of the statement, see *Ekonomika i zhizn'*, no. 9 (February 1991), p. 1. For the grievances of the group, see *Sovetskaia Rossiia*, March 23, 1991; *Sel'skaia zhizn'*, March 19, 1991; *Sovetskaia Rossiia*, March 23, 1991; and *Krasnaia zvezda*, March 14, 1991.

4. *Argumenty i fakty*, no. 9, March 1991, p. 3.

5. For such a charge that included a detailed scenario involving the hated regional soviets on the eve of the Congress, see the interview with Sergei Shakhrai in *Komsomol'skaia pravda*, March 27, 1991, p. 2.

March and the beginning of April. Khasbulatov had reiterated the request on February 15.

The difference between pro-Yeltsin forces and conservatives over the timing of the Congress was surely related to the referendums on the preservation of the Union and creation of an elected Russian presidency that were scheduled for March 17. The pro-Yeltsin forces wanted a congressional session immediately after the referendum, when Yeltsin presumably would be strengthened by the results. Conservatives wanted the Congress held before the referendum.

In fact, the Third Congress was to be scheduled for March 28, essentially when Yeltsin wanted it. This decision was passed by both houses of the Supreme Soviet with majorities of 58.4 percent and 52.8 percent, respectively.[6] These figures were typical of Yeltsin's ability to achieve a majority within the Russian parliament during 1990 and 1991 if he worked with centrist forces, but they showed how little hope he had of getting the two-thirds vote he needed for an elected presidency.

Yet the Third Congress of People's Deputies that the conservatives had been advocating to censure Yeltsin ended with a resolution announcing a presidential election on June 12, the anniversary of the Russian Declaration of Sovereignty. At the Fourth Congress, held from May 21 to 25, the Congress passed the necessary constitutional amendments.[7] As anyone would have predicted, Yeltsin won the election handily. But how had he managed to win the two-thirds vote in the Russian parliament that had seemed impossible to obtain in February and even in the first days after the Third Congress opened on March 28?

The first sessions of the Third Congress were a scene of wild disarray, even in comparison with previous congresses.[8] Democratic Russia had organized large demonstrations in Moscow, and a USSR decree to enforce order there with federal troops produced a strong reaction. Once again the agenda became the subject of intense debate. The primary concerns were

6. *Sovetskaia Rossiia*, March 23, 1991, p. 3.

7. On May 22 the Congress confirmed with 690 votes in favor the Law on the President worked out by the Supreme Soviet. But on May 23 and 24 the Congress made the necessary amendments on the clauses of the Constitution that were individually affected. *Chetvertyi s"ezd narodnykh deputatov RSFSR (21–25 maia 1991 goda): Stenograficheskii otchet*, 4 vols (Moscow: Supreme Soviet RSFSR, 1991). The vote on the law is in vol. 1, p. 137.

8. The best descriptions are found in the conservative press. See, for instance, *Pravda*, March 29, 1991, p. 1; and April 1, 1991, p. 2.

whether the six Supreme Soviet leaders could give a report on Yeltsin at the beginning of the Congress and whether the question of an elected president should be on the agenda. Early votes were ominous for Yeltsin. The report was put on the agenda but not the discussion of the presidency. The issue was raised repeatedly, and often the inclusion of the presidency on the agenda received a narrow plurality, but never a majority. Then on March 31 anti-Yeltsin forces achieved an actual majority for their proposal to postpone the discussion until the next Congress.

On April 1 the pro-Yeltsin newspaper *Izvestiia* said there was "no sense" in convening the Congress, and the next day the radical newspaper *Komsomol'skaia pravda* reported that Democratic Russia knew no important decision could be made at this Congress. On April 3 *Komsomol'skaia pravda* repeated that "obviously" the question of the presidency would not be decided at the Congress.[9] But by a 576 to 322 vote on April 2 the Congress placed on the agenda the resolution "On the Redistribution of Powers between High State Organs of the RSFSR to Implement Anticrisis Measures and Implement Congressional Decisions." This resolution expanded the powers of the more liberal Supreme Soviet vis-a-vis the Congress and gave Yeltsin as its chairman the right to issue obligatory orders, including emergency ones.

In addition, the resolution endorsed an elected presidency by saying that extra powers of the chairman of the Supreme Soviet would expire when an elected president took office. The resolution mentioned an election for president on June 12 and called another session of the Congress for May 21, implicitly to discuss constitutional amendments to create a presidency. Because this resolution did not itself create a presidency, it did not require a two-thirds vote—and did not receive it. On April 5 the Congress passed the bill 607 to 228 with 100 abstentions.

The resolution seemed to solve nothing. The constitutional amendments required from the May 21 Fourth Congress would have to receive nearly 700 votes to pass, far more than Yeltsin had been able to gather on any important issue. Even if a presidency were established, the Fourth Congress was far too close to the scheduled June 12 election date for a properly organized election and campaign. And, of course, the Moscow Communist party first secretary made eminently good sense when he asked how politi-

9. *Izvestiia*, April 1, 1991, p. 1; *Komsomol'skaia pravda*, April 2, 1991, p. 1; and April 3, 1991, p. 1.

cians could be talking about the mechanisms of an election for an office whose powers had not been defined.

Yet on April 6 the respected newspaper *Nezavisimaia gazeta* ran the confident headline, "Russia Will Receive a President at the Beginning of the Summer." Everyone acted as if the election would take place on June 12, and everyone organized for it. On April 17 Nikolai Ryzhkov officially agreed to be the candidate of the Communist party, and the party formally nominated him on the day before the Congress opened.[10] And on May 25 the Congress did pass the necessary amendment.

How had the impossible happened? How had Yeltsin managed to win over two-thirds of the deputies? First, of course, he had been helped by the referendums of March 17. Paradoxically, the vote in the referendum in favor of the preservation of the USSR was perhaps even more useful to Yeltsin than the referendum on the presidency. If the conservatives and centrists saw this vote as guaranteeing the continuation of the Union, the need of a strong leader for Russia was obvious and the danger that he could do great harm was reduced. Moreover, by enacting laws establishing the Russian presidency, conservatives and centrists hoped to legitimate both the referendums and make it difficult for Yeltsin to repudiate the referendum on the Union.

Almost no evidence has been published about the negotiations that led to his victory on an elected presidency, but considering the pattern of subsequent events, it must have rested on two agreements Yeltsin negotiated: one with Gorbachev's forces on the Union Treaty, and one with a most interesting figure in the Supreme Soviet—Aleksandr Rutskoi, a forty-four-year-old air force colonel—that involved his selection as Yeltsin's vice presidential running mate. Moreover, through Ruslan Khasbulatov, an ethnic Chechen who was first deputy chairman of the Supreme Soviet, the former autonomous republics were able to insist on a presidency with limited powers inside Russia.

The Alliance with Aleksandr Rutskoi

The action that broke the deadlock in the early days of the Third Congress was the April 2 announcement by Rutskoi of a new deputies' faction:

---

10. N. I. Ryzhkov, *Desiat' let velikikh potriasenii* (Moscow: Kniga-Prosveshchenie-Miloserdie, 1995), p. 401.

170 "Communists for Democracy" who supposedly were defecting from the Communists of Russia faction to support Yeltsin. Rutskoi accused the Communists of Russia of being too conservative and too inflexible and asserted that his group would urge reform. The Communists for Democracy spoke out for "an end to the disintegration of the Union . . . to the anarchy and chaos in the country," but declared full support for the Supreme Soviet and its chairman.[11]

As was often the case, the size of the new faction announced to the press did not correspond to the number of deputies registered to it with the Secretariat of the Congress. Only ninety-five were on the official list.[12] *Sovetskaia Rossiia* reported with scorn that the list included just eleven deputies who were members of Communists of Russia, and then the list that was published included only seven. The list included deputies from a broad political spectrum.[13]

Nevertheless, Rutskoi's claim of support was closer to the truth than the number of members of the group indicated: a substantial number of centrist and conservative deputies had, in fact, decided to vote to give Yeltsin a Russian presidency if the circumstances were right. No quid pro quo was ever acknowledged, but it surely was not a coincidence that on May 18 Yeltsin announced Rutskoi would be his running mate. As Yeltsin himself emphasized, Rutskoi was a perfect choice to balance the ticket: sixteen years younger, more conservative and nationalist, a member of the Communist party, and a soldier with close ties to the generals who had fought in Afghanistan and were unhappy with Yeltsin's position regarding the Baltics and the Union.

Rutskoi was a career air force pilot who had flown more than 530 military missions in Afghanistan, was shot down twice and captured once, and had been awarded the Soviet Union's highest medal—Hero of the

---

11. *Tretyi (vnecherednoi) s"ezd narodnykh deputatov RSFSR (25 marta–5 aprelia): Stenograficheskii otchet*, vol. 3 (Moscow: Respublika, 1992), p. 98; *Izvestiia*, April 4, 1991, p. 2; and *Trud*, April 3, 1991, p. 1.

12. *Sovetskaia Rossiia*, April 19, 1991, p. 2.

13. The factions represented were Social Democrats, 4; Democratic Russia, 14; Radical Democrats, 3; Smena, 8; Left Center, 13; Independent Trade Union, 10; Independent Deputies, 8; Cooperation, 8; Workers' Union, 7; Organizers of the Economy, 9; Russian Union, 4; Rossiia, 10; and Communists of Russia, 7. The faction of which the largest number of deputies were members was the Autonomous Territories with 16. *Krasnaia zvezda*, April 5, 1991.

Soviet Union—along with an Order of Lenin and a Gold Star.[14] In his second tour in Afghanistan in 1988, he served as deputy commander of the Air Forces of the Fortieth Army, which was commanded by Boris Gromov, who became first deputy minister of internal affairs.

Rutskoi first achieved national awareness with a front page article in *Krasnaia zvezda* (*Red Star*) in January 1989. He began by admitting, "I am speaking loud words." He repeatedly emphasized "our military pride in heroism, in the fulfillment of our warrior's duty with honor and with true allegiance, and that means to the Motherland." He singled out Boris Gromov, his last commander in Afghanistan, as one of three men to whom he was closest. "We are fighting brothers, people with identical ideas. We are tied together by dedication to our military duty."[15]

Rutskoi had been sent to study at the Academy of the General Staff in Moscow, a mid-career military training institute designed for those slated to become generals. While there, he entered politics. He unsuccessfully tried to run for the USSR Congress of People's Deputies in Kuntsevo District on the northwest edge of Moscow in a bitterly fought race.[16] After graduation from the academy in the spring of 1990, Rutskoi was offered promotion to general and an appropriate post.[17] Instead he ran for the Russian parliament in his native Kursk in the large national-territorial district that embraced the entire oblast. On the first round he was a distant second with 12.8 percent of the vote behind a radical priest who had 33.0 percent. On the second round he was supported by the local party organs, and the various moderate and conservative forces rallied around to give him a victory. Rutskoi became the deputy head of the fifty-five-person faction of deputies who were military or KGB officers.[18] Then at the First Congress he was named

---

14. Rutskoi interview in *Izvestiia*, June 14, 1991, p. 3. See also *Komsomol'skaia pravda*, April 6, 1991; and "Moscow TV Interviews Vice President Rutskoi," Moscow television, December 30, 1991, in Foreign Broadcast Information Service, *Daily Report: Soviet Union*, December 31, 1991, p. 44 (hereafter FBIS, *Soviet Union*). For Rutskoi's description of this period in his life, see Aleksandr Rutskoi, *O nas i sebe* (Moskova: Nauchnaia Kniga, 1995), p. 242.

15. *Krasnaia zvezda*, January 8, 1989, p. 1.

16. In the first race, the electoral commission, dominated by radicals, refused to register him because only two radicals were placed on the ballot. When neither won and a second race was required, Rutskoi did make the ballot and the runoff, but lost the latter. *Rabochaia tribuna*, May 24, 1991; and *Komsomol'skaia pravda*, April 6, 1991, p. 2.

17. *Izvestiia*, June 14, 1991, p. 3.

18. *Krasnaia zvezda*, May 18, 1990, p. 1; and May 20, 1990, p. 1. In 1996 Rutskoi was to be elected governor of Kursk.

chairman of the Committee for Veterans, Invalids, and Social Protection of Servicemen.

As has been noted, in June 1990 the founding Congress of the Russian Communist party was convened shortly after the Russian First Congress of People's Deputies. The party congress was held in two sessions, one before the July 2 All-Union Party Congress and one in September. Only 28 deputies of the Russian Congress of People's Deputies were elected to the 272-member Central Committee of the Russian Communist party, and most were regional officials who were not active legislators. Rutskoi was one of the few active deputies elected to the Russian Central Committee.[19]

Rutskoi had a reputation for being direct and honest, but in mid-1990 he seemed to be positioning himself very carefully and thinking about his political future. He generally voted on the center-conservative side, but he managed to be absent on the three crucial early votes—the right of Russian laws to override Soviet laws and the prohibition of party units in the police and the military—that would likely have made him unacceptable either to the conservative Communist party leadership or to Boris Yeltsin.

Rutskoi kept a fairly low profile during the first eight months of the Russian parliament, but in early 1991 he suddenly appeared as one of Boris Yeltsin's strongest supporters. On January 21 he spoke out passionately in the Supreme Soviet against Soviet actions in the Baltics. He denounced the "lawlessness when laws taken by the Congress and Supreme Soviet of the Russian Federation are not ratified by the Center."[20] (Presumably he had in mind the law that forbade the use of Russian troops in ethnic conflicts in other republics without the permission of Russian authorities.) Most of all, however, Rutskoi seemed intensely angry at Gorbachev and even contemptuous of him for failing to acknowledge his own role in ordering military actions in Lithuania (and earlier Georgia) and for letting the military be unfairly blamed for independent action: "Nagorno-Karabakh—was Gorbachev there or not? Tbilisi, Baku, Yerevan, and finally Vilnius. . . ."

When eleven members of the Supreme Soviet Presidium supported Yeltsin against the six Supreme Soviet leaders who denounced him on February 21, Rutskoi was among the supporters. Given that the other ten were all on the radical side of the spectrum, he found himself in company

---

19. The Central Committee membership was listed in *Sovetskaia Rossiia*, September 7, 1990, p. 1.

20. The speech was republished in *Argumenty i fakty*, no. 4, January 1991, p. 2.

very different from that at the plenary sessions of the conservative Russian Communist Party Central Committee.

The path that Rutskoi took in April 1991 was not lightly considered. The striking thing about the factions in the Russian parliament is that their leaders made no effort to extend them outside the legislature. Rutskoi, by contrast, spoke not simply of a parliamentary group, but of a "movement." Indeed, when he gave an interview to the radical newspaper *Argumenty i fakty* almost immediately after the formation of Communists for Democracy, the interview ended with the address, telephone number, and fax number of the movement's organization committee. When the correspondent asked Rutskoi whether rank-and-file Communists were ready "to rise under your banners," he answered, "These are not my banners, but ours."[21]

Communists for Democracy was an effort not only to counterbalance the Communists of Russia faction, but also to take the leadership of the Communist Party of Russia from conservatives such as Ivan Polozkov, its first secretary. At the beginning of July, Rutskoi joined with seven of the most distinguished supporters of perestroika in signing a manifesto in favor of a broad-based Association of Democrats.[22] The other signers included Aleksandr Yakovlev and Eduard Shevardnadze, the two leading liberals of Gorbachev's Politburo, who had long advocated a split in the Communist party; Nikolai Petrakov, Gorbachev's last radical economic adviser; Gavril Popov and Anatoly Sobchak, the mayors of Moscow and Leningrad; and Ivan Silaev, the premier of Russia.

During the June presidential campaign, Rutskoi and his movement were obviously meant to make it easier for the reform movement in the Communist party to support Yeltsin comfortably even though Yeltsin was outside the party and taking a strong antiparty position. The real question was the long-term significance of the movement. Some spoke of its being a vice presidential party, but *Pravda* charged that it was really a presidential party.[23]

Pravda's analysis seemed plausible if Yeltsin was going to have a cooperative relationship with Gorbachev. Of course, when the relationship deteriorated further and Yeltsin abolished the Communist party in Russia

---

21. *Argumenty i fakty*, no. 17, April 1991, p. 2.
22. *Nezavisimaia gazeta*, July 2, 1991, p. 1. Another leading economic radical, Stanislav Shatalin, was originally announced as a signer, but this proved to be a mistake.
23. *Pravda*, August 12, 1991.

after the attempted August coup, Rutskoi had real reason to wonder about his own relationship with the Russian president. But by that time Rutskoi was vice president and in the official line of succession, and Yeltsin could not change that without a new constitution and new elections when Russia became independent.

The Union Treaty and the Russian Presidency

After Yeltsin demanded Gorbachev's resignation in February, his relationship with the USSR president became extremely tense. Gorbachev was still the country's leader, and he commanded the support of many political moderates. Even the conservatives who detested him still had to support him against Yeltsin's attempts to destroy the authority of the Union and its institutions.

Gorbachev had more than enough influence in the Russian Congress of People's Deputies to deny Yeltsin the two-thirds support he needed for a constitutional amendment to create a Russian presidency. But on April 24 it became clear how Yeltsin was going to obtain Gorbachev's support. *Pravda* reported that on April 23 Gorbachev met with the leaders of nine of the Union republics in the Moscow suburb of Novo-Ogarevo and officially pledged to sign the Union Treaty in the "immediate future." The leaders of the Baltic republics, Armenia, Georgia, and Moldavia did not sign the document, but Boris Yeltsin was present. During the previous four weeks, leading reformers, including Aleksandr Yakovlev, had been urging an alliance of reforming forces and a reconciliation of Gorbachev and Yeltsin; the statement about the Novo-Ogarevo meeting seemed a breakthrough in that direction.

Yeltsin's statement of April 24, if given credence, represented his full acceptance of the supremacy of the Union. It termed the Union Treaty the key step in resolving current crises, and the republics pledged unconditional fulfillment of the 1991 economic and financial commitments and respect for Union legislation. By vowing to fight "extremist groups" who called for the overthrow of the existing elected organs of state power, Yeltsin implicitly withdrew his demand that Gorbachev resign and his denunciation of the USSR Congress of People's Deputies.

When the law on the Russian presidency was presented to the Fourth Congress in May, it included the clause that obeying the laws of the USSR was obligatory for the Russian Republic and its president. Sergei Shakhrai asserted, "No ambiguity remains."[24] At the end of the Congress Yeltsin reported on the session of the Federation Council held on May 24. He said that it had been agreed to call the country the Union of Sovereign States, but asserted that "it was firmly agreed, and this was a united position, that this is a federal state, not a confederation. In this there was full unanimity."[25]

Merely by holding the Novo-Ogarevo meeting and signing the statement, Gorbachev made a major concession to Yeltsin. A key to the meeting was the invitation list. For a year the main threat to the integrity of Russia had been the recognition of the autonomous republics as equal to the Union republics. Because the former autonomous republics were not invited to Novo-Ogarevo, the negotiations on the Union Treaty that continued there after April 23 excluded them. It appeared Gorbachev was willing to sacrifice the interests of the autonomous republics to cut a deal with the former Union republics, particularly Russia.

Although it cannot be documented, part of the agreement between Gorbachev and Yeltsin involved Gorbachev's support for creating the office of Russian president. While Yeltsin has claimed he was surprised by Gorbachev's proposal to meet at Novo-Ogarevo, the Supreme Soviet was drafting the law on the presidency to present to the Fourth Congress, and Khasbulatov was to claim that the drafting process was collegial.[26] Virtually all decisions were made by a two-thirds vote, with 90 percent of the many proposals of the Communists of Russia accepted by the Supreme Soviet.[27] It could not be a coincidence that the centrist pro-Gorbachev forces in the Russian parliament were voting with Yeltsin on the creation of the Russian presidency, and the condition was driven home when the Supreme Soviet adopted the law on the presidency on April 24, the day after the meeting in Novo-Ogarevo.

If Gorbachev's memoirs are to be believed, he had nothing to do with the compromises of April in the Russian Congress or any knowledge of them. He even suggested that the Russian Communist party and the Communists of Russia supported Yeltsin on the presidency issue out of pique at Gorbachev.[28] Nevertheless, everyone understood how many votes were

---

24. *Chetvertyi s''ezd narodnykh deputatov*, vol. 1, p. 78.

25. *Chetvertyi s''ezd narodnykh deputatov*, vol. 4, pp. 62–63.

26. Boris Yeltsin, *The Struggle for Russia*, trans. Catherine Fitzpatrick (Random House, 1994), p. 26.

27. *Chetvertyi s''ezd narodnykh deputatov*, vol. 1, pp. 130–31.

28. Mikhail Gorbachev, *Zhizn' i reformy,* vol. 2 (Moscow: Novosti, 1995), p. 520; *Memoirs* (Doubleday, 1996), p. 587.

necessary to pass a constitutional amendment in the Russian Congress, and someone was extracting a promise from Yeltsin about the Union Treaty. It is virtually impossible to believe that Gorbachev and his men were not involved. If he was not, it was because he had indeed become so incompetent as to deserve removal for health reasons. It is easy to think that the deal had been cut earlier when the referendum on the Union was combined with a referendum on the Russian presidency.

On April 24–25 Gorbachev also fought off a challenge from within the Central Committee on the much more liberal party program that he was forcing through. On April 2 a number of regional party officials, like Yeltsin, had sharply criticized Gorbachev because of the price increases being introduced at the time. On April 13 Gorbachev scheduled a Central Committee plenum for April 24. When he was severely criticized at the plenum, he threatened to resign. With his hand strengthened by the Novo-Ogarevo agreement, however, the Central Committee voted almost unanimously not to consider the resignation.[29]

When the Congress of People's Deputies was convened on May 21, it was a foregone conclusion that it would pass the constitutional amendments necessary to establish the presidency. Even the Communist party had already nominated its candidate. However, the Congress featured an interesting political dynamic. On the one hand, because the campaign was already under way and because Yeltsin could renege on his promise to sign a Union Treaty if he were denied his presidency, the Congress could scarcely fail to pass the law establishing the presidency. On the other hand, the Yeltsin forces did not want to appear to insist on too authoritarian a presidency lest they frighten the electorate into voting against Yeltsin or frighten the military into a coup. Even if they could defeat constitutional amendments limiting the power of the president, they were in a difficult political position to do so.

The central matter on the floor of the Congress was the power of the Congress to overturn the decrees and executive orders of the president. The autonomous republics under the leadership of Ruslan Khasbulatov were unhappy about their exclusion from Nove-Ogarevo, and they were eager to limit Yeltsin's power. When the Supreme Soviet had drafted the law on the presidency in April, it had given itself the power to annul such presidential

---

29. For Gorbachev's acknowledgement that the date of the Novo-Ogarevo meeting was chosen to strengthen his position in the Central Committee, see *Zhinzn' i reformy*, vol. 2, p. 523. Not in *Memoirs*.

actions if the Constitutional Commission (the equivalent of the U.S. Supreme Court) said that they were unconstitutional, but it had given the Congress of People's Deputies the right to do so on its own initiative for any reason.

The Legislation Committee headed by Yeltsin's close adviser Sergei Shakhrai had the right—or at least assumed the right—to make minor changes to clarify the language of legislation. In this particular instance the committee made the "minor" correction of dropping altogether the right of the Congress to overturn presidential decrees on its own initiative. At the congressional session the deputy chairman of the Supreme Soviet several times protested against this change. When the congressional leadership failed to respond, the Congress on its own initiative enacted the limitations on the president's power by a vote of 591 to 344 with 18 abstentions.[30]

On other issues, however, the Congress was more accommodating to Yeltsin's position. Proposals that it have the right to confirm the appointment of each cabinet member (rather than just the premier) and that the Supreme Soviet have the right to suspend presidential orders until the Congress could meet received only 403 and 408 votes, respectively.[31]

The long-term question about the Gorbachev-Yeltsin agreement concerned the nature and durability of the agreement on the Union Treaty. Yeltsin and some of the more radical newspapers publicly claimed that Gorbachev had accepted "all proposals made by Russia," and Yeltsin said in his memoirs that Gorbachev's speech at the session was more than he expected.[32] In the examples he cited, however, Gorbachev's concessions seemed of little significance. Other than agreeing to the new status of the autonomous republics, which was a card Gorbachev was always willing to give to Russia in the end, his concessions were the kind of decentralization that he had always declared his eagerness to institute.

Various important matters remained unresolved. The primary legal one concerned the power of taxation. The USSR government wanted a system of taxation similar to that followed in the United States: each level of government could levy its own taxes (or at least the USSR and republican governments could exact their own—the so-called two-channel system of taxation). Russia insisted that the USSR government should not have the right to levy taxes, but should be allocated money by the republican govern-

30. *Chetvertyi s"ezd narodnykh deputatov*, vol. 1, pp. 120, 137; and vol. 2, pp. 6, 15.
31. *Chetvertyi s"ezd narodnykh deputatov*, vol. 1, pp. 23–24, 32.
32. Yeltsin, *Struggle for Russia*, p. 26.

ments. This insistence had been a central obstacle to Gorbachev's acceptance of the Shatalin 500-Day Plan, and if Gorbachev had accepted this "proposal made by Russia," then he had made a major concession indeed. However, Yeltsin hinted that Russia might have to make concessions on this point, and the draft of the Union Treaty published in June had a taxation clause that essentially adopted Gorbachev's position.[33]

Another unresolved matter was the real position of Ukraine and the relationship of its leader, Leonid Kravchuk, to Yeltsin. Yeltsin had taken a very confrontational position with Gorbachev and then had seemed to back down at key points. Kravchuk had been deferential to Gorbachev and the USSR, but he always found more or less plausible excuses not to make final commitments. Although he had signed the Novo-Ogarevo agreement on the Union Treaty, he insisted that he could not sign any Union Treaty, at least until the Ukrainian parliament met in September.

Earlier Kravchuk had said passage of a Ukrainian constitution was a precondition to signing. Because the constitution was held up by such extremely difficult issues as which language would be the state language of Ukraine, there was no reason to expect that it and therefore the Ukrainian signing of a Union Treaty was in the immediate offing. (The Ukrainian constitution was finally adopted by the Ukranian parliament, the Supreme Rada, on June 28, 1996.) If Yeltsin knew that Ukraine was going to keep postponing a decision, he could agree to support the Union Treaty without any fear it would be approved. One could even imagine that Yeltsin and Kravchuk were playing a fairly well coordinated game of good cop–bad cop.

A third problem was the interpretation of the treaty. The draft published in June was to engender diametrically opposed hysterical responses. Conservatives proclaimed it meant the complete and final end of the Union; radicals (for example, Yury Afanasev, one of the coordinators of Democratic Russia) and nationalists demanded it not be signed because it meant the end for any autonomy for the Union republics. Many of the clauses were actually ambiguous, but the nationalists seemed to have more to fear than the conservatives. The radicals were often judging the Union Treaty by a very high standard of autonomy indeed: the editorial staff of *Moscow News*, for example, criticized it for implying that the USSR as well as the Union republics might have embassies abroad.[34]

33. *Izvestiia*, June 27, 1991, p. 2.
34. "Ob etom mechtal Sakharov?" *Moskovskie novosti*, no. 33 (August 18, 1991), pp. 1, 8.

At any rate, each of the clauses would be the subject of continuing conflict between the central and republican governments. What was unexpected by those not privy to the secret understandings—certainly including radicals such as Afanasev—was the interpretation Yeltsin would put on the clauses immediately after the presidential election.

The Election for President

The campaign for the Russian presidential election is easy to describe because it was so short. The Law on the President was passed on May 22, 1991, but the registration of candidates ended on May 18 and the candidates were confirmed by the Congress on the twenty-second.[35] The election was held on June 12. Although the date had been set in April, except for several fringe candidates, no one except Yeltsin did any serious campaigning until the second half of May. The election was clearly timed to give him a major advantage, part of the bargain to ensure him the presidency in return for concessions he was presumably offering Gorbachev on the Union Treaty.

The Russian Communist party, Yeltsin's major opposition, was in a particularly difficult position. It had a much more conservative reputation than Gorbachev's all-Union Communist party, and it was certain to have grave problems finding a moderate liberal to run under its banner, even if it were to choose that alternative. Its first secretary, Ivan Polozkov, came from the conservative grain regions of the South and was unlikely to be an attractive candidate in the industrial North.

With no time to build up a credible alternative to Yeltsin, the Russian Communist party chose former USSR premier Nikolai Ryzhkov as its candidate. Ryzhkov had the needed industrial background and the northern base, and he was associated with the Abalkin economic reform policy that had been denounced by Yeltsin. He chose Boris Gromov, the last Soviet commander in Afghanistan, as his running mate to exploit Yeltsin's weakness among the more traditional patriotic elements of the population.

However, Ryzhkov had enormous weaknesses as a candidate. He was from Yeltsin's own base of Sverdlovsk and could not effectively challenge him there. As the manager of a huge all-Union plant, the Urals Machinery Works (Uralmash), who had become a first deputy minister of machine

---

35. *Chetvertyi s"ezd narodnykh deputatov*, vol. 1, p. 224.

building, then first deputy chairman of the USSR Gosplan from 1975 to 1982 under Brezhnev, and then USSR prime minister from 1985 until January 1991, he was the personification of centralized power and was not very credible as the person to lead the fight for greater Russian autonomy from USSR direction. He had been unfairly smeared in the press for more than a year and a half.

Worst of all, Ryzhkov was personally identified with a policy of deliberate price increases as a first step in economic reform. Although radicals understood their policy of freeing prices would lead to sharp increases, they were silent about this when they denounced Ryzhkov's and Pavlov's policies. Yeltsin had been able to exploit Ryzhkov's policies in May 1990 when he was elected chairman of the Presidium of the Supreme Soviet. Now when people were deeply disturbed at the sharp increase in inflation and the sharp drop in production, Yeltsin could charge that all their suffering resulted from Gorbachev's and Ryzhkov's refusal to adopt the painless 500-Day Plan.

The other candidates were even less of a challenge for Yeltsin. Vadim Bakatin might have been a formidable candidate if he had been nominated by the Communist party. A construction manager from West Siberia, he had been regional first secretary in Kirov and Kemerovo and then Gorbachev's minister of internal affairs. He had been replaced in December 1990 when rumors swirled that Gorbachev was moving in a conservative direction, and this had strengthened his reputation for being somewhat liberal.[36] Yet Bakatin's police experience also made him credible as a president who might introduce greater order.

Bakatin was admired among educated and professional centrists, but he was little known outside those circles. He was a lackluster candidate who began his campaign late and did little to establish himself. Even within his natural constituency, he was seriously compromised by the three-way race. Because the Communist party continued to have a strong organizational base in the countryside, Ryzhkov was guaranteed a good proportion of that vote. If he had convinced a substantial proportion of the workers that Yeltsin was too radical, he could have made a serious contest of the race. For moderate liberals, then, a vote for Bakatin was a vote taken away from Yeltsin and an indirect vote for Ryzhkov, and many who preferred Bakatin and what he stood for voted for Yeltsin as the most viable reform candidate.

36. The reputation seems to have been deserved. Mikhail Nenashev, *Poslednee pravitel'stvo SSSR: Lichnosti, Svidetel'stva, Dialogi* (Moscow: Krom, 1993), p. 73.

The other three presidential candidates were less serious contenders. General Albert M. Makashov was commander of the Volga-Urals Military District and unabashedly hard-line. Vladimir V. Zhirinovsky was leader of the Liberal-Democratic Party of Russia but generally occupied a populist, fascist position. Aman-Geldy M. Tuleev, chairman of the Kemerovo Oblast Council of People's Deputies, had been a leader in the coal miners' strike in Siberia.

It was almost universally expected that Yeltsin would win the election, but many thought he would not win 50 percent of the vote on the first round and would be forced into a runoff. He received 57.3 percent. Ryzhkov received 16.9 percent and Bakatin 3.4 percent. The hard-line Makashov also did poorly with 3.7 percent, while the more populist Zhirinovsky and Tuleev received 7.8 percent and 6.8 percent, respectively.[37] The other 4.4 percent of the voters either voted against all candidates or somehow spoiled their ballot. Thus Yeltsin did even better than 57.3 percent if measured only against the votes cast for other candidates.

The size of Yeltsin's vote and the weakness of his opponents had a dramatic impact on perceptions. The *New York Times* had covered the election sporadically on its inner pages, and it had reported correctly that Yeltsin's powers as president would not be much greater than those he had as chairman of the Supreme Soviet. The actual victory, however, produced a large front-page story and an editorial, "Russian Revolution."[38] And that is what it turned out to be.

The August Coup D'État

Anyone who knew the history of Boris Yeltsin and his relationship with Mikhail Gorbachev would have predicted that the relatively warm relations between the two men from April to July 1991 would not last long. Yeltsin had bought the presidency by accepting a number of amendments limiting the power of the office and a Union Treaty that remained ambiguously worded. It seemed highly likely that Yeltsin's concessions were tactical and temporary: once Yeltsin won a popular mandate, he would try to modify them.

37. *Izvestiia*, June 20, 1991, p. 1.
38. "Russian Revolution," *New York Times*, June 14, 1991, p. A26.

Meanwhile, Gorbachev had scheduled more radical price liberalization for January 1, 1992, and the liberalization already undertaken was spurring inflation. Yeltsin had a long history of increasing wages, pensions, and payments to peasants unilaterally with money he did not and could not have and then of blaming "the center" for inflation and all economic hardship. He and Gorbachev had agreed on only one thing: the desirability of taking credit for the success of economic reform and blaming the other for all the pain. Each would follow this course with respect to the inflation. The continuing Ukrainian resistance to accepting the Union Treaty was certain to provide Yeltsin with ample opportunity to reopen all the ambiguous clauses and informal deals in the treaty and insist that the Ukrainian position be accepted.

Nevertheless, from mid-April through June many believed that Gorbachev and Yeltsin were moving away from the confrontation of the fall and winter of 1990–91 and toward greater cooperation.[39] Although any modus vivendi would be uneasy, Gorbachev had the dominant governmental position and the support of the military. Yeltsin appeared to have little choice but to honor the agreements he had made. With a general from the Afghanistan war as Russia's new vice president, it would be easy for the military to remove Yeltsin for unconstitutional acts and have one of its own succeed to the presidency.

As a consequence, as the August 20 date for signing the Union Treaty approached, nationalists feared that the agreement ended all hope of republican autonomy. From this perspective the conservative coup d'état launched against Mikhail Gorbachev on August 19 seemed a tragic mistake. Things seemed to be going reasonably well for the conservatives, but they panicked and produced the very destruction of the Communist party and the Soviet Union that they had most feared.

This assumption, however, neglects the events in the weeks before the coup. The basic problem for the conservatives was not the Union Treaty itself but the interpretation Yeltsin put on it and the unilateral actions he began to take on the basis of his interpretation. Far more disturbing was Mikhail Gorbachev's inability or unwillingness to respond effectively to Yeltsin's actions.

39. This was true, for example, of the successive analyses of the Russian political system published in the spring of 1991 in *Trends*, an "official use only" report of the Central Intelligence Agency that is automatically declassified six months after its publication.

In the late spring Sergei Shakhrai, Yeltsin's chief legal counselor, warned publicly that a number of the clauses of the Union Treaty were unacceptable. On July 1, just two weeks after the presidential election, Yeltsin himself stated that "this Union Treaty destroys Russian statehood, thus eliminating the very foundations of democratic transformations."[40] A week later, however, the republican presidents, including Yeltsin, came to a basic agreement on the treaty. The version of the treaty agreed to on July 23 was little different from the draft published on June 27 that Yeltsin condemned (and that his chief assistant, Gennady Burbulis, was to call "completely unacceptable" in late September).[41]

Sometime during July, Yeltsin became convinced that the treaty could be used not to bring the Union back together but to tear it asunder. He became its insistent proponent, asserting that Russia could become truly sovereign only if it were signed. In early August, even before it was signed, he began interpreting the treaty in a way that left the USSR government with virtually no power. Moreover, he took actions that had no subtlety or duplicity whatsoever. He seemed intent on being as provocative and offensive to Gorbachev as possible.

The draft of the Union Treaty published on August 14 had purportedly been initialed on July 23, but the only major change involved a seemingly obscure rewriting of the provision on taxation agreed to after July 23. On July 30 Radio Rossiia reported that Gorbachev had accepted Yeltsin's position on taxation.[42] Gorbachev, Yeltsin, and Kazakhstan President Nursultan Nazarbaev had met secretly on the night of July 29–30 in what was said to be a difficult meeting. The Union Treaty was not supposed to be signed until the fall, but in exchange for Yeltsin's agreement to sign the treaty on August 20, Gorbachev agreed not only to accept his position on taxation, but also to give Russia immediate control over all economic enterprises on its territory, including oil fields and their foreign currency revenues.[43]

It is not clear whether these agreements were ever incorporated into the Union Treaty, for the published record on last stages of negotiation of the Union Treaty is muddled. Gorbachev claims in his memoirs that everyone

40. *Rossiiskaia gazeta*, July 2, 1991.
41. For the drafts of the Union Treaty, see *Izvestiia,* . For Burbulis's statement, see *Rossiiskaia gazeta*, September 28, 1991, p. 1.
42. Radio Rossiia, July 30, 1991, in FBIS, *Soviet Union*, July 31, 1991, p. 77.
43. For Yeltsin's description of this meeting see *Struggle for Russia*, pp. 38–39.

agreed on a federal tax, but not on its size. However, the *Financial Times* was told, likely by the Ukrainians, that Gorbachev, Yeltsin, and Nazarbaev had agreed the center would receive a fixed 10 percent of taxes collected.[44] In his memoirs, Gorbachev claims that a "compromise" agreement on taxation was reached on July 29. However, the compromise he cites was, in fact, the clause published in the Soviet press on August 14, and it did, indeed, accept Yeltsin's position. In his memoirs, Gorbachev says nothing about Russia's assuming control of all-Union enterprises.[45]

The clause on taxation in the draft Union Treaty published in June had been obscure. As Georgy Tarasevich had noted in late February, the Russian representatives had moved away from their insistence that only republican taxes be permitted. But in conceding that there would be Union taxes, they had insisted that their level be decided on the basis of coordination with the republics.[46] However, the nature, frequency, and timing of the coordination remained unspecified.

The "compromise" on taxation adopted on July 29 seems just as obscure to an outsider. "For the new financing of the expenditures of the Union budget connected with the realization of the powers transferred to the Union, unified (*edinyi*) taxes and dues are established with fixed percentages determined in agreement with the republics on the basis of an expenditure budget (*statei raskhodov*). Control of expenditures of the Union budget is realized by participants of the Treaty."[47]

In actuality, however, the phrase "in agreement with the republics on the basis of an expenditure budget" had a specific meaning in the Soviet context. For decades, the expenditure budgets of the various ministries and departments of the republics and regions had been established on a ministry-by-ministry basis, and then the republics were assigned whatever tax receipts were necessary to cover the expenditures. The agreed-upon compromise seemed to reverse the old pattern. The Union government would have to negotiate out its detailed expenditure budget with a large number of republics, and then they would graciously supply the tax money necessary

44. Chrysta Freeland and John Lloyd, "Soviet Republics Win Concessions," *Financial Times*, August 5, 1991, p. 2.

45. Gorbachev, *Zhizn' i reformy*, vol. 2, pp. 549–53, 556. Incredibly, Gorbachev's description of the meeting with Yeltsin is excised from the English-language memoirs, and the tax clause, which is printed in *Memoirs,* p. 628, is treated as a Yeltsin concession.

46. *Izvestiia*, February 22, 1991, p. 2.

47. Gorbachev, *Zhizn' i reformy*, vol. 2, p. 552; *Memoirs*, p. 628.

to finance the already negotiated budget. If no budget were negotiated, then there would be no taxes. That was precisely what was to happen in the fall of 1991.

Not only does Gorbachev describe a full renunciation of any independent taxing and budgeting power for the Union as a compromise, but he claims the Supreme Soviet and Council of Ministers were satisfied, which patently was not the case. Their officials were so dissatisfied they launched a coup d'état. Premier Valentin Pavlov claimed that he was given the draft of the Novo-Ogarevo treaty only on August 12, and not as premier but as a member of the Security Council. He was shocked. He claimed he managed to break all rules of secrecy and have the draft published in the *Moscow News*. His version seems right: the draft was published in the *Moscow News* on August 14 and then in *Izvestiia* the next day.[48] The version published on August 14 included the phrase "agreed on July 23," but it included new taxation language that was accepted at the July 29–30 meeting, and then by only two of the republic presidents.

An even greater problem than the new language, however, was the interpretation Yeltsin was giving the language, an interpretation in line with the secret July 30 agreement. The striking feature of the days before the Union Treaty was to be signed was the decisiveness with which Yeltsin was acting and the passivity of Gorbachev in the face of the challenges.

One line of Yeltsin's attack was launched against the Communist party. On July 20 he issued a Decree on Ending the Activity of Organizational Structures and Mass Social Movements in State Bodies, Establishments, and Organizations of the RSFSR.[49] The decree forbade forming political party groups at state-owned places of employment "regardless of their subordination," in effect banning the Communist party organizations that had been centered in the enterprises from the first days of the Soviet regime. (Officially it also banned them in places of employment owned by other republics or countries in Russia.)

Yeltsin's legal basis for banning this political activity was dubious in the extreme. The USSR Law on Public Association said that only the courts could outlaw a party, and this would seem to apply to outlawing branches

---

48. The *Moskovskie novosti* issue was officially dated August 18, but as TASS reported at the time, it was published on August 14. TASS, August 14, 1991, in FBIS, *Soviet Union*, August 14, 1991, p. 31.

49. *Izvestiia*, July 22, 1991, p. 1.

of a party.[50] But besides this challenge to USSR laws, which was scarcely new for him, the prohibition of this or any activity at industrial enterprises was a direct attack on the power of the central government. These enterprises were overseen by all-Union ministries; Yeltsin's assumption of authority to regulate the enterprises' inner life on this matter was an implicit claim to regulate all their actions.

The decree of July 20 was to go into effect in two weeks, which intentionally or unintentionally gave Gorbachev time to react and allowed Yeltsin the possibility of retreat. But Gorbachev did not respond to this challenge to central authority, and when the two weeks passed, Yeltsin went a step further. On August 5, during a trip to the oil fields of Tiumen, Yeltsin declared that the new Union Treaty would give the Russian government complete control over Russia's oil, the prices the fields were to charge, and the taxes to be levied against them. He criticized the USSR government for not paying oil workers high enough wages or giving the fields sufficient control over the hard currency they produced.

The Interfax news agency reported that Yeltsin even taunted Gorbachev as he announced his decision to turn Tiumen into a free economic zone, that is, one free from any central economic influence except for that of the USSR Ministry of Railroads. "The industrial enterprises of the Tiumen region [including the oil fields] will be freed from paying the 40 percent so-called [USSR] presidential tax, Boris Yeltsin said, and expressed hope that the Soviet President would not be hurt by this forced measure because [it increases] the Tiumen oil and gas industry workers' interest in enhancing their labour productivity."[51]

Yeltsin could not have chosen a more crucial field of battle. The Tiumen fields generated the hard currency needed for foreign purchases and repayment of the Soviet foreign debt. In addition, pricing policy with respect to petroleum was a momentous decision in economic policy and relations toward the non-Russian republics. Yeltsin thus asserted that Russia would be setting the oil prices. It would charge market prices for petroleum and gas to those republics that did not join the Union Treaty, and it would negotiate the prices with the other republics. Because all the other republics were importers of oil and gas and could not afford to pay market prices,

50. See the discussion in *Moscow News*, May 21 and May 24, 1992; and *Izvestiia*, May 4 and May 25, 1992.

51. "Promises Decree," Interfax, August 8, 1991, in FBIS, *Soviet Union*, August 9, 1991, p. 60.

they would be at the mercy of the Russian government within the new Union. There would be almost nothing for the Union institutions to do.

On August 10 Yeltsin had generalized his statements about Tiumen: "On 20 August the Union Treaty is to be signed . . . and the authority of Union departments comes to an end. . . . We will abandon the services of these ministries immediately. . . . Enterprises come under the jurisdiction of Russia." [52] On August 15 he announced the takeover of three more huge factories: the Cherepovets and West Siberian Metallurgical Works and the Urals Machinery Works in Sverdlovsk. Although he always left himself room to retreat if Gorbachev and the army began to resist his actions, Yeltsin gave the appearance of a man who knew what he wanted.

Surely it was these actions and statements that aroused alarm in Pavlov and others, not simply the draft of the Union Treaty he received on August 12. On August 16 Moscow's Radio Rossiia Network reported a "sharp difference" between Yeltsin and Pavlov on how to interpret the Union Treaty. [53] For example, the first deputy premier of the Russian government was unsuccessfully trying (for the last time on August 17) to get Pavlov to agree to transfer the USSR State Committee for Supply to the control of the Russian Republic. [54]

The moderates and conservatives in the government agreed with Pavlov that the inevitable result of Yeltsin's interpretation of the Union Treaty and Gorbachev's acquiescence would be the disintegration of the country and severe economic difficulties. In this, they were correct.

Two days before Gorbachev was to return from vacation to sign the Union Treaty, the top officials of the government launched a coup d'état against him. At 4:32 in the afternoon of August 18 all telephone communication to his summer residence at Foros in the Crimea was cut off. A few minutes later five high Soviet officials entered his home unannounced. They included Oleg Baklanov, deputy chairman of the Defense Council and Gorbachev's chief lieutenant for supervising the military-industrial complex; Oleg Shenin, senior secretary for personnel for the Communist party and the person in charge of the party in Gorbachev's absence; Valentin Varennikov, deputy minister of defense and commander of the ground forces; Valery Boldin, the president's chief of staff who has been quoted in

---

52. Radio Rossii, August 10, 1991, in FBIS, *Soviet Union*, August 12, 1991, p. 47.
53. "Yeltsin, Pavlov, 'Sharp Differences' on Treaty," Radio Rossiia Network, in FBIS, *Soviet Union*, August 16, 1991, p. 39.
54. *Rossiiskaia gazeta*, September 4, 1991, p. 2.

this book because of his intimate ties to the president for more than a decade; and Oleg Plekhanov, head of—in American terms—the Secret Service that guarded the president.[55]

The visitors to Foros came as representatives of an even more senior group: the Emergency Committee (the so-called GKChP), composed of Baklanov; Gennady Yanaev, the vice president; Valentin Pavlov, the premier; Vladimir Kriuchkov, chairman of the KGB; Dmitry Yazov, the minister of defense; Boris Pugo, the minister of internal affairs; and two more ceremonial figures—the heads of an industrialists' and a collective farmers' group, respectively. Anatoly Luk'ianov, chairman of the Supreme Soviet, was deeply involved, although he has unconvincingly denied it,[56] and virtually the entire cabinet tacitly endorsed the action after the fact. When General Aleksandr Lebed learned the names of the conspirators, allegedly for the first time, from a top Yeltsin adviser when Lebed was already in the White House, he reported, "I was shaken. How can these men be seizing power? They already were the embodiment of power."[57]

The delegation sent to Foros presented their case to Gorbachev. They proposed that he turn over power to Vice President Yanaev, who would proclaim an emergency situation (martial law in American terms) and introduce order. Baklanov told Gorbachev, "Nothing is required of you. Stay here. We will do all the dirty work for you."[58] Some of the group seemed to think Gorbachev might agree, but he reacted hostilely and aggressively. The exchange was emotional until the end, but all agree that he shook hands with them when they left , and some professed to see this as tacit encouragement.

At 6:00 the next morning the Emergency Committee announced on television that it had temporarily assumed power because Gorbachev was ill and that Vice President Yanaev would exercise the powers of the president until he returned. Troops and tanks were sent into Moscow, but the

---

55. Vladimir Kriuchkov, *Lichnoe delo* (Moscow: Olimp, 1996), p. 149, is the source for the information that Shenin was in charge of the party while Gorbachev was in Foros.

56. Luk'ianov has written little, but a number of his interviews are collected in A. Lukianov, *Perevorot mnimyi i nastoiashchii* (Moscow: Manuskript, 1993).

57. Aleksandr Lebed, *Za derzhavu obidno . . .* (Moscow: Moskovskaia pravda, 1995), p. 390.

58. V. Stepankov and E. Lisov, *Kremlevskii zagovor* (Moscow: OGIZ, 1992), p. 13. Gorbachev agrees. However, the fact that his memoirs are not cited in the second half of this chapter reflects their lack of meaningful information on the coup or its prelude.

conspirators acted very indecisively.[59] Because they claimed to be awaiting Gorbachev's return to power, they announced no policy change, but emphasized patriotic themes and the restoration of order. They even said nothing about the Communist party.

The leaders of the coup did little to control the Russian government. The entire Russian leadership, legislative and executive, including Yeltsin, had spent the night at the dacha village of the Russian government at Arkhangelskoe-2 in the Moscow suburbs, but the security troops loyal to Kriuchkov who surrounded the village were not ordered to seal it off. Several hours after the Emergency Committee made its announcement on television, Yeltsin and other leaders were allowed to drive to the Russian government building, the White House (*Belyi Dom*, in Russian), where they organized resistance.

CNN was allowed to continue to broadcast and to focus its cameras on the White House, thereby magnifying the impression of resistance. (Other than at the White House, there was little resistance throughout the Soviet Union.) Neither telephone communications, electricity, water, nor access to the White House was cut off. Key military officers were allowed to talk with White House officials by phone and even to visit there. When the head of the air force told several people that he opposed the coup, the news was on the foreign radio broadcasts the next day.[60]

On the evening of the nineteenth, most of the leaders of the coup held a press conference for foreign and Russian journalists. Premier Pavlov was not present, and the journalists were told he was ill. At the time the minister of defense thought he was drunk, but Pavlov claims he had a nervous breakdown. Those who were there showed signs of nervousness.

The leaders of the coup took no action that evening or the next day, but the Russian leaders succeeded in building more solid barricades around the White House and worked to win the allegiance of army officers and the rank-and-file soldiers sent into Moscow. Meanwhile, the passage of another day added to the impression of the coup leaders' indecisiveness and incompetence. Those who originally were inclined to obey them because of

59. Yazov has testified that he only intended for troops to come from the airport to guard a number of buildings and that it was a surprise to him that they brought tanks with them.

60. Yevgeny Shaposhnikov, *Vybor*, 2d ed.(Moscow: Nezavisimoe izdatel'stvo PIK, 1995), p. 29.

personal conviction, career considerations, or fear of arrest had increasing reason to rethink their position.

The crucial moment of the coup came on the night of August 20–21. The leaders of the Emergency Committee had decided to storm the White House at 3:00 in the morning and drew up plans involving troops of the Ministry of Defense, the KGB, and the Ministry of the Interior. But, as the prosecutors phrased it, "the last hours passed in tense expectation. Everyone looked at each other: the army at the KGB, the KGB at the troops. Would they move to the starting points? The MVD glanced at both." The commander of the parachute troops, Pavel Grachev, has asserted that "if I had gone, then everyone would have gone after me."[61] Grachev claims that he was already cooperating with the Russian government during the day of the twentieth, but Kriuchkov's bitter comment seems closer to the truth: Pavlov "shot balls in both baskets so that he would be prepared for any circumstance, depending on how events developed."[62] General Lebed's memoirs about Grachev are no more reassuring.

Once doubts arose about the participation of any unit, the plan quickly unraveled: no one wanted primary responsibility and blame. Shortly after midnight, the minister of defense decided he had to call off the attack. Kriuchkov and Baklanov argued with him for two hours, but without success. At 9:00 A. M. on August 22 the collegium of the Ministry of Defense decided to withdraw troops from Moscow.[63] The coup, in effect, was over.

Five of the leaders of the coup flew to Foros, apparently to try to persuade Gorbachev to act decisively to counteract the Russian government and to convince him that the coup had shown how little effort would be needed to restore order.[64] Gorbachev, however, refused to meet them, and they were returned to Moscow under arrest.

Of all the astonishing developments that occurred between 1985 and 1991, none was more unexpected to absolutely all observers than that the KGB and the military would launch a coup that simply collapsed because of a refusal to use any force. Kriuchkov was in the Soviet embassy in Hungary when the 1956 revolution was crushed, and for a quarter of a

---

61. Stepankov and Lisov, *Kremlevskii zagovor*, pp. 174–76.
62. Kriuchkov, *Lichnoe delo*, pt. 2, p. 199.
63. Stepankov and Lisov, *Kremlevskii zagovor*, pp. 180–86.
64. This is Kriuchkov's explanation, and it is as reasonable as any for what always has seemed a bizarre action. *Lichnoe delo*, pt. 2, p. 202.

century he was one of Andropov's closest lieutenants for Eastern Europe and then foreign intelligence. He more than anyone else in Moscow should have known how to organize a coup.

For this reason, hundreds of hypotheses have been advanced about the thinking of the conspirators and the extent of Gorbachev's and Yeltsin's prior involvement and knowledge about the coup. The events were so strange, even in hindsight, as to give rise to countless rumors and conspiracy theories. The best analysis of the coup, that of John Dunlop, is organized around a series of riddles. This discussion will follow the same course, but it is organized differently from Dunlop's chronological arrangement. The reader is referred to his book for a more detailed account of individual aspects of the coup.

The Mystery of Gorbachev

The most obvious explanation for the actions (or rather nonactions) of the Emergency Committee is that the leaders thought Gorbachev would eventually legitimate what they had done and that they did not want casualties that would complicate the process of reconciliation. From such a hypothesis, it is a small step to the suspicion that Gorbachev had given a signal he would so respond. The second most obvious explanation for the lack of military action is that the chief beneficiary of the events, Boris Yeltsin, had found out what was going on and had subverted the military beforehand. Given the attraction of Russians to conspiracy thinking, both hypotheses found much support in Russia, with Premier Pavlov supporting both in his memoirs.[65]

Several days after the end of the coup, even Eduard Shevardnadze suggested in public that Gorbachev had somehow been involved, and many Russians agreed this must have been the case. Westerners have been quite skeptical, Archie Brown being the latest to express contempt for any such accusation.[66] Not only did Gorbachev seem to be putting himself and his

---

65. Pavlov charged that Gorbachev organized the coup and that Yeltsin learned about it and took it over. Valentin Pavlov, *Avgust iznutri: Gorbachevputch* (Moscow: Delovoi mir, 1993), pp. 73, 124. Of course, the true conspiracy theorists think that George Bush and the CIA masterminded everything in Russia, including the coup attempt, to achieve the dissolution of the Soviet Union.

66. Archie Brown, *The Gorbachev Factor* (Oxford: Oxford University, 1996). Dunlop avoids conclusions about Gorbachev's involvement, but he structures his riddles in such a way as to indicate that, at a minimum, he has suspicions. John B. Dunlop, *The Rise and Fall of the Soviet Empire* (Princeton University Press, 1993).

family in grave danger, but he did not appear to be planning anything else in a sophisticated manner after the summer of 1990 and was not likely to be doing so this time either.

Any hypothesis that Gorbachev explicitly approved of the coup can be rejected out of hand. The various participants were testifying and writing while still under arrest, and they had every incentive to use their best possible defense: "we were not overthrowing Gorbachev, but carrying out his will." No one makes this first-hand charge in a direct manner. Nevertheless, now that virtually all the memoirs have been published, the issue seems more complex than many Westerners, including me, originally thought. The real question is whether Gorbachev, intentionally or not, left the impression he desired a coup to be carried out or even expected one. This possibility cannot be totally dismissed.

Everyone knew that Gorbachev had a pathological desire to avoid responsibility for harsh actions and to maintain deniability, which inevitably could leave doubt about the meaning of his words. For example, as shall be discussed in the next chapter, then Minister of Defense Yevgeny Shaposhnikov has written that in November 1991 Gorbachev had told him that a military coup was the best of hypothetical variants. When Shaposhnikov objected that this could lead to prison, as it had in August, Gorbachev answered that, of course, he was not recommending such an action, only speaking hypothetically.[67] Shaposhnikov had opposed the August coup and had no reason to misreport the conversation. It is, however, easy to understand how a top adviser might not interpret such a presidential statement as hypothetical.

Beyond any reasonable doubt, Gorbachev had authorized the severe public warnings of Kriuchkov and the top generals in December 1990 that were discussed at the end of the previous chapter. Kriuchkov is convincing in his insistence that Gorbachev had authorized the sending of militarized units to Lithuania in December and their use in January.

Another esoteric action in December strongly suggested that someone was thinking about serious military action against someone. The commander of the parachute troops normally was supervised by the deputy minister of defense for the air forces, but in December 1990 the head of those troops, Vladislav Achalov, was promoted to deputy minister overseeing them. The commander of the air forces was thus taken out of the line of

---

67. Shaposhnikov, *Vybor*, p. 138.

command between the paratroopers and the minister of defense (and president). In his memoirs, the commander, Yevgeny Shaposhnikov, describes the decision as peculiar.[68] But all agree that Shaposhnikov was the most proreform of the deputy ministers and that Achalov was conservative. Shaposhnikov was being put in a position where he did not have to organize any action involving the paratroopers and could not directly interfere. Such an appointment obviously required Gorbachev's approval, and it is hard to believe he did not understand its implications.

In an off-hand remark to the prosecutors, Yanaev suggested that his lack of agreement had prevented a coup d'état in April 1991 (actually a good time for one).[69] However, the first clear sign that the future leaders of the coup were thinking of independent action came on June 17. Premier Pavlov went to the Supreme Soviet to speak about the economic situation of the country, allegedly without the knowledge of Gorbachev. He called for additional powers for the government (that is, the Cabinet of Ministers, not the president), and then in closed session Kriuchkov, Pugo, and Yazov, the heads of the two police ministries and the military, discussed the security situation in ominous terms. The session was held five days after Yeltsin was elected president of Russia, and these men were clearly thinking of strong actions to control him.

Pavlov has described his speech in detail, and while he treats it in a matter-of-fact manner, it called for a drastic restructuring of government.[70] After removing Nikolai Ryzhkov as premier, Gorbachev had pushed the Cabinet of Ministers out of the government's Kremlin office and was strengthening the role of what Americans would call the White House staff. Pavlov implied that the Cabinet of Ministers—or really the Presidium of the Cabinet of Ministers—would become a real cabinet. It would have the right to issue obligatory decrees on economic matters, subject to the veto of the president or Supreme Soviet. Moreover, the government would have the right to coordinate the police, army, and procuracy in a centralized struggle against organized crime. These agencies had not been subordinated to the premier in the past, but only to the general secretary or the president. Now they were to be brought under the premier's direction, and it was hard to imagine this would be limited to a struggle against organized crime.

Finally, Pavlov proposed that the Supreme Soviet reestablish the control of the government over the banking system that Gorbachev had let the

---

68. Shaposhnikov, *Vybor*, p. 25.
69. Stepankov and Lisov, *Kremlevskii zagovor*, p. 159.
70. Pavlov, *Avgust iznutri*, pp. 76–78.

republics, particularly Russia, take over. He also asked for permission to create "a centralized, independent, single tax service for the whole country." In effect, Pavlov was demanding that the USSR Supreme Soviet take back the legal authority that Gorbachev had ceded to the negotiators of the Union Treaty and exercise it to reject the position of the Russian and Ukrainian governments. Without doubt, the leaders of the Supreme Soviet, and especially its chairman, Anatoly Luk'ianov, supported Pavlov strongly.

Because Yeltsin had just won a convincing victory in the Russian presidential election, the Pavlov program was not directed so much against Gorbachev as against Yeltsin. It promised a major confrontation with Russia and its newly legitimated leader. The heads of the police and military were essentially telling the Supreme Soviet in closed session that they were willing to back up Pavlov and Luk'ianov in this confrontation.

As U. S. Ambassador Jack Matlock commented, "it was as if the secretaries of state and defense, along with the director of central intelligence and the head of the FBI, had gone to the U.S. Congress without the knowledge of the president and asked that they be allowed to overrule the president."[71] Gorbachev reacted to this defiance in a most peculiar manner. Essentially, he did nothing. Three days later, after the speeches had been reported in the Moscow press, the Moscow mayor in a highly conspiratorial manner wrote a note to Ambassador Matlock saying that "a coup is being organized to remove Gorbachev. We must get word to Boris Nikolayevich" and that Kriuchkov, Luk'ianov, Pavlov, and Yazov were the men involved. He asked the Americans to warn Yeltsin, who was in the United States. The Americans warned Gorbachev, and on the twenty-first he went to the Supreme Soviet to say calmly that, while he understood Pavlov's concern, the steps he was proposing were not necessary.[72]

Popov has suggested that Gorbachev approved of the moves of his chief lieutenants (a point with which Pavlov, of course, agrees[73]), but that Bush's phone call destroyed his deniability and forced him to repudiate them. Popov's argument ignores the fact that Pavlov's proposals would require

71. Jack Matlock, *Autopsy on an Empire: The American Ambassador's Account of the Collapse of the Soviet Union* (Random House, 1995), p. 540.

72. Gavril Popov, *Snova v oppozitsii* (Moscow: Galaktika, 1994), pp. 203–11. For Matlock's description of the meeting, see his *Autopsy on an Empire*, pp. 539–46. So far as can be judged, it is the Supreme Soviet session alone that led the Bush administration to warn the Russians of a coup and to claim knowledge for foresight. Matlock is scathing of Bush's "reckless" handling of the incident. (p. 545).

73. Pavlov, *Avgust iznutri,* pp. 79–81.

legislative and perhaps even constitutional action and that Gorbachev would eventually be forced to declare himself and lose deniability—indeed, that on June 18 he had already signaled this position to the Supreme Soviet. The newspaper *Kommersant*, which emphasized this fact, speculated that Gorbachev was trying to pressure the upcoming G-7 meeting into providing aid.[74] Perhaps the Bush administration was playing the same game.

Kriuchkov reports that Gorbachev repeatedly approved the drawing up of plans for what Americans would call martial law and the use of harsh steps to prevent economic collapse. Others agree. Then, according to Kriuchkov, Gorbachev would always say it was necessary "to wait for the right moment." Kriuchkov reports that just before Gorbachev left for vacation at Foros on August 4, he again instructed Yazov, Pugo, and Kriuchkov to analyze the situation and prepare measures in case martial law had to be introduced. In his last conversation with Kriuchkov before leaving, Gorbachev said in a "weighty" manner, "Anything can occur. If there is a direct threat, then we will have to act."[75]

According to second-hand testimony, several participants said they had been encouraged by Gorbachev. Boldin has commented that "Shenin was taken aback [by Gorbachev's hostile reception at Foros]. Only the day before, he had been expecting a friendly discussion and a mutually agreed solution, in the spirit of previous conversations. In fact, the trip had been made on the condition that there would be a mutual agreement and a decision by the president." When the group left, Boldin has written, "Baklanov, clearly puzzled by what happened, said, 'But he thought that was the only solution. What has changed?'"[76] The chauffeur who was driving the three men from the airport to the presidential residence and back reported that they were in a good mood on the way, but very upset and irritated on the way back.[77]

Whenever Gorbachev spoke ambiguously, his lieutenants probably had been inclined to take him seriously because of his evident distaste for Boris Yeltsin. Gorbachev's more radical advisers and his most conservative critics actually describe him in the same way—as a man who had become convinced the system could not be reformed and must be overthrown. The

---

74. *Kommersant*, June 17–24, 1991, p. 1.
75. Kriuchkov, *Lichnoe delo*, pt. 2, pp. 146–47.
76. Valery Boldin, *Ten Years That Shook the World: The Gorbachev Era as Witnessed by his Chief of Staff*, trans. Evelyn Rossiter, (Basic Books, 1994), pp. 26, 28.
77. Stepankov and Lisov, *Kremlevskii zagovor*, p. 18.

radicals say that he had experienced a heroic internal revolution in adopting democratic values, the conservatives that he was a traitor; but this was a difference in normative interpretation, not an analytical difference. There is also, however, universal agreement that Gorbachev was highly emotional in his hatred of Yeltsin. When he seemed bent on surrendering virtually total power to Yeltsin, few could believe he really meant it. It is a major puzzle for the historian as well.

Basically there are three explanations for Gorbachev's behavior. First, he may have become tired and depressed and essentially gave up. Second, he may have made a conscious decision to create a confederation such as Switzerland or the European Economic Community and to serve as a president with limited powers, even, as some said, such powers as the Queen of England had. He may have maneuvered to destroy the USSR government with maximum stealth and deception to prevent a conservative reaction. Third, he may have cynically accepted Yeltsin's most extreme suggestions in the belief that this would provoke a coup d'état he could use to his benefit while preserving deniability.

Unfortunately, none of these explanations is really convincing, at least if Gorbachev had carefully thought through his position. Without question he was tired, and a Western psychologist might have diagnosed clinical depression. He had not given up, but he surely was not thinking very clearly. Certainly the concessions he made to Yeltsin on July 29–30, and the steps Yeltsin began taking in Tiumen, were so sweeping that a rational man could not have expected a confederation as strong as the Swiss arrangement to result or himself to be left a meaningful role of any type. At some level Gorbachev must have hoped that the accelerating collapse of political order and the economy would lead the "force ministers" to get rid of Yeltsin for him, and he may not have greatly cared whether he would be retired or left with some role.

The Mystery of the Conspirators' Plans

Most of the memoirs and testimony of those involved in the coup emerged while they were under arrest. Their lawyers were, no doubt, working with them to build the best legal case.[78] Even today it would not be

---

78. For example, one of Pavlov's memoirs has a very long section arguing that Gorbachev was not kept isolated at Foros but could have communicated outside or left. The section contains much interesting information, but it reads like a good lawyer's brief for a weak case rather than a convincing historical document. Pavlov, *Avgust iznutri*, pp. 32–66.

legally wise to talk about an intention to arrest Yeltsin or storm the White House. Thus Kriuchkov, who has said in retrospect that the coup definitely should have moved decisively against Gorbachev from the beginning, implausibly denies there were plans against Yeltsin and does not express regrets on the subject. One should understand Kriuchkov's legal situation before condemning him too strongly for what must be a lack of frankness on this point.

The real problem for the historian is the claim by all participants that planning for the coup began only a few days before and even that many key decisions were made only after Gorbachev refused to cooperate. The claim is self-serving and cannot be fully true, but the coup was so disorganized that it may be partially true.

It is clear from many sources that Gorbachev had at times authorized planning for martial law and that it was undertaken. Both Kriuchkov and the prosecutors agree that the last detailed planning began on August 6, with the work being done by high representatives of the KGB and the Ministry of Defense. The military's representative was Pavel Grachev, commander of the parachute troops. The prosecutors imply, but do not say, that the planning was begun at the initiative of those who conducted the coup, but Kriuchkov, as has been seen, says it was undertaken at Gorbachev's initiative.

Over the previous year the top officials of the government and the Communist party had become alarmed by the course of events and by Gorbachev's decisions (or nondecisions), and they had every right to be. They were thinking about what to do if the president did not correct course. They must have been cautiously sounding each other out. And whatever the intentions of the future leaders of the coup when they went to the Supreme Soviet on June 17 to call for additional powers for the government, they were thinking of some major change.

According to the standard interpretation of the August coup, its planning began seriously early in the month. As has been seen, Gorbachev met with Yeltsin and President Nazarbaev of Kazakhstan at the end of July, conceded Yeltsin's position on taxation, and agreed to remove Pavlov and Kriuchkov from their posts. Yeltsin said in his memoirs that he had found transcripts of this conversation in Kriuchkov's safe.[79] In this view, Kriuchkov and Pavlov had launched the coup to save their jobs.

---

79. Gorbachev had made the same charge in a November 1991 BBC interview. Dunlop, *Rise of Russia*, pp. 194–95.

It is, however, not clear that this interpretation rests on fact. Kriuchkov categorically denied that he had ever bugged the conversation or knew its substance. He noted that the prosecutors had never charged him with such an activity. The prosecutors reprinted Kriuchkov's denial in their white paper on the coup; because they did not refute it, they thus seemed to confirm it.[80] On such matters, one should not rely on Yeltsin's testimony alone.

Kriuchkov and Pavlov suggest that the triggering event for the coup was their receipt of the latest copy of the Union Treaty on August 12. Pavlov focused immediately on the one major change made since June: the clause on taxation approved by Gorbachev on July 30.[81] Surely, however, they were also watching with alarm Gorbachev's failure to respond to Yeltsin's prohibition of the party in the army and his claim to the Tiumen oil fields. One of the middle-level officials who had been making a detailed plan for martial law stated that Kriuchkov told him on August 14 that martial law would be introduced against Gorbachev's will.[82]

Troop leaders were told on the morning of August 17 to begin preparations, but if the testimony of the memoirs is to be believed, the conspirators first met that evening, and even then they did not have the final agreement of Vice President Yanaev or even Interior Minister Pugo. Yanaev had to be pressured to become acting president at this late stage. Minister of Defense Yazov and Minister of Internal Affairs Pugo both told their wives that they had been drawn in the plot and foolishly so, and they seem to have given it little thought. When Supreme Soviet Chairman Lukianov asked about the group's plan on the evening of August 18, after Gorbachev's communications had been cut off, Yazov answered that they had no plan.[83] Kriuchkov denied this, but no one has claimed there was a meaningful contingency plan if Gorbachev did not agree to support the Emergency Committee. Gorbachev's chief of staff, Valery Boldin, who was ill and seems to have been a marginal participant in the coup, returned to the hospital for the night of August 18–19. His testimony is likely to be reliable, and it is devastating in its description of the chaos both in the evening and in the morning when

80. Stepankov and Lisov, *Kremlevskii zagovor*, p. 260.
81. Indeed, Kriuchkov claims there would not have been a coup if *Moscow News* had not published the leaked treaty on August 14. This position is very far-fetched, because both he and Pavlov had received the treaty as members of the Security Council on August 12, and Pavlov was the leaker. Kriuchkov, *Lichnoe delo*, pt. 2, p. 133.
82. Stepankov and Lisov, *Kremlevskii zagovor*, p. 84.
83. Stepankov and Lisov, *Kremlevskii zagovor*, p. 102.

he returned.[84] The military units never received any clear orders or even information that the Emergency Committee had been established. They had to learn it from the Muscovites with whom they came in contact.

There are several possible explanations for the lack of a plan. One, suggested by the prosecutors, is that the coup leaders had the 1968 Czechoslovakia scenario in mind.[85] The Soviet Union sent troops into Prague, but they did not use force. The top reformers were arrested but quickly released. The government and media were allowed to denounce the invasion, and Aleksandr Dubcek remained party first secretary for seven months. The original reform program, although not the changes and hopes of the summer, remained substantially in place and was modified as its proponents were gradually removed. Indeed, although Czechoslovakia became much more conservative in the 1970s, it still remained freer and more market oriented than many communist countries, including Brezhnev's Soviet Union.[86]

If the coup leaders envisioned such an unfolding of events, they ignored the fact that Czechoslovakia was not a huge country with republics refusing to obey central laws and with an economy out of control. It had a functioning Communist party and government structure, as well as a minority Slovak elite that was more than willing to take the top posts and move against a Czech majority that had been treating them badly. All the Czechoslovakian elite understood that the Soviet Union was capable of severe repression and quite determined, and they could use this attitude as a justification for nonresistance. The Soviet Union of 1991 was in a very different position. Only if it had a strong, united military and KGB might politicians adjust, and the military and KGB would have to prove they were willing to repress to ensure this outcome.

A second explanation for the chaos of the August coup, an explanation not inconsistent with the first, is that the participants disagreed about Gorbachev's motivations and his likely response. Was he, in Gennady Yanaev's words, a man "ill with indecisiveness" who after a few days would fly at once to the Supreme Soviet to sanction the actions of the Emergency Committee after the situation was stabilized?[87] Would he agree

84. Boldin, *Ten Years That Shook the World*, p. 29–30.

85. Stepankov and Lisov, *Kremlevskii zagovor*, p. 121.

86. See Fred H. Eidlin, *The Logic of "Normalization": The Soviet Intervention of Czechoslovakia of 21 August 1968 and the Czechoslovak Response* (Columbia University Press, 1980), pp. 28, 69.

87. Andrei Karaulov, *Vokrug Kremlia* (Moscow: Slovo, 1993), pt. 2, p. 426.

to serve as party secretary like Dubcek? Or was he a traitor who should be treated, at best, as Nikita Khrushchev was in 1964, which was seemingly the position of General Valentin Varennikov, commander of the ground forces.

The problem with Yanaev's vision was that it was unrealistic. Given an almost pathological desire for deniability, Gorbachev would never have sanctioned what was done during his confinement. Once he returned as president, he would have been under severe pressure from intellectuals and the West to remove and arrest those who had held him illegally. If he had the powers of president, he would change personnel. If he did not have such powers, who was going to maintain order and conduct a consistent reform policy? And what would have happened with Yeltsin? If he was still the elected president of Russia, he scarcely would be compliant. If he had been removed, Gorbachev would be even more hard-pressed to deny and reverse the actions of his lieutenants.

Yanaev's reluctance to become acting president must show that he was acutely aware of this possibility. Pavlov's drunkenness or nervous breakdown, his memoirs suggest, occurred when he realized the logic of the situation after Gorbachev rejected the offer at Foros. Pavlov, as usual, sees things in terms of a plot: in his view, Gorbachev had deliberately drawn his lieutenants into a coup and wanted them to get rid of Yeltsin with bloodshed so that he could get rid of them. But one need not attribute such planning to Gorbachev to agree with Pavlov about the likely consequences of such a coup and the return of Gorbachev to Moscow.

Kriuchkov's memoirs show he never had much faith that Gorbachev would go along with the coup, and he may have agreed to the Foros strategy to obtain the agreement of the other members. He was, however, extremely vague in his memoirs about his own plans in the future. In several cryptic lines he noted that the Congress or Supreme Soviet might have legally removed Gorbachev. That, indeed, was an option in people's minds, but by the second day of the coup, Luk'ianov was saying it would be impossible to obtain a two-thirds vote.

The most serious problem for the coup—and in analyzing its likely consequences if it had been successful—was that it did not contain a natural leader who inspired respect. Who was supposed to run the country and what would be his policy? Gennady Yanaev, the acting president, was the most unwilling member of the team, and neither he nor anyone else thought he would make a credible president. No one could envision the military participants in the coup, both nearly seventy years old, as the equivalent of

General Augusto Pinochet of Chile, and Kriuchkov was a foreign policy specialist with no domestic political or administrative experience.

It is very possible that the leaders of the coup had given little serious thought to the future. Kriuchkov, Pavlov, Pugo, and Luk'ianov were not reactionaries in the usual sense of the term but moderate reformers. John Dunlop's hypothesis that Kriuchkov had the intention of soon instituting mass arrests seems unlikely.[88] The leaders probably had a vague hope that the Congress of People's Deputies or the Party Central Committee, which had moderate reforming majorities, would select a strong, moderate reforming leader and that he would return to the perestroika policy of early 1987, but with a Ryzhkov-like economic policy. They probably did, indeed, have vague memories of how easily things had gone in Czechoslovakia in 1968 and had not thought out the probable consequences when the repressing troops and government are domestic rather than foreign.

But having such hopes and realizing them were two entirely different matters. There were certain to be some arrests, if for no other reason than that some radicals were glad to be martyrs. It is easy to imagine many scenarios in which the leaders of the coup, even against their will, would find themselves becoming ever more repressive. Certainly, establishing order and restoring economic growth were going to require a strong, effective leader with strong powers. Like general secretaries in the past, such a leader would have wanted to free himself from the control of the men who brought him to power. Once he had done that, no one—including the leaders of the coup—had any idea what he would do.

Events such as the August coup become defining moments in a country's mythology, and they come to be seen as the struggle of good and evil. If evil had prevailed, mythmakers say, it would have been extremely evil. Serious historians have a duty to be more skeptical. The forces at work in Soviet society that were described in chapter 2 were extremely powerful. Gorbachev came to power with the support of the nomenklatura in the Central Committee, and the more conservative members of the 1985 nomenklatura were retired or dead. The social, economic, and political factors pushing for a more liberal system than the one in 1985 or even 1987 would be stronger than they were in 1985, and any leader had a strong incentive to respond to them.

88. Dunlop, *Rise of Russia.*

The West would likely have pushed for a more liberal society. The first reaction of the Bush administration was to accommodate the coup: the administration had made crucial foreign policy achievements, especially in Eastern and Central Europe. They were its top priority, and this gave any new Soviet leaders great leverage if they were willing to use this card. The West would also have been under great pressure to adjust to the new regime to keep its friends of the perestroika period out of jail, and the coup leaders would have been wise to use this bargaining chip to moderate the Western response. To repeat, it is easy to write scenarios in which things went very wrong, but one should not forget there were other scenarios.

The Military and The Logic of Collective Action

In immediate terms the August coup failed because its leaders could not find troops to storm the White House on the night of August 20–21 and because the next morning the collegium of the Ministry of Defense voted to withdraw troops from Moscow. Everyone agrees that there was no significant resistance outside Moscow and that the storming of the White House would have been a relatively easy military operation. But although the White House could have been stormed on August 19–20 with few casualties, scholars agree that the number would have been considerably higher the next night, even though Lebed suggested they would largely be limited to fire and smoke deaths inside the White House itself.[89]

Why were the leaders of the Ministry of Defense, the KBG, and the Ministry of Internal Affairs—all core leaders of the coup with divisions at their command—unable to bring the minimal force to bear at the crucial moment? Memoir evidence on this question is very untrustworthy. Several of the officers most deeply implicated have not written memoirs and were not even indicted. Besides Vladislav Achalov, the deputy minister of defense in charge of the parachute troops and surely an active coup supporter, Boris Gromov, the commander of the MVD troops, is a mystery. Minister of Internal Affairs Pugo was an active participant in the coup (and committed suicide afterwards), but the internal troops that were his main potential contribution were never used.

89. Lebed, *Za derzhavu obidno*, pp. 400–01. See also *Spektakl nazyvalsia putch 1993* (Tiraspol: Rekliz-Edis, 1993).

Gromov's appointment as first deputy minister of internal affairs in December 1990 had been treated as one of the signs of Gorbachev's sharp turn to the right. Gromov then became the Communist candidate for vice president in the Russian election and, less than a month before the coup, one of ten signers of a page-long conservative manifesto that called out for a movement to end to "the fatal collapse of the state, the economy, and the individual."[90] In 1992 a commission said that the fate of the coup had been decided when Gromov and Grachev decided not to apply force. The prosecutors' testimony is that Gromov was against the use of MVD troops from at least the day of August 20.[91] At the time, however, Grachev referred to Gromov's role more ambiguously and Gromov was relieved of his post in what clearly seems to have been a punishment.[92] In one of Pugo's last conversations before his suicide, he asked that his regards be given to Gromov.[93] Moscow analysts all assumed in the fall of 1991 that he was an unindicted coconspirator.

Officers who did write memoirs all testified that they were democrats, that they never would have agreed to use force against the people, and that their resistance had saved the country. A certain skepticism is warranted. Even Air Force Commander Yevgeny Shaposhnikov, the one general the coup leaders never trusted and who most clearly was an early opponent of the coup, portrays himself as resolute on the morning of the nineteenth, but the presidential official with whom he spoke—a lieutenant colonel—describes him as supportive on the shedding of blood but less forthcoming on exchange of information and contacts.[94] Shaposhnikov also quotes the Military Statute: "The order of a superior is law for the subordinate. An order should be carried out unconditionally, exactly, and on time."[95]

---

90. Two of the signers were the conservative writers Yurii Bondarev and Valentin Rasputin, and one (Gennadii Zyuganov) was the first secretary of the Russian Communist party. Three were leaders of the coup: Valentin Varennikov (the ground forces commander), Aleksandr Tiziazhov (the leader of the defense industry managers), and Vasily Starodubtsev (the chairman of the Peasant Union). *Sovetskaia Rossiia*, July 23, 1991, p. 1.

91. Stepankov and Lisov, *Kremlevskii zagovor*, p. 174.

92. *Krasnaia zvezda*, August 31, 1991, p. 3; and September 6, 1991, p. 1. After the collapse of the Soviet Union, Gromov suddenly reappeared as first deputy commander of the ground forces.

93. Stepankov and Lisov, *Kremlevskii zagovor*, p. 251.

94. Shaposhnikov, *Vybor*, pp. 23–24. Interview with V. A. Burkov in M. Zabylin, *Istina momenta* (Moscow: Respublika, 1992), bk. 1, p. 65.

95. Shaposhnikov, *Vybor*, p. 24.

The most interesting military memoirs covering the coup were written by General Aleksandr Lebed. A person not knowing that the book referred to real events would assume the chapter titled "The Spectacle That Was Called a Coup" was a very well written humorous novel. Lebed commanded the Taman division that was brought into Moscow on August 19, and he paints an extraordinary picture of confusion in the orders he received or did not receive from his superiors, notably Achalov and Grachev. He himself moved back and forth between the two sides in battle fatigues. He claims both to have drawn up (in ten minutes) the plan to storm the White House for Defense Minister Yazov and to have recommended that Yeltsin declare the troops were under his command as Russian president. Lebed says all the right words about not firing on the people but also refers to the obligation to carry out orders. When Grachev asked him if he was ready, he answered "I am ready," but then thought to himself, "I am always ready if only I knew for what."[96] Clearly, Lebed was weighing his options, and other generals were following the same course.

This is, of course, precisely what a rational actor would do. Mancur Olson, it may be remembered, insisted that the crucial element in maintaining authoritarian rule is the logic of collective action. Rational military officers, unless they are in a very small group in a position to conduct a coup, should respond to the incentives of money and promotion and to the threat of punishment when asked to carry out an unpleasant order. When an attempted coup d'état occurs, key subordinates must make a rapid judgment as to who will have the ability to reward and punish. Will the old leaders hang on and ruthlessly punish the disloyal, or will the leaders of the coup win and react as strongly with respect to friends and opponents? It is a decision on which not only one's career but one's very life may depend. Any rational person will weigh options if given an opportunity.

The first rule of a successful coup, therefore, is not to give subordinates an opportunity for reflection but to present them with an apparent fait accompli so that any opposition seems suicidal. The leaders of a coup must show absolute self-confidence. The fundamental error of the leaders of the August coup is that they did not act to cut off options for commanders. They did not issue clear orders at a time when the orders could have easily been carried out and when commanders would not have dared to refuse. The coup leaders should have sealed off or arrested Yeltsin in his dacha; once he

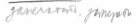

96. Lebed, *Za derzhavu obidno* pp. 383–411.

made his way to the White House, they should have immediately cut its communications and prevented barricades from being built. It was madness to let generals such as Shaposhnikov, Lebed, and Grachev talk with the Yeltsin government and to bargain with, and no doubt mislead, both sides. It was even worse to let young soldiers, many of whom voted for Yeltsin, to be brought into the streets of Moscow to do nothing but be subject to the appeals of other young people from the capital. As Shakespeare, who lived in a time of coup d'états and understood them, wrote, "If 'tis be done, best that it be done quickly."

A second major mistake of the coup leaders was not being frank from the beginning that Gorbachev would be removed. Even if they did not accuse the president of unconstitutional actions—and certainly the process of achieving the Union Treaty was a gross violation of the existing constitution—and of undemocratic failure to follow the people's will after the March referendum on the Union, everyone understood that the situation was spinning out of control. They could have said that Gorbachev, while good-hearted, was incapable of coping with the crisis, a position everyone would have accepted.

Instead, at the time the crucial actions were being ordered, the troop commanders were being asked to attack the democratically elected Russian government to bring an "ill" Gorbachev back to power. If the leaders of the coup were, in fact, going to allow Gorbachev back, then there was every possibility that he would find a way to punish those who had supported the coup. If Yeltsin were not arrested or removed, it was certain he would try to do so.

Third, it never was clear what was to come later if the coup was successful and Gorbachev was not brought back. Who was to be the leader and what was to be his policy? Was the Communist party to return as a leading party? Would the system be turned into a parliamentary one with its speaker, Anatoly Luk'ianov, becoming a real prime minister. Even Shaposhnikov, who had basically turned against Yazov by this time, reported a conversation with his chief deputies on August 20: "We shared our confusions about the USSR Supreme Soviet and the Central Committee of the Communist party. Why were they silent? Were they for or against? Or were they waiting to join the victor?"[97] He said in his memoirs that it was a moral decision to support the courageous Yeltsin against the cowardly

97. Shaposhnikov, *Vybor*, p. 28.

Central Committee or Supreme Soviet, but Mancur Olson would completely understand the rational aspects of the decision. The disappearance of Pavlov, the nervousness of Yanaev and others at the press conference, the failure to take decisive measures of any kind—all this added to the impression there was no anti-Yeltsin person or force on whom to bet.

Fourth, the lines of command were never clear. Soviet leaders had divided troops among the Ministry of Defense, the KGB, and the Ministry of Interior as a defense against a coup. August 1991 showed that this system could work against a coup even when the three ministers all agreed. Each ministry was given a role. Deputy Minister of Defense Achalov had overall command of the paratroopers sent into Moscow, while the troops guarding the Yeltsin compound were KGB. If there had been a precise set of orders, this posed no real problems, but on the night on which the White House was to be stormed, the commander of each type of troops had to worry whether the others would act. No one wanted to be the first to go.

Finally, there was a deep generational division within the military that probably was a factor in the outcome of the coup. Several years before, virtually the entire top military command had been born around 1923 and thus had been junior officers during World War II. By the time of the coup, the minister of defense and the deputy ministers who commanded the ground forces, the air defense forces, the strategic rocket forces, and the civil defense were still of this generation (all five were born in 1923 or 1924), while almost all the other deputy ministers were born between 1925 and 1935. (The exception was Mikhail Moiseev, the head of the General Staff, who was born in 1939.) The older commanders in particular were especially unhappy at Gorbachev's abandonment of the hegemony in Eastern Europe that was so hard-won in World War II.

Almost all the military officers mentioned in this chapter were veterans of the Afghanistan war and men who knew each other well. They were overwhelmingly in their mid-forties at the time of the coup. Vice President Rutskoi was the member of the group who had been politically most successful, but the last commander in Afghanistan, Boris Gromov, seems to have been the most respected. Whatever their views and calculations, this generation of generals saw the world differently from Yazov and Varennikov and others who had fought in World War II. The Afghanistan veterans ultimately used the coup and then Russian independence to take over the Ministry of Defense from the older generation of generals, and the thought must have entered their minds during the coup that this might be the result if it failed.

As shall be seen in the next chapter, the new defense minister, Yevgeny Shaposhnikov, continued strongly to favor the Union, and Vice President Rutskoi was to speak out loudly in its favor in November and December. The army newspaper, *Krasnaia zvezda*, was to support the same line, and the conservative generals such as Gromov obviously were even more alarmed after August than before. The failure of the coup left in power a man who, for whatever reason, had not been willing to resist the disintegration of the Soviet Union. Now he was even more demoralized and much of the state apparatus had been discredited. His chief rival had not only renewed self-confidence, but a heroic worldwide image as a man who had defended Russian democracy against tanks. The processes of disintegration were likely to accelerate, and the question was whether the younger generation of the military would be willing to act against Yeltsin.

CHAPTER FOURTEEN

Economic Options and the Breakup of the Union

THE BREAKUP of the Soviet Union can be understood on many levels. Most directly the breakup occurred because Boris Yeltsin saw no other way to replace Mikhail Gorbachev and because Gorbachev and the military refused to defend the Union with force. In a less direct sense, it occurred because the elite had lost faith in the centralized command-administrative system and adopted a new faith that dismantling the government was the secret of economic growth and efficiency.

Yeltsin succeeded brilliantly in employing a Marxist image of the state and a Marxist insistence on the crucial role of property in his "anticommunist" attack on the centralized state. In this image the state loomed above society and the republics, repressing them in the interests of a ministerial nomenklatura, a class that managed and in effect owned the means of production. This state became "the center," and the only way to democratize society was to socialize—to give back to society through universal privatization—the property controlled by the ministerial class.

The campaign to overthrow the communist system was a masterpiece of populist politics. Non-Russian radicals successfully mobilized local nationalism against the Soviet Union by calling it a Russian Empire, while Boris Yeltsin successfully mobilized Russian nationalism against the Soviet Union by asserting that it deprived Russia of political and economic power. The campaign was also a masterpiece of international politics. A West that was deeply concerned about the disintegration of a nuclear superpower was brought along by the adoption of an antistate, antisubsidy free-trade eco-

449

nomic policy that, it was argued, could only be enacted within the boundaries of Russia itself.

Gorbachev after the Coup

Gorbachev arrived in Moscow from Foros at 2:00 a.m. on August 22 and was taken directly to his dacha outside Moscow. As Yeltsin addressed a huge "rally of the victors" outside the White House at noon, Gorbachev stayed at the dacha rather than attend, express his thanks to the participants, and share in the victory. He met with senior academic advisers, and Leonid Abalkin reported that he seemed in control of himself and the situation.[1] Trusted men had been appointed as minister of defense, chairman of the KGB, and minister of the interior. That evening he emerged at a long press conference in which he pledged to purge the Communist party of reactionaries, thereby indicating his belief that the party was reformable.

On the morning of August 23, however, Gorbachev met for ninety minutes with Yeltsin and agreed to clear all major appointments with him. In particular, he removed his temporary appointees to head the military and the police ministries. Yevgeny Shaposhnikov became USSR minister of defense, Vadim Bakatin chairman of the KGB, and Viktor Barannikov (the Russian minister of interior) USSR minister of interior. When Shaposhnikov came to the Kremlin to hear of his appointment, Yeltsin was the first to greet him and to make clear that the real lines of command were far more complicated than the formal ones.[2] Arkady Volsky later claimed in an interview that if Gorbachev had stood up to Yeltsin on these appointments, the army would have supported him and the Union would have been saved.[3]

Shortly after noon on the twenty-third, Gorbachev went to the Russian Supreme Soviet and permitted Yeltsin to humiliate him before the nation on live television. Yeltsin violated the secrecy of his agreement with Gorbachev and told the Supreme Soviet he had gained the right of veto on all central government appointments. Then he pulled out a memorandum on the Cabinet of Ministers meeting of August 19 that showed nearly all

---

1. Leonid Abalkin, *K tsely cherez krizis: spustia god* (Moscow: Luch, 1992), p. 122.

2. Yevgeny Shaposhnikov, *Vybor*, 2d ed. (Moscow: Nezavisimoe izdatel'stvo PIK, 1995), pp. 60–63.

3. Jerry Hough, interview with Arkady Volsky, December 28, 1991.

ministers had either supported the coup or had been neutral.[4] He bullied
Gorbachev into reading it aloud before the country. Finally Yeltsin dramatically presented and signed a decree suspending the activity of the Communist party in front of its general secretary even though he had no right to do
so. The acting chairman of the Russian Supreme Soviet, Ruslan
Khasbulatov, finally ended the torment by telling Yeltsin he felt sorry for
Gorbachev and that things should be brought to an end.

Yeltsin tried to consolidate his position on August 24 by placing not only
the USSR economic ministries, but also the USSR State Supply Committee, the successor to the USSR State Planning Committee, the USSR State
Bank, and the Foreign Economic Bank under the control of the Russian
government. The Russian Ministry of Communications took over the
USSR Ministry of Communications, including its control over top secret
Kremlin communications.

Within a few days, those defending the central government struck back.
The first deputy ministers were put in charge of the old USSR ministries,
and Yeltsin's decrees were revoked. Gerashchenko was reappointed chairman of the USSR State Bank, and it remained fully a central organ.[5] Until a
new constitution was adopted, political power was given to the State
Council composed of Gorbachev and the heads of ten Union republics.
Economic power was officially placed in the hands of the new Interrepublic
Committee for Operational Economic Management. Because five of the ten
republics were Central Asian and strongly supported Gorbachev, he
seemed to be in a very powerful position within the State Council, especially vis-à-vis Yeltsin, who had one vote.

The Committee for Operational Economic Management was headed by
a group of four presumed equals. Gorbachev's representative, and thus the
de facto chairman, was Arkady Volsky. The official chairman was Ivan
Silaev, the chairman of the Russian Council of Ministers, while the deputy
chairmen were Arkady Volksy (Gorbachev's representative), Grigory
Yavlinsky, and Yury Luzhkov, deputy mayor of Moscow. Luzhkov supervised distribution of food, fuel, and other supplies, and Yavlinsky was in
charge of economic reform. Yavlinsky was often described in the Western

---

4. For the memorandum, see *Izvestiia*, August 23, 1991, pp. 1, 3.
5. Or so it seemed at the time. However, Gerashchenko remained a key figure in the
Yeltsin government even after the abolition of the Russian Congress that allegedly was
directing him to follow an inflationary policy. He was serving not only as a scapegoat
for the West but as a key financial figure. In the fall of 1991 he must have been acting
in a way that earned Yeltsin's trust.

press as Yeltsin's chief economic adviser, and his and Silaev's presence on the committee was considered a sign of Yeltsin's power on it. In reality, Yeltsin was pushing both out of power.

Nevertheless, Gorbachev made no effort to follow up on these first steps. No new prime minister was appointed and no deputy prime ministers. Most of the USSR ministers who were dismissed in the wake of the coup were not replaced. The USSR Congress of People's Deputies was forced to dissolve itself, and a new Supreme Soviet was selected by unconstitutional means, with the republics choosing delegates who were responsible to them. At Yeltsin's "categorical" insistence, no new chairman of the USSR Supreme Soviet was selected, only chairmen of the Soviet of the Republic and the Soviet of Nationalities.[6] (Several republics, including Ukraine, refused even to name delegates.) Andrei Grachev, who became Gorbachev's press secretary, says that administratively Gorbachev was interested only in building a presidential staff. Yeltsin's vice president, Aleksandr Rutskoi, was to write contemptuously that "instead of introducing order in the country in September, Gorbachev was working on his book, *The August Putsch: Reasons and Consequences.*[7]

The Committee for Operational Economic Management had little ability to control economic events, and Yegor Gardar is contemptuous of the lack of effort of its top officials.[8] As was planned even before the coup, the industrial ministries were being replaced by ministerial-like institutions— ''holding companies'' and ''stock corporations,'' for example—and related banks. The situation in the automobile and agricultural machinery industry was typical. The Ministry of the Automobile and Agricultural Machinery Industry was replaced by Avtosel'khozmash-kholding, the Automobile and Agricultural Machinery Holding Company.[9] The counterparts to this holding company in other industries had various designations. Some—for example, that for the rocket industry ("general machine building")—were holding companies. The Ministry of the Electrotechnical Industry became an "interrepublican stock corporation," while the Petrochemical Industry

6. Vadim Medvedev, *V komande Gorbacheva: Vzgliad iznutri* (Moscow: Bylina, 1994), p. 206.

7. Andrei Grachev, *Kremlevskaia khronika* (Moscow: EKSMO, 1994), p. 169; and Aleksandr Rutskoi, *O nas i o sebe* (Moscow: Nauchnaia kniga, 1995), p. 165. In English, Gorbachev's book is *The August Coup: The Truth and the Lessons* (Harper Collins, 1991).

8. Yegor Goidar, *Dni porazhenii i pobed* (Moscow: Vagrius, 1996), p. 142.

9. *Pravitel'stvennyi vestnik*, no. 39 (September 1991), p. 2.

and the Machine Tool Industry each became an "interrepublican stock company."

In the few instances in which the internal structures of these new institutions were revealed, they looked familiar. Roschermet (the Russian ferrous metallurgy industry), Spetsstal (special steel industry), Truboprom (steel tube industry), and so forth were names that had long been given to the administrative subdivisions (*glavki*) of the old Ministry of Ferrous Metallurgy.[10] The former minister remained head of the new corporation.

At the beginning of 1990 the Gorbachev government had started to create branch "commercial banks." These corresponded in scope to the old industrial ministries, and indeed they were stock societies that were ostensibly formed by the plants of the various ministries. In early 1990 the new Bank for the Development of the Automobile Industry of the USSR (Avtobank) was described both as a stock society whose stockholders were almost all enterprises of the automobile and agricultural machinery branch and as "a component part of the state apparatus." The mission of the branch banks was to perform the short-term banking functions for the branch, but (as their name implied) they were also to provide long-term investment in their own plants and their suppliers.[11]

The new holding companies were formally private—"'private wholesale trading firms'' they were later called. Therefore they could and did include the former enterprises of a given ministry in the non-Russian Union republics even after the breakup of the Soviet Union. The Automobile and Agricultural Holding Company, I learned in an interview in October 1992, was staffed by five hundred people who acquired supplies and then sold them to their plant for a 5 to 6 percent commission, a pattern that seems to have been typical.

The holding companies and banks were meant to be closely controlled by the government, at least at first. Abalkin had written in 1991 about the attractiveness of Japanese ideas, and these Soviet banks had the appearance of the quasi-official banks that had been at the heart of the Japanese conglomerates made up of corporations, banks, and MITI, the Japanese Ministry of International Trade and Industry.[12] The new quasi ministries,

10. "Metallurgy Industry Declining in 1991," Interfax, January 6, 1992, 1934 GMT, in Foreign Broadcast Information Service, *Daily Report: Soviet Union*, January 9, 1992, p. 27 (hereafter, FBIS, *Soviet Union*).

11. *Argumenty i fakty*, no. 3, January 20–26, 1990, p. 8.

12. *Der Spiegel*, July 6, 1987, in FBIS, *Soviet Union*, July 10, 1987, pp. S1, S2.

first seen in 1989 in an experiment that created Gazprom (the successor to the Ministry of the Gas Industry), were intended to be the corporate component of this conglomerate.[13] At first, they would essentially be state enterprises, but gradually they would become more autonomous.

Such an evolution of the ministries seemed an intelligent step. What was inexplicable was that they should be subordinated to the Russian government. They were, in fact, interrepublican. If Roschermet included Ukrainian steel plants, if the holding company for the rocket industry included the Ukrainian plants producing the SS-20 rocket and its electronic components (as the director of the plant in Kharkov reported in an interview in November), why should they be "Ros" (Russian)?

Yet it was the Russian government that came to control them in the fall of 1991. In 1992 the Russian Ministry of Industry had departments, often staffed by twenty-five to fifty officials, to correspond to the old ministries. When I visited the Department of the Tractor and Agricultural Industry in 1992, Avtoselkhozkholding turned out to be located on the same floor, four doors away from the office of the department head. Nikolai Pugin, the former minister of the automobile industry, was head of the holding company.

Russian control meant that the taxes of the new entities and the money they generated from sales no longer went to the USSR government. Whatever the theoretical power of the USSR State Council and the Interrepublican Committee for Operational Economic Management, they had no administrative tools to enforce their decrees on these holding companies and banks, and they had no independent financial resources.

Why didn't Gorbachev insist loudly on the creation of a new USSR government that would oversee and tax these semimarketized institutions? It was an argument that not only would have been attractive to conservatives but hard to answer by nationalists outside Russia. Instead, the institutions were practically invisible to the casual observer. Russia was reported to be taking over plants in its territory, not multirepublican holding companies.

The calculations of the so-called conservative bureaucrats, even the industrial ministers, were clear enough. Property was being privatized, and they were going to get their share, regardless of the subordination of the holding companies. The more chaotic the government arrangements, the less the control over the seizure of property there was likely to be. The top officials of the non-Russian republics were in a position similar to those of

13. Leonid Abalkin, *Ne ispol'zovannyi shans: Poltora goda v pravitel'stve* (Moscow: Politizdat, 1991), pp. 65–66.

the USSR, and they had no interest in mentioning that they were often obtaining the appearance of independence in the industrial realm and that their plants were really subordinated to Russian holding companies that were subordinated to the Russian government.

But what was Gorbachev thinking? There is no evidence that he was significantly involved in the decisions to change ministries into holding companies. That was the reform of Leonid Abalkin, Valentin Pavlov, and others like them. These men had been swept away in the previous year, and Gorbachev may never have thought through the implications of the creation of the new Russian holding companies and the arguments he could have used against them in the non-Russian republics.

Surely, however, he understood the broader constitutional changes: the abolition of the Congress, the granting of extraordinary rights of veto over appointments to one republican president instead of a collective body, the gradual Russian takeover of all central institutions. He accepted these without a fight as well, just as he allowed himself to be humiliated at the Russian parliament on August 23. Basically, of course, he simply was continuing the policy of overthrowing the constitutionally established order and abolishing the central government that he had followed since at least April and that had produced the coup. If he had become eager to sign a Union Treaty that bypassed and abolished the Congress and to give Yeltsin control over taxation and the enterprises in early August, why should he reverse his policy a month later after he had less reason to trust USSR officials? Unfortunately, such an explanation only returns us to the mystery of why he had acted as he had in July and August.

Memoirs provide little help in clarifying matters. Gorbachev had told Cherniaev on the eve of the coup that he was hellishly tired, and he reports in his memoirs that after the coup he "was devilishly tired."[14] Andrei Grachev, his press spokesman, reported that it took several weeks for Gorbachev to regain his old form.[15] Yet even then he focused his efforts on negotiating a new Union Treaty and receiving a steady stream of foreign dignitaries. Although Gorbachev may not have noticed it, the visitors were primarily coming to meet and size up Yeltsin and fruitlessly to advocate the preservation of the Union.

---

14. Mikhail Gorbachev, *Zhizn' i reformy* (Moscow: Novosti, 1995), vol. 2, p. 587; *Memoirs* (Doubleday, 1996), p. 650.

15. Grachev, *Kremlevskaia khronika*, p. 164.

Gorbachev's memoirs on this period are bland and primarily deal with the Union Treaty and the foreigners. They provide no evidence he was following Yeltsin's moves closely and thinking about how to deal with him. Yeltsin was on vacation in the South and, according to Grachev, Gorbachev persuaded himself that Yeltsin would not take an active role and posed no direct threat. "We have no disagreements with Boris Nikolaevich about the Union," he said.[16]

Radical Muscovites and Westerners echoing their position asserted that the USSR presidency was going to be turned into a ceremonial position such as exists in Germany. They made the point in as offensive a way as they could: Gorbachev was going to be turned into the Queen of England, although their subtext was that he was already playing such a role and was well suited for it by personality. The best explanation for Gorbachev's behavior is that he did not see this as a threat or insult but as the goal he was pursuing. He was willing to concede almost anything to obtain the Union Treaty that would preserve and legitimate the post of USSR president. He seemed to believe that he would still have the key role in foreign policy and in dealing with foreign countries, but no one who knew anything about Yeltsin's history or who was reading the newspapers about the conflicts within the Russian government would have concluded that Yeltsin willingly would have given Gorbachev what he wanted.

Gorbachev may also have been consistent about his old assumptions about the social consequences of price increases. He may have thought Yeltsin's price liberalization would produce such unrest that he, Gorbachev, needed only to be around to pick up the pieces. His press assistant, Grachev, attributed the following statement to him:

Let the ambitions of the republican leaders "burn themselves out." Give them the chance to show themselves in practice. Let them try to do somewhat real. Otherwise they will again put the blame on the center, which, they will say, is only interfering with their ability to act. When they come face-to-face with real problems, then their worth . . . in the eyes of the people will be evident.[17]

The Two Economic Strategies and Russian Independence

From Gorbachev's point of view and from that of Western governments and economic institutions, the most urgent item on the USSR agenda was

---

16. Grachev, *Kremlevskaia khronika*, pp. 169, 170, 174. Gorbachev's memoirs make the same point; *Zhizn' i reformy*, vol. 2, p. 585; *Memoirs*, p. 649.

17. Grachev, *Kremlevskaia khronika*, p. 174.

the creation of "a common economic space," an economic union that would provide a common currency, a central bank, and a common market. If such an economic community were established and the military remained centralized, the Soviet Union would, it was hoped, inevitably come to have a federal system or a strong confederative system.

In early September 1991 the Soviet government began drafting an economic treaty to guide relations among the republics, a task assigned to Grigory Yavlinsky. While visiting British Prime Minister John Major, Yeltsin declared on September 4 that "with certain reservations, we must return to [Yavlinsky's] program" (that is, the old 500-Day Plan).[18] Yavlinsky favored a strong economic union within the boundaries of the former Soviet Union, and when the draft treaty was completed, Yeltsin allowed Deputy Premier Yevgeny Saburov to go to Alma-Ata, Kazakhstan, to initial it, apparently with his blessing. On October 8 Russia and seven other republics formally signed a new economic pact, and on November 6 Ukraine and Moldavia added their signatures as well.

An economist such as Stanislav Shatalin might think a common market was economically inevitable and that it would automatically produce the needed political superstructure. But a political scientist or a politician might think of another possibility: If there was no meaningful USSR government, why should there be a USSR? At the beginning of 1990 almost no one had thought of an independent Russia, but by the end of the year the idea was gaining currency, and by September 1991 it was the subject of open discussion.

It is still not known when the argument favoring an independent Russia crystalized in the Yeltsin camp. By the time of the August 1991 coup, however, two groups of Yeltsin advisers, each led by men who came from Yeltsin's home base of Sverdlovsk, had developed sophisticated arguments about the link between successful economic policy and Russian independence and had begun to articulate them.

One group was based on followers who had been lower-level obkom party secretaries when Yeltsin had been obkom first secretary. Led by Oleg Lobov and Yury Petrov, they favored maintaining strong ties with the other republics. Lobov had been a defense industry manager who had moved into the party apparatus and was second secretary in the last year of Yeltsin's tenure in Sverdlovsk. He had served as party second secretary in Armenia

18. *Rossiiskaia gazeta*, September 5, 1991, p. 2.

and was the liberal candidate (in essence the Yeltsin candidate) for first secretary of the Russian Communist party in the summer of 1990. He became first deputy premier of the Russian government, Yeltsin's top representative. Petrov had also risen out of the defense industry into party work and had served as an obkom party secretary from 1977 to 1982 before being brought into the Central Committee apparatus. He returned to Sverdlovsk as obkom first secretary to replace Yeltsin in 1985. When Yeltsin fell out with Gorbachev in late 1987, Petrov was exiled to Havana as ambassador to Cuba. In 1991 Yeltsin appointed him head of the presidential administration, a position comparable to chief of the White House staff in U.S. administrations.

The Lobov-Petrov group of advisers included the top economic officials in the Russian Council of Ministers: Yevgeny Saburov, deputy premier and minister of economy; Igor T. Gavrilov, deputy premier for the environment; Mikhail Bocharov, head of the Supreme Council on Economic Reform and founder of Democratic Russia; and Gennady V. Kulik, minister of agriculture. They drew in former Deputy Premier Grigory Yavlinsky to draft an economic program and were supported by Premier Ivan Silaev.

The second group of Yeltsin advisers was led by Gennady Burbulis, who had been chairman of the Scientific Communism Department at the Urals Polytechnical Institute in Sverdlovsk before entering politics as a victorious candidate in the 1989 USSR elections. Burbulis did not meet Yeltsin until 1989, but became acquainted with him in Moscow in the USSR Congress of People's Deputies and soon became one of his chief political advisers.[19] He served as Yeltsin's liaison in the USSR parliament when Yeltsin moved into the Russian political arena and served as Yeltsin's campaign manager in the 1991 presidential campaign. After becoming president, Yeltsin had created a new State Council that he seemed to envisage as a kind of policymaking Politburo; he appointed Burbulis to head it as state secretary.

Burbulis's chief allies came from the democratic camp and included a large number of the heads of the more political ministries—Foreign Affairs, Internal Affairs, Justice, and Labor—as well as Mikhail Malei, the deputy premier for administering state property. This group did not, however, have much economic expertise, and because the political battle was going to be fought out on the issue of economic reform, Burbulis needed credible advisers. He allied himself with a team of young economists led by Yegor

19. On their first meeting, see *Komsomol'skaia pravda*, January 21, 1992.

Gaidar and Aleksandr Shokhin, both of whom had long been associated with Stanislav Shatalin, and soon placed them in dacha 15 in suburban Arkhangelskoe to draft an economic plan.[20]

Yegor Gaidar was born in 1956 in Moscow in one of the elite families of Moscow, the son of a rear admiral and the grandson and great-grandson of famous writers. In the late 1970s he wrote his dissertation on upper government policymaking under Shatalin's supervision. He became the head of a laboratory in Shatalin's Economics Department in the Institute of Systems Research, an institute that was headed by Prime Minister Aleksei Kosygin's son-in-law and that worked closely with the most elite officials.

In the Gorbachev years Gaidar became a frequent contributor to the Central Committee journal, *Kommunist*, and in 1987 was named the head of its Political Economy and Economic Policy Department by its chief editor, Ivan Frolov.[21] He continued to work with Shatalin during these years and moved with him to the Institute of Economic Forecasting, again as head of a laboratory. When Frolov became chief editor of *Pravda*, the leading newspaper of the Communist party, Gaidar followed him and became economics editor. In this capacity he served on the commission drafting the 500-Day Plan. He left in December 1990 to found his own Institute of Economic Policy. In October 1991 a journalist wondered with awe at how Gaidar had been transformed from one of "the most cautious and politically 'delicate' analysts" into the leader of the most radical economic and political elements in a "struggle of titans in the Russian leadership."[22]

Gaidar's closest associate was Aleksandr Shokhin, born in 1951, who also worked as the head of a laboratory in Shatalin's institute, but whose specialization was social policy.[23] In 1988, when Foreign Minister Eduard Shevardnadze was looking for an assistant to help him on Politburo duties associated with domestic policy questions, Shokhin was selected. When Shevardnadze resigned in December 1990, his last official decree was to appoint Shokhin as head of the Foreign Economic Administration of the

20. *Rossiiskie vesti*, no. 31, December 14, 1991, p. 8.
21. For the post see *Kommunist*, no. 10 (July 1987), p. 87. For Gaidar's life before 1989, see *Dni porazhenii i probed*, pp. 11–48.
22. *Nezavisimaia gazeta*, October 9, 1991, p. 1.
23. Gaidar's relations with Shokhin were, Shokhin has reported, destroyed in December 1992, presumably because Shokhin decided to stay in the government when Gaidar was forced out. "Shokhin Discusses Reforms, New Appointments," Moscow Television, February 1, 1994, 1953 GMT, in FBIS, *Soviet Union*, February 3, 1994, p. 29.

Ministry of Foreign Affairs. At the same time Shokhin was offered the post of minister of labor and social questions in the Russian government. He refused the first time, but in the summer of 1991 he accepted.

To a large extent the policy prescriptions of the Burbulis-Gaidar group were the standard monetarist package of the International Monetary Fund: liberalize prices, conduct a free trade policy, control inflation through a tight money policy, privatize and reduce the role of government. If these policies were followed, it was assumed, private economic actors would take the steps necessary to improve the economy.

Gaidar's plan was a variant of the Polish shock treatment (indeed, Jeffrey Sachs, who sponsored the Polish treatment, was a close and vociferous supporter of Gaidar), and its goal was a major reduction in the size of the bloated and inefficient state industrial sector. Immediate introduction of market prices (price liberalization) would force managers to adjust quickly, dismiss surplus labor, and produce goods attractive to the market.

Privately, both proponents and opponents of the policy acknowledged that its effect and its intention were deindustrialization. The huge state heavy industries, especially the defense industry, would be drastically reduced in size, and with nowhere else to go, the redundant work force would stream into the understaffed services sector. Shokhin commented that 30 percent of the Italian work force was employed in small enterprises and service jobs, implying that Russia's unemployment problem would be easy to solve because it lacked a service sector.

Gaidar and his associates believed that the manufacturing sector other than the defense industry was thoroughly noncompetitive in the world market. And to rely on arms sales seemed incompatible with the close relationship with the West that would be required to open the economy to the outside world. For these reasons they turned to the export of petroleum, natural gas, and raw materials as the only source of the hard currency that was needed to buy the equipment to modernize industry. Domestic market prices for these raw materials, especially petroleum, were necessary to minimize their wasteful use inside the Soviet Union as well as increase the incentives for their production.

Opponents found Gaidar and his followers unbearably arrogant. In public at least they tolerated no criticism, and they would not acknowledge the legitimacy of compromise. They had the right answers. In November 1991 Andrei Nechaev, also a former head of a laboratory in the Central Mathematical Institute who became first deputy minister of economics and finances (the de facto minister of economics), emphasized the importance of their group's being a team and having the proven answers of economic theory and practice.[24]

Nechaev reported that Burbulis originally intended "to put old cadres of the type of Malei in charge of the economy and give us the ministries [to head]." (Mikhail Malei was fifty years old and in September had been identified by the economist Yevgeny Yasin as one of two members of the Russian government who were too radical to talk with rationally.)[25] Burbulis insisted that he and his followers be put in full charge of the economy or they would not serve in the government at all: "We said, 'Do the reform yourselves. If those people know how to do it, let them do it.' 'In the end,' Nechaev said, our "putsch" was successful.'"[26] Yeltsin commented in his memoirs that he valued the self-confidence of Gaidar because he wanted to be free to focus on immediate political strategy and tactics.[27]

Meanwhile, the Lobov-Petrov group argued that Russia could not, as they put it, be Kuwaitized—it could not rely exclusively on the production and export of petroleum and raw materials. Russia had a sophisticated manufacturing sector with a highly trained labor force. Manufacturing might be inefficient, but this meant only that it needed to be protected and eased into the world market slowly. Like the Pacific Rim countries of recent decades, they said, Russia should begin exporting lower-quality products at low prices to subject manufacturers to foreign competition and give them incentives to improve quality.

In the second half of the 1980s former premier Nikolai Ryzhkov from Sverdlovsk had supported more market-oriented prices than Gorbachev was willing to tolerate, and the Lobov group of industrialists from Sverdlovsk Region was even less afraid of movement toward market prices. Big business knew that it often had a monopoly in the production of goods and that it could survive and thrive in an inflationary environment. The industrialists, however, wanted price controls to keep inflation, and especially price increases of monopolistic producers, within limits. At a time when the exchange rate bore no relationship to real value, they believed that

24. *Rossiiskie vesti*, no. 27, November 16, 1991, p. 3.
25. *Rossiiskaia gazeta*, September 27, 1991, p. 2.
26. *Rossiiskie vesti*, no. 27, November 16, 1991, p. 3. Aleksei Golovkov, Burbulis's chief assistant, later confirmed that everyone in the group—presumably including Burbulis—agreed that the members would be appointed on an all-or-nothing basis.
27. Boris Yeltsin, *The Struggle for Russia* (Time Books, 1994), p. 151.

freeing the prices of petroleum and other commodities would have a disastrous impact on the manufacturing sector.

The policy of the industrialists reflected the classic argument in favor of infant industries, although the Soviet industrialists were infants only as competitors in the world market. Because, it was said, Soviet industry was technologically more backward, it needed protection until it could compete at world levels. Like Count Sergei Witte, who engineered the Russian industrialization drive of the 1890s, Lobov and his associates welcomed large-scale foreign investment.[28] Indeed, this was their answer to the need for the capital that Gaidar sought in commodities sales. They also believed that the investment would be facilitated by high tariff walls that would protect foreign as well as domestic producers from foreign competition. Anyone who has talked seriously with American corporations will recognize that this often is, indeed, a real consideration in investors' calculations. The argument could be supported by references to the successes of the Chinese model of reform, the importance of the manufacturing sector for anchoring Russian power, and the political instability that a shock treatment would produce.

The conflict between the two groups of Yeltsin's advisers was expressed in macroeconomic terms, but it had the most profound implications for Russia's relations with the non-Russian Soviet republics. The tightly integrated character of the Soviet economy meant that the Lobov-Petrov position depended on the continued existence of the Union—certainly "a common economic space." The monopoly suppliers of components were spread throughout the Soviet Union, and economic collapse in the non-Russian republics was certain to be reflected in the health of the manufacturing sector in Russia.

Yevgeny Yasin, one of the leading economists associated with the group, declared that when the Soviet Union introduced world prices into trade with Eastern Europe, trade volume dropped 30 percent. He expected worse in the tightly integrated Soviet Union. He estimated a 20 percent drop in the volume of production in 1991 and a further 10 to 15 percent in 1992. A dissolution of the Soviet Union, he thought, would produce an additional 20 percent decrease. "That is virtually a catastrophe."[29] Yasin was to be

28. Evelyn Davidheiser, "The World Economy and Mobilizational Dictatorship: Russia's Transition, 1846–1917," Ph.D. dissertation, Duke University, 1990.

29. *Rossiiskaia gazeta*, September 27, 1991, p. 2.

minister of economy in the mid-1990s when the economic decline reached 50 percent from the 1990 level.

The proponents of this position within the Yeltsin government were often deeply offended at the low prices that the non-Russian republics paid for such products as petroleum, all the more so because of the republics' complaints about Russian exploitation.[30] However, they believed that the introduction of market prices for petroleum and other Russian raw materials would have a disastrous impact on industry in the non-Russian republics because of their total dependence on Russia for these products. They did not want the mass closing of non-Russian factories because their components were needed in Russia.

In contrast, the Burbulis-Gaidar economic policy implied that the Union was unnecessary. If Russian exportation of petroleum, natural gas, and raw materials was to be at the core of economic strategy, selling these products to the non-Russian republics at subsidized prices was prohibitively costly and should be ended. If it was desirable to subject the manufacturing sector to harsh market forces quickly, it might not matter so much if the planned economic ties between the republics were broken. Thus a policy of full independence of Russia from the other republics coincided with the Gaidar group's optimal economic policy. Indeed, when Gaidar was appointed first deputy premier in October, the *Financial Times* emphasized his "uncompromising views" on the subject.[31]

Proponents of Gaidar's economic approach bolstered their position with political arguments. Foreign Minister Andrei Kozyrev asserted that the International Monetary Fund had a proven program for helping countries undergoing economic reconstruction, but it had a precondition: "the presence of a government that enjoys popular support and is ready to conduct tough reform, including unpopular measures at first." Such a government,

---

30. See, for example, Saburov's complaint that "Russia cannot act forever as a dairy cow." *Komsomol'skaia Pravda*, August 30, 1991, p. 2. Vice President Aleksandr Rutskoi used the same phrase and was particularly annoyed that other republics would import Russian oil at subsidized ruble prices and then export it (perhaps refined) at world market prices for hard currency. See his interview in "Rutskoi: Russia's 'Big Brother' Role Is Over," *Le Figaro*, September 14–15, 1991, p. 3, in FBIS, *Soviet Union*, September 19, 1991, p. 54; and "Rutskoi Interviewed on Fate of Russia," Moscow Television, October 1, 1991, 2120 GMT, in FBIS, *Soviet Union*, October 3, 1991, p. 46.

31. John Lloyd, "Russian Republic Must Take Responsibility for the Soviet Debt," *Financial Times*, November 4, 1991, p. 4.

Kozyrev said, could be formed in Russia only under Boris Yeltsin.[32] Others insisted that Russia could conduct thoroughgoing economic reform only if it did so alone because many of the other republics were so conservative that they would hold Russia back.[33] A group of young economists who were to become the core of the Gaidar government argued that Russia had no real choice in any case. The other republics, they said, would not carry out decrees of any new superrepublican agencies any better than they carried out those of the old agencies.[34]

Because the differing macroeconomic policies had such profound consequences for the structure of political power, the character of the country, and Russian national identity, it is difficult to judge whether the proponents of either position accepted the implications for the Union because of their acceptance of a particular economic strategy or whether they adopted an economic strategy because of its implications for the Union.

The latter suspicion is especially strong of the Burbulis-Gaidar team, and particularly Burbulis. First, Burbulis had little economic expertise; for him, an economic program was effective insofar as it served political purposes. Second, he had long been one of Yeltsin's advisers in the fight with Gorbachev over the Union Treaty. His goal had been the political and economic independence of Russia, and he came to the conclusion that it should be achieved through the liquidation of the USSR. In choosing his economic advisers, he considered willingness to accept the breakup of the Soviet Union a primary criterion for inclusion. They were instructed "to work out options for action on the supposition that a commonwealth will not be created."[35]

The Victory of the Burbulis-Gaidar Position

The great drama after the failed August coup took place in the Russian government as contending camps fought for Yeltsin's ear. The battle spilled over into the press and was fought out on the economic issues discussed in the previous section. Beneath the surface, however, the future of the Union was the real issue.

32. *Nezavisimaia gazeta*, October 12, 1991, p. 2.
33. *Izvestiia*, September 25, 1991, pp. 1–2.
34. *Nezavisimaia gazeta*, September 28, 1991, p. 4.
35. *Nezavisimaia gazeta*, January 22, 1992, p. 1.

Moscow was tense in September and October 1991, but the drama may well have been a play whose ending had already been written. If Gorbachev had resigned in September as USSR president, the Union would almost surely have been saved, for a Yeltsin who became president of the Soviet Union would have strived to save it. Otherwise, however, Yeltsin had little hope of replacing Gorbachev as USSR president until 1995 because he did not have the support of the military for an anti-Gorbachev coup. Meanwhile, Gorbachev's September constitutional reforms gave Russia little power within Union organs. Yeltsin's temptation to get rid of Gorbachev by abolishing his job must have been irresistible from the beginning.

But if the ending of the play was foreordained before late September, many actors did not know it. According to Yury Petrov, who worked with Yeltsin for more than fifteen years, Yeltsin had a decisionmaking style that involved little give-and-take discussion with his subordinates. Instead, he listened carefully to everyone, mulled over their suggestions, made his decision, and then announced it. As a result, even his closest associates might not understand, except through inference, his thought processes. His decisions could come as a surprise.[36]

Certainly one thing was clear. Yeltsin had provoked the August coup by starting to take over all economic enterprises in Russia and by denying the central government the right to collect taxes. He was unlikely to reverse himself on these actions, and the Russian Supreme Soviet strongly supported him. Even when hopes for an interrepublican economic agreement remained high, the Russian Supreme Soviet under Yeltsin's ally, Ruslan Khasbulatov, passed a law declaring that the decisions of any interrepublican agency would only have the force of recommendations for Russia.[37]

The nature of Yeltsin's thinking quickly became evident by late September. When in August Russian Premier Ivan Silaev moved to the USSR Interrepublican Committee for Operational Administration of the Economy in addition to heading the Russian government, he wrote Yeltsin a letter questioning the transfer of institutions, such as the news agency, Novosti, from all-Union to Russian control and insisted that the decisions of the

---

36. These observations were made by Yury Petrov in seminars on April 25, 1993, at Duke University. In an interview Burbulis said that he talked more intimately with Yeltsin, but in his memoirs Yeltsin indicated that this was one of Burbulis's characteristics that strongly irritated him.

37. *Rossiiskaia gazeta*, October 15, 1991, p. 1.

committee be obligatory for all republics. He received a devastating response. At the Russian Council of Ministers meeting of September 24, Deputy Premier Mikhail Malei read Silaev's letter and criticized the premier severely. The reaction of the ministers on the Council of Ministers showed that the "liquidationist" position had "far more" support in the cabinet than the integrationist one.[38] On September 26 Yeltsin's press and information minister also criticized Silaev in an interview in the Russian government's newspaper and did not object when the interviewer characterized the premier as a new Pavlov. The next day Silaev resigned as premier.[39]

Yeltsin had dropped out of sight on September 18, first allegedly for health reasons and then for his official vacation, leaving none of the economic or jurisdictional issues resolved. With the conflict between the Burbulis-Gaidar and the Lobov-Petrov groups continuing, as a Soviet paper expressed it, to be a "primitive struggle," the tension became unbearable.[40]

Yeltsin himself acted in ways that increased the uncertainty. A conference was scheduled for October 1 in Alma-Ata, Kazakhstan, to sign the agreement he had been advocating to establish an economic union among the republics. At the last moment he decided not to join the other presidents there, sending his economics minister, Saburov, instead. But he told Kazakhstan President Nursultan Nazarbaev that Saburov was authorized to sign for Russia. The agreement was duly signed, but the next day the Russian Council of Ministers officially declared that the government had not authorized Saburov to sign and that his signature was therefore null. Because, as first deputy premier, Lobov was the highest official in the Council of Ministers and was supported by virtually all the top economic officials in the government, the decision was "like thunder in a clear sky." Burbulis's supporters on the council had outvoted the economic ministers in a meeting marked by shouting and high emotion.[41]

It was hard to believe Yeltsin disagreed with the outcome. Burbulis had become much more open in supporting the breakup of the Soviet Union. In early September he had pointedly refused to answer a question about his

38. The phrase is that of the *Izvestiia* government correspondent. See *Izvestiia*, September 26, 1991, pp. 1–2; and *Sovetskaia Rossiia*, September 25, 1991, p. 1.

39. *Rossiiskaia gazeta*, September 26, 1991, p. 1; and *Izvestiia*, September 28, 1991, p. 1.

40. *Komsomol'skaia pravda*, October 11, 1991, p. 1.

41. The best reporting of developments at this time is found in *Nezavisimaia gazeta*. See especially October 5, 1991, p. 1; and October 10, 1991, p. 1.

image of Russia a year hence. On October 2 he talked about Russia's being the legal successor to the Soviet Union. On October 8 he met with a group of Russian deputies and baldly asserted that "Russia should declare its independence and proclaim itself the successor state of the former Soviet Union."[42] During this time, Burbulis had flown to see the vacationing Yeltsin for "short consultations."[43] Indeed, in his memoirs Yeltsin commented that both Burbulis and Silaev had visited him in Sochi and that he had made his final decision in favor of Burbulis in September.[44]

The decision was almost surely made by the time of Silaev's resignation on September 27. Already on September 20, Minister of Labor Aleksandr Shokhin had come to the airport to meet Anders Aslund, the scholar of Soviet affairs. He told Aslund that Russia would be independent, named the important members of the new government, and agreed to accept the help of the economist Jeffrey Sachs and his associates once the Russians were in office.[45] Shokhin may have been bluffing about the certainty of his victory, but other officials soon acted as if they too were certain about the outcome. On September 30 Mikhail Bocharov, Yeltsin's candidate for premier in 1990 and chairman of the Council for Economic Reform, resigned, complaining that none of the council's ideas was being accepted.[46] On October 8 Igor Gavrilov, the deputy premier for the environment, resigned. The next day Saburov followed.

Nevertheless, when Yeltsin returned to Moscow on October 10, he behaved as if he might support Lobov and Petrov's advocacy of economic union. He had a five-hour meeting with Gorbachev and the leaders of nine other republics on October 11 and called for an agreement that would guarantee the " common economic space."[47] A week later he signed such an agreement. The major Western newspapers did not mention Yegor Gaidar, but concentrated attention on Yavlinsky, who preferred an economic union.

When the financial ministers of the G-7 countries met in Bangkok in mid-October to discuss the issue, U.S. Secretary of the Treasury Nicholas Brady said that an interrepublican economic agreement was a condition for

---

42. *Rossiiskaia gazeta*, October 9, 1991, p. 1.
43. *Rossiiskaia gazeta*, October 10, 1991, p. 1.
44. Yeltsin, *Struggle for Russia*, pp. 151–52. Burbulis confirmed this in an interview with the author in March 1995.
45. Anders Aslund, *How Russia Became a Market Economy* (Brookings, 1995), p. 17.
46. *Pravda*, October 2, 1991, p. 2.
47. *Izvestiia*, October 12, 1991, p. 1.

substantial Western aid.[48] This position must previously have been made privately. The West was concerned about the repayment of the Soviet debt if the USSR disintegrated or its economic performance worsened, or both. As was often the case from 1992 to 1994, "the whole spectacle," as a Russian television commentator stated, "was conceived to show rich but incredulous foreigners that a new community exists, that the situation is under control, and that it is time for the West to help."[49] (No doubt Yeltsin was also trying to keep the situation ambiguous for Gorbachev and the military as long as possible.) The American ambassador was not fooled: he noted that Russia was against a common ruble zone, while Ukraine was against a coordinated budget.[50]

If there were any doubts as to whether Burbulis essentially spoke for Yeltsin, however, they did not last long. On October 15 Yeltsin gave a television interview in which he called for a radical economic reform based on the liberalization of prices. He pledged "to complete the destruction of the center" by cutting off payment to all central ministries performing functions that he did not consider necessary.[51] On October 28 he proclaimed before the Fifth Russian Congress of People's Deputies his intention to conduct radical reform "decisively and without wavering." He spoke not only about a liberalization of prices, but "free prices": "a one-time transition to market prices—a difficult, forced, but necessary measure."[52] He pledged rapid privatization (at least of small-scale enterprises in services, trade, and industry, where 50 percent were to be privatized in six months) together with a tight money policy and a sharp reduction in government expenditures. He claimed that after six months of inflation and a decline in living standards, prices would fall and living standards would start to rise.

---

48. See Francis X. Clines, "Soviet Republics Agree to Create an Economic Union," *New York Times*, October 12, 1991, p. A1; James Sterngold, "Group of Seven Edges toward Soviet Debt Relief," *New York Times*, October 13, 1991, p. A12; Sterngold, "Brady Says Social Pact on Union Is the Key to Aid," *New York Times*, October 15, 1991, p. A3; Clines, "Delay in Election Urged by Yeltsin," *New York Times*, October 17, 1991, p. A3; and Clines, "8 Soviet Republics Sign Economic Pact," *New York Times*, October 19, 1991, p. A3, for the sequence of events.

49. Fred Hyatt, "8 Soviet Republics Sign Economic Union Treaty, Many Complex Issues Left for Negotiation," *Washington Post*, October 19, 1991, p. A20.

50. Jack F. Matlock, *Autopsy on an Empire: The American Ambassador's Account of the Collapse of the Soviet Union* (Random House, 1995), pp. 622–23.

51. Michael Dobbs, "Yeltsin Vows to Begin Broad Economic Reform; State Controls on Prices to Be Lifted," *Washington Post*, October 16, 1991, p. A29.

52. *Izvestiia*, October 28, 1991, pp. 1–2.

But if the overt focus of the October 28 speech was radical economic reform, its subtext was the independence of Russia from the Union and the other republics. Yeltsin began by stating that "in practice, we have been living in a new country for two months," and he casually referred to "the sovereign states of the former Union." He accused the other republics of finding Russian fixed prices "superattractive" and taking advantage of them. This situation, he asserted, was to end. "Interrepublican organs can play only a consulting and coordinating role. . . . Russia will proceed from the norms of international law in its relations with the former members of the Union. The economic ties with these states will be based on world prices. Such a policy, first of all, is the way to recognize the real independence of any state. . . . If this process is unsuccessful for any reason, Russia will be able to take responsibility as the successor to the USSR on itself."[53]

Yeltsin talked as if the economic agreements recently reached with the non-Russian republics were as nonexistent as the USSR institutions. He announced that Russia would take control over imports and exports and responsibility for Soviet foreign obligations (the foreign debt) and that it would introduce the free competitive sale of foreign currency. He gave the other republics two weeks to accept an interstate bank for the ruble zone that in effect put Russia in control of their money supply. If they refused— which he clearly expected—the Russian Bank would independently take over production of money.

On November 6—surely not by coincidence the anniversary of the Bolshevik Revolution—Yeltsin announced his new government. It ended all doubt about the outcome, for he stated that he would take over the premiership while remaining president. Burbulis became the first deputy premier, in effect the real premier. The idea of Yeltsin's officially serving as premier was Burbulis's and was motivated, Yeltsin later said, by the desire to circumvent the need to have Burbulis confirmed by the Congress if he were premier.[54] Yegor Gaidar became a deputy prime minister, not only overseeing all the ministries in the economic sphere, but serving directly as the minister for the economy and finances. It was the first time in Russian history that these ministries were combined. Shokhin became the deputy premier in charge of social policy, including education and health.

53. *Izvestiia*, October 28, 1991, pp. 1–2.
54. Yeltsin, *Struggle for Russia*, p. 157.

Professionals were chosen for the more technical ministerial portfolios, but many sensitive posts were given to young associates of Gaidar. Abalkin noted with pride in his memoirs how "green" and young the Gorbachev-Ryzhkov government of 1989 was when it averaged fifty-five years of age.[55] Yeltsin, following Stalin's practice in the late 1930s, went to a qualitatively younger generation. Burbulis and the first three deputy premiers (Gaidar, Shokhin, and Sergei Shakhrai) were scholars who averaged thirty-nine years of age and had no high-level administrative experience. The ministers in charge of the fuel and energy, industry, agriculture, state property, foreign economic relations, justice, and foreign affairs averaged thirty-nine years old at the end of 1991 (that is, they were born in 1952 on average).[56] The Gaidar group saw itself as a team and insisted on full responsibility. It took over many of the important posts of deputy ministers.

Dilemmas of the Democrats about Democracy

Yeltsin's confrontation with the Union seemed certain to reignite his conflict with the Russian Congress. At the time the presidency was created in May, he had reached a gentlemen's agreement with the legislative leaders that he would consult with them when he planned a decree that seemed outside the law. Although his decrees taking power from the central government after the coup had virtually no legal basis, he did little such consulting.[57] He did not even make an effort to be tactful. When the Russian Supreme Soviet reconvened on September 19, he suddenly canceled his scheduled speech, claiming illness. Because no medical report was issued and he soon traveled to the Nagorno-Karabakh Region in Azerbaidzhan, it was widely assumed that his illness was political and was designed to demonstrate his independence from the legislature.

Nevertheless, the Supreme Soviet did little to try to restrain Yeltsin's attack on the central government. Almost all its leaders who had opposed Yeltsin in February had been removed.[58] When Ruslan Khasbulatov was elected chairman of the Supreme Soviet in October, there were signs

55. Abalkin, *Ne ispol'zovannyi shans*, p. 27.
56. Their biographies are in *Kto est' kto v Rossii i v blizhnem zarubezh'e* (Moscow: Novoe vremia, 1993).
57. *Nezavisimaia gazeta*, November 23, 1991, p. 1.
58. For Svetlana Goriacheva's bitter description of how she was treated, see *Izvestiia*, November 20, 1991, p. 2.

Yeltsin wanted a stronger supporter, but in late November, Khasbulatov was still called "Boris Yeltsin's most consistent supporter."[59]

Some of the most severe strains in the legislature were occurring in the democratic camp. One cause was simply generational. Most of those who had been leading the fight for democratization and economic reform through the 1980s were in their fifties and sixties. But Yeltsin was selecting men in their thirties and forties who were not old enough to have had a significant role in the events of the 1980s. This inevitably produced resentment among the older men.

In addition, Democratic Russia had always been an uneasy alliance of radicals and moderates, and their conflicts were intensified by the collapse of communism in August, as the faction's three cochairmen were frank to acknowledge in October. "We were united," Yury Afanasev said, "by the active rejection of the totalitarian system with the undivided power of the CPSU and the KGB, MVD, and army that stand guard over its interests. That is, the activity of 'Democratic Russia' until the August events was primarily of a destructive nature. If that word frightens you I have put it another way: dismantling." Another cochairman, Gleb Yakunin, then added that the differences "appeared only when a positive program was required."[60]

In particular, the democratic parliamentary leaders found themselves in a very ambiguous position on two fundamental questions: the relation of political and economic reform and the relation of democracy and the power of the democrats themselves. The democrats wanted rapid introduction of the Western political and economic system. But a Western political system that gives citizens the right to vote also gives them the right to reject painful economic reform. Public opinion polls showed just 15 to 20 percent popular support for radical economic reform, and the radical party, Russia's Choice, was to receive only 15 percent of the vote in the December 1993 election. A truly democratic system was not likely to produce majority support for those who wanted immediate market reform, let alone for the urban intellectual radicals.

---

59. *Nezavisimaia gazeta*, November 27, 1991, p. 3.

60. *Izvestiia*, October 7, 1991, p. 2. At the Fifth Congress Afanasev was one of the most adamant critics of the compromises that the democratic deputies had been making with "the representatives of the partocracy." *Piatyi (vneocherednoi) s''ezd narodnykh deputatov RSFSR (10–17 iulia, 28 oktiabria–2 noiabria, 1991 goda): Stenograficheskii otchet*, vol. 1 (Moscow: Respublika, 1992), pp. 310–11.

What was the solution to this dilemma? "If Democratic Russia is a political organization," its cochairman Lev Ponomarev said, "then naturally it has the right to claim that its representatives possess power." Another cochairman, Gleb Yakunin, was frank in asserting that "I am prepared to close my eyes to the excessive strengthening of executive power. . . . If we have taken power, we must implement it, even by tough methods, for the benefit of society." However, the third cochairman, Yury Afanasev, objected strenuously: "Gleb Pavlovich, that leads straight to Bolshevism."[61]

The first signs of this conflict in the democratic camp had become visible even before the August coup attempt. Yeltsin's election as president required the election of a new chairman of the Supreme Soviet, and it was assumed that his loyal first deputy chairman, Ruslan Khasbulatov, would be named as his successor at the Fifth Congress of People's Deputies in mid-July. However, Democratic Russia unexpectedly split on this succession.[62] The organization nominated Khasbulatov, but other democratic factions nominated two other candidates and a fourth democrat nominated himself. Khasbulatov received 342 votes against 435 for the moderate conservative candidate, Sergei N. Baburin. Sergei M. Shakhrai received 124 votes, Vladimir P. Lukin 71, and Nikolai M. Arzhannikov 4.[63]

The election rules required a runoff between the top two candidates. If Khasbulatov had picked up all 199 votes that had gone to the other democrats in the first round, he would have had 10 more (541) than required to win. In fact, however, Baburin gained 50 votes on the second round to receive 485 votes and Khasbulatov added only 45 votes to reach 387. In subsequent ballots, Baburin's support eroded to 460, but Khasbulatov's total never rose above 414.[64] Because the deputies voted for Supreme Soviet chairman by secret ballot, the voting patterns are uncertain. But 984 deputies cast a ballot in the first round, while subsequent totals were more than 150 short of this. All observers agreed that radical democrats were refusing to vote for Khasbulatov, mostly by not voting, even though they were in the hall.[65]

61. *Izvestiia*, October 7, 1991, p. 7.
62. For the surprise this gave Khasbulatov's conservative opponents, see *Sovetskaia Rossiia*, July 23, 1991, p. 2.
63. *Piatyi s''ezd*, vol. 1, pp. 204–05.
64. *Piatyi s''ezd*, vol. 1, pp. 229–30.
65. In particular, see *Sovetskaia Rossiia*, July 18, 1991, p. 1.

The major division within Democratic Russia was between deputies led by Khasbulatov and those led by Shakhrai.[66] Shakhrai was a strong supporter of Yeltsin and quickly became the president's legal adviser and later his deputy premier in charge of the security agencies. He often advocated a powerful executive in Moscow as a protection of the integrity of Russia. Khasbulatov, by contrast, was a Chechen supported by the autonomous republics.[67] It was not difficult to predict that any effort by Yeltsin to strengthen the hand of Moscow vis-à-vis the regions would push Khasbulatov into opposition. The radical democrats' behavior suggested that they expected Yeltsin to try to increase the influence of Moscow.

A leader of the moderate conservative faction, Rossiia, accused the radical democrats of being cynical and undemocratic.

> We don't believe that the Congress is in such a blind alley that it cannot elect the chairman of the Supreme Soviet. But we see how certain forces push us to this. In the first months of the Russian presidency, some find it useful to have a Congress that is compromised with the voters, a weakened Supreme Soviet, and no Constitutional Court at all. . . .
>
> [Neither] Baburin nor Khasbulatov are proponents of extreme political positions. In fact, each frightens the radicals and the conservatives with their independence and dedication to principle. The *Rossiia* group appeals . . . to Democratic Russia [and other deputies' groups] . . . to form the leadership of the Supreme Soviet on the basis of a great coalition. To allow the work of the present Congress to be wrecked means to give authoritarian forces the possibility of discrediting the representative organs of government and of accusing them of an inability to work together constructively.[68]

Whatever the reason, and opposition from each end of the political spectrum was certainly important, the effort at compromise failed. Eventually the Fifth Congress was adjourned until the autumn and the election of a chairman postponed until then.[69]

In the October session Khasbulatov was easily elected chairman of the Supreme Soviet. On October 3, just after the Russian Council of Ministers repudiated Saburov's signature on the Alma-Ata agreement, Khasbulatov

66. TASS, July 17, 1991, in FBIS, *Soviet Union*, July 18, 1991, pp. 76–77. Also see *Sovetskaia Rossiia*, July 23, 1991, p. 2.

67. Some rural agrarniki apparently voted against Khasbulatov on principle because he was a Chechen, believing that the chairman of the Supreme Soviet should be an ethnic Russian. *Rossiiskaia gazeta*, July 16, 1991, p. 1.

68. *Piatyi s"ezd*, vol. 1, pp. 307–08.

69. As a result, the Fifth Congress was to meet in two widely spaced sessions, July 10 to 17 and October 28 to November 2.

lashed out at Burbulis and Shakhrai at a press conference and demanded their resignations.[70] This emotional outburst never was explained and remained an isolated event, but it clearly expressed frustration at the course of events. Khasbulatov was later to say that he disagreed with change in the Union Treaty negotiations at Novo-Ogarevo in April and refused to participate (he presumably was expressing the discontent of the former autonomous republics), that he refused to convene an emergency Congress after the August coup to abolish the system of soviets, and that he rejected the idea of dissolving the Soviet Union.[71]

It is likely Khasbulatov's demand for the resignations of Burbulis and Shakhrai was a signal that a repetition of July's conflict over the chairmanship would drive him into opposition to Yeltsin's program. But once Khasbulatov received what he wanted, he was content to sit back and wait, except on matters such as Yeltsin's proposed takeover of the Central Bank. No one could be certain about what would to happen in the conflict between Gorbachev and Yeltsin, and especially about what the military would do. If Yeltsin really was going to have power to enact his economic program, there would be plenty of time to debate its consequences.

The problem of the relationship of democratic reform, economic reform, and the power of the democrats arose in sharp form over the power of Yeltsin to appoint the state governors. When the principle of direct election of the USSR president and then the Russian president was accepted, it was taken for granted that the chief executives of the regions and cities would become elected governors and mayors as well. Immediately after his election as president, Yeltsin won the right to appoint his own representatives in the provinces, but they had little power. In the wake of the coup, however, he also assumed the right to appoint provincial governors (*glava administratsii* or heads of administration) until local elections were held.

On September 6 the Presidium of the Supreme Soviet set November 24 as the date for the elections, but Yeltsin wanted to postpone them for a year and to retain the right of appointing governors that he had assumed in August in the wake of the coup.[72] Instinctively the democrats favored elections. They knew that without them the old regional elite would remain

70. "Khasbulatov Trashes Shakrai, Burbulis at Meeting," TASS, October 3, 1991, in FBIS, *Soviet Union*, October 7, 1991, p. 51.

71. "Khasbulatov Views Collapse of Union, New Ties," *Den'*, no. 35, September 5–11, 1993, pp. 1–2, in FBIS, *Soviet Union*, September 8, 1993, pp. 47–48.

72. *Rossiiskaia gazeta*, September 20, 1991, p. 1.

in place. Yeltsin's authoritarian ways also raised serious concerns. In September a TASS correspondent reported that "many deputies from the democratic camp intend to make a protest at the session against the tendency of executive power to predominate over the legislative power. . . . Viktor Sheinis [told her that] 'a truly serious problem has arisen, though it is a solvable one.'"[73]

Yet the best analysts of Democratic Russia told them what they already suspected: that they would not do well in the provincial elections. It was estimated that the democrats probably would win in twelve regions, were likely to win in ten more, had an outside chance in ten, and virtually no chance in thirty-six.[74] Aleksandr Sobianin and Dmitry Yur'ev, the leading analysts of the Democrats, wrote that they considered new elections "catastrophically dangerous for the fate of Russia" and that this was why the president was so opposed to them.[75]

Thus the democratic movement had a strong political interest in supporting Yeltsin in his desire to appoint regional governors, at least if he appointed the right kind. But Yeltsin often appointed the wrong kind. Except in a few regions whose leaders were utterly discredited by the coup (such as Krasnodar, the home of Russian Communist leader, Ivan Polozkov), Yeltsin usually came to an accommodation with the local soviet and appointed a head of administration acceptable to it. In some areas, such as Novosibirsk and Ul'ianovsk, this was the conservative Communist party first secretary who had been soviet chairman. Yeltsin often tried to satisfy Democratic Russia—and create a system of checks and balances—by appointing a radical out of the Russian parliament as his presidential representative, but the representatives had little power.

The same Fifth Congress that elected Khasbulatov chairman of the Supreme Soviet also passed a decree giving Yeltsin emergency powers for one year. He could appoint regional governors during that period and all ministers. He could essentially introduce by presidential decree whatever economic reforms he wanted. On October 28, when he announced his intention to assume the premiership and introduce radical economic reform, the Congress voted almost unanimously to support him. Even the Communists of Russia voted affirmatively.

73. "Extremely Stormy Atmosphere," TASS, September 19, 1991, in FBIS, *Soviet Union,* September 20, 1991, p. 48.

74. For the decree, see *Rossiiskaia gazeta*, October 10, 1991, p. 1.

75. *Nezavisimaia gazeta*, October 17, 1991, p. 2.

Only once, on November 22, was there a warning that the Congress would not always back Yeltsin when an action involved the relative power of the executive and the parliament. Yeltsin had initiated most of his policy by executive decree. The USSR Central Bank was being taken over, and Yeltsin's decree would have given him control over the bank and, in effect, over the entire financial policy of the republic. This was too much. By a 182-1 vote, the Supreme Soviet suspended the decree.

The thinking of the congressional leaders in October 1991 is hard to analyze, but in retrospect their grant of extraconstitutional powers to Yeltsin was a monumental mistake. The crises of late 1992 and 1993 in the relationship between Yeltsin and the Congress did not, as the president's spokesmen claimed, result from an attempt of the Congress to change the Constitution and usurp the power of the president. When the year passed and the emergency powers expired, Yeltsin treated them as his by right. Instead of accepting a return to the Constitution or accepting a compromise new constitution, he moved toward dissolving the Congress and imposing a constitution that gave him the emergency powers he already had.

Perhaps the congressional leaders believed in the fall of 1991 that if they tried to stand up to Yeltsin, he would dissolve the Congress immediately and call new elections that he could win. Perhaps they still could not really believe that the military would not intervene to save the Union and wanted to strengthen Russia's position in a new federation or confederation so that they themselves would have some power.[76] Perhaps they believed that Yeltsin should be given the chance to take radical steps so he would create such popular opposition that he would be easy to handle. Perhaps they simply were so uncertain and confused by the rapid pace of events that they lacked ideas about what else to do. Perhaps they were afraid of any solution involving negotiation with the military or were in such despair about Gorbachev that they thought anything else would be better.

If the majority in the Russian legislature had come together in defense of democracy and the Union at this time and had worked with the forces around Gorbachev, history could have been very different. But the uncertainties for the analysts reflect the confusion in the thinking of the participants as well. All the beliefs mentioned in the previous paragraphs were probably part of the thinking of the legislative leaders. No doubt, each

---

76. At year's end Khasbulatov said, "The characteristic feature of the beginning of the year was that we effectively had no power at all." Moscow Central Television, December 29, 1991, 1300 GMT, in FBIS, *Soviet Union,* January 2, 1992, p. 63.

believed one of them one day and another the next. That is the definition of revolution: old bearings are gone and few people have a sense of what the new ones will be.

The Dissolution of the Soviet Union

In retrospect, the movement of events in the autumn of 1991 seems straightforward. Gorbachev, as has been seen, took no serious step to reestablish the central government, and few countries had such a need for a strong central government if they were to survive. In the wake of the August coup, the Baltic republics took formal steps to establish their independence, and this independence was quickly recognized both by Moscow and the West. Except for Russia, Kazakhstan, and Turkmenistan, other republics followed with their own declarations of independence.

On the surface, little changed from the war of laws that had increasingly featured the Soviet Union for the last two years. Yet now the economy was deteriorating rapidly. Moreover, the disintegration of central power was increasingly accompanied by civil war in the republics. Armenia and Azerbaidzhan had been torn apart for three years by conflict over Nagorno-Karabakh, and the war heated up in the fall of 1991. Serious civil war broke out in Tadzhikistan and Georgia and threatened in Moldavia.

The striking event of the fall of 1991, however, was the relentless takeover of central functions and institutions by the Russian government. The most important, although the least reported in the press at the time, has already been discussed: the replacement of the industrial ministries by "holding companies," "stock corporations," and "stock companies" and their subordination to the Russian rather than the USSR government. This action essentially deprived the central government of its finances and set the stage for its further disintegration.

The industrial ministries were only the first step. On October 26 Yeltsin issued a decree specifying that the USSR Gosplan would have no authority in Russia. Gorbachev countermanded this order but took no action to enforce his veto. On October 28 Yeltsin announced his radical economic reform, which assumed Russia had full control of all economic and financial levers on its territory. On November 17 he issued a series of decrees that gave the Russian government control of all foreign currency and gold and the coinage of money in Russia and the central institutions in Russia.

All these actions flatly contradicted the economic agreement he had signed with Ukraine ten days earlier.

Memoirs are filled with little details about the practical meaning of the collapse of the Soviet Union in the fall of 1991 even before the country was formally dissolved. Those in prison because of participation in the August coup quickly noticed that control of their prison was transferred from the USSR Ministry of Internal Affairs to the Russian Ministry of Internal Affairs and that personnel from the warden to the guards were changed.[77] The USSR Council of Ministers became so impoverished that it began renting government dachas to private businessmen, and ministers found themselves eating in the same dacha dining halls as businessmen—but only able to afford much less expensive meals.[78] Most newspapers refused to publish the communiques about the meetings Gorbachev was having with the major foreign officials visiting him.[79] The man who was appointed USSR ambassador to France in November was also offered the post of Russian ambassador. He accepted, and no one treated the resulting situation as unusual.[80]

When Yeltsin proclaimed in this speech of October 28 that the staff of the USSR Ministry of Foreign Affairs would be reduced by 90 percent, he indicated that his ambitions were not limited to economic sovereignty. Behind the scenes his men were demanding not that secret police functions be decentralized to the republican level, but that the USSR secret police be placed under Russian control, that the sign on the building simply be replaced.[81]

But equally important were the steps Gorbachev did not take. Not only was no effort made to appoint key figures in the central government, but no 1992 budget of any consequence was being drafted. Defense Minister Yevgeny Shaposhnikov reports that in practice no one was really concerned with a military budget for 1992. When he sent documents to the Committee for Operational Economic Management, he received no meaningful response.[82] When eight republics signed an economic treaty on October 18,

77. Nadezhda Garifullina, *Tot, kto ne predal: Oleg Shenin: stranitsy zhizni i bor'by* (Moscow: Vneshtorgizdat, 1995), p. 140.

78. Mikhail Nenashev, *Zalozhnik vremeni: Zametki, razmyshleniia, svidetel'stva* (Moscow: Progress, 1993), p. 8.

79. Cherniaev, *Shest' let s Gorbachevym: po dmevmikovym zapisiam* (Moscow: Progress-Kul'tura, 1993), p. 505.

80. Boris Pankin, *Sto oborvannykh dnei* (Moscow: Sovershenno sekretno, 1993), p. 8.

81. See the discussion by the last chairman of the USSR KGB, Vadim Bakatin, *Izbavlenie ot KGB* (Moscow: Novosti, 1992), pp. 120–21.

82. Evgeny Shaposhnikov, *Vybor*, 2d ed. (Moscow: Nezavisimoe izdatel'svo PIK, 1995), p. 91.

one of the last amendments was removal of the December 31 deadline for producing a budget for 1992.[83] A careful reader might have noted Georgy Yavlinsky's claim in mid-October that the Foreign Economic Bank (Vneshekonombank) would run out of funds in two months and might have reflected that this too pointed to a severe crisis at the end of the year.[84]

Gorbachev kept acting as if the Union Treaty was still a solution to his problems. He talked insistently about "a union (*soiuzynoe*) state," rejecting the concept of "a union of states," but in practice he accepted almost any weakening of the powers of the central government in the Union Treaty that the republics wanted. After insisting on a "union government," he accepted the characterization "democratic confederative state" in the Union Treaty that he was willing to sign in November, even though individual paragraphs had not been agreed upon.[85] As in August, he seemed to think that almost any formal agreement about the Union would be worthwhile, that the imperatives of economic integration would eventually lead to real functions and power accruing to the central government.

Yeltsin continued to say there would be a Union, and Belorussia, Kazakhstan, and most Central Asian states talked as if they were ready to sign. In mid-November, however, *Financial Times* correspondent Chrystia Freeland was reporting that "Ukrainian leaders . . . have a new, irresistible view of themselves as autonomous, respected members of the world community" and were driving for independence. They had, she and Gillian Tett stated frankly, "prevaricated throughout the negotiations on an economic union treaty."[86]

Yet everyone understood that words such as *sovereignty* and *independence* were being used in ill-defined ways. After the Ukrainians voted for independence on December 1, Gorbachev could call President Leonid Kravchuk and say with some justice:

Why are you deciding to interpret independence as obligatory exit from the Union? There are republics which previously declared their independence and

83. Leyla Boulton, "Eight Republics Sign Soviet Treaty," *Financial Times*, October 19, 1991, p. 2.

84. Peter Norman and Stephen Fidler, "G7 Bitterly Divided over How to Handle Soviet Crisis," *Financial Times*, October 15, 1991, p. 8.

85. The treaty to be initialed on November 25 was published in *Pravda*, November 27, 1991. See Medvedev, *V komande Gorbacheva*, pp. 221–22.

86. Chrystia Freeland, "Ukraine Builds Its Independence," *Financial Times*, October 21, 1991, p. 7; and Gillian Gett and Chrystia Freeland, "Ukraine Rejects Treaty on Economic Union," *Financial Times*, October 18, 1991, p. 2.

still participate in the creation of a new Union. It is fully natural that a majority of the people of Ukraine voted for independence. Who wants to vote against it? However, approximately as many people spoke out in March for the preservation of the Union and the participation of Ukraine in it. This means that if the question on independence was asked differently—outside or inside the framework of the Union—the result would have been different.[87]

Everyone also understood that Ukraine could not maintain real independence if Russia meant what it said about charging world prices for its petroleum, natural gas, and raw materials to Ukraine and made acceptance of some kind of federation or confederation a condition for subsidized prices. Ukraine simply could not maintain industrial production if it suddenly had to pay market prices for raw materials and fuel, and it could not maintain the loyalty of the Russian-speaking industrial areas if it rejected the offer of strong confederation in return for subsidized goods.

Yeltsin's actions in forming his government, his persistence in taking over Union functions, and the frank language of his chief adviser, Gennady Burbulis, pointed in the direction of an independent Russia. However, Yeltsin's continual words of reassurance pointed toward maintenance of some type of confederation, and many noted that Canada and Switzerland were confederations. A number of observers, including the chairman of the KGB, Gorbachev's press secretary, and the American ambassador to the Soviet Union, have reported that they were very slow in thinking that the Soviet Union would actually disintegrate.[88] This was the result of Yeltsin's skillful obfuscation.

As November progressed, however, Yeltsin became increasingly insistent. The fourth-quarter USSR budget was covered only by the printing of money. In mid-month he irritably agreed to prolong the life of the USSR Ministry of Finance and Ministry of Economics (the old Gosplan) for two weeks, but no longer.[89] On November 14 the State Council seemed to agree on governmental arrangements for the Union Treaty, and Gorbachev announced that initialing of the treaty would take place on November 25. He brought in live television, but with the nation watching, Yeltsin refused to sign. Gorbachev was publicly humiliated once more and made no effort to hide his disappointment in talking with the press.

87. Grachev, *Kremlevskaia khronika*, p. 323.
88. Grachev, *Kremlevskaia khronika*, p. 274; Bakatin, *Izbavlenie ot KGB*, p. 211; and Matlock, *Autopsy on an Empire*, p. 622.
89. Grachev, *Kremlevskaia khronika*, pp. 293–94; and Gardar, *Dni porazhennii i pobed*, p. 114.

Yeltsin then moved quickly. He cut off the financing of central ministries. The Russian parliament, strongly supporting him in his drive for independence, refused the USSR government's emergency request for 92 billion rubles in tax money. By the end of November the USSR State Bank had no money to pay for central functions, and on November 29 its chairman announced that the country only had money to pay its bills for two or three days. On November 30 Yeltsin and Gorbachev met, and Yeltsin agreed to assume the financial responsibilities of the USSR government. The Russian government took control of the USSR Ministry of Finances, and it also announced it was taking control of the Ministry of Foreign Affairs buildings and embassies "temporarily" so their employees could be paid.

All this was carefully timed. The Ukrainian referendum on independence was scheduled for December 1, and it was widely expected to pass. In practice, nearly 90 percent of those participating in the election voted for independence. Even a majority of those in the Russian eastern and southern areas voted affirmatively. Yeltsin quickly recognized the independence of Ukraine, acting as if Russia were an independent state. The withdrawal of funding from the USSR government meant that the Soviet Union was brought to the brink of default on its international loans at precisely the time Yeltsin wanted to move. This minimized the possibility that the West would object.[90]

On December 7 Yeltsin and the presidents of Ukraine and Belorussia went to Minsk for discussions about the new situation. No official indication was given that this would be a historic meeting, but the lead headline in *Izvestiia*, a newspaper very close to the Yeltsin forces, suggested its editors were not surprised by what was to happen: "On the Eve of the Meeting in Minsk: Will a 'Trilateral Union' be Concluded?[91]

The general intention of the presidents was clear enough, but so too was their nervousness about what they were doing. They were overthrowing the president, the government, and the state more surely than had the organizers of the August coup. The minister of defense and the chairman of the KGB had powerful military forces at their disposal, and they had to consider the possibility that Gorbachev had been deceptively pliant in order to lure them into some illegal action so that he could arrest them.

90. This is emphasized in Serge Schmemann, "The Soviet Shell," *New York Times*, December 2, 1991, p. 10.
91. *Izvestiia*, December 7, 1991, p. 1.

As a result, the presidents did not come to Minsk with a detailed agreement in hand. Indeed, they did not even have a photocopy machine at their meeting place in Belovezh Forest to reproduce the documents for the three of them to sign. Fortunately, they had fax machines, and they copied the required documents by sending them from one machine to another in the same room.[92] Even then the documents were phrased carefully: they did not dissolve the Soviet Union or even state it had ceased to exist. Instead the presidents said that "since the USSR is ceasing to exist" they were forming a new Commonwealth of Independent States. It was a legalistic formulation the presidents hoped to use if they were arrested: they could say they were not overthrowing the state, but were trying to prevent chaos.

The details of the Commonwealth structure were not important. The crucial fact was that the state Gorbachev headed was being dissolved. Yeltsin was to make clear that the Commonwealth would not have a president, a ministry of foreign affairs, or a flag.[93] If the decision was carried out, Gorbachev would be out of a job. Even at the end, however, the Yeltsin regime was not confident. Yeltsin refused to come to the Kremlin after the Minsk meeting, giving the excuse that he might be arrested. It may have been a real reason instead of a pretext.

Both Gorbachev and Yeltsin met with the top military officials, and Arkady Volsky insisted in an interview that the military would have supported Gorbachev even at this stage if he had been willing to impose martial law.[94] Anders Aslund met the members of the Yeltsin government at a reception the evening of December 10, and to his surprise found them very tense. The next morning "the contrast in mood could not have been greater."[95] The military had agreed to support Yeltsin. The Russian Supreme Soviet also was not confident. It issued a declaration of independence only on December 12—after the military had decided. The point was made dramatically when U.S. Secretary of State James Baker came to Moscow. Yeltsin insisted they meet in St. Catherine's Hall in the Kremlin—the place where Gorbachev had met heads of state—and he had the minister of defense sitting at his right hand. Russian Foreign Minister Andrei Kozyrev explained to a reporter that this was a deliberate signal. In the words of *Izvestiia*, "President Yeltsin thus demonstated to Baker and

---

92. Yeltsin, *Struggle for Russia*, p. 112.
93. *Izvestiia*, December 17, 1991, p. 1.
94. Jerry F. Hough, interview with Arkady Volsky, December 28, 1991.
95. Aslund, *How Russia Became a Market Economy*, p. 20.

also to opponents inside the country that he enjoyed the support of the army, in any case its highest leadership."[96]

The Belovezh agreement had been highly offensive to the leaders of the non-Slavic republics that had been excluded from the decision to break up the Soviet Union. The presidents of Kazakhstan and the Central Asian republics met on December 12 and indicated their willingness to join with the Slavic republics. The next week was spent preparing for a meeting on December 21 at Alma-Ata that would bring the presidents of all the republics together to approve the change. All but the Georgian president attended, and they officially declared that the Soviet Union had ceased to exist. They informed Gorbachev that the same was true of the institution of the USSR president. Russia was to be the legal successor of the Soviet Union on such matters as holding the Soviet seat on the Security Council and assuming responsibility for its foreign debts.

This was the decision for which Gorbachev and the world were waiting. Russia occupied the Soviet seat at the United Nations on December 24. Gorbachev agreed to resign at 7:00 p.m. on December 25. But even this process did not go gracefully. He and Yeltsin had agreed that Yeltsin and Defense Minister Shaposhnikov would come to Gorbachev's office to pick up the "nuclear button" immediately at 7:20 p.m. Instead Yeltsin insisted at the last minute that Gorbachev come to a "neutral" spot. When Gorbachev refused, Shaposhnikov picked up the technical apparatus without Yeltsin. Then, although Gorbachev had been told he could retain his office until December 30, he discovered the next day that a scheduled meeting in his office had to be moved because his office had already been cleared out.[97]

The Mystery of the Soviet Military

Thus the actual breakup of the Soviet Union went as smoothly for Yeltsin as the preceding months. Yet there had been strong reasons for the general nervousness. Although the democrats and the moderates in the Congress generally supported Yeltsin's decrees and even his authoritarian

96. *Izvestiia*, December 16, 1991, p. 1. Baker understood all the symbolism: James A. Baker, *The Politics of Diplomacy: Revolution, War, and Peace, 1989–1992* (Putnam, 1995), p. 569.

97. Gorbachev, *Zhizn' i reformy*, vol. 2; *Memoirs*, pp. 671–72; and Shaposhnikov, *Vybor*, p. 136.

manner, Vice President Aleksandr Rutskoi denounced the steps Yeltsin was taking. Rutskoi was one of the generals in their mid-forties who had fought in Afghanistan, and he seemed to be a personal friend of the most powerful of them, Boris Gromov. If in his public censure Rutskoi were speaking for the generation of officers who had served in Afghanistan (the so-called Afghantsy), anything was possible.

As a Russian newspaper columnist later noted, Yeltsin and his entourage expected Rutskoi to disappear into the shadows after the election, like an American vice president. To their astonishment he did not.[98] He vigorously opposed the coup and organized the military defense of the Russian parliament sitting in the White House. He flew to Gorbachev's vacation home in Foros in the Crimea, leading the group that was going to liberate the USSR president. As a reward, he was promoted from colonel to major general, the Soviet equivalent of the American rank of brigadier general.[99]

In the fall Rutskoi traveled widely inside Russia and abroad, giving one interview after another. His constant theme was the need not only for a common economic market but also for political union. He was obviously disappointed with Burbulis's victory and almost immediately began attacking him, first indirectly in references to "the same people who had devoted their lives to teaching 'scientific communism'" and then directly.[100] He savagely attacked the competence of the Gaidar team and the harshness of its price liberalization program. By November 30 he had become vitriolic. Gaidar, he said, would make a splendid deputy minister of finances, but his team consisted of "little boys in pink trousers, red shirts, and yellow shoes" who had no idea what they were doing.[101]

Rutskoi continued writing articles and granting interviews into January 1992. He emphasized three themes: the disastrous impact of Gaidar's economic program on the population and the incompetence of its drafters, the importance for Russia—however defined—to be a great and proud

98. *Nezavishimaia gazeta*, February 12, 1992, p. 2. For a discussion of the steps that offended Rutskoi, see the discussion by his former press secretary in *Moscow News*, no. 20, May 17–24, 1992, pp. 6–7. Yeltsin also wrote in his memoirs as if he thought Rutskoi would be like an American vice president. *Struggle for Russia*, pp. 30–33.

99. John B. Dunlop, *The Rise of Russia and the Fall of the Soviet Empire* (Princeton University Press, 1993), pp. 216–17, 221, 250, 252–53.

100. *Nezavisimaia gazeta*, December 18, 1991, pp. 1–2.

101. Radio Rossii, December 1, 1991, in FBIS, *Soviet Union*, December 2, 1991, p. 4.

power (he favored strong action against Chechnia when it first declared independence in November), and the need to enforce the laws.

Rutskoi's all-out press campaign against the government was often treated as irresponsible populism and was attributed to his ambition.[102] This accusation may well have been true, but commentators were leery of discussing the really interesting aspect of his criticism: the extent to which he was expressing publicly what the military was thinking privately. To judge by the headlines in the military newspaper, *Red Star*, in early 1992, Rutskoi's views certainly had a good deal of support in the military: "Officers Demand Clear and Well-Considered Decisions from Politicians," "The Officer Meetings: No to the Disintegration of the Armed Forces," "While Politicians Argue about the Army, Economic Problems Intensify," "The Army Doesn't Want to Become an Independent Political Force—But Circumstances and Politics Push It to It."[103]

By all the evidence, Rutskoi was considerably more moderate than Boris Gromov, the leader of the Afghantsy and future head of the Russian ground forces. In the summer of 1991, when Rutskoi signed a liberal political manifesto with persons such as Aleksandr Yakovlev, Eduard She-vardnadze, Gavril Popov, and Anatoly Sobchak and served as Yeltsin's vice presidential running mate, Gromov, as may be remembered, signed a nationalist proclamation with several strongly nationalistic writers and three of the men who would join the August coup. He ran with Nikolai Ryzhkov as the vice presidential candidate on the Communist ticket in the Russian presidential election of June 1991.

If Rutskoi was so unhappy, what was likely to be the frame of mind of more conservative members of the Afghantsy such as Gromov? They had fought for their country in Afghanistan, and for them the threat to Russia came from the kind of fundamentalism they had encountered there and

102. See, for instance, Lev Ovtrutsky, "Rutskoism," *Moscow News*, no. 12, March 22–29, 1992, p. 7.

103. *Krasnaia zvezda*, January 11, 1992, p. 1; January 15, 1992, p. 1; January 16, 1992, p. 1; and January 22, 1992, p. 1. When the armed forces were divided and the Russian Ministry of Defense was created on March 17, 1992, *Red Star* was made the official organ of the ministry. Its editor was replaced by a forty-one-year-old naval captain. A colonel who had been on Yeltsin's staff became its first deputy editor. The newspaper's coverage of the government immediately became favorable. (See, for example, the two front-page stories on Yegor Gaidar on April 1 and April 4.) It was unlikely that the military had suddenly become enthusiastic about the disintegration of the Soviet economy and the continuing decline in industrial production, let alone the creation of separate armies in the different republics.

from nuclear powers such as China and Pakistan that had supported the Afghan rebellion.

For men with such a perspective, Boris Yeltsin should have been anathema. They had left Afghanistan in stable Communist hands, but Yeltsin not only let the southern buffer states of Soviet Central Asia and Transcaucasus become independent, but had also ended financial support for Afghanistan. The Afghan stability for which they had fought for a decade collapsed, and the chaos spread into Soviet Central Asia. Men such as Yegor Gaidar were following a policy that could be—and was—described as a Western-directed effort to turn Russia into a semicolonial supplier of raw materials. At a minimum the Gaidar policy was not kind to the defense industry and the heavy industry with which the military had been traditionally allied. Moreover, while the Chinese model of economic reform was producing growth of 10 percent a year, the Soviet model was producing little but pain and chaos in the short run.

Why didn't the Afghan generals intervene to impose the policy that Rutskoi was propounding? The KGB chairman, Vadim Bakatin, reports in his memoirs that he was a strong supporter of the Union, and he reprints an impassioned article he wrote in *Izvestiia* on October 25. And, as Bakatin notes, the stream of high-level foreign officials were coming to Moscow not only to learn about the situation but to tell Soviet leaders, in the words of British Foreign Minister Douglas Herd, "In general, we in the West think in this way: 'Disintegration is not needed.'" Bakatin wrote that "at time I formed the impression that the guests manifested more concern about the situation in the Soviet Union than some of our eminent politicians. In the fall of 1991, practically all of them were characterized by a desire to facilitate the preservation of the unity of the republics in some form."[104]

Aleksandr Rutskoi reports that he went to Gorbachev after the signing of the Minsk agreement and begged him to use his power and arrest the three republican presidents.[105] Minister of Defense Yevgeny Shaposhnikov, for his part, reports that in mid-November Gorbachev had indirectly asked the military to intervene. According to Shaposhnikov, Gorbachev called him to the Kremlin. The conversation was extremely congenial, and Gorbachev talked about the various options for getting out of the crisis. "The most appropriate was the following: 'You military take power in your own hands, install a government convenient to you, stabilize the situation, and

---

104. Bakatin, *Izbavlenie ot KGB*, pp. 199, 203–08, 177-78.
105. Rutskoi, *O nas i o sebe*, pp. 153–54.

then go to the side.'" Shaposhnikov answered that something like that was attempted in August and that the path leads to prison. Gorbachev then responded, "What are you talking about, Zhenia? . . . I wasn't proposing anything to you, but simply *stating* variants, thinking aloud." "The cordiality and hospitality began to wane. The conversation, which began so well, came to an end."[106]

Shaposhnikov saw himself as a reformer, but he was to approve Yeltsin's military attack on the Russian Congress in 1993.[107] He credibly describes himself as being dubious about the August coup from the beginning, but he also talks about the duty of the military officer to carry out orders.[108] His post-1991 memoirs still testify that he was a strong supporter of a common economic space and a confederation at a minimum and that he was deeply disturbed about the movements of Ukraine toward military independence. He says he often talked with Gorbachev about the republics. On September 22, 1991, the Ministry of Defense sent an official memorandum about the problems of republican independence.[109]

Many explanations have been advanced for the lack of military action. Some have posited that the troops would not have obeyed and the army would have been unable to fire on the people, but this is scarcely so. In 1988, 37 percent of the troops from the emergency forces came from Central Asia and Transcaucasus, and 97 percent of the officers were Russians, Ukrainians, Belorussians, and Tatars.[110]

Most have focused on the presumed demoralization and personal corruption of the military leadership. This was probably more important at a later period, but even in the fall of 1991 Shaposhnikov reports he had to intervene against members of the military selling weapons abroad, and he vehemently denies charges that he himself sold weapons to the Chechens.

Yet even Shaposhnikov asserts that in the name of the struggle against "privilege" (high generals using expensive state dachas while in office), he proposed to Gorbachev and Yeltsin that the state dachas be privatized, that they be given to particularly worthy marshals and generals who would become very privileged indeed by the action.[111] "Worthy" surely had a

---

106. Shaposhnikov, *Vybor*, pp. 137–38.
107. Shaposhnikov, *Vybor*, pp. 274–78.
108. See chapter 13.
109. Shaposhnikov, *Vybor*, pp. 90–91, 103–08.
110. *Nesokrushimaia i legendarnaia: O ogne politicheskikh batalii, 1985–1993* (Moscow: Terra, 1994), pp. 40, 63.
111. Shaposhnikov, *Vybor*, p. 69.

political meaning, and those benefiting from the new order had to worry that their dachas or other gains would be renationalized if political change occurred.

In the short run, however, the crucial questions were ones of alternatives and responsibility. Shaposhnikov clearly saw Yeltsin as a more attractive leader than Gorbachev:

> I was struck by [Yeltsin's] unique capacity to work, by his accessibility. I could phone Yeltsin at practically any time of the day. If it was necessary to meet, it was enough to phone once to set a time. . . . "Strong" expressions, that is curse words, were completely absent in his lexicon. . . . And what energy, what a *life-force* he had.[112]

In his memoirs Shaposhnikov expressed the opinion that Gorbachev should have resigned in favor of Yeltsin after the August coup. "Many people did not want the disintegration of the Union, but they did not want Gorbachev."[113]

The issue of responsibility was even more crucial. Shaposhnikov had to suspect that the organizers of the August coup had been treated to a similar abstract discourse about appropriate variants and that they then had found themselves betrayed by the proposer of the variants. But the thing that the military and others found maddening about Gorbachev was precisely that he would not take responsibility and act decisively to save the Union and his government. If as commander in chief Gorbachev had provided the political cover and authorized the introduction of martial law as Rutskoi was pleading, Arkady Volsky is most probably right that the military including Shaposhnikov would have carried out orders.

Thus once again, as throughout this book, one comes back to Gorbachev's thinking. No doubt he was tired of the burdens of office, believed he had played his historic role, and did not know what to do next if he did not seize the levers of power. Valentin Pavlov, always a man attracted to a conspiratorial interpretation, has another explanation for Gorbachev's behavior: he deliberately destroyed the USSR state so that there would be no USSR institutions to bring him to legal responsibility for initiating the August putsch.[114]

---

112. Shaposhnikov, *Vybor*, p. 130. The chairman of the KGB, Vadim Bakatin, had a similarly high opinion of Yeltsin (*Izbavlenie ot KGB*, p. 16), and his contemptuous judgment of "prominent politicians" cited on pp. 177–78 refers to the USSR president.

113. Shaposhnikov, *Vybor*, pp. 138–39.

114. Valentin Pavlov, *Avgust iznutri Gorbachevputch* (Moscow: Delovoi mir, 1993), p. 6.

Whatever else is to be said about Gorbachev, however, he was to remain true to basic assumptions or principles to the end. He had never believed in the exercise of force in foreign or domestic policy, and when he had used it in domestic policy, he had been so concerned about deniability that he had condemned himself to ineffectiveness. Even as he saw power ebbing away, he could not bring himself to try to act.

History judges men and events in terms of ultimate results, and it is kinder on those who articulate great ideals. Long periods of torment become condensed in memory into one or two sentences. Fourteen years elapsed between the battle of Lexington and Concord and the installation of George Washington as U.S. president. In retrospect, it is as nothing, but fourteen years from 1989 would take us to 2003. If the consequences of the economic hardship bring most of the republics voluntarily back together and Russia quickly moves to become a normal market, democratic state, then Gorbachev may come to be seen as a man with great psychological insight into the need to eschew the use of force.

But in the interim decades, the judgment that will be made of him was expressed in the famous proverb about the nature of the paving material on the road to Hell. If anything goes wrong from a long-term perspective, this will be the judgment of history as well. Richard Pipes has written that Russians are doomed to either authoritarianism or anarchy,[115] and Gorbachev will be cited as a prisoner and victim of the Russian intellectual tradition. Gorbachev had none of the sense that democracy was a state that involves some repression. Let us hope that the great suffering of Russia will not continue too much longer because of it. Let us hope that the tragedy of the Gorbachev years does not ultimately visit some great catastrophe on the world as a whole.

115. "Response to Wladislav G. Krasnow," *Russian Review*, vol. 38 (April 1979), p. 196.

CHAPTER FIFTEEN

Conclusion

MIKHAIL GORBACHEV was not riding an uncontrollable tiger. China affords convincing proof that communist systems can be reformed in an evolutionary manner for fifteen years at least, and such a period would have brought the Soviet Union to 2000 and Gorbachev to his sixty-ninth birthday. Moreover, there is no such thing as a pure planned or pure market system, and countries in middle stages of industrialization normally have more government regulation and intervention than they do at later stages. Modern Western economies always combine market and regulation: they are "mixed economies," we used to say. Similarly, democracy at its early stages normally is only half-democratic. Transition to a fuller market and more comprehensive democracy is always evolutionary and managed and takes decades.

In explaining why events in the Soviet Union *evolved* in a more liberal, market-oriented direction, one must look at changes in society and at the imperatives of postindustrial society and the global economy. But in explaining why events in the Soviet Union took a *revolutionary* course, I follow Crane Brinton, Mancur Olson, and Theda Skocpol in pointing to the attitudes of those at the very top of the system and the decisions they made or did not make, not pressure from below. Most who advance this interpretation of the last years of the 1980s and the first of the 1990s focus on Gorbachev's ostensible indecisiveness or his weakness of character. But as Yegor Ligachev has contended, Gorbachev was not inherently indecisive. He showed astonishing decisiveness in consolidating power within the Communist party, spurring democratization, abandoning Eastern Europe, and destroying the leading party organs and the party apparatus.

The reason for Gorbachev's indecisiveness on economic reform and federalism was intellectual. He had no theory of how transition was achieved. He distrusted the bureaucracy that would have to manage a transition, and he had an exaggerated fear of its power. He did not understand that a functioning market depends on government and law. Least of all did he have a feel for what Crane Brinton once called the subtle "line in actual practice of government between force and persuasion . . . not to be drawn by formulas, by 'science' or textbooks, but by men skilled in the art of ruling."[1] Because any theory of transition must require strong government action, Gorbachev's beliefs also prevented him from accepting others' theories of transition, notably those of Nikolai Ryzhkov and the economists associated with him.

Gorbachev's views and those of his closest advisers seemed to flow from the anarchism in Marxism and from the Russian intelligentsia's traditional distrust of government, business, and the military—even the nihilistic features of the intelligentsia's tradition.[2] Marx never recognized that management and entrepreneurship were useful in creating and maintaining capitalism, and his vision of socialism was also noninstitutional in its vague combination of planning and the withering away of the state. Lenin understood the importance of organization, but his vision of the communist future was as anarchistic as Marx's. Both understood that democracy was a state, that it ultimately rested on the use of force. But in rejecting any state, they were left with the anarchist conception of democracy.

Marxism-Leninism was victorious in Russia in large part because it was so congenial to the mind-set of the Russian intelligentsia. American intellectuals developed and propagated the concept of a broad and good middle class that included professionals, businessmen, civil servants (not "bureaucrats"), military officers, and even skilled workers. Whatever one may say about this as a realistic view of American social structure, American intellectuals were building a coalition. They were emphasizing the similarity of the interests and values of various elite groups with one another and with the broader population, and they were including themselves among the elite groups. By so doing they were offering cooperation with the other elite

---

1. Crane Brinton, *The Anatomy of Revolution* (Norton, 1938), p. 66.
2. Jonathan Steele of the *Manchester Guardian* emphasizes the nihilism in the Russian tradition and in Gorbachev's reform in *Eternal Russia: Yeltsin, Gorbachev, and the Mirage of Democracy* (Harvard University Press, 1994), pp. 269–73.

groups rather than confrontation. This has proved a farsighted political strategy that has been very beneficial for American intellectuals.

Members of the Russian intelligentsia, by contrast, have seen themselves as superior and isolated, alienated from all other groups in society. They have spoken of a conflict between state and society, but they have included only themselves and professionals in society. Capitalists (or the economic nomenklatura), bureaucrats, and the army have been described as enemies, and the *narod* (the people) as contemptible. A century ago the peasants were "the dark people," but by the 1980s the workers were viewed in similar terms. A perceptive American journalist reported in 1981:

> My friends are convinced that sixty years of Soviet rule, which has taught schoolchildren to lie and destroyed civic virtue, have turned the Russian people into a rabble, ripe for envy, violence, and demagogy, but not for responsible citizenship. If the hated regime were to collapse overnight, fierce nationalists would be more likely than enlightened liberals to replace it, if only because few enlightened liberals manage to develop in that soil, and few understand or want them. Even if something more humane were to arise, it would be torn apart by the dumb anger Soviet rule has incubated.[3]

In political terms this world view implicitly denies the broad coalitional strategy needed for evolutionary reform. It leads instead to the situation bemoaned by Leonid Abalkin in the late 1980s: economists and government officials saw each other as enemies (*vragi*). The view is compatible only with a policy of trying to destroy the position of other groups in the elite and hoping a good new society will emerge. For more than a hundred years this political strategy has been disastrous for Russian intellectuals.

There are many lessons to be drawn from the story told in this book. The first, of course, is for Russian intelligentsia. In 1996 they were once more disillusioned with what they had created through their struggle in the 1980s. From their perspective, businessmen are Mafia, property is owned by the nomenklatura, bureaucrats are corrupt, and workers and peasants cannot be trusted to elect state governors because they would vote for the wrong candidates. Regions cannot be given powers of taxation because this would lead to the disintegration of Russia. Agricultural reform is impossible because the cities would starve.

As a consequence, Russian intellectuals still are not thinking of coalitions. They still are not developing reasonable strategies of transition to a

---

3. George Feifer, "Russian Disorders," *Harper's*, February 1981, p. 54.

democratic market society with reasonable concepts of the trade-offs and compromises needed in such societies. They still are not studying the experiences of China and the third world because they recognize only the most advanced countries in their most idealized form as models worthy of their attention. And once again other groups are thoroughly disillusioned with the intelligentsia, whom they now call democrats, besmirching a word that should connote responsiveness to people's wishes—the opposite meaning from the one it has acquired in Russia. Although the intellectuals are beginning to be ignored and expelled from power, Russia will not become a normal country until they become a constructive force in society.

But there are also lessons for the West. The insensitivity of Gorbachev and his advisers to the institutional bases of the market and democracy had its counterpart in influential policy communities in the West, particularly among economists in the international economic organizations and the technical assistance organizations promoting democracy. The West lionized those Russian intellectual reformers who criticized all other groups as communists and nomenklatura and who espoused contemporary American institutions and theories. It encouraged them in all their worst characteristics.

Moreover, it was Westerners who assured the Russians that the abrupt destruction of the old system would lead automatically to the rise of a good society with a fully functioning market. They talked of leaping a chasm in a single jump or the impossibility of moving from a British to an American traffic pattern by first having trucks driving on the right side and then cars. When at the end of 1991 Yegor Gaidar talked sensibly about taking a year to introduce changes, it was Westerners who insisted that he accelerate his program.[4] The radical Russian reformers learned that it was necessary to lie to Westerners, to keep a double set of books, and to find scapegoats for the failure of their own (self-proclaimed wise) decisions. The result was that many Westerners retained ideas far more naive than those of the Russian radicals themselves, who were learning from mistakes.

The basic problem for American analysts was that Western society has been too stable since World War II. Its institutions, rules, laws, and incentive systems have come to be taken for granted. Economists and other social scientists assumed the permanence and stability of the macroeconomic

4. Anders Aslund, *How Russia Became a Market Economy* (Brookings, 1995), p. 65.

rules within which the actors played.[5] Once it was concluded that the explanation for the slow economic growth in the West after 1970 was excessive government interference in the market, the invariable prescription was to privatize, reduce the role of government, get the prices right, and ensure fiscal stability (or, perhaps, control the money supply). The governing assumption seemed, indeed, to be the one expressed by the president of the CATO Institute in 1990 in Moscow: "Introduce freedom, and the market will take care of itself." The decline in overall rates of economic growth in the 1970s, 1980s, and 1990s has not changed that perception.

Similarly, as the great American political debates on the role of government and federalism that surrounded the New Deal and the desegregation movement receded from memory, the concepts of democracy and democratization also became very noninstitutional and ahistorical. Democracy was defined as individual freedom and free elections with competitive parties, and the implicit model was an idealized version of contemporary American democracy. The vision was not of democracy as it existed in nineteenth century England and the United States, let alone many of the democratizing countries of Asia and Latin America, which would have been more appropriate for Russia. Indeed, it had little correspondence to real American democracy that scarcely solves problems such as entitlements or the deficit through shock therapy.

Although the word *anarchism* is discredited in the United States and has become essentially synonymous with *terrorism*, much of Western analysis, in fact, became anarchistic or semianarchistic if taken literally. The analysis was, of course, not meant to be taken literally; the rules, laws, and incentives found in the United States were taken for granted. But when such a system had to be introduced from scratch, the need to give priority to the establishment of rules, laws, and incentives was forgotten. The same advice was given to Russians as was given to third world countries where these rules, laws, and incentives in large part already existed. In the Russian context the implicit anarchism of the analysis became all too real. Westerners tacitly assumed that rules, laws, and incentives would emerge like Athena from the head of Zeus. When the Russians asked for help on the transition to a market economy, Americans forgot the first crucial advice:

---

5. This was not always true at the microeconomic level. There was a keen awareness that changes in the tax and depreciation laws would affect incentives and therefore business decisions in major ways.

get the laws right, get the court system right, get the political system right, think about incentives.

Eventually the Robespierres of the Second Russian Revolution will finally be pushed from the scene. People are likely to come to power who understand the importance of the state, of clear and enforced rules, and of incentive systems that give managers a long-term perspective oriented toward production rather than seizure of property at any cost. In theory this is all to the good. A real market economy and a real democracy will never be established in Russia until the basic principles understood by the new rulers are introduced.

Yet the so-called reformers in Russia and their Western supporters have defined the market and democracy in very noninstitutional, antistatist terms. To the extent their opponents adopt the definitions of the reformers, they may be led to reject the general concepts of market and democracy. This would be a tragic mistake. It is for the West to begin developing theories that reflect the reality of Western and third world history, not doctrinaire models based on the precorporate world of the early nineteenthth century. The West must put special emphasis on devising theories of economic and political development that apply to countries at middle levels of development, for these countries in Asia will pose the greatest threats to peace in the first half of the twenty-first century.

The Character of the Second Russian Revolution

Neither the liberalization in the Soviet Union nor the Second Russian Revolution was caused by the military buildup of the Reagan administration.[6] They were caused by changes in the attitudes and values of the Soviet elite and the rest of the population that were decades in the making, by the greater attraction for an educated population of what are called "Western values" and what Gorbachev called "universal human values." As early as 1959 Edward Crankshaw noted major differences in attitudes between those in administrative work who were younger than age thirty-five and those who were older. As the young men of the 1950s aged and rose into the middle and top levels of the elite, they brought with them their dissatisfac-

6. By the same token, of course, events also proved wrong those American liberals who said that a hard-line American policy would make liberalization in Soviet domestic and foreign policy impossible.

tion with the old system, political culture, and values. Those who were younger were still more disenchanted.

Many Westerners found it difficult to accept that the Russians were a normal people and that education, urbanization, and occupational differentiation would change the attitudes of both the elite and the people as they had elsewhere in the world. The strong pressures being created in support of liberalization and democratization not only within the intelligentsia but even among the so-called partocrats were given far too little attention.

American conservatives in particular had profound misconceptions about the attitudes of those high in the Communist party and military hierarchies. The conservatives did not see an economically underprivileged and politically repressed middle class or business class, but instead a privileged nomenklatura that was united in protecting its power and position. They did not see the differentiation that had occurred within the bureaucracy and failed to understand that individual bureaucrats often had fundamentally different interests from those of their institutions and would have unusual and attractive opportunities to pursue their individual interests in a time of change.

In fact, the Russian people strongly supported democratization after 1989. When they finally turned against the "democrats," their responses in public opinion surveys made it clear they were rejecting authoritarian dictatorship masquerading as democracy, not democracy itself. They were disillusioned by continued control of the regions by an economic policy that did not reflect public opinion and by the continued rule of the regions by the center, which Yeltsin had promised to end. The non-Russian republics have gained some independence, but not the Russian provinces, and that was and is a source of great resentment.

Neither did the party and economic nomenklatura prove a solid bulwark defending the old system. Most of Gorbachev's radical advisers had worked for years in the Central Committee apparatus. Moreover, as Mancur Olson predicted, the hearts and minds of the people were less important to effecting revolution than the local Soviet government officials who controlled the purse and had the power to hire and fire. The war of laws between the Soviet and republican governments and the chaos it produced was created by local Communist party officials, not revolutionaries in the street. And the defiance of the Baltic republics began in 1988 and 1989 when the Communist first secretaries were still in power, while the Ukrainian drive for independence was conducted by a party apparatus in which very little turnover in personnel had occurred or was to occur in the first years of independence.

There were many causes for discontent among the elite. The most prominent included the corrosive effect of education in destroying support for the restrictions on freedom found in the Soviet Union, and the growing dissatisfaction of the upper and middle elite with the gray egalitarianism of Soviet society and the low level of privilege in their lives in comparison with their counterparts in the West. The widespread travel abroad in the 1970s, including that of Gorbachev himself, was crucial. The exchange programs of the West were far more crucial in destroying communism than the military buildup of the early 1980s. An increasingly differentiated elite was also restive under the political dominance of those employed in the defense and heavy industry. The experience of the West and the Pacific Rim countries demonstrated to the elite that depression was not inherent in capitalism and that integration into the world economy was better for technological advance than was Soviet autarchy. Finally, the elite despaired of the Soviet system's ability to achieve a smooth and rapid transition to a service economy and the consumer benefits and social mobility associated with it. Their children and those of workers found upper mobility blocked by a system that best served the social mobility interests of peasants streaming into the city.

A final Western misconception of the Soviet elites' state of mind was that Marxism-Leninism had indoctrinated them in the need for authoritarianism.[7] In fact, the doctrine actually was multifaceted. The young in the Soviet Union had, of course, not been told that Marxism-Leninism was authoritarian and that authoritarianism was needed. Instead, they were taught that communism was democratic and that the essence of Lenin's nationality policy was the right of secession. Older leaders repeated such concepts cynically, but for the young they were the ideals that government was supposed to serve, and the ideals against which Soviet reality and later policy choices were judged. The young of the 1940s and 1950s were to become the middle-aged of the 1980s.

The changes in people's attitudes obviously did not lead directly to revolution or even liberalization. Soviet society in the mid-1980s was little different from what it had been at the beginning of the 1980s, but the social pressures of the earlier period had been only marginally reflected in

---

7. Most pointed to Lenin's *What's to Be Done*, with its image of a centralized party, its contempt for workers' "trade union consciousness," and its insistence that the party had the obligation to follow its understanding of the laws of history rather than reflect the workers' view of their interests.

Brezhnev's policy. Radical political change required a change in the people in power, which generally meant leaders with a younger outlook. A leader much older than Gorbachev could have introduced radical change (this happened in the Catholic Church with Pope John XXIII), but it was more likely to be introduced by a person whose values had been shaped in the 1940s and the 1950s rather than in the 1910s and 1920s.

Why did liberalization give way to Gorbachev's transformation of the system and lead to its destruction in such a short time? The immediate reason was that Gorbachev refused to use enough force to ensure obedience to Sovies laws and to suppress separatism. An enormous amount has been written about the handful of deaths Soviet security forces caused in Tbilisi, Baku, and Vilnius, as if these acts somehow destroyed perestroika. But continuing such limited applications of force would surely have preserved the Union. After all, the Soviet population was thoroughly cowed in 1988.

Intellectuals responded to the Nina Andreeva letter of March 1989 with retreat until the letter was attacked in *Pravda*. If the momentum toward separatism had been stopped and obedience to central laws enforced, stability could have been maintained with few deaths or arrests. Martial law was imposed successfully and with little bloodshed in Poland in December 1981, even though public pressure against the government was much greater, workers better organized, strikes more widespread, and the political and administrative chaos much more serious. It was crucial for Gorbachev to be firm about the limits of protest if he wanted perestroika to succeed.

If any leader in any country indicates that he will not enforce laws or central authority, events will surely spin out of control. The logic of collective action is based on the assumption that individual attempts to seize goods or power will be opposed by police and, if necessary, the army. If individuals and local government officials learn this resistance will not materialize, they have a strong self-interest to seize more and more goods and power. Edward Banfield's "rioting for fun and profit" is not far from Steven Solnick's "colossal bank run in which local officials rushed to claim their assets before the bureaucratic bank closed for good."[8] Until the rioters and the officials seizing property and power are stopped, they will be joined

8. Steven L. Solnick, "Growing Pains: Youth Policies and Institutional Collapse in the Former Soviet Union," Ph.D. dissertation, Harvard University, 1993. The quotation is from the abstract on the computerized dissertation abstracts at the Library of Congress. The quotation from Banfield is in *The Unheavenly City: The Nature and Future of Our Urban Crisis* (Little, Brown, 1968), pp. 211–34.

by others. It was Gorbachev's refusal to take responsibility for the minor application of force, not the use of the force itself, that undermined perestroika.

One reads Crane Brinton's words from 1938 with a feeling of familiarity.

> The Russian ruling classes, in spite of their celebrated Asiatic background, were by the late nineteenth century more than half ashamed to use force, and therefore used it badly, so that on the whole those on whom force was inflicted were stimulated rather than repressed. . . . One of the best signs of the unfitness of the ruling class to rule is the absence of this skill among its members. When those of them who [have] positions of political power [do] use force, they [use] it sporadically and inefficiently.[9]

The most interesting question is why Gorbachev and his closest advisers refused to act to save the system. At one level, the answer seems simple: they had lost faith in communist ideology, Lenin, and the command-administrative system. Moreover, it was not only the reformers who had lost faith. The so-called conservative leaders had ample opportunity to remove Gorbachev when the political situation in the Baltic republics deteriorated and when he tolerated the war of laws with Boris Yeltsin. If they had been as convinced of the virtues of socialism as earlier Soviet leaders, they would have intervened to prevent him from losing Eastern Europe. And, of course, no political behavior was more telling than that of the men who organized the August 1991 coup. They were the most conservative members of the Politburo and Soviet leadership, but even they did not believe enough in the system and the country to use force to preserve it.

Crane Brinton pointed to abandonment of the system by intellectuals as a crucial element in successful revolutions. However, hundreds of dictators from Stalin to General Augusto Pinochet in Chile demonstrate that one can rule handily with intellectuals in opposition. Revolution occurs when the elite begin to believe the disaffected intellectuals.[10]

---

9. Brinton, *Anatomy of Revolution*, pp. 66, 67.

10. In addition, the causal arrows between intellectuals and elite can go in both directions, for intellectuals may be driven by a desire for access to power and funding. This book has commented that many economists curried favor. In the early 1980s it was a shock for me to discover the director of the Soviet Institute of the International Workers' Movement beginning to focus the work of his institute on the Pacific Rim and integration into the world economy. At the time this seemed a clear sign that the director thought the post-Brezhnev leadership was not likely to fund the kind of work done by the institute in the past and there was little danger in the position he was taking.

At what point did Gorbachev lose faith and what were the reasons? In retrospect, his policy after 1986 was basically consistent and its outcome predictable, whether or not he understood where his decisions were leading. Once he rejected retail price increases in December 1986, once he was repelled by the use of force that might be required if demonstrations broke out, once he thought that administered price increases would allow the bureaucracy to throttle reform, any kind of evolutionary transition was out of the question.

It is likely that Gorbachev at first thought the changes he was instituting could be kept within bounds. Yeltsin was probably right in suggesting that at some point Gorbachev became demoralized. But the evolution in Gorbachev's thought will probably never be understood with complete confidence. He has written that he destroyed his annotated appointment books in December 1991 out of a fear of arrest. Vladimir Kriuchkov was calling Aleksandr Yakovlev a CIA agent, and many moderate reformers and conservatives wrote of being betrayed. The memoirs of Gorbachev and his advisers—Gorbachev's most of all—reveal little about their interrelationships, and concern for their mutual safety must be one reason. It is much safer for Gorbachev and his advisers to say now that they were committed to democracy and that they were surprised by everything that happened except democratization.

The complex relationship of leader and adviser makes analysis of Gorbachev's state of mind particularly difficult. It is possible that he was being honest when he told the Poles in 1988 that he had not originally thought of political reform as the central component of his program. But if his first priority was economic reform, that of Yakovlev, Anatoly Cherniaev, Georgy Shakhnazarov, and Ivan Frolov, his closest political advisers, was political. As discussed in earlier chapters, in December 1985 Yakovlev wrote a memorandum to Gorbachev calling for a split in the Communist party, and therefore for a multiparty system. In 1988 he told a new assistant that he thought Marx had been fundamentally mistaken. He later commented that he never thought the East European Communist parties would survive democratization. Cherniaev's first advice when he became Gorbachev's personal assistant was that Germany should be allowed to reunite. It is possible that at early stages some of these advisers deliberately proposed actions that they were convinced would destabilize the system but hid these expectations from Gorbachev, who was more naive. And by the same token, it is likely that Gorbachev was hiding many of his inner thoughts from his advisers as well as from conservatives.

Yet ultimately Gorbachev chose his advisers and decided whom to keep and whom to let go. It was he who made the decision to cast aside relatively radical reformers such as Leonid Abalkin and Oleg Bogomolov, let alone the highly qualified reformers in the financial community who associated with Nikolai Ryzhkov. It was he who was attracted to the idea of full democratization rather than the more authoritarian economic reform that was found in Asia (and that he cryptically mentioned in his memoirs without evaluating).[11] And when in late 1990 he became demoralized about the course of events and essentially shed Yakovlev, Eduard Shevardnadze, and Nikolai Petrakov, he could not bring himself to embrace the conservatives or even the moderate reformer Valentin Pavlov, whom he appointed as premier. As late as December 1991 Gaidar and his colleagues were extremely worried that the military would support the Union, but Gorbachev still would not pay the price of declaring martial law.

Gorbachev increasingly considered democratic processes the way to find difficult answers to the problems he did not know how to resolve. Defining democracy in very noninstitutional and consensual terms and believing the use of force was incompatible with it, he found himself helpless before those who defined politics and government in other ways. He was seeking consensus where consensus was impossible and had no sense of Brinton's "line in actual practice of government between force and persuasion."[12] The result was inevitable once he faced a rival who was certain what he wanted and was decisive in seeking it.

The summer of 1990 was when the situation became revolutionary, and two factors were critical: Gorbachev's failure to insist on central control of finances and his emphasis on privatization. Gorbachev was at first oblivious to the dangers of rising deficits and then was uncertain how to handle Yeltsin as the latter skillfully extended the central government's financial difficulties. His failure to oppose Yeltsin's attack on the treasury and to defend the central government's power of taxation created serious doubts within the military and bureaucracy about the desirability of supporting him against Yeltsin.

Valentin Pavlov was correct in considering as a turning point the conference in the summer of 1990 at which Gorbachev refused to fight the newly elected republican governments over control of taxation. Historians are virtually unanimous in emphasizing financial difficulties of the old govern-

11. Mikhail Gorbachev, *Memoirs* (Doubleday, 1995), p. 494–95.
12. Brinton, *Anatomy of Revolution*, p. 66.

ment as a crucial element in all revolutions ("a rich society with an impoverished government" was Brinton's phrase).[13] Never, however, has a government with total control over "taxation" because of its ownership of all property fallen into financial bankruptcy because it allowed local governmental units under its control to take control of tax revenue. (As Brinton's model suggested, the economic problems at this stage were minimal— an end to growth, yes, but nothing like the depression that began in mid-1991.) That is what happened from the summer of 1990 and the late summer of 1991 in the Soviet Union.

Yet in the long run the emphasis on privatization that began with Abalkin's (and Ryzhkov's) 1989 plan and reached its height with the 500-Day Plan in the summer of 1990 was just as important. The Chinese privatized little state property, and even agricultural land was leased rather than privatized. Essentially they let the market grow up around the state sector, beginning first with agriculture and the services. In their enterprise zones, they permitted new cities to evolve out of small villages. Once Gorbachev refused to have the price adjustments (or the combination of rationing and market forces) of the Chinese model that was necessary for agricultural reform and instead concentrated on decentralization of power to enterprises, he was driven almost inexorably to privatization as the path to market reform.

Critics of the 500-Day Plan focused on the wild utopianism of its insistence that privatization be finished in the first 100 days or so, but the mere idea of universal privatization had a profound psychological impact on everyone. They took it for granted that the plan's timing was utopian, but if it and the Abalkin plan, which also emphasized privatization, were being defined as the two poles of the discussion, Gorbachev's centrist position was certain to feature radical privatization spread over a longer period. If Yeltsin won, privatization would likely be more rapid.

This had a particularly significant effect on the officials of the state apparatus. Once those with managerial experience saw that economic reform was probable, most had a strong interest in it.[14] The introduction of a private sector would at the very least raise managerial wages throughout the country. An opening to the world economy would give managers access to

---

13. Brinton, *Anatomy of Revolution*, pp. 40–41.

14. For an analysis and documentation of this attitude in banking reform, see Joel Scott Hellman, ''Breaking the Bank: Bureaucrats and the Creation of Markets in a Transitional Economy,'' Ph.D. dissertation, Columbia University, 1993.

foreign currency and foreign bank accounts. (The absence of access to bank acounts was the major disincentive for the large-scale corruption often found in the third world and in Russia after 1991 but generally lacking in the Soviet Union before 1988.) Privatization would permit the accumulation of unprecedented wealth.

Once the alternatives were limited to the Abalkin plan and the 500-Day Plan, any official could see what was coming and begin to position himself to exploit it. In the early stages, directors of enterprises took advantage of their increased independence to sell off "excess" and "outdated" equipment, often to the newly legalized cooperatives in which, not entirely by coincidence, they or their relatives had a controlling interest. The rewards from these takeovers were so much greater than they were from normal investment and production that, not surprisingly, these latter were neglected.

The drumbeat of press criticism of the bureaucracy contributed to the speed of the change in attitude. Middle-level officials had long been keenly aware that their salaries were low even by Soviet standards and that their living standards, even with some nonmonetary supplements, were not remotely comparable to those of their counterparts in the West.[15] As first secretary of the Stavropol Gorkom in 1967, for example, Gorbachev had a one-bedroom apartment, which was not unusual.[16] The man in charge of all construction in Leningrad lived in a two-bedroom apartment in the 1980s. However, as he commented to me, he and other officials like him valued the prestige and sense of accomplishment they received. But once the state-owned media began to denounce the command-administrative system as well as the "conservative" and "privileged" bureaucrats, the bureaucrats not only lost this psychic income but had no reason to be loyal to the state and party that controlled the media.

In short, the vaunted Soviet bureaucracy turned out to be a collection of "bureaucrats" with very different interests from those of the bureaucracy. Mancur Olson did not sufficiently recognize this point in his *Rise and Decline of Nations*, but he emphasized in "The Logic of Collective Action in Soviet-type Societies" that it applies even to officials who are loyal to the regime:

15. Yegor Ligachev reported in 1989 that the average salary of party officials was 216 rubles a month, little more than the average salary in the country. *Pravda*, July 2, 1988, p. 11.

16. Mikhail Gorbachev, *Zhizn' i reformy*, vol. 1 (Moscow: Novosti, 1995), pp. 111, 118–19; *Memoirs*, p. 78.

Just as it does not normally pay a typical individual to rebel, so it also does not pay for the typical policeman or soldier or bureaucrat who happens to be believe in the regime to go out of his way to help the regime survive simply because he favors the regime. It does not pay the typical official of a regime to carry out the orders of the leadership unless there is some incentive for him to do that separate from his belief in the established system.[17]

If a person has no possibility of leaving the bureaucracy for other bureaucracies or the private sector, his or her self-interest is intimately tied to the job. The employee's supervisor controls the incentives and coercive weapons that will determine the person's future. The distinctive thing about bureaucrats in the communist world was their limited ability to get away, which dampened their political behavior.[18] When they acquired the freedom to leave, their behavior changed.

The Importance of Institutions and Incentives

"The victors are never judged," a Russian proverb insists, and the lessons of the Second Russian Revolution will be drawn by those who see its ultimate consequences. If Russia quickly evolves into the normal country that Anders Aslund already envisions and if its foreign policy remains peaceful, the suffering of the 1990s will seem no more significant than that in the Great Depression of the 1930s in America seems to Americans fifty years later. The same would have been true of the suffering during Soviet collectivization if it had produced an efficient agricultural system. Those Westerners who see the Revolution of 1990–91 as successful are already quite callous about the enormous suffering it has caused.[19]

But if pre-1996 economic policy produces some political disaster, Western advice will be damned as severely in retrospect as Western policy toward Germany at the Versailles Conference and in the 1920s. The same

17. Mancur Olson, "The Logic of Collective Action in Soviet-type Societies," *Journal of Soviet Nationalities*, vol. 1 (Summer 1990), p. 15.
18. See Albert O. Hirschman, *Exit, Voice, and Loyalty: Responses to Decline in Firms, Organizations, and States* (Harvard University Press, 1970).
19. For example, between 1990 and 1994, an extra 1.5 million people died who would have been alive if only the already very heavy mortality rates of 1990 had been maintained. Jerry F. Hough, Evelyn Davidheiser, and Susan Goodrich Lehmann, *The 1996 Russian Presidential Election* (Brookings, 1996), p. 94.

is true if post-1996 prosperity is seen as having been produced by a change in economic policy, not by the pre-1996 policy.

If one excludes the extremely unlikely possibility that Gorbachev was determined to destroy the Soviet system from the beginning, however, one can at least draw lessons on the reasons that the path he chose did not result in the radical transformation within the system that he seemed to want. One can point to mistakes in the steps he took to achieve his goal, be it optimal or misguided, and draw lessons for others who attempt policy change in other situations.

First, it is clear that Gorbachev believed the defects of the Soviet economic system were the result not of rational responses of officials to the incentives it embodied but of the warping power of those who benefited from the system. Thus he came to see the problem of reform not in terms of constructing a new incentive system but of overcoming the resistance of those fattening off the old one. And he fundamentally misjudged the individual interests and concerns of officials within the economic and state bureaucracies. He did not understand that these interests would be decisive.

Second, because he was insensitive to the role of rules, laws, and incentives in shaping the behavior of individuals, Gorbachev was far too cavalier in assuming that new institutions, rules, laws, and incentive systems would spontaneously emerge to guide people to efficient and effective behavior. It was as if he assumed that the market was a part of the state of nature that needed only to be released from government fetters to function properly. It existed already formed on the other side of the chasm if the leap were only made.

In fact, a modern market is very unlike the bazaars of traditional society where a simple exchange of goods and money takes place. Bazaars may be able to develop more or less spontaneously, but a modern market depends on long-term investment and on contracts in which goods are delivered and paid for at a later date. These in turn require a comprehensive legal code, precise definitions of property, an efficient and predictable system of taxation, an effective enforcement mechanism, a well-functioning and just judicial system, and appropriate regulatory laws. A modern market is created by government and maintained by government. Serious foreign or domestic investment is impossible if government, democratic or nondemocratic, is not strong enough to govern and to enforce laws in a predictable way.

The relationship between government, especially democratic government, and the market is complex. Government must not feel free to change laws at its whim, or participants in the economy will lose all sense of predictability. Yet a democratic government that cannot change its laws is a government in which the people have no power. Because most political struggle involves efforts by people to protect themselves from the market, the logical outcome is obvious: the majority in a democracy must develop some sense of restraint.[20] This precondition is the crucial reason that democracy is so difficult to achieve in societies with uneducated populations traumatized by transition to the city.

The assumption that the complex market system that developed over centuries in the West would develop spontaneously and quickly in what had been a nonmarket economy ignores all the problems that stem from the lack of correspondence between rational individual action and collective action. Individuals respond to incentives, but they have little incentive to establish a collective good such as a framework of incentives unless they have the opportunity to set up one that is designed to provide them some particular advantage rather than serve the common good.

In addition, the assumption that real progress comes only from most drastic destruction of institutions is profoundly ahistorical. The experience of Germany and Japan after World War II is often cited, but in both cases occupying troops prevented radical communist action and then the Marshall Plan, a major program of state-directed economic assistance, provided help in restructuring (Lincoln Gordon, a top administrator in the Marshall Plan, has estimated that U.S. assistance from 1948 to 1952 totalled $78.5 billion in 1996 dollars, $290 billion in terms of a comparable percentage of American GDP).[21] The truly radical revolutions, whether they come from the right as in Iran or the left as in Cambodia, normally have economic consequences that last for decades. The destruction wrought by the American Civil War left the southern states economically backward for three-quarters of a century.

It is for this reason that a large number of comparative political scientists have been writing about "bringing the state back in." The economist these political scientists have found most instructive is Douglass North, who emphasizes the impact of institutions—the laws, organizational forms, and norms of behavior that shape human interaction.[22] The political scientists

20. V. O. Key, *Public Opinion and American Democracy* (Knopf, 1961), pp. 3–26.
21. Jerry Hough, interview with Lincoln Gordon, October 4, 1996.
22. Douglass C. North, *Institutions, Institutional Change, and Economic Performance* (Cambridge University Press, 1990), pp. 3, 33, 47.

advocating a rediscovery of the state have been highly critical of the work of Marxists and neoclassical economists and have insisted that the role of the state is crucial in furthering economic performance. Adam Przeworski, speaking for an international group on studying East-South systems transformation, was typical in asserting concern at the antistatist bias of reforms in Latin American and Eastern Europe.

> Repeatedly we have been sounding an alarm at the prospect of a further weakening of state institutions. Indeed, we have become convinced in the course of these analyses that several of the dangers facing new democratic regimes are due to the inability of state institutions to guarantee physical security, to establish conditions for an effective exercise of citizenship, to provide moral leadership, to mobilize public savings, to coordinate resource allocation, and to correct income distribution. The principal mistake of neoliberal prescriptions is that they underestimate the role of state institutions in organizing the public and the private life of groups and individuals. Without an effective state, there can be no democracy.[23]

These analyses, however, remain very general. First, those talking about the state often fail to define it, and the phrases *strong state* or *effective state* are ambiguous. Sometimes they denote an efficient administrative system, in other contexts an authoritarian regime that can suppress unrest, in still others a political leader with a successful economic policy. North, for example, has made little effort to examine the politics that form and change the institutions. Indeed, despite his attack on neoclassical economics, he has insisted that "fundamental changes in relative prices are the most important source of [institutional change]."[24]

Second, the analyses are ahistorical. Observers recognize that markets function differently in early stages of industrialization from the way they do in later stages, with the pressures for protectionism usually much stronger in earlier stages. Full-fledged Western democracy of the late twentieth century is very difficult to achieve at early stages of industrialization. Yet the analyses lack guidelines for what kinds of political and economic measures are appropriate at which stage, let alone information on how to implement them. The West does not have good theories of transition any more than Gorbachev had, and this is true for democratization as well as marketization.

23. Adam Przeworski and others, *Sustainable Democracy* (Cambridge University Press, 1995), p. 110. Also see p. 12.
24. North, *Institutions, Institutional Change, and Economic Performance*, p. 84.

To begin to remedy the deficiency, scholars can become more specific in their discussion of the state and of institutions. To this end, it is often conceptually more useful to define rules and laws as incentive systems, for this provides observers with greater awareness of the effect of concrete measures on the behavior of individuals. Incentives are, of course, not simply created by government action. Tradition or culture can be defined as rules and incentive systems, usually rational (or functional) at one time, that became imbedded in habit. Development or modernization can be seen as a transition from rules and incentive systems appropriate at one stage of economic development (or established by force or tradition) to other rules and incentive systems appropriate in other economic circumstances (or established by force or the political process).

There are many reasons the process of development is so complex, but one certainly is that it confronts individuals with rules and incentive systems that are changing and often conflict with each other. People must constantly decide how to balance them or choose between them. The incentive systems learned during childhood often diverge from those encountered later, and a person may act either according to learned rationality or according to newly created incentives. Finally, of course, a far-sighted person in such a society can respond to existing incentives or try to decide which may be changed through legislation or revolution. On long-term decisions (education, career, or investment choices), the latter considerations may be crucial.

The continual adjustment in incentive systems, let alone the breakup of an entire old incentive system, multiplies choices. A person is often forced to decide whether to play in the old game, or bet on a new one being established, or engage in collective action to try to change the rules of the game.[25] Small wonder that during a time of very rapid change many people may feel so anxious that they seek to escape from freedom. And small wonder that in revolutionary times leaders may be so overwhelmed with new information and new choices that they function in ways whose overall rationality is difficult to discern, even in retrospect.

The uncertainties created as people decide when to be guided by the old incentive system and when by new opportunities make analysis intellectually fascinating but difficult. Scholars have many choices. They may analyze the effects of incentive systems on individual behavior, or they may

25. This is most obvious in microeconomic decisionmaking where politics and economics most often intersect—the tax code.

seek to determine the conditions likely to lead to one incentive system's superseding another, either in an existing political process or through revolution. The latter analyses obviously can and should lead to further analysis of the best ways to change or reinforce incentive systems to effect desired changes, such as how to transform communist and other systems into democracies with effective economic systems.

In recent decades the rational-choice political scientists have concentrated on how individuals respond to a preexisting incentive system, yet they have a natural comparative advantage over psychologists and economists in analyzing the effort to change the rules, laws, and incentive systems. Rational-actor analysis that takes the existing rules for granted closes the door on analysis of change in the rules of the game and leads to a bias in favor of the status quo. However, any analysis that assumes collective action is never rational without side payments and coercion leads to the conclusion that the key determinant of societal decisions is that by which people reach a position in which they can provide side payments and exercise coercion.

Since the struggle to change incentive systems inherently has a greater impact on outcomes than decisions made within them, it inherently is of more scholarly importance. The bigger the politics, the more basic the rules and incentive systems being challenged. The biggest politics, that producing great revolutions, affects the most basic rules and incentive systems. These are the natural subjects of study for political scientists.

From a policy point of view, the clear implication is that when one thinks of change, one needs to give even greater attention to the consequences of incentives for individuals during the dismantling of the old system. Too often economists focus on some ideal set of incentives in the new system— or even in the ideal system, not the economic system that exists in the United States, let alone western Europe and Japan.[26] One cannot assume that the immediate introduction of the ''ideal'' rules will have an optimal effect. For this reason analysts must always begin with the individual incentives within the existing institutional framework. Russia, China, and Poland all began from different starting points, which should properly have affected the strategy followed. The Polish shock treatment is blithely

26. Milton Friedman is more honest than many economists who are closer to his views about government than they would like to admit. He was frank in telling Russians that they should not adopt "American socialism" (his phrase), but should introduce real capitalism.

praised without any thought that Poland always had private agriculture and developed a small private service and industrial sector in the 1970s. Poland went through ten years of painful price adjustments and privatization between the Solidarity revolt of 1979 and the fall of East European communist regimes in 1989, an adjustment that required it to introduce martial law. Indeed, even since 1989 the shock treatment has been applied to industry very gingerly, and much of the shock was administered not by governmental policy but by the unwelcome decision by the Soviet Union abruptly to end its long-term trade relationships in the Council on Mutual Economic Assistance (Comecon).

Democracy and Democratization

No problem is more difficult to analyze from a rational-actor perspective than the character or even desirability of democracy, democratization, and dictatorship. I have turned repeatedly in this book to the work of Mancur Olson for illumination, for he has been peculiarly willing to think about the most fundamental questions and to accept the consequences of his logic wherever it seems to lead him. He makes an enormous contribution even when one disagrees with him. His analysis of democracy, dictatorship, and development provides an excellent starting point, but it also illustrates the problems that are encountered.

Olson's view of government is not romantic. Revolution occurs, he argues, not because of revulsion against oppression or injustice, but because rulers lose control of the system of incentives and coercion. Government will arise not because of some voluntary social contract, but because it is "a stationary bandit," more efficient and acceptable than "roving bandits."

> If the stationary bandit successfully monopolizes the theft in his domain, then his victims do not need to worry about theft by others. If he steals only through regular taxation, then his subjects know that they can keep whatever proportion of their output is left after they have paid their taxes. Since all of the settled bandit's victims are for him a source of tax payments, he also has an incentive to prohibit the murder or maiming of his subjects. It will also pay him to provide other public goods whenever the provision of these goods increases taxable income sufficiently.

Later Olson expands this vision: "An autocrat who is taking a long view will try to convince his subjects that their assets will be permanently protected only from theft by others, but also from expropriation by the autocrat himself. If his subjects fear expropriation, they will invest less, and in the long run his tax collections will be reduced.''[27]

The logic of this argument seems to lead toward a defense of dictatorship: "Any individual who has autocratic control over a country will provide public goods to that country because he has an 'encompassing' interest in it. . . . The larger or more encompassing the stage an organization or individual has in society, the greater the incentive the organization or individual has to take action to provide public goods for society."

Yet Olson rejects this conclusion. The problem, he contends, is that the autocrat has an interest in maximizing taxation to the point that revenues fall. That equilibrium point can be high. Moreover, the autocrat may have a short time horizon and, if so, "it is in his interest to confiscate the property of his subjects, to abrogate any contracts he has signed in borrowing money from them, and generally to ignore the long-run economic consequences of his choices."[28] Only democratic societies, Olson suggests, will have a time span that extends across generations and will have an incentive to protect investment and keep taxes at an optimal level. Thus democracy is not only morally but economically superior.

Olson's analysis is comforting, but unfortunately it has two obvious problems. First, the level of taxation is not the only relevant variable in an analysis of democracy, dictatorship, and development. The real question is the purpose for which money gathered through taxation (and corruption) is used. Does it go principally to government expenditures that are consumed by the population or into foreign villas and foreign bank accounts for the autocrat, his friends, and family? Or does the extra money acquired by those close to the autocratic regime go primarily into domestic investment? If so, it may be extremely beneficial for economic growth even if the ways in which capital is acquired would not be countenanced in ethics textbooks. The fact that government is an efficient accumulator of large amounts of money may make it a natural source of early investment capital and growth.

Marxists see the state arising as an instrument of the propertied class to protect their ill-gotten wealth. Olson's image of the stationary bandit essentially reverses this image, at least if the stationary bandit and his men use their ill-gotten wealth in substantial part for investment. Instead of being

27. Mancur Olson, "Dictatorship, Democracy, and Development," *American Political Science Review*, vol. 87 (September 1993), pp. 568, 571.
28. Olson, "Dictatorship, Democracy, and Development," p. 572.

hired by the owning class, the enforcers themselves become the first large-scale owners.[29] This may, indeed, explain why rapidly industrializing countries often have strong governments with large-scale corruption.

Second, Olson's analysis of democracy is much too optimistic. Virtually all politics in a country such as the United States centers on people trying to use the state to obtain more resources than the market would give them. As Olson emphasizes in *The Rise and Decline of Nations*, large interest groups may function as roving bandits who either seek subsidies from the public treasury or protection from market forces. They may achieve their aims through helping the representatives maximize their personal wealth. Olson contends that the accumulation of concessions to powerful interest groups in a long-lasting democratic state harms growth. But it is unclear why, in principle, these concessions are less harmful to economic growth than excessive extraction of wealth by the autocrat.

Although Olson emphasizes the power given large interest groups by the logic of collective action, a major purpose of democracy is to overcome this logic. No action is more irrational than voting, especially in national elections, for no political action is less likely to have an impact on the outcome. Yet the costs of voting, especially in presidential elections where information costs are minimal, are so low that moral suasion and a sense of collective duty can usually overcome rational calculation. If the political leaders are driven by the desire for reelection to respond to the will of the voter, the worst problems of collective action are solved.

The problem is that there is no guarantee that the democratic electorate will have a long time horizon. The voter may look for a maximization of current consumption over investment and thus seek lower taxes and condone higher government expenditures and a foreign trade deficit. The aged in particular have a strong interest in focusing exclusively on social security and medicare. In fact, political science models generally show that the success of an incumbent party in presidential elections is correlated with an increase in per capita personal income. The success of a Ronald Reagan, who provided high short-term consumption at the cost of a deficit that restricted long-term growth, suggests that politicians often inherently understand the validity of these models.

29. For Soviet scholars who made this argument in the Brezhnev period, see the discussion of Leonid Vasilev's work in Jerry F. Hough, *The Struggle for the Third World: Soviet Debates and American Options* (Brookings, 1986), pp. 52–53.

The time span of the voter may be particularly short at early and middle levels of industrialization when standards of living and levels of education are low. Thus the populist tendencies of democratically elected leaders in the third world are legendary. Democracy at such stages is traditionally associated with inflationary policies, subsidies, and the protectionism of an import substitution policy. Some Latin American autocrats such as Augusto Pinochet in Chile have promoted economic growth, while others such as Anastasio Somoza in Nicaragua have been rapacious. Elected rulers, at least before the 1980s, have more consistently followed the model of Juan Peron in Argentina.

Finally, a basic assumption of democratic theory—that elected representatives are driven by the desire for reelection—is too little subjected to examination. A representative driven by economic rationality will not find the salary of a representative compelling. Rather, the money to be earned through corruption, legal graft, and pleasing rich men or organizations who will provide more highly paid positions after government service may be far more decisive in influencing legislators than the fear of being defeated in the next election.

Small wonder that Douglass North is found to complain,

> One gets *efficient* institutions by a polity that has built-in incentives to create and enforce efficient property rights. But it is hard—maybe impossible—to model such a polity with wealth-maximizing actors unconstrained by other considerations. It is no accident that economic models of the polity developed in the public choice literature make the state into something like the Mafia—or, to employ its terminology, a leviathan. The state then becomes nothing more than a machine to redistribute wealth and income. Now we do not have to look far afield to observe states with such characteristics. But the traditional public choice literature is clearly not the whole story.[30]

Rousseau rightly said that a ruler must make every effort to convert might into right, and the same point must be made in the economic sphere. The institutional framework that North has emphasized must be internalized in individual actors, with long-term interest, morality, and fear of punishment interlaced in a way that the individual does not distinguish among them but simply thinks "ought." The Protestant ethic may well have

---

30. North, *Institutions, Institutional Change, and Economic Performance*, p. 140. The paragraph, however, illustrates the problem with conventional and nonconventional definitions. The meaning of the first sentence is unclear when examined closely. Leaving aside other fundamental problems, it certainly does not mean simply "privatization." North defines "property rights" as "the rights individuals appropriate over their own labor and the goods and services they possess" (p. 33).

been crucial in the early stages of marketization not simply because of its promotion of work and saving, but also because it emphasized the concepts of calling and professionalism. Communism also heavily inculcated the concept of duty. To tell Russians that they should simply follow self-interest, and to give them the opportunity to follow such self-interest on the most basic of questions about property acquisition when their time horizon is extraordinarily short is a fundamental mistake. Moreover, to think that emotion is never part of daily life or politics is scarcely believable.[31]

Because the individual vote will never have an impact on the final outcome of a contest, it is perhaps rational for voters to satisfy psychological needs with their vote rather than to try to advance their economic interests. Whatever the reason, matters such as abortion, crime in the distant inner cities, and gun control play a far greater a role in politics than their "real" significance in the world would justify. Clearly, however, they have a symbolic importance that is very real for the voters.

Thus the logic of democracy and dictatorship is inherently ambiguous, for it is uncertain whether a given dictator or a given electorate will take a short-range or long-range view of its self-interest, whether emotion or symbolism will have a crucial impact. One is, therefore, left with ancient wisdoms. The best ruler is an enlightened despot who sees his interest as improving the economic performance and security of his subjects (and thus his long-term tax returns). Unfortunately, despots as a group cannot be trusted to be enlightened, and the problems of collective action make it very difficult to remove one who proves to be unenlightened. Democracy, therefore, is the worst of all the forms of government except for all the others, but not when extreme populists seem likely to come to power who will end democracy and conduct an aggressive foreign policy.

This is scarcely a satisfying intellectual analysis, but we are also left with the historical record. One feature of this record is that countries such as Haiti with a population that is 75 percent illiterate and desperately poor are particularly unlikely to have an electorate that makes long-term economic growth and the security and well-being of the owning classes their top priority. In the early stages of industrialization when a business and middle class is being formed, the members of that class often support dictatorial

---

31. Harold D. Lasswell, *Psychopathology and Politics* (Viking Press, 1930), pp. 183–84, needs to be reread. "It is becoming something of a commonplace that politics is the arena of the irrational. But a more accurate description would be that politics is the process by which the irrational bases of society are brought out into the open."

regimes, although the regimes are "constitutional" dictatorships that will protect property and establish impartial judicial systems to enforce contracts and protect individual rights. As the experiences of Chile and some of the Pacific Rim countries illustrate, the economic growth record of these regimes can be impressive.

A second feature of the historical record, as Samuel Huntington has reemphasized, is that the movement toward democracy has not been a straight line. Instead, there have been waves: the first long wave of democratization from 1828 to 1926 (although as the experience of France indicates, scarcely one without interruptions); the first reverse wave from 1922 to 1942; a second, short wave from 1943 to 1962; a second reverse wave from 1958 to 1975; and a third wave of democratization since 1974. Huntington wrote before the democratization in Russia, but even in the other cases, he cautioned that one cannot know whether the third wave of democratization will be followed by a third reverse.[32] Moreover, democracy has sometimes been replaced by relatively benign constitutional dictatorships, sometimes by those in which rulers seek only to enrich themselves, and sometimes by those of the character of Hitler's Germany or Stalin's Russia.

A third feature of the historical record is that a century of study of political systems has used definitions of democracy that focus on elite conflict, elite isolation from the masses, and the use of democratic institutions to keep the masses quiet.[33] Indeed, this definition of democracy is one on which, to some extent or another, the entire American pluralist school in the twentieth century has agreed.[34] For reasons analyzed by William Riker, the approach strongly supports a liberal definition of democracy, one emphasizing restraints on leaders rather than a populist or a Rousseauian definition based on leaders' representation of the people.[35]

32. Samuel P. Huntington, *The Third Wave: Democratization in the Late Twentieth Century* (University of Oklahoma Press, 1991), pp. 16–26, 280ff.

33. The seminal study for this line of analysis is Joseph Schumpeter, *Capitalism, Socialism, and Democracy* (Harper, 1942). The two classic works in political science are Key, *Public Opinion and American Democracy*, and Stein Rokkan, *Citizens, Elections, Parties: Approaches to the Comparative Study of the Processes of Democracy* (New York: McKay, 1970).

34. See Robert R. Alford and Roger Friedland, *Powers of Theory: Capitalism, The State, and Democracy* (Cambridge University Press, 1985), for the argument that this viewpoint has been dominant.

35. William H. Riker, *Liberalism against Populism: A Confrontation between the Theory of Democracy and the Theory of Social Choice* (San Francisco: W. H. Freeman, 1982).

An examination of the relationship of democratization and economic reform in Russia is more appropriate in a study of the period from 1991 to 1996. Yet two points can be made. First, scholars must not simply extend to other places the transition-to-democracy analysis that currently focuses on the mechanisms of transition in countries at an advanced stage of development in Latin America and southern Europe. Elite interests and calculations in earlier stages of economic development need to be explored. In the process, the ways the problems of collective action are resolved within an elite, whatever it is, need more exploration. Second, much more attention should be given to the role of the state in democratization as well as economic development, but definitions must be more precise in the discussion of its role and particularly of the relationship of the interests of individual bureaucrats (be they military officers or economic planners) to the collective interests of their own bureaucracy, the state as a whole, and the economic elite.

Despite the lip service given to the rediscovery of the state, the state has disappeared from literature not devoted to economic development. This is true even in the models of a scholar working on democracy such as Samuel Huntington, who used to take institutions seriously (figure 15-1). There is no state in Huntington's model, and thus it leads to no questions about what best promotes economic development, education, and democratic values.

It is often said, for example, that Ghana had a higher per capita income than did South Korea in the 1950s and that the subsequent flowering of South Korea is the product of more effective market-oriented policies there. No doubt South Korean economic policy has been more effective than Ghana's (although the Korean policy scarcely was based on the assumptions of the economic advice given to Russia). Yet in the 1950s virtually the entire Korean population was literate when virtually the entire population of Ghana was illiterate. Surely this difference is more important than the similarity in their reported per capita income.

Finally, the work both on the social roots of democracy and the process of transition to democracy is marked by the relative superficiality of the analysis of the political system to which the transition is being made. Democracy is almost invariably defined in procedural terms: the choice of leaders in competitive elections in which most citizens can vote and in which participants can speak and campaign freely. Yet anyone who knows history and the contemporary third world understands there is no clean line between democracy and nondemocracy. Many dictatorships have legislative bodies, and these bodies, like the first European parliaments, are not

Figure 15-1. *Economic Development and Democratization*

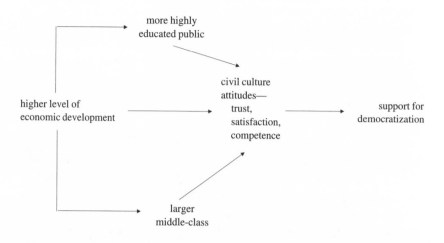

Source: Samuel P. Huntington, *The Third Wave: Democratization in the Late Twentieth Century* (University of Oklahoma Press, 1991), p. 69.

totally without influence. But like the early parliaments, they are more advisory bodies to the ruler than institutions with real power.

Similarly, in some countries whose political systems meet the formal definition of democracy, the bureaucracy seems to rule; in others the military has a silent (and not always so silent) veto power. In countries that are formal democracies, elected politicians may respond very little to public opinion and may be absorbed with enriching themselves and serving those who can help them achieve this goal. It is not enough to define democracy in broad and loose terms that implicitly seem close to that found in American suburbs.

From a policy perspective, the crucial questions of democratization are not those that deal with relatively benign stages of political development, but the democratization through which nuclear and potential nuclear powers such as China, India, Indonesia, Pakistan, and Russia are passing. Democratization at that stage requires a sophisticated examination of the interaction of the processes of establishing democracy and constitutional restraints on the majority, as well as those of national identity, delineation of country boundaries, and federalism. At a time when free trade has become a dogma, it is necessary to look at the experience of European countries that came to industrialization late, many of which developed totalitarian or semitotalitarian regimes at least in part in response to the exposure of urban villagers to the changes and competition of the world economy.[36] The dangers are simply too great to allow the political and security issues involved in nation building to be abandoned to economists whose models do not include political considerations.

The Implications for American Policy

It is difficult to draw implications for American policy on the breakup of the Soviet Union because the breakup has been treated by many observers as an American triumph. Presumably the only lessons to be drawn are how to destabilize some other competing power or powers, and such a subject is politically too sensitive to discuss openly. The problem, however, is that the retrospective claims of the 1990s remind one of Senator Patrick Leahy's advice about Vietnam: declare victory and withdraw. Those observers who quietly said that the Soviet-American confrontation was useful in preserving European security now hail as a consequence of their farsighted policy the reunification of Germany they tried to stop. Those who created a huge American budget deficit for a military buildup they claimed was needed to stop a Soviet juggernaut heading for the Persian Gulf or the English Channel now say they alone knew the Soviet Union was near collapse and that the Soviet military would not forestall Ukraine's independence.

Similarly, the spokesmen for the Bush administration, while conceding they supported Gorbachev, did not loudly proclaim that their goal was to help him preserve the territorial integrity of the Soviet Union. Yet as Bruce Berkowitz and Jeffrey Richelson have written,

> By the late 1980s, U.S.-Soviet relations had improved significantly . . . and Gorbachev was seen as being largely responsible. The Bush administration wanted to take these improvements in U.S.-Soviet relations even further. Under its policy of "moving beyond containment," the Soviet Union would be "integrated into the community of nations." . . . It was clear that U.S. leaders wanted Gorbachev to remain in power. . . . [The objectives were] establishing a long-term partnership with Gorbachev and preserving the integrity of the Soviet Union. . . . Had [President Bush's speech in Kiev in early August 1991] dissuaded the Ukrainians from total secession, it would now be viewed as a classic

36. Evelyn Davidheiser, "The World Economy and Mobilizational Dictatorship: Russia's Transition, 1846–1917," Ph.D. dissertation, Duke University, 1990.

example in which the United States demonstrated leadership and influenced events.[37]

Finally, there is no guarantee the ultimate political outcome will be benign. In December 1993, by a two-to-one margin, Russians were convinced that the West's economic advice represented a deliberate effort to weaken Russia. This margin rose to three to one in 1995 and more that that in 1996.[38] It is not in American interests that Russians have this perception, whether it is true or not.[39] Politicians such as Gennady Zyuganov and Aleksandr Lebed play to this popular feeling and feed it. There is no guarantee about their policies if they come to power.

It may well be, of course, that the breakup of the Soviet Union will indeed some day be seen to have been best for long-term American interests. Just as the road to hell sometimes takes a circuitous route, so the road to heaven can be paved with bad intentions and wrong assumptions. But even if the outcome turns out to have been the best possible, the analogy with Russian roulette is appropriate. In Russian roulette, one wins five times out of six—maybe more if gravity makes it less likely that the bullet will stop at the top chamber. But if one loses, the result is catastrophic. Even if the likelihood of a reasonable long-term outcome from the course of events in Russia is fairly high—as I believe it to be—America took a substantial chance that control of nuclear weapons would be lost or that a Russian leader not unlike Hitler would be produced by the kind of national humiliation and economic disaster suffered by Germany in the 1920s. This outcome is still possible, and there has been no reason to take the chance.

It is often said that the United States did not and does not have the ability to affect domestic policy in a country such as the Soviet Union. That is wrong. To the extent that the decisive factor in a disintegrating situation is the mind-set of the leader, the West can wield influence, especially when, as in the Soviet Union, the leader is eager to win Western approval. When stabilization funds are provided, the West is, in effect, often able to bribe

37. Bruce D. Berkowitz and Jeffrey T. Richelson, "The CIA Vindicated: The Soviet Collapse *Was* Predicted," *National Interest*, no. 41 (Fall 1995), pp. 41, 38, 44-45.

38. Jerry F. Hough, Evelyn Davidheiser, and Susan Goodrich Lehmann, *The 1996 Russian Presidential Election* (Brookings, 1996), p. 41.

39. This is the subject of another book. But so there will be no misunderstanding, I think that the IMF advice had the absolutely predictable result of weakening Russia—likely for many years. Those giving the advice, however, were deeply convinced that it would lead to the best results for Russia.

officials to take certain actions, especially if the officials can find ways to obtain part of the money themselves.

It is impossible to imagine Gorbachev following the policy he did if he were told by Westerners he respected that the Far Eastern models on economic reform and democratization were the correct ones. It is impossible to imagine a domestic coalition that would have formed in Russia to support the economic policy of the Russian government under Boris Yeltsin unless it were supported by the West financially. The West was not powerless to affect developments in Russia; it was decisive.

But even if we assume that this judgment is correct, what are its implications? The policies of the Bush administration and the Clinton administration were very similar. The State Department in both administrations followed policies similar to those of "from Vladivostok to Vancouver" (in Secretary James Baker's words) under the Bush administration and of "strategic partnership" under the Clinton administration.[40] These policies essentially defined the task as reintegrating a healthy Russia back into the West, much as Germany was reintegrated after World War II. It was assumed that this required a democratic political system in the Soviet Union as well as a change in its foreign policy.

The Treasury Department—or the economists specializing in foreign economics who moved back and forth between Treasury, the International Monetary Fund, and the World Bank—basically argued that the Soviet Union and then Russia must end government regulation, privatize immediately, introduce market prices immediately through the release of controls (price liberalization), engage free trade in foreign economic relations, and institute very tight monetary controls and a balanced budget. Whatever the virtues of that advice from an economic point of view (and this book has, of course, been very doubtful about those virtues), it clearly meant the destruction of the USSR, the dismantling of the state system of managing the economy before a new system could be introduced, and the possibility of a popular reaction in the streets that could have the most unpredictable political results. It was scarcely what would have been recommended if political stability in a democratic society were the main priority.

---

40. "At East West Crossroads, Western Europe Hesitates," *New York Times*, March 25, 1992, p. A10; and Elaine Sciolino, "Reassuring Eastern Europe, Christopher Praises Hungary's Reforms," *New York Times*, October 22, 1993, p. A8.

Faced with these two sets of advice, the Bush and Clinton administrations accepted both. The Treasury Department and the economists in the international economic organizations defined the economic policy. Under Secretary of the Treasury Lawrence Summers went to Moscow in 1993 when Yeltsin wanted to dissolve the Russian Supreme Soviet and reappointed Yegor Gaidar as first deputy premier and support for a harsh economic policy, by all outward appearances an attempt to ensure American support of Yeltsin's political actions.[41] When the fascist Vladimir Zhirinovsky won the ensuing 1993 Duma election, Strobe Talbott of the State Department spoke of "too much shock and too little therapy," but when the president went to Moscow in January, he supported the retention of the extreme monetarists (Gaidar and Boris Fedorov) and a continuation of shock therapy.[42]

The State Department policy, with various deviations and inconsistencies, defined the strategic relationship with Gorbachev and Yeltsin, respectively, subject to the domestic political pressures for including Poland, Hungary, and the Czech Republic in NATO. When President Clinton traveled to Moscow in April 1996, he said that America's first priority was control over nuclear weapons and the safety of the nuclear materials.[43] The economic collapse and the precipitous drop in investment was, of course, the chief threat to nuclear safety, but this point was not made.

Throughout this period the debates on American policy almost never dealt with potential contradictions between strategic and economic policy. President Bush was criticized for supporting Gorbachev for too long and President Clinton for the same sin vis-à-vis Yeltsin, but both criticisms were misplaced for lack of any reasonable alternative. Yet neither president was criticized for the policy to which he pushed his counterpart in Moscow. Both presidents were criticized for having excessive trust in the future foreign policy of Russia—but by the very people that were most insistent Russia follow the economic policy most likely to bring a fascistlike leader to power.

41. Steven Greenhouse, "I.M.F. Delays $1.5 Billion Loan to Russia Because Reform Is Stalled," *New York Times*, September 20, 1993, p. A3.

42. Peter Passell, "Russia's Political Turmoil Follows Half Steps, Not Shock Therapy," *New York Times*, December 30, 1993, p. D2; and Steven Erlanger, "Leading Russian Reformer Quits, Questioning the Cabinet's Policies," *New York Times*, January 17, 1994, p. A1.

43. Michael R. Gordon, "Summit in Moscow Urges A-Test Ban," *New York Times*, April 21, 1996, p. A1.

Similarly, neither the scholarly nor intelligence community was useful in helping their country and government follow a different policy. Specialists on the Soviet Union have been criticized for mistakes in prediction, but their greater sins are to be found elsewhere. Scholars were almost always asked to be court astrologers, making predictions in a politically acceptable manner. If they accepted, they and the editors with whom they dealt had to function within the court's rules, and the rules are as complicated as those in Brezhnev's Soviet Union. They were and are also very restrictive in their way. Scholars too often—and this is self-criticism as well as criticism of others both in the past and at the present—were attracted to this role and allowed it to affect the way they studied the Soviet Union, the questions they asked and did not ask, and the conclusions they drew and the way they phrased them.

Generalist scholars have been even less helpful. Political economists have largely adopted the perspectives and methodologies of the classical economists and have had little to add about the role of the political. Theorists on democracy have focused only on the late stages of democratization found in Latin America of the last two decades, while theorists of revolution focus only on revolutions at the early stages of industrialization. The very geostrategists who wrote thousands of articles and books about the dangers to the United States of retaliating with nuclear weapons if the Soviet Union attacked Western Europe or even Minutemen missiles in South Dakota never say anything about placing a nuclear umbrella over Warsaw and Prague. Multiculturalists have damned the effort to compare countries at different times but at similar stages of development (Asia and Africa today and Europe in the eighteenth and nineteenth centuries). The paradoxical result is that they define standards of democracy and human rights as those found in the contemporary West.

Although the desire of those in the political sphere to make predictions for reasons of psychological self-assurance or political legitimacy is extraordinarily strong, it is striking how seldom these predictions are useful. All observers comment on the problem of a flood of contradictory or Delphic predictions, but the example of this book shows how the problem goes more deeply.

Thus from mid-1990 to mid-1991 any fool could see that the continuation of Gorbachev's toleration and even encouragement of chaos would lead to the collapse of the Soviet system. The question was whether his policy would continue, and it was on that question that analysts differed. I thought Gorbachev would use his presidential power to institute some form of martial law. The analysts of the CIA associated with Robert Gates, who had always been skeptical about Gorbachev's intention to reform and then about his ability to do so, believed the military and the KGB would overthrow him. Those in the intelligence community who published *Trends* believed that the compromises struck between Yeltsin, Gorbachev, and Aleksandr Rutskoi would hold, perhaps ultimately because they assumed Rutskoi spoke for the military. The striking thing about these three predictions was that they all led to the same policy-relevant and misleading prediction: the territorial integrity of the Soviet Union was relatively safe.

But what if the Bush administration had been told in January 1991 that during the following year Gorbachev would simply let Yeltsin take over industrial plants and all taxation, that the Soviet military would conduct a coup without using force, and that Russia would leave the Soviet Empire? Neither the administration nor any serious specialist would have believed such a prediction. By the time the prediction became credible in late summer, it was too late for the administration to do anything, except perhaps encourage the military to stage a coup d'état.

What the administration needed in 1989 and 1990 was contingency analysis. It needed to be told that the economic shock therapy advocated by the IMF, coupled with the American condemnation of the type of action taken by the Chinese in Tiananmen Square in June 1989 and the Western threats against Soviet action in the Baltic states, would, if Gorbachev heeded them, almost surely lead to the disintegration of the Soviet Union.

In my opinion, the president should have been told that, if his priority was to avoid this disintegration, he should have tried to educate Gorbachev about the nature of American federalism and the slowness with which any country (including the United States) moves to democracy. He should have pointed to the success of the Asian model of industrialization (and that of Europe in the past), with its high protectionist trade barriers, as the most appropriate industrial strategy until Soviet plants became as technologically sophisticated as Western ones. He should have warned that excessive privatization would focus all attention on takeover politics and would destroy the system of taxation, which was based on state ownership of industry. He should have denounced the 500-Day Plan for the nonsense that it was and warned for the reasons laid out in this book that destroying the power of the local party organs would have terrible consequences for the economy. He should have promised American aid if an incremental plan of transition were adopted, and he should have said that Premier Ryzhkov was closer to such a plan than was his radical economic adviser (whom, as may be remembered, Ed Hewett correctly called a man with the views of Milton Friedman).

This posture in 1989 and 1900 would almost surely have educated Gorbachev and his advisers about the problems of democratization and marketization enough to enable to them to find a path to reform that would have avoided the heavy economic costs of the policy that was followed (and the danger of a fascist leader) and that would have achieved the administration's goal of preserving the territorial integrity of the Soviet Union.

Without any doubt, the last two paragraphs have produced dangerously high blood pressure among many readers. First, not everyone would agree that the advice I have prescribed was the best reform strategy for the Soviet leaders. The editorial writers of the *New York Times, Financial Times, Washington Post,* and *Wall Street Journal* were giving the Soviet Union starkly different advice on economic reform, and they were not praising the gradual political liberalization in China. The West did not have a consensus theory of transition for communist countries, and the theories with the most support featured much of the anarchism to which Gorbachev was already attracted.

Second, even if one assumes that President Bush agreed with everything I have said, he could not have advocated such action in public, and he could not have given such advice in private without seeing it quickly leaked to the press. To praise Japanese protectionism, to quote Abraham Lincoln's views on secession as relevant for Soviet behavior toward Estonia or Ukraine, to say the Communist party apparatus should be dismantled carefully, or to warn against rapid privatization would have been political suicide.

The best President Bush could have done would have been to talk about the need for gradualism, the dangers of populism, the advantages of a strong president, the lessons of American federalism, the importance of the sanctity of laws, and the like. He should probably be criticized for not doing so earlier and more consistently. But when he did speak in gradualist terms in Ukraine in August 1991 and described the American political tradition in moving terms, he was severely derided for giving a "chicken Kiev" speech that did not promote Ukrainian independence.

Only the most naive would argue that American leaders can isolate their efforts to influence developments abroad from their domestic political concerns in the United States. It would be equally unrealistic to suggest that they can develop theories of transition, as Gorbachev often said, "on the march." To alter the advice of the International Monetary Fund, President Bush would have had to force through a general change in its approach to dealing with the third world, and that would have involved a terrific battle. President Clinton was successful in pressuring the IMF to lower its standards in granting Russia loans, but that was an entirely different matter than obtaining a change in the words and analysis that accompanied the money.

Lord Keynes once said that those who most consider themselves practical minded are the prisoners of some defunct economist. The point needs to be emphasized and generalized. Frameworks of analysis have a powerful impact upon events; they are part of the rules about which Douglass North has written. Whatever criticism may be made of those in the international economic community, they unquestionably have concrete advice to give and an understandable justification for that advice. Whatever praise may be given those who emphasize the importance of the role of the state in economic life and who discuss the difficult relationship of democracy and market, they talk in very general terms and have not developed concrete theories of transition that have concrete implications that can be explained in politically viable ways. The ancient wisdom is correct: you cannot beat something with nothing.

It is the job of scholars to develop frameworks of analysis with specific implications for policymakers and to try to ensure that they are constantly revised so as to remain as useful as possible. It is too soon to make definitive judgments about the long-term consequences of the Russian Revolution of 1990–91 and the Western policy toward it. But as those consequences become clearer, they will have the most profound theoretical results. They will become the center of a great scholarly debate on the relation of state and economy and of democracy and the market.

In that debate it is necessary to move from generalities about the role of the state to more specific and useful analysis. Asia and Africa in the first half of the twenty-first century will be facing the same kinds of strains that Europe faced in the nineteenth and first half of the twentieth century, and it is vital that the lessons represented by Russia be absorbed. India and China have the same potential to disintegrate as the Soviet Union or the Austro-Hungarian Empire. Iran's experience shows that fascistlike leaders can come to power as easily in Asia as they did in Europe, and now it is possible for them to come to power in countries with nuclear weapons. It is only with historical perspective and insight, generalized in terms of the logic of the gradual development of constitutional restraints on government and elite support for democracy that the world will have some hope to avoid many of the same problems in the twenty-first century that tore it apart in the twentieth century.

Index

Abalkin, Leonid, 117, 126, 134–36, 212, 455; economic reform plan, 263, 347–49, 354, 357, 359–60; in Ryzhkov's cabinet, 341, 343–44
Abkhazian Autonomous Republic, 246–47
Acceleration program, Gorbachev and, 107
Accounting money, 111–12; versus transferable money, 343
Achalov, Vladislav, 434–34, 443, 447
Administrative system, Soviet: destruction of Communist party and, 272; subordination within, 255–56. *See also* Central administration, USSR; Command-administrative system, USSR
Adomeit, Hannes, 208
Afanasev, Yury, 172, 419, 471–72
Affirmative action policy, Soviet, 224, 238
Afghanistan War: Gorbachev and, 193n; veterans, 485–86
Afghanistan, Yeltsin's policy on, 486
Aganbegian, Abel, 95, 137–38, 347, 370
Ageev, Genii E., 290n
Agrarian party, 297–98
Agrarniki, in *1990* Russian Congress, 302
Agriculture: economic reform, 16–18, 137–38, 356–57; subsidies, 114, 114n
Akhromeev, Marshal Sergei, 209
Alcohol, campaign against, 124–25
Algeria, *1991* elections in, 251
Aliev, Geidar, 57
Alma-Ata agreement, 457, 466, 473
Anarchism: of communist ideology, 491; of Western analysis, 494–95
Andreeva, Nina, 147, 498
Andropov, Yury: background, 67, 88; Gorbachev and, 68, 70–71, 86–87;

lieutenants, 57–58, 68, 90; and military, 78; political career, 85, 88, 89–90; and reform, 19, 96–97, 124
Antimodernization theories, 10
Apple, R. W., 206
Arbatov, Georgy, 121, 121n, 182, 191
Armenia: and Azerbaidzhan, 234; education in, 236, 243; national identity, 234; position in Soviet Union, 235. *See also* Nagorno-Karabakh conflict; Transcaucasus
Armstrong, John, 228
Article 6 of USSR Constitution, 266–67; removal of, 268, 270
Arutiunian, Yury, 239
Arzhannikov, Nikolai M., 472
Arzhinba, Vladislav, 246
Asia, Central. *See* Central Asia
Aslund, Anders, 123, 349, 467, 482, 504
Association of Democrats (political group), 414
August *1991* coup d'état, 428–32; chaotic nature, 439–41; conspirators, 437–43; events preceding, 422–28; Gorbachev's role, 432–37; lack of leadership in, 442; military in, 443–48; passivity of masses, 12; possible scenarios, 442–43; triggering event, 439; U.S. response, 443
Authoritarianism: economic reform and, 141; Gorbachev's retreat from, 142; versus totalitarian system, 18, 143. *See also* Dictatorship
Autonomous oblasts, 227
Autonomous republics, 227; in *1990* Russian Congress, 303; ethnic composition, 246t; lack of sovereignty, 383–84; legal transformation of, 381–82, 390–92;

527

political unrest, 247; sovereignty demands, 245–48; and Union republics, 246–47, 392; and Union Treaty renegotiation, 381, 392–93; Yeltsin's policy on, 385. *See also* Republics, USSR

Azerbaidzhan, 235–36; and Armenia, 234; national identity, 234. *See also* Nagorno-Karabakh conflict; Transcaucasus

Baburin, Sergei N., 222, 244, 311, 387, 472

Bakatin, Vadim, 329, 395, 421–22, 450, 486

Baker, James, 134, 341, 482, 520

Baklanov, Oleg, 428–29, 431, 436

Baku, Azerbaidzhan, 235

Baltic republics, 232–34; declaration of independence, 477; education in, 243; ethnic composition, 232–33; incorporation in Soviet Union, 232; passivity, 11; population, 228t; and reform, 331; relaxation of controls on, 148; sovereignty demands, 386; and Union Treaty, 377. *See also individual republics*

Banfield, Edward, 498

Bangladesh, secession of, 374

Banks: after August *1991* coup, 453; crisis of, 479

Barabanov, Vladimir A., 289

Barannikov, Viktor, 450

Bashkirs, 227, 282

Basis of Economic Relationship between the Soviet Union, the Union Republic, and Autonomous Republics (law), 381

Belorussia: assimilation in, 229; and dissolution of Soviet Union, 481–82; ethnic composition, 229; nationality problems, 377n; population, 228t; UN membership, 217, 221

Belovezh agreement, 481–83

Beria, Lavrenty, 144n, 234

Berkowitz, Bruce, 518

Berlinguer, Enrico, 74

Bessarabia, 233

Bialer, Seweryn, 108

Biriukova, Aleksandra, 125

Black-earth region: in Bolshevik Revolution, 27–28, 29t

Bobkov, Filipp D., 290n

Bocharov, Mikhail, 300, 314, 328, 335; and economic reform, 354, 458

Bogoliubov, Klavdy, 156

Bogomolov, Oleg, 119n, 136–37, 347

Boldin, Valery, 72n, 75, 104–05, 207; in August *1991* coup, 428, 436, 439–40; on Gorbachev, 104–05, 114–15, 207–08, 259

Bolshevik Revolution of *1917:* ethnic support for, 239; paradoxes, 317n; social base of, 24–30, 32–34

Book publishing, liberalization, 145–46

Bourgeoisie: communist disdain for, 39–40; Marxist definition, 1n; in Soviet Revolution, 1–2

Bovin, Aleksandr, 154

Brady, Nicholas, 467

Branch institutions in USSR, 374–75

Brass, Paul, 252

Bratishchev, Igor, 311

Bread prices. *See* Prices

Breslauer, George, 59

Brezhnev, Leonid: background, 30, 32, 34; last years in power, 41, 61–62, 89; lieutenants, 87–89; and national identity issue, 226; political career, 85; and power structure, 375; reforms, 19, 41–42, 143

Brezhnev era: changing social structure, 44–51; stability, 41–44, 58, 61; Western perception of, 42–44, 59

Brinton, Crane, 2, 15, 490–91, 499, 502

Brown, Archie, 432

Brzezinski, Zbigniew, 59

Budgetary process, Soviet, 36, 111

Bukharin, Nikolai, 53, 144–45, 400

Bulgaria: political reform, 205. *See also* Eastern Europe

Burbulis, Gennady, 367; and dissolution of Union, 466–67; economic reform vision, 458, 461, 463; and Union Treaty renegotiation, 424; in Yeltsin's government, 469–70

Bureaucracy: attitude changes in, 502–04; and Bolshevik Revolution, 28–30; composition, 52–53; and economic reform, 20–21, 62, 105, 375; generational cleavage in, 55–56, 65–66, 67t; Gorbachev's distrust of, 491, 505; levels, 57; occupational cleavage in, 53–55; privileges in Soviet system, 34–35; radical economists' view of, 122; regional cleavage in, 56–58; as ruling class, 52; and Soviet Revolution, 1–2, 25; understaffing, 48

Burlatsky, Fedor, 82, 90, 98, 180, 185; and economic reform, 126–27, 137; political career, 90, 187

Bush administration: and August *1991* coup, 443; and Gorbachev's reform, 253–54, 518; Russian policy of, 518, 520–21, 524

Capitalism, Lenin's condemnation of, 39–41

Ceausescu, Nicolae, 199t, 206

Censorship, relaxation of, 144

Central administration, USSR: disorder in, 394; 500-Day Plan and, 365–67; Gorbachev's reform and, 106; versus provincial governments, 56–58; reorganization, Gorbachev and, 394–95

Central and Eastern Europe. *See* Eastern Europe

Central Asia: and dissolution of Union, 483; ethnic composition, 236; population, 228t. *See also individual republics*

Central Committee. *See* Russian Central Committee; USSR Central Committee

Chebrikov, Viktor M., 88–89, 91, 201, 265

Chechen-Ingush Autonomous Republic, 247

Chechnia, 485

Checks and balances: Brezhnev's policy of, 87–89; Gorbachev's policy of, 94

Chernenko, Konstantin: death, 76–77; Gorbachev and, 71–74; political career, 70–71, 84–85, 88–89

Cherniaev, Anatoly, 125–26, 180, 260; background, 184; and foreign policy, 195–96, 500; political career, 184–85

Chernobyl nuclear disaster, and liberalization, 144

Chernomyrdin, Viktor, 34

Chiesa, Giulietto, 170, 172

China: American investment in, 204, 205t; disintegration potential, 525; economic reform, 17–18, 20, 22, 95–99, 104; Gorbachev's visit, 204; nationality policy of, 219–20; political reform, 18; privatization, 17–18, 502; as reform model, 16–17, 19, 106, 118–19, 135–37; Soviet democratization and, 203–04

Christianity, and democracy, 4n

Chubar, Vlas, 224

Circular flow of power, 80–86; Gorbachev and, 273; institution of, 81; Lenin and, 81; origin of term, 63; Stalin and, 81–82

Civil wars, in Soviet republics, 477

"Civilized Relations: A Necessity, a Reality, or a Utopia?" (Yakovlev), 192

Class hatred in USSR, 32, 39

Clinton administration: and Gorbachev's reform, 253–54; Russian policy, 520–21, 525

Coal miners' strike of *1989,* 135, 168, 263, 345, 422

Coalition formation in *1990* Russian Congress, 306

Cockburn, Patrick, 110, 116, 126–27

Collective action, logic of, 498; and August *1991* coup, 445, 447; and democracy, 512; Gorbachev's misunderstanding of, 372;

and resistance to change, 62; and revolution, 7

Comecon. *See* Council on Mutual Economic Assistance

Command-administrative system, USSR: dismantling of, 122; and economic reform, 118–22

Commonwealth of Independent States, formation, 482

Communism: appeal of, 28, 31–34, 39; campaign to overthrow, 449; as disease of transition, 25–26; and economic security, 34–37; ethical basis, 514; loss of faith in, 499–500; and psychological security, 37–41

Communist Manifesto (Marx), 35, 39–40; historical setting, 26, 31

Communist party: in *1989* election, 160–61, 164–69; in August *1991* coup, 447; benefits from rule of, 252–53; and democratization, 261; and economic reform, 255–58, 356–57; end to power, 249–77; evolution possibilities, 257–58, 271; Gorbachev and, 102, 250, 258–62, 272–77, 404; incentive system, 20, 255, 257; leading role of, 266–67, 271–72; liberalization of, 147–48, 151, 154; membership, 256; as parliamentary party, 273–77; power, 254; reorganization under Gorbachev, 273–77; split in, 414; structure, 255–56; and Union Treaty renegotiation, 378; USSR Constitution and, 266–67; Yeltsin's attack on, 426–27, 439, 451. *See also* Russian Communist party

Communist regimes: instability, 9–10; Soviet, 14n

Communist revolutions: industrialization and, 26. *See also* Bolshevik Revolution of *1917*

Communists for Democracy (political group), 411, 414

Communists of Russia (political group), 303–04; in *1990* Russian Congress, 311–12; versus Democratic Russia, 304; split in, 411, 414

Congress of People's Deputies. *See* Russian Congress of People's Deputies; USSR Congress of People's Deputies

Conservative economists: and price reform, 117–18; views, 354–55; virtues, 136–37

Conspirators in August *1991* coup d'état, 428–29, 437–43; mistakes, 446

Constituent Assembly, *1917* elections for, 26–27, 29t

Constitution, USSR: *1936,* 376; *1977,* 376, 383; Article 6 of, 266–68, 270; Gorbachev and, 376–77
Constitutional democracy, steps leading to, 141
Consumption: economic hysteria and, 264; policy of maintaining, 348
Control, loss of, Gorbachev's reform and, 140–42, 249–51, 272
Cook, Linda, 43
Corporations, economic model of, 118, 121
Corruption: effects, 511–12; privatization and, 503
Costa Rica, *1948* revolt in, 8
Cost-plus pricing, 112n
Council on Mutual Economic Assistance (Comecon), 510
Coup d'état of August *1991. See* August *1991* coup d'état
Crankshaw, Edward, 55–56, 65–66, 495
Czechoslovakia: *1968* invasion of, 440; economic reform, 98–99; instability, 196; political reform, 206

Daniels, Robert, 63
Decentralization of power: Communist party and, 255; Gorbachev's reform and, 101–02; Khrushchev's reform and, 253; obstacles, 227; and privatization, 388
Democracy: American assumptions about, 37; analysis of, 510–14; anarchist conception of, 491; and Christianity, 4n; constitutional, steps leading to, 141; definitions, 213, 298, 501, 515; factors producing, 6; and force, 139; Gorbachev's definition, 501; historical record of, 514–18; Leninist definition, 298; naive definitions, 213; Olson's view, 511–12; psychological problems in, 38; Russian misrepresentation of, 493; Soviet, intellectuals and, 23; in third world, 513; use of term in Soviet system, 149. *See also* Democratization
Democratic Russia (political group), 293–94, 300–301, 303–04; in *1990* Russian Congress, 304–05, 309; call for Gorbachev's resignation, 398; collapse of communism and, 471–72; versus Communists of Russia, 304; division in, 471–74; formation, 300; and Moscow demonstrations, 408; and Yeltsin, 474–75
Democratization: Communist party and, 261; economic reform and, 140–41, 341; as evolutionary process, 9; Gorbachev and, 103, 126–28, 142, 148–55, 171–72; industrialization and, 5–6, 13, 507;

inevitability, 146–47; intermediate stages, 4; models, 516–17, 517f; and price reform, 128, 138; recent theories of, 8; revolution and, 3–8; in Russia, beginnings of, 14n; Russian character and, 514; and Soviet federalism, 215; time factor in, 14
Demonstrations: Moscow, 321–22, 408; Tiananmen Square, 18, 135, 169, 203–04; 253; Timisoara, Romania, 206
Deng Xiaoping, 135, 373
Destabilization, Gorbachev and, 140–42, 249–50, 272
Detente, Soviet debate on, 190
Deutsch, Karl, 9
Developing countries. *See* Third world
Di Palma, Guiseppe, 8, 13, 59
Dictatorship: appeal of, 37; and democracy, 516–17; economic growth under, 515; and fear of Gorbachev's rule, 394–98, 404–05; logic of, 511, 514; Soviet, 142–43; stability, 7–8; totalitarian versus authoritarian, 143
Dissidence, incentives for avoiding, 257
Dissolution of Soviet Union, 477–83; causes, 449; economic reform and, 367–68, 462–64; events preceding, 405; factors leading to, 128; implications for U.S. policy, 518–25; and military, 482–89; passive acceptance of, 12–13; Russia and, 374, 462–64, 481–82; unpredictability, 23–24, 373–74; Western perception of, 449, 467–68, 486, 518–25; Yeltsin and, 465–66
Districts. *See* Territorial base
Dobrynin, Anatoly, 104–05, 180; background, 179; and foreign policy, 178–79, 201
Dolgikh, Vladimir, 95, 201, 201n
Domestic policy: foreign policy and, 175–76. *See also* Economic reform; Political reform
Duma: composition, 292n; typical nature, 151; under Yeltsin, 262
Dunlop, John, 432, 433n, 442

East Germany: instability, 196; political reform, 205
Eastern Europe: collapse of communism in, 250; communist leadership, 199t; economic relations with, 196, 208; economic shock therapy in, 208, 509–10; Gorbachev's policy on, 186, 193, 195, 198–209; multiparty systems in, 150–51; political importance, 196; political reform, 202–06, 250; as reform model, 16–17, 106, 118–19; Soviet analysis of, 194; Soviet domestic policy and, 196–97, 208

Economic performance, USSR: in *1989,* 263–64; after August *1991* coup, 452–55, 477; public hysteria and, 264

Economic reform, USSR, 20–22; beginnings, 95–99, 106–10; versus Chinese experience, 17–20, 22, 95–99, 104, 118–19; command-administrative system and, 118–22; Communist party and, 255–58, 356–57; and democratization, 140, 341; disregard for previous experience, 118–19; and dissolution of Union, 367–68; early success, 107; financial problems, 112–14; and foreign policy, 196; 400-Day Plan, 354, 360; Gorbachev and, 19, 21, 103–10, 114, 119–20, 342–45; institutions and, 20–21; peculiarities, 345–48; and political control, 140–41; presidential dictatorship and, 253; and Russian independence, 457–58, 462–64; social consequences, 120; steps, 16; supporters, 24–25, 26–27t; tragedy, 103–39; USSR Congress and, 263–64; weaknesses, 103–05. *See also* 500-Day Plan

Economic security in Soviet system, 34–37

Economic shock therapy: arguments for, 21n; in Eastern Europe, 208, 509–10; Gorbachev and, 11, 105, 131, 133, 375; radical economists and, 122

Economic sovereignty, 387

Economists, USSR: compartmentalization, 136; pecuniary motivations, 138. *See also* Conservative economists; Radical economists

Education, Soviet: changes, 44–45, 46t; egalitarian nature, 35; government policy on, 24, 65

Efficiency, in Soviet system, 36–37

Egalitarianism, in Soviet system, 34–35; economic reform and, 120

Elections, Russian. *See* Russian election of 1990; Russian presidency, election for; Russian Supreme Soviet

Elections, USSR: alternatives for conducting, 251; control over, 251, 254; economic reform and, 140; format, 154, 165–66; Gorbachev's speech on democratization and, 154–55; of leadership, 81–83; nature, 143, 152–53; *1987* experimental, 153–54; *1988* mandate, 141; presidental, 270. *See also* Republican elections of *1990*; USSR election of *1989*

Elections-*90,* 293

Elites: cleavages among, 53–58, 65–66, 67t; democratic political activity, 11; and dissolution of Soviet Union, 449;

divisiveness, 492; and intellectuals, 499n; and revolution, 4–5, 6–7, 10, 12–13; Soviet, 51–58; and Soviet Revolution, 497; Western, 51. *See also* Bureaucracy

Empire, versus multiethnic country, 373

Engels, Friedrich, 54–55

Entente: definition, 190; Gorbachev and, 193; Soviet debate on, 189–92

Entrepreneurship: in China, 18; in Soviet Union, 502–03

Equilibrium of mid-*1970s,* 41–42, 58, 61; American perception of, 42–44, 59

Escape from Freedom (Fromm), 38–39

Estonia: declaration of independence, 376; ethnic composition, 232–33; language law, 376; sovereignty demands, 386; Soviet controls, 148. *See also* Baltic republics

Ethnic conflicts, in Union republics, 247, 262–63. *See also* National identity *and under individual republics*

Etika (political group), 303

Europe, Eastern. *See* Eastern Europe

Europeanization, debate on, 194

Europe, Western. *See* Western Europe

Factions: in *1990* Russian Congress, 312; Soviet parties as, 12; in Soviet power structure, 86–87

Falin, Valentin, 201

Federalism, Soviet: centrifugal forces in, 238; democratization and, 215; Lenin's concept, 217–20; peculiarities, 216–21; versus U.S. federalism, 222

Federation Council, USSR, 248, 376, 402

Fedorchuk, Vitaly, 57

Fedorenko, Nikolai, 362

Fedorov, Boris, 3, 333

Fein, Esther, 264

Fil'shin, Gennady I., 244

Financial planning, Soviet, 36, 110–14. *See also* Price reform

First Russian Congress of People's Deputies, 279–83; agenda, 304–05, 307t; coalition formation in, 306; composition, 286, 287t, 291, 295, 296–97t; conflict with Yeltsin, 470; democratic features, 282–83, 292; disorder, 276, 308–12; dissolution, 385, 406, 476; distribution of forces in, 312–14; members, 299t; political groups in, 299–304; and Supreme Soviet, 281; and USSR Congress, 279, 282–83, 294, 299. *See also* USSR election of *1989*

First USSR Congress of People's Deputies: candidates, 161–64, 162–63t; composition, 159–60, 164–69, 168t; conservative nature, 299, 327–28, 379; and economic reform, 350; Gorbachev's control over, 399–400; idea of, Gorbachev and, 157–58; purpose, 160–61, 172; social impact, 169–74; television coverage, 170–71, 250, 254, 298–99; work, 262–66. *See also* USSR election of *1989*

500-Day Plan, 105, 117, 361–72; criticism of, 502; Gorbachev and, 212n, 213, 370–71; origin, 354; and privatization, 363–64, 364n; radical nature, 117, 245; and taxation, 364, 366–69; and Union republics, 390; and Union Treaty renegotiations, 390–91; Yeltsin's political goals and, 213, 333–34, 339

Food prices. *See* Prices

Force: August *1991* coup, 431–32; democracy and, 139; Gorbachev's reluctance to use, 332, 489, 498–99; as government function, 21–22; Western tolerance for, 253–54

Foreign policy, USSR: and domestic policy, 175–76; Gorbachev and, 175–89, 192–96, 204, 209. *See also under individual politicians*

400-Day Plan, 354, 360

Freedom, problems of, 38–39

Freeland, Chrystia, 479

Friedman, Milton, 509n

Frolov, Ivan T., 150, 185–86, 194, 329, 459; ideological views, 260

From Truman to Reagan (Yakovlev), 191

Fromm, Erich, 38–39

Frunze, Mikhail, 224

"Fuku" (Yevtushenko), 144n

Gaidar, Yegor: background, 459; career, 186, 213, 362; economic reform vision, 105, 348, 458–61, 463, 493; as revolutionary, 3; in Yeltsin's government, 122, 469–70

Garibaldi, Giuseppe, 315

Gates, Robert, 523

Gavrilov, Igor T., 458

General secretary: power, 81–84, 93n, 99, 255; selection, 99; threats to power of, 84–85, 100, 261

Generation gap: in military, 447–48; in Soviet elite, 55–56, 65–66, 67t; in political views, 4–5

Geneva summit (*1985*), 194

Georgia: civil war, 477; and dissolution of USSR, 483; education, 236, 243; ethnic conflicts in, 262–63; national identity, 234; position in Soviet Union, 235. *See also* Transcaucasus

Gerashchenko, Viktor, 132, 344–47, 451, 451n; and economic reform, 354–55

Gerasimov, Gennady, 205–07

Germany: division of, 190; reunification, 179, 184, 195, 208–09; in *1920*s, 519. *See also* East Germany

Ghana, 516

Gidaspov, Boris V., 274

Gierek, Edward, 118

Glasnost, and democratization, 141, 143–44

Glushkov, Nikolai, 110, 115

Gomulka, Wladislaw, 118

Gorbachev, Mikhail: and *1989* USSR election, 167; and *1990* Russian elections, 279; advisers, 210–13, 327; alternatives to actions of, 251–54; ascent, 61–102; after August *1991* coup, 448, 450–56; before August *1991* coup, 399–403, 455; in August *1991* coup, 432–37; background, 57, 64–66, 258, 258n; career, 66–71, 85–86; centrist position, 252, 329–32, 334, 359, 371, 399; and Communist party, 102, 250, 258–62, 272–77, 404; conservative position, 110; consolidation of power, 266–68, 404–05; and 500-Day Plan, 370–71; and democratization, 103, 126–28, 138–39, 142, 148–55, 171–72; and destabilization, 140–42, 249–50, 272; disillusionment with, 397–98; and dissolution of Soviet Union, 478–79, 488–89; East European policy, 186, 193, 195, 198–209; and economic reform, 103–10, 114, 119–20, 342–45, 349–52; election as general secretary, 62–64, 69–70, 74–80, 148; foreign policy, 175–76, 189, 192–96, 204, 209; foreign policy team, 176–89; generation of, 65–66, 70; ideological beliefs, 259–60; inconsistency, 132, 368–69; indecisiveness, 490–91; and legislative reform, 156–61; lieutenants, 90–91, 94–95, 176–89; loss of faith in communism, 499–500; mistakes, 21–22, 171–72, 372, 405; and national identity, 238, 240–41, 247–48; personality, 315, 317, 329, 433, 490; and political reform, 103, 126–28, 143–47, 341; power, 83–84, 94, 100, 139, 350; and price reform, 123–25, 130–38, 342–43; and radical economists, 135–39, 360; radical views, 73–74, 103, 106–07; and reform, 19, 21, 79, 96–99, 173, 266; resignation, 415, 483; situation inherited by, 60; source of power, 63–64; style, 119, 139; tactical maneuvers, 68, 86–87, 131–33, 357–58, 369–71; threats to power of, 100–102; and Union Treaty renegotiation, 378–81, 383, 393, 404, 455–56, 479; and USSR Congress, 166–67,

171; West European policy, 193–95; Western perceptions about, 99n. *See also* August *1991* coup d'état

Gorbachev, Mikhail, and Boris Yeltsin: alliance, 359–61, 415–20, 422–24; break-up, 141–42; Gorbachev humiliation by Yeltsin, 450–51, 480; similarity of views, 4–5; struggle between, 12, 146, 315–40, 403, 415; Yeltsin calculations about Gorbachev, 329–32

Gorbachev, Raisa, 259, 321

Goriacheva, Svetlana, 313, 339

Gosplan, 111; in Soviet power structure, 374

Government: and market, 505–06; Olson's analysis of, 510–11. *See also* Central administration; Provincial governments

Grachev, Pavel, 431, 438, 444

Great Purge of *1936–39,* 149

Grishin, Viktor, 73–74, 82, 318–19

Gromov, Boris, 156, 395, 485; in August *1991* coup, 443; in Russian presidential election, 420

Gromyko, Andrei: and foreign policy, 183, 190–91, 194–95; Gorbachev's election and, 76–77; political career, 68, 147, 158, 177

Grosz, Koroly, 200

Group politics: development, 298–304; Rutskoi and, 414. *See also* Factions; Independent political groups; Interest groups

Gulf War. *See* Persian Gulf War

Havel, Vaclav, 206

Health care system, USSR, 35; collapse, 208, 251

Heavy industry, Soviet preferential treatment, 34, 54

Herd, Douglas, 486

Hewett, Ed, 11, 119, 352–53, 524

Hill, Ronald, 187

History, reconsideration of Soviet, 144, 145n

Holding companies: industrial ministries as, 452–55, 477

Honecker, Erich, 199t, 205

Horowitz, Donald, 373

Hu Yaobang, 203

Hungary: *1988* unrest, 200; inherent instability, 196; political reform, 203, 205; Soviet perception of economic reform, 95–99

Huntington, Samuel P., 4n, 515; and model of democratic transition, 516, 517f

Hurst, Steve, 268

Husak, Gustav, 199t, 206

Ideological advisors, power of, 84–85

Ideology: Brezhnev regime and, 59; communist, loss of faith in, 499–500; and economic reform, 109–10; Lenin's, 299–300; and Soviet federalism, 226

IMEMO. *See* Institute of the World Economy and International Relations

IMF. *See* International Monetary Fund

Imperialism: The Highest Stage of Capitalism (Lenin), 40, 218

Incentive systems: change, 508–09; of Communist party, 20, 255, 257; and economic reform, 103–04; importance for reform, 505, 508–09

Independent Deputies (political group), 303

Independent political groups: in *1989* USSR Congress, 166, 172–73; in *1990* Russian Congress, 299–304; political liberalization and, 146. *See also* Factions

Independent Trade Unions (political group), 303

India: disintegration potential , 525; ethnic policy, 221–22, 252

Industrial ministries, transformation into holding companies, 452–55

Industrialists, in *1990* Russian Congress, 302

Industrialization: and communist revolutions, 26; and democratization, 5–6, 13, 507; stage of and political regime, 507, 514–15

Industrializing countries: peasants, 31; workers, 31–32

Industry: communist, 48–51; modernization plan for, 460; reform, 16, 120; preferential treatment of, 34, 54

Inflation: factors in controlling, 346; first signs, 263; *Law on State Enterprise (1987)* and, 342–43; radical economists' approach to, 345–48

Institute of the World Economy and International Relations (IMEMO), 182, 188

Institutions: Soviet branch, 374–75; destruction of, 22; importance, 493–95; and reform, 20–21, 505–07, 516

Intellectuals and democracy, 23; and elites, 499n; and revolutions, 499; Russian, 23, 491–93; U.S., 491–92; and Yeltsin, 335

Interest groups: in democracy, 512; in Soviet Union, 52–53, 302

International Monetary Fund (IMF), in Russia, 519n, 520

Interregional Group of USSR Deputies, 172–73, 293, 298–99, 327–28; formation, 166; and Union Treaty, 377

Investment, in Soviet Union, 346–48

Isakov, V. B., 378n

Ivanova, Tatiana, 304

Jaruzelski, Wojciech, 169, 198, 199t, 203
Job creation, in Soviet system, 34, 36–37
John Paul II (Pope), 145
John XXIII (Pope), 498

Kadar, Janos, 95, 199t, 200
Karelo-Finnish Republic, 227n
Kashmir, U.S. policy on, 254
Kazakhstan: and dissolution of USSR, 483;
    ethnic composition, 237; population, 228t;
    and reform, 331; riots in, 127. See also
    Central Asia
Keller, Bill, 333
Keynes, John Maynard, 525
KGB: and attack on Lithuania, 396–97; in
    August 1991 coup, 447
Khasbulatov, Ruslan, 306, 313; background,
    473; political views, 367; in Russian
    Supreme Soviet, 451, 465, 470–74; and
    Yeltsin, 335, 339, 407, 410, 417
Khrushchev, Nikita: political career, 85;
    reforms, 44, 62, 96, 253
Kirgizstan: Communist party, 148. See also
    Central Asia
Kirilenko, Andrei: background, 34, 87;
    Gorbachev and, 85; and military-industrial
    complex, 78; political career, 68, 84, 86.
    See also Kirilenko political machine
Kirilenko political machine, 86–90;
    Gorbachev and, 90–100
Kirkpatrick, Jeane, 42
Kirov, Sergei, 318
Kolesnichenko, Tomas, 197
Komin, A. N., 115–16
Komsomol. See Young Communist League
Korea, South, 516
Kornai, Janos, 111
Kortunov, Andrei, 361
Kosygin, Aleksei, 68; and economic reform,
    19, 44, 362
Kovalev, Vladimir A., 291–92
Kozyrev, Andrei, 463–64, 482
Kravchenko, Leonid, 170
Kravchuk, Leonid, 372, 479
Kremlin floor plan: Gorbachev and, 401; and
    power structure, 351
Kriuchkov, Vladimir, 193n, 201, 266, 369n;
    in August 1991 coup, 431–32, 434, 436,
    438–39, 441–42; background, 432, 442;
    and hysteria of 1990–91, 396–97
Kuchma, Leonid, 34
Kudriavtsev, Vladimir, 363, 376
Kulakov, Fedor, 68–69, 85; background, 67
Kulik, Gennady V., 458

Kunaev, Dinmukhamed, 127
Kurds, 220
Kuwait, national identity, 221–22

Laitin, David, 222
Land, Russian peasant structure and, 27–28.
    See also Territorial base
Land leasing program, 108–09;
    shortcomings, 104–05
Lange, Oskar, 115
Language, and national identity, 221–22
Latvia: ethnic composition, 232–33; and
    Union Treaty renegotiation, 378. See also
    Baltic republics
Law on Local Self-Government and the
    Local Economy, 382
Law on State Enterprise (1987), 243–44;
    effects, 342–43
Law on the Division of Powers between the
    USSR and the Subjects of the Federation,
    381, 384
Law on the Division of Powers between the
    USSR and the Union Republics, 377–78,
    392
Leadership, Soviet: age of, 80; Brezhnev era
    and, 61–63; and dissolution of Soviet
    Union, 374; and price reform, 123–35;
    secrecy in communications, 207; selection,
    81–83
Leahy, Patrick, 518
Lebed, Dmitry, 223
Lebed, General Aleksandr, 234, 519; in
    August 1991 coup, 429, 445
Left, use of term, 321n
Legislative elections, 1988 mandate of, 141
Legislature: reform, 156–61, 174; Russian,
    336–38; Soviet, democratic rules of, 301.
    See also Russian Congress of People's
    Deputies; USSR Congress of People's
    Deputies
Lenin in Zurich (Solzhenitsyn), 260
Lenin, Vladimir: anarchism of, 491; and
    circular flow of power, 81; concept of
    government, 143, 157, 497n; denunciation
    of Stalin, 84; fear of reformism, 121; and
    federalism, 217–20; and foreign policy,
    175; Gorbachev's attitude toward, 259–60;
    ideology, 299–300; as moralist, 31, 40;
    and national identity, 218–19, 222,
    238–39; personality, 315; social policy,
    28, 30, 36
Leninism, appeal of, 39
Li Peng, 204
Liberal Democratic party, 296, 422
Liberalization: and economic reform, 140;
    political, 143–48; and revolution, 15n

Ligachev, Yegor: background, 57, 91; career, 90–92; denunciation of, 147, 200, 259; and economic reform, 95, 98, 124, 126; Gorbachev and, 71–72, 75, 78, 83, 86, 94; memoirs, 11, 82, 169; and party system, 252; and political reform, 79, 146–47, 155–56; Yeltsin and, 319, 321–22, 327
Lithuania: attack on (*1991*), 339, 396–97, 400, 403; ethnic composition, 232–33; religion issue in, 145. *See also* Baltic republics
Living standards, Soviet, 16t
Lloyd, John, 264, 328
Lobov, Oleg, and economic reform, 457–58, 461–63
Logic of Collective Action, The (Olson), 20, 503–04
Luk'ianov, Anatoly, 87, 150, 330, 442; in August *1991* coup, 429, 439; career, 156; and political reform, 156–57
Lukin, Vladimir P., 393, 472
Luzhkov, Yury, 451
Lysenko, Trofim, 185

Major, John, 457
Makashov, General Albert M., 422
Malei, Mikhail, 458, 461, 466
Malenkov, Georgy, 44, 361
Manaenkov, Yury A., 307
Managers, Soviet, 36–37; class of, 30; privatization and, 502–03
Mannheim, Karl, 2
March, James G., 316
Market, requirements, 505–06
Marshall Plan, 506
Martial law and August *1991* coup, 438–39
Marx, Karl: criticism of, 260; historical period of, 26; as moralist, 31, 39–40; on private property, 35; on role of state, 2
Marxism: anarchism of, 491; and neoclassical economics, 5
Maslennikov, Nikolai I., 244
Masliukov, Yury D., 266, 354, 357
Masses, passivity of, 11–13
Matlock, Jack, 435
Mazow:ecki, Tadeusz, 204
Mazurov, Kiril, 68–69
Meat: consumption, 113; prices, 113
Media. *See* Press; Television coverage
Medical care. *See* Health care system
Medvedev, Roy, 70n
Medvedev, Vadim, 87–88, 107, 182–83; background, 183; and economic reform, 125, 129, 132, 183, 211–12; and foreign policy, 183; and price reform, 136, 355; and Yeltsin, 319–24

Mensheviks, ethnic support for, 239
Middle class. *See* Bourgeoisie
Mikhailov, Aleksei, 354, 360
Military: in *1989* USSR election, 167; in *1990* Russian Congress, 302; in August *1991* coup, 443–48; demoralization of, 487; and dissolution of Soviet Union, 482–89; Gorbachev's policy on, 252–53; grievances, 54–55; and political reform, 209
Ministries: dismantling of, 122; industrial, 452–55; and provincial governments, 56–58
Minorities, in Union republics, 247
Minsk agreement, 481–83
Modernization theory: and democratization, 5–6; and revolution, 6; shortcomings, 13–14; on Soviet future, 8–10
Moiseev, Mikhail, 447
Moldavia: civil war, 477; ethnic composition, 233; population, 228t
Money: accounting, 111–12, 343; in Soviet economic system, 111–12; transferable, 343
Money supply: control of, 346–48, 366–67; expansion, 343, 344t, 345–46; nature, 346
Moore, Barrington, 10
Mortality, in Russia, 22
Moscow, centralization of power in, 56–57
Moscow demonstrations: and Third Russian Congress, 408; Yeltsin's toleration of, 321–22
Mozhin, Vladimir P., 93
Multiethnic country, versus empire, 373
Murakhovsky, Vsevolod, 125

Nagorno-Karabakh conflict, 186n, 236, 247, 477
Nagy, Imre, 203
National districts, 227
National identity: Lenin and, 218–19, 222, 238–39; of non-Russian republics, 227–38; problems involving, 221; Russian, 238–41, 388; in Soviet Union, 221–25; Stalin and, 222–26, 239. *See also* Ethnic conflicts
Nationalism: Gorbachev and, 371–72; Russian, 216; Soviet disregard for, 145, 218–19; Yeltsin and, 273
NATO, expansion, 521
Nazarbaev, Nursultan, 237, 331–32, 424–25
Nechaev, Andrei, 460–61
Neoclassical economics, and Marxism, 5
New Economic Policy (NEP): Gorbachev and, 73–74, 78–79, 141; return to, 106, 109
Nikolai II (Tsar), 251

Nikonov, Viktor, 125
Nomenklatura: use of term, 3. See also
  Bureaucracy
Non-Party (political group), 303
North, Douglass, 20, 506–07, 513
Novo-Ogarevo agreement, 415–17, 419, 426

Obkom first secretaries: power, 100–101; in
  Russian Republic, 101–02, 274–76, 275t;
  selection, 85; in USSR Supreme
  Soviet, 285
Obkom, definition, 285
Occupational structure: bureaucratic
  cleavage and, 53–55; changes, 45, 47t,
  48–50, 50t; and destruction of communist
  system, 50–51; of 1985 Russian Supreme
  Soviet, 287t; and 1989 USSR elections,
  161, 162t, 163–64, 164t; and 1990 Russian
  elections, 286–87, 287–88t, 295–96; of
  Russian Congress, 302
Odom, William, 42
Ogarkov, Marshal Nikolai, 54–55, 78
Olson, Mancur, 278, 445, 490, 495, 503–04;
  on collective action, 7, 20–21; on
  government, 7–8, 15, 510–12
Ordeshook, Peter, 4n
Otkhodniki, role in Bolshevik Revolution,
  27–28, 29t

Pankin, Boris, 181–82n
Pan-Slavism, 388
Parliamentarism: Soviet view, 300; Yeltsin's
  view, 310
Parliamentary system: Soviet, 269. See also
  Congress of People's Deputies
Parsons, Talcott, 9
Partocracy. See Bureaucracy
Parties: as factions, 12; liberalization of
  Soviet system and, 146, 150–51; and 1990
  Russian election, 292–94; prohibition of,
  426–27, 439. See also Factions;
  Independent political groups
Passivity, of Russian people, 11–13
Pavlov, Nikolai, 311
Pavlov, Valentin, 115, 123–24, 126, 128,
  455; in August 1991 coup, 429–30,
  434–35, 437n, 438–39, 441–42; on
  Gorbachev, 488; as premier, 400–401,
  426; and price reform, 131, 344, 354; and
  Yeltsin, 428
Peasants: in Bolshevik Revolution, 24,
  26–30, 32; in bourgeois revolutions, 1–2;
  and democracy, 38; in industrializing
  countries, 31
Pechenev, Vadim, 96
Peel, Quentin, 348

Pelshe, Arvid, 68
Perestroika: definition, 106; Gorbachev's
  vision of, 109; origins, 74n; positive
  influence of, 107
Perestroika: A History of Betrayals
  (Ryzhkov), 79
Persian Gulf War: Soviet policy, 188–89;
  U.S. policy, 253
Petrakov, Nikolai, 116–17, 213, 414; and
  economic reform, 345, 352–56, 360
Petrov, Yury, 241–42, 465; economic reform
  visions, 457–58, 461–63
Pipes, Richard, 42, 489
Plant management, Soviet, 36–37; financial,
  111–12
Plekhanov, Oleg, 429
Plekhanov, Sergei, 361
Poland: border with Ukraine, 231–32;
  economic reform, 118; instability, 196;
  lessons of, 118, 138; 1988 unrest,
  199–200; 1989 election, 169; political
  reform, 202–05; shock treatment in,
  509–10. See also Eastern Europe
Politburo: end of power, 250, 271, 278;
  general secretary's control of, 82–83; and
  Gorbachev's election, 62–64, 69, 74–77;
  and political reform, 156; reorganization,
  Gorbachev and, 266, 330–31; and Russian
  Supreme Soviet election, 307; socializing
  in, 86–87; Yeltsin's resignation from,
  322–24
Political groups. See Factions; Independent
  political groups; Parties
Political hierarchies, similarity of views in,
  4–5
Political illiteracy, Soviet, 211
Political reform: Chinese, 18; Soviet, 16–17.
  See also Democratization; Liberalization
Political sovereignty, 387–88
Political system, Soviet, 142–43; proposed
  changes, 156–57
Politics: and emotion, 514; group, 298–304,
  414. See also Populist politics
Polozkov, Ivan, 272, 307–08, 414, 420, 475
Ponomarev, Aleksei A., 338
Ponomarev, Boris, 179
Ponomarev, Lev, 472
Popov, Gavril, 122, 212, 414, 435–36
Population, Soviet: in Brezhnev era, 44; in
  republics, 227, 228t
Populist politics: and dissolution of Soviet
  Union, 449; of Yeltsin, 252, 306–07
Power. See Circular flow of power;
  Decentralization of power; Power
  structure

Power structure, Soviet, 63, 80–86, 93n, 374–75; Brezhnev's reforms, 61–64; factions in, 86–87; Kremlin floor plan and, 351; Lenin's reforms, 81

Predictions, political, 522–23

Premier, Soviet, 93n

Preservation of Union: desire for, 12, 406, 484–85; referendum on, 406

Presidency. *See* Russian presidency; Soviet presidency

Press: controls on, 144, 146–47; exaggeration of economic problems by, 254; in *1990* Russian elections, 291

Prices: economic reform and, 123–24; political effect of increases, 330

Price reform, Soviet: Abalkin plan and, 349; alternative methods, 115; beginnings, 110; conservatives' position on, 355; controversy over, 114–18; criticism of, 250; democratization and, 128, 138; imbalances requiring, 111–14; leadership and, 123–35; political rivalries and, 357–58; Western perception of, 117

Primakov, Yevgeny, 188–89

Private property: communist perception of, 35, 110; alternatives to, 108; as revolution incentive, 2. *See also* Privatization

Privatization: attitudes toward, 501–04; Chinese model for, 17–18, 502; control over, 245–47; and corruption, 503; 500-Day Plan and, 363–64, 364n; decentralization of power and, 388; Russian advantage in, 454–55

Privileges, in Soviet system: bureaucracy and, 34–35; distribution, 54; proletariat and, 30–34

Proletariat: bureaucracy and, 29–30; privileges under communism, 30–34. *See also* Workers

Provincial governments: and central administration, 56–58; Yeltsin's appointments, 474–75

Przeworski, Adam, 507

Psychological security, communism and, 37–41

Pugin, Nikolai, 454

Pugo, Boris K., 266, 395; in August *1991* coup, 429, 434, 439, 443

Radical economists: and command-administrative system, 120–22; and Gorbachev, 135–39, 360; and price reform, 116–18, 351; and Ryzhkov's economic plan, 345–48; views, 352–54

Rakhmanin, Oleg, 186

Rakovsky, Khristian, 223–24

Rakowski, Mieczyslaw, 202

Razumov, Yevgeny, 90–91

Razumovsky, Georgyy, 83, 92, 94

Reagan, Ronald, 127, 193–94, 512

Referendums of *1991,* 406; Gorbachev and, 404; and Russian presidential election, 410, 417

Reform, Soviet: versus Chinese, 19–22; imbalances in, 209–13; intellectual assumptions about, 16–22. *See also* Economic reform; Political reform

Reform models: Chinese, 16–17, 19, 106, 118–19, 135–37; East European, 16–17, 106, 118–19; intellectual assumptions and, 16–22

Regimes. *See* Communist regimes; Dictatorship

Regions. *See* Territorial base

Reisner, Mikhail, 219

Religion: and ethnic assimilation, 230–32; and secession movement, 232; and Soviet stability, 145. *See also* Christianity

Rent, economic reform and, 112–13

Republican elections of *1990,* 280n; East European events and, 250; insufficient control over, 251, 254; and Soviet Revolution, 278. *See also* Russian election of *1990*

Republics, Soviet: civil wars, 477; collapse of communism and, 214–15; concentration of power in, 375–76; declarations of independence, 477, 479–80; and dissolution of Union, 483; ethnic boundaries, 219, 221; 500-Day Plan and, 364–65, 390; Gorbachev's policy, 101–02, 145, 174, 331–32, 385; legal rights, 216–17; political leadership, 100–101; Russian declaration of independence and, 469; types, 227. *See also individual republics*; Autonomous republics; Union republics

Revenko, Grigory, 363

Revolutions: from below, 7; characteristics, 316–17; and democratization, 3–8; economic consequences, 506; immediate cause, 4; individuals as determinants of, 315–17; irreversibility, 249, 251; liberalization, and 15n; modernization theorists' view, 6; Olson's view, 510; pragmatic definition, 5; recent theories, 6–8; social base, 32–33; success, 2. *See also* Bolshevik Revolution of *1917;* Communist revolutions; Soviet Revolution of *1990–91;*

Reykjavik summit, 127

Richelson, Jeffrey, 518

Riga, Latvia, 232
Right, use of term, 321n
Riker, William, 515
Rise and Decline of Nations (Olson), 21, 503, 512
Rodionov, Yury, 263n
Romania: political reform, 206; Soviet reaction to executions, 207–08. *See also* Eastern Europe
Romanov, Grigory: background, 57, 65, 69; and Gorbachev, 76, 97; political career, 69–70, 72–73
Rostow, W. W., 10, 25
Rousseau, Jean Jacques, 513, 515
RSFSR (Russian Soviet Federated Socialist Republic). *See* Russian Republic
Rukh movement, 230
Ruling class. *See* Bureaucracy; Command-administrative system; Elites
Rural areas, and *1990* Russian election, 296–98
Russian Central Committee, 413
Russian Communist party, 258, 272–73; founding congress, 276, 413; and Gorbachev, 404; in Russian presidential election, 420. *See also* Communist party
Russian Congress of People's Deputies: Third, 407–09, 417–18; Fourth, 408–10; Fifth, 472–73, 475–76; Yeltsin and, 278–79, 300–301, 335–40. *See also* First Russian Congress of People's Deputies
Russian election of *1990,* 290–98; candidates, 283–90, 285t, 288t; defects, 292–94; democratic nature, 298; factors determining results, 295–98; results, 294–95; turnout, 290
Russian Patriotic Bloc (political group), 293
Russian people: assimilation of, 239–40, 241–42t; attitudes, 10–11; changing status in republics, 240; and democratization, 496, 514; national identity, 238–41; passivity, 11–13; patience, 138; Western prejudice regarding, 496–97
Russian presidency: creation, 269, 279, 404–10, 417–18; economic reform and, 253; election for, 420–22; referendum on, 406; Yeltsin and, 338, 373, 417–18
Russian Republic: autonomous republics of, 245–46, 246t; declaration of sovereignty, 386–90, 391t; and dissolution of Soviet Union, 374, 462–64, 481–82; economic grievances, 241–45, 463n; economic reform, 457–58; formation, 219; Gorbachev's policy, 330–31; independence and economic strategies, 456–64, 469; obkom first secretaries in,

101–02, 274–76, 275t; political grievances, 248; population, 228t; privatization and, 454–55; size, 227; status in USSR, 215–16, 241–42; takeover of Union functions, 451–55, 477–78; and Union Treaty renegotiation, 385, 415–16; Yeltsin's bet on, 328
Russian revolutions. *See* Bolshevik Revolution of *1917*; Soviet Revolution of *1990–91*
Russian Soviet Federated Socialist Republic (RSFSR). *See* Russian Republic
Russian Supreme Soviet, 280–81; budgetary problems, 338; and Congress, 281; and dissolution of Union, 465; election of deputies, 313–14, 336–37; election of Yeltsin as chairman, 304–08, 327–28, 336, 385, 405–06; Gorbachev's humiliation before, 450–51; legislation, 337; *1985,* composition, 284–86, 287t; versus Yeltsin, 253, 339, 407, 470; Yeltsin as chairman, 332–35
Russification policy, 222–23; in autonomous republics, 247, 384
Rutskoi, Colonel Aleksandr, 207n, 294, 311, 398, 463n; background, 411–12, 447–48; political career, 412–13, 484; and Union preservation, 484–85; and Yeltsin, 410–11, 413–15
Rybkin, Ivan, 311
Ryzhkov, Nikolai: background, 34, 92–93, 95; cabinet, 263, 341–44; and Communist party, 168, 254; economic program, 306, 330, 349–52, 523; and economic reform, 120, 130–31, 210, 252, 263–66; and foreign policy, 176; Gorbachev's election and, 75–76, 78–79; memoirs, 86; political career, 90–91, 93; political destruction, 352–53, 355–61, 394; and price reform, 123–25, 131, 134, 155–56; and reform, 19, 54, 95, 97–98; in Russian presidential election, 410, 420–22; and Yeltsin, 319, 325

Saburov, Yevgeny, 457–58, 466–67
Sachs, Jeffrey, 460, 467
Sakharov, Andrei, 144, 160; in USSR Congress, 170, 328
Savings, in USSR, 346–48
Schmemann, Serge, 74, 140–41
Schurz, Carl, 40
Second economy, 143
Secrecy, in leadership communications, 207
Secretaries. *See* General secretary; Obkom first secretaries

Security, Soviet, economic reform and, 120. *See also* Economic security; Psychological security

Senchagov, Viacheslav, 344

Services: economic reform in, 16–17; Soviet transition to, 48

Shaimiev, Mintimer, 392

Shakhnazarov, Georgy, 186–88; and foreign policy, 201–02; on Gorbachev, 260, 402; and political reform, 150, 152, 157, 260, 319, 354; and Union Treaty renegotiation, 379–80

Shakhrai, Sergei, 313, 415, 418, 424, 470; in Supreme Soviet elections, 472

Shanin, Theodore, 135

Shaposhnikov, Yevgeny, 448, 450, 478; in August *1991* coup, 433–34, 444–47; and dissolution of Union, 486–88

Shatalin, Nikolai, 361

Shatalin, Stanislav, 213, 350, 356, 360; background, 361n, 361–62; economic reform plan, 362–63, 457

Shchepotkin, Viacheslav, 291–92

Shcherbakov, Vladimir, 400

Shcherbitsky, Vladimir, 91, 101

Sheinis, Viktor, 475

Shelepin, Aleksandr, 181

Shenin, Oleg, 428, 436

Shevardnadze, Eduard: background, 177–78; and economic reform, 126; and foreign policy, 176–78, 205; Gorbachev and, 94, 432; ideological beliefs, 414; resignation, 395

Shock therapy. *See* Economic shock therapy

Shmelev, Nikolai, 116, 116n, 121n; economic policy, 348

Shokhin, Aleksandr, 362; background, 459–60; economic reform vision, 459–60, 467; in Yeltsin's government, 469–70

Silaev, Ivan S., 314, 335, 339, 354, 414; and economic reform, 458; political career, 451; resignation, 465–67

Simon, Herbert, 316

Simoniia, Nodari, 189n

Sitarian, Stepan, 360

Skocpol, Theda, 6–7, 490

Slavic republics, 228, 228t; and dissolution of Soviet Union, 481–82

Slavophilism, 388

Sliun'kov, Nikolai: and economic reform, 125, 129, 263, 355; political career, 90–91, 93

Smena (political group), 303

Sobchak, Anatoly, 414

Sobianin, Aleksandr, 475

Social base: of Bolshevik Revolution, 24–30, 32–34; for change in Soviet system, 78; of Soviet Revolution, 24–25

Social contract, Soviet regime as, 43

Socialist Revolutionaries (political group), 27

Soiuz, meaning of term, 377

Solidarity (political movement): impact on Soviet Union, 197–98; legalization, 202; victory, 204

Solnick, Steven, 498

Solzhenitsyn, Aleksander, 216, 260, 388

South Korea, 516

Sovereignty: definitions, 387–88; Russian usage of term, 386

Soviet, meaning of term, 280n

Soviet of Nationalities (USSR), 280–82

Soviet of the Republic (USSR), 280–81

Soviet presidency: versus American presidency, 269; creation, 132, 152, 250, 266, 269–73

Soviet Revolution of *1990–91:* causes, 15, 495–504; characteristics, 315–16; conventional interpretation of, 2–3; hysteria preceding, 394–98; impression of irreversibility, 249; lessons for U.S., 5; nature, 1–2, 373; prelude to, 23–60; prevention, 251–54; social base, 24–25; theoretical perspective on, 8–13; unpredictability, 23–24

Soviet system: economic security in, 34–37; egalitarianism in, 34–35, 120; legitmacy, 58–59. *See also* Soviet system change

Soviet system change: American skepticism about, 42–43; in Brezhnev era, 44–51; bureaucratic inability to resist, 62; factors favorable for, 43–44; need for, 80; social base for, 78

Soviet Union: desire for preservation, 12, 406, 484–85; formation, 220–21. *See also* Dissolution of Soviet Union

Sovnarkhozy: economic reform and, 130, 252; establishment of, 62

Stalin, Joseph: bureaucrats and, 29–30; and circular flow of power, 81–82; and democratism, 149; denunciation of, 84, 144n, 148; on foreign exploitation, 40–41; and national identity, 222–26, 239; and Transcaucasian Federation, 234–35

Stanley, Alessandra, 189n

State: definitions, 507; and democracy, 507, 516; and society, 53; in Soviet Revolution of *1990–91,* 15; and revolution, 7

State and Revolution (Lenin), 28, 36, 217

States and Social Revolution (Skocpol), 6–7

Status decline, Soviet, 45–47, 47t

Stavropol: in *1989* USSR elections, 287–89; political importance, 67, 89, 178; and reform, 152–53

Steele, Jonathan, 150

Stepan, Alfred, 4

Strategic Defense Initiative, 193

"Subjects of the federation," 381

Subsidization, 112–14

Summers, Lawrence, 521

Supreme Soviet. *See* Russian Supreme Soviet; USSR Supreme Soviet

Suslov, Mikhail, 67, 84

Szporluk, Roman, 388

Tadzhikistan: civil war, 477; ethnic composition, 236. *See also* Central Asia

Talbott, Strobe, 521

Tarasov, Boris, 311–12

Tarazevich, Georgy S., 377n; and Union Treaty renegotiation, 377–78, 380, 425

Tatariia: demand for sovereignty, 282; ethnic group in, 227; and Union Treaty renegotiation, 378

Taxation: in analysis of democracy, 511; and August *1991* coup, 438–39; 500-Day Plan and, 364, 366–69, 393; power of, 418–19; and Soviet Revolution, 501–02; Union Treaty renegotiation and, 424–26

Tbilisi, Georgia, 235

Television coverage: criticism of, 250; of Russian Congress, 309; of USSR Congress, 170–71, 250, 254, 298–99

Territorial base: of *1990* Russian Congress, 296–98, 303; of Bolshevik Revolution, 27–28, 29t; of bureaucratic division, 56–58

Tett, Gillian, 479

Third world: democracy in, 513; and Gorbachev's policy, 179

Tiananmen Square demonstrations, 18, 135, 169, 203–04; U.S. response to, 253

Tikhonov, Nikolai, 34, 93

Time factor: in democratization process, 14; in Gorbachev's reform, 107–08; in Union Treaty renegotiation, 379–80

Timisoara, Romania, demonstrations, 206

Tiumen oil fields, 405, 427–28, 439

Tolkunov, Lev, 70n

Totalitarian system, versus authoritarian system, 18, 143

Trade, Soviet: with Eastern Europe, 208; opening to world economy, 244–45

Trade unions: in Soviet power structure, 374; Soviet view, 300

Traditional values, versus Western values, 39–40

Transcaucasus, 220, 234–36; population, 228t

Transferable money, versus accounting money, 343

Transition theory, 120–21, 132; Gorbachev and, 491; Western, 507

Travkin, Nikolai, 303

Trotsky, Leon, 28–29, 52, 144–45, 400

Tsinev, Grigory, 88–89

Tsipko, Aleksandr, 260–61

Tsvigun, Semen, 88–89

Tucker, Robert, 225

Tuleev, Aman-Geldy M., 422

Ukraine: assimilation in, 230, 231t; border with Poland, 231–32; declaration of independence, 479–81, 496; and dissolution of Soviet Union, 481–82; ethnic composition, 229–30; etymology of name, 222; population, 228t; nationalism, 230–31; religions, 230–32; status in Soviet Union, 100–101; and Union Treaty renegotiation, 419; Ukrainianization, 223–24; UN membership, 217, 221

Unemployment: economic reform and, 120; Soviet system and, 36–37

Uniate Church, 230–32

Union (political group), 400

Union of Soviet Socialist Republics. *See* Soviet Union

Union republics, 227–28; versus autonomous republics, 246–47, 392; declarations of sovereignty, 386; ethnic conflicts in, 247; legal transformation of, 381–82, 390–92; population, 227, 228t; privatization and, 245–47; size, 227; sovereignty, 383–84; and Union Treaty renegotiation, 381, 419

Union Treaty renegotiation, 250; and August *1991* coup, 423–28, 439; economic reform and, 362–63; events leading to, 376–81; first draft, 390–94; 500-Day Plan and, 390–91; Gorbachev and, 383, 404, 455–56; Gorbachev's draft, 404; last stages, 424; participants, 381, 391–92; republics and, 381–85; and Russian presidency, 415; Yeltsin and, 334

United States: and dissolution of Soviet Union, 518–25; federalism, 222; Gorbachev's view, 193–94; presidency, 269; response to August *1991* coup, 443; Soviet perception of, 191–92; and Soviet reform, 493–95; tolerance for use of force, 253–54. *See also* West

Upward mobility: and Bolshevik Revolution, 30, 32–34; and destruction of communist system, 50–51, 497; and political stability, 45

Urban peasants, in Bolshevik Revolution, 24, 26–30, 32
Urbanization: in Brezhnev era, 44; and destruction of communist system, 50
USSR Central Committee: and economic reform, 107–08, 110, 265–66; functions, 84; general secretary's control over, 83; Gorbachev's election and, 77–78, 79t; International Department of, 178–79, 182, 184, 201; power, 261, 278; reorganization under Gorbachev, 200–201; Socialist Countries Department of, 182–83, 187, 198, 201; in Soviet power structure, 374
USSR Congress of People's Deputies: dissolution after August *1991* coup, 452; and Russian Congress, 279, 282–83, 294, 299; two-tier legislature in, 281; and Union Treaty, 377. *See also* First USSR Congress of People's Deputies
USSR election of *1989*, 11; candidates, 285t; control of, 142; criticism of, 250; Gorbachev's response to, 251; results, 164–69, 168t; in Stavropol region, 287–89
USSR Supreme Soviet, 158–59; Gorbachev and, 158; composition, 159n, 285; and economic reform, 350
Ustinov, Dmitry, 34; political career, 68, 70–72

Values, traditional, versus Western values, 39–40, 495
Varennikov, General Valentin, 369n, 428, 441
Vice presidency, USSR, 401–02
Vid, Leonard B., 347
Vilnius, Lithuania, 232
Virgin Land program, 237
Vlasov, Aleksandr, 279, 305, 307–08
Volsky, Arkady, 150, 450–51, 482
von Clausewitz, Karl, 175
Voronin, Lev, 132
Vorotnikov, Vitaly, 294; background, 57; and economic reform, 125; political career, 90
Voslensky, Mikhail, 42
"Votes against all," 292–93, 293n
Voting: and democracy, 512–14. *See also individual elections*

Weber, Max, 10
Weiner, Myron, 216
West: and Brezhnev era, 42–44, 59; and dissolution of Soviet Union, 449, 467–68, 486, 518–25; economic advice of, 519; effect on developments in Russia, 519–21; Gorbachev's reforms and, 213, 253,

264–65; lessons for, 493–95; prejudiced views of Russians, 496–97; and price reform, 117; Russian attitudes toward, 39–41, 51; Russia's policy toward, 175, 193; status decline in, 45–46; theories of transition, 507
Western Europe: Gorbachev's policy, 193–95; Soviet policy, 192, 194. *See also* West
Western values: Russian attraction to, 495; versus traditional values, 39–40
What's to Be Done (Lenin), 497n
White House, Russian, 430–31
Witte, Count Sergei, 119, 462
Women, in Communist party, 256
Work. *See* Job creation; Occupational structure
Worker-managers, 30
Workers: in *1989* USSR election, 169; disillusionment with communist regime, 47–48, 49t; in industrializing countries, 31–32. *See also* Proletariat

Yakovlev, Aleksandr, 179–82, 369n; background, 57–58, 181; and economic reform, 19, 126, 211, 353–54; and foreign policy, 191–92, 199, 206–07; ideological views, 260–61, 414; and media control, 251; and political reform, 127, 146–47, 150–52, 155, 157; and Yeltsin, 320, 325
Yakunin, Gleb, 471–72
Yalta Conference, 217
Yanaev, Gennady, 401–02; in August *1991* coup, 430, 439, 440–42, 447
Yaroslavl national-territorial election, 291–92
Yasin, Yevgeny, 360, 462–63
Yavlinsky, Grigory: and economic reform, 354, 360, 457–58; reappointment, 451; resignation, 339, 366
Yazov, Dmitry, 429, 430n, 434, 439
Yeltsin, Boris: and August *1991* coup, 12, 430–31, 465; background, 30, 34, 256, 317; as chairman of Russian Supreme Soviet, 332–35; comeback, 325–28; consolidation of power, 450–51, 469; decisionmaking, 465; and dissolution of Soviet Union, 465–66, 477–83; and economic reform, 105, 122, 333–34, 339, 348, 367; election as Russian president, 405–10, 420–22; election as Russian Supreme Soviet chairman, 304–08; emergency powers, 475–76; financial policies, 403, 423; and national identity, 273; in *1989* USSR election, 162–63, 165, 278; in *1990* republican election, 278–79; personality,

320, 325, 328, 336; political career, 72–73, 91, 94, 147–48, 317–18; political genius of, 215; and political reform, 64n, 146, 323; populist policy, 252, 306–07, 316, 319, 322, 332; power, 272; pre–coup actions, 405, 426–28, 439; provincial governors appointment by, 474–75; pursuit of power, 340; and radical economic reform, 468–69, 477; removal as first secretary, 324–25; resignation from Communist party, 334; resignation from Politburo, 322–24; as revolutionary, 3, 249; and Russian Congress, 278–79, 300–301, 335–40; and Russian independence, 469; and Russian presidency, 273, 338, 373, 417–18; versus Russian Supreme Soviet, 253, 339, 407, 470; and Rutskoi, 410–11, 413–15; and

Union Treaty renegotiation, 385, 393; in USSR Congress, 279, 327–28. *See also* Gorbachev, Mikhail, and Boris Yeltsin
Yerevan, 235
Yevtushenko, Yevgeny, 56, 144n
Young Communist League, 374
Yur'ev, Dmitry, 475

Zadornov, Mikhail, 354, 360
Zaikov, Lev, 125, 167, 262
Zaslavskaia, Tatiana, 57, 137, 375
Zhao Ziyang, 204
Zhirinovsky, Vladimir, 422; in *1993* election, 296–97, 521
Zhivkov, Todor, 199t, 205
Zimianin, Mikhail, 180n
Zyuganov, Gennady, 258, 273, 519